Delinquency and Justice

A Cultural Perspective

Mary S. Jackson

East Carolina University

Paul Knepper

East Carolina University

Boston   New York   San Francisco
Mexico City   Montreal   Toronto   London   Madrid   Munich   Paris
Hong Kong   Singapore   Tokyo   Cape Town   Sydney

Series Editor: Jennifer Jacobson
Series Editorial Assistant: Beth Lee
Marketing Manager: Krista Groshong
Production Administrator: Anna Socrates
Editorial Production Service: Matrix Productions Inc.
Electronic Composition: Omegatype Typography, Inc.
Composition Buyer: Linda Cox
Manufacturing Buyer: JoAnne Sweeney
Photo Researcher: Katharine S. Cook
Cover Administrator: Kristina Mose-Libon

For related titles and support materials, visit our online catalog at www.ablongman.com

Between the time Website information is gathered and then published, it is not unusual for some sites to have closed. Also, the transcription of URLs can result in unintended typographical errors. The publisher would appreciate notification where these occur so that they may be corrected in subsequent editions.

Library of Congress Cataloging-in-Publication Data

Jackson, Mary S.
    Delinquency and justice : a cultural perspective / Mary S. Jackson, Paul Knepper.
        p.   cm.
    Includes bibliographical references and index.
    ISBN 0-8013-3307-5
        1. Juvenile justice, Administration of—United States.   2. Juvenile delinquency—United States.   I. Knepper, Paul.   II. Title.

HV9104 .J27   2002
364.36'0973—dc21   2002020846

Printed in the United States of America

10 9 8 7 6 5 4 3 2 1   07 06 05 04 03 02

Photo Credits: p. 8: Hannah Gal/CORBIS; p. 47: David and Peter Turnley/CORBIS; p. 57: Key Color/Index Stock Imagery, Inc.; p. 72: National Library of Medicine; p. 86: Jeff Greenberg/PhotoEdit; p. 121 (all 5 photos): AP/Wide World Photos; p. 152: AP/Wide World Photos; p. 156: Bill Aron/PhotoEdit; p. 174: A. Ramey/PhotoEdit; p. 182: A. Lichtenstein/Corbis/Sygma; p. 201: Getty Images Inc.; p. 217: Michael Newman/PhotoEdit; p. 245: Michael Newman/PhotoEdit; p. 271: Joel Gordon/Joel Gordon Photography; p. 303: A. Ramey/PhotoEdit; p. 329: © CORBIS; p. 354: AP/Wide World Photos; p. 388: Chuck Savage/Corbis/Stock Market.

CONTENTS

PREFACE

At few other moments during the American juvenile justice experience has so much been at stake. The juvenile court began as an experiment, an effort to find a better response to the wrenching dilemma of what to do about troubled youth. A hundred years later, that experiment has become part of the public bureaucracy that is criminal justice, and yet so many issues remains unsettled. Judges, legislators, professors, practitioners, and citizens have questioned nearly every aspect of the experiment. No part of juvenile court, police work with juveniles, juvenile corrections, and delinquency theory has not been considered.

The founders of juvenile justice offered the juvenile court as the solution to the challenges surrounding delinquent youth. Finding the proper response to an illegal act is a weighty matter; to meet the concerns of victims, promote domestic order, and consider the human problems of individual lawbreakers in an effort to do justice is not easy to begin with. Add to these concerns the youthfulness of the lawbreaker and the task becomes weightier. The underage lawbreaker necessarily brings into consideration a range of issues less clearly delineated in criminal cases—family, school, and peers, for example. It adds heft to every aspect of the decision about what to do—youthfulness presents the hope for change, the tragedy of wasted life, and the troubling question of adult complicity. The juvenile court, with its special authority and distinct procedures, was the answer the founders thought to offer. After a century, nearly every aspect of that answer has been subject to re-thinking.

Everyone who intends to work in criminal justice, even in those professions not attached to the juvenile court, needs to know about juvenile justice. Police officers spend a great deal of their energy on young people, and few who have worked in a criminal courtroom or prison have not wondered, when looking at the individuals before them, about what might have been. Knowledge of the issues, policies, and rationales of the juvenile court is essential. It may be even more important simply to know that others have confronted the same dilemma; to know what they thought, why they pushed the policies they did, what they expected, and what they hoped to avoid.

So much of understanding juvenile justice comes through culture. Young people bring their culture to an agency of government that retains its own legal culture. People who work together, whether police officers, attorneys or social workers, develop their own organizational culture. All of this shapes activities already formed by the cultures of the people that make up the United States: the religious, political, economic, ethnic, and racial identities of Americans.

This book tries to understand the cultures at work in juvenile justice without being overwhelmed by academic culture. Textbooks follow certain conventions and this text adheres to them. It follows a style of organization that university students and faculty find comfortable. At the same time, we have endeavored to offer an understanding of juvenile justice that takes particular notice of culture at work. We devote entire chapters to gender and ethnicity; other chapters include international, religious, and political material. This text also devotes entire chapters to delinquency prevention and the future of the juvenile court.

Acknowledgments

In any undertaking like this one, authors become indebted to the ideas, encouragement, and just plain hard work of others. This is certainly the case for us. A number of people contributed to this project in various ways, but no one contributed more than Allyn and Bacon's Jennifer Jacobson. Jennifer brought her energy to the project that carried us from drafts to publication, and we are grateful. There is a saying, attributed to Henry Frye, Chief Justice of the North Carolina Supreme Court, that applies here: "When you see a turtle sitting atop a fencepost you can be sure it did not get there by itself." We would like to thank the following reviewers for their helpful critiques: Gerald Bayens, Washburn University; Eugene E. Bouley, Jr., Georgia College and State University; Vanessa A. Brown, Southern Illinois University, Edwardsville; M. Reid Counts, University of North Carolina, Wilmington; Gloria Fennel, University of Wisconsin–Eau Claire; Casey Jordan, Western Connecticut State University; Elizabeth L. Lewis, Waycross College; Christine Ludowise, Georgia Southern University; Samantha Mannion, Housatonic Community College; Donna M. Massey, University of Tennessee, Martin; Charles Ousley, Seminole State College; and Krishna Samatrai, Smith College.

M. S. J.

P. K.

1 Explaining Delinquency

CHAPTER OBJECTIVES

On completing this chapter, students will have tools to:

- Provide an overview of the juvenile justice system
- Compare the juvenile justice system and the adult criminal justice system
- Examine factors that impact serious violent juvenile delinquent behavior
- Describe the processing of children through the system
- Examine race and gender issues in juvenile justice

The Roots of Juvenile Justice in the United States

The terrorist attack that destroyed the World Trade Center on September 11, 2001, in New York City brought to the citizens of the United States an acute awareness of the country's vulnerability. However, the culture of the United States historically is marked with violence in the struggle to survive. The belief and the accepted norm has been that although violence exists, careful consideration must be given to the impact it has on youths, delinquency, and justice in U.S. society.

As an historical overview of the juvenile justice system, this chapter comments about issues dealing with violence among young offenders: Are young offenders more violent today than ten years ago, or are they simply committing more violent crimes? This question continues to elicit debate throughout the United States, as lawmakers and educators grapple with the question of whether delinquents should be treated or punished. This chapter considers the question of violence and discusses treatment versus punishment in the context of *parens patriae* (protecting children). It traces parens patriae to the Hammurabic Code and shows how it was reflected in ancient Roman law as *patria potestas* (paternal authority), in English common law, and in a very broad modern interpretation in the United States today.

The chapter describes the creation of the U.S. juvenile court system, profiling a major challenge to the authority of the court system in *Commonwealth v. Fisher.* In discussions of culture and history, philosophy and goals are seldom discussed, thus not providing the whole picture. This chapter demonstrates how the philosophy of the juvenile justice system incorporates many aspects of U.S. culture (including race and gender issues, especially the treatment of females and minorities). The chapter describes processing the delinquent through the system because it is important for students to see early in their study the inter-connection between how delinquents are processed and the philosophical shift in justice. Initial arrest, adjudication, and final disposition are strongly related to the particular mod-els of justice that permeate the court hearing the case. Students need to understand the crime control, due process, rehabilitation, and nurturing models of justice. The chapter ends as it begins with a discussion of treatment versus punishment and concludes with a speculation about the future.

Justice for Juveniles?

Juvenile justice has been debated hotly by the public. Youths have assumed many of the activistic roles once held by their baby boomer parents and by their grandparents, the hip-pies, rebels, and dropouts of the 1960s and 1970s. Youths today proudly display pierced bodies, baggy clothes, and unique hairstyles; communicate in monosyllables; and listen to loud and violent music. The violent nature of the lyrics and drug innuendos that they echo have prompted some adults to try to have certain record albums legally prohibited.

Adolescents criticize the school systems for not teaching anything relevant, schools blame parents for not taking more interest in their children, and parents feel helpless and wonder, "What's wrong with my child—why can't someone help?" Child advocate organi-zations and others, such as the Office of Juvenile Justice Delinquency Prevention (OJJDP), focus primarily on prevention of juvenile delinquency and diversion.

The OJJDP was created as a result of the Juvenile Justice and Delinquency Preven-tion Act of 1974. Its primary responsibilities are to assess the effectiveness of the juvenile justice system, to develop and implement alternatives to prevent juvenile delinquency, and to assist with the diversion of status offenders from training schools. Serious and violent juvenile offenders (SVJ) have been a top priority of OJJDP, and they have created a study group to initiate efforts to prevent serious and violent juvenile offending. The study group provides guidance to jurisdictions across the country that are implementing OJJDP's com-prehensive strategy (OJJDP 1998 and 2000). Some politicians, however, insist that juvenile court systems must get tougher on juvenile offenders because of the increase in the violent nature of juvenile crimes.

Violence is the major issue that emerges from all of this debate. Between 1985 and 1994 OJJDP reported an increase in the number of juvenile offenders involved in violent crimes (crimes resulting in personal injury, identified in the crime index as murder, forcible rape, robbery, and aggravated assault) and crimes with weapons—weapons violations reportedly increased 156 percent (OJJDP 1997). Violent crime rates for juveniles decreased by 3 percent between 1994 and 1995 (OJJDP 1997:4) but the Uniform Crime Reports (UCR) indicates that in 1995, 18 percent of violent crimes in America were committed by youths under the age of 18 (UCR 1996, table 38, 218). The UCR contains statistical arrest information sent monthly by local law enforcement organizations to the FBI, which compiles and distributes the information throughout the country in a yearly volume titled *Crime in the United States.* Politicians have won elections based on "get tough on violent juvenile offenders" platforms using UCR data.

Another issue is whether the solution to the violence lies in the administration of harsher punishment of adults, or whether the violent nature of society itself might be changed by focusing on television, movies, and media.

Wheeler (1993) contends that adolescent violence has increased by 16 percent primarily because of the amount of television and movie watching done by youths (Brownstein 1996, 32–44). The Federal Communications Commission (FCC) has imposed ratings from R (restricted) to G (general audience) on television shows and movies in an attempt to regulate viewing. Corporate leaders in the entertainment industry feel that such government intervention is a first amendment infringement on their industry's rights. Recording artists have broken away from large recording companies that succumbed to government intervention and have formed their own record companies (e.g., Death Row Records). The entertainment industry argues that its products do not necessarily enhance violence in youths because they merely depict society from a historical perspective, and by its very nature, America historically has been a violent society.

Amid this debate lies the question of whether juvenile crime actually has increased. Albanese (1993) suggests that delinquency is not on the increase as a whole, but that the publicity given to specific violent delinquent situations may give the appearance that it is on the increase. Schwartz (1992) suggests that the U.S. juvenile population is decreasing and that by the year 2000 will have decreased to such a degree that delinquent crime, accordingly, will decrease sharply.

The juvenile justice system makes the final judgement on the juvenile offender. Appropriately referred to as a "system," all of the components of juvenile justice are interrelated and, ideally, should work together in support of juveniles. However, the most politically powerful components dominate policy issues. For example, the most powerful of the subsystems in juvenile justice, the juvenile court systems, tend to support personal political aspirations as they formulate and implement policies affecting juvenile offenders. One such example is the Violent Crime Control Act of 1994 (the Crime Bill).

The Crime Bill, one of the most sweeping anti-crime laws in contemporary U.S. society, not only focuses on adult criminal behavior and on women as victims of crimes, but also includes punishment for delinquent offenders. Although this bill contains provisions for prevention programs, it provides harsher sanctions for youthful offenders who commit violent acts. The Crime Bill appears to be facilitating a move in America away from the concept of *parens patriae,* as interpreted in nineteenth-century English common law to meet the needs of children under its care, to a more punitive philosophy as was dictated by the Hammurabic Code.

Historical Perspective

Parens Patriae and Its Legacy

In examining the juvenile justice system it is vital to consider its origins, and in considering the origins, it is important to discuss the evolution of the *parens patriae* doctrine. Although the doctrine has been used as the legal and moral foundation for the American juvenile justice system, it has raised concern regarding its theory as well as its practice (Pisciotta, 1982). Theoretically, *parens patriae* is intervention by authority, usually imposed on those considered unable or unwilling to make their own decisions. The authority is mandated to decide what is best for youths. Sometimes decisions have not worked out well for youths or society. Some critics of the justice system say that the best interests of youths are not served because the system has failed to protect their rights and to provide needed services. Other critics argue that the system has failed because youths are not held accountable for their delinquent acts and society is not being protected (Moore & Wakeling 1997), and hence, they call for harsher punishment.

The central premise of *parens patriae*—that parents are societal agents in child rearing—rests on the political environment of the society (Blustein 1983), and child-rearing practices are defined by society. Therefore, the doctrine has historically promoted a specific perception of parenthood: The application of parenthood provides an acceptable or unacceptable theory of child rearing that is determined by the state or by a person who holds authority to make the decision. The beginnings of *parens patriae* can be traced back to ancient Babylonia.

Hammurabic Code.   During the eighteenth century B.C., King Hammurabi of Babylonia, in an effort to create social order, established a set of laws for his subjects. The Hammurabic Code is considered by most criminologists to be the first written effort to codify laws (Allen & Simonsen 1992). *Parens patriae* grew out of these social control laws. The political environment during this period was based on a conservative ideology and the prevailing climate was one of societal protection. Children received harsh punishment. The laws did not separate delinquent acts of children from criminal acts of adults. Consequently, children who had committed only minor delinquent acts were treated as adults. They were not separated from adults in prisons, and were not given preferential treatment. If the act committed was punishable by sanction, then punitive measures, even hanging, were imposed based on the act itself, with no consideration for the age of the offender. There were no clear distinctions between the most serious crimes (felonies), and less serious crimes (misdemeanors). In addition, acts considered illegal only when minors display the behaviors—status offenses—did not go unpunished.

The Hammurabic Code specified that children should be severely punished if they disobeyed their parents or did not attend school. These status offenders were dealt with immediately: The expectation was that they would not commit the act again after receiving serious punishments ranging from whippings to mutilations. Children were expected to be obedient to their parents, and the father was regarded not only as the head of the household but as the primary punisher when the child misbehaved (Kramer 1963). This notion of fathers having unlimited, unquestioned control over children was a child-rearing practice that evolved into a central premise of *parens patriae,* which evolved with the Romans into *patria potestas.*

Patriae Potestas.   The Greek and Roman empires contributed much to the evolution of the concept of *parens patriae.* The Greeks as a democratic civilization encouraged individualism, freedom, and protection of rights and due process (the theory that a person is innocent until proved guilty). Contemporary U.S. society borrows much of its political ideology and architectural concepts, as well as many philosophies on government and family, from ancient Greek culture. As medical doctors continue to take the Hippocratic Oath, students of philosophy search for truth as they ponder over the wisdom of Socrates, Plato, and Aristotle, and students of military science study the strategies of Alexander the Great, American society continues to struggle with Draconian laws in discussions of issues of juvenile justice. The fifth and sixth centuries B.C. in ancient Greek history were considered a culturally intellectual and just period. However, during the seventh century, Draco, an Athenian statesman and lawmaker, felt that the Greeks were getting out of control. Draco imposed legal codes that were considered extremely severe and harsh: As applied to youths, Draco's laws ranged from beatings to public mutilations and even death.

U.S. philosophy still supports the belief in freedom and protection of individual rights, but increased numbers of violent acts by juvenile offenders in the United States has caused more punitive measures to be considered to control and reduce violence. Although mutilations are out of the question, the death penalty has been approved for youths seventeen and older based on a 1989 Supreme Court decision (*Wilkins v. Missouri*). And although public beatings have not been approved, some school systems still administer corporal punishment under the *parens patriae* doctrine.

The Romans, too, believed in ***due process:*** They were very much concerned about protecting each individual's rights. They prided themselves in formulating and religiously implementing laws that they deemed were the basis of a good republic. Roman law descends from a written code, the Twelve Tables (Abadinski 1991). The Twelve Tables underwent constant interpretation from Roman scholars. The constant revisions were meant to ensure that Roman laws were responding to the needs of their citizens (15). The Romans felt that their laws were fair to all classes of people within the Roman Empire, but some citizens received more "fairness" than others. For example, lawbreaking men received greater sympathetic consideration than did women and children. Men legally could sell family members (including children) into slavery when they deemed it necessary. Fathers could beat and mutilate their children. The father's absolute power over his family, ***patria potestas,*** meant to the Romans the power of life and death. This concept was modified slightly as it was adopted by English kings and translated into English common law. England, lacking a constitution, is bound even today by common law.

English Common Law.   Both ancient Roman law and English common law have had a great impact on U.S. society. In Rome, *parens patriae* had been extremely arbitrary and based primarily on harsh punishments, with the father as primary authoritarian. The tradition of fathers having authority over family continued in England but was not absolute. Two major factors in English culture interfered: the king and the Church of England. The people were guided by both in matters of punishment for children.

In England, the king was considered divine and was viewed as the father of the entire country. He thus assumed royal power and authority over every citizen. The English rewrote Roman laws to reflect justice in the name of His Majesty. The monarch's authority aroused great concern in the Church of England as royal sovereigns attempted to extend their powers to include dominance over the Church. The king's law became universal or "common" throughout the country in every aspect of life. English common law involves the customs and traditions that are used by the English courts in making decisions.

The king seized ultimate power as guardian over the destinies of children, and all youths were considered his wards. It was during this period that the idea of *parens patriae* was interpreted by the king (he made the laws and interpreted them) to allow his intervention into the lives of children as necessary, legitimate, and just.

Under English common law, although each family was responsible for its children, the king's responsibility was for all of his subjects. This role of responsibility was *parens patriae:* the king, as father of the country, assumed responsibility for the protection and conduct of his subjects. In this role, he ultimately was responsible for caring for children if there was disintegration of the family system. Monarchs took on this responsibility zealously when wealthy families were affected because the kingdom could inherit the wealth if the children became wards of the sovereign. The earliest recorded legal example in England of the use of *parens patriae* can be traced to *Wellesley v. Wellesley* (1827).

In *Wellesley v. Wellesley* the significant issue was whether the Court of Chancery could intervene and allow the Duke of Beaufort's children to be placed with their aunt after the death of their natural mother. It was the mother's last request that the three children be placed with their maternal aunt, Misses Long. The Duke attempted to get custody, citing the fact that they were his children. Misses Long's argument was that the Duke's adulterous affair with Helen Bligh and his move to Paris with her had created a separation between the Duke and his wife prior to her death. The court ruled in favor of Misses Long's claim to care for the children. The court's decision was based on the best interests of the children. Although this was one of the first recorded cases of the court's intervention on behalf of children, it started a legal tradition that would continue under *parens patriae* that had been passed from the Roman *patria potestas* and legally interpreted by the English Chancery court.

> The Court of Chancery has jurisdiction to appoint a guardian for infants, being Wards of the Court, excluding the father; and upon evidence that the father was living in a state of adultery, and had encouraged his children in swearing, keeping low company, etc. [sic], it was held a fit case to exercise the power to exclude him from the guardianship. (1078)

Undoubtedly, remnants of Roman law prevailed throughout colonial America and today in contemporary U.S. society. For example, one of the basic assumptions of the crime control model—guilty until proven innocent—can be traced to Roman law, whereas, according to English common law, in which the due process model prevails, a person is considered innocent until proven guilty. Thus, current examples of *parens patriae* have incorporated both Roman and English common law into the current U.S. legal structure (Pisciotta 1982).

Houses of Refuge. The ***houses of refuge,*** also called "houses of reformatory" and "reform schools," like other institutions that followed, were intended as shelters for impoverished children guilty of delinquent acts and as sanctuaries to shelter homeless children from the dangers of the streets. The first house of refuge, which is considered the first reformatory for youths, was built in 1825 in New York City, followed in 1826 by the establishment of a house of refuge in Philadelphia. Both were privately operated. The first public institution for juvenile offenders was established in Boston in 1826—the Boston House of

Reformation (McCarthy & Carr 1980). Houses of refuge soon appeared throughout the United States. The philosophy that inspired the development of the houses of refuge is similar to the theory behind a diversion program in contemporary society. Refuge houses were to be used primarily for children who committed minor delinquent acts, such as running away. The houses of refuge were also used as group homes, much like foster homes in contemporary society. They would provide a family-like atmosphere for children considered salvageable. Many of these children were committed to refuge houses for status offenses. Status offenses are less serious deviate acts committed by minors such as school truancy, curfew violation, and noncompliance to parental supervision.

Although the concept of refuge houses became popular and widespread, there were some legal challenges to their continued use. One landmark challenge to the state's right to commit children to refuge houses was the case of *Ex Parte Crouse* in 1838 in Philadelphia. Mary Anne Crouse was a child who refused to abide by the rules and regulations set forth by her mother. According to her mother, she was incorrigible and totally out of control and thus, the state committed her to the Philadelphia House of Refuge:

> . . . that the said infant by reason of vicious conduct, has rendered her control beyond the power of the said complainant, and made it manifestly requisite that from regard to the moral and future welfare of the said infant she should be placed under the guardianship of the managers of the House of Refuge. (p. 24)

Her father challenged the decision on the grounds that Mary Anne had not committed a crime, received no legal representation, and had not been given a jury trial. The appellate division, however, upheld the decision on the basis of *parens patriae,* ruling that the state has a responsibility to care for and protect children when parents fail to do so. The court's decision was based on the fact that the Philadelphia House of Refuge was established under provisions of a March 23, 1826, act that stipulated that the state had a right to lawfully place children in the House of Refuge when they were beyond the control of their parents:

> The House of Refuge is not a prison, but a school. Where reformation, and not punishment is the end, it may indeed be used as a prison for juvenile convicts who would else be committed to a common goal; and in respect to these, the constitutionality of the Act which incorporated it, stands clear of controversy. (24)

This was the first time in U.S. court history that the concept of *parens patriae* was used to resolve a court case dealing with children (Binder *et al.* 1997).

Another landmark case that challenged the use of the houses of refuge was *People Ex Rel. O'Connell v. Turner* (1870). Daniel O'Connell, age fifteen, was placed in the Reform School of Chicago. His father requested his release from the school because the youth, according to state statute, had not been convicted of a crime and had been imprisoned without due process of law. Robert Turner, superintendent of the house of refuge, was named as defendant in the case. The state's argument in the case was that according to the City Charter of Chicago, which had been approved by the legislature on February 13, 1863, it had a right to place Daniel in the reform school. The significant issue in this case was whether the Chicago legislature had the right to pass a law that would allow the arrest and confinement of a youth who had not committed a crime under state law. The court questioned why minors should be imprisoned if they had not committed a crime, and whether minors were afforded due process under the Charter Statute. They specifically referred to violations of the sixth (speedy trial) and seventh (public trial by an impartial jury) amendment rights. This landmark case raised a number of issues surrounding the reform school's ability to incarcerate youths who had not committed crimes and some researchers believe it was this case that led to the change in admittance policies of reform schools. The houses of refuge not only brought attention to the need to institutionalize some youths, but also focused attention on the need to protect juveniles and their rights.

Protecting Juveniles

Child Savers Movement.   The Child Savers were prominent middle-class citizens who, during the nineteenth century, advocated strongly for children's rights. The group included writers, doctors, legislators, and female activists. They believed society was mistreating children and actively campaigned to stop such atrocities as long work hours and poor treatment in houses of refuge. They focused on poor children because they believed poverty contributed to delinquent behavior. Therefore, they set out to elicit change in these children through government intervention (e.g., establishment of facilities that could change and care for these lower-class children).

Children in need of protection.
Hannah Gal/CORBIS.

The Child Savers formulated policies and lobbied against cruel treatment of these children. They viewed the placement of juvenile offenders with adult offenders not only as cruel, but as nonproductive. They felt that these children should be given an opportunity to continue to grow and develop their strengths in controlled environments appropriate to their maturity level so that they would not contaminate the rest of society. They also believed that placing youths with adult offenders would not deter delinquent activity but would promote it.

Today, some critics question the motives of the Child Savers, and accuse them of being concerned primarily with keeping the poor out of sight and contained. Among the most vocal critics of the Child Savers have been Sanford Fox, professor of law at Boston University, and Anthony Platt, professor of social work at California State University in Sacramento, both of whom believe that the Child Savers were not as humanitarian as they professed to be (Platt 1969). Platt depicts the Child Savers as stringent believers in crime control, which emphasized that social progress could not emerge without efficient law enforcement and strict supervision of children (p. 14). Delinquent youths were pathological, dangerous, and a threat to society, according to the Child Savers. It was their aim to get these misfits off the streets so that society would be protected.

Whatever their underlying motives, the result of their philosophical beliefs and legislative actions led to the creation of the first reform schools for youths in the United States. Reformatory schools helped to improve the behavior and attitudes of juveniles placed there. The earliest reform schools for children were established in New York City in 1825 and Boston in 1826. These early reformatories were designed with a cottage-style format and offered the most serious offenders an opportunity to amend their ways.

Elmira Reformatory (opened in 1876 in Elmira, New York) under its first superintendent, Zebulon Brockway, is considered to have led the way for other reform schools. Elmira has been hailed as one of the most progressive reform schools in early history because of its holistic approach to education (Eggleston 1989). This marked the first time in juvenile justice that education was considered important for incarcerated youths.

The reformatory was run in a military style, much like contemporary boot camps. It emphasized discipline, neatness, and special diets. Behavior modification was a primary treatment component, and youths were expected to work and drill long hours. Elmira was said to have prepared the youths for military duty by military "in your face" tactics—many of the former inmates served in World War I (Smith 1988). Personal attacks were made on Brockway's reputation because inmates were said to have been beaten severely. Brockway's techniques were recognized as questionable and, as a result, the Child Savers rallied for the development of a court system for youths.

The Creation of the Juvenile Court

The establishment of the juvenile court system should be considered one of the most revolutionary events relating to children's rights to occur in U.S. history. Although some critics would suggest that the legislation that created the court system was no more than political policy designed to control and further oppress children (Regoli & Hewitt 1997), others would suggest that any system is far better than no system at all. Like all major issues, the establishment of the first juvenile court is debatable because there is no general agreement as to which state had the very first special tribunal for children (Platt 1974). Some states, like

New York in 1872 and Massachusetts in 1874, had a special children's tribunal that was designed primarily to hear cases that dealt only with children and youths (McCarthy & Carr 1980). There is general agreement that the Illinois Juvenile Court Act of 1899 was the first official enactment that established the current juvenile court system in U.S. society.

The Illinois Act of 1899.   The first juvenile court was established in Cook County, Illinois, in 1899. The court emerged as the brainchild of members of the Chicago Women's Club in 1895 (Empey & Stafford 1991:58). Although these women initially had the idea for the establishment of a juvenile court system, many legislators did not think it was constitutional until a few attorneys who were members of the Chicago Bar Association considered the idea. They then wrote the Illinois Juvenile Court Act, which was presented to and passed by the legislature in 1899. It was strongly felt that juveniles should be heard in a system separate from the adult criminal system. Thus, the Women's Club along with the Chicago Bar Association set out to create a legal atmosphere that would guarantee the just treatment of juvenile offenders. The process began with a philosophy and goals different from those of adult court. Careful scrutiny of terminology to be used when dealing with youthful offenders became a priority. The first time the term "delinquent" was used legally was in the Illinois Act to describe a minor who committed serious behavioral acts punishable by law.

Six years after its establishment the juvenile court was faced with its first constitutional challenge.

Commonwealth v. Fisher.   The first landmark challenge to the powers of the juvenile court system was the case of *Commonwealth v. Fisher* (1905). Greg Fisher, who was 14 years old at the time of adjudication on a larceny charge, was committed to a house of refuge by the court. Fisher and his attorney alleged that he was being held unconstitutionally because the court had no authority to commit him. The U.S. Supreme Court ruled that the juvenile court did have a constitutional right to detain him based on his age and the notion that the juvenile court system was primarily established to rehabilitate and treat children, not to punish them.

This landmark ruling strengthened the philosophy and goals that had been defined by the Illinois Act that distinguished youthful offenders' treatment from that of adult criminals. It strengthened the child advocate's position that children should be rehabilitated and not punished. The implications of this ruling still stir controversial debate in contemporary society as the trend seems to be shifting in the direction of punishment. However, the goals and philosophy of the juvenile court system have not yet been changed to reflect the current climate in the country. They only have received modification by different states.

Philosophy and Goals.   The philosophy of the juvenile court system is derived from *parens patriae,* and treatment rather than punishment is a primary goal. In conjunction with rehabilitation and treatment, a primary objective is to protect children and create a safe environment for them during the rehabilitative process. Revenge, as used in the criminal system in the form of retribution, which implies "eye for eye," is not considered a useful or necessary tool in the juvenile system.

The juvenile court system is not a criminal system. As created by legislation, it is considered statutory and civil in nature. Most juvenile court systems are separate entities and located in the lower jurisdiction levels of the state court systems. There are many differences between the juvenile court system and the criminal system.

Differences and Similarities between Juvenile and Criminal Court Systems. Among the numerous differences and similarities between the juvenile and criminal systems, one major difference is the age factor: Minors are considered persons who are under the age of majority. Any violation of a penal code by a minor is considered a delinquent act, not a criminal offense. Although states differ widely in their definitions of delinquent acts, most states define such acts as offenses committed by children under the age of eighteen, although other states set the limit for delinquency at fifteen and under. Another major difference between the two systems is the terminology that describes their functions and participants. In the juvenile system, for example, children are not arrested—they are taken into custody; they do not go to trial—they are adjudicated delinquents; they are not sentenced—they are committed; and finally, they are not on parole—they receive aftercare. Other differences and similarities are delineated in Table 1.1.

Juvenile Courts in the Twentieth and the Twenty-First Centuries

Juvenile justice has changed a great deal, yet in many ways there has been little change. Theoretically the philosophy has always remained the *parens patriae,* but in practice the philosophy has been interpreted according to the needs of the particular culture. It has changed from one of protection to one of punishment during its evolutionary process.

Philosophical Changes. Prior to the twentieth century, juveniles were treated the same as adult offenders. There were no separate holding facilities and little attention was given to age differences of offenders. Youths of all ages who committed different levels of serious offenses simply were dealt the same consequences as their adult counterparts. Many of the

TABLE 1.1   **Differences and Similarities between Juvenile and Criminal Court Systems**

Differences	Similarities
age	components the same in both systems
terminology	plea bargains
no bail for youths (most states)	proof beyond reasonable doubt standard
no capital punishment for youths	Miranda warnings mandatory
parental involvement required for youths	right to counsel extended
referees may hear youth cases instead of judges	right to hearing
children's identity safeguarded	probation/aftercare option

youths who were involved in delinquent acts did not attend school and many were forced into horrendous child labor situations.

Juvenile court did not exist until early in the twentieth century, with the enactment of the Illinois Juvenile Court act of 1899. As a result, its creation marked the beginning of the separation of juveniles and adult offenders. Equally, it provided a philosophical foundation for basic assumptions that guide policies and decisions made about the juvenile delinquent. This philosophy of treatment and rehabilitation has been the topic of much criticism and reform during the twentieth century.

Criticism and Reform.   By 1925 almost every state had developed juvenile courts by legislative acts, and because juvenile courts were created legislatively, they were considered statutory. As juvenile courts emerged, each began to acquire unique aspects. For example, states differed on the age that a youth is deemed to be delinquent—most states define a minor as a person younger than 18, but there is a far greater difference in the definition of a juvenile delinquent among individual states. A generic term for *juvenile delinquent* is a minor who violates penal codes, but because states have the latitude to define what a minor is, the definition of juvenile delinquent varies from state to state. In Ohio, a juvenile delinquent is a youth 17 or younger who violates penal codes; in New York, Connecticut, and North Carolina, a juvenile delinquent is a person younger than 16 who violates penal codes.

The juvenile justice system has been much criticised by child advocates, media, and special interest groups. The criticism has focused on many areas, but major points have been (and continue to be): who is responsible for the juvenile delinquent's behavior (parents or the delinquent), the issue of offenders becoming younger and more violent, and finally, the disproportionate overrepresentation of minorities in the juvenile justice system.

North Carolina revamped its juvenile justice system with the passage of the Juvenile Justice Reform Act of 1998. One of the major provisions of this bill was to modify their undisciplined (status offender) category to include 16 and 17 year olds. In addition, many states have revisited their transfer of jurisdiction (sending the case to adult court) age to include younger offenders, and every state in the Union is grappling with considerations for offenders who are younger and younger. A major issue facing reform in the juvenile justice system is what to do with young offenders. Issues for the debate include discussions of

TABLE 1.2   Age Limits for Juvenile Court Jurisdiction

Age	States
15	Connecticut, New York, North Carolina
16	Georgia, New Hampshire, Illinois, Louisiana, Massachusetts, Michigan, Missouri, South Carolina, Texas, Wisconsin
17	All other states and the District of Columbia

Source: OJJDP, 1997 Statistics Summary, p. 30.

whether they are responsible for knowing right from wrong, and whether they should be incarcerated, as opposed to receiving treatment/counseling.

The juvenile justice system remains in a state of flux as attempts are made within the system to make modifications based on needs of the younger offenders and their families. Family courts are emerging in an attempt to provide holistic perspectives for the young offenders and their families. The goal is to address the needs of the family simultaneously with the needs of the youths in the family.

Another example of the issues that the system faces in light of increased violent actions on the part of younger offenders is continued gross violence portrayed in the media. Some youths emulate what they see on television or in the movies and often express limited understanding of why their acts were wrong, but also why there are negative consequences for their behavior. For example, a 12 year old in Florida killed his 7-year-old friend by inflicting wrestling moves on her while they were playing. The youth said that he saw the techniques while watching World Wrestling Federation wrestling matches. He methodically demonstrated the techniques on national television as he explained his defense.

The juvenile system is in the midst of a struggle to figure out what direction to take. It was originally created to provide rehabilitative services including protection, care, and safety for youths, but as delinquent offenders are becoming younger and are committing serious violent acts, the philosophy appears to be changing, leaning toward that of the adult system of punishment.

Although there have always been youths committing delinquent acts, violent youthful offenders seemed to emerge during the 1970s and 1980s and persisted throughout the 1990s. Juvenile reform in the 1970s focused primarily on deinstitutionalization of status offenders. A push by the federal government placed funds in communities that developed community-based programs. These programs seemed to divert youths from becoming involved with the juvenile system and with community correction programs. Some states, such as Massachusetts and Utah, closed their training schools and created a few treatment facilities for violent offenders (Drowns & Hess, p. 67).

Drug Economy.   The 1970s marked the beginning of large scale involvement of juveniles in the drug subculture. Youths were look-outs, watching for police officers as drug deals took place, runners delivering drugs to buyers, and mules carrying drugs to distributors. The 1980s extended juvenile involvement in the drug subculture as their roles increased to buying and distributing drugs. The thinking by "drug lords" that the introduction of youths into the drug world was a great investment was correct, primarily because they did not have to pay youths as much money, and if arrested they would not be committed for as long as an adult would be for the same offense.

With the widespread notoriety of the re-emergence of gangs and their involvement in the drug economy, juveniles, drugs, and violence soon gained great media coverage, a second major factor that influenced the shift to a crime control model for juveniles.

Media.   Television is a primary socialization agent in U.S. society (Marger 1996). As the nation watched more television with news stories focusing on drugs and youthful offenders, citizens became alarmed at the notion that youths were becoming increasingly violent. The media created believers and nonbelievers—some critics of the media suggested that the exaggeration and glamorizing of the drug subculture influenced more youths to become involved in selling and distributing drugs, because a large percentage of youths watched television and frequented movies.

The television and movie industries cater to this young audience by focusing on their subculture. For example, Ice T, a former rapper notorious for the controversial lyrics in his album "Cop Killer," has risen to Hollywood star status, appearing in numerous movies and a television series. Likewise Will Smith, another former rapper, rose to become a television series star (*Fresh Prince*) and moved on to become a movie star (*Ali*).

Along with converting rappers into movie stars to hold on to young urban viewers, the movie industry also suggests to youths that nudity, profanity, and sex are acceptable behaviors as they cast clean cut young stars such as Leonardo DiCaprio in sexually explicit leading roles (*Titanic*).

Not only do the media immediately alert the public to what is going on but they also serve as a vehicle for the public to voice their opinions (Gallup polls) about delinquents. Many media critics feel that reporters tend to focus only on the most heinous situations and on very young violent offenders, as when every major morning news show in America focused on the Jonesboro, Arkansas, incident in which five students and a teacher were killed in school by two young males (13 and 14) with guns. A third major factor influencing public opinion about youthful offenders and the shift to a "get tough" crime control model has been the accessibility, use, and misuse of guns.

Guns.   According to the OJJDP, between 1985 and 1994 the number of juvenile court cases involving violence and guns increased greatly. OJJDP reports crime against person up by 93 percent and weapons law violations up by 156 percent (OJJDP 1997:3). Although the UCR (1996) indicates that the violent crime rate declined in 1996 and was at its lowest since 1987 (p. 11), the proportion of violent crimes where firearms were used have remained essentially the same. But UCR reports that more persons under the age of 18 are using firearms. Firearms were the weapons of choice used in approximately seven of every ten murders committed by persons under 18 (UCR 1996).

The subject of youths and guns has caused many states to revisit their **bind over** (certify to the adult criminal system) age. Bind over occurs when the juvenile judge transfers jurisdiction of a juvenile case to the adult criminal system. More young offenders are committing crimes with guns because of easy access to firearms. Prior to the 1980s, the concern had been for the rehabilitation of young offenders, but now, as they become even younger, citizens wonder if there is a need for more citizen protection from the young offender and support the need for more stringent measures to stop violent behavior.

Public attention to youths with guns has been exacerbated by school incidents. Within a period of one recent year, five major incidents involved teens who used guns to murder students, teachers, and parents. In Springfield, Oregon, 15-year-old Kip Kinkel was considered unruly by his parents. On May 21, 1998, he killed both of his parents. Police reports indicated that the adolescent had been expelled from school because he had a gun on campus. In an argument with his father, the teenager became enraged and shot his father to death. When his mother returned home, he shot and killed her, too.

The Jonesboro Incident

Mitchell Johnson (13) and Andrew Golden (11), armed with pistols, opened fire on classmates and teachers at their middle school in Jonesboro, Arkansas, on March 24, 1998. In four minutes of firing 22 rounds of ammunition, they killed one teacher and 4 fellow students.

Jonesboro is in a rural area of northeastern Arkansas. Golden's mother is a postmaster and Johnson's father is a long-haul trucker. Both families are considered middle class. The children were taught how to shoot at a very young age. Arkansas law provides that these two children cannot be tried as adults. A major debate in Arkansas today is about changing the current minimum bind over age, now 14.

Do you believe that children are more violent today? Discuss issues of treatment versus punishment. Consider issues of parental liability. Should parents be held responsible for their child's easy access to guns?

In Pearl, Mississippi, 16-year-old Luke Woodham received three life sentences for killing his mother and two students in October 1997. In West Paducah, Kentucky, 14-year-old Michael Carneal killed three students at his high school. In Jonesboro, Arkansas, 13-year-old Mitchell Johnson and 11 year-old Andrew Golden shot and killed five students and one teacher at their middle school.

The five teens killed 14 people and wounded 44 others. These horrendous incidents have brought national attention to the use of guns by children, leading several states to begin reevaluating their gun laws, especially in relation to minors. Mississippi has made murder on school property a capital offense; Oregon is considering changing its bind over laws; and the entire Congress is seeking harsher penalties for people who sell firearms to children. The five incidents that spurred this reevaluation of minors with guns, however, were instigated by minors who acquired guns from their parents' homes. The powerful National Rifle Association (NRA) lobbies against such legislation (citing violation of the third amendment right to bear arms) and legislators seem to be staying away from passing laws that focus on parents with guns.

Some critics of the NRA suggest that the NRA is weakening politically. Intraorganizational power struggles, the passage of the Brady Bill (1993)—which requires a five-day waiting period to purchase a permit to carry a handgun—and decreased support by law enforcement officers when the NRA suggested that bullets that were capable of penetrating police vests should be available to the public are three factors that have contributed to this weakening.

One strategy a number of states use to control the increase in crimes by juveniles with guns is to decontrol guns, allowing for the passage of concealed weapon laws. These laws allow citizens who do not have a criminal history to purchase firearm permits and carry their guns. States with laws permitting concealed weapons have increased to 31.

A Burlington, Wisconsin, teenager got "cold feet" and informed school authorities of a plot to kill students, teachers, and school administrators on November 16, 1998.

Five 15- and 16-year-old high school students had planned to kill specific students and teachers from a hit list. The guns were from the home of one of the youths. This potentially violent school incident was stopped before anyone was killed, but other places, like Jonesboro, have not been so fortunate. Major concerns are not only the violent nature of the offenses but also that many targets are schools and that white, middle-class youths perpetuated these crimes. Many citizens in these communities voice disbelief that such violence could happen in their community. Such incidents have alerted the United States to the fact that violent juvenile behavior occurs throughout the country, not just in urban ghettos. Violence among youths has influenced the need for special provisions to be included in the Crime Bill.

Violent Crime Control and Law Enforcement Act of 1994.   The Violent Crime Control and Law Enforcement Act of 1994 called for the distribution of federal funds over a period of five years. More than $15 billion were allocated for this bill. It is one of the largest anti-crime bills that has been passed in the history of the United States—it represents the country's largest commitment of federal dollars to address the country's crime problem.

Although this bill is unique, containing a broad range of provisions emphasizing harsher punishment for serious offenders, gang members, and drug offenders, it is limited in its provisions for prevention programs for youthful offenders who may not be involved in drug or gang activities.

This bill strongly endorses ***community policing***—proactive policing in partnership with community residents—and makes over 60 federal crimes subject to the death penalty. Specific provisions of this crime bill relate to delinquent offenders:

1. The three strikes provision for youthful offenders prohibits adults from transferring a handgun to a person less than 18;
2. Offenders 13 years old and older can be tried as adults;
3. State funds are available for juvenile correctional facilities in an effort to ensure space for violent repeat offenders. These funds can be used for boot camp, "shock incarceration," weekend incarceration, and community service;
4. Funds are available specifically for programs to address youthful offenders who commit gang- and drug-related crimes; and
5. Funds are available for prevention programs such as drug courts and anti-gang activities.

Although opponents of the bill suggest that there is too much money in it and too few ways to evaluate outcomes, supporters argue that no amount of money is too much to stop the violence.

Juvenile Justice Today

Juvenile justice today is in a continual state of flux. How will the younger offender and the violent nature of offenses impact juvenile justice today and the future of justice in this millennium? Two major areas that will be influenced are parental liability and the disposition of young offenders.

Parental Liability.   Although some states have changed their laws to address the needs of younger offenders, many have considered parental liability as a means to control guns in the hands of youths. ***Parental liability laws*** provide consequences that parents or legal guardians must face as a result of their child's delinquent behavior. Parental liability laws have been used extensively by divisions of human services in instances of abuse and neglect from the outset. But they have become more prominent in cases of delinquency in recent years, probably influenced by the fact that the offenders have become younger and more violent.

In the school incidents, youths took guns from their parent's homes. California, in an effort to curtail gang violence, placed sanctions on parents of gang members who were involved in delinquent activity. The parents' sanctions could result in fines or prison time. North Carolina extended the application of its parental liability laws to the authority of the probation officer in October 1998. Whereas only a judge could cite parents and hold them responsible for their children's behavior, now probation officers can cite parents for contempt. Pennsylvania imposed parental liability in 1967. Speck (1968) reported, however, that there was no proved correlation between parental liability and lower delinquency rates.

A criticism of parental liability laws is that children might use these laws vindictively against their parents. They can commit an act knowing that the parents will receive punishment. Some critics believe that state intervention has gone too far when it punishes parents, yet offers the parents few options and little support when the youth is unwilling to abide by parental supervision.

Proponents of parental liability laws believe that children are the victims and that they act out in a delinquent manner in response to poor, limited, or no adult supervision. Many professionals believe that blaming these victims will not reduce delinquent behavior, and that adults interacting with troubled youths should take a closer look at their own behavior. Children often emulate adult behavior, although they lack a true understanding of the consequences of such behavior. Two examples for consideration are the father who killed an official at a children's hockey scrimmage and the mailing of anthrax-laced letters.

Thomas Junta, the "hockey dad," was convicted January 11, 2002, of involuntary manslaughter in the beating death of Michael Costin. The men had fought after Junta disagreed with Costin's call and Costin was killed. Junta claimed self-defense. The issue here is the impact of this assault on the children who witnessed it. Will the youngsters perceive such confrontational and aggressive behavior as an acceptable solution to disagreement?

After letters contaminated with anthrax spores arrived in legislators' offices in October 2001, a number of adolescents perpetuated anthrax hoaxes, such as leaving a white, powdery substance in a high school classroom. Irresponsible acts like this might once have been considered mere pranks, but in the aftermath of terrorist attacks, they affected people beyond the immediate communities. The people of the United States were more alert to perceived threats. Children and adolescents saw adults display new and different behavior, that of a people coming to grips with their country at war. In homes and schools people discussed violence and retaliatory measures—war planes bombing foreign lands—and terrorism. After the attacks, youths heard discussions of a new violence beyond the usual talk of violence on television, in the movies, and in their music, as well as face-to-face. The impact on youths of this new violence was not immediately measurable, but experts anticipated that whatever change the violence created in U.S. culture would become evident in the country's youths.

Young Offenders.   The U.S. system of jurisprudence adopted three underlying assumptions about age-related responsibility of children and youths from English common law: that children less than 7 years of age were presumed incapable of criminal intent; that 8- to 14-year-old offenders should not be held responsible for their behavior unless the state could prove that they knew right from wrong; and that offenders over the age of 14 can assume responsibility for their acts and deserve punishment (Allen & Simonsen 1998:317).

As younger children become delinquent offenders the court system has had some interesting challenges. Juvenile courts have not been equipped during the dispositional hearing phase to render traditional decisions because many programs have not geared up to effectively treat offenders under the age of 12. In many instances the courts simply order psychological or psychiatric counseling, and sometimes parents are not included in the counseling.

With cyberspace technology, the U.S. juvenile court system may conduct hearings over the Internet. Some states already videotape young offenders in the detention center. Child advocates question whether these techniques guard the confidentiality of the youths.

Confidentiality for juveniles has been a sensitive issue. To protect the identities of children involved in delinquent activities, using their faces in news stories was prohibited, and police officers were not allowed to photograph or fingerprint youths. In a move toward the integration of youth and adult offenders, these practices are being eliminated in some states.

With cyberspace technology, the courts may impose more home confinements in conjunction with electronic monitoring, with classroom instruction supplied over the Internet. Thus, the juvenile offender of the future may be more isolated. With this access, however, more Internet-related delinquent behavior may result in more white-collar delinquent offenses.

As the Internet becomes an integral part of the juvenile justice process, equal treatment of male and female offenders could occur because computer programs can be written without paternalistic program components. Cyberspace will have its impact on juvenile delinquency to an unimaginable extent.

Race, Ethnicity, and Gender: Historical Perspective.   Researchers seem to be in general agreement on issues of race and gender disparity in juvenile justice. Yet, although there is agreement, the circumstances and problems continue to persist. Since the time of the Hammurabic Code throughout subsequent history, consideration and attention were given to delinquent males; little attention was paid to delinquent females until the late twentieth century. Differences in treatment according to race have coexisted with those of gender. The Romans attempted to treat all of their citizens fairly, regardless of race: They just enslaved and otherwise punished citizens who did not pledge allegiance to the Roman empire or who were not wealthy.

Racial and Cultural Issues.   Researchers have documented differential treatment in the juvenile justice system based on race. The UCR continues to report that African-American

TABLE 1.3   1995 Arrests of Juveniles under the Age of 18

Charge	Estimated Number of Arrests	Age 12 & Younger	13–17	White	Black
Total	2,745,000	9%	23%	69%	28%
Crime Index Total	885,100	12%	20%	66%	31%
Violent Crime Index	147,700	8%	26%	48%	49%
Murder	3,300	3%	39%	39%	58%
Forcible Rape	5,500	11%	24%	54%	45%
Robbery	55,500	6%	26%	38%	60%
Aggravated assault	83,500	9%	25%	56%	42%
U.S. Population Ages 10–17	29,929,000	38%	12%	79%	15%

Source: OJJDP Juvenile Offenders and Victims Update on Violence 1997, p. 17.

youths are disproportionately over-represented in arrest rates. The arrest rate for African-American youths is higher in the violent crime category than for white youths in the same category: In 1995 African-American youths represented 15 percent of the American juvenile population although their arrest rate was 28 percent of all juvenile arrests (OJJDP 1997:17).

Empirical data suggest that police officers are likely to stop and arrest African-American youths more often than any other racial group. Race of police officers has been of little consequence in the high arrest rates among African-American youths. This phenomenon is explained by Nicholas Alex's thinking that African-American police officers arrest just as many (maybe even more) African-American youths as white because they do not want to be viewed by their colleagues as favoring African Americans. Also, they may receive more resistance from African-American youths because the youths view them as "selling out" or "Uncle Toms." Thus, the African-American youth views the juvenile justice system as adversarial beginning with the point of arrest.

African Americans who have committed delinquent acts enter the system with the added burden of knowing that they can expect a very negative experience. This attitude makes it very difficult for the probation officer to make a positive assessment of these youths and to make recommendations to the judge. Some probation officers recommend training schools because they want to change a youth's negative attitude and teach him a lesson. Others will ignore a youth's demeanor and try diversion programs, but fewer minority youths are referred to diversion programs than are their white counterparts.

Latino delinquents are next in disproportionate arrest rates. Their arrest rate is lower than that of African Americans, but not as low as white delinquent youths. Although not considered primarily a racial minority (based totally on physical characteristics), but as an ethnic minority (based on cultural differences), Latino youths are one of the fastest growing populations in U.S. society.

The language barrier is a major area of concern when working with Latino youths in the juvenile justice system. That so few police officers or court personnel speak Spanish creates communication barriers for the youths and their families. Minority youths from age

TABLE 1.4   **Ethnicity of Youths in Custody**

Race/Ethnicity	All Facilities	Public	Private
Total juveniles in custody	100%	100%	100%
White, non-Hispanic	37%	32%	53%
Minorities	63%	68%	47%
Black	40%	43%	34%
Hispanic	19%	21%	10%
Asian/Pacific Islander	2%	3%	1%
Native American	2%	1%	2%

Minority youth outnumber nonminority white youth in public custody facilities by more than two to one; in private facilities nonminority white youth slightly outnumber minority youth (1995).

Minorities were more than two-thirds of all juveniles in custody in public facilities and were just under one-half of juveniles in private facilities.

Source: OJJDP Juvenile Offenders and Victims: 1997. Statistical Summary, p. 42.

10 to 17 in 1995 comprised 32 percent of the U.S. population, yet they represented 68% of youths locked in detention centers (OJJDP 1997:42).

Gender.   American society has traditionally been paternalistic. Females have existed in the background, living in the shadow of males, almost invisibly. American society is uncomfortable about arresting and locking up female offenders. Male juvenile offenders are arrested twice as often as females for violent offenses and for status offenses. Yet, females have a higher incidence of runaway, a highly rated status offense. This disparity has fueled discussions around *selective law enforcement,* in which law enforcement officers use their discretion in making arrests.

Throughout history and within every recorded civilization, females have been the primary care providers. This has had an impact on decisions made by enforcers of laws. For example, many juvenile justice officers (traditionally a male-dominated occupation) believed that female delinquents needed to be protected—thus females received leniency in the system.

Perhaps the only period in American history when females were dealt with more harshly than males occurred during the Salem witch hunts (1647–1692), when females who were suspected of witchery were stoned to death or hanged. Regardless of age, females suspected of witchcraft were shown no mercy. Witchery was seen primarily as a female phenomenon, and although warlocks were reported, many more females were punished than males.

Witchcraft historically has been viewed as a crime punishable by death: "Thou shalt not suffer a witch to live" (Exodus 22:18), and witches have been viewed traditionally as people who practice crimes against nature. During the seventeenth century, witch-finding was a lucrative profession: Witch finders searched throughout Salem for females who had the "mark" of the witch and brought them to trial, before special judges and jurors. Between 1647 and 1692 in Salem, many females were accused of practicing witchcraft.

From the Salem witch period to today's United States, male decision makers have handed down selective justice. As a result of an amended civil rights act (1991) and antidiscrimination laws, more females have been able to enter the juvenile justice system in decision-making roles. The implication is that there may be less of a protective demeanor and one of more equal treatment in juvenile justice. Evidence suggests that nontraditional treatment methods are needed as female arrest and incarceration rates increase. It is possible, however, that if female arrest rates continue to increase, the treatment versus punishment pendulum might swing back to the treatment end of the continuum.

Processing a Juvenile Offender

The National Juvenile Justice Clearinghouse outlined methods for handling juvenile delinquents. These procedures, which can be viewed as phases of processing, are used throughout the United States and may vary minimally from state to state. For example, some states do not have a post-dispositional hearing, and other states may simply use different terminology, but the process entails application of the same methods. Most juvenile court proceedings function according to the same phases: pre-adjudicatory, adjudicatory, dispositional, and post-dispositional.

Pre-adjudication

The pre-adjudication phase occurs after the juvenile commits a delinquent act. An adult files a petition with the juvenile court intake worker who decides to take the case or refer it to another social agency. The *petition* is the legal affidavit that alleges the charges against the youth; it can be filed by any adult, parent, teacher, minister, or police officer. The **intake worker** assesses cases to determine which can be screened out of the system, referred to another agency, or assigned to a probation officer. Probation officers begin to gather data on the juvenile and the charge(s). They interview the juvenile and the juvenile's parents. In some states the intake worker may have these responsibilities as well. Written notifications of the charges are sent to the parents along with notification of any scheduled hearings. The probation officer prepares a report to present at the youth's hearing. Some court systems use referees to ease the court's backlog. Referees are hearing officers in the juvenile court system, and although they are not judges, they are used as judges' designees to sort cases. Although referees have authority to make placement decisions, judges do not relinquish all authority because they must sign off on all court orders.

Adjudication

The adjudication phase parallels the trial period in the criminal system. This is the phase in which the evidence is presented before the court and the judge determines whether a delinquent act has occurred. Delinquent acts are divided into three categories: felony, misdemeanor, or status offense. A **felony** is a serious offense such as murder, aggravated assault, or rape; a **misdemeanor** is a less serious offense such as vandalism. **Status offenses** include acts that would not be considered offenses if committed by an adult. For example, acts such as truancy, curfew violation, incorrigibility, and runaway are status offenses. Status offenders are further delineated into categories such as CHINS (children in need of supervision); PINS (persons in need of supervision); JINS (juveniles in need of supervision); YINS (youths in need of supervision); and FINS (families in need of supervision). The adjudication phase in the juvenile system is less formal than its counterpart in the criminal system. In the juvenile system, the judge may call upon other civilians to testify or provide evidence. Hearsay evidence is admissible in this situation. There usually is no jury and the juvenile is allowed to address the court on his or her own behalf even with legal representation present. It is the judge's responsibility to review the evidence and accept or reject the allegations on the petition.

Disposition

The dispositional hearing is held after the adjudicatory process. This is the time when the judge decides whether and how the child will be sanctioned. In this phase, the juvenile court judge has the flexibility to decide specific sanctions against the youth. Some choices include return placement into the home with the parents, restitution (the offender pays money or provides services to victims of the offense or to the community), dismissal of case, foster home placement, group home placement, institutionalization, drug rehabilitation, probation, and training school. At the dispositional hearing others such as ministers, teachers, and relatives are allowed to express their concerns about the sanctions and make additional recommendations. Many juvenile court judges will rely not only on the probation officers' recommendations as they make their dispositional decisions, but will also seek input from the *guardian ad litem*. The guardian *ad litem* is a person appointed by the court to act primarily for the best interest of the youth. Although the *guardian ad litem* investigates the youth's situation much like the probation officer, the major difference is that the former is usually a volunteer who is not bound by court rules and policies when making recommendations to the court.

Post-disposition

The post-dispositional stage parallels parole in the adult system and is known as aftercare in the juvenile system. *Aftercare* is supervision provided by the juvenile court system for children who have been returned to the community from juvenile correctional facilities. This period is important in that the transition is made from an institutional lifestyle to community readjustment. Many children and their families need support and encouragement during this phase, especially with school reentry and employment. Although readjustment to community living is an important process, some states do not provide this post-dispositional phase. Delinquent children return to the community from training schools (correctional facilities) ill-prepared and usually unable to make a satisfactory community adjustment, thus, the recidivism rate is extremely high.

According to Costellano (1986) many states have opted to move away from the *parens patriae* philosophy to a "justice" model. The provisions of law under these models can include determinate sentencing, increased due process rights, and formalized diversion processes with a focus on accountability as opposed to treatment.

Models of Justice

In the study of the treatment of juvenile offenders, it is important to consider various models of justice and their impact on the offender and on society as a whole. Models of justice simply are values underlying the juvenile justice system. Herbert Packer, a well-known criminologist, developed two prominent models of justice, crime control and due process.

Other more contemporary models that have been used to expand Packer's model are the rehabilitation model and the nurturing model.

Crime Control Model

The belief in the crime control model is based on the presumption that if police officers arrested more serious violent offenders and if the courts incarcerated them expeditiously, that would reduce serious violent delinquent offenders. This expectation relies heavily on selective law enforcement and speedy trial aspects of justice. The crime control model carries the presumption of guilt, implying that the delinquent is guilty until proved innocent. This does not presuppose that the police officer acts as judge, but the department's focus is on high efficiency rates and repression of the delinquent behavior (Inciardi 1998:11). The delinquent behavior is repressed by emphasizing law and order, high arrest rates, controlling crime, getting tough on crime, and greater reliance on police officers' needs to control crime better. This model is influenced greatly by the presiding political climate. The United States could be considered a strong advocate of the crime control model when one reviews the laws that have recently been enacted (e.g., Crime Bill). The media have also influenced the expansion of this model with programs, such as "America's Most Wanted," that call upon citizens to get involved in the fight against crime.

Due Process Model

The basis of the due process model is embedded in the belief in the formal structure of equality and individual rights. This would ensure limited constitutional violations. The due process version stresses that an individual is innocent until proven guilty. It emphasizes compassion for the rights of the juvenile delinquent and considers procedural rights its primary consideration. This paradigm was bolstered in the 1960s and 1970s as the U.S. Supreme Court ruled in favor of the individual rights of delinquent youths. *In re Gault,* a 1967 case in which the Supreme Court held that juveniles may not be denied basic due process rights (see Chapter 10 for more details), is a typical example of the Court's focus on ensuring delinquents the same rights under the constitution as adults.

Rehabilitation Model

The rehabilitation model stresses the need for treatment. The thinking is that even though a delinquent act may have been committed, the delinquency is simply a symptom of a greater problem that should be addressed. This model is based on the medical model, which places emphasis on illness and on the need for finding a cure for the illness if the person is to heal. This approach involves, to a great extent, family participation, and is often used with drug-related offenders.

Nurturing Model

This model originated in Colorado in 1989 and currently is used in mental health and school systems in numerous states. The contemporary nurturing model is emerging through partnerships between police officers, probation officers, parents, community residents, teachers, and social service workers. This approach embraces the notion of "it takes a village to raise a child." It is unique in that it takes into consideration issues of diversity, such as race, gender, religion, and sexual preference. The presumption is that in order for the youth to stop the delinquent behavior, a holistic treatment approach must be adopted that is inclusive of the child, parents, teachers, arresting officer, probation officer, and any other significant person in the child's life. Most traditional models focus only on the delinquent, and seldom on all the people who play a significant role in the life of the child. This model makes it possible not only for the child to take responsibility for the behavior, but also for adults to share the responsibility. The key components in this model are responsibility, accountability, and cultural competence (i.e., how diversity impacts the juvenile delinquent).

Although these models of justice all seem to have a "just deserts" premise, they have not been effective in significantly reducing delinquency. Perhaps the doctrine of *parens patriae* is outdated and there is a need to modify statutes involving justice models (Junger, 1981). Regardless of the model adopted, the juvenile court should be clear about its role either to treat or to punish the delinquent offender.

Treatment or Punishment

Some researchers (Feld 1992) believe that the problems and issues experienced by juvenile court systems throughout America will not be resolved with adversarial debates such as the treatment versus punishment argument. The pendulum seems to be swinging in the direction of punishment of juvenile offenders. Just as some Hammurabic laws were meant to control crime, so, too, are new laws and legislation passed in contemporary society. Many laws have been expanded to hold parents responsible for the delinquent behavior of their children. More children are placed in jails with adult inmates, and the accepted age for placing children in adult facilities is becoming increasingly lower. In many states the age at which a child can be tried in an adult criminal court is now 13.

Lowered Age Requirement

Many states have already lowered their minimum age requirement for bind over of offenders to the adult system. This change is a result of a sharp increase in the number of violent acts committed by younger and younger children. The transfer issue was heatedly debated in Michigan when 11-year-old Nate Abraham, the youngest offender to be tried as an adult, was found guilty of murder and sentenced to the adult system. This case heightened the debate across the United States about transfer age.

The uproar over increased juvenile crime has convinced legislators that there is a need to get tough on juvenile offenders. The Crime Bill (1994) signed by President Clinton specifically stipulates harsher punishment for youthful offenders and explicitly focuses on children who are gang members. With the tougher laws and harsher punishment, there may be little room for rehabilitation or treatment. Even though it would seem that there are fewer and fewer "child savers" as we approach the dawn of the twenty-first century, the good news is that not only is juvenile delinquency decreasing, but numerous diversion programs are emerging that focus on young serious offenders and their needs.

Summary

Initially, juveniles who committed criminal acts were whipped, mutilated, isolated to repent, or placed with adult offenders to be subjected to adult sanctions. There was no consideration for the need to rehabilitate until the Child Savers reform movement stimulated enough interest to establish the Illinois Juvenile Court Act of 1899.

The juvenile court system is statutory and was created primarily to provide treatment and rehabilitation and to separate delinquent offenders from adult criminals. As a result, two systems of justice emerged: the juvenile system and the adult criminal system. Though the two systems serve many of the same purposes, there are several distinct differences between them. Similarities and differences between the two systems are so closely related that points such as terminology and due process, as guaranteed by the Constitution, are closely scrutinized in both. Of major concern in the juvenile system is the development of uniform agreement upon factors such as age and definition of terminology.

The methods of processing a juvenile offender through the system are generally the same from state to state, but once juveniles enter the system, undergo treatment, and return to society, in some states there is no provision for an aftercare component. The present outcry to get tough on crime affects the juvenile offender as well as the adult offender. Many juvenile offenders are products of adult mentoring and often emulate adults who are involved in criminal acts. Yet, there is a constant attempt to blame the children. Even though it is difficult to locate children who can supply drugs and guns to the public without adult assistance, there is still a growing tendency to blame the children for the ever-increasing violence and criminal behavior in American society.

Although it is understandable that citizens and legislators may call for tougher laws that will inflict harsh punishment on youthful offenders, it is not comprehensible that 11- and 12-year-old children should be incarcerated with adult criminal offenders. Nor is it logical and sound reasoning to believe that harsh laws will deter young offenders from committing seriously violent acts.

It would appear that criminologists and other social scientists have taken a back seat to politicians in the debate. Perhaps social scientists should reclaim their position as trailblazers and return to the real issue of protecting children and their rights.

KEY CONCEPTS

adjudicate	felony	*parens patriae*
adjudication	*guardian ad litem*	*patria potestas*
aftercare	houses of refuge	referee
Child Savers	Illinois Act of 1899	reformatory
Commonwealth v. Fisher	juvenile delinquent	selective law enforcement
community policing	liability laws	status offender
delinquent child	minor	Violent Crime Control Act
Ex Parte Crouse (1838)	*O'Connell v. Turner*	*Wellesley v. Wellesley*

DISCUSSION QUESTIONS

1. Explain the concept of *parens patriae* and apply it to contemporary juvenile justice.

2. Discuss the landmark case that challenged the authority of the juvenile court system.

3. Discuss the Child Savers and the controversy that went along with their emergence. Are there child savers in contemporary U.S. society? If so, identify them. If not, why not?

4. What are some of the indications that contemporary American society is reverting to punishment philosophy as opposed to the rehabilitation model?

5. Identify the similarities and differences between the juvenile justice system and the criminal justice system.

EXERCISES

1. Talk with a juvenile offender and an adult criminal offender. Discover how they perceive the two different systems.

2. Form two groups. One group must defend the argument for treatment of juvenile offenders and the other group must defend the argument for punishment.

3. List some complications that child abuse reporting laws may create for children, parents, professionals, and social service organizations.

2 Patterns of Delinquency

CHAPTER OBJECTIVES

On competing this chapter, students will have tools to:

- Understand widely used methods for measuring delinquency
- Examine and describe patterns and trends in delinquency
- Identify methods used to measure chronic violent offenders
- Examine delinquency patterns in other nations

Juvenile Violence

When newscasters report about children who kill, people worry. News coverage of murder and violent crimes by adults raises fear and concern, but when the murderer, the mugger, or the rapist is a young person, it raises even greater concern. Juvenile violence invites questions about U.S. society and culture, deep questions about what's wrong with the way children grow up, with the places they live, with the kinds of things they learn. Each headline about young people committing violent acts raises concerns about the extent of the problem and the future.

Government statistics provide one source of answers to the problem of delinquency in America. Public officials, criminologists, and social workers are among those who look to statistics to find trends, to understand patterns, and to forecast issues. Juvenile crime statistics, along with primary research conducted by professional criminologists, represent the primary means of studying delinquency. The Federal Bureau of Investigation has provided arrest statistics since 1930; juvenile court statistics have been available since 1926. Juvenile crime can also be studied by surveying young people about their experiences as victims and perpetrators and by tracking groups of young people over time to explore the difference between delinquent and nondelinquent careers. A deeper understanding of American delinquency can be had by exploring patterns and trends in juvenile crime in other countries of the world. An understanding of delinquency in other nations allows for a broader understanding of domestic problems.

The first part of this chapter introduces the controversy over "superpredators" and collection of the first crime statistics in nineteenth century France. The second part explains the major sources of juvenile crime statistics: the Federal Bureau of Investigation's Uniform Crime Reports, Juvenile Court Statistics, and the National Crime Victimization Survey. The third part reviews the major strategies for primary research—self-report studies and cohort studies. The fourth part reviews patterns and trends in delinquency in the United States including geography, victims and offenders, trends over time, and the segment of chronic, violent offenders. The fifth part considers the problem of delinquency in Japan, Germany, and Russia.

Superpredators and Statistics

Juvenile crime statistics are a double-edged sword. One edge makes the social scientific study of delinquency possible. Government statistics furnish the basis for information about patterns and trends in juvenile crime. The other edge limits social scientists' knowledge. No source of information about juvenile crime is perfect; each source of official statistics has limitations. Official statistics both present and distort the understanding of delinquency in the United States, and this is nowhere more apparent than in the issue of superpredators.

The Coming of the Superpredator

In 1995, John J. DiIulio published an article in the *Weekly Standard* titled "The Coming of the Super-Predators." DiIulio, a Princeton political scientist with appointments at the Brookings Institution and the Manhattan Institute, wrote, "On the horizon . . . are tens of thousands of severely morally impoverished juvenile super-predators. They are perfectly capable of committing the most heinous acts of physical violence for the most trivial reasons . . . they fear neither the stigma of arrest or the pain of imprisonment." Many officials in the system, from prosecutors to police officers, reported experiencing this new generation of juvenile criminals. Some public officials, including members of the U.S. Congress and state and local legislators heard what DiIulio had to say, and took legislative action. Others, including those at the Office of Juvenile Justice and Delinquency Prevention (OJJDP) doubted that a new generation of chronic and violent young offenders was on the way. They took steps to dispel the "myth of the superpredator."

Drawing on the observations of juvenile justice professionals and earlier research, DiIulio wrote that a small percentage of young people committed the bulk of juvenile crime. He noted that the earliest research dealing with delinquent careers reported that about 6 percent of the delinquents were responsible for about 50 percent of the delinquency. Using this "6 percent to 50 percent" formula, DiIulio predicted a steep increase in the amount of juvenile crime based on demographic changes. By 2000, the U.S. population would include 500,000 boys between 14 and 17 years of age, or about 30,000 additional serious juvenile offenders. Using age shifts in California's population, DiIulio forecast that juvenile arrests would increase 30 percent by 2004. But that, he insisted, was only half of the story.

The other half of the story was that each generation of juvenile criminals proved themselves about three times as dangerous as the generation before. Later generations went on to commit more serious crimes than the previous generation. "It's not what's happening now," DiIulio warned, "but what's just around the corner—namely, a sharp increase in the number of super crime-prone young males" (DiIulio 1995, 24). He theorized that while most Americans grew up in stable homes with responsible parents, some came up in conditions of moral poverty. Moral poverty, as DiIulio defines it, is the lack of loving, capable, responsible adults who teach young people right from wrong. In the extreme, moral poverty means to grow up surrounded by deviant, delinquent, and criminal adults in abusive, fatherless, and jobless settings. Superpredators represent a generation of "radically present-oriented" and "radically self-regarding" young people who live for the moment with no sense of the future to guide them, who show no remorse for wrongdoing, who only regret being caught (DiIulio 1995, 26).

The OJJDP doubted the emergence of superpredators. "Earlier this decade," wrote OJJDP Administrator Shay Bilchik, "certain researchers promoted a theory of the emergence of a generation of young, violent 'superpredators' in the next century . . . Fortunately, however, these concerns have been greatly alleviated as juvenile crime indicators have persistently dropped over the past several years. The FBI's recently released 1998 crime statistics showing a one-year, 8-percent drop in juvenile violent crime arrests offer further reassurance that the day of the superpredator is not at hand" (Snyder & Sickmund 2000, 1). Cindy S. Lederman, presiding judge of the Miami–Dade Juvenile Court, has also observed: "Today's youth do not commit more acts of violence with greater regularity than their predecessors, but more juveniles are being arrested for violent acts . . . This means that the 'superpredator epidemic' does not exist" (Lederman 1999, 23).

To enable administrator Bilchick to make this observation, OJJDP researchers Howard Snyder and Melissa Sickmund analyzed juvenile crime statistics collected by the FBI and the Bureau of Justice Statistics. They pointed out that arrest rates increased during the 1990s for all age groups. The crime index increased due in large part to increases in aggravated assault, and the highest arrest rates for aggravated assault were found for people between the ages of 35 and 45. Arrest rate trends between 1981 and 1997 for juveniles reflected changes in public attitudes and law enforcement policy. The increase in juvenile arrests for curfew violations, for example, reflected a greater willingness on the part of law enforcement to enforce curfew laws and not an increase in the number of young people willing to break curfew laws. Increases in violent crime by juveniles can be explained by an increased law enforcement response to the crime of domestic violence. Society has become more sensitive to the problem of domestic violence, and juveniles involved in family violence are more subject to arrest. In addition, the OJJDP researchers pointed out that the growth in murders between 1987 and 1993 could be explained by the greater availability of firearms (Snyder & Sickmund 1999, 1–5).

Finally, Snyder and Sickmund challenged the basic strategy of predicting future violent crime trends based on the size of the juvenile population. They found that the juvenile arrest rate is unrelated to the size of the juvenile population. The juvenile arrest rate for violent crimes soared between 1987 and 1994 while the juvenile population increased only slightly; the juvenile arrest rate for violent crimes dropped dramatically between 1994 and 1997 while the juvenile population increased only slightly. "It is a fool's errand to try to predict future crime trends . . ." Snyder and Sickmund conclude, "No one has been able to predict juvenile violence trends accurately. It is clear, however, that the nation is not doomed to high levels of juvenile violence simply because the juvenile population will increase. As Attorney General Janet Reno has said, 'demography is not destiny'" (Snyder & Sickmund 1999, 6).

Quetelet and the First Crime Statistics

How could juvenile justice experts disagree so acutely about juvenile crime? In part, the disagreement over superpredators reflects the politics of juvenile justice policy making. Claims about trends and patterns in juvenile crime typically preface suggestions for changes in the response to juvenile offenders, and DiIulio and Bilchik represent two very different perspectives. DiIulio doubts that the government can have much impact on juvenile crime and relies instead on churches. Bilchik's OJJDP has offered a comprehensive strategy for dealing with juvenile crime based on the coordination of government agencies and community resources. The superpredator controversy is about more than politics, however. It also reflects something very basic about statistics: They conceal as much as they reveal.

The French government published the first national crime statistics in 1827. Annual publication of French crime statistics revealed that the incidence of criminality followed predictable patterns. L. A. J. Quetelet, a Belgian mathematician and astronomer, analyzed these statistics and noted several patterns. In his book, *Research on the Propensity for Crime and Different Ages,* Quetelet found a statistical correlation between age and crime that defined the contemporary study of delinquency. Quetelet reported that some people were more likely to commit crime than others, specifically young, poor, unemployed, and uneducated males (Bierne 1993, 78–79). Quetelet's analysis gave a scientific basis for observations that might otherwise have been attributed to the prejudices of an aristocratic Belgian critic of French society (Bierne 1993, 75, 79).

Quetelet observed that the annual number of homicides varied little from year to year, making it possible to forecast not only the number of homicides, but also the number of murder trials, convictions for murder, and sentences for murder. He also understood that the accuracy of his prediction relied on an assumption about what the statistics actually revealed. Any scientific analysis of crime must assume "a relationship pretty nearly invariable between offenses known and judged and the unknown sum total of offenses committed" (Bierne 1993, 80). In other words, Quetelet recognized that government statistics did not reflect every crime. Some unknown amount of crime was not reflected in the official records because the offenses remained secret or because the perpetrators had avoided appearing in court. For predictions based on statistics to be meaningful, it was necessary to assume that the amount of crime *known* to the authorities did not change relative to the amount *unknown* to authorities. If this were true, then it could be said that the trends observed in official statistics also occurred in society, in social behavior that could not be observed. **Quetelet's assumption** paved the way for much current statistical analysis in criminology.

Quetelet himself became interested in the normal distribution and its implications for criminal behavior. The normal distribution (or Gaussian distribution, after mathematician Karl Friedrich Gauss who formulated it) is an abstract mathematical concept describing the distribution of a variable within an infinite number of cases. When plotted on a graph using vertical (x) and horizontal (y) axes, the curve resembles a bell. The largest number of cases falls in the middle, around the statistical mean or average, with few exceptions at each end. A graph showing the height of women in the United States would show an average height of five feet seven inches, with most women within a inch or so of the average height and a few very tall women and a few very short women. Quetelet theorized that the typical or average person had propensity to break the law to greater or lesser extent that rarely resulted in criminal action. But some individuals represent unusual deviation that results in criminal behavior. These were persons of inferior moral stock, Quetelet said, such as vagrants, gypsies, and other inferior classes. Quetelet took the view that moral defectiveness was revealed in biological characteristics, particularly in the appearance of the face and head (Bierne 1993, 90–91). As clever as he was, Quetelet committed the most fundamental mistake in analyzing statistics. He could not resist the temptation to go beyond what the statistics actually revealed to argue his position.

Two important lessons can be learned from superpredators and statistics. One, meaningful interpretation of juvenile crime statistics depends on an understanding of the sources and methods of collection. Two, meaningful interpretation of juvenile crime statistics does not stray beyond what the statistics actually reveal.

Sources of Official Statistics

The sources of official juvenile crime statistics in the United States are the Uniform Crime Reports (UCR) published by the FBI; Juvenile Court Statistics (JCS) published by the National Center for Juvenile Justice (NCJJ); and the National Crime Victimization Survey (NCVS) published by the Bureau of Justice Statistics.

Uniform Crime Reports

The premiere source of crime statistics is, formally, *Crime in the United States: Uniform Crime Reports*. The FBI has published the UCR every year since 1930, when Congress authorized the FBI—known then as the Bureau of Investigation—to collect and publish national crime statistics and create the Division of Identification and Information within the Bureau.

Hoover and the UCR Program.   In 1925, J. Edgar Hoover, who had been appointed a year earlier to head the Bureau, told the House Appropriations Committee that the country needed a system for assembling uniform crime statistics. Congress did not agree. Hoover found an ally in the International Association of Chiefs of Police (IACP), an organization concerned with national crime statistics since its inception in 1894. The IACP had appointed a Committee on Uniform Crime Reports in 1927. After reviewing state criminal codes and evaluating record-keeping practices, the IACP committee completed a plan for crime reporting. In 1930, Hoover received Congressional approval and the Bureau began its reporting activities along the lines laid out by the IACP. The first report appeared in August 1930 with the director's name displayed prominently at the top of page one (IACP 1929).

The UCR is compiled by FBI statisticians from reports submitted by about 16,000 law enforcement organizations across the United States. Local law enforcement agencies submit crime data directly to FBI headquarters in Washington, D.C., or through state-level programs. In North Carolina, for example, the Division of Criminal Information of the State Bureau of Investigation (SBI) collects the information from law enforcement agencies throughout the state, then forwards this information to the national program. A number of states publish a Uniform Crime Report each year that is similar to the national report published by the FBI (NCSBI/UCR 1997).

Interpreting UCR Statistics.   Interpreting UCR statistics requires an understanding of distinction between **index** and **non-index crimes.** In 1929, when the UCR program was developed, the Committee on Uniform Crime Records of the International Association of Chiefs of Police recognized that not all crimes were reported to police. The committee evaluated various crimes based on their seriousness, frequency of occurrence, pervasiveness in all geographic areas of the country, and likelihood of being reported to law enforcement. The committee selected seven crimes to serve as an index for measuring fluctuations in the overall volume and rate of crime. Known as the crime index or Part I offenses, these seven crimes are: homicide, forcible rape, robbery, aggravated assault, burglary, larceny, theft, and motor vehicle theft. Congress added arson to the index in 1979.

The UCR contains less information for 21 less-serious crimes; these are the non-index or Part II offenses. Part II offenses include other assaults, offenses related to stolen property, vandalism, weapons offenses, sex offenses, drug abuse violations, liquor law offenses, disorderly conduct, and vagrancy. Part II offenses also include offenses of curfew, loitering, and runaway for persons under age 18.

The UCR program collects information on the age, race, and sex of persons arrested for both Part I and Part II offenses. Law enforcement agencies also report the number of Part I clearances that involve only offenders under the age of 18. Crimes are cleared in one of two ways: (1) at least one person is arrested, charged, or bound over for prosecution; or (2) when some element, by exceptional means and beyond the control of law enforcement, precludes arrest of the offender.

Technical Criticisms of the UCR.   How accurate is the UCR? Criminologists have noted several technical shortcomings with the UCR approach (McCleary, Neinstadt, & Ervin 1982, 361–372; Seidman & Couzens 1974, 457–493; Sherman, Christensen, & Henderson 1982):

1. *The dark figure of crime.* An unknown, but probably large, amount of delinquency goes unreported and therefore does not show up in UCR statistics. This is referred to as the "dark figure of crime."
2. *Limited participation.* The UCR program is voluntary. Not all law enforcement organizations submit reports and, therefore, UCR figures do not cover all jurisdictions within the United States. In 1966, the National Sheriff's Association established a committee on Uniform Crime Reporting in order to encourage sheriff's departments across the country to participate in the program. Coverage is about 93 percent for metropolitan areas and 89 percent for rural areas.

3. *Clerical error.* Among reporting departments, record-keeping varies from efficient to poor, and some delinquency may be lost due to clerical error. The UCR program relies on completion of "time-consuming and error-filled" summary reports by contributing agencies (NCSBI/UCR 1997, 7).

Incident-Based Reporting. In 1985, the FBI announced an enhanced UCR program featuring the National Incident-Based Reporting System (NIBRS).

NIBRS will collect data on each incident and arrest within 22 crime categories. For each offense known to police, incident, victim, property, offender, and arrestee information will be gathered when available. The goal of the UCR redesign is to modernize crime information by capturing the information presently maintained in law enforcement records. Incident-based reporting eliminates the monthly reports of contributing agencies; agencies submit a copy of their own crime reports and may submit automated reports on disk, on tape, or by electronic transfer.

To begin NIBRS, the FBI awarded a contract to develop new offense definitions for the enhanced system. This involved revising definitions of certain index offenses, identifying additional offenses to be reported, and developing data elements (incident details) for all UCR offenses. The FBI studied various state systems to select an experimental site for testing the programs and selected the South Carolina Law Enforcement Division. FBI computer experts designed automated data capture specifications for use in adapting South Carolina's data processing system to the UCR redesign. The FBI began receiving NIBRS data in 1989, and by 1997, 10 state systems and 3 individual agencies in Texas began supplying NIBRS format data (FBI/UCR 1997, 2–3).

Juvenile Court Statistics

Juvenile Court Statistics (JCS) have been available for about as long as UCR statistics. The Children's Bureau, then part of the U.S. Department of Labor, initiated the JCS in 1926 to provide information about the nature and extent of problems faced by juvenile courts. In 1952, responsibility was transferred from the Department of Health, Education and Welfare to the Law Enforcement Assistance Administration. Since 1975, the National Center for Juvenile Justice has had responsibility for the program. The National Center for Juvenile Justice collects, analyzes, and stores the information presented in the JCS as part of the National Juvenile Court Data Archive (Butts & Sickmund 1992, 11).

JCS is the primary source of information about the activities of the nation's juvenile courts. JCS contains information about the kinds of delinquent behavior that bring youths into juvenile court, about the characteristics of youths who appear before juvenile court, and about the court's response to delinquency cases. The data can be used to depict trends in referrals to juvenile court over several decades. JCS statistics provide a judicial source, rather than citizen reports to police, for measuring crime. The statistics furnish information about juvenile offenders. The most information that can be obtained about offenders is obtained in cases in which there has been a conviction. Curiously, judicial records were considered originally as the preferred source of information for what became the UCR program. Several of the consultants suggested judicial records before the IACP's committee decided on complaints to police (Maltz 1997, 34).

The National Juvenile Court Data Archive collects demographic, legal, and dispositional information on more than 600,000 delinquency and status offenses annually. JCS uses data from the archive, which are provided by state and county agencies responsible for collection of information about the processing of youths through juvenile courts. The juvenile courts that contribute information to the archive represent jurisdiction over 96 percent of the juvenile population. The archive receives two forms of data:

1. *Automated case-level data.* This information describes case characteristics such as age, gender, race, source of referral, offense charged, and type of disposition.
2. *Aggregate court-level data.* This information describes court activity, case flow characteristics, and the frequency and types of services offered by juvenile courts (Butts & Sickmund 1992, 10).

National estimates of court activity are developed using the case-level database, the court-level database, and county-level estimates of juvenile population.

JCS, like other official measures of delinquency, has limitations. The information contained in JCS reports is not the result of a census, a scientific sampling procedure, or a uniform data collection effort.

1. JCS statistics reflect the portion of juvenile crimes that comes to the attention of the juvenile court. The dark figure of crime—or the portion of unreported delinquency—limits JCS as well as UCR.
2. JCS statistics do not reflect every reported delinquent act. Cases involving multiple offenses are categorized according to the most serious offense. Similarly, multiple dispositions are categorized according to the most serious disposition (Butts & Sickmund 1992, 10).

National Crime Victimization Survey

The National Crime Victimization Survey (NCVS) measures the amount of crime by asking people in the United States whether they have been victims of crime. The NCVS began in 1972 as the National Crime Survey, a statistical program established by the Law Enforcement Assistance Administration (LEAA). In 1979, the program was transferred from LEAA to the Bureau of Justice Statistics (BJS). Data collection is conducted by the Bureau of the Census for the BJS under an interagency agreement (Lehnen & Skogan 1984, v).

The NCVS is based on a national sample of about 80,000 households across the United States. In 1992, 166,000 interviews were conducted in 84,000 housing units. NCVS has obtained a response rate of 95 percent or higher for households selected for these interviews. Households stay in the sample for three years; household members are interviewed seven times during this period. The initial interview is conducted in person; five of the next six are conducted by telephone. The interview begins with a brief screening questionnaire to determine if any crimes have occurred within the past 12 months. If crimes are reported, detailed questions are asked about the incident including time and place of occurrence, medical treatment, extent of economic loss, characteristics of the victim(s) and offender(s), and whether the crime was reported to the police.

NCVS measures rape, robbery, assault, burglary, personal and household larceny, and motor vehicle theft. NCVS does not measure murder, nor does it include "victimless crimes" of drunkenness, gambling, drug abuse, and prostitution. NCVS also does not measure crime where victims may have a reason to conceal activity, such as buying stolen property and fraud and embezzlement (BJS 1993). The NCVS collects information from victims about the age, race, and gender of offenders. NCVS also contains information about victims of crime and about the relationship between victims and offenders.

Technical Criticisms of NCVS.   Not everyone in the United States can be interviewed. Therefore, the NCVS is based on a random sample. That random sample provides a representative count of crime in the United States. NCVS also provides information about victims that could not be collected any other way. Nevertheless, researchers have noted several technical shortcomings:

1. *Memory loss.* The information is subject to the accuracy of recall and memory loss. Forgotten incidents are not reported.
2. *Telescoping.* Telescoping has to do with inaccurate reports about when incidents occurred. Events may have taken place later in time (forward telescoping) or earlier (backward telescoping) than the victim recalls.
3. *Compression.* There is a tendency for victims to compress events into more recent time periods. Victims tend to report incidents that occurred during the end of the six-month reference period.
4. *Blurred events.* Victims who repeatedly experience the same crime often blur these events. The memory of series crimes, such as household burglary or assault (domestic violence), cannot always be untangled into separate incidents (Taylor 1989, 3–5).

NCVS Redesign.   After an evaluation of NCVS in 1979 by the National Academy of Sciences, the BJS began a research program to redesign the survey. This redesign effort led to several improvements. BJS revised the screening strategy to aid respondent recall and provide additional information on the situations in which victimizations are likely to occur, resulting in improved reporting. The new screener asks about various life domains such as work and leisure and provides short cues to evoke memory. BJS has also used computer-assisted telephone interviewing (CATI) and computer-assisted personal interviewing (CAPI) developed by the Census Bureau. These techniques eliminate hand-coding of data, reduce the possibility of clerical error, and improve the speed of preparation (BJS 1989).

The Research Enterprise

None of the official sources of delinquency statistics represents an accurate measure of delinquency. In addition to the technical limitations of the various official data, there are conceptual limitations. Conceptual limitations are factors that make the information unsuitable for testing delinquency theory. For this reason, delinquency researchers have developed their own methods of data collection.

Conceptual Criticisms

In addition to technical limitations of various sources of official statistics, researchers have identified several aspects of official statistics that limit their usefulness as measures of delinquency. These conceptual criticisms make the application of delinquency theory problematic because they interfere with conventional social science methods.

1. *Official statistics record only legally defined categories of crime.* The definition of delinquent acts used in official crime statistics reflects prevailing social, cultural, and political influences. The conception of delinquency changes over time.
2. *Official statistics reflect the organizational priorities of the government agencies responsible for them.* Quite apart from the amount of delinquent behavior are changes in reporting practices, in statistical procedures and technology, in national and local campaigns against specific crimes, and in fluctuations in the ratio of police to citizens.
3. *Aggregation of data conceals significant characteristics of delinquency.* Official statistics capture trends, such as increases and decreases in the volume of delinquency over time. But these same statistics also conceal aspects of the delinquents themselves: Is an increase due to a few youths committing many delinquency acts, or many youths committing a few delinquent acts?

Major Research Strategies

The limitations of official sources of data have prompted delinquency researchers to develop their own methods for measuring delinquency. Self-report and cohort studies are two of these approaches.

Self-Report Studies. Unlike victimization surveys, which ask victims about delinquent acts committed against them, self-report surveys ask youths to report delinquent acts they themselves have committed. To collect this information, researchers distribute written survey forms to a group of young people and ask them to report the number of times they have engaged in particular delinquent acts. They also are asked whether these acts came to the attention of police and the juvenile court. The surveys ask youths for characteristics about themselves, such as age, race, gender, and family income, which are used to explain variations in delinquency.

In 1946, Austin Porterfield published the first self-report study of juvenile delinquency. He found that over 90 percent of the college students he surveyed admitted to having committed at least one felony crime (Porterfield 1946). The following year, James Wallerstein and J. C. Wyle extended Porterfield's study with a population of 700 juveniles. Of those surveyed, 91 percent admitted to at least one offense punishable by a year or more in prison and virtually all—99 percent—admitted to at least one offense for which they could have been arrested had they been caught (Wallerstein & Wyle 1947, 107–112).

In 1976, Suzanne Ageton and Delbert Elliott initiated the National Youth Survey (NYS), a nationwide self-report survey of more than 1,700 youths between the ages of 11 and 17. The youths resided in about 100 cities and towns across the nation, and included people of various economic and ethnic backgrounds. Elliott has collected information from this sample for more than 20 years (Ageton & Elliott 1978).

Cohort Studies.   The cohort study is a specific kind of longitudinal study. In a *cohort study,* a group of people who have something in common—they were born the same year, they graduated from high school the same year, they were arrested the same year—are studied over a period of time. Delinquency cohort studies include all people born in a particular year in a city or county. Researchers track their activities for a period of years. Using a combination of archival research (local police records, county records) and self-report surveys, cohort studies chronicle the delinquent careers of a group of people. By comparing those arrested with those not arrested, researchers can compare the life courses leading to delinquency.

Sheldon and Eleanor Glueck pioneered the cohort study of delinquency. To explore the array of biological, pyschological, and sociological factors that contribute to delinquency, the Gluecks compared 500 boys in a Massachusetts reformatory to a matched sample of boys from the Boston area. They matched the delinquents and the nondelinquents by age, race/ethnicity, neighborhood characteristics, and intelligence to help ensure that the two groups were similar. They tracked the two groups, beginning in 1939, for nearly two decades. They found that whereas the majority of those in the nondelinquent group remained law-abiding, the majority of those in the delinquent group continued to commit all sorts of crime between the ages of 17 and 25 (Glueck & Glueck 1950). Nearly 50 years after the Gluecks published the study, Robert Sampson and John H. Laub found their original computer cards while looking around in the basement of a library at Harvard University where the Gluecks' papers had been stored. They reanalyzed the Gluecks' data to explore links between juvenile delinquency and adult criminality. They concluded that although the Gluecks' conclusion about the continuity of illegal activity over the life course is essentially true, some change is possible (Sampson & Laub 1993).

Other important cohort studies have been conducted in Philadelphia, Pennsylvania; London, England; and Racine, Wisconsin. In 1972, Marvin Wolfgang, Robert Figlio, and Thorsten Sellin at the University of Pennsylvania published the results of a cohort study in Philadelphia. The cohort consisted of 9,945 males born in 1945 who resided in the city of Philadelphia from at least their tenth to eighteenth birthdays. The researchers collected information from official police records and from school records. They found that 3,475 of the boys had at least one contact with the police before they reached the age of 18. Compared to the nondelinquents, delinquents received less education and lower grades, came from lower class backgrounds, and had a greater probability of being arrested as an adult. Wolfgang's research coined the term "chronic offender." The researchers found that the 626 boys—6.3 percent of the total cohort—who committed five or more offenses were responsible for 51 percent of the total number of delinquent acts. Specifically, this fraction committed 71 percent of homicides, 73 percent of rapes, 82 percent of robberies, and 69 percent of aggravated assaults (Wolfgang, Figlio, & Sellin 1972).

Donald J. West and David P. Farrington studied a cohort of 396 boys from a working-class area of London who were born between 1951 and 1954. They counted convictions up to the twenty-fifth birthday (official statistics in England do not include arrests). They found that 132 of the boys had been convicted; they included 23 chronic offenders with 6 or more convictions who accounted for about half of all the convictions. When interviewed at age 18 or 19 and asked about offenses committed during the past 3 years, the chronics admitted to 30 percent of the burglaries, 32 percent of all thefts of vehicles, and 24 percent of all thefts from shops. Compared to the nonchronic offenders, the chronic offenders tended to have been convicted at an earlier age, to come from lower-income families, and to have had behavior problems at school (Blumstein, Farrington, and Moitra 1985, 187–220; West & Farrington 1977).

Lyle Shannon carried out a study involving three cohorts of people, both males and females, born in Racine, Wisconsin. Of a total of 6,127 people, 4,179 had resided in Racine from age 6 through age 32 for those born in 1942, through age 25 for those born in 1949, and through age 21 for those born in 1955. The researchers used about 6,000 police and court records. The researchers found that 90 percent of the males in each cohort had engaged in youthful misbehavior, as had 65 to 70 percent of the females. White females had the fewest contacts with police; black males had the most contacts with police. Police contacts occurred most frequently in the city of Racine. The researchers also found that although the pattern of delinquent behavior declined after the teenage years, increase and frequency of misbehavior typically occurred after instances of court sanction. Those with police contacts as juveniles were less likely to have police contacts as adults (Shannon 1982).

The National Longitudinal Survey of Youth (NLST).   The NLST combines self-report and cohort research methodologies. Information for the study comes from self-report surveys and includes information about behavior that does not come to the attention of juvenile justice authorities. The first wave of the study interviewed a national sample of 9,000 youth who were between the ages of 12 and 16 at the end of 1996. The first interviews were conducted during 1997 and 1998. The researchers found that about 22 percent had smoked cigarettes and 21 percent had drunk alcohol. About 14 percent had engaged in an assault, and a smaller proportion reported carrying a handgun (7 percent), belonging to a gang (2 percent) or selling drugs (1 percent). The prevalence of deviant behaviors did not vary by sex, race, or residence. Males and females, whites and nonwhites, and rural and urban youth were equally likely to report that they had engaged in most delinquent activities although there were significant exceptions. Males were more likely than females to have carried a handgun, purposely destroyed property, and engaged in assault. Whites were more likely than blacks to report they had smoked cigarettes and carried a handgun; blacks were more likely than whites to report that they had stolen something worth more than fifty dollars. Those living in rural areas were more likely than those in urban areas to report that they had drunk alcohol (OJJDP 2000).

Delinquency Patterns and Trends

What do the statistics reveal about delinquency? What do criminologists think they know about delinquent behavior?

Delinquency Rates

Rates are used to compare the incidence of delinquency through time and across jurisdictions. The fact that Los Angeles, New York City, and Miami have the highest numbers of violent juvenile crimes does not say much because these are among the nation's largest cities—more juveniles reside there. In order to compare the amount of delinquency in two or more jurisdictions of varying populations, researchers use rates. The delinquency rate shows the incidence of delinquency within a specific population. Rates are typically calculated annually, and usually for 100,000 juveniles. Rates may be calculated for several offenses or for a specific offense; rates can be calculated for regions of the country, for states, for counties, for cities, and for other jurisdictions.

To find the rate of violent juvenile crimes in the United States for 1997, for example, it is necessary to know the number of violent crimes reported and the number of juveniles living in the nation in that year. The total number of violent crimes (juveniles arrested for murder and nonnegligent manslaughter, forcible rape, robbery, and aggravated assault) is divided by the number of juveniles (the number of people in the United States between the ages of 10 and 17) then multiplied by 100,000. The result is the violent juvenile crime rate, the number of juvenile arrests for violent crimes per 100,000 juveniles.

The rate of violent juvenile crime for 1997 would be calculated as follows:

$$\frac{123,400}{30,640,000} \times 100,000 = 402.7$$

$$\frac{\text{number of violent juvenile arrests}}{\text{number of juveniles ages 10–17}} \times 100,000 = \text{juvenile crime rate}$$

The Geography of Delinquency

Violent juvenile crime is geographically concentrated. The FBI's violent crime index includes murder, forcible rape, robbery, and assault. The rate of arrests per 100,000 juveniles, ages 10 through 17, varies by state. In 1995, the District of Columbia had the highest rate (1,528). New York (996) and Florida (764) had the highest juvenile violent crime arrest rates of all states, followed by New Jersey (704), Maryland (674), and California (621). The states with the lowest rates were West Virginia (89) and Vermont (29) (OJJDP 1997, 23).

Within these states, the rate of juvenile crime arrests varied substantially from community to community. In New York, for example, about a dozen counties near New York City had rates of 500 or above, although about the same number of counties, in the northern portion of the state, had rates between 0 and 100. In California, about 24 counties had rates of 500 or higher, 17 counties had rates between 300 and 500, about 8 counties had rates between 100 and 300, and about 5 counties had rates between 0 and 100.

The FBI's Supplemental Homicide Reports reveal that in 1995, about one-third of all murders of juveniles in the United States were geographically concentrated in 10 counties. The major cities in these 10 counties (in order of highest number of murdered juveniles) are Los Angeles, Chicago, New York, Detroit, Dallas, Houston, Phoenix, San Bernadino,

Philadelphia, and St. Louis. No juveniles were murdered in 84 percent of more than 3,000 counties. In about 9 percent of counties nationally, only one juvenile was murdered (OJJDP 1997, 2). Similarly, 84 percent of counties in the United States reported no juvenile homicide offenders in 1995. Another 10 percent reported only a single homicide offender. About 25 percent of all juvenile homicide offenders were reported in just five counties: the major cities in those counties are Los Angeles, Chicago, Houston, Detroit, and New York City (OJJDP 1997, 11).

However, states with low violent crime index rates tend to have high rates of juvenile property crime. The FBI's property crime index calculates the number of property crimes (burglary, larceny, motor vehicle theft, and arson) for 10– through 17-year-olds per 100,000 10– through 17-year olds in the population. Delaware had the highest property crime index rate at 4,438. Other states with high property crime index rates included Wisconsin (4,613), Idaho (4,106), Oregon (3,987), South Dakota (3,894), and Utah (3,735) (Snyder 1997, 10).

Juvenile Victims and Offenders

Juveniles are more likely than adults to be victimized by violent crime. NCVS data show that the victimization rate for violent crimes for juveniles between the ages of 12 and 17 is nearly three times that of adults (116.3 per 1,000 juveniles compared to 43.1 per 1,000 adults) (OJJDP 1997, 4).

- Juveniles had higher victimization rates than adults in all types of communities (urban, suburban, and rural).
- The violent victimization rate for juvenile males was about 50 percent greater than for juvenile females.
- The overall victimization rate for white juveniles was similar to black juveniles.
- More than two-thirds of violent victimizations were not reported to law enforcement.

Higher rates of violent victimization of juveniles is explained partially by another pattern of juvenile crime: young people who are victimized typically are victimized by other young people. In 1994, about 74 percent of assaults on victims from 12 to 19, and 61 percent of robberies were committed by offenders from 12 to 20 (Clarke 1998, 6). Almost one-third of all violent victimizations against juveniles 12 or older were committed by schoolmates (5).

For all violent crimes, juveniles are most likely to be victimized by someone they know. About 60 percent of violent crimes were perpetrated by acquaintances, 35 percent by strangers, and 5 percent by family members. This same pattern is true for rape/sexual assault and for assault. In about 77 percent of rape/sexual assault victimizations and in about 61 percent of assaults, the assailant is an acquaintance. This pattern is not true for robbery, however. In about 51 percent of robberies, the assailant is a stranger. In about 36 percent of robberies, the offender was an acquaintance and in about 12 percent, the offender was a family member (OJJDP 1997, 5).

The pattern of youth-on-youth crime is clear with murder. UCR statistics show that a juvenile, either alone or with other juveniles, were the offenders in 14 percent of all homicides for which an offender was identified in 1995. The FBI estimates that 21,600 people were murdered in the United States during 1995. According to the FBI's Supplementary Homicide Report (SHR) data, law enforcement agencies were able to identify the offender in 13,400, or about 62 percent, of these homicides. In the remaining 8,200 homicides, no offender was identified (OJJDP 1997, 12). This includes single- and multiple-offender murders (1,900 homicides, 2,300 juvenile offenders). Who did juvenile murderers kill in 1995? About 27 percent of victims were younger than 17, and about 57 percent of victims were younger than 24. Most (85 percent) of homicide victims were male. Slightly more (49 percent) were black than white (48 percent). About 79 percent of the victims of juvenile homicide were killed with a firearm (12).

When Delinquency Occurs

For years, police have suspected that after-school hours represent prime time for juvenile delinquency. Reports of crime to law enforcement agencies occur most frequently during late afternoon hours on school days. Information from the FBI's NIBRS indicates that juveniles are at greatest risk of becoming victims of juvenile crime at the end of the school day. The four hours following school, from 2 PM to 6 PM, represent the most dangerous time for young people. About one in five of all violent crimes with juvenile victims occurs between three in the afternoon and seven at night on school days (Snyder & Sickmund 1999, 34–35).

The amount of juvenile delinquency during after-school hours is likely even higher than that captured by police reports. Juveniles do not report a significant portion of victimizations to adults, and when they do tell an adult, they are more likely to choose some authority other than the police. When they report after-school victimizations, they are likely to report the victimization to school officials and may handle the matter themselves and not involve law enforcement. Because crimes in and around school are likely to be reported to school officials and not to police, such crimes may be less frequently reported than crimes occurring during other periods of the day (Snyder & Sickmund 1999, 34–35).

Delinquency Trends

Both UCR and NCVS statistics indicate that juvenile violent crime remained constant through most of the 1970s and 1980s, increased during the early 1990s, and has began to decrease in recent years.

UCR statistics reveal that during the 1980s, the rate of violent juvenile crime remained constant. In 1988, the juvenile violent crime arrest rate was nearly identical to the 1980 rate. In fact, this rate had changed little since the 1970s. In 1989, the rate began to increase. The rate increased 64 percent from 1988 to 1994, when it began to decrease. The juvenile violent crime arrest rate declined 12 percent from 1994 to 1996. Juvenile arrests for murder have shown the greatest decline in recent years. Between 1993 and 1996, juvenile murder arrest rates decreased 31 percent. Juvenile arrests for property crime have remained constant. From 1987 to 1993, when violent crime arrests increased significantly, juvenile arrests for property crimes remained about the same. In 1994, the juvenile property crime index began to fall as well. In 1996, the rate of 2,400 property crime arrests for every 100,000 youths in the United States between the ages of 10 and 17 years of age was the lowest in a decade (Snyder 1997, 6).

NCVS statistics reveal a similar pattern. Victim reports indicate that the juvenile violent crime rate changed little between 1973 and 1989. From 1989 to 1993, the rate at which juveniles committed violent crimes increased 43 percent. Then, from 1994 to 1995, the number of violent victimizations dropped 20 percent, the largest decline in the 25 year history of the NCVS statistical program. In fact, the rate of juvenile crime in 1995 had returned to the 1989 level. The largest decrease between 1994 and 1995 occurred in aggravated assaults, which fell by 32 percent (OJJDP 1997, 16).

Why did violent juvenile arrest rates rise in the 1980s? What explains the decline in arrest rates for violent juvenile offenders in recent years? Crime is extremely age-sensitive and fluctuations in the overall crime rates in recent years are explained by shifts in the age structure of the U.S. population. Young people from 15 to 24 commit most of the crime, and criminal activity decreases with age. Crime rates fluctuate with the portion of people in the U.S. population in their crime-prone years. Crime rates increased in the 1960s, then decreased during the 1980s, as the baby boom population (that is, the generation of people born in the years after World War II) reached and then aged out of their crime prone years (Steffensmeier & Harer 1991; Wilson 1985, 13–25).

The decline in violent juvenile crime cannot, however, be explained by a declining population of young people. The number of young people increased during the period that violent crime perpetrated by young people decreased. According to the U.S. Bureau of the Census, the estimated proportion of the national population from 10 to 19 remained about 14 percent from 1990 to 1996 (Clarke 1998, 6, 8).

It is likely that the rise and fall in the rate of violent juvenile crime had to do with drugs and guns. Alfred Blumstein and Erik Jonsson, researchers at Carnegie Mellon University, have explored juvenile violence and its relationship to illegal drug markets. They explain that during the 1980s, "crack" cocaine became popular in the nation's large cities. Crack had a powerful influence over drug markets because of its low price; it brought many users into the cocaine market because many low-income people could afford to purchase it, one "hit" at a time. In order to accommodate the increase in sales, drug sellers recruited larger numbers of sellers. Young people became the new sales force. They worked for less than adults and were more willing to take risks. As sellers recruited more juveniles to sell crack, juveniles armed themselves with guns for protection while transporting drugs or money—obviously they could not call on police for protection. As drug dealers armed themselves, more teenagers not involved in the drug trade armed themselves, either for protection or for enhanced status. As more teenagers carried guns to school and in their neighborhoods, firearms spread throughout the community, and with firearms came violence and murder (Clarke 1998, 8, 9; NIJ 1995).

Exactly why crack use declined in the mid-1990s is difficult to determine. More research is needed before it can be said which of the varied responses reduced crack use, or when its popularity fizzled on its own. Research conducted by the National Institute of Justice (NIJ) confirms that crack use has declined. In 1987, the NIJ began a study to measure drug use among people arrested in most large cities. The research relies on urinalysis to detect the use of cocaine within the previous 48 to 72 hours. Of 24 of the nation's largest cities, 10 showed a 10 percent decline in cocaine use among people of all ages who were arrested (Clarke 1998, 8, 9; Golub & Johnson 1997). Crack cocaine use did not decrease in all cities, and some small cities have reported no crack cocaine epidemic at all. It may be that the crack epidemic will bypass some cities. Or it may mean that the epidemic arrived in smaller cities later than larger cities (Clarke 1998).

Chronic Violent Offenders

Are juvenile offenders more violent than they were decades ago? Concern about the increase in juvenile crime arrests between the mid-1980s and the mid-1990s has led to concern that juvenile delinquents have changed. Does the United States face a new generation of violent, predatory juvenile criminals?

Howard N. Synder at the NCJJ researched this question. Using court records from Maricopa County, Arizona (Phoenix), he analyzed the delinquent careers of more than 151,000 juveniles who turned 18 between 1980 and 1995. He looked for changes across the 16 years in average number of referrals per offender and in the average number of violent referrals per offenders. If juvenile offenders are changing, the characteristics of those delinquents who graduated in 1980 should differ from those who graduated in more recent years. Synder's research did not find such differences (OJJDP 1997, 24–25).

Synder found that 15 percent of youths who had come to court had four or more delinquency referrals before they turned 18 and were responsible for 59 percent of each graduating class' serious referrals. The proportion of chronic offenders (those who had four or more referrals) in each graduating class remained constant throughout the 1980s, averaging 13 percent of all graduating class members. The graduating classes of the 1990s displayed an increase in chronic offender proportions, averaging 17 percent from 1992 to 1995. Although the number and proportion of chronic offenders grew over the cohorts, the nature of the individual offender's career remained the same (OJJDP 1997, 25).

He found that 8 percent of the youths in the graduating classes were charged with a violent offense by the time they reached the age of 18, and for most (83 percent) this was the only violent episode in their careers. A greater proportion of graduates in recent years had a violent offense referral (between 6 percent and 8 percent in the 1980s and 11 percent in the 1990s). The number of violent referrals in each career did not change across the classes. For most of the youths charged with a violent crime, this was the only violent episode in their delinquent careers. Today's violent youths commit the same number of violent acts as the violent youths of 15 years ago. What has changed is that a greater proportion of juveniles are committing violent acts (OJJDP 1997, 25).

Delinquency in Other Nations

Much delinquency research and theory deals with the United States. In other countries of the world, youth crime reveals patterns that place the United States in perspective. Japan, Russia, and Germany represent nations with economic and political systems comparable to the United States, but each has different social and ethnic divisions. Japan has one of the lowest crime rates among nations with an industrial economy and a democratic government, but a relatively high juvenile crime rate. Although the Soviet Union had a low crime rate, Russia experienced an increase in juvenile crime. Germany, which has a juvenile justice system comparable to that of the United States, also experienced an increase in juvenile crime following unification in 1990. Despite the differences, patterns of delinquency in all four nations share common aspects that place U.S. patterns in broader perspective.

One of the challenges to comparative juvenile delinquency study is finding comparable statistics. Some nations do not collect or publish juvenile crime statistics. Other nations collect the statistics, but because methods of data collection differ, the statistics cannot be compared directly. As is true of delinquency statistics in the United States, meaningful interpretation relies on an understanding of what the statistics represent. In Japan, the National Police Agency collects crime statistics and publishes a white paper on juveniles. The white paper includes the number of reported offenses per 100,000 people (crime rate) and the number of reported offenses cleared by police. The Soviet Union began collecting national crime statistics in 1928, but this information was not available to the public until 1989. During the Soviet period (1917–1992), delinquency statistics represented a government secret. In Russia, the Ministry of Internal Affairs of the Russian Federation collects crime statistics that show the number of crimes known to police. Crime data for the Federal Republic of Germany are collected by the Federal Police Office. Unlike UCR statistics, German police statistics count suspects and not arrested offenders. A suspect is someone who has been identified by the police through police investigation or from victim reports. Neither Japan, Russia, nor Germany conducts national victimization surveys comparable to the U.S. NCVS.

Japan

Japan provides an interesting example of a nation with one of the world's lowest crime rates, but a relatively high rate of delinquency.

Crime and Delinquency in Japan.   Of all the nations in the world with industrial economies and democratic forms of government, Japan has one of the lowest rates of crime. For almost every type of crime, the rate in the United States far exceeds that of Japan. Compared to Japan, the incidence of rape is 18 times higher and the incidence of homicide 8 times higher. The robbery rate in New York City is 270 times that of the rate in Tokyo. In fact, the only areas in which Japan's crime problem come anywhere close to the United States' is in the incidence of organized crime and juvenile offenses (Thornton & Endo 1992, 2).

Unlike the statistics for adult crime, the statistics for juvenile crime are relatively large and increasing. In 1982, police reported a "third wave" of juvenile delinquency with previous spikes occurring in 1951 and 1964. In 1995, two offenses, larceny and embezzlement increased (Thornton & Endo 1992, 107). In 1995, larceny, the largest category of juvenile crime, accounted for 66 percent of offenses under the Juvenile Penal Code, followed by embezzlement at 18 percent. (Most of the larceny cases were theft of parked bicycles.) Bodily injury accounted for about 5 percent. The largest category of juvenile Special Law offenders referred to public prosecutors (other than road traffic violators) was violations of the Law for Control of Poisonous and Powerful Agents, which accounted for 67 percent (Government of Japan, 1997, 8), including a small amount of glue sniffing and paint thinner abuse (Thornton & Endo 1992, 2).

A study of crime in one Japanese city, Kawagoe, found traffic offenses to be the most numerous violations. The local police confront hot rodders, *bosozoku*, a persistent problem. The majority of bosozoku are under 20 years of age and about half are dropouts from high school. They operate automobiles, as well as motorcycles, in a reckless manner, usually in swarms (Thornton and Endo 1992, 165). After the road traffic law was amended in 1978, the problem seemed to abate, but it persists. There are other large street gangs in Japan besides *bosozoku*. The *chinpira* are found in Japan's major cities. They wear bell-bottom trousers and short jackets. Their illegal activities include breaking into automobiles, auto thefts, rolling drunks, and extorting money from other adolescents (106).

Explaining Japanese Delinquency. Explanations for Japan's relatively low crime rate typically rely on the homogeneity of Japanese society. Japan is a closely knit society with a strong sense of community. This sense of community is tied to cultural values of respect for authority, a strong work ethic, and hierarchy (Thornton & Endo 1991, 28–33; Westerman & Burfeind 1991, 21–24). From this perspective, the explanation for Japan's delinquency problem begins with a discussion of the erosion of this traditional sense of community. The Japanese work ethic has produced a tremendous trade surplus for Japan, and world-wide sales of Japanese products. Recent opinion surveys among Japanese workers has shown that attitudes are changing. The "new breed" (*shinjinrui*) are abandoning the ethic of "all work and no play" to less work and greater pursuit of leisure (Thornton & Endo 1992, 29, 184–185).

Although there are distinctive features of Japanese society, the homogeneity of the Japanese people is a myth. Japan has no problems with ethnic conflict because the Japanese government refuses to acknowledge the presence of ethnic minorities in Japan. The Japanese government insists that there is only one race in Japan, Japanese, and simply overlooks Japan's other ethnic populations. Despite official ideology, Japan does have ethnic minorities; these include the Ainu of Hokkaido, resident Koreans and Chinese, and the Okinawans. The census contains no data on racial or ethnic minorities; ethnic minorities are invisible in census publications (Potter & Knepper 1996, 103–118). There is no minority crime problem in Japan because the Japanese government simply does not collect crime statistics for ethnic groups (Knepper & Potter 1998, 2–12).

Rather than the absence of conflict, the method of dealing with conflict explains Japan's low crime rate. Japan's criminal justice system operates on two tracks. The first is the formal process of apprehension, prosecution, and correction. Japan's criminal justice system was influenced by German law and legal institutions and U.S. concepts of due process and constitutional protections. Each stage of proceedings involves the usual roster of decision-makers: police, prosecutors, attorneys, and judges. The second track, which parallels the first, is an informal process for which there is no Western analog. A pattern of confession, repentance, and absolution dominates each stage. The players include not only the public officials, but offenders, victims, and their families. From the initial police interrogation to judicial sentencing, the vast majority of the accused confess, display repentance, seek forgiveness from their victims, and plead for mercy from the authorities. In return, offenders are treated with leniency: They are dropped from the formal process altogether. By any standard, Japanese criminal justice is extraordinarily lenient (Haley 1989, 195–196).

Russia

Changes in Russian society have numerous implications for delinquency. Since 1992, Russian society has experienced tremendous social, political, and economic change, placing tremendous strain on young people.

Social Change and Crime.   During the years of the Soviet Union, the people of Russia enjoyed a very low crime rate. Official figures made available in 1989 revealed that the Soviet Union had relatively little crime. In 1987, the Soviet crime rate was 558 crimes reported for every 100,000 people, compared to the U.S. rate that year of 5,550 crimes reported per 100,000 people. In other words, the United States had ten times more crime than the Soviet Union (Finckenauer 1995, 16).

In 1985, Mikhail Gorbachev became the leader of the Communist Party in the former Union of Soviet Socialist Republics. As president of the USSR, he initiated a series of fundamental changes in Soviet society including *glasnost* or "openness" and *perestroika* or "restructuring." These changes precipitated the breakup of the USSR in 1992 into separate republics, the largest being Russia. They also led to other changes in Russian society—the ugly side of *glasnost*—including pornography, homelessness, nationalist groups (such as the Russian *Pamyat* or "memory" society), black market profiteering, and organized crime (Finckenauer 1995, 12–13). During the first six months of 1992, following the breakup of the USSR, there were 1.3 million crimes in Russia alone. This figure represented about a 30 percent increase over the 1 million reported in 1991. The largest increases occurred in burglaries and property theft (Finckenauer 1995, 17).

During this period in 1992, juvenile crime increased by about 19 percent, and juvenile crime accounted for a larger portion of Russia's overall crime. In 1980, about 10 percent of Russian crime was attributed to juveniles; by 1992, this figure had increased to 18 percent. The largest categories of juvenile crime included theft of personal property, theft of state property, and hooliganism (a catchall category). The number of juvenile crimes in 1992 also included intentional homicides, intentional grave bodily injury, and rape—a larger portion of violent crimes among juveniles than earlier in the decade (Finckenauer 1995, 73). Russian public officials and Russian citizens feared that law enforcement had broken down and there was little to deter young lawbreakers (Finckenauer 1995, 17).

The amount of juvenile delinquency in Soviet successor states and former nations of the Soviet bloc in Eastern Europe increased as well. Government statistics showed an increase in juvenile crime in Bulgaria, Croatia, the Czech Republic, Estonia, Latvia, and Poland between 1992 and 1996 (Asquith 1998, 39). The level of increase raised concern, as did changes in particular categories of juvenile crime. The Estonian, Hungarian, Latvian, Moldovan, Polish, Slovak Republic, and Ukranian reports showed an increase in violent crimes committed by young people. Not only did murder by juveniles appear to have increased, but officials note an increase in the brutal and violent nature of murder, robbery, and rape (Asquith 1998, 40).

Explaining Russian Delinquency.   Although many Russians only recently have learned the extent of juvenile crime in Russia, the nation had a delinquency problem prior to *glasnost* and *perestroika*. From 1960 to 1970, juvenile crime represented the Soviet Union's biggest crime problem, particularly in the medium-sized, industrializing cities in the North, Siberia, and the Far East, which have a youthful male work force.

In fact, the Soviet Union had a gang problem. The first youth gang appeared in Kazan in 1978. After assaulting several citizens, 27 members (8 underage) were arrested and convicted: The gang's leader was executed by shooting. But for the city's teenagers, the gang had become legendary and wannabe groups formed first in Volga cities, then across the

Russia inherited the Soviet Union's juvenile gang problem. David and Peter Turnley/ CORBIS

country. The groups organized on a territorial basis. Each included the "peel" (12 to 14 years old) and "elder" (above 18 years old) members. The primary aim of each gang appeared to be fighting against other gangs. In Kazan, this became a war. In 1986, 1,700 teenagers' fights were reported by the city militia and in 1987, over 500. The war spread across the Volga region, and the gangs began to visit Moscow, where they acted like hooligans, robbed other teenagers, and assaulted passers-by at random (Sergeyer 1998, 102–104). The Lyubera gangs appeared shortly after the Kazan groups. First identified in Lyubertsy, a Moscow satellite city, these youths spent time in body-building clubs. They wore T-shirts and loose pants, cut their hair short, and were united by their hatred of foreign things. They, like the Kazan groups, used the commuter trains to make raids into Moscow, where they sought to "beat up punks and heavy metal fans" (Sergeyer 1998, 106).

The portrait of the typical Soviet delinquent, in fact, resembled a picture familiar in the United States. With a few exceptions, such as thieves of socialist property, most criminals in the USSR came from broken homes, alcoholic parents, and family incomes below the Soviet poverty level. The average educational level of offenders lagged behind that of the average Soviet citizen, and most were employed in jobs that relied on physical skill rather than specialized training (unemployment was not officially recognized) (Shelley 1980, 220–221). The breakup of the Soviet Union has intensified this pattern. In Russia, Poland, Ukraine, Latvia, and Moldova, the number of single-parent families is increasing.

A substantial portion of juvenile offenders in these countries have experienced family dissolution (Asquith 1998, 41–42).

In 1985, a Soviet decree against alcohol use provided for the restriction of alcoholic beverages, reduction of vineyards, closing of distilleries, and strict prohibition of alcohol use during working hours. All of these measures helped reduce the crime rate by half during the next two to three years (Sergeyeu 1998, 73).

Germany

Germany also experienced dramatic political change toward the end of the twentieth century. In 1990, the Federal Republic of Germany (West Germany) reunited with the German Democratic Republic (East Germany). The division occurred after World War II when the Allied powers divided the German Reich. A wall went up in the city of Berlin, dividing the eastern portion from the western portion. In 1990, the Berlin wall came down and the two Germanies became the Federal Republic of Germany. As a consequence of German unification in 1990, the criminal justice system had to be established in East Germany according to West German standards.

The German juvenile justice system resembles that of the United States. In 1923, the Youth Court Law provided a legal framework for dealing with juvenile offenders (14 to 17 years old) who formerly had fallen under the jurisdiction of the adult system. The youth court movement, beginning with creation of a separate youth department in Frankfurt in 1908, led to the creation of a separate system for responding to youth crime (Albrecht 1997, 236–239). The sanctions provided by the Youth Court Law used educational measures in conjunction with punishment. Although there is no German counterpart to the U.S. practice of police diversion into specific programs, German youth courts do practice diversion—exemption from a judicial sentence. Juvenile district attorneys and juvenile court judges attempt to adhere to a nonstigmatizing and informal approach (Kaiser 1992, 189).

Delinquency in Germany.   Crime rates in West Germany increased after World War II, then leveled off beginning about 1960. The juvenile crime rate remained relatively stable until the end of the 1980s and beginning of the 1990s, when there was a marked increase in juvenile crime. Crimes of violence, which had increased since the 1950s, increased as well.

At the same time, the proportion of juvenile offenders within the criminal population actually decreased. Whereas juveniles accounted for 15 percent of all suspects in 1980, their share dropped to 9.5 percent by 1991. Serious violent crimes, as well, remain rare events. Violent offenses accounted for about 15 percent of juvenile crimes in 1994; the largest categories of juvenile crime were theft (42 percent), aggravated theft (23 percent) and criminal damage (15 percent) (Albrecht 1997, 224). The increase can be explained by rise in petty theft. Property and nonviolent offenses far outweigh violent offenses in the population of female offenders. Among males, theft and criminal damage offenses comprise the largest categories of delinquency; serious violent offenses and drug offenses are few (Albrecht 1997, 243).

The geography of German delinquency resembles that of the United States. In West Germany, the highest rates of juvenile crime are reported for urban areas. Although the majority of Germans live in small cities (20,000 or fewer inhabitants), the highest number of offenses are recorded in the largest cities (32 percent in big cities compared to 21 percent in small cities) (Kaiser 1992, 187).

Explaining German Delinquency.   The incidence of crime among ethnic minorities in Germany provides a focus for understanding German delinquency. Unlike in crime statistics in the United States, crime suspects in Germany are identified by nationality. Official statistics kept by the government revealed higher rates of crime among ethnic populations in West Germany, including Italians, Greeks, Spaniards, and Turks. In 1960, the total suspect rate for non-Germans was more than twice as high as that of Germans, and by 1990 was more than four times as high (Chilton 1995, 330). The Turks, the most significant numerically, had murder and assaults between two and four times as high as Germans. Property crime rates for all ethnic minorities, including Turks, were lower. In 1993 almost half the police suspects (46 percent) were traced to foreign minority members and about a third (34 percent) of all juvenile offenders (the population of foreigners in Germany is about 8.7 percent) (Yeager 1997, 153–154). Police statistics reveal a greater prevalence of delinquency among ethnic minorities. By age 14 about 14 percent of ethnic minority youths have been suspected at least once of having committed a crime, compared to about 5 percent of German youths (Albrecht 1997, 244).

Unofficial statistics indicate that German youths are more frequently delinquent than ethnic minority youths. A self-report study of delinquency in one German city, Mannheim, found that German youths aged 14 to 21 were more likely to be involved in property, violent, and drug offenses (Yeager 1997, 154). Similarly, self-report information for the city of Bremen in the 1980s found no significant differences between foreign juveniles' and German juveniles' involvement in delinquency (Albrecht 1997, 244). The skinhead movement, which appeared in Hanover in 1984, also involved German youths between the ages of 14 and 21. The movement spread across both East and West German cities including Leipzig, Dresden, Munich, Wittenburg, and Cologne. "Skins" congregate in taverns, then search train stations in major cities in search of *kanaken*—people with darker skin color. Skinheads attacked a group of Vietnamese asylum-seekers in 1991 and set fire to homes of Turks near the northern town of Moellen in 1992 (Albrecht 1997, 245). Although skinheads style themselves as a Nazi political organization and have attracted international attention, the majority of skinheads know very little Nazi ideology. Skinheads also operate alongside juvenile gangs without skinhead rhetoric. One social worker estimates that gangs account for 90 percent of youth crime in Berlin (Douglas 1992, 113).

The pattern of ethnic involvement in delinquency in Germany is explained by patterns of immigrants. First-generation immigrants generally experience lower rates of offending than natives owing to improved conditions of living, housing, and medical care. Second-generation immigrants—the children of immigrants—generally have higher rates than their parents, especially in the area of property crimes. This occurs as the lowest segments of society fill up with immigrant groups and, relative to German natives, experience unemployment, bad housing, poverty, and insufficient vocational skills and training. As assimilation occurs, the criminality of immigrant groups tends to take on the crime rate of their adopted country (Yeager 1997, 156–157).

A similar pattern has unfolded in eastern Germany, the former German Democratic Republic. Delinquency information for eastern Germany, the *new länder,* have been collected, but because the criminal justice system there had yet to be fully developed, they are not wholly reliable. The statistics previously obtained in eastern Germany, which showed a lower rate of convictions than in western Germany, have been viewed with a great deal of skepticism. Statistics gathered since unification indicate an increase in juvenile crime along with an increase in crime in general. Statistics from 1993 and 1994 indicated the trend in delinquency rates in eastern Germany to converge with those in western Germany. Young people in the east are exposed to risks thought to produce delinquency and are more apt to break the law, particularly in auto theft (Albrecht 1997, 240). Crime and delinquency among ethnic minority youth can be explained by the same theories applied to German youth. These include poverty, family dissolution, absent/poor parenting, school problems, unemployment, and the prevalence of violence in movies and television (Albrecht 1997, 199).

Summary

The controversy over whether a new generation of superpredators is about to hit the streets reflects in part the difference in sources of information about juvenile crime. There are three sources of official statistics: the Uniform Crime Reports (UCR), collected by the Federal Bureau of Investigation; Juvenile Court Statistics (JCS), collected by the National Center for Juvenile Justice; and the National Crime Victimization Survey (NCVS), conducted by the Bureau of Justice Statistics. In addition, criminologists study crime through research. There are two primary research strategies for studying delinquency: self-report surveys, in which youth are asked to report their involvement in illegal activities, and cohort studies, in which researchers track groups of young people over time. Some research methodologies combine these approaches, such as the National Longitudinal Survey, a self-report survey of a cohort of 9,000 youths, which began in 1996.

The rate statistic is a prevalent statistic in delinquency research. It is useful for comparing the incidence of juvenile crime across years and jurisdictions. Delinquency rates vary by geography, time of day, and over time. Juvenile murder is concentrated in about 10 counties across the United States. After-school hours are the most frequent time of day for delinquent acts to occur. On the whole, delinquency rates remained constant during much of the 1970s and 1980s, increased during the 1990s, and have declined slightly during the past few years. Juveniles are more likely than adults to be victims of violent crime and most often the perpetrator is another juvenile. A small portion of youth—fewer than 15 percent—commit violent crimes, although that percentage may be increasing.

Compared to other nations, the United States has a higher rate of violent juvenile crime. At the same time, gangs and other juvenile crime problems appear in other counties. Japan has one of the lowest crime rates in the industrialized world, although it has relatively high rates of juvenile delinquency. Traffic offenses, involving Japanese "hot rodders," is a common offense. Juvenile crime increased in Russia following the restructuring of the government in 1992. Gangs, which appeared during the later years of the Soviet era, are also a problem, as they are in Germany. Juvenile crime in Germany increased during the 1990s after stable rates during the 1970s and 1980s. Most likely, this reflected the period of uncertainty following reunification. In each society, delinquents represent a similar portrait of young people from impoverished backgrounds, broken families and those with alcohol problems, and school problems. Juvenile crime represents a major issue for public officials in each nation.

KEY CONCEPTS

cohort studies	Juvenile Court Statistics	self-report studies
delinquency rate	National Crime	superpredator
incident-based reporting	Victimization Survey	Uniform Crime Reports
index and nonindex crimes	Quetelet's assumption	

DISCUSSION QUESTIONS

1. Which is the best source of delinquency statistics: the UCR, JCS, or NCVS? Why?

2. Make a list of three things "everybody should know" about delinquency based on the patterns and trends revealed in statistics and research.

3. Do young people in other countries engage in delinquent behavior for the same reasons as young people in the United States, or are delinquents in other countries motivated by a different set of causes?

LEARNING ACTIVITY: SMALL GROUPS

In the United States, delinquency statistics are provided for four races: white, black, Asian Pacific Islander, and American Indian/Alaskan Native. Not only is the United States the only nation in the world to use these categories, it is the only nation to collect and publish official statistics using racial categories.

Break into small groups. After reading the paragraphs that follow, decide if the federal government should continue to use the same racial categories, add to or change the categories in some way, or end the practice of race-coded delinquency statistics. Draft a policy statement for consideration by the U.S. Congress. Be prepared to defend it.

Juvenile arrest statistics disproportionately involve minority populations. According to the U.S. Bureau of the Census, in 1996 the juvenile population of the United States was 80 percent white, 15 percent black, and 5 percent other races (Hispanics are counted as white). According to the Federal Bureau of Investigation, in 1996, blacks and other races accounted for 61 percent of arrests for murder, 45 percent of arrests for rape, 60 percent of arrests for robbery, and 42 percent of arrests for aggravated assault (Snyder 1997, 3). These statistics have the appearance of objective statistical information, but they are not, because race cannot be objectively defined.

The categories used in UCR statistics follow the official scheme promulgated by the Office of Federal Statistical Policy and Standards (OFSPS), Office of Management and Budget, in 1978. There are four racial categories (white, black, American Indian/Alaskan Native, and Asian/Pacific Islander) and two ethnic groups (Hispanic Origin, Not of Hispanic Origin). The categories have no scientific or anthropological basis. The Office of Management and Budget and the Census Bureau insist that the categories reflect prevailing social perceptions of race, not science. Physical anthropologists have themselves all but abandoned the idea of race in their textbooks; one recent survey found only 2 of 22 physical anthropology textbooks used race to classify humans. Rather, these categories were conceived in cooperation with the U.S. Census Bureau in order to standardize collection of race data by federal data-collection agencies as well as by state agencies, which must comply with federal data collection requirements. Yet by attempting to provide a way for U.S. citizens to describe themselves, the categories reinforce popular misconceptions about an anthropological basis for race and links between race and criminality.

Race is a fluid, elastic, social, and political designation, not a discrete, mutually exclusive category of humankind. The majority of visible minorities in the United States, for which official statistics reveal disproportionate arrest rates, do not fall neatly into racial categories. A person with ancestors in the Dominican Republic, for example, may choose to identify as Dominican, be thought to be black, and be officially counted as Hispanic. People who identify as mixed or biracial may identify as African American, American Indian, or white. There are black people who look white, white people with black ancestors, as well as a growing number of people who have one white parent and one black parent. There is no Jewish race, for example, and presumably this is why no official statistics are broken down for Jewish Americans. But there is no identifiable black or African race either, no Asian or yellow race, no Indian or red race. Why are there official categories for these groups? It is a violation of the equal protection under law for the government to classify people according to arbitrary distinctions of skin color and ancestry (Knepper 1996, 104).

Yet flawed as they are, these categories are bases for official estimates of race and delinquency in the UCR. The UCR is the only official source for longitudinal delinquency data by race, yet coding changes over the years make it impossible to construct trend data for Latinos, Asians, and American Indians. There was no category for American Indians prior to 1953, and since then it included Alaskan Natives. Mexican Americans were defined as a separate race prior to 1942, then joined the white category between 1942 and 1980, after which they became part of the Hispanic ethnic group. Similarly, Japanese and Chinese Americans started out as separate races in 1953, then became the Asian race along with Pacific Islanders. The white and black categories have remained, however; given the historic "one drop" rule (all persons with a trace of African ancestry are considered black), black is a catch-all statistical category that includes persons of mixed white, Indian, Asian, and Spanish descent (Knepper 1996, 99–100).

The lack of an objective definition of race makes interpretation of current delinquency statistics problematic as well. It is impossible to determine racial background by appearance, yet no one knows what percentage of those identified in UCR statistics are based on the police officer's perception, or whether the arresting officer asked the individual to identify to which racial category they belonged. Did the arresting officer guess the race from the color of the person's skin, from the way the person spoke, or from the sound of the person's name? If the officer asked the person, did they choose black or some other category because there simply was no category to reflect their real racial and ethnic identity?

The NCVS has the same problems. In the NCVS, the race of offenders is determined by appearance. Information about the offender's race come from the victim's perception of the offender's race in personal crimes of violence. Violent personal crimes are often traumatic experiences resulting in general disorientation. Many of these crimes occur under vague circumstances, often at night, and criminal assailants do make attempts to conceal their identity. BJS statisticians acknowledge that "it is possible that victim preconceptions, or prejudices, at times may have influenced the attribution of offender characteristics." Not surprisingly, the NCVS includes only two racial categories: black and white. This is because victims simply cannot distinguish racial identity beyond these simple categories. Further, there is research indicating that victims over-identify black offenders; matching survey data with police records indicates that victims overestimate the number of incidents involving black suspects in comparison with police estimates of whether the suspect was white or black (Knepper 1996, 96–97).

The United States is the only country in the world to collect and publish crime statistics for race. When Statistics Canada, the branch of Canada's government responsible for its national crime statistics, attempted to introduce racial categories into the Canadian UCR in 1990, the Toronto police refused to collect them. Questions raised in Toronto and other provinces of Canada about the rationale and accuracy of the statistics led the Department of Justice in Canada to declare a moratorium on their collection in 1992. The Department of Justice Canada concluded that the statistics should not be used because data collection procedures rendered the figures unreliable and would distort analyses based on them. Some argue that the United States should follow Canada's lead and declare a similar moratorium. This would not prevent research into delinquency and race, but would improve it. Researchers would need to use classification schemes based on self-identity, which is the only valid measure of race (Knepper 1996, 111–112).

3 Theories of Delinquency: Biopsychological Explanations

CHAPTER OBJECTIVES

On completing this chapter, students will have tools to:

- Understand biological theories that explain delinquent behavior
- Understand contemporary thought about biological theories
- Apply biological theories to specific cases
- Gain a contemporary understanding of Lombroso's body type theory
- Consider genetic experiments conducted in the United States and their implications

Why Study Theories?

Discussion of theories may be boring to students because theories generally are presented in the abstract, which makes them difficult to understand and remember—there is nothing to tie them to real life. So why are theories important? In juvenile delinquency studies, familiarity with many theories places students in a better position to develop a keen understanding of delinquent behavior. Delinquents, like other sociological groups, differ in gender, race, religion, and age. To attempt to apply one theoretical conceptualization to all delinquents is analogous to trying to make every person in the United States attend only operas. Some would enjoy it but many would object and not attend. If crime increased each time there was an opera, it would be necessary to determine who was committing crime, why they were committing crime, and how to stop or reduce crimes during opera performances. Immediately, a variety of theories about the who and why of opera-performance-related crime would be advanced, and would be followed by proposals of theories about what to do to stop or reduce the crime rate. If crime continued to escalate without explanation other than the untested theories that were posed immediately, the options for solving the problem would be limited. The more theories that are available, the more options that are available for devising a solution.

Accordingly, theory is important in helping us to understand, explain, and predict delinquent behavior (McConnell 1994). Understanding many theories of delinquency is necessary because delinquents themselves are diverse and one theory cannot be applied effectively to all. If social scientists can explain why children pick up guns and shoot others, then perhaps these children can be helped to understand their own behavior. Perhaps changes in policies and laws will not only help these children to understand and change their behaviors, but may prevent or limit similar occurrences in the future. This chapter introduces three broad theoretical frameworks—biological, psychological, and sociological—only to provide an initial overview of all three. When social scientists understand (via theory) why youths behave a certain way, it is easier to explain their behavior and to assist them to make positive changes. Social scientists must be able to understand their own behaviors and attitudes, especially when they interact with youths, because although youths may not be able to academically label adults' reactions and actions, they can "read" adults very well. Adults who understand themselves more effectively can help children to understand themselves.

In today's society, young people are challenged by the pressures they experience: societal conflict and personal and interpersonal issues. They are dizzy with their internal struggle with issues of identity, with sorting out what they are supposed to do about domestic violence, with the discrepancy between parental examples and society's expectations about drug use, with whether it is okay that their household includes two mothers or two fathers. As they progress developmentally, youths may feel that it is useless to discuss these conflicts with their parents and may attempt to resolve them on their own. And some, no matter how hard they try, may not find the answers they seek and may begin to release their frustration in the form of delinquent behaviors.

Although McConnell (1994) divided all theoretical frameworks into sociological, psychological, and biological, sometimes they overlap so that delinquent behavior may be explained by one or more of these factors, or perhaps by a combination of all three.

Sociological explanations of delinquency hold that it is caused by external forces that have an impact on behavior. External forces include anything in the environment with which the individual has contact, such as peer groups, or intangibles such as poverty. During the 1970s and 1980s some people believed that subliminal messages in television programs and musical lyrics caused juvenile delinquency. The "subliminal" theory has been largely abandoned: Television and music at the end of the first millennium and the beginning of the second explicitly depict sex and violence, leaving little need for subliminal messages. But certain kinds of music play an influential role in the lives of youths. Researchers have concluded that heavy metal and rap music have a negative effect on youths as it stimulates them toward violence and fosters a negative involvement with school work (Roe 1996). Singer *et al.* (1993) reached similar conclusions in their study of 715 suburban high school youths, finding that heavy metal, specifically, had an effect on delinquency, especially when parental supervision was low. Theorists have also discussed how music can lead to serious psychological problems in addition to delinquency (Singer, Simon, Levine, *et al.* 1993) The victimization of youths by corporate U.S. culture in setting standards for what's "cool" and what's not through television advertisements has been a major concern for study in the causes of delinquent behavior.

Psychological explanations of delinquency portray the individual as becoming delinquent due to internal forces such as depression, lack of self-esteem, or weak ego. In search of answers to the emotional state of youths, these explanations focus on motivational drives. This approach is gaining more and more popularity because of the reported increase in the violent nature of youthful offenses. In seeking answers to why youths pick up guns and shoot their classmates and teachers, researchers look to youths' mental state for answers. If youths are unable to discuss and express, in an acceptable manner, feelings of isolation, rage, anger, or frustration, they may act out their violent emotions by substituting actions for their feelings. These feelings may have built up for so long that when they release them, youths become out of control and extremely deadly. They may not be able to control their behavior and actions because they have not had an opportunity to express them in an acceptable manner. Their personalities may have developed around the frustrations, leading to the evolution of a personality that they are unfamiliar with and cannot control and they unleash these energies through violent acts.

Biological explanations of delinquent behavior focus on factors such as genetics, chemical imbalances, neuroscience, and even food ingestion. Some researchers are taking a closer look not only at foods consumed but at pesticides used in the growing of those foods as possible factors that impact behavior. This theory receives closer scrutiny as answers are sought about why children commit serious delinquent acts at very early ages. Foods contain so many chemicals, preservatives, and artificial ingredients that the ingredients that may be imposing a negative effect on other bodily chemicals cannot be determined. The Environmental Protection Agency (EPA) placed a ban on most uses of some farm pesticides primarily to protect children For example, the pesticides organophosphate and methyl parathion can no longer be used on many fruit and vegetable crops such as apples and turnips. Organophosphate, used as a chemical nerve agent during World War II, is one of the most commonly used pesticides for killing insects. When DDT was banned in 1972, it became the substitute of choice. The pesticide methyl parathion, a household insecticide, was responsible for the deaths of children in Tunica, Mississippi, in 1984 and for the severe illness of some in Pascagoula, Mississippi, in 1996 (Weld 1993, 1, 7a). Another speculation is that the feeding of small amounts of arsenic to chickens not only creates larger, fatter chickens, but expedites the growth and physical maturation of children who consume them.

Biological explanations for delinquency have been among the most debatable among social scientists because they have focused primarily on IQ, race, and gender as major variables. Negative contexts of these variables include biological explanations such as Murray's theory of the bell-shaped curve, in which he depicts minorities as predisposed to delinquency because of their lower test scores on standardized tests; Adolf Hitler's fantasy of making the world a better place by creating superhuman Germans and eliminating the "inferior Jewish race;" Lombroso's theory that criminals and delinquents can be easily identified by physical appearance; and Freud's rationale that females are inferior beings who are prone to commit delinquent acts because of their weak egos and their sexual deficits. A contemporary "time of the month" theory, based on hormonal research, was proposed by some theorists, such as Karen Horne and Katherine Dalton, who concluded that Pre Menstrual Syndrome (PMS) is associated with delinquent behavior.

This chapter on biopsychological explanations for delinquent behavior includes the classical models of traditional biological explanations and introduces contemporary perspectives in neuroscience.

Biopsychological Theories

Biological explanations of human behavior focus on genetic factors that make assumptions about human activity that has occurred in the past, is presently occurring, or is predicted to happen in the future. Students theorize about professors to help predict how well they will perform in a particular class. The first time they enter a class, they decide that maybe the professor is cool or think, "Oh boy, not another boring semester!" Such thinking is based on assumptions about the professor from the initial contact. The decision may be based on the professor's appearance, their ability to communicate, and the amount of work they expect in the class. The first two factors are easily explained in a biological perspective, because appearance will reveal race, gender, and physique, and communication can reveal nationality or speech impediments. Students may question why the professor's syllabus indicates so much hard work for them over the semester—why so many tests and so many chapters to read? If students look to a biological explanation for the professor's behavior, perhaps it can be found in the Freudian reasoning that the professor's growth and development as a child did not resolve a childhood crisis as delineated by one of the Freudian developmental stages. It is, of course, left up to the student to decide which of the stages in the professor's life went unresolved!

Freudian Theory

Sigmund Freud (1856–1939), considered the grandfather and creator of psychoanalysis, is perhaps the most renowned psychological theorist of modern time. Freud was born in Freiburg, Moravia (now Pribor in the Czech Republic), one of seven children of a Jewish

Sigmund Freud 1856–1939
Key Color/Index Stock Imagery, Inc.

wool merchant. He died in England of cancer of the jaw. He spent the majority of his life-time in Vienna, Austria, where he married and had a lucrative medical practice in neurology and neuropsychiatry. He was considered by some to be radical in his approach to treatment. He believed that all humans have secrets that are hidden in deep, dark corners of the mind. In his quest for answers to questions of the mind, he studied and practiced the art of hypnosis, interpreted dreams, experimented with self-analysis, and experimented with cocaine. He developed the psychoanalytic approach using such methods as free association.

Free association is based on the patient's willingness to spontaneously express ideas, and on a fundamental rule of an agreement of honesty (Thompson 1998, 697–715). The patient must be able to enter into an associative dialogue with the therapist that not only will unveil or reveal important information about the patient but also will assist the therapist in helping patients to resolve some of their conflicts (Hadar 1999, 109–127).

Freud revolutionized thinking related to growth and development of humans as he posited five primary stages of human development to explain behavior. He theorized behavior as phases of a psychosexual developmental process that involved conflicting traumatic episodes that needed to be resolved. He delineated five specific stages of human development—oral, anal, phallic, latency, and genital—which occur sequentially. Each stage was associated with a crisis.

Oral Stage (0 to 2 years).   This stage is dominated by innate reflexes that discharge *libidinal energy.* This libidinal energy is satisfied through sucking. Although the libidinal energy is considered sexual energy, the baby does not recognize this energy as sexual, but simply as a means of satisfying a need.

Anal Stage (18 months to 3 years).   A striving for self-mastery develops during this stage. The libido is organized around the anus. The child learns that retention and expulsion of feces is associated with pleasure. Children are pleased with the discovery and may want to handle and play in their urine and feces. During this stage, children discover that they can control some situations by their behavior—by producing or not producing a bowel movement in the little round container on which they are placed. Even though it is pleasurable to expel the bowels, children also experience pleasure and displeasure from the struggle with the parent during the toilet training process. The struggles associated with pleasure and displeasure between parent and child will continue throughout the growth and developmental periods. How they resolve the conflicts during toilet training and subsequent stages will impact the child's adult life and life choices.

Phallic Stage (4 to 6 years).   At the start of the fourth year, the libido becomes organized around genital stimulation. This stage encompasses the Oedipal and Electra complexes. During the Oedipal period (the male sexual experience in which the son falls in love with his mother because she is the one who has tended and cared for him for most of his life), the son perceives his father as a primary competitor for the mother's attention. That his father can sleep with his mother but he cannot, becomes a major basis for contention for the child to try to resolve. The child experiences love and hate for his father for being his rival and for his mother for taking the father's side. To resolve this struggle, the child uses a coping mechanism that Freud termed *repression* in which he represses, or does not think about this on a conscious level. A strong ego helps the child through this crisis.

The Electra complex is similar to the Oedipal complex but girls experience strong emotions—a love/hate relationship—toward their fathers. Wilkinson (1993) describes this as a genital dress rehearsal in which girls first experience genital femininity, masturbate, and hold sexual fantasies about their fathers (Wilkinson 1993, 313–330). The female's quest for her father's affection and attention continues as a major crisis in her life if not resolved.

Penis envy is Freud's explanation for teen pregnancy. The female is upset and angry that she does not have a penis and the baby is a reasonable substitute for this deficiency. G. B. Johnson (1966) as reported by Skinner (1997) concluded that female college students who kept pencils after a test, although in situations where male students returned theirs, were demonstrating their penis envy. Some contemporary psychoanalytic researchers have rejected the penis envy theory (Dahl 1996) and have substituted a feminist perspective. They maintain that the notion of penis envy is of little "mutative value" when preschool females discover that they do not have a penis because they do not become "shocked" as Freud speculated. Freud labeled the love/hate feelings for parents of opposite sex from the child's perspective. What happens in similar situations when both parents are of the same sex? What happens when there is only one parent and the child does not experience competition with the perceived lover or nemesis? When there is no male with whom to compete does society then become the nemesis? Does a specific male or female teacher earn that role from the child's perspective? Based on societal laws, the child learns that relationships between males and females are more acceptable than same sex relationships, so if the child experiences sexual feelings for a same-sex parent, are those, too, likely to be repressed?

Latency Stage (6–onset of adolescence). Children enter a period of sexual latency in which the libido is suppressed. It is a period when the child experiences more control over the id impulses and strives to build a stronger ego through learning and experiences. This is when puberty begins.

Genital Stage. Having experienced puberty, the child is sexually capable of reproducing the species but because of laws, policies, values, and beliefs, it becomes a struggle. Youths not only fantasize but their bodies now physically respond to their fantasies. The struggle is to find acceptable release for the sexual struggle.

Freud speculated that as humans leave one developmental stage and enter the next, problems continue to occur and escalate; if the individual is unable to resolve them, they carry over to the next stage, making smooth progression to the next phase difficult. He speculated that the id, ego, and superego all assist in development of the human personality.

Personality Structure (Id, Ego, and Superego). Personality is the condition or the traits that make individuals who they are. It is further described as individual inner qualities that provide lucidity in behavior (Leary 1999, 3–26). These qualities are consistent and change very little regardless of situation, which makes it possible to predict and understand human behavior (Shoda 1999, 155–181). Personality defines the person and contributes to making each individual distinctively different from others. These differences are a composite of heredity, environmental, and psychological factors. Freud theorized that the psychological factors that helped to explain personality were two-dimensional components of the mind (Zastrow & Kirst-Ashman 1994). Thus, his dichotomous construct of the mind consisted of two major components, each with sub-units of three parts. The first unit consists of three different levels: conscious, preconscious, and unconscious. The conscious level is the awareness area in which individuals are cognizant of conceptualizations and emotions. The preconscious level can be elevated to conscious; however, if not stimulated to become conscious, the ideas will remain in the preconscious state. The unconscious level is a level where secrets may be hidden that can be unleashed through dreams and, by some youths, in delinquent activities. For example, some delinquents may indicate that they did commit a delinquent act but also that they do not know why they did it. Probing into their unconsciousness may provide answers to the reasons.

Freud's explanation of personality proposed a second component of the mind that also consisted of three parts, the id, the ego, and the superego. The *id* is the intuitive, uncontrollable force that occurs sporadically. It is an instinctual drive that seeks immediate gratification. It functions purely on the need to achieve pleasure and receive immediate gratification regardless of the price to self or others and is referred to as the ***pleasure principle.*** Infants function primarily on the pleasure principle. They want things "right now" and nothing matters beyond instant satisfaction—all of their needs should be taken care of immediately. This narcissistic, self-centered thinking is a function of the id. If youths are not exposed to the reality that others exist in their world and that there are consequences for their id outbursts, then they may expect to do whatever they want without thought of consequences or of the well-being of others. Freud named the conscious act of thinking before acting or reacting the *ego.*

The ***ego*** is the force that suggests that thought should be given to the actions of the id. Primarily, it functions as an inhibitor to id responses as it attempts to process the actions of the id and make sense of those actions. It focuses on the need to understand laws, policies, and procedures and to gear the individual's behavior accordingly. Freud called this the reality principle (Brunetiere, Leguay, & Depond 1986, 99–102). The ego seeks appropriate or acceptable solutions to the needs of the id. The ego solves problems and is more rational than the id, attempting to shed light on situations that are instinctual behaviors for the id. It uses defense mechanisms, such as repression (blocking out something from consciousness) and regression (reverting back to a more primitive cognitive process) in its struggle with the id. The ego does not have an easy job, for it can enter into conflict with the id. If the id wins, the youth is said to have a weak ego. Treatment will focus on strengthening the ego to overpower the id when there is a conflict between the two. The ego has assistance from the conscience in this struggle.

The ***superego*** is the conscience that identifies what is morally and ethically correct. It governs guilt and shame and helps the individual to formulate a self-perception. The superego can be likened to a law enforcement officer in individuals' minds that alerts them to warnings and punishments. The struggle occurs when individuals are forced to adapt to larger societal norms that are different from their cultural norms. The superego is a repository for many thoughts that may have been repressed. Dream therapy, in which dreams are interpreted, is an important resource that can contribute to gaining insight and modifying the individual's behavior by bringing repressed information about a person's thoughts and behaviors to the surface (Berube 1999, 88–101). Freud theorized that dreams are helpful in explaining behavior and releasing stress and tension in the superego's effort to dispel or release some of the individual's drives.

Dream interpretation is a major focal point of Freud's psychoanalytical method. According to Freud, everyone dreams. Not all dreams are remembered, but those that are remembered are significant and can be interpreted as symbolic truths of past or future events. Morris (1998) used case examples to demonstrate the accuracy of dreams in uncovering what she termed "unconscious conflict" during the pre-Oedipal relationship between mother and daughter. The dreamer might not understand some of the dreams and might cope by repressing them (blocking them out of conscious memory) because their significance may be too painful. Psychoanalytical theorists believe it is necessary to bring the repressed information from the preconscious to the conscious level for the purposes of acknowledgment and resolution. Other coping strategies that Freud identified as defense mechanisms include denial, regression, rationalization, reaction formation, identification, compensation, projection, and sublimation.

Denial is a mechanism used often by delinquent youths. In an attempt to escape reality, they reject or withhold information under the pretense that they do not know the truth. Although they may very well understand and know, they find that not admitting the truth is less painful than admitting it, regardless of the consequences.

■ *Regression* occurs when adolescents are faced with situations that are too painful to bear. They bury the problem and their thoughts and feelings about it deep in the infantile unconsciousness. Children who experience sexual abuse tend to regress because they feel safer in an infantile state in which they once were safe and happy. Regression differs from repression in that the individual reverts to an earlier stage of development and functions according to characteristics unique to that stage. In repression, the painful thoughts simply are blocked out of the conscious mind.

■ *Rationalization* is demonstrated by delinquents in their effort to make sense of their behavior to themselves and to others by hiding their real intentions or purposes, concocting excuses for their behavior, perhaps explaining that they stayed out late because the movie did not end until late.

■ *Reaction formation* is seen in delinquents' efforts to act the way they are expected to in specific circumstances, turning their attitudes and behaviors on and off based on the situation. For example, if ordered to see a psychologist for evaluation, they may react opposite from the way they ordinarily behave. Or they may overreact in an effort to be committed to a mental health unit instead of a juvenile facility.

■ *Identification* is a coping device in which adolescents take on the attitudes and behaviors of their idols or role models. For example, some delinquent youths will emulate drug dealers in mannerisms and attire.

■ *Compensation* takes effect when youths are not successful in one endeavor and focus on another area in which they may find success. Delinquent youths who experience few or no successes in school may seek success in the illegal world, perhaps discovering success in stealing cars even though they cannot experience it in math, science, and English.

■ *Projection* is the ploy of casting blame on someone else in an effort to shed responsibility for their own behavior and make someone else the scapegoat. Delinquent youth may claim that they became delinquent because their parents did not love them or spend enough time with them, when in fact, the parents were always available.

■ *Sublimation* is the mechanism in which negative behaviors are turned into positive ones, as in the example of a delinquent youth who sells drugs then using his newly acquired mathematics skills in class to calculate equations.

The Freudian approach may be useful when working one-on-one over long periods with delinquent children who have experienced physical and sexual abuse, rather than with groups of delinquent children. Other children may not respond as well to this approach and may be in need of a shorter-term approach.

A major contemporary criticism of Freud's work is related to his belief that females have weak egos and are guided by sexual promiscuity and penis envy. Freud came to these conclusions because many of his patients were women who were experiencing problems resolving some of their conflicts. This was his baseline, but he did not perform comparative research to determine if "well" women experienced similar concerns, issues, and problems. Despite Freud's possibly short-sighted generalization, his work and discoveries about the human mind revolutionized treatment of mental illness and provided a theoretical foundation that others could expand upon. It can be an effective approach for working with some delinquents, but other theories may be more applicable for some youths.

Erik Erikson

Erik Erikson (1902–1944) was born in Frankfurt, Germany. Erikson reportedly struggled with identity confusion about his Jewish heritage as he matured. He never knew his natural father, and, believing that his stepfather was his natural father, bore the stepfather's surname, Homberger, until he changed his last name to Erikson on becoming a U.S. citizen.

Erikson was a Freudian follower who expanded on Freud's psychosexual stages of development to include three additional crucial stages. Erikson's theory that the strengths found in the earlier stages offer a firm foundation for the later stages are supported by data he and his colleagues collected in interviews (Erikson, Erikson, & Kivnick 1989). Erikson posited eight stages of development that are progressive and are determined by the individual's ability to resolve crises at each of the levels. Each stage of development is distinctive and individual and carries responsibilities that are unique to that stage. The responsibilities of each stage can be viewed as counter-differences for the stage. For example, in the first stage, trust is countered by mistrust. Erikson believed that a life should be balanced and the task of reconciling the dilemmas with the corresponding responsibilities further demonstrate the need for balance. Teaching children to trust parents and other responsible adults and to mistrust strangers is an example of the balance between trust and mistrust.

Trust versus Mistrust.   This stage is equivalent to Freud's oral sensory stage. The child's responsibility is to develop the ability to strike a balance between trusting responsible adults and knowing when not to trust them. The child must understand that adults are neither all good nor are all adults bad, but must realize that adults will possess characteristics of good and bad, and must be able to make the distinction.

Autonomy versus Shame and Doubt.   In this stage of development, children seek the balance between the struggle to discover on their own as opposed to relying on parents. This stage offers children the opportunity to build self-esteem and become more confident in decision making and problem solving. They discover their ability not only to control other situations, but to control themselves as well.

During this stage, parents or guardians provide verbal interference such as harshly scolding children for asking a question, or physical interference, such as slapping their hands for picking up a toy in a store, will hinder children's explorative instinct to self-discovery. Children thus experience shame and become further confused—the beginning of doubt and insecurity.

Initiative versus Guilt.   This is the responsibility stage of development in which children become future-oriented in thinking and actions. For example, although they do not yet attend school, now is the time to begin to think and plan for the big day. They may consider what it is going to be like to go to kindergarten with other children and leave their parents at home. Although they may eagerly look forward to going to school, they may not want to leave the parents and may experience guilt about having to do so. Some creative children may even feign illness so they will not have to leave.

Industry versus Inferiority.   Children's ecological systems now consist of much more than just parents—they may include, for instance, a conglomeration of church members and a peer group at school. Children now enter the "real" world of education where activities may be rigorously structured and expectations are greater than at home. They are expected to assume responsibility for their behavior and actions, are expected to remember and follow rules, and are now able to identify and label sexism and racism. This is where they discover that sometimes regardless of how hard they work and apply their skills it may all boil down to who they are. For example, students who are laughed at because their reading skills are not as keenly developed as those of others are unlikely to want to read in class and may do almost anything to avoid reading aloud. Some very industrious children may become so devastated in the school setting that they become insecure in their abilities and skills, cease to show any enthusiasm, and fear to try. The struggle is to maintain a positive balance between industry and inferiority, for if children become conditioned to believe that only hard work breeds success, they may eventually achieve success, but may lack the humility necessary to create a well-balanced individual. Any number of competent individuals may be able and willing to perform a task to textbook perfection, but if they never have achieved balance, they may be lacking in the development of self-identity or people skills. The competent individual who acknowledges limitations but constantly strives to improve on them reflects a successful balance between industry and inferiority.

Ego Identity versus Role Confusion.   This stage is critical because it is the point from which the "who am I" search evolves. Victor Frankl referred to "who am I" as a search for meaning (Frankl 1963). The search for meaning is a result of physical and psychological changes within the individual. For most human experiences there are instructions and guidelines, but no such help exists for this search. Adolescents have no formula to explain what is happening to them and how they should react to these physical and psychological changes. Adolescents are bombarded with many different messages from their ecological systems, which integrate the physical, psychological, and social environments to improve the individual as well supply environmental needs (Zastrow & Kirst-Ashman 1994, 10–11). This flood of messages leads adolescents to a state of confusion and uncertainty about the present as well as the future. In the search for meaning and methods of overcoming the many obstacles that stand in their way, some may resort to delinquent acting out as they attempt to grow and mature to adulthood in society without losing sight of who they are. This is the point at which many adolescents want to "make their statement," which may be accomplished by bizarre changes in their appearance as seen in their clothing, unusual hair colors and styles, body piercing, and tattooing.

Intimacy versus Isolation. This stage signals the beginning of mental maturity—young adulthood. Young adults make career choices and seek a sense of stability in relationships, community, and career. This interaction reflects various levels of intimacy. For example, people can be intimate with their family, friends, and lovers, but the degree of intimacy differs. If adolescents are unable to experience intimacy among their family relationships, they tend to establish the necessary intimacy with their friendship groups, perhaps joining gangs to find the family intimacy that they seek. The extent and amount of intimacy at one time could determine the amount and extent of the individual's isolation. In the aftermath of extensive technological advances people have become more isolated and are experiencing less and less intimacy. Computers and the Internet allow people to remain in their homes however; with no need to venture out. A great many human needs, such as education, shopping, and social chatting (to name a few) can be acquired by using a computer. Thus, intimacy and isolation, as Erikson foresaw, may be viewed from the perspective of a computerized society.

Generativity versus Stagnation. Erikson's middle adulthood stage is a period of intergenerational sharing and for attempting to contribute to society. The computer revolution offers a hint that the stagnation concept may need to be modified; individuals' feelings of caring may not be readily evident because they may communicate largely through computers and may seldom venture outside their homes. Erikson theorizes the midlife crisis in which individuals begin to question the aging process and want to do something to slow the process down in this stage. Some will take proactive measures and begin to watch their diets, exercise, and initiate or increase preventive medical care. Others may radically change their lifestyles and appearance, trying to behave as young people—purchasing fast cars or dressing in the mode of young adults, and seeking intimate relationships with younger women or men.

Ego Integrity versus Despair (Late Adulthood). This stage of development has undergone some interesting metamorphoses in the 1990s; as baby boomers reached maturity, the definition of *elderly* took on a different meaning and a more vibrant concept than it had when Erikson defined it. Although Erikson considered retirement from work as the beginning of this stage, he did not account for the buyouts and early retirements experienced by baby boomers. A number of retired people around age 50 seem to have found the balance between ego integrity versus despair (i.e., the aging process). They seek to eliminate the detachment that Erikson spoke of as part of this stage by becoming involved in community activities and continuing to work part time. Some companies respect the experience of mature individuals and rehire them as consultants or trainers. Retired individuals volunteer to work in schools as hall monitors, tutors, and recreational staff. Thus, many baby boomers demonstrate ego integrity in reviewing their lives and continuing to grow and develop.

Jean Piaget

Jean Piaget (1896–1980), a Swiss psychologist, respected Freud's psychosexual stages of development, but believed that epistemology (the study of knowledge) played a crucial role in understanding behavior. Piaget explained how a person acquires the penchant for cognitive crisis resolution as he described how one comes "to know."

The way humans cognitively process and communicate information has an impact on behavior. Communication theorists, in their effort to explain behavior, use a communications model that is useful in discussions of how people come to "know" things. Their model (shown at the end of this paragraph) explains that an individual can process only what goes into the mind (input). As information is sent to the brain, the brain's responsibility is to make sense of the information (cognitive processing) and then to send it to be acted upon. The act or outcome (output) is a result of the processed information. The type of feedback received from others about the output will determine the need for modifying or changing the input.

Input——→Cognitive or Interval Processing——→Output——→Feedback

Piaget focused on the internal processing component. Seeking to discover how an individual comes to know things and understand information, he proposed four cognitive processing stages of development.

Sensorimotor (0 to 24 months).   This stage emphasizes knowing how, not what or why. Children know instinctively how to take in food, initially through sucking, then through assimilation (making sense of new experiences), and accommodation (adjusting) to experiences. Reflexes dominate, because children experience the world solely through reflexes.

Pre-operational (2 to 7 years).   Language gives children the ability to deal with many aspects of the world with verbal (talking) and nonverbal symbols.

Concrete Operations (8 to 11 years). Children can perform mental transformations. They give up the egocentric view, raise questions, and can draw maps that others can understand.

Formal Operations (12 years through rest of life).   People can think abstract thoughts, solve problems, and reason.

According to Piaget, children pass through these stages at their own pace but once the stage has been completed, it cannot be revisited or reversed. He speculated that passage through the cognitive stages was either hindered or enhanced by factors of assimilation and accommodation. He discussed assimilation as a process of decoding environmental input. He suggested that infants, who lack a well-developed intellect, attempt to figure things out in their environment orally, that is, everything that they are given or that they discover goes into their mouths—their way of seeking knowledge or discovering what makes up their world. Accommodation, however, is the attempt to understand by adaptation.

Piaget believed that interaction with the environment was an important component in the cognitive process. When children are able to link their experiences to intellectual abstractions, they are better able to understand concepts. Piaget emphasized that an essential teaching mechanism was for children to undergo an experiential learning process.

All certified teachers in U.S. school systems have been exposed to the theories of Piaget. Might students do better in school if experiential learning, in which they are challenged to seek knowledge actively from their environment and to communicate that knowledge in the classroom, were a major part of teachers' classroom planning? As Piaget postulated, children seem to learn better by doing. (See Chapter 5 for more discussion of schools and delinquents.)

Lawrence Kohlberg

Lawrence Kohlberg (1927–1987) was born in the Bronx. Kohlberg believed strongly that issues of morality and ethics are important factors in decision making and problem solving, and his theory of moral development has helped in the understanding of children and adolescents' behavior. He delineated stages of moral development using underpinnings from Freud's and Piaget's concepts. He believed, as did they, that life span growth takes place in developmental stages that occur in an orderly sequence. Kohlberg believed, with Piaget, that as children grow and develop not only does cognitive processing become more difficult but moral and ethical issues present more of a dilemma.

Kohlberg's stages of moral development are categorized into three major levels with two stages in each level. He considered morality from age four to adulthood.

Level I: Preconventional Morality (4 to 10 years).   The child has narcissistic views at this level.

Stage 1: Obedience and Punishment.   In this stage, the moral world is black and white, with little room for gray. Obedience is rewarded and rebellion is punished. The individual is either good or bad. Children believe that if they do what is right they will not be punished and that a "bad" act, even with good intent, will be punished.

Stage 2: Instrumental–Relativist Orientation.   Children seek self-satisfaction. Children believe that they deserve to do whatever they desire and therefore it is right to commit the act. Although they now understand that others may think differently, children do not care because they are concerned primarily about their own gains, as exemplified in the phrase, "I will do this because I want to do it."

Level II: Conventional Morality (10 to 13 years).   Children consider others in the scheme of things and no longer focus totally on themselves.

Stage 3: Good Boy and Nice Girl Orientation.   Children want to please others, so they display the demeanors that they feel are advantageous. They also begin to make judgments about the behaviors of others.

Stage 4: Law and Order Orientation.   Children are aware that society has laws that assist with order and that law and order are important essentials in a free society.

Level III: Postconventional Morality (adolescence to adulthood)

Stage 5: Legalistic Orientation.   Individuals consider the rights of others within a legalistic framework. They consider issues of intent and mitigating circumstances to be important. The individual citizen's responsibility for making society just is as important as the notion that active participation in the legal system by citizens is a moral responsibility.

Stage 6: Universal Ethical Orientation.   Individuals who have reached this level of morality voice the notion that all humans are equal and should be treated with respect and dignity. They believe that immoral laws should be eliminated and replaced with laws that dictate equality for all citizens. People do not fear dying for the rights of their fellow humans who seek equality. Few individuals completely attain this highest level of morality in a lifetime.

Kohlberg's work has been criticized as antiquated and too seriously flawed to be taken seriously (Rest *et al.* 1999). Some criticize Kohlberg's ethics as monological, representing one segment of the population of the world, and therefore, not universal (Sigurdson 1997). Morality needs to be conceptualized from a multifaceted aspect of existence with an interdependence perspective (Walker & Hennig 1997).

Kohlberg's theory of moral development provides insight into the issues of morality and ethics that many adolescents face as they grow and develop. In addition, the questioning of the moral and ethical dilemma of behavior is a major issue in discussions of eugenics in U.S. society.

Eugenics

The historical perspective of eugenics and genetic testing began with early concerns about poverty and the belief that the poor exhausted societal resources and gave nothing of relevance back to society. Preacher–economist Thomas Malthus (1766–1834) believed that the poor should be limited in their ability to reproduce children because their children would also be poor and the poor eventually would outweigh the food supply. Sociologist Herbert Spencer (1820–1905) took up Malthus' argument and vehemently professed the need to consider that nature provides an orderly schema for the elimination of things that are not relevant and that to eliminate criminals and poor people, who were of no benefit to society, was not wrong.

Sir Francis Galton was intrigued by this concept and attempted to explain scientifically how the poor and criminals were of no value to society through heredity. He not only postulated reasons but suggested eugenics (selective mating) as a means of eliminating the problem. He believed that poverty and criminal behavior could be resolved by selective marriages between people of good background, that only these well-bred individuals should be allowed to have children, and that others should be sterilized (Galton & Benjamin 1998).

Discussions of eugenics turn to Germany during the time of Adolf Hitler and the racial hygiene laws that forced hundreds of thousands of people to undergo sterilization

(Reilly 1999, 2). Some argue that Hitler was influenced by the practice in the United States of sterilizing the mentally ill.

The U.S. Supreme Court ruled in the landmark case *Buck v Bell* (1927) that the eugenic sterilization of Carrie Buck, a mentally ill female, was constitutional, upholding a Virginia law and setting the standard for all the other states. It heralded a victory for the practice of eugenics in U.S. society (Lombardo 1985). After *Buck v Bell* more than 60,000 mentally retarded individuals were sterilized in the United States (Smith 1993). The manipulation of heredity in the United States is not merely an intellectual exercise that fits into the framework of Social Darwinism. The United States has supported subtle eugenic practices through miscegenation laws, the immigration laws of 1921 and 1924 (Reilly 1999), and the contraceptive implant, Norplant®, which some consider a satisfactory method of reproductive control for females under seventeen and for poor women (Clarke, Schmitt, Bono, *et al.* 1998).

IQ and Delinquency

The notion that some minors engage in delinquent activity because of low intelligence has sparked spirited debate. Add specific minorities to the equation and the debate becomes even more spirited. Twentieth-century researchers have considered the link between IQ and delinquency, and several schools of thought have emerged from their research. Hirschi and Hindelang (1977) and Wilson and Herrnstein (1985) found indications that IQ and delinquent acting out might be significantly correlated. Their work suggests that youths with low IQs are at more risk of becoming delinquent than youths with higher IQs. Opposers contest that IQ testing is not exact because many of the tests used to measure IQ are culturally biased (Grenfield, 1998; Livingstone, 1995). Most IQ tests were designed by middle-class white males, thus many of the items might not be recognized by youths from poverty-stricken environments, whose parents might be from a different culture, or who might not speak English. Some researchers argue that many of the designers of IQ tests might not be able to pass a test of these youths' survival mechanisms. Excluding culturally specific methods of demonstrating intelligence by minority youths does not produce a representative sample.

Studies by Jensen (1998), Shockley (1968), and Herrnstein and Murray (1994; 1996) have promoted and expanded upon the idea that minorities are prone to delinquency because of their genetic composition, postulating that minorities are intellectually inferior and thus more likely to commit delinquent acts.

William Shockley.   In the continuing theoretical debate regarding IQ, race, and delinquency, William Shockley, who received the 1956 Nobel Prize in Physics, played a major role. His 1968 presentation to the National Academy of Sciences reported that his study of children of several races who were adopted by white families showed a significant correlation between race and IQ. He attributed an IQ gap between racial groups purely to genetics (Pearson 1992).

Arthur Jensen.   Jensen (1969) developed his theory from the Spearman (1904) notion of a "*g* factor." Jensen believes it accounts for differences in intelligence between races (www.debunker.com/texts/jensen.html). The *g* (general intelligence), according to Jensen, is the cause of a fifteen-point difference between blacks and whites on IQ test scores (Jensen, 1998). *g* is the primary mental source, functioning like a computer's CPU, which speeds up or slows down individual performance and has an impact on mental ability. Jensen explains that *g* is not a cognitive process and suggests that the concept of individual intelligence is indefinable and should not be used. Jensen correlates brain size and IQ and concludes that low *g* is the cause of delinquent behavior in youths. Jensen's latest foray purports to show how Jews, too, are genetically different.

Herrnstein and Murray.   *The Bell Curve: Intelligence and Class Structure in American Life* (1994), in which Herrnstein and Murray, too, report an intelligence gap between races and argue that intelligence is based on heredity, created debate among academicians in U.S. society. The authors assert that blacks score much lower on IQ tests than whites. They attribute social problems, such as poverty and delinquent behavior, to low IQ. They maintain that black people have a mental deficiency that cannot be changed. Herrnstein and Murray argue for the elimination of such programs as Head Start and Fresh Start that would enhance the opportunity of minorities to learn better or to improve their academic skills because, they believe, the programs will do nothing to alter the mental deficiency.

Biological Theories

Some theorists believe that external factors, such as environment, cause children and adolescents to become delinquent. Yet few of these researchers explain why not all youths who experience similar external forces—poverty, slum neighborhoods, or drug-infested urban homes—become delinquent.

On the whole, only a small percentage of U.S. youths become delinquent. Often, the spotlight is on poor black urban youths. Other children and adolescents in the same impoverished areas also display delinquent behavior, but some have greater access to available social resources and are deferred more often from the juvenile justice system. Still, why is delinquency not higher among youths and why do youths who do not live in poverty commit delinquent acts?

Biological theorists might respond by suggesting that regardless of external factors youths must face, individual youths have to make decisions based on personal perceptions and internal factors of personality and heredity, which are key elements in decision making. When youths commit delinquent acts, whether they are rich or poor, are from an urban area or a rural area, or are black or white, the decision to commit the act is based on values, goals, motivation, and biological composition.

Individual decisions to engage in delinquent activities are based on choice theory. ***Choice theory*** supposes that youths who commit delinquent acts do so because they have made a decision that the acts are purposeful, meaningful, and necessary at the time they commit them. The youths are temporarily guided by their individual desires and instincts and do not consider the outcomes or the consequences of their actions. The concept of free will is a major component of choice theory: A youth independently decides to steal a car without any external threat or pressure because of an intrinsic personal desire. The decision is a rational choice because the person considers the consequences and determines that there would be none because no harm would be done. "I taught him better, he just decided to do what he wanted to do." Parents, regardless of racial or ethnic background, say these words in court when they have no other explanation for their child's delinquent behavior. They suggest that the youth made a decision and freely choose to commit a delinquent act despite knowing better and instead of relying on the values the parents had taught.

Beccaria and Classical Criminology

Philosophers Cesare Beccaria (1738–1794) and Jeremy Bentham (1748–1832), were leading theorists of the classical school of thought and advocates of the utilitarian notion that individuals behave a certain way and make choices based on free will as a result of their perception of the outcome of their behavior. Utilitarian philosophers believe that punishment is the major factor in deterring delinquent and criminal behavior. Without punishment social disorder would reign and more and more individuals would commit crimes. The assumption of utilitarian thinking is that individuals are essentially bad and, given the opportunity, will commit crimes, and must be threatened with punishment to deter bad behavior and catalyze good behavior. Laws must be an ever-present threat to keep these individuals in check and mindful of the punishment for lawbreakers.

Beccaria and Bentham believed that through free will, people rationally choose to become delinquent. They believed that delinquent act would surely be committed if the potential criminal thought that the immediate gratification outweighed the consequences of that act.

Underlying Assumptions of Classical Criminology

Free will, choice, determinism, capital punishment, and the belief that the punishment should fit the crime are basic assumptions of classical criminology that are derived from Beccaria's early writings. He outlined the principles of classical thought in his *Essay on Crimes and Punishments*. Barnes and Teeters (1959, 322) listed these principles of Beccaria:

1. All social action should be based on the utilitarian concept of the greatest good for the greatest number.
2. Crime is an injury to society, the only rational measure of which is the extent of the injury.
3. Preventing crime is more important than punishing the people who commit the crime. To do so the public must be educated about what the laws are, their support for the law enlisted, and virtue rewarded.
4. Secret accusations and torture should be abolished. People accused of crimes should have speedy trials and be treated humanely before, during, and after the trial.
5. The purpose of punishment should be to deter crime, not to obtain revenge for an offended society. It is not the severity of the punishment but its certainty and swiftness that will deter crime. Penalties must fit the crime: Crimes against property should be punished by fines or by imprisonment for people who cannot pay the fine. Capital punishment should be abolished because life imprisonment is a better deterrent.

Beccaria argued that crime and delinquency could be stopped if punishments were severe enough to make youths desist from their delinquency: Incarceration would be an appropriate sanction should they not desist. The classical view dominates today, as lawmakers advocate harsher and more stringent laws for juvenile offenders, and states build more training schools to incarcerate the higher numbers of juveniles who are becoming delinquent at a higher rate. U.S. society views youth crime from a classical perspective of delinquency, considering whether offending youths knew better or knew right from wrong. For instance, National Rifle Association (NRA) members question whether a youth who shoots another with a gun obtained from home has been taught the dangers that guns pose and how to appropriately and safely handle the gun. The issue for the NRA is not the gun in the hands of the minor, but whether the child had been taught firearm safety. Weapons manufacturers now produce guns that include safety switches and trigger locks: If youths use such guns, the public can deduce that they knew what they were doing and can more easily decide to punish youths for such violent acts. Classical theorists believe that the punishment should fit the crime and that all delinquent acts should not incur the same punishment—a youth who steals a car for a joyride should not receive the same treatment as a youth who sells drugs. This is an impetus for initiating behavioral modification programs in detention centers and training schools and for creating prevention and diversion programs.

The Positive School of Criminology

Emerging from the ideas of Auguste Comte (1798–1857), positive thinking was further promulgated in the middle to late 1800s by Cesare Lombroso, who is considered the father of criminology. Theorists of the positive school of criminology believed that external as well as internal forces over which the individual had no control caused delinquency. Positivists believed that because the individual had little, if any, control over these forces, punishment should fit the individual delinquent and not necessarily the delinquent act. Capital punishment was not considered positive punishment. Positivists believed that the scientific method and the study of personality and body types could explain delinquent behavior, and that delinquent and criminal behavior occurs because of individual, predetermined characteristics.

Lombroso

Cesare Lombroso, a medical doctor for the Italian Army, became interested in why some soldiers committed criminal acts and others did not. As he monitored the soldiers and performed medical examinations, he concluded that their physical characteristics were the major distinguishing factor. He observed that men who engaged in criminal activity had atavistic characteristics, and concluded that he could identify criminals by their large ears, protruding foreheads, long jaws, wide nostrils, and slouched physiques.

Lombroso believed that the configuration of the individual body determined its owner's criminality or delinquency. William Sheldon (1949) reported the results of his examination of the relationship between somatotype (body type) and delinquency. Body type theory suggests that body type reflects personality and determines behavior. Sheldon described three basic body types: mesomorph, endomorph, and ectomorph.

Cesare Lombroso 1835–1909
National Library of Medicine

Mesomorphs have bony, muscular, athletic bodies. Sheldon theorized that people with such bodies appear to be confident, outspoken, and able to map out a plan of action and carry it out. They seem to demand respect and seemingly can manipulate others easily. They may be admired in the delinquent subculture although their behavior may be reactive and impulsive.

Endomorphs are soft and obese. Sheldon described them as insecure and prone to be followers. He described them as loyal, conscientious, methodical, and insecure, requiring clear and explicit explanations. Structure is beneficial to endomorphs. Although very loyal, they will succumb to great pressure. Sheldon said that in the delinquent subculture, endomorphs are included in illegal activities but seldom participate in the original planning and usually only perform specific tasks and are given only the information needed to execute the activity. Because they have usually been excluded or isolated from legal activities because of their physical appearance, they may participate eagerly in illegal behavior such as being a lookout for the group or may function as mules (transporting drugs) when asked to do so by mesomorphs whom they admire. Sheldon said that endomorphs are least suspected of involvement in delinquent illegal activities by law enforcement because of the way they look. Sheldon reported that endomorphs may be pedophiles.

Ectomorphs, according to Sheldon's schema, are intellectuals or masterminds. Their bodies are tall, thin, and fragile. They are secure, able to assess situations and individuals accurately, and to formulate long-range plans. They are impatient, arrogant, and intolerant of mistakes, but may deal well with people. They may view the aggressive tendencies of mesomorphs as challenge to their authority, control, leadership, or intelligence. As leaders, Sheldon said that ectomorphs will identify and delineate roles clearly so that they are understood by all.

Lombroso believed that genetics played a major role in creating criminal behavior. His ideas laid the framework for other genetic theories. His scientific explanation of the cause of delinquent and criminal behavior was hailed as a major breakthrough in criminology during his time.

Discussions of theories fit into three distinct paradigms:

1. Belief in the theory as originally proposed;
2. Belief in some aspects of the theory, but not all;
3. General opposition to the theory.

Researchers such as Raffaele Garofalo (1851–1934) and Enrico Ferri (1856–1929), who agreed with Lombroso's biological theory, emerged. Garofalo believed in Lombroso's theory as Lombroso proposed it. Ferri believed in Lombroso's theory, but added an important modification, the dimension of consideration of social factors, which he believed would strengthen the theory. Charles Goring (1870–1919) completely rejected Lombroso's thinking and indicated that regardless of an individual's physical characteristics, mental processing really determined criminal and delinquent behavior. Goring reasoned that if criminals, who possessed what he called "defective intelligence," had children, those children could become delinquent because the parent transmitted the defective intelligence gene.

Goring believed that sterilization, which eliminated the possibility of people deficient in intelligence having children, was one method of controlling illegal behavior. Some students of criminology would consider this thinking barbaric or inconceivable in contemporary society, as others would consider it a plausible alternative and look to the numerous such genetic experiments conducted in the United States. Much research on human subjects was performed in the United States in the second third of the twentieth century. Revelations of unethical research tactics, such as those used in the Tuskegee experiment, caused reluctance, mistrust, and skepticism among people who might otherwise participate in studies.

Tuskegee Experiment.   The Tuskegee experiment, in which the U.S. Army and the U.S. Public Health Services performed research on a group of African American men without their knowledge from 1932 until 1972 (the longest nontherapeutic human experiment in medical history), is one of the United States' most blatant and despicable examples of racial experimentation (Thomas & Quinn 1991, 1498–1505). The more than three hundred men, all infected with the syphilis virus, were neither informed of nor treated for the degenerative disease. The federal research project revealed a total disregard for people who were racially different because they are not valued and not viewed as humans and therefore used to advance a scientific ideology: "The men's status did not warrant ethical debate. They were . . . not patients; clinical material, not sick people" (Jones 1981, 179).

Other Experiments in the Name of Research.   Prison inmates are asked to volunteer for scientific experimentation and are studied for a variety of reasons, including cancer and genetic research. Early studies that related to Goring's ideas were Richard Dugdale's genealogical study published as *The Jukes: A Study in Crime, Pauperism, Disease, and Heredity* (1877) and Arthur Estabrook's reanalysis, *The Jukes and the Kallikaks* (1912).

Lombroso's body-type theory not only opened the door for greater research in this area but set the stage for the creation of opposing theories. A criticism of his work is that he only studied Italian military men, so his theory might not be applicable to other populations, such as women and delinquents. Although Lombroso offered hypotheses about female criminals, they were negative. Lombroso's discussion of delinquents was limited.

Regardless of the limitations or criticisms of his work, Lombroso formulated a biological theoretical conceptualization that had a strong impetus in the twentieth century and is destined to become even more relevant in the twenty-first.

Contemporary Traditional Biopsychological Theories

By the twentieth century, Lombroso and his followers had laid a firm foundation for biological theory. Researchers concentrated more on Ferri's integration of biological and social factors and Goring's intellectual factors than on Lombroso's physical traits as primary causes of delinquent and criminal behavior.

Neurological Abnormalities

Contemporary researchers speculated that although observable physical factors might have bearing on the individual's risk of delinquency and criminal behavior, other salient biological factors, such as a youth's sugar intake, hormones, DNA, or chromosomes might be of equal or greater importance. As criminologists speculate on the causes of delinquency from a biological perspective, genetic, neurological, and biochemical factors receive equal consideration. Neurological functioning encompasses anything dealing with the body's nervous system. The nervous system is a network consisting of the central nervous system and the peripheral nervous system. The neurological (nervous) system tells the body what it needs, what is going on inside and outside it, and when it is experiencing pain, cold, and hunger. When the nervous system does not function properly, it causes changes in behavior that can manifest themselves in depression, hyperactivity, aggression, or violent acting out.

Neurological dysfunction can slow the functioning of the brain, a condition labeled minimal brain dysfunction (MBD), which interferes with language development and negatively affects IQ. Numerous studies have considered the effects of neurological dysfunction and delinquency. Attention Deficit Hyperactivity Disorder (ADHD) characterizes a child who is hyperactive and displays aggressiveness, isolationism, and impulsive behavior. Hyperactivity has been studied extensively in children and adolescents and ADHD is so popular a diagnosis for children that many children may be wrongly diagnosed as hyperactive. Ritalin® (methylphenidate) has been used to reduce the amount of hyperactivity among youths and has been prescribed in such great quantity for so many children that it has earned the nickname of "child's crack" (Smith 2000; Kissinger 1998).

Learning Disabilities

Youths experiencing learning disabilities (LDs) can be misunderstood and incorrectly labeled. Only recently have attention and research focused closely on this condition. The National Institute of Mental Health (NIMH) defined learning disability as a mental disorder in which afflicted people experience consistent limited ability to interpret what they hear and see, possibly throughout their lives. To learn more about ADHD, go to the Web site for government publications (www.nimh.nih.gov/publicat/learndis.htm).

The causes of LD are not clear, although neurological speculations and associated theories of genetics, drug abuse, and toxic chemicals abound. The Diagnostic Statistical Manual of Mental Disorders (DSM) classifies LD into three distinct categories: developmental speech and language disorders, academic skills disorders, and "other," a suitcase category for such problems as out-of-control behavior. NIMH cautions about labeling children as LD when they may be simply a bit slower in their developmental skills than other children.

Children and adolescents with LD may display difficulties in comprehending and expressing language. They may function like other youths physically, but may experience problems in reading, writing, and conceptualizing and may be labeled mentally retarded. They may become the class clown or class bully or may aggressively act out with the intention of being removed from class because they do not want to experience the embarrassment of peers discovering that they cannot read or write or perhaps merely can't understand what they have read. Such severe acting out may occur during class time, when students have to read aloud or orally work math problems. Students with LD may turn in homework late or not at all. On the other side of the coin, adolescents with LD may be very verbal, innovative, and creative artistically.

Teachers of large classes may write off youths with LD because they do not have the time necessary to devote extra attention to such students. Teachers may perceive children with LD as children who do not want to learn. Youths with LD sometimes go undetected in the classroom by not saying anything (Root 1994).

Drug dealers know the value of time investment theory in the recruitment and retention of youths in their drug businesses. Youths with LD are not as easily written off as failures in the drug world as they are in most academic settings. In the school setting, loud and disruptive students may be suspended after numerous disruptions. Alone and bored, with no parental supervision, such a youth may be spotted by the neighborhood drug dealer and a scenario like this simulated one might occur.

DRUG DEALER: Hey, what's up, bro'?

YOUTH: Not much. I just can't seem to do anything right.

DRUG DEALER: Hey, you look like a smart dude. What say we go and kick it a bit?

YOUTH: Oh, I don't know [hanging his head as he contemplates the situation]. I just seem to mess up everything [frustratedly kicking a tin can on the street].

DRUG DEALER: Hey it's all right man [putting his arm around the youth's shoulder]. You look cool to me. Since you don't have anything else to do right now how 'bout a little favor for me?

YOUTH: Well . . . I don't know. . . .

DRUG DEALER: Come on man. You smart. You got the time and I give you a few bucks 'cause I know you cool.

YOUTH: Well . . . all right.

> DRUG DEALER: Take this package to [names a street address] for me. They'll phone me after they get it.
>
> YOUTH: All right. [Takes the package reluctantly. Goes to make the delivery.]

Later, the youth returns to their designated meeting spot and the dealer has had news about the drop.

> DRUG DEALER: Yo, what happened little bro'? You took the package to the wrong apartment.
>
> YOUTH [despondent demeanor]:   See, I told you. I can't do nothing right.
>
> DRUG DEALER: Hey, it's all right big man. I messed up the first time, too. But look at me now. You can do it. You will be all right. You are a smart dude. Come on with me. I will show you how it's done and you'll be as good as me one day.
>
> YOUTH [beaming with delight]:   You mean it. One day I'll be as successful as you?
>
> DRUG DEALER: Right, smart man. We going to make a good team, you and me. Come on! I'll show you how it's done. We'll do this thing together.

The drug dealer accomplished two things that the classroom teacher could not. First, he invested time with the youth and listened to him. Second, he built the youth's self-esteem by providing him with positive enforcers that he could do it and by using positive adjectives describing the youth as "smart man" and "big man." The dealer made the youth understand that he was not unique in "messing up"—everyone does—as the dealer informs him, "I messed up the first time, too." Equally important, the dealer invested time in the youth by showing him how to do the job, walking through the process with him.

Advancement of Science and Technology.   Advanced technological methods have popularized the genetic theories of delinquency. Technical advances have made it possible to move forward with the study and implementation of genetic alterations of humans. Surrogate mothers and test-tube babies proliferate. Successful cloning of large mammals has been publicized, and more research into not only the cloning process but toward the elimination of specific genetic flaws will be a priority in the twenty-first century. Scientists may discover and isolate a particular gene that causes delinquency.

Biochemicals and Delinquency

Environmental pollutants can still be a major problem in the future as we consider biochemical links to delinquency. Adults question why children seem to physically mature faster today than years ago. Early physical maturity might be related to chemicals that are inhaled via the air or ingested through the food supply, for example, toxic pollutants are in the air and foods have been treated with hormones to increase their size. Fish, if not farm-raised in a controlled atmosphere, suffer from polluted waters where some die from pfisteria. Even vegetarians are not safe from polluted food—many vegetables are saturated with pesticides that also pollute the soil and water supplies.

Another dietary issue to consider is the daily intake of sweets. Children and adolescents in U.S. society are taught to be cognizant of diet, with parents encouraging them to eat properly and to avoid fast foods and sweets, which are popular with adolescents. Even so, preprepared breakfast foods and cold cereals that are common in U.S. households are saturated with sugar. School lunch programs have dietitians and nutritionists to try to ensure that youths get some balanced, nutritious meals.

Genetic researchers continue to study the effects of toxic chemicals on behavior. Herbert Needleman (1991) concluded that lead poisoning negatively affects children's learning in school and can lead to delinquent acting out.

Contemporary adults observe that they would not want to be a child or adolescent growing up in today's society because it is too difficult. Youths not only have to deal with baby boomer parents and grandparents who grew up in the confusing, socially disordered world of the 1960s, but must face the temptations of a healthy economy.

Personality Theory and Testing

Personality theory suggests that adolescents become delinquent as a result of personality flaws that may have occurred during the developmental stage The Minnesota Multiphasic Personality Inventory (MMPI-2), which is used to measure the degree of abnormal mental functioning in individuals, is, perhaps, the most widely used method for testing delinquent personalities. The 566-item instrument, normed on adult males and females (18 to 80 years old) was devised by Hathaway and McKinley in 1943. It should not be used to test the personality of youths. The 478-item MMPI-A, which was specifically designed for testing youths between the ages of 14 and 18 years, is the more appropriate test. Among the other tools that assist clinicians with their interpretation of the results of the tests are the International Statistical Classification of Diseases manual (ICD-10) and the Diagnostic Statistical Manual of Mental Disorders (DSM-IV). The ICD-10, first published in 1893, is one of the oldest manuals for interpretation of diseases. Its primary purpose is to provide a global classification system for human diseases. It is used extensively by medical doctors. The DSM-IV is used extensively by psychologists, criminologists, and social workers.

The DSM was first published in 1952 and has undergone four revisions. It provides a classification of mental disorders and is unique in that it also offers insight into cultural influences, as well as organic factors, that may have an impact on behavior. Some of the strengths of this manual are that it is universal, its conclusions were empirically tested, it provides a classification system with specific symptoms, and it is culturally sensitive.

Debate on personality testing may be anticipated to continue throughout the coming decades. Some believe that minorities are intellectually inferior to the majority population and that the majority of the delinquency is committed by minorities. Others argue disparities in the data, racial bias, racism, and that the data indicate that race alone does not determine high or low intelligence or criminality. A third group claims that a combination of factors must be considered when discussing race, IQ, and criminality.

Summary

Criminal justice students may frown on the notion of theoretical discussions because they are unable to see the fruits of knowing and understanding biological theory. They may become emotionally repulsed by the notion of genetic predisposition to delinquency and expression of racist attitudes. They may think that biological theory is simply another way to give delinquents a way to "cop out" of responsibility for their actions. It is important to understand biological explanations and their roots because this theoretical perspective provides a stronger foundation for making and improving on the argument for the biological perspective. It provides another perspective to consider when working with delinquent youths and their families, because what works with one youth may not be applicable or acceptable to working with another youth. Knowledge of a variety of theories will provide the students with a variety of knowledge, which can lead them to numerous mechanisms and alternatives for working with youths and families who have very little trust in the system. Biological explanations of delinquency may help students to understand a little more about themselves. Understanding of self is extremely important when working with children and adolescents, because they constantly present challenges not only to the system, but also to the individual psyche. Youths understand individuals who are working with them very well and use that understanding for their own purposes. Thus, if individuals who work and interact with youths understand how biological explanations of behavior can have an impact on themselves, youths win because they have people interacting with them who are secure and have no need to compete with them. The juvenile worker wins because youths are usually very cooperative and willing to work with knowledgeable, challenging, and positively responsible adults. The system and parents win because youths may receive the assistance they need.

KEY CONCEPTS

classical criminology	free association	positive criminology
ectomorph	id	repression
ego	mesomorph	superego
endomorph	personality types	
eugenics	pleasure principle	

DISCUSSION QUESTIONS

1. Why is it important to consider biochemical factors when discussing delinquency?

2. Discuss the concepts of positive eugenics versus negative eugenics and the impact they may have on the study of delinquency?

3. What is the impact of classical thinking about delinquency? How will classical and positive perspectives affect juvenile justice in the future?

EXERCISES

1. Consider the following thoughts by Martin J. Niemoeller and discuss the implications.

   In Germany they first came for the communists and I did not speak up.
   Then they came for the Jews and I did not speak up.
   Then they came for the trade unionists and I did not speak up.

Then they came for the Catholics and I did not speak up because I am Protestant.
Then they came for me—and there was no one left to speak up.

2. Considering the theories you have studied in this chapter, write a brief discussion addressing these three questions: Beyond the IQ, race, and delinquency discussions, what remains? Do we enter into a eugenics program that kills off all individuals with low IQs? After we have killed off all known and potential delinquents based on genetic composition and IQ scores, who is next?

Sociological Theories of Delinquency

CHAPTER OBJECTIVES

On completing this chapter, students will have tools to:

- Understand theories that focus specifically on sociological theories
- Gain skill in the application of sociological theories
- Apply sociological theories to case examples
- Examine the impact of sociological theories on delinquency prevention
- Consider the impact of the environment on delinquent behavior

Sociological Factors in Delinquency

Some researchers believe that external factors, such as environment, play a vital role in the delinquency process. Environmental factors include peer pressure and poverty. In a sense, the sociological theory of delinquency promotes the idea that youths become delinquent because of things they are taught and learn and experience as they grow and develop. Unlike biological theory, which focuses on the individual, sociological theories stress the interaction between the individual and the environment. To delineate sociological theories so they can easily be comprehended and remembered, this chapter considers the theories from micro- and macroperspectives, the two broad categories in which the theories have been divided. The microperspective introduces sociological theories from the view of interactions with peers, parents, and teachers. The macroperspective is from the view of interactions with conditions, such as poverty, which exist in the environment. Those macro factors that exist in youths' worlds that have an impact on them, but over which they have no direct control, are powerful forces that influence their behavior. For example, youths would have difficulty getting their families out of poverty because they are not responsible for the poverty, but they may react to it by committing delinquent acts that they believe will assist the family's economic situation (e.g., robbery, drug dealing, and so forth, for money).

This chapter focuses on traditional sociological theories: opportunity theory, social disorganization theory, strain theory, and conflict theory. It uses contemporary examples in considering traditional theories so that the student can understand more easily the importance of the theories and also apply them in contemporary context. Table 4.1 (page 115) summarizes major traditional theorists, their theories, and the major premise of each.

Columbine: A Sociological Perspective

Eric Harris and Dylan Klebold armed themselves with two sawed-off shotguns, a semiautomatic handgun, a semiautomatic rifle, and a dozen homemade bombs as they entered school on April 20, 1999, in Littleton, Colorado. They fired more than 200 rounds of ammunition before the day ended. They were middle-class teens (one drove a BMW to school) who were described by their classmates as Hitler fanatics who dressed in black and were members of an ostensible organization called the "Trenchcoat Mafia."

Columbine High School Shooting Timeline: April 20, 1999

11:14–11:17 A.M.	Eric Harris and Dylan Klebold take bombs into Columbine High School and plant them in the cafeteria.
11:19 A.M.	Harris and Klebold start shooting from the top of a stairwell.
11:23 A.M.	911 is called to the Sheriff's office from the school.
11:24 A.M.	School Resource Officer Neal Gardner responds to the problem in the school and trades shots with Harris.
11:25 A.M.	The first sheriff's car arrives at the scene. Jefferson County Sheriff's Deputy Scott Taborsky is the driver of the car.
11:27 A.M.	A pipe bomb explodes in the cafeteria.
11:27 A.M.	Harris and Klebold go to the school library.
11:30 A.M.	Police blockade school perimeters.
11:34 A.M.	Gunshot kills last of the thirteen victims.
11:36 A.M.	Harris and Klebold leave school library.
11:44 A.M.	Harris and Klebold return to the school cafeteria and fire shots at bombs, trying to ignite them.
11:45 A.M.	Harris stops temporarily in the cafeteria to sip a drink left in a Styrofoam cup. The two teens leave the cafeteria.
11:46 A.M.	Ten SWAT officers use a fire truck for cover to enter the school building.
11:47 A.M.	A fire bomb goes off in the cafeteria.
11:56 A.M.	Harris and Klebold, still carrying guns, go back into the cafeteria.
Noon	Harris and Klebold leave cafeteria and later return to the library where they commit suicide. Ambulances take the first of the wounded students to hospitals.
12:06 P.M.	A second SWAT team enters the school building.
12:30 P.M.	SWAT team sweeps the building.
3:30 P.M.	Police find the twelve bodies, including Harris and Klebold.
4:00 P.M.	Sheriff's spokesman, Steve Davis, announces the two teens, Harris and Klebold were found dead.
4:30 P.M.	Building declared under control.
6:15 P.M.	Explosives found in teens' car.
10:30 P.M.	All dead victims identified and taken from school.

Source: Special Report: The Littleton Massacre. *Time.* May 3, 1999, 28.

As Columbine High School was evacuated, 15 people, including one teacher, 12 students, and the 2 gunmen, did not leave the building alive; 22 others reportedly were injured in the mayhem. What made Klebold and Harris shoot their classmates and teacher? Did they do it because of behavior they had learned? Did they do it because of weak established bonds with social systems (e.g., schoolteachers, students, and parents)? Did they do it because they had been labeled a certain way? Did they do it because they had been oppressed? Did they do it because they lived in poverty? Did they do it because it was expected by some of their peers? The two adolescents are dead and only speculation remains to offer explanations for the attack.

Delinquent youths are a minority among youths: The majority of youths do not become delinquent. What explanations can be offered for the nondelinquent majority in the adolescent population? Observing the individual microsocialization process that children experience in their homes, their lack of delinquent behavior might be a result of the influence of their parents. From a structural, macroperspective, it might seem that all children born in the United States are at risk of becoming delinquent. Why? Because the United States has a long history of innate violence and because violence still deeply permeates and ripples through U.S. society. The brutality of children with guns is seen more and more often. The National Rifle Association (NRA), as it lobbies against gun-control legislation, boasts that guns have made the United States the great nation that it is today. From the macrosociological perspective, delinquency in the United States should be an expected phenomenon.

Macrosociological Perspectives

Macrosociological perspectives are structural theories. They are the theoretical conceptualizations that focus primarily on inanimate environmental factors that may influence youths to engage in delinquent activities. These inanimate environmental influences include poverty, neighborhoods, and capitalism.

Poverty

According to the 1998 U.S. Census Bureau Report, more than 13.3 percent of U.S. citizens are considered poor and living below the poverty level. The greatest percentages of the poor were among minorities: African Americans were 26.5 percent (9.1 million) and Hispanic were 27.1 percent (8.3 million); whites were only 11.0 percent (24.4 million). Although poverty has declined greatly, a large percentage of the poor are children and adolescents—19.9 percent in 1997 (Bureau of the Census 1998).

Poverty, as defined by the federal government (the Office of Management and Budget sets the standards in Directive 14 authorizing the Census Bureau to collect and disseminate data on poverty), is an income of less than $16,954 annually for a household of four. Poverty is not defined for military personnel, correctional inmates, or children under age 15 in foster care with nonrelatives (Bureau of the Census 1999).

Oscar Lewis coined the phrase *the culture of poverty* (Lewis 1966) after his research revealed that more often than not, poverty clearly could be a vicious, unbreakable cycle. He described intergenerational poverty as creating feelings of hopelessness and powerlessness, and a fatalistic outlook in people unlucky enough to be caught in its grip. Lewis theorized that this attitude, engendered from continual existence in impoverished conditions, creates an impoverished mind. Therefore, even if programs are made available to the individual or if the economic situation changes positively, the individual will continue to think that poverty conditions still prevail and they are still impoverished.

William Ryan (1976) sharply criticized the culture of poverty theory in *Blaming the Victim*. He indicated that the poor are victims of societal ills and should not be blamed for their misfortune. He suggested that blaming the poor for their inability to escape poverty is a convenience for policymakers, when, in fact, the poor are poor simply because they do not have money (Zastrow & Kirst-Ashman 1994) Many of the poor are children, not adults, and may be at risk of becoming delinquent because they do not have access to resources to improve their quality of life. Cloward and Ohlin called this unavailability of access *blocked opportunity*.

Blocked Opportunity Theory

Richard Cloward and Lloyd Ohlin (1960) developed opportunity theory. This theory proposes that when no legitimate means are available for youths to experience success, they will find other ways to achieve their goals through illegal means and delinquent activities. Cloward and Ohlin describe youths who are without adequate social and economic resources and supports as driven toward delinquency in an effort to gain some of the things that they want. Some youths become involved in illegal activities to provide financial support for their family. If no adult male supports the family, the oldest sibling, who may be 12 years of age or younger, may assume that responsibility. Laws in most states require youths to be at least 16 years old to get a work permit, so unlawful activities may be the only resources for them to provide financial support in their homes.

Opportunity theory can also be applied to street gang subcultures. Some youths may join gangs to gain some financial success through illegal gang activities. Initially, they may consider the enhanced possibility of success rather than the danger and risk involved because they have not experienced achievement legally or legitimately.

Financial gain is not the only success youths seek: Youths who join gangs may additionally be seeking love, security, and protection. The gang subculture offers these things when the opportunities for them otherwise are blocked (e.g., at home and at school). They experience personal and group success, as well, when they find in the gang the opportunity to advance in rank because of their skills and their willingness to take risks.

Older gang members and adults (OGs) invest time explaining and demonstrating to younger gang members to aid them in the successful completion of their assignments. From the novice gang members' perspective, the teaching and modeling role assumed by OGs reduces some of the stress that they experience. From the perspective of the OGs, who may have been anxious about how well their young protégés would complete their tasks, it is rewarding when the younger gang members demonstrate their ability to perform successfully. OGs are then able to role model for other, younger members.

Slum Neighborhood Theory

When children and adolescents do not receive the protection they so desperately need from society and their family structure, the community social structure should be able to assist. But when youths live in deteriorating, low socioeconomic conditions, which they share with the community, there is nowhere to turn for help. Clifford Shaw and Henry McKay recognized this zonal impoverished area as a contributor to high delinquency rates. They theorized that slum neighborhoods and neighborhood disorganization were major causal factors of delinquent behavior among youths.

Robert Park is attributed with being the first to describe the ecological model of delinquency. With Ernest Burgess and Roderick McKenzie (1928), he considered crime rates in relation to city composition and development. They focused on urban city living, specifically termed "concentric zones." Clifford Shaw and Henry McKay (1942) also explained an ecological perspective as they considered the causes of delinquency among 25,000 youths over a 30-year period in Cook County, Illinois. They considered delinquency from a macrostructural level, rather than a microstructural level. They considered the impact of external institutional influences on delinquent behavior as opposed to focusing on the individual delinquent. They theorized that slum neighborhoods in a state of disintegration and disorganization caused youths to become delinquent.

They described slum neighborhoods as disintegrated and transitional and used the slum areas of Chicago as their model to support their disorganization theory. They noted that the inner city sections of Chicago showed the highest measure of delinquency while neighborhoods far away from the inner city had less reported delinquency, regardless of the population profile of the area. Based on that data, they concluded that the localities, and not the type of people living there, produced delinquent behavior (Shaw & McKay 1942).

Predicated on their analysis, Shaw and McKay created a neighborhood project to test their theory. They devised the Chicago Area Project, which was a treatment program located in a slum neighborhood in Chicago. The primary purpose of the program was to determine if delinquency in the areas where the project was operating would decrease if the areas were provided with adequate resources. Thus, community residents were employed in the program to provide counseling, rap sessions, recreation, tutoring, and other community activities deemed important to the specific community. The community organization model was a popular social work model that thrived in the 1960s and 1970s during the social unrest in U.S. communities. Zastrow and Kirst-Ashman (1994) note that prior to the 1960s, the Freudian medical model, which focused on the individual who was perceived as ill and seeking a cure, was the prominent model.

Shaw and McKay's ecological approach to delinquency stresses the importance of the interaction among behavior, economic and social factors, and delinquency. It also suggested that a change in the economic condition of youths could bring about changes in their propensity to become involved in illegal acts. One area that requires a closer review as consideration is given to this theoretical approach, is the presumption about individuals who reside in slum areas. Shaw and McKay formulated their theory around disorganization, and thus presumed that all individuals in these areas are disruptive and disorderly and in dire need of assistance to get their lives in order. Many of these individuals are second and third generations of impoverished people. They live in the environment simply because they cannot afford to live anywhere else. They do not like living under these conditions, but they must do what it takes to continue to survive from one day to the next. The environment is a hostile one, largely because many of these people have been victims of gentrification. When a city or a private company purchases slum holdings for development, the minorities who live there are forced to move out and into another impoverished area deeper in the inner city, so the area can be rebuilt as condominiums or shopping centers and can become profitable real estate. This forced move does much to contribute to the generation of continued hostility. For example, as minorities began to move into the urban area they witnessed "white flight" from the community and watched the people who left relocate in surrounding suburban areas. Thus, the new inhabitants, most of whom were impoverished minorities who lacked the resources to relocate, continued to live in the area, year after year observing it deteriorating and feeling angry and helpless to stop it. Each generation becomes more infuriated. The anger is further compounded among the community residents with the implementation of a "beautify downtown" project.

The newly renovated downtown condominiums and shops bring middle and upper class tenants into the area. The minorities who were displaced still live in the city and may be able to visit—if they have transportation or bus fare—their old neighborhoods, which are now luxurious housing, condominiums, and specialty shops. Experiencing this type of transition fuels feelings of anger, helplessness, and powerlessness. A neighborhood that had been labeled disorganized (a slum) is now perceived as organized (affluent).

Disorganization

Shaw and McKay's theory is referred to as social disorganization theory. The implications are that impoverished neighborhoods lack organization and that middle- and upper-class socioeconomic neighborhoods are more organized. Criminal justice students should use caution when considering disorganization and organization in a structural framework. In identifying a community as disorganized, the implication is that it lacks major positive components or attributes, such as community leadership; lacks parental supervision of minors; or is overwhelmed with deviant behaviors, with parents participating in illegal activities.

Disorganization in impoverished neighborhoods should not suggest that leadership is lacking in these communities. From such communities have emerged strong leaders known not only in U.S. society but around the world. In addition, the community churches act as major catalysts in fostering and developing leadership skills in the communities' children and adolescents. It is not practical to label one community as disorganized simply because it lacks consistent parental disciplinary guidelines for youths. Another community that lacks parental disciplinary guidelines may be labeled organized simply because of a little diversity in the mix of the neighborhood. Parents in lower socioeconomic areas expect their children to follow rules and respect those expectations, as well as themselves, just as any other parent does. Is it reasonable to label communities of impoverished households in which a small percentage of youths are delinquent and may lack proper or adequate parental supervision as disorganized? In communities of middle- and upper-class households, youths also lack proper adult supervision, but the neighborhoods are not labeled disorganized because the youths have been able to evade the juvenile justice system through the use of more available resources.

Disorganized neighborhood.
Jeff Greenberg/PhotoEdit

Impoverished neighborhoods are labeled in many ways and there are many perceptions about the people living in the areas. For example, these areas are considered disorganized because of reported high crime rates and the public belief that many of the adults in these areas are uncaring people who also participate in criminal activity. The majority of the people living in these areas are responsible citizens who are simply not fortunate enough to have an income that is above the poverty level.

Many of the inhabitants of impoverished neighborhoods are domestic workers or hold other menial, low-skill jobs. They report to work every day, expect law enforcement officers to protect them and their homes, pay their bills as far as their pay checks will extend, and have the same desires for their children as middle- and upper-class people. Their social values are no different, but the means to attaining values may differ because of a different type of strain placed upon them.

Robert Merton

Strain theorists believed that adolescents become delinquent because they do not have access to resources that others have and therefore become frustrated. Because they cannot gain access to these resources legitimately, they resort to delinquent activities to relieve the strain.

Robert Merton (1957), who greatly admired Emile Durkheim, expanded on Durkheim's theory of anomie, which is also called strain theory. Anomie, according to Durkheim, occurs when individuals remove themselves from societal conformity because they are fed up with the rules and policies that reflect societal norms (Durkheim 1933). Merton (1957) placed Durkheim's concepts into a perspective based on the U.S. value system of the Anglo Protestant work ethic that every U.S. citizen can be successful if they work hard. Merton pointed out that U.S. citizens who do work hard and still do not achieve success experience severe strain. His position was rife with hints of the Marxist theory that class values play a major role in creating delinquent behavior (Messner & Rosenfeld 1997). For example, strain occurs not because social values are different but because the means to obtaining these values differs by economic status. But most U.S. citizens, throughout their formative years, are told that if they work hard they will succeed. Strain enters when the distortions and confusing messages of the reality of being a minority in U.S. society are added to the equation.

Minority children are told stories of how past generations worked to the extent of human endurance as slaves, toiling all day and well into the night helping to build a strong U.S. economy. They continued this hard work ethic as free people employed as domestics in the homes of the rich, scrubbing floors, windows, and walls and returning home exhausted, but somehow mustering the strength to care for their families. Confused minority children wonder, when mother and father work so hard, why the family is still poor. Children learn the lessons of being a minority in U.S. society very early in life.

The responses to the real world that children learn are taught to them by their parents, and are directly related to the racial background of the parents. White, middle-class children are taught that police officers are their friends and the first persons to seek out when they need help. African American mothers, regardless of their socioeconomic class, teach their sons that they must take precautions in the presence of white police officers. The youths are not taught to seek out police officers readily, but are taught safety measures to adhere to when they are stopped by police officers.

Hard work, which supposedly leads to the achievement of success, is without question based on majority values, so for people of minority extraction the job is much more difficult. The majority population determines who among the minority are designated to join in the fulfillment of the U.S. dream. As they function in the schizophrenic society described above, many youths—especially minorities—are at high risk of experiencing strain.

Agnew (1992) expanded on Merton's work and specifically provided a framework for understanding the sources of strain among delinquents. He theorized that the more strain adolescents experienced in school, for instance, the more apt they were to lean toward displaying delinquent behaviors. Strain could emanate from parents who may compare siblings negatively to one another, perhaps expecting a youth who gets failing grades to be more like a sibling in the family who does well in school. Strain can be experienced by children in school whose teachers have high expectations of them without supporting them in meeting the expectations.

Agnew's theory of strain is extremely relevant to contemporary society because it offers a feasible explanation for incidences of students killing in schools all over the country. Agnew and White (1992) posit three primary stimuli that evoke strain on adolescents:

1. Prevent them from achieving positive valued goals.

Adolescents feel tremendous strain when they struggle to reach a goal, and are unable to do so because they feel that others have gotten in the way and prevented them from doing so. This type of strain can be seen in students who truly believe that education is the key to success. They work very hard, but, like many others, may experience a slump. When they need individualized assistance, the teacher may not have the time to give and the students may receive failing grades. They then display anger toward that teacher, act out, and disrupt the class. Some students may go to the extreme and kill the teacher because of the bad grades.

2. Eliminate positively valued stimuli.

A positively valued stimulus can be animate or inanimate. For example, the removal of an adolescent from one school to another as a result of family relocation may present a great deal of strain on the youth. Moving can be especially stressful depending on the time of relocation. In the middle of the school term it could cause greater stress than moving during the summer months, because during summer there is time to establish new friendships without the burden of also trying to adapt to the new school environment.

3. Give them negative stimuli.

Some believe that if adolescents are subjected to harsh physical and emotional treatment and are punished often and severely, they will commit crimes (Agnew 1995). Punishment is often a cause of strain. Even when adolescents suggest verbally ("It does not matter.") or nonverbally (continued negative acting out behavior) that they do not care, in reality, they really do care. Suggesting to the adult that they do not care is a coping strategy used to reduce the level of strain that they are experiencing. Adolescents use numerous coping mechanisms to deal with the frustration, depression, and suicidal ideations that can result from strain. Delinquency is one mechanism in reaction to that stress.

Albert Cohen

Cohen, like Merton and Agnew, also believed that social and economic factors are fundamental causal ingredients in delinquent behavior. In *Delinquent Boys* (1955), he discussed specific economic and social influences that create strain that leads to frustration, which eventually leads to boys committing delinquent acts. He explained that boys from lower socioeconomic conditions who had been socialized in U.S. society would usually strive for middle- and upper-class values. When they can not attain them legitimately, they become angry and frustrated and demonstrate their feelings by acting.

Cohen called their frustrations "status frustration" because they were helpless and could do very little to change their lower socioeconomic status. Unable to effect change, many attempt to gain prestige and status through gang activity and delinquent acting out. This conduct is exactly opposite that of middle and upper class youths whom they try so hard to emulate. Thus, according to Cohen's theory, these youths create a subculture that imitates societal norms, but make rules that apply to themselves and their situation. This subculture becomes, in their estimation, the legitimate culture of which others must take note and prove themselves worthy to enter. For example, youths who cannot accomplish the required task (gang initiation) are not allowed to enter the gang, an experience quite similar to the one they experienced in trying to enter middle-class culture.

Cohen viewed the cause of delinquent behavior as a reaction by lower-class boys to social and economic deprivation, which forces them to create a subculture of their own where they can experience success and achievement even if it is considered negative under societal rules. Cohen, however, later recognized the need to expand his work (Cohen & Short 1968). He considered the application of his theory to middle- and upper-class boys who became involved in delinquent activity. He theorized that they, too, rebelled against societal norms, not because they were excluded from being part of it, but because they were a part of it and the demands were too much for them to bear. Thus, they experienced strain and frustration when unable to meet the constraints of being middle class. Because, however, they were already members of the middle class, they had no need to form gangs but might join them simply to make a statement against middle-class norms.

Walter Miller

Miller, like Cohen, taught that lower socioeconomic status youths were more prone to delinquency because of their economic situation. However, unlike Cohen, Miller does not teach that lower-class boys are delinquent as a result of rebelling against middle-class values, but that they seem to seek pleasure from the delinquent experience.

Miller (1958) viewed the matriarchal unit as problematic for these youths. Not only did he identify poverty as a major cause of delinquency in U.S. society, but he also believed that matriarchal family situations contributed to the delinquent process. His reasoning was that many of the boys in his study grew up in single parent-homes where the mother was forced to assume the role of primary care provider in the household. Miller questioned whether these boys would have been socialized differently had there been two parents in the household, as he compared them with middle-class families in his control group in which households had two parents. He theorized that boys in single-parent households did not have the advantage of male bonding or the male figure to emulate, factors that, according to him, could lead them to economic success.

Miller's belief in the disadvantages of single-parent homes is a major cause of criticism of his theory. Antiquated even in the1960s when it gained popularity, his rationale is even more antiquated today, more than forty years later. Even in two-parent households, both parents usually work and contribute equally to the financial and emotional success of the household. Middle- and upper-class parents may work endless hours to maintain their particular lifestyles and may not have a great deal of time to spend with their children. The opposite applies to lower-class single parents, who by virtue of their inconsistent employment history may have quite a bit more time to spend with their children. However, Miller points out that even the quality time spent with the child may not be quality time at all if parents' social skills are questionable. If parents are unable to read or write, they cannot read to their children or assist them with homework.

Miller seems to have applied a majority-based value system to these families. Although some single parents may not be able to read or write, they have elicited assistance from others who can. Some older children read to each other, church deacons and church volunteers spend after school hours reading and assisting these children.

Miller believed that there were no males in single-parent households. He described these situations as "family life dominated by females" (Miller 1958) in which youths were unable to formulate meaningful bonds with their mothers. Miller felt that males played no significant role in the lives of these adolescents. Black family theorists would reject this notion, as they have described the relationships in these families as close-knit. In addition, they discuss how others, extended family, including neighbors and church members, have acted as positive substitutes for black male adolescents where fathers are absent (Billingsley 1992; Hill 1992; McAdoo 1988).

Finally, single-parent households, especially headed by females, are more common in the twenty-first century than ever before. Thus, statements about households headed by women must take into consideration that African Americans no longer are alone in bearing the stigma of that condition. More research is needed in this area to produce more definitive answers.

Conflict Theory

Karl Marx (1818–1883) theorized that capitalism was a major cause of criminal and delinquent behavior. His theory was that under capitalism, those in power (the haves) establish laws within their value system that allow them to remain in power while negating behaviors displayed by the poor (have nots). He explained that in a capitalist society, this was justified and entirely necessary, because such a society thrives with those in power making the decisions and the lower-level individuals carrying out the tasks the powerful deem necessary.

Marx perceived lower-level workers as laborers whose tasks are primarily to produce services and goods for the general welfare of society. In a capitalist society, these laborers must remain in their positions, but there is a constant struggle between the elite and the laborers. According to Marx, the laborers will eventually win the struggle, which will bring an end to capitalism.

Marx and his contemporaries believed that the powerful elite would continue to create and implement laws specifically designed to keep the poor in their place. An example of the application of Marxist theory to juvenile justice is the disproportionate number of minority youths arrested and incarcerated in the juvenile justice system. It can be argued that even though youths from the middle and upper classes commit and are caught in delinquent acts, for social control, minorities are overrepresented among the youths incarcerated.

Walker, Spohn, and Delone (1996) discuss in great detail the usefulness of Marx's conflict theory as applicable to racism and prejudice practiced in the juvenile justice system. According to Marxism, it is not by accident that minorities are overrepresented in the juvenile justice system; it is a methodical plan designed by the ruling class to keep them in their place. This rationale leads to the speculation that after all the funds are provided to states for research projects to study the problem of minority overrepresentation, and after all the published studies, overrepresentation of minorities should decrease, but it has not decreased and shows no signs of doing so. It will not decrease because, as Marxist theory projects, overrepresentation is an ideal mechanism for social control and can only be eliminated if there is an overthrow of capitalism.

Social control is perpetuated by the "get tough" rhetoric and tougher legislation supported by the fear of citizens that juvenile delinquency is on the increase and more violent than ever. Those in power and in fear of losing their wealth because of delinquency push for harsher juvenile laws. The elite implement laws that are tougher on delinquents and authorize spending on the construction of more training schools and detention centers. Although their numbers are increasing, detention centers and training schools will continue to experience overcrowded conditions as the struggle for control continues between the classes.

Marx theorized that this conflict would remain as long as unequal distribution of power among the classes existed.

Systems theoretically designed to help prevent delinquent behavior or divert youths from delinquent behavior seem often to fall short of their goals. For example, training schools, which are supposed to offer rehabilitation and treatment, offer little rehabilitation and treatment. The majority of youths entering these facilities are able to read and write minimally (and, in some cases, not at all), with achievement in school far below the level that corresponds to their chronological ages. When they are discharged from the facilities, they perform at the same poor level of reading and writing. The youths are warehoused; they are confined, clothed, fed, and given no opportunity to prepare for reentry into the community with any type of improved skills. If not attending the institution's school, they are permitted to watch television all day. Although certified school programs exist within juvenile correctional facilities, these students do not excel or even perform at the academic level appropriate for their ages (Miller 1998).

Many programs look great in facilities' year-end reports. In reality, these facilities are interestingly different from their year-end reports: The average day of a youth would likely be spent watching television after completing minimal morning chores of taking care of personal hygiene, making the bed, and having breakfast (Miller 1998).

Little training goes on in training schools, because little more is available than basic medical, school, and psychological services, and many of these are voluntary, or for youths who are considered dangerous, violent, or suicidal (Miller 1988). Marxist thinking would have it that federal and state dollars will be adequate for funding administrative positions in social programs, but limited for providing services that delinquent youths and their families need.

Few prevention programs are located in the delinquents' communities, and most neighborhood programs cannot provide transportation for youths and their families so that they can enter prevention programs. Child care is seldom provided for families that may have transportation, but have younger children in the family that cannot be left alone. Marxist conflict theorists speculate that many juvenile delinquent programs are designed to fail or at best to provide services to a minimal number of youths and their families.

Contemporary Marxist Theory

Richard Quinney discussed criminal and juvenile justice systems as modern-day contradictions. He notes that the very concept of "justice" is misleading and that Marx never used the term because he viewed it as "ideological twaddle." The concept implies equality, although equality does not exist in a capitalist society in which primarily the elite define and interpret the implementation of justice to be administered primarily to the oppressed class (Quinney 1977, 26).

Quinney speculates that the "get tough" punishment philosophy practiced on juvenile offenders was developed to advance capitalism (Quinney 1977, vi). Power brokers do not attempt to reduce delinquency, because it is a natural and normal occurrence that has a meaningful role in a thriving economy.

Like Marx, Quinney views delinquency as a mere manifestation of end products of capitalism (Quinney 1977, 35) based on the promotion of "poverty, inequality, and unemployment" (32). Criminal and delinquent behaviors are fostered activities in a capitalist society and are very necessary to the continuation of capitalism. The criminal and juvenile systems are designed to control the underprivileged: The primary mechanism for that control is the correctional facility. Capitalistic society must control the behavior of the masses, so when delinquents refute that control, their behavior is characterized as deviant. When youths' behaviors deviate from the norm, control theory offers a means of regaining control of them.

Social Control Theory

Travis Hirschi is one of the foremost contemporary control theorists. Hirschi authored *Causes of Delinquency* (1969), in which he discussed in great detail the relationship between delinquent youths and their societal bonds. He viewed delinquents as individuals who had gone astray primarily because the bonds between them and societal systems had either broken or weakened (16), thus creating a situation to which youths react in a negative manner (i.e., delinquent behavior). Hirschi postulated four major areas where social bonding is necessary: attachment, commitment, involvement, and belief (16–30).

Attachment is the association that the delinquent has with individuals, groups, and organizations. These associations form very important emotional relationships for youths. When youths experience difficulty interacting with one or more of these entities, the bond is said to have weakened, causing conflict for the youths and creating societal control issues with which the youths must cope by forming other attachments as substitutes for the weakened or lost ones. A classic example is the youth whose home environment lacks the family experience joining a gang that becomes the surrogate family.

Commitment reflects the motivation and drive that the individual is willing to invest in achieving an outcome or goal. When delinquents are allowed to plan, develop, and participate in programs, the programs are more apt to be successful because the youths have committed to their success by investing their thoughts, time, and ideas into the process. Delinquents who will not display or verbalize a commitment to societal values that have kept them from achieving success legitimately may commit to a delinquent subculture.

Involvement implies being a part of something and participating in activities. When delinquent youths are not involved in traditional activities, they may engage in illegal activities. If their time is dominated by traditional lawful activities, quite naturally, they will have less time to engage in unlawful acts.

Belief is the knowledge and understanding of the values, morals, and legal system that impose the standards of right and wrong on individuals. When adolescents no longer believe in adults or place trust in the legal system, they turn to acts of delinquency. The acts may be of a less intense or less serious nature if the individuals believe in values from family teachings that may be religiously rooted. When youths have limited or no moral or religious belief, it is likely that their delinquent acts will be more serious. All of the aforementioned factors, individually or together, delineated by Hirschi can be causes of delinquency. Strong bonds or ties can decrease the risk of youths becoming delinquent.

Hirschi expanded on his theory by considering not only the causes of delinquency from a macroperspective but also how individual fortitude may also play a pivotal role. With his colleague, Michael Gottfredson, Hirschi formulated a self-control theory that focused on youths' behavior in classical perspective. Self-control theory considers how youths enjoy pleasure and avoid pain. Thus, Gottfredson and Hirschi (1990) theorized that adolescents who were able to maintain self-control were not likely to become delinquent, whereas quick-tempered youths, who act impulsively out of need for immediate gratification, are more at risk for engaging in delinquent behavior.

Self-control theory differs from Hirschi's social control theory because the focus shifted from macrosystemic factors, which are based on societal institutions such as school, church, and Boy Scouts, to a micro- or self-perspective, in which the emphasis is on the individual's ability to manage self.

Microsociological Perspectives: Social Learning Theories

The macroperspective focuses on structural theories of delinquency, considering organizational or institutional factors that cause delinquent behavior. Institutional factors, such as poverty, have to be attacked from a systemic perspective that calls for policy and legal changes and modifications. However, the consideration of delinquency from a microperspective examines individuals and groups and contends that children learn their behavior from others. Thus, change can be effected on a smaller, individualized scale but can have a great impact on large groups.

Social learning theory is based on the premise that behavior is a learned process that involves socialization. Under social learning theory, individuals behave the way they do because they have observed others and are mimicking what they have seen. Therefore, deterrent factors, such as punishment, can make individuals alter their behavior. Under social learning theory, many adolescents would not commit delinquent acts for fear of the punishment they might suffer as a result of their delinquent behavior.

Albert Bandura

Bandura (1977) postulated the rationale that children learn by observing and imitating the behavior of others and taking on the values and the beliefs of those they imitate. Thus, children are socialized to behave a certain way as they grow and develop. This socialization begins in the home, as children observe and imitate the behaviors of their parents. They act it out, dressing in parents' clothes, using makeup, and playing house. Families in which children witness criminal behavior, such as domestic violence, abuse, and other bizarre behavior, may consider it normal and acceptable and go on to emulate that behavior. Some parents, wondering where they went wrong, comment that they raised their children to be respectable and God-fearing, yet those children choose to become delinquent.

As children grow and develop, they are exposed to many different mechanisms of the socialization process. The entertainment mediums of television and movies are two of the most dangerous socialization agents in contemporary society. Youths spend many hours watching their favorite heroes, television and movie stars who enact the violent aggression that many children and adolescents imitate. "Rambo" and "Terminator" were popular 1980s movies whose heroes used sheer violence, unmercifully killing their nemeses to achieve their goals. In the 1990s, violence and aggression became airborne with movies such as

"Independence Day." Television took no back seat to airborne violence with science fiction killers such as "Cyborg." Television and movies moved violence into the second millennium with fictional alien battles, information contained in secret "X-Files," and "Farscape space" characters.

Despite the concern of parents, who advocate regulating violence in the media, media corporations have taken minimal action to limit the amount of violence they portray. Comedy shows are filled with messages of violence and sex as standup comedians, such as Chris Rock and Adam Sandler, use profanity, and entertainer Michael Jackson fondles his groin as part of his performance. Cartoons meant to entertain the younger television audience are as violent as other television programs. For some children, early Saturday and Sunday morning cartoons begin the day with fistfights witnessed over a bowl of breakfast cereal. This violence reinforces the violence that youth engage in, as well as validating their behavior.

Other learning theorists who expanded on Bandura's social learning perspective were Edwin Sutherland and David Matza. They believed, as did Bandura, that youth become delinquent because they have learned how to engage in delinquent activity from others who have influenced them (e.g., family members and friends).

Differential Association

Edwin Sutherland formulated differential association theory (DA). DA theorizes that youths become delinquent as a result of behavior learned from acquaintances, friends, and relatives. Sutherland clearly indicated that this learned behavior becomes a skill that youths acquire through interactions with others who assist them to make refinements. Sutherland and Cressy (1955, 77–79) posit nine principles of criminology that can be applied to delinquency:

1. Criminal behavior is learned.

    Delinquent behavior does not come about because of genetic or inherent predisposition, but occurs because children have been taught and learned the behavior from others.

2. Criminal behavior is learned in interaction with other persons in a process of communication.

    The implication is that youth participate in delinquent behavior because they have not only observed it in others but have been guided through the delinquent process and taught, as well as discovered for themselves, what works and what does not work as they commit their delinquent acts.

3. Learning of criminal behavior occurs principally within intimate personal groups.

    The importance of peer group influence is relevant to explaining delinquency. The peer group exerts more influence on the adolescent, in some instances, than the family. Youths may become involved in delinquent activity because their friends are doing it, or simply because their friends encouraged them.

4. Learning of criminal behavior includes techniques of committing the crime, which are sometimes very complicated and sometimes very simple, and the specific direction of motives, drives, rationalizations, and attitudes.

    The culture of delinquency has to be taught, learned, and eventually mastered by the adolescent. Even as they were taught the family culture as children, they must also be taught the delinquent culture.

5. The specific direction of motives and drives is learned from various favorable and unfavorable definitions of the legal codes.

   Because everyone interprets the law differently, youths have their perspectives and are able to hear different views about the justice system from others. They can also develop for their own personal use many reasons for doing what they do.

6. A person becomes delinquent if definitions favorable to violating the law exceed definitions favorable to obeying it.

   When youths are continually exposed to success stories about delinquent acts, they are not only entertained, but gain new insight into techniques for committing some of these acts.

7. Differential associations may vary in frequency, duration, priority, or intensity.

   Youths become involved in delinquent activities based on their acquaintances and friendships or the extent of the relationship. For example, how important a person is in their lives will influence the degree of delinquency youths will participate in as well as determine how deeply their involvement will be. The youths' ages, as well as the ages of the acquaintances with whom they have relationships, also will have an impact on the delinquency.

8. The process of learning criminal behavior by association with criminal and anticriminal patterns involves all the mechanisms incorporated in any other learning.

   Sutherland suggests that becoming delinquent is a skill that must be acquired and not something that merely can be taught in the abstract. Like any other career skill, the delinquent must constantly practice in order to become adept. Delinquent youths continue to perform delinquent acts although they know they are going to be caught because they do not think of getting caught but of successfully accomplishing the delinquent act.

9. Criminal behavior is an explanation of general needs and values; it is not explained by those needs and values, since noncriminal behavior is an explanation of the same needs and values.

   The art and skill of being successful at a craft (in this case, delinquency) is a primary motivation behind delinquent behavior. Sutherland argued that the same motives for nondelinquent behavior are the motives that stimulate delinquent behavior.

Sutherland's contribution to the field of criminology has been of great assistance in the study of the causes of delinquency. His principles have been beneficial in considering all delinquent youths, regardless of age, race, gender, or nationality. This global perspective allowed others, like Matza, to expand on his conclusions.

Neutralization or Drift Theory

David Matza (1964) postulated a drift theory that expanded Sutherland's differential association theory. Like Sutherland, Matza believed that youths learn delinquent behavior, but he considered the impact of youths' individual value and belief systems. Matza speculated that the values and beliefs developed in early childhood play a significant role in their delinquency.

Matza theorized that delinquent youth were able to move into and out of delinquent roles, a process he termed "drift," by using neutralization techniques that allowed the drifting capabilities. He developed his theory from the classical school of criminology, primarily considering the role of free will (Matza 1964, 181). He explained that free will allows the neutralization or drift process, which has two components, preparation and desperation.

Youths do not become involved in delinquent behavior if they are ill-prepared. Matza identified a number of methods for preparing for delinquency. They may consider the strengths and limitations of the law enforcement unit in the area in which they will operate. In their review of police competence levels, they determine which officers are assigned, how visible the officers are, and the officers' reputations. They consider their own proficiency, to get "hyped up." They consider how well they executed other delinquent acts without being caught, talk about how good they are at what they do, and become excited about the next job. In their cognitive processing about the juvenile system, they consider that juvenile sanctions will be minimal compared to adult sanctions. Finally, the level of preparedness resulting from reflections on past experiences enables youths to learn from past mistakes. "If drifting boys [or girls] are too scared, too apprehensive about repeating an old offense because they recall the fear they experienced last time, the will to engage in crime is obviously discouraged" (1964, 186). Therefore, using past experience to prepare for future delinquency becomes crucial, according to Matza. The will to enter into new delinquent experiences must be activated by feelings of desperation.

Desperation.   Matza suggested that desperation offers the delinquent "the will to commit delinquent acts" (1964, 189). He goes further to state: "Subcultural delinquents experience desperation when caught in the mood of fatalism . . . they seek to restore the mood of humanism in which the self is experienced as cause . . . the delinquent is rejoined to moral order by the commission of the crime!" (189)

Matza's explanation suggests that when youths drift toward delinquency, environmental factors influence their decision to become delinquent. He stresses the classical notion that delinquents make the decision of their own free will. Neutralization occurs when they begin to justify their delinquent behavior. Matza and Gresham Sykes (1957) identified the following neutralization techniques that delinquent youths use:

> *Denial of Responsibility.* Delinquents place blame on others. For example, a friend (or perhaps an unnamed source) is behind the whole thing. Perhaps it is the fault of their parents who made them angry.
> *Denial of Injury.* Delinquents justify actions by questioning the rightfulness or wrongfulness of others. For example, "If she had not left her keys in the car, I would not have stolen it."
> *Denial of Victim.* Delinquents justify actions by suggesting that victims were really not victims but instigators.
> *Condemnation of the Condemners.* Delinquents justify their delinquent behavior by citing the violent nature of society: "It's a jungle out there. You must get them before they get you."
> *Appeal to Higher Loyalties.* Delinquents justify their delinquent behavior by citing the number of corrupt law enforcement officers on the streets, and complain that they are trapped.

Neutralization explains how youths may drift in and out of delinquency. As with other theories, the unanswered question remains: Why can some youths drift back and forth into delinquency while others never drift? One response is that some children may drift into delinquency because they are labeled delinquent and must behave as delinquents.

Labeling Theory

Howard Becker wrote that regardless of the reasons for delinquency, youths who become delinquent and youths who are not yet delinquent are given labels that psychologically mark them and that some are not able to dispel. Thus, delinquency is an end result of labeling (Becker 1963, 9).

Labeling usually begins with parents, early in children's lives. Parents either praise or show disfavor with children by labeling them as good or bad. They seldom distinguish between children's behavior as good or bad, and the children themselves as good or bad. When parents say "bad," children think that they themselves are bad and do not understand that only their behavior is inappropriate or unacceptable.

Gordon Allport, in *The Nature of Prejudice* (1954), suggested that when people continuously are labeled in a specific way, they soon begin to act that way. Thus, when children are labeled "bad," "mean," or "uncooperative," they try to live up to these negative labels just as youths who are labeled "smart," "intelligent," and "good" try to live up to these labels. Living up to labels and making the predictions true is called "self-fulfilling prophecy" (Becker 1963; 1997).

Others expect youths to act according to their labels and treat them according to their labels even if they do not display the expected demeanors. Youths become confused when they attempt to straighten up and do the right thing and still are ridiculed for prior behavior. They may decide that it is pointless to change. Labeling theory has been of particular interest to researchers studying the disproportionate representation of minorities in the juvenile justice system. Some researchers suggest that the disproportionate representation of minorities in the system can be attributed to labeling and that it not only has influenced greatly arrest rates among this group, but has had a negative impact on judges' decisions. The Office of Juvenile Justice Delinquency and Prevention (OJJDP) has sponsored programs to study the overrepresentation of minorities in the juvenile system. The programs have found that minority youths are arrested and sent to training schools more often than their white counterparts (Hsia & Hamparian 1998). Some researchers, however, indicate that labeling theory is on the demise, primarily because of the conservative political environment of U.S. society. Siegel and Senna (1997) suggest that labeling theory should not be completely tossed out or ignored because:

1. It provides insight into functioning of systemic controls,
2. It considers and emphasizes the social factors prevalent in influencing adolescent behavior,
3. It demonstrates an explicit difference between delinquent acts and consistent careers of delinquent behavior. (223)

Labeling theory offers an explanation as to why youths act "bad" when in fact they are really not bad but simply scared to death of becoming bad or scared of having to continue to maintain the "front" of acting bad. Cases have been reported in which hostile, violent, abusive, uncooperative, delinquent youths have been reached by therapists who did not label them, but treated them with honesty, patience, and accepting attitudes.

Labeling is not only one of the simplest explanations for delinquency but one that people commonly use consciously and unconsciously. Adolescents who are constantly labeled will assume the role of the label. Children who constantly are told that they are "bad" or "good," and are treated as such, will respond to their labels and act accordingly.

Nature versus nurture is an age-old controversy that occupies a place of prominence in the minds of many theorists and researchers and precludes all other ideas in their reasoning as to why adolescents commit delinquent acts. Was the commission of an act of delinquency the result of a person's genetic makeup or was it due to the learning of negative socialization and the release of negative energy that emerged as a result of adverse socialized interactions? Alternative theories are explained in the context of socialization: Delinquent children act as they are socialized to be. Delinquency is a coping reaction to their belief that they are inferior, a belief that results from the youths' inability to take responsibility for their behavior or as a result of oppression.

Differential Oppression Theory

Differential oppression (DO) is postulated by Regoli and Hewitt (2000), who believe that children, very early in life, become casualties of oppression as a result of their victimization by macro- and microsocietal systems. They reason that oppression, in the form of victimization by adults, causes some children to commit delinquent acts regardless of their socioeconomic status. Regoli and Hewitt described four principles of DO theory:

1. Adults emphasize order in the home and school.

    Adults rely on the structure that defines their own lives and provides them with the organization that they need to endure their daily routines. When the order becomes disorder, it interferes with their everyday routines and unbalances their behavioral patterns. Disorder (or distraction) for adults occurs when children deviate from the ordered behavior pattern that adults have set for them. The responses that these distractions elicit are based on the amount of deviation and the intensity of the emotional agitation the adults experience as a result of the distraction.

2. Adults perceive children as inferior, subordinate beings and as troublemakers.

    Many adults expect children to stay in their places because they do not view children as equals. Adults may recognize that children have needs and rights, but adults' needs and rights are at the forefront of consideration and adults may consider what is significant to the child inconsequential if the adult does not see its utility. When children venture outside the realm of adult-set peripheries, they are perceived as in need of immediate control and are labeled as troublemakers or children at risk.

3. The imposition of adult conceptions of order on children may become extreme to the point of oppression.

    Any change in order is viewed as a threat and may be met with hostile and oppressive action from the adult. Oppressive action can occur in varying degrees from verbal threats to very serious physical abuse, such as whipping.

4. Oppression leads to adaptive reactions by children.

    The two adaptive behaviors identified in this theory are illegitimate coercive power and retaliation. Children learn the exercise of **illegitimate coercive power** from their parents and use it for their own benefit. Adults do not accept such mimicry by children and perceive it as illegitimate. Children perceive the coercive power used against them by adults to be unnerving and intimidating, but when children use coercive power against adults, it immediately becomes illegitimate. The concept of youths exerting power over others is illegitimate because children are not supposed to possess power: Because they do not know how to handle power legitimately, it can only create disorder. Hence, the belief that the wielding of power is not to be shared with youths. (158–159)

Regoli and Hewitt describe the second adaptive behavior, **retaliation,** as the circumstance under which children learn to use power by seizing control of something important in the lives of their parents, such as their daily schedules. By creating disorder in school, children are able to establish the need for parent–teacher conferences. Parents then must alter their schedules to meet school officials to discuss their children's behavior. Children may fail to show up at mealtimes or stay out late. These actions not only cause disruptions to the parents' schedules, but they create situations that can be corrected only if the child chooses to change the negative behavior.

In the United States today, violence and hostility exist on all levels. On the large scale, in corporate industry, the power and the hostility in corporate takeovers clearly are escalating. On a smaller scale, the intensity of today's children's power base has also changed. Children, in an effort to assert their dominance in the power struggle, no longer are satisfied with petty truancy or acting out, and the stakes become higher and more dangerous as they become involved in extremely violent behaviors. They demonstrate their aggression through the killing of classmates, teachers, parents, and themselves.

DO theory offers a relevant perspective that should not be overlooked in light of the increase in serious, violent, delinquent acts perpetrated by children. Some people believe that violence perpetrated against the community by children cannot happen in their neighborhoods because they live in middle- or upper-class communities. They believe that their children have everything they need for normal healthy lives. Yet, these children may be the unsuspecting victims of oppression because adults expect that children will not change the order of things and will maintain the status quo as they grow and mature. These children may experience as many coercive threats from their parents as do children of lower socioeconomic status. Children on the low end of the scale may be taught from birth that they are oppressed and should, for their own survival, strive to create disruption in the order of things. More research in this area with white middle- and upper-class children could be interesting, because these are the children who have committed mass murders of classmates.

Feminist Theory

Feminist theory is not really a contemporary theory, but a traditional way of thinking that has been accepted by contemporary intellectuals. Feminist theory is a set of ideas and assumptions that focuses primarily on women, and specifically highlights the impact that these ideas and assumptions have on U.S. society and societal changes.

Pollock-Byrne indicates that Lombroso's *The Female Offender* (1894) is one of the earliest publications that tried to explain female criminal behavior, but suggests that female offenders had been studied even earlier (1990, 10). However, female offenders were not taken seriously because their delinquencies were considered less serious and related to sex. Although much of this rationale has not changed in contemporary reasoning, the underlying causes suggested to explain the behavior have changed.

The inducement to consider that females become involved in delinquency because of gender oppression came to fruition in the 1960s and 1970s during the Civil Rights revolution in U.S. society. With the passage of the 1964 Civil Rights Act came the quest for equality for all citizens, including women, and the recognition that women had long experienced oppressive behavior from a societal macroperspective and a male microperspective.

Although a civil rights precedent had been set in the 1800s with the passage of the first civil rights act in U.S. history, women did not receive equal rights under that act. More often than not, the issues of civil rights, equality, and justice had been discussed only in terms of the oppression of black U.S. citizens. However, during the 1960s and 1970s, through marches, research, and court challenges, females and female advocates spoke up loudly to try to make the United States accountable for wrongs inflicted on its female population. Thus, the United States saw the birth of the contemporary feminist movement.

This movement stimulated numerous changes politically, economically, and in the world of scientific research. More research dollars were allocated to studies on women and women's issues. As more research developed on female offenders, this body of knowledge became categorized into separate and distinct paradigms identified, overall, as feminist theory. Five distinctive theoretical foundations emerged: They are identified by Kourany, Sterba, and Tong (1991) as liberal feminist theory, radical feminist theory, psychoanalytic feminism, Marxist feminism, and postmodern feminism.

Liberal Feminist Theory.   Elizabeth Cady Stanton (1815–1902), a strong advocate of women's equality, once stated that the major reason women seek and should be granted equal opportunity in all aspects of life is "the solitude and personal responsibility of her own individual life" (Kourany, Sterba, & Tong 1991, 270). Her belief was that women are responsible beings and, like men, should have the opportunity to take responsibility for the direction in which their lives move.

The scope of liberal feminist theory encompasses the feminist movement by focusing on Stanton's views for achieving equality for females. Women have been able to rise above remaining in their place, which was usually at home, and away from the work force and especially away from the executive machinery and decision making. The prevailing nineteenth century rationale was "keep 'em barefoot and pregnant." But once they had attained equality, women also had to accept the responsibility and consequences that are an important part of it.

Equal opportunity for women has been the major tenet of liberal feminist theory because women have long been discriminated against morally, ethically, socially, and legally. Moral discrimination in the form of the "double standard" historically has plagued women. Women have been expected to remain subservient, stay in the home, care for children, and maintain a household, while men work outside the home and are free to come and go at leisure, completely unrestricted. Ethically, societal norms continue to sanction the inequalities by consciously perpetuating them, or making little or no effort to effect changes in them. Socially, in interpersonal relationships, females are expected to exhibit nonaggressive behavior, and may be labeled negatively if they go after what they want. Finally, legally, women historically have received lower pay for doing the same work as men, and even in light of antidiscrimination laws, this policy has changed very little.

Liberal feminism's primary focus is on equalizing opportunities for women. Its vision is future-oriented, in that it does not focus on past atrocities inflicted by males in the way of radical feminism. Its goal is to ensure that if females choose to explore a course of action that they find appealing, they will have the opportunity to do so, and if denied the opportunity, it will not be simply because of their gender.

Radical Feminist Theory.   Radical feminist theory believes that women, having been oppressed for so long by a male-dominated society, have no choice but to resort to violent delinquent behavior as an inevitable response to this domination. Radical feminist theorists believe that male domination of females has created a dichotomy of oppressor and oppressed. Firestone (1991) uses Marx and Engels' rationale further to describe that perspective as a historical evolutionary struggle between, not only the classes, but between the genders (282–287). However, Firestone is quick to note that the oppression that women experience is not simply an economic struggle but agrees that it goes beyond economics, as Marxist feminist theorists suggest (284). Females have experienced oppression in all areas of society because males, as Firestone observed, have had the power to limit females' access to resources and their use and to define their roles and responsibilities for them. Power is determined by the accessibility to resources and the use of those resources. Males historically have held the primary power positions in U.S. society and it has only been recently that a female, Janet Reno, was appointed the chief law enforcement officer in the country and another female, Madeline Albright, was chosen Secretary of State. Even with these notable advances, the major power positions have been and still are held by males who define roles, which add to females' feelings of psychological insecurity.

Radical feminism is not only viewed as a psychological (i.e., socialization or conditioning) process, but also as a physical one, as when females are physically abused: raped, beaten in domestic violence, forced into prostitution and pornography, and sexually harassed (MacKinnon 1991, 295–308). Many female adolescents who run away from home because of sexual abuse unwittingly end up in lives no better than those they left behind. Once again, they may fall into oppression, as in forced prostitution, but they may reason that it is better because they imagine that they are in control, that their male mentors really care about them. This form of sexual oppression causes a great deal of physical and emotional harm to the youths' psyches.

Psychoanalytic Feminism.   One major area that is seldom addressed in feminist theory is the female personality. Chodorow suggests that women have different psychological qualities from men and that the development of gender differences over the life span should be subjected to more scientific exploration by researchers (1991, 309–332). She explains that children's social relationships are critical in formulating their personalities (230) and therefore greatly influence their behavior. Gender issues become a part of children's conscious and unconscious personality very early in life. Chodorow's developmental cycle begins with infancy, when children are totally dependent on adults for care. She notes that the primary care-giving adult who has a major influence on a child's developmental characteristics is usually female. Many mothers and female caregivers have been conditioned to accept male domination and perpetuate the oppressive state by training children to follow the same teachings.

Chodorow also discusses an "oral incorporative" stage (1991, 331) in which the child begins to form attachments, usually bonding and closely identifying with the primary care provider. She calls these early stages of development the primary identification stages. Often, according to Chodorow, adolescent females will repeat the primary care techniques they received from their mothers or their primary care providers. In repeating what their mothers did, they experience double identification, in which mothers begin to identify with daughters and with their own mothers because they have had both experiences.

In the United States, after the age of three, male children are treated differently from females and adult male figures begin to take on a more active role in their socialization. It is believed that by the age of three males and females have an understanding of the concept of gender and realize that they are either boys or girls. Chodorow says, however, that boys have to readapt, and in doing so, they replace the primary identification that they experienced earlier with their mothers, although girls have no need to readapt. Chodorow developed her rationale around psychoanalytical feminism; Spellman (1991, 322–342), however, criticizes Chodorow's failure to consider class or race as variables in psychoanalytic feminism. She suggests that Chodorow has done what male psychoanalytic theorists have always done by rejecting or simply not including discussions of feminism in their reasoning.

Marxist Feminism. Marxist, or socialist, feminism posits the notion that Hartmann (1991, 343–355) delineates as a progressive initiative for feminism. Women are thought to be in need of liberation, and the liberators should be the females themselves, because they cannot expect that their oppressors will become their emancipators. Because men are in the top positions in the societal hierarchy, they will not relinquish their power easily. They will, however, allow women to achieve some gains, but only gains that men do not perceive as detrimental to themselves or to their societal goals. For example, females may assume relatively few decision-making positions and in them are closely scrutinized and monitored by males. Their decisions could not be independent of male scrutiny, because females might make nurturing decisions for the good of all without regard to monetary concerns, and that would threaten capitalism (Belknap 2000). Hartmann explains Marxist feminism as women's struggle against patriarchy and capitalist idealism, which males have created. In her theory of a Utopian society, womanhood is respected, acknowledged, and not oppressed (355).

Postmodern Feminism. Leclerc (1991) perceives the contemporary feminist as a female awakening from a deep sleep (1991, 362–371). Another analogy is of a frozen female in a time capsule. When the capsule is opened, the female species has evolved into a new and different being. No longer a quiet, submissive person who is heavily dependent on males for everything, this new species does not even need the male of the species for procreation, because this can be accomplished in a laboratory with the assistance of modern technology.

Modern feminist thought does not suggest role reversal such as oppression or enslavement of males, but it does suggest the continued liberation of females and encourages more use of female-based knowledge and the inclusion of female perspectives into all aspects of life. In the classroom, for instance, just as students are taught delinquency theories of male theorists, they should receive exposure to feminist theories, too.

Feminist theory, regardless of which of the five foundations that one argues, has emerged as a convincing alternative theory when discussing female delinquent behavior.

Reality Therapy

Reality therapy, which is closely related to choice theory, is the reality-based assumption that juveniles alone are responsible for their behaviors and therefore must accept the consequences of that behavior. Choice theory emerged from traditional classical thinking, which focused on free will. William Glasser popularized the notion of reality therapy and specifically demonstrated its effectiveness for use with juvenile delinquents and the at-risk population of children.

Glasser postulated that juveniles respond best to immediate gratification to meet their needs or to achieve their goals, so he focused on the here and now in therapeutic conditions. What youths want and what adults think they need may be radically different and may generate hostility between the two. The ways in which adolescents go about accomplishing their goals or satisfying their needs may be much different from the way adults feel they should go about these tasks. Thus, Glasser's theory cautions adults about imposing ironclad, no-option plans of action on youths if they want to achieve positive results.

Glasser's reality therapy strongly emphasizes the need to have adolescents, and to some extent their parents, involved in the therapy from beginning to end. It is the adolescents' responsibility to guide the process, which Glasser called the "doing" component of reality therapy (1965). Reality therapy stresses the importance of self-control and focuses on methods of assisting adolescents to understand the importance of being in control of their own behavior. The underlying assumption is that youths must come to the understanding that they are fully responsible for their behavior and that no one else shares that responsibility with them. When they do lose control and resort to extreme anger or do physical harm to others or themselves, then they can blame only themselves for that behavior.

Making excuses and placing blame on others are not acceptable rationalizations for adolescent misbehavior (Glasser 1965). For example, for youths to claim that they beat up another who laughed when the teacher embarrassed them in class is not acceptable. Reality therapy would focus on the aggressive behavior, considering how the aggressor could have handled the situation differently and still have accomplished two distinct goals, feeling good about themselves during an embarrassing moment and letting the other student know that that they were dissatisfied with being laughed at in class.

Reality therapy does not admit social, political, or economic factors as viable rationalizations for delinquency. Reality therapy acknowledges the inconsistencies and inequalities in life, but does not allow adolescents to dwell on them or use them as an excuse. Past experiences are not allowed as excuses for current behavior. What happened in the past cannot be changed in the present, which is the focus of attention, and only what is happening now and in the future can be shaped by adolescents if they choose to do so. The implication is not that the past should be forgotten, but that it should be placed in perspective and remembered so that the same misbehavior is not repeated.

Reality therapy briefly considers past events, but this area of discussion will not be allotted much time. In this therapy, the majority of time is used to examine what currently is happening and how adolescents can make choices to control their present behavior, regardless of the past. According to the principles of reality therapy, the present behavior will not change by dwelling on the past. Only by doing something about now can change be achieved (Wubbolding 2000). Reality therapy is analogous to giving adolescents a new lease on life and not using past misbehavior as the yardstick for measuring their future.

Reality therapy corresponds with the ideas in the initial development of juvenile justice and the evolution of the juvenile court system in U.S. society in the early 1900s, when the major goals were treatment and rehabilitation of delinquents.

Paradoxical Reality Therapy

Robert E. Wubbolding's (2000) notion of paradoxical reality therapy is a treatment-oriented therapy in which paradoxical instances can be used effectively to motivate behavioral change when working and interacting with adolescents. Paradoxical reality therapy's basic assumption is to use contradictory reasoning that will lead to adolescents changing their thinking about behavior and situations. All humans want to have control of most of life's situations, or at least to create the perception that they have. Although few enjoy giving up that control, some thrive on being in control. Adults may struggle with adolescents who want to do things their way, which is not the adults' way. A common scenario occurs when adolescents stay out beyond their curfew. Adults repeatedly admonish the adolescents for that behavior, and the adolescents repeat it over and over, to the adults' dismay. The adults argue the merits of the curfew and the need to adhere to it. The youths perceive this as criticism and distrust and run away, believing that the adults want to run their lives. When the adolescents return, the adults may resort to closer supervision, stricter house rules, and more monitoring of the youths in an attempt to gain the needed control, and behavior and attitude change.

Reality therapy suggests that it is permissible for adults to give up some control; paradoxical reality therapy suggests that allowing adolescents to take control and accept responsibility for their behavior will help the youths to better understand the behavior and decide what needs to happen for the situation to change. As an added dividend, this provides the sense of autonomy that the youths seek. Wubbolding (1984) suggests that in situations such as this, paradoxical reality therapy—doing the opposite of what the adolescents expect—is likely to show the best results. Avoiding argument is important because argument is expected by youths. Heated arguments in the past did nothing to resolve the problem and resulted in the more serious behavior of running away, so argument can be expected to do nothing more than escalate the situation.

Wubbolding explains that paradoxical reality therapy is rooted in the basic assumption that primary human needs such as power, freedom, belonging, and enjoyment are stimulated by internal drives and that doing, thinking, and feeling are useful for the task of changing behavior (1984, 4–6). Wubbolding explains how, by adhering to specific guidelines, paradoxical reality therapy can be effectively used with youths who are considered hostile and uncooperative.

Juvenile correctional facilities use reality therapy extensively as the primary mode of treatment. One of the major limitations to the use of reality therapy in treatment facilities is the importance of understanding the principles and steps in reality therapy, for example, knowing when to apply reality therapy and when it may not be the most appropriate methodology. Wubbolding cautions against immediate use in violent death crises, such as suicide, and in tumultuous and chaotic family situations. He suggests that individuals should come to terms with these circumstances before reality therapy begins because reality therapy, like other therapies, is not a panacea to be used with every adolescent in every situation. Reality therapy should not be used for shock, but with an understanding of why it may be the effective model to achieve the desired outcome with the adolescent.

Nurturing Theory

Do adolescents behave a certain way because of their inherent genetic makeup or because of what they have learned through exposure to external environmental factors? Nurturing theorists (Bass & Moody 1993; Bavolek 1988) have formulated the theory that little can be done about genetic composition short of radical surgical procedures. Therefore, they suggest that the best plan of action is to make the best of what the individual is and utilize strengths within the individual to bring about individual change. This change comes as a result of focusing on how youths feel and think about themselves (Bavolek 1988, 1). In addition, the entire family participates in small nurturing group sessions. They must make three commitments:

1. To attend all of the sessions;
2. To participate in group activities by expressing their thoughts and feelings;
3. To complete weekly home assignments during the family home nurturing hour (Bavolek 1988, 1).

Nurturing theory was developed in 1983 in Utah at the Family Development Resources Center, a privately supported program. Nurturing philosophy is based on a belief model that emphasizes empathy as a key component; an underlying assumption of the theory is that personal experiences shape and exacerbate human behavior. Adolescents act the way they do because of events and circumstances encountered in past as well as current situations. What they stand for (self-awareness) and what they believe in (belief system) are variables that help youths to make decisions. Adolescents who possess strong values and a strong sense of self can make acceptable decisions: relatively few adolescents who live in areas infested with criminal activity become delinquent, although criminal activity is going on all around them. Adolescents with low self-esteem and negative belief systems are more prone to engage in delinquent behavior, regardless of their socioeconomic status or living environment. Harris and Klebold, who masterminded the Littleton, Colorado, school massacre, were from middle-class, suburban households. Yet they were social isolates who verbalized and acted on negative beliefs that athletes and minorities caused them pain and should therefore be eliminated.

Nurturing theory is a proactive strategy in which the clinical foundation focuses on the family as the beginning point for treatment. Of notable importance to the success of the theory is the notion of "reparenting" the adult (Bass & Moody 1993), that is, teaching them positive parenting skills, which will lead them to a more intense awareness and knowledge of societal parental role expectations. Empowering the adolescent in the family provides opportunities for both the parent and the adolescent to learn about each other's anxieties and interpretations of their experiences. Reparenting carries the expectation that positive change should occur from all family members and not just from the adolescent who may be acting out. Understanding the family's behavior and significant environmental factors (e.g., school, social activities, church, significant others, etc.) are prerequisites to change (Bavolek 1988).

Nurturing theory is based on three major tenets: philosophy, clinical foundation, and practical application. The philosophy of the nurturing theory is that each individual's personal outlook or epistemology of life is important; therefore, knowing and understanding one's own philosophy is essential. Accordingly, youths are asked to consider and verbalize what they stand for and believe in, and are discouraged from apologizing for beliefs that may contradict societal norms. They are encouraged to discuss those beliefs based on their life experiences.

The clinical foundation assumes that people, if given the opportunity, would choose to be kind to one another. Sometimes the kindness does not happen because of circumstances such as chaotic family situations, but the rationale is that the kindness (or positive thinking) can be regained. One method of regaining positive attitude is to come to a better understanding of self. To accomplish this, adolescents are asked a series of "what" questions: What do you want in life that would satisfy you if you could give it to yourself? What image would you like to portray to others? What image do you think others have of you? What method do you now use to handle your anger? What method would you like to be able to use to express your anger? Through this process of inner self-examination, youths can gain a better understanding of their behavior and move in a positive direction to make favorable changes. When adolescents are able to describe experiences and define themselves positively, they experience positive feelings.

Self-awareness is a prerequisite to change, thus the facilitator or clinician's ability to be honest and nonjudgmental is of vital importance—as is understanding the nurturing principles. Nurturing principles emphasize adolescents' need to feel responsible for their behavior whether it is acceptable (i.e., good) or deviant (i.e., bad). Another important principle for the clinician to remember is that it is imperative that adolescents be included in the process of either establishing or defining the rules as they apply to them.

Nurturing theory emphasizes the notion that all behavior is purposeful and all individuals undergoing the process of nurturing have an agenda. For the adolescent and the family, the agenda is to get better or to make positive change. For the facilitator, the agenda is to assist

Five Nurturing Principles for Helping Adolescents Manage Their Behavior

1. Adolescents need to feel responsible for their behavior—good or bad.
2. In establishing any type of rules or expectations, adolescents must be included in the process.
3. Negotiate with adolescents. Work out compromise to the satisfaction of both youths and parents.
4. Parents and adolescents must be able to listen and communicate their views without feeling threatened, criticized, or blamed.
5. Adolescents' opinions, feelings, and needs are no less valid than those of the parents. Equality breeds respect, and respect breeds cooperation.

Source: Bavolek, Stephen. (1988). Nurturing Program for Parents and Adolescents. *Adolescent Handbook.* Park City, UT: Family Development Resources, Inc., p. 44.

with the reinforcement of strength within the individual and the family unit to a point of functioning autonomously without the need of a nurturing facilitator. Therefore, the process (family bringing about change) and the product (clinical application) are interdependent.

The practical application component is as important as the initial components, for in the practical application process, facilitators or clinicians must realize that their roles are not to provide information to individuals, but to bring the individuals to reveal the knowledge that they already possess. Nurturing theory suggests that practical application is a sequential process with a beginning and an ending. The process begins with facilitators asking, "Tell me something about yourself." This opening statement allows adolescents opportunity to self-discover. Discovery of self is more effective than facilitators giving adolescents information or telling them what to do. Eventually, individuals ask: "What should I do?" and facilitators might not have an acceptable answer. During the practical application phase, adolescents become receptive to the clinicians' thoughts and begin to understand and to practice what they come to realize, that their behavior is not making them feel better or helping their situation. Facilitators then ask the youths what they would like to do rather than maintain the negative behavior.

Most adolescents experience a great deal of anger and have not been taught healthy ways to channel it. Many youths do not understand that feeling anger is a normal and healthy experience. They need assistance to find appropriate ways to express the anger. The nurturing therapists delineate some exercises for youths to express anger without harming others (Bavolek 1988, 48):

> *Angry Letter.* In this exercise, youths express their anger and hurt in letters to the people with whom they are angry. They place their letters in envelopes where they can easily see them, and when they feel angry again, they should go open their letters, and read them. They should repeat this as often as the angry feeling occurs. Soon the youths will discover that their letters are no longer needed and they can dispose of them.
>
> *Angry Shreds.* In this exercise, the youths write the name of the person with whom they are angry in large lettering on a piece of paper, tear it in as many small pieces as possible, burn the shreds, and flush the ashes down the toilet.
>
> *Angry Cry and Scream.* In this exercise, youths, alone in rooms with doors closed, shout as loudly as they can the worst possible thing, real or imagined, about the person who is upsetting them. After doing this several times, the youths should exercise energetically.
>
> *Anger Role Play.* In this exercise, youths should imagine that the person who has upset them is seated across from them in an empty chair. As they face the imaginary person, they verbalize their thoughts. Then they move to the empty chair and respond as if they were the person. Repeat the exercise until the youth has resolved the issue.
>
> *Physical Exercise.* Youths should engage in physical exercise, such as jogging, situps, basketball, swimming, or tennis until they are extremely tired and need to rest (Bavolek 1988, 48).

In nurturing theory, it is essential to include all of the youth's family members and significant others as much as possible in the change process. This involvement creates anxiety among family members because they not only feel the pain that they are now suffering, but also develop fear and anxiety about the pain they anticipate as a result of the process.

They fear the therapeutic environment, especially when significant others are included, because they don't know what to expect from them. In some instances, they may have warned their adolescent against interacting with the significant other because of delinquent behavior and illegal activity.

Facilitators must be clear about their own role in this process, because expectations and roles may overlap if definite parameters are not observed. Roles must be clearly defined and facilitators must not become so involved in the process that they lose sight of the goal. They must remember that just like the adolescent and family, they are performing in a role, but that their goal is quite different from that of the family. The goal of facilitators is to assist the family members to become empowered and ready to make necessary changes voluntarily to resolve their crisis without outside help.

Although facilitators should exhibit a caring demeanor, they also must remember that people care on three levels—family, job, and community—that can be translated into interactive roles. As they facilitate the nurturing process, helpers must keep in mind their own backgrounds and areas of caring, but should not let their personal roles affect their work with adolescents and their families. In the nurturing capacity, it becomes quite easy for the facilitators to unconsciously assume parental roles when working with adolescents. Facilitators must remember that they are not these adolescents' parents and must remain in the facilitating role. Nurturing theory suggests that human beings learn on two levels, cognitive (thoughts) in the head and affective (feelings) in the heart. Facilitators can allow themselves to feel empathy for the people with whom they work, but should not take their problems home. They must take time for themselves to be strong for the family during the next session.

Although reparenting is an essential tool in nurturing theory, facilitators must be careful not to attempt to reparent the entire community of which they are part. Facilitators have to separate their time as facilitators from their time as individuals in the community.

Nurturing theory takes a commonsense approach to working with adolescents and their families. Its ecological attitude takes into consideration all things and all individuals involved in the adolescents' milieu in interactions with youths and their families. A major strong point of this perspective is that the family as well as the other components of the adolescents' world (e.g., school, court, church, etc.) must be involved in the process. The theory embraces the concept that "it takes a village to raise a child" and involves all the key individuals in the youths' lives to help to bring about change. The change for adolescents and their families is achieved through community intervention as opposed to individual therapeutic intervention.

Since their inception in 1983, nurturing programs have been field tested with more than 2,000 adults and 6,500 adolescents throughout the United States and in workshops in Germany, Austria, and Canada (Bavolek 1990). Pre- and post-test inventories measure treatment effectiveness. The Adult-Adolescent Parenting Inventory (AAPI), developed specifically for this program, is used to assess high risk behaviors and attitudes of parents and adolescents and to evaluate the success of the program itself (Bavolek 1984, 1989, 1990).

Multisystemic Therapy

Multisystemic therapy (MST) has been described as a family-, home-, and community-based, present-oriented intervention that can be used effectively to reduce delinquent behavior (Henggeler 1997). It is designed to work with youths between the ages of 12 and 15 and their families. MST was developed in the late 1970s at the Family Services Research Center at the Medical University of South Carolina. The initial focus of MST was on adolescents experiencing mental health problems. MST was designed to address issues such as lack of services, and to create services that would, in the long term, render more effective solutions. To focus on effective long-term solutions, all social ecological factors had to be considered. For example, family, school, peer group, and neighborhood, as well as the adolescent's behavior, all have some influence on attitude, values, and social skills. This premise for MST grew out of the basic assumption that delinquent behavior exhibited by adolescents is multicausal and should be addressed multisystemically. However, because each adolescent is unique, MST is an individualized process that is customized to meet the needs of youths and their families. Nine basic principles for practitioners are delineated in the MST process:

1. Understand the "fit" between the identified problems and their broader circumstances.

    The practitioner's initial role is to review all of the material and discern what is happening based on the social ecological factors identified. Then the practitioner meets with youth, family members, teachers, and so forth, to listen to their perspectives in an effort to put all of the information into a workable framework. The practitioner determines, along with the adolescent and other support systems, which factors have impact on the others and the intensity of the impact, to help prioritize strategies for intervention. After a schema is figured out and approved by the youth, and the other concerned people, the plan is implemented. If the plan seems to work and behavioral changes occur, the practitioner continues to monitor the youth; if it does not work, then the practitioner revises the plan.

2. Therapeutic contacts should emphasize and use systemic strengths to levels for change.

    The practitioner should focus on strengths and not on pathology, emphasizing protective factors such as supportive family, attendance at school, and attendance at church, to assist youths and their families to reach their goals. This process builds self-esteem within the youth as well as within the family, which may also feel hopeless and frustrated.

3. Interventions should be designed to promote responsible behavior and decrease irresponsible behavior among family members.

    One of the major goals of MST is to change the behavior so that youths act more responsibly. For instance, one goal for youths might be to avoid physical conflicts in school, so strategies to assist them to refrain from fighting in school would be considered. Parents also might need to adjust some of their adverse behaviors that may influence the youths' negative behavior. Intervention strategies should not only focus on designing strategies for the youth, but also on developing strategies (such as structuring more effective and consistent disciplinary process for their youths) for the parents.

4. Interventions should be present focused and action-oriented, targeting specific and well-defined problems.

    The focus of the entire process is reality—that is, what is occurring now in the youths' lives. To stay focused on the here and now, therapists consider intervention strategies that will render immediate results. Other approaches have not been very effective with serious offenders because they focused on the past and the youths and their families are present-oriented and want to see and feel immediate results.

5. Interventions should target sequences of behavior within or between multiple systems that maintain the identified problems.

This principle targets empowering the parents. Many parents have been unable to act as agents or advocates for their children, especially in the school system. Research has proved that parents who assume an active role in the education of their children will realize greater benefits than parents who do not. One method of assisting youths to change their behavior at school is to aid their parents to become more active in school activities and to share positive input in discussing issues related to the welfare of their children.

6. Interventions should be developmentally appropriate and fit the developmental needs of the youth.

This principle strongly supports the belief that age appropriate strategies are the most effective for dealing with youths. For example, it may be appropriate to give 5-year olds timeout periods when they display inappropriate behavior, but 15 year olds may need more age appropriate sanctions, such as restriction of telephone privileges.

7. Interventions should be designed to require daily or weekly effort by family members.

Many families and youths may have the notion that MST will perform similarly to other agencies with which they have had unrewarding experiences. One difference between other agencies and MST is that MST recognizes that situations with multiple problems are also multidimensional and initially require many hours of contact with clients. Simply identifying some problem areas may require numerous hours. To ensure that the youths and their families receive emotional support and are provided the essential, ongoing evaluation, requires hours of monitoring. This principle recognizes that problems that have existed for a long time cannot be resolved without intense, consistent oversight.

8. Intervention effectiveness is evaluated continuously from multiple perspectives with providers assuming accountability for overcoming barriers to successful conclusions.

Evaluation, a crucial component of the intervention process, is important to determining whether or not the strategies are working so practitioners and youths and their families and other support systems readily can modify them. Evaluation is fundamental to effective interventions; in some programs, if the initial strategy does not work, the rationale is that the youth is not trying hard enough to change. MST recognizes that the underlying problem may be the result of a systemic issue that should be addressed in the process. For example, one strategy may be for a youth to attend reading class every day with no absences. Investigation of the school's report that the youth missed a reading class might result in the discovery that the youth was in a meeting with another teacher who provided an excuse slip, but forgot to give the school office a copy.

9. Interventions should promote treatment generalization and long-term maintenance of therapeutic change by empowering caregivers to address family members' needs across multiple systemic frameworks.

The outcomes of MST should be long-term behavioral change within youths and their family environment. This principle emphasizes that the responsibility for "doing" belongs to youths and their families because it is not the role of practitioners to do things for them. Practitioners are neutral. They primarily act as advocates for youths and their families as they try to empower the youths and change their behaviors (Henggeler, Schoenwald, *et al.* 1998).

MST begins with assessment. Here the identification of adolescents' problem behaviors involves everyone with whom they interact—parents, teachers, probation officers, and so forth. The focus of the session is to eliminate or reduce the antisocial behavior and its objective is to build on the collective strengths of everyone participating in the session. How these strengths can facilitate termination of the problem is carefully considered. For example, although a teacher may be excellent, the student is doing poorly in class. The teacher does not have time to review with one youth, but one of that teacher's strong points, is flexibility and willingness to assign a classmate who is doing well in the class to tutor the student with the difficulty.

The next major phase of MST treatment is assessment of the risk factors—obstacles or barriers to resolving the problem. Practitioners identify the fit between the problem and the broader systemic conditions, define the targets of intervention, and clarify whether the measures taken were effective (Henggeler *et al.* 1998; http://www.mstservices.com/text/treatment.html#core). Risk factors may include lack of parental discipline and supervision, poor study habits, poor communication skills, or chaotic home environment.

Practitioners identify the risk factors and focus on the protective factors with the youths and others who will be involved in the process. Practitioners should not use diagnostic labels. They should create a realistic situation in which the youth and family feel comfortable, so the first session may take place in the family home. Early contacts are frequent, but over time, contacts decrease, until, eventually, the family no longer needs the practitioner. The ultimate goal is for the family and the youth to successfully employ the strategies themselves.

Some youths, as identified by Henggeler, are ineligible for this approach. They include:

1. Youths whose parents will not participate in the sessions.

    Because MST is a family-oriented approach, it is imperative that parents be involved in the process. If the youth is in foster care, the foster parents must be involved in the sessions. In other words, the youth's primary care providers are expected to participate, and are told in the beginning that their participation is mandatory.

2. Suicide risks.

    Adolescents who are suicide risks are not eligible because MST is a here and now, reality-based therapy and youths who display suicidal ideation need individualized care. However, after they have received treatment and are no longer in the care of a therapist, they may be considered for MST.

3. Sexual offenders.

    Sexual offenders, like suicide-prone adolescents, initially need more individualized therapy. Because a community-based approach is incorporated in the framework of MST, it is not appropriate to include sexual offenders in MST.

4. Drug abusers who are not involved in other delinquent behaviors.

    Even though drug abuse is considered delinquent behavior, the drug abuse alone does not make the adolescent eligible for MST. Parents and youths both must agree to participate in the program, even if they are referred by the court.

MST is a relatively quick process: The treatment period is usually four months. Although MST has proved effective with other populations, such as Canadian youths, the majority of youths who have benefited from MST have been African American males from single-parent households (Brondino *et al.* 1997), primarily because they usually have comprised a large percentage of the incarcerated juvenile population. Henggeler suggests that MST has been effective with African American youths for several reasons:

1. Practitioners include family members in the treatment process from onset to termination.
2. MST focuses on the extended family as well as the family's informal support networks.
3. MST does not use diagnostic labels or jargon, and the practitioner uses terms and concepts from everyday language. Culturally appropriate practices are used and valued because the multicultural treatment teams reflect the ethnic composition of the population served.
4. Families are seen in their homes so that therapeutic barriers, such as sterile clinical offices, can be removed and because they feel more comfortable in a familiar environment.
5. Youths and their families are involved in constant, ongoing evaluations and feedback.
6. MST has proved to be effective with this population through a number of clinical trials (Brondino *et al.* 1997).

MST has been described as a "treatment theory" (Henggeler 1998). This social ecological model is deeply rooted in the conviction that all systems involved in youths' lives are interconnecting and related. This theory includes the belief that cultural issues must be addressed because they are a very crucial component to youths' deviant acting out. Thus, the aim is to assist the young people in bringing about change in their environment so that they can function appropriately even in chaos.

Afrocentric Perspective.   Some Afrologists suggest that MST is a creative approach with the infusion of culturalism into the framework of the theoretical underpinnings. However, they argue that there appears to be no one moment when the youths can reflect on self and discover their identity. This dimension especially is needed for African-American youths, and an Afrocentric approach adds it.

Asante (1988) discussed Afrocentrism in the context of a need for a philosophy that would provide a theory based on the cultural heritage of individuals who have an African heritage. Murray and Herrenstein boldly have provided a clear message to criminal and juvenile justice systems that the systems are overcrowded with minorities (specifically African American) because intellectually, minorities are genetically inferior and prone to criminal activity (Murray & Herrenstein 1994). Others have attempted to disguise their rationale (even though they agree with Murray and Herrenstein) by proposing different tactics, yet fostering the same thinking. The difference in tactics is not to clearly and explicitly state that minorities are inferior, but to ensure limited methods of rehabilitation in juvenile correctional facilities. Some educators who agree with Murray and Herrenstein have practiced limiting the scope of knowledge to which criminal justice students are exposed in colleges and universities.

Historically, criminal justice students in the United States take a course that focuses on theories that have an impact on criminal and juvenile delinquent behavior. Theories not only shed light on delinquency but also can assist in the prevention of delinquent behavior. Yet, with statistics pointing to overrepresentation of minorities in the juvenile justice system, few textbooks include culturally competent theories as a framework for students to consider. Most juvenile justice texts begin with the biological perspectives of Lombroso, Sheldon, and Murray and Herrenstein, include insights from psychological giants such as Freud and behaviorists such as Skinner, and end with the sociological theories of Shaw and McKay, Ohlin and Cloward, or Sutherland. Some are beginning to break the cycle and include feminist theory because of the increase in arrest rates of female delinquents.

Asante's (1988) Afrocentric theory is included in this chapter as one response to the overrepresentation of minorities in the juvenile justice system. Unlike traditional, classical theories of criminology, its focus is on a positive perspective for providing minority clients in the system—as well as those interacting with these minority clients—a positive mechanism that may promote a reduction in delinquency and the high rate of recidivism among this population.

A major underlying assumption of Afrocentrism is the opinion that individuals are responsible for their behavior, but there is also a collective responsibility to ancestors. If individuals do not understand who they are, it becomes difficult to maintain positive behavior and display positive values. Accordingly, Asante suggests that understanding heritage instills respect in the individual for himself as well as his culture. Afrocentric theory suggests that coming to an awareness of self through an understanding of heritage will afford the delinquent less time and opportunity to engage in negative, self-destructive, delinquent activities. When youths are able to understand their heritage, they will gain more respect for their parents, community, and society. Afrocentric theory teaches that it may take a village to raise a child, but the village must first teach the child self-awareness, so that respect and consideration for others may follow.

Afrocentric theory is deeply rooted in the notion of the importance of the clients' understanding who they are. A key element that brings about that understanding is knowledge of historical events that frame the present and shape the future. Although Asante (1988) suggests that Afrocentric theory can be applicable to all adolescents, it seems to be very relevant to African American adolescents during the twenty-first century because incarceration and arrest rates have increased among this group and prevention and diversionary programs have begun to focus on Afrocentric principles. Some of those principles, as delineated by Asante, are:

1. Because individuals are products of their heritage, teach adolescents to be proud of their ancestral contributions to society.
2. Assist adolescents to understand what they have to offer their community and society.
3. Focus on the adolescents' strengths and show them how to use them positively to accomplish their goals.
4. Assist adolescents and families to understand the importance of community and of working together as a community to resolve conflicts and other issues.
5. Help them to understand the importance of learning about others and how the information can be helpful to their own growth and development.

Afrocentric theory postulates two major, basic propositions: that Afrocentric theory embraces people of African heritage and not just African Americans, and the value of diversity in which numerous perspectives are valued and practiced (Asante 1988). Any scholar can practice and understand Afrocentric theory: Asante contends that some black people do not understand Afrocentric theory although many white people do. Degrees from universities are not indications of a person's capabilities, that is, their sensitivity and responsiveness to black cultural data (63). It is not a "blacks only" theory. It is an alternative perspective that can be used especially with children who are hostile, uncooperative, noncompliant, hard to reach, and lost in the juvenile justice system "because it is neither a matter of color nor theme . . . it is the Afrocentric method which makes Afrological study possible" (60). Asante identifies three underlying assumptions of Afrocentric theory: competency, clarity of perspective, and understanding (60).

Competence is the individual's ability to assess the delinquent's situation from a holistic perspective. This should a macroecological perspective (e.g., systems that include not only justice systems but church and spirituality) as well as the microecology of the adolescent (e.g., adolescents' perceptions of self, community, society, and the world).

Clarity of perspective implies the need to be able to see things through the eyes of adolescents so that the youths can be helped to reframe negative perspectives to become more positive realities. This warrants clear understanding that people working with the youths must put aside their value systems temporarily in order to gain a better understanding of the youths.

Understanding implies the ability to focus on the situation or problem, not in judgment but in relation to implications. The delinquent's issues are not one problem but are a multitude of interrelated activities to consider in relation to consequences and the impact they have on other people—not merely on the youths, but on their families, community, and society. Cases have been reported in which angry clients, with whom psychoanalytic and behavioral therapies had failed, responded favorably to therapists who showed them respect, were honest with them, and seemed to understand them.

Health care professionals working with delinquent youths can become more effective by incorporating an entire battery of theoretical perspectives (including an Afrocentric perspective) because all adolescents are different and each may need many different approaches. Showing respect and understanding their culture appears to be one effective method when working or interacting with African American youths.

Summary

Sociological explanations for the causes of delinquency are grounded in the notion that environmental factors are primary forces that have an impact on delinquent behavior. Environmental factors can be viewed in a dichotomy of microsystems and macrosystems, both of which have an impact on delinquency. For example, from the moment children are born, they are influenced by sociological systems. They begin with the microsystem of the family unit in which children observe the individuals around them and begin to imitate the behavior of adults. As the children grow and develop into adolescents, they continue to observe and imitate the adults around them, but they also become involved with peer groups where all they say and do is measured by their peers.

Sociological theories are based on the premise that behavior is learned. Thus, children and adolescents learn their delinquent attitudes and behavior from those around them.

TABLE 4.1 **Summary of Traditional Sociological Theories**

Theorist/Proponent	Theory	Premise
Cloward and Ohlin	Blocked opportunity	Lack of legitimate means to success can lead to engaging in illegitimate means to success.
Shaw and McKay	Social disorganization	Slum neighborhoods in a state of disorganization cause delinquency.
Robert Merton	Strain theory	Adolescents become delinquent because of the lack of availability of resources.
Albert Cohen	Status frustration versus middle-class measuring rod	Boys from lower socioeconomic conditions seek middle- and upper-class values. Delinquency is a reaction to social and economic deprivation by lower-class boys.
Walter Miller	Matriarchal family units	Boys in single-parent households in which the female is dominant are more prone to delinquency.
Karl Marx	Conflict theory	Capitalism is a major cause of delinquency based on an unequal distribution of power
Richard Quinney	Conflict theory	Adolescents become delinquent because of their low socioeconomic status.
Travis Hirschi	Social control theory	Adolescents become delinquent because of weak or broken bonds between them and other systems.
Travis Hirschi	Self theory	Youths become delinquent when they are unable to control their anger and aggression.
Albert Bandura	Learning theory	Adolescents become delinquent through observation and imitation.
Edwin Sutherland	Differential association	Youths become delinquent because of their relationships with others.
David Matza	Neutralization theory	Youths drift into and out of delinquency by using neutralization techniques.
Howard Becker	Labeling theory	Adolescents become delinquent trying to live up to a label, such as "bad."

Shaw and McKay theorized that children and adolescents become delinquent because of their slum environment, which produces neighborhood disorganization and transitional disintegration. The question then becomes, if that is the case, why are there fewer delinquents than nondelinquents? Gottfredson and Hirschi formulated the idea that some children and adolescents do not become delinquent because they have the free will to make choices and the ability to exert self-control. Other youths who become delinquent, but who may reside in the same neighborhoods, may become delinquent because they have not mastered the ability to control their impulses and their need for immediate gratification.

Labeling theory describes a powerful force that places a stigma on children that they feel they must live up to achieve acceptance. Adolescents are often the recipients of labels, and the labels can have many kinds of impact on them, making them want to live up to their labels and initiating within them the determination to become successful in their delinquent quests. The ability to engage in delinquent activity is not based solely on labels. Some adolescents drift in and out of delinquency. In delinquency, they discover success that they were not privy to prior to their delinquency. As they discover that they can be successful delinquents, they continue to prepare for it and desperation urges them to continue their deviance. They use neutralization techniques to rationalize their delinquency and feel better about it.

Students of criminal justice must be aware of the many theories that explain the causes of delinquency, understand them, and be able to apply theoretical conceptualizations to their assumptions. Sociological theories will not be applicable in all situations and with all delinquent adolescents, but knowledge of the theories is important. Cyberspace has unlocked the doors to unidimensional thinking. As adolescents are exposed to more and more, society must continue to seek new and diverse methods of addressing their needs. No one theory is the panacea that will reduce delinquent behavior. With the increase in population diversity in the United States and the increase in serious, violent delinquent acts by young children and adolescents, it is important to develop, discuss, and implement theories that may increase understanding of the causes of children's delinquency. These theories will be foundations for practice and treatment models as we struggle to prevent, reduce, and eliminate serious, violent behavior among young children and adolescents.

KEY CONCEPTS

Afrocentric
Afrology
anomie
Chicago Area Project
culture of poverty

differential association
macrofactors
microfactors
multisystemic therapy
nurturing

poverty
reality therapy
self-fulfilling prophecy

DISCUSSION QUESTIONS

1. Explain some strategies you would use in working with delinquent adolescents.

2. Identify some factors that are important to remember when working with delinquent adolescents. Discuss why you feel these factors are important.

3. What is your theory about why adolescents become delinquent? If your theory is not sociological, compare and contrast the different thoughts. If your theory is sociological, specify whether it is a macroperspective or a microperspective and identify a theorist who may agree with your particular theory.

4. Did you or a friend ever participate in delinquent behavior when you were growing up? If so, explain. If not, explain why not and identify a theory that supports the explanation.

5. Did the Columbine students who shot fellow classmates and a teacher learn the behavior? Did they act because they were socialized to do so? Did they act because they were labeled social isolates? Discuss, using theoretical arguments.

EXERCISES

1. Form small groups and debate whether microfactors or macrofactors cause youths to become delinquent. Quote theorists to validate your debate.

2. Design a community program to reduce or eliminate delinquency in your community. Present your program design to the class and discuss ways to improve it.

3. Discuss how a community program that already exists in either your community or a community that you are aware of could reduce delinquency in the area.

4. Talk with someone in your community who works with delinquents. Ask them to explain the strengths of their program, some of the obstacles they face, and how they overcome the obstacles. Submit your written comments for discussion in class.

CHAPTER

5 Schools and Delinquent Behavior

CHAPTER OBJECTIVES

On completing this chapter, students will have tools to:

- Understand issues related to school violence
- Consider constitutional issues that schools and students face
- Consider factors that cause schools to fail students and communities
- Gain insight into the roles and responsibilities of police officers in schools
- Consider positive actions to reform schools

The Proliferation of Violence in the United States

Schools and violence are linked in contemporary U.S. culture. Television, magazines, movies, and newspapers recount stories of school violence. Regardless of the geographical location or the socioeconomic status of a community, more and more citizens discuss school violence and their fear that it eventually will occur in their schools. On every level of education—elementary, middle school, high school, college—many educational facilities experienced some degree of chaos—and those that did not, prepared for it, believing that in time, violence would occur. The September 11, 2001, attacks on the United States added another dimension to the violence students and teachers in U.S. schools have to face. These attacks placed schools in a vulnerable position and demonstrated the need for a plan to protect students and teachers from all types of violence, whether created externally by terrorists or internally by students.

School violence committees emerged throughout the United States to study the phenomenon and make recommendations to local boards of education on methods to reduce, control, or eliminate violence in their communities' schools. A prevention strategy that emerged as a result of the disorder is the assignment of police officers to neighborhood schools. The officers' roles, however, are preventive. The officers are visible to present a positive presence and to communicate with students to help resolve problems before violence occurs. This chapter focuses on questions about how violent the schools and the students attending them are. Looking at the evolution of the U.S. education system from a historical perspective, it considers dilemma-evoking issues that concern parents, educators, and students, such as sexuality, freedom of expression, privacy, and respect. It considers pressures that may lead children to perform poorly in school, such as tracking and irrelevant curricula, and pressures on teachers, such as merit pay increases based on the number of students who pass year-end exams, and then pursues a speculative look at the future of U.S. schools.

School Violence

Is youth violence in schools greater than ever before in the history of the United States? The average citizen was bombarded with news about school shootings before and since the deadly Columbine incident (see Chapter 4). The media, through sensationalism, made violence in the schools fodder for anyone seeking office, funds, or attention as U.S. citizens wait for the next school catastrophe to occur.

Timeline of School Shootings

March 7, 2001	A fourteen-year-old girl wounded another girl in the cafeteria of Bishop Neumann High School in Williamsport, Pennsylvania.
March 5, 2001	A fifteen-year-old boy shot up his high school in Santee, California. It was described as the worst school shooting in the United States since the Columbine massacre two years earlier. Two were left dead and thirteen other students were wounded with the youth's .22 revolver.
May 26, 2000	A thirteen-year-old boy shot another at Lakeworth Middle School in Lakeworth, Florida.
February 29, 2000	A six-year-old boy fatally wounded a sixteen-year old girl at Buell Elementary School near Flint, Michigan. A nineteen-year-old was charged with involuntary manslaughter for allowing the boy easy access to the .32-caliber handgun.
December 6, 1999	A thirteen-year-old boy wounded four students (another was severely bruised in the chaos) at Fort Gibson Middle School in Gibson, Oklahoma. He used a 9mm semiautomatic handgun.
November 19, 1999	A thirteen-year-old randomly shot and killed a seventh grader at Deming Middle School in Deming, New Mexico. The killer, a dual citizen living in Mexico and commuting to school, was struggling with depression after the death of his mother.
May 20, 1999	A fifteen year old injured 6 students at Heritage High School in Conyers, Georgia. The assailant was depressed after breaking up with a girlfriend.
April 20, 1999	Two youths killed 14 students, including themselves, and one teacher and wounded 23 others at Columbine High School in Littleton, Colorado.
June 15, 1998	A fourteen-year-old boy wounded a teacher and a guidance counselor in a hallway at Richmond High School in Richmond, Virginia.
May 21, 1998	A fifteen year old killed 2 students and wounded 22 others at Thurston High School in Springfield, Oregon.

(continued)

Continued

May 19, 1998	One student shot and killed another in the parking lot at Lincoln County High School in Gayetteville, Tennessee, three days before graduation. The victim was dating the former girlfriend of the shooter.
April 24, 1998	A fourteen-year-old boy killed one teacher and wounded two students at a dance at James W. Parker Middle School in Edinboro, Pennsylvania.
March 24, 1998	Four students were wounded as Westside Middle School in Jonesboro, Arkansas, which was emptied during a false fire alarm.
December 15, 1997	A fourteen year old, hiding in nearby woods, shot and wounded two students in Stamps, Arkansas, as they stood talking in the parking lot.
December 1, 1997	A fourteen-year-old boy killed three students and wounded five at Heath High School in Paducah, Kentucky, as they participated in a prayer circle.
October 1, 1997	A student killed two students and wounded seven at Pearl High School in Pearl, Mississippi. The shooter also killed his mother.
May 5, 1997	One student was shot on the steps of City-as-School in New York City.
February 19, 1997	A sixteen year old shot and killed the principal and a student and wounded two others at his high school in Bethel, Alaska.
April 15, 1996	A twenty-three-year-old alumnus was shot in the gym at McKinley High School in Washington, D.C.
February 2, 1996	A fourteen year old shot and killed two students and a teacher and wounded another in his algebra class in Moses Lake, Washington.
April 8, 1994	A seventeen-year-old student shot his teacher at Largo High School in Maryland.
May 24, 1993	A fifteen year old shot and killed a sixteen-year-old schoolmate at Upper Perkiomen High School in Pennsburg, Pennsylvania.
March 25, 1993	A ninth-grade girl was shot by another girl in the hallway of a high school in St. Louis, Missouri.
January 18, 1993	A student shot and killed a teacher and a janitor in East Carter High School in Grayson, Kentucky.
January 12, 1993	An eighteen year old died from multiple gunshot wounds after a dispute with schoolmates in Norland Senior High School in Miami, Florida.
May 1, 1992	A former student shot and killed four students and injured nine others in Lindhurst High School in Olivehurst, California.
February 9, 1992	A student shot and killed two others in Thomas Jefferson High School in Brooklyn, New York.
January 17, 1989	A man randomly opened fire and killed 5 children and injured 29 more in Cleveland Elementary School in Stockton, California.

Sources: ABC News: Recent School Shootings: www.archive.abcnews.go.com/sections/us/shootings_side1205; Elissa Haney: lycos.infoplease.com/spot/schoolviolence1.html; *Time,* March 19, 2001, pp. 22–31.

School violence has become a major political issue, as candidates stress how much they abhor the violence in the nation's schools. Former President Clinton attempted to get Congress to pass gun control legislation that would limit the availability of guns in the hands of children. The National Rifle Association (NRA) countered that slack gun-control laws are not the reason children commit violent acts with guns in schools, arguing that

Eric Harris

Kip Kinkel

Andy Williams

Dylan Klebold

Luke Woodham

AP/Wide World Photos

citizens have a constitutional right to bear arms and that stringent gun control legislation is not the answer.

The American Academy of Pediatrics (AAP) created tension among the ranks of the American Medical Association (AMA) when they released a statement supporting gun control. The AMA and the NRA have powerful lobbies in Washington, but the AMA had never taken a position on gun control. After the AAP released this statement supporting gun control the AMA declared that it was inappropriate because gun control is not a medical issue. The AAP took the position that gun control is a medical issue because they spend a great deal of time in emergency rooms caring for young children with injuries from guns (AAP 1999).

Others describe the focus on violence as "much ado about nothing," and as media hype. They entertain the notion that there has always been violence in schools, and they disagree with the idea that violence by juveniles is on the increase (Ewing 1992; Miller 1992; Schwartz 1992). Schwartz suggests that the media mislead the public with inaccurate information gathered and provided to them by the government and they make no attempt to correct their statistics even when mistakes are called to their attention (50). These researchers have attempted to dispel numerous myths about youth violence with data. Schwartz (51–53) identified eight popular myths:

> Myth 1: Delinquency is on the increase. Schwartz says that delinquency rose in the 1960s and early 1970s but stabilized in the late 1970s and showed a decline between 1979 and 1984. He notes that in 1985, statistics showed another slight increase. He suggests that U.S. society should not panic and overreact to a perceived juvenile crime epidemic in the United States.
>
> Myth 2: Juveniles commit more serious crimes than any other segment of the population. Schwartz argues that crime rate statistics do not support this statement because juveniles account for only a small percent of the serious crimes (Kaufman *et al.* 1999).
>
> Myth 3: Juveniles commit more crimes against the elderly than other groups. Schwartz maintains that only a very small percentage of crimes against the elderly are committed by juveniles. He contends that fewer than 30 percent were committed by an individual 20 years or younger (Schwartz 1992, 53).
>
> Myth 4: Females commit more serious crimes than their male counterparts. Schwartz argues that although statistics indicate an increase in female crime rates, the increase closely mirrors the small increase in the male crime rate, leading him to reason that the female crime rate has not skyrocketed.
>
> Myth 5: Juveniles are prone to commit delinquent acts against strangers. Schwartz contends that adolescents do not usually attack total strangers for no reason (unless the juveniles are undergoing gang initiation or they and the strangers are gang affiliated). He notes that most adolescent assaults or physical attacks are perpetuated against other teens with whom they are familiar, and usually the reason for the violence is known to all parties involved in the mayhem (Schwartz 1992, 52).
>
> Myth 6: Juveniles commit more serious violent crimes than adults. Schwartz argues that generally they do not have the resources that adults have to secure weapons and he emphasizes their limited ability to inflict monumental financial losses upon the economy as adults do (Schwartz 1992, 52).

Myth 7: Minority youths commit the most serious juvenile crimes. Schwartz claims that minority youth are arrested and committed at a greatly disproportionate rate and consequently the statistical data is disproportionately generated. He further argues that the data do not include information on unreported crimes, or the high arrest rates of minority youths, and crimes in which youths with greater access to available resources have been diverted from the juvenile justice system.

Myth 8: If you lock up juvenile offenders, the crime rates will decrease. Schwartz insists that "there is little or no relationship between the rate of serious juvenile crime and the rate at which youths are being incarcerated" (Schwartz 1992, 53). He argues that states that incarcerate youths at a high rate also have high juvenile crime rates.

Schwartz argues that for political reasons, the government and the media mislead the public into thinking that juvenile delinquency is steadily and rapidly increasing and that juvenile offenders are by far more violent than adults. He suggests that juvenile delinquency is a problem, and advises that it does not need a "quick fix" (53). He reasons that violent serious crimes committed by youths can be reduced by careful, well thought-out, ongoing planning.

Historical Perspective: How Far Have We Come?

In seventeenth-century colonial America, formal education was made available to all children but was not regarded as compulsory. Children who were required to help their families on farms, unruly children, slaves, and females were viewed as individuals who did not need education: Schooling for them would be a waste of time. The law dictated that children should be able to read and write by age 12. By 1918, all states had adopted mandatory schooling for children as compulsory school attendance laws were enforced throughout the country (*Brown v. Board of Education;* Cubberley 1962). The Amish have been the only exception to mandatory school attendance. In *Wisconsin v. Yoder* (1972), the Supreme Court ruled that Amish children are exempt from compulsory school attendance beyond the eighth grade.

By the dawn of the nineteenth century, all U.S. school districts were required by law to have an official advisory body to monitor them and make academic recommendations to improve the educational success of district schools. This body, previously known as the town council, was now called the "board of education" and its sole responsibility was matters pertaining to the schools (Powell 2001).

Certification guidelines and the methodical separation of children into levels based on chronological age were introduced in the nineteenth century. Prior to this time, children were educated based on their level of maturity, with disregard for chronological age. The schoolteacher was an extension of the town council, and just as the town council wielded its power over the town, the teacher exercised absolute power and authority in the classroom. Decisions on textbooks, the type of books that students would read, the length of the school day, the rules and policies, and the methods of discipline that would be employed—all were decided and implemented by the teacher.

Contemporary school policies have a "zero tolerance" approach toward disruptive behavior. Zero tolerance implies that the school system takes swift action against students who violate rules and are disruptive in or on school property. Adams (2000) identifies six problems with zero tolerance:

1. The majority of adolescents who are suspended or expelled from school are the students most in need of education.
2. Procedural due process issues are not necessarily a major consideration to school personnel.
3. The nurturing component of education is greatly reduced or eliminated.
4. Racism, unintended or intended, is practiced.
5. Students can be removed from school for minor infractions of school policy.
6. Research does not prove that zero tolerance effectively reduces disruptive behavior.

Some results of zero tolerance have been the stringent implementation of disciplinary tactics, such as corporal punishment, suspension, expulsion, and medication of youths.

Corporal Punishment

Corporal punishment was used in school systems by teachers who had a strong religious background. They believed that it was ethically and morally right for children to show respect for adults and they had zero tolerance for children who misbehaved in the classroom. Corporal punishment was sanctioned by all as a disciplinary tool, and teachers had the permission of parents as well as the council to properly discipline children in the classroom. (Adams 2000; Kaestle & Foner 1983; Rothbard 1999).

Corporal punishment is the inflicting of pain on children by physical force, such as beating them with a switch or paddle. Corporal punishment and the death penalty are the only violent, legal, state-sanctioned punishments that exist today as remnants of colonial times. The Emancipation Proclamation of 1863 did away with legal whipping of slaves, domestic violence laws have eliminated the condoning of spousal beatings, and the U.S. military has placed a moratorium on hazing of military personnel, with the court martial of officers who sanction the practice. Corporal punishment, however, remains authorized and legal in some school districts in the United States.

The Legality of Corporal Punishment.   The legal issues dealing with corporal punishment are confusing and can be contradictory. Sometimes when parents are concerned about violence in the schools, the state may sanction corporal punishment by teachers at school, but may not sanction corporal punishment by parents in the home. Who monitors the degree of corporal punishment to assure that it does not become abuse? All 50 states have mandatory reporting laws under which health care professionals and teachers are required to report any suspicion of child abuse to authorities. Parents may be reported and held accountable, but there is no specific requirement to report suspicion of abuse if teachers use corporal punishment unreasonably.

Sweden was the first country to pass a comprehensive law against anyone who used corporal punishment as a disciplinary tool on children (Block 2000). Adults are subject to criminal prosecution if they are found guilty of using corporal punishment. Block identifies two major impacts of the Swedish law, first, that child abuse declined and second, that other countries (Germany, Ireland, New Zealand, Switzerland, and United Kingdom) used it as a model.

Arguments Opposing Corporal Punishment.

- Corporal punishment exacerbates the notion that violence is an acceptable means of settling disputes. Adults are role models for children, and when adults use physical force on children, they communicate that force and pain are alternatives to settling differences through reasoning. Adolescents who have this example will resort to physical violence to resolve differences rather than reaching a solution by communicating and talking about a problem. Corporal punishment can lead to serious physical injuries. Hitting a child on the buttocks with a wooden paddle could cause injury to muscles, could fracture the coccyx, or could cause pelvic injuries that could result in serious medical problems. Some adults reason that corporal punishment is permissible if they do not use paddles. Other methods, too, can cause serious injury: Spanking the hands can result in nerve damage or broken bones in the fingers, pulling a child's ears can lead to deformities, and shaking can cause brain damage (Behrman, Kliegman, & Jensen 2001, 79).

- Corporal punishment can cause emotional damage. Children may become fearful in anticipation of the physical force. Some children exhibit overwhelming fear by bedwetting. Some withdraw or isolate themselves from others and live in a dream world where physical force is not practiced. Corporal punishment is not an effective deterrent. Corporal punishment in the presence of a child's peers can cause the child great embarrassment. The beaten child may misbehave again to an even greater degree to retaliate for the embarrassment suffered in front of peers. The corporal punishment may allow the misbehaving adolescents an opportunity to demonstrate to peers how really tough they are because they can take the punishment without showing that they feel it by crying. In some instances, adolescents may seek corporal punishment as a form of initiation, which demonstrates their toughness to their peers.

Arguments Supporting Corporal Punishment.
The U.S. Supreme Court has ruled in favor of corporal punishment. *Ingraham et al. v. Wright et al.,* raised questions about corporal punishment to maintain order and discipline in the school setting in relation to the use of cruel and unusual punishment and whether the Fourteenth Amendment's due process clause requires prior notification and a hearing.

Other views expressed in favor of corporal punishment include:

- *Tradition.* As long as there have been children, they have to some degree been beaten by adults and usually they have fared well. Some believe in hitting to get the child's attention. The practice started at birth, when doctors would spank the infant after it emerged from the womb. The cry after the spank was an indication of the infant being alive and healthy. The practice of spanking may continue through the

Ingraham et al. v. Wright et al. **430 US 651, 97 S. Ct. 1401 (1977)**

Certiorari to the United States Court of Appeals for the Fifth Circuit

The case argued November 2–3, 1976

Decision reached April 19, 1977

The parents of two Charles R. Drew Junior High School students in Dade County, Florida, filed a lawsuit against the principal, the assistant principal, an assistant to the principal, and the superintendent of the Dade County school system, for using paddling as punishment in the school. The students were hit more than 20 times with a paddle because they did not follow a teacher's instructions. One boy developed hematoma and had to receive medical care. The other was unable to use his arm for about a week. The students alleged that their eighth and fourteenth amendment rights had been violated. They claimed that they were not only subjected to cruel and unusual punishment but that it was inflicted without prior notification or a hearing in violation of the due process clause of the fourteenth amendment. The court concluded that:

1. The use of paddling in public schools did not constitute cruel and unusual punishment. The justices agreed that the cruel and unusual punishment clause of the eighth amendment was applicable to criminals for their own protection but not to students who received corporal punishment and that if the paddling was unreasonable, children could file civil and criminal liability. The justices, therefore, saw no justification for a ban on paddling.
2. The use of corporal punishment in schools was minimal and common law safeguards were adequate to provide the students with due process. (The common law right of a child recognizes the need to exercise carefulness and not to use excessive force when disciplining children.) Therefore, the due process clause of the Fourteenth Amendment does not require prior notification and a hearing before rendering corporal punishment on students.

---

child's developmental years, although the purpose changes from determining if the child is healthy to teaching the child to discriminate right from wrong. "My parents whipped (or spanked) me and I turned out all right," is a common argument for hitting children.

■ *Bible.*   The Bible has been quoted as the definitive source that advocates corporal punishment. Proverbs 23:14, "You shalt beat him with a rod, and deliver his soul from hell," is quoted in support of corporal punishment. Religious people argue Biblical verses that appear to favor the use of physical punishment against children.

■ *Tough Love.*   Parents who tell their children that they beat them out of love provide distorted and confusing messages. Children cannot understand why loving parents would inflict physical pain on them. They assume that people who love them will protect them from danger and harm. Beaten children's interpretation now is that parents will protect them against everyone except themselves as parents and teachers who are authorized to use physical force.

■ *Cultural Acceptance.*   Some immigrants to the United States feel that they are experiencing cultural intrusion when they are criticized for utilizing corporal punishment. Their justification is that corporal punishment has been a part of their cultures for countless generations and they do not see a need to change the practice now. Many parents willingly describe how corporal punishment was employed in their immediate families and in their extended families as well.

Corporal punishment continues to be an issue with which parents, teachers, legislators, and the court systems in many states grapple. More than 20 states have not only sanctioned the use of corporal punishment in schools, but also have passed legislation to ensure compliance. Only Massachusetts and New Jersey prohibit any type of corporal punishment in their school systems. Many states rely on the common law privilege (where reasonable force is acceptable in the discipline of children in schools) as long as the child's procedural rights are not taken away.

Contemporary School Disciplinary Practices

Adams (2000) has described the zero tolerance approach adopted by school systems for handling behavioral problems as having two dimensions, detection and punishment. Detection involves substantive monitoring and assessing students during the school day. Detection can be financially costly for a school system, because it requires increased security measures, equipment, and additional personnel, such as resource officers.

Punishment, the other dimension of zero tolerance, is driven by the get tough philosophy that is the core of many decisions made about children and adolescents in the United States. The punishment can be expulsion or suspension. Adams identifies this dimension as a return to Draconian practices, in which the motivations were to inflict punishment, not to make changes that might correct the problem. Suspension and expulsion are two widely accepted forms of discipline universally practiced in the United States' school systems. Although neither is as controversial as corporal punishment, they have become a focal point of public debate because of zero tolerance. When a student is suspended or expelled from school, the implication is that the student has violated school policy. How does suspension differ from expulsion?

Suspension.   The two types of school suspensions are in-school suspension (ISS) and out-of-school suspension (OSS). Suspension constitutes either the student's removal from the classroom to an alternative class setting (ISS) or the student's removal from school property for a specified period of time (OSS). ISS programs are used for adolescents who commit minor infractions. Adolescents are allowed to remain in specified areas on school property with school staff monitoring their activities. OSS sanctions are applied to youths who commit serious school policy violations. OSS sanctions last longer and a parental conference is usually required before adolescents can return to school. Each school system uses its individual school policy to define the seriousness of infractions.

Goss v. Lopez 419 U.S. 565 (1975)

Decided January 22, 1975

Lawsuit filed by Central High School student, Dwight Lopez, who had been suspended from school for approximately 10 days without a hearing.

The student contended that the 10-day suspension was unconstitutional because he was not allowed a hearing. He requested the removal of the suspension from his records.

Dwight Lopez stated that at least 75 other students were involved in the lunchroom incident for which he had been suspended and that he was not involved in the incident.

A three-judge panel declared that Lopez had been denied due process of law because school officials did not allow his version to be heard. The panel ordered all references of suspension removed from the student's record.

The school appealed the panel's ruling. However, the U.S. Supreme Court affirmed the ruling and indicated that the school principal might have been correct on the merits but was inconsistent on due process, because Lopez should have been given an opportunity to explain his side.

Browne (1999) used data from a study by the Applied Research Center (ARC) to suggest that minority youths may receive the most school suspensions. He found that school suspensions demonstrated racial disparities between African-American and white students. Adams (2000) supports Browne's analysis and states that many teachers suspend youths because they cannot or do not want to deal with difficult students. He suggests that the majority of students who are suspended are minority students. Adams noted the disparities in the use of ISS and OSS sanctions in his 1994 presentation to the annual meeting of the Eastern Sociological Society. He stated that schools with large numbers of minority youths are more likely to use OSS than ISS and without regard to procedural rights.

Procedural rights should be a consideration in out-of-school suspensions and must be safeguarded when youths are expelled.

Expulsion. Expelling students, officially removing them from the school environment for an extended period of time, which can be for an entire academic year, is a serious action resulting from a significant school infraction. Expulsion can occur when students have been involved in fights or have weapons or drugs on school property.

Expulsion made headline news in 1999 when the Reverend Jesse Jackson and the Rainbow/PUSH coalition attempted to persuade the authorities to rescind the expulsion of the "Decatur Seven," seven Decatur, Illinois, high school students who were involved in a fight after a football game. The fight, termed a "brawl in the stands," left three students facing criminal charges. One withdrew from the school, and the remaining six were expelled for up to two years, with a review at the end of the first year. Jackson considered the punishment unjust because the seven were grouped for punishment, and he cited a U.S. Department of Education Report that harsher punishments are rendered to minority children—"Our youths are being driven from the educational process and into the streets."

Expulsions are handled differently from suspensions because they involve more serious behavior. Authorities must follow some of the general procedural guidelines of due process in expelling youths from school.

Medication.   Adams (2000) cites overuse of medication as another type of frequently used disciplinary measure in the schools system. He refers to it as "medicalization of disruptive youths." When students consistently act out in the school setting, they are viewed not only as delinquents but are also given a medical label. The medical label allows treatment under medical conditions and implies the use of prescription drugs.

Attention deficit disorder (ADD) and attention deficit hyperactive disorder (ADHD) are medical disorders that have been diagnosed for many adolescents who display "disruptive" behavior in the classroom. A commonly used medication for children and adolescents is Ritalin®, the use of which has stimulated debate about its overuse and minimal monitoring of dosages by physicians. Another major concern is the use of Ritalin for younger and younger children. According to Smith (2000), the *Journal of the American Medical Association* (*JAMA*) published a review of HMO and Medicaid prescription records from 1991–1995 that revealed an increase in stimulant prescriptions for two to four year olds. Smith surmised that soon, "we will be prescribing Ritalin for toddlers!"

Lack of appropriate community services for children who have acquired a medical label is a further concern. Some states have developed programs as a result of litigation. North Carolina, for instance, defines a category of children and adolescents who display severe, disruptive classroom behavior and cannot tolerate a regular classroom environment because of emotional stress. These children and adolescents are placed in Willie M centers that are designed specifically to address their special needs. These centers were mandated as a result of a class action lawsuit, *Willie M v. Hunt* that was filed on behalf of four youths who had been expelled from school because of their disruptive behaviors. The suit alleged that the four youths were denied their rights to treatment and to an education. The suit was settled out of court in 1980. All parties agreed that the state should provide services based on the needs of youths, and not on what was available within the state. An agreement to establish Willie M centers to address the special needs of the state's disruptive children was a major provision of the settlement.

The idea of addressing the needs of children who require special attention is commendable. However, some of the implications are teachers and other referral agents over-labeling or mislabeling youths to get them into a Willie M program so that they do not have to deal with them. These youths are tarred with a label that will remain with them throughout their adolescence. Many will not be reintegrated into the regular school classroom and will not graduate from high school. Adams (2000) suggests that this intervention provides adults who work with disruptive youths a method of control in which they do not have to adhere to procedural due process.

Disciplinary measures are one of many issues that school systems have to face in the twenty-first century. Other issues that create educational dilemmas are sex education and constitutional rights issues such as freedom of expression and the right of search and seizure.

Sex Education

Should schools be held responsible for teaching students about "the birds and the bees" or should parents provide sex education at home? Pediatric HIV infections and teen pregnancies have risen, and school systems recognize that adolescents need to be informed about sex and that many parents do not feel comfortable discussing sex with their children. In some schools, physical education classes lightly touch the issue, and some schools offer sex education classes. On the other end of the spectrum are legislators who suggest that merely telling adolescents to practice abstinence is a good strategy for prevention of teen pregnancy.

Some school systems have condom dispensers in the bathrooms, encourage open discussions about sex-related issues, and have formed teen support groups. Charles Ballard, of the Institute of Responsible Fatherhood and Family Revitalization, is a leading expert on teen fathers and a pioneer of programs to empower teen fathers in and outside of the school system. Ballard believes that teen fathers have been overlooked, and has been a strong advocate for government intervention on their behalf.

Systemic Factors That Cause School Failure

Many individuals speculate about the reasons for the high percentage of students who are unable to pass exit exams, drop out, and cannot read and write well after graduation, and about violence in the schools. Some contend that instead of blaming the adolescent victims, the public should examine systemic causes, issues that are endemic to the school system itself. Is it possible that some factors within the school system cause student failure that can lead to deviant or delinquent behavior?

Schaefer and Polk (1972) identified factors that they believed contributed greatly to the poor performance of many adolescents in U.S. school systems. The same factors are just as relevant or even more relevant today as when Schaefer and Polk first identified them.

Irrelevant Instruction and Inappropriate Teaching Methods

Irrelevant instruction focuses on teaching materials, content, and subject matter. Adolescents often wonder how or why the classroom content relates to their own plans and goals. The teacher's responsibility and obligation is to show students how classroom work can help them reach their goals. Teachers can usually accomplish this task easily.

Effective educators seek innovative teaching techniques, but lesser teachers become burned out and fall into routine patterns that bore students—especially students who are at risk or delinquent. On one extreme, these teachers take a hard-line approach and are perceived as strict disciplinarians who may have negative verbal and physical interactions with students. Teachers who use this disciplinary approach must control their own feelings as they maintain control of their classes. They target adolescents whom they deem troublemakers and take a tough attitude with them. The rationale is preventive—taking care of problems before they start.

Other teachers use a laissez-faire approach, in which the adolescents control the classroom and the teacher is an adult figurehead. The students make all major decisions and the teacher carries out the plans. Course content may be discussed periodically but the students do not feel a real responsibility to complete or submit homework assignments. The teacher seems to be there to collect a paycheck, according to students (Rothbard & Murray 1999).

Between the two extremes are teachers who are neither disciplinarians nor slackers. They enforce rules and teach, but they appear to care only about students who are self-motivated and high achievers. Other students are left to flounder or fall through the cracks. They make no effort to capture the attention of students who are average or below average performers, and their teaching methods remain the same regardless of the students' learning styles.

Testing, Grouping, and Tracking

Many school districts use standardized tests to determine if students comprehend subject matter adequately to graduate. Schools resort to standard tests to determine whether students should be promoted to another grade, and as a consequence of failing standard tests, many students drop out of school.

Grouping and tracking have long been associated with school failure. Students who are grouped or tracked remain in that group or track throughout their matriculation in that school system. People who are labeled inappropriately and assigned to lower tracks throughout their academic careers may carry the stigma into their college and professional lives.

Grouping and tracking occur when students are placed in specific academic sections and are kept there until they graduate. Each group follows a specific curriculum. Seldom do students from one group take courses that are designed for another group.

Although cognitive and experiential skills are both important commodities, all students do not have the opportunity to develop equally in both areas in some school systems and with some teachers. Such students may develop feelings of superiority if they are successful in the college preparatory group, but others in the same group may experience anxiety over the possibility of not succeeding, which could lead to intense stress and acting out. Some females in college preparatory tracks have stated that they feel stressed out because they are uncertain that they will succeed, especially when they find themselves in a calculus class with primarily male students. They say that they feel "less smart" and begin to question their intellectual capacity. According to Stinchcombe (1964), to many students in the college preparatory track, the thought of failure induces a predisposition toward delinquent behavior more so than to students in the vocational track.

Students in the vocational track may never develop to their full potential because they are not expected to accomplish at a high level and are not encouraged to set high goals.

Inadequate Compensatory and Remedial Education

Many school systems include compensatory and remedial education in their teaching curriculum. Some students, however, do not seem to reap the benefits of remediation. Students may find the way remediation is conducted degrading. Teachers may not have ample time to spend with remedial students. They may give remedial students their old assignments to correct, but may have limited discussion with them about what they did not understand. So although the students correct their work, they may not understand the material.

Some schools recommend private learning centers to assist students with remedial learning. Because the private centers are not free, students from families of lower socioeconomic status may be unable to take advantage of them. Sometimes the centers are in areas that students whose families do not have cars may not be able to reach.

Inadequate Teachers and Facilities in Low-Income Schools

Members of the general public in the United States want their automobiles repaired by the best mechanic available and their medical problems diagnosed and treated by the best doctor in the field, but ironically, this same demanding public does little to provide troubled and failing students with the best teachers. Seldom are innovative, highly qualified teachers placed in schools in low-income districts. Frequently, teachers in these areas may be educators who are ready to retire, educators whose records are unacceptable to other school districts, or educators who were not successful in passing state certification tests. These teachers may receive fewer pay incentives, may have to work with lower quality books, may have access to limited technological equipment, and may teach in leaky, dilapidated school buildings. These substandard conditions place students who have to endure them at great risk not only of experiencing academic failure, but also of dropping out of school and becoming delinquent.

Distant Schools

The distance from home to school is an important factor in students' failure or success. Students who live far from school are less likely to be able to participate in extracurricular activities than those who live nearby. Parents, especially in low socioeconomic households, may not have access to transportation or cannot afford transportation fees so their children can participate in after school activities.

Families who live far from their children's schools may lack frequent communication with teachers. They experience little contact with school personnel, have limited input to school policies, and consequently have little information about what is going on at the school. They have few opportunities to participate in parent–teacher associations (PTA). If their children have problems, these parents have limited information at teacher–parent conferences because they have not been able to engage in ongoing dialogue with teachers about their children. This weak bond between parents and school staff increases the youths' chances of failure.

Economic and Racial Segregation

Wilson (1985) considers class as a factor that affects inequality more than race. Wilson's rationale suggests that regardless of race, disadvantaged students are likely to experience school failure because they live in lower socioeconomic neighborhoods and are assigned to school systems, many of which are racially segregated and are not as thriving as the middle- or upper-class school systems.

The class argument explains that if students in segregated systems have the same technical equipment, the same quality of books, buildings in mint condition, and competent, motivated, innovative teachers, they should be successful. Diversity then becomes a major consideration. Segregation limits the social interaction among diverse students and creates a unidimensional cognitive spectrum that lacks a variety of input, which could be detrimental when graduates enter the workforce. Diverse ideas resulting in a stronger United States was a strategy that was an impetus to forced school busing, which was implemented as a stipulation in the *Brown* decision.

As a result of forced busing, many U.S. parents educated their children in home schools. Home schools are permitted to operate only if they met strictly enforced, specific state education requirements. Charter schools were another innovative idea that was a result of forced busing. Charter schools are well-established neighborhood schools intended specifically for neighborhood children. Like the home schools, charter school programs

Brown v. Board of Education of Topeka Kansas 349 U.S. 294 (1954)

Case decided May 17, 1954

Linda Brown, a black third grader, had to walk a mile or more across railroad tracks to reach her school. A white elementary school was closer to her house. Linda's father attempted to enroll his daughter in the white school, citing that it was closer and he feared for his daughter having to walk such a long distance to school, but the school refused to admit her.

The defendants cited the separate but equal clause of *Plessy v. Ferguson* (1896) as case precedence.

The Supreme Court struck down *Plessy* and stated that "separate educational facilities are inherently unequal."

The *Brown* decision ordered school districts to desegregate, which resulted in forced busing of students to create integrated schools.

---

also must meet state requirements. The debate over whether school systems cause students to fail and to become delinquent continues in the twenty-first century. As the United States turns its attention to solving systemic problems and assigning its best, most creative, and most passionate teachers to work with children who are at risk of becoming dropouts and delinquent, it is extremely important to focus on the preparation of educators for the classrooms. Are the expectations different for teachers today than they were many years ago?

Changing Roles of School Personnel

The notion of police officers in the schools was not common until recently. Now school systems from the elementary level through high school consider it. In some states, police officers who work in schools are referred to as School Resource Officers (SROs) and undergo rigorous, specialized training before they are placed. They study juvenile policy, juvenile law, and how to create positive interactions with students. They learn collaborative strategies, effective team approaches, conflict resolution, and mediation to use with students.

As law enforcement officers' roles evolve and become more specialized in working toward prevention, so might the roles and preparation of educators change. Schools of education may require college students to take criminal justice courses to gain better understanding of the laws, the legal system, and deviant adolescents. Adolescents may be more familiar with their rights and the court system than are their teachers. Some insecure teachers lash out at unruly students, sending them to the principal's office, having them expelled, or engaging in verbal encounters that may escalate to physical assault.

College students seeking education degrees might broaden their educational preparedness if a juvenile justice course were part of their preparation. Such a course might help them gain a better understanding of the juvenile system and develop greater empathy toward their students, as well as an understanding of legal issues of the student–teacher relationship.

Legal Issues

Heavy media coverage of school violence by students has increased the public's awareness of youths' rights. Some schools hire police officers for security and install metal detectors to protect students and teachers from weapons being brought into the school.

Some argue that metal detectors and other scanning devices are not necessary in school buildings; others argue that students should be protected at all cost. Although the U.S. Supreme Court has not yet ruled on the use of magnetometers and scanning devices in school buildings, some state supreme courts have ruled.

Because metal detector searches are deemed "administrative" searches that target specific groups or individuals and are designed primarily for public protection, a warrant for the search is not required. Accordingly, the question of probable cause is not an issue with the use of metal detectors. In Pennsylvania, the court also ruled in favor of the school's decision to use metal detectors for the safety of the students.

The major issue, again, was whether the school system was conducting illegal searches that students believed constituted a violation of their fourth amendment right. In this case, as in *Dukes,* the students did not have a choice.

People v. Dukes **(151) Misc.2d 295, 580 N. Y. S. 2d 850 (1992)**

Case decided January 31, 1992

Judge Bruce Allen, presiding

On May 17, 1991, police officers placed metal detectors in the lobby of Washington Irving High School in Manhattan. They posted signs outside the school building that a search for weapons would occur. At the beginning of the school year, students had been told that searches would be conducted without advance notification because the school wanted to eliminate weapons on school premises.

All students were subject to the search but officers could use their discretion. The school principal stood next to the officers conducting the search. The students were scanned by officers of the same gender, who used hand-held scanners.

Tawana Dukes was scanned by Officer Jessica Wallace. Officer Wallace asked Tawana to open her school bag when the scanner indicated the presence of a metal object. She complied and the officer discovered a black switchblade knife with a five inch blade. Tawana indicated that the knife was for her protection. She was arrested and charged with criminal possession of a weapon, a fourth-degree, Class A misdemeanor.

Tawana alleged that her fourth amendment right was violated.

The court ruled that there was no violation because this was an administrative search that required not the probable cause standard but the reasonable standard. The search was reasonable and the officer was not intrusive.

In the Interest of F. B., 658 A. 2d. 1378 (1995)

Superior Court of Pennsylvania

Judges: Johnson Cirrillo and J. J. Saylor

Case argued April 4, 1995

At University High School in the Philadelphia school district, school officials used metal detector scans to search students in an attempt to reduce or eliminate the trafficking of drugs and weapons on school property. Parents received written notification at the beginning of the year about this policy and received ongoing reminders throughout the school year. School officials made the students aware of the policy by putting up signs and posters throughout the school. The procedure of going to a specific area and emptying their pockets upon entering the school was made clear. It was understood by all the students. A Swiss folding knife was found on F. B. during the scan.

F. B. stated that the search was unreasonable, violating his fourth amendment right, and cited *T. L. O.* as a basis for his argument.

The court ruled that the search was reasonable because all of the students were searched, and because of the school's high rate of violence and the need to protect the students, the *T. L. O.* reasonableness standard had been met.

Search and Seizure

Conducting searchs in school systems was tested in *T. L. O.,* the landmark case that set the precedent for school searches.

The Supreme Court not only issued a ruling on the case but also suggested some guidelines for schools systems to follow. The court ruled that for the safety of all students,

New Jersey v. T. L. O. 105 S. Ct. 733 [1985]

The case involved two teen girls (T. L. O. was fourteen) who were caught smoking in the bathroom at Middlesex School in Piscataway County, New Jersey. In the principal's office, the vice principal asked T. L. O. to empty her purse. In the purse were cigarette rolling papers, a pack of cigarettes, a small amount of marijuana, a pipe, empty plastic bags, a large number of one-dollar bills, and a list of student names. The parent and police were notified. T. L. O. admitted that she had been selling marijuana.

T. L. O. argued that the fourth amendment does not allow unreasonable searches in public schools by school officials and that students have the expectation of the right to privacy at school. In addition, she argued that the probable cause standard should be the same for students in school as for other people.

The U.S. Supreme Court, in an opinion by White, ruled that the search was not unreasonable, that school officials do not need search warrants to search students in their schools, and that school officials can conduct searches based on "reasonableness" and do not need probable cause.

school personnel have a right to protect students and therefore do not have to adhere to the probable cause clause.

School personnel can, therefore, conduct searches where there is "reasonable suspicion." The reasonable suspicion guideline implies that any information provided can be used to conduct a search on school property. The searches, however, must be conducted by school personnel and not police officers. Police officers, although housed in the school, are still bound by the probable clause standard. Police officers can conduct legal searches on school property without a search warrant only when the infraction is in plain view, in connection with a criminal act, a canine search, or with the student's consent.

Freedom of Expression

Young people receive many confusing and distorted messages, and the school system should be accountable for its part in this. For generations, children and adolescents have been taught that when they are in the home they should be seen and not heard, and that adults lead by example. In the learning environment of the school, among their peers, students believe that they should be able to freely express their thoughts and feelings. They read about individuals in history who have given their lives for causes such as democracy, so they become confused when they are told that they are restricted from expressing themselves in school about issues that may be considered too political, politically incorrect, or unpopular. They reason that the school environment is one place where they should be able to express themselves without fear of retaliation.

When youths enter the school environment, the public anticipates that they will learn and that they will be administered to within approved guidelines. School personnel are expected to perform as substitute parents from school opening until dismissal at the end of the day. The Latin term that describes their role is *in loco parentis* (in place of the parent). Along with substituting for parents go many of the responsibilities associated with parenting: School personnel are responsible for the care and protection of youths and have been granted power and authority to do what they think is best for them in the school environment. As with natural parent-child relationships, sometimes student and teacher relationships experience strain and youths need to express themselves. The boundaries, however, are not so clearly defined in the school environment as in the home.

Do students have a right to freedom of expression as guaranteed in the first amendment? Should their rights to express themselves be limited, to afford the school staff the opportunity to maintain order and create an atmosphere of less conflictual activity, making the school environment more conducive to learning?

The Supreme Court has ruled on cases involving what students can wear as well as what students can say. An example is the case of *Tinker, et al. v. Des Moines Independent Community School District, et al.*

Another case that the Supreme Court heard in 1986 illustrates the more conservative side of the court. In the Bethel School District case, a student had made a speech that contained numerous obscenities.

Student–teacher relations experience strain just as parent–child relationships undergo stress and strain with verbal self-expression or style of dress. Students may continue to test the first and fourteenth amendment rights in the school environment.

Tinker, et al. v. Des Moines Independent Community School District, et al. 393 U.S. 503, 89 S. Ct. 733 (1969)

Supreme Court of the United States

Argued November 12, 1968

Decided February 24, 1969

Three students, 16, 15, and 13 years of age, wore black armbands to school in Des Moines, Iowa, to protest the war in Vietnam. They were suspended from school from December 16 until after New Year's Day for wearing the armbands. They alleged that the suspension was unjust, citing that it violated their first amendment right of freedom of expression. They argued that there was no disruption of their classes and their attendance in class was in a normal quiet manner.

School officials claimed that the wearing of the arm bands by the students caused disruption in the educational process, therefore they prohibited them. The Supreme Court ruled in favor of the students, stating that as long as the students did not cause disruption, the school did not have a right to forbid them from expressing themselves peacefully.

Since school shootings have become a national issue, school personnels' concerns about student dress and personal ornamentation may have become overzealous in their actions. One young student was expelled from school because he was wearing a Star of David, a revered symbol of the Jewish faith. Although he explained that his family was Jewish, school officials still prohibited him from wearing it because they believed it was a gang-related symbol. The increased sensitivity to students' dress is a result of frequent gang activity and violence in the schools and has led to the implementation of dress codes in some public schools. In the Columbine attack, the killers had worn long black trench coats that were thought to mark them as part of a group of loners and outsiders.

Bethel School District No. 403 v. Fraser 478 U.S. 675, 106 S. Ct. 3159 (1985)

On April 26, 1983, Matthew N. Fraser, a 17-year-old senior at Bethel High School in Tacoma, Washington, made remarks that were considered obscene and offensive in a nominating speech at a school assembly.

The day after the speech, Fraser was charged with disruptive conduct and suspended for three days. His name was removed as graduation speaker. The authorities said that his nominating speech had a "disruptive effect on the educational process" in the school.

Fraser was a member of the debate team, had been given a top speaker award, and was an honor roll student.

The court ruled that the school district had not violated his first amendment rights by the action taken. The court stated that schools had a right to "prohibit the use of vulgar and offensive terms in public discourse." Fraser was, however, allowed to give the graduation speech at his school.

Some school districts, after much consideration, require uniforms in public schools. The rationale is to reduce tensions occurring in student–teacher relationships, to lessen the anxiety among peers who feel that they have to wear designer clothes to compete for popularity, and to ward off or decrease gang activity in the schools. The U.S. Supreme Court has not heard a case challenging the constitutionality of uniform dress codes.

Are Schools Really as Violent as They Are Portrayed to Be?

Parents, teachers, and students all expect to feel safe and be safe when they enter a school building. Ironically, some juvenile correctional facilities may be safer to walk through than some public schools. It is increasingly difficult to distinguish between a public school and a training school. Armed guards and metal detectors protect public schools, but most training schools do not employ armed officers or have any type of scanning devices. Detection and disciplinary measures that range from weapon scans to disallowing their freedom of expression are methods of dealing with violence in our schools. But just how violent are the schools? Public schools have become veritable fortresses; they brim with security measures that could withstand the scrutiny of adult or juvenile correctional institutions' security inspection. Schools have chains and padlocks on their doors, metal detectors, and security cameras, and may require students to carry identification badges and display them upon request by a teacher. U.S. public schools appear to be in severe chaos that is rooted in the public's fear of school violence. School districts, responding to political pressure to find answers, are collecting more federal dollars to implement safer schools and to reduce violent acts in the schools.

How violent are the schools? Some people agree with the position of the National Education Association (NEA), that the schools have become havens for drugs, gangs, and violent, delinquent adolescents. The NEA suggests that U.S. urban schools are "steeped in violence." The NEA describes high school students as frustrated, hopeless, and angry, and suggests that they act out these feelings violently and aggressively.

Others agree with Greenberg (1999), who suggests that "in every era, American schoolchildren—especially teenagers—have been unruly and destructive . . . preteens swore, drank, had sex and even dueled with guns. If school violence wasn't a problem back then, it was only because fewer children went to school" (Adams 2000, 2). Greenberg (1999) further suggests that not only has there always been school violence but that the only difference now is that today's students are better armed.

Finally, there are those who believe, as Adams (2000) does, that there will always be violence in U.S. schools because of the nature of U.S. society. But, according to Adams, what is more harmful is the establishment of an environment that induces such fear in children that it creates in them the need to become violent. "Perhaps doing the most harm is the anxiety that is running rampant and so prevalent and pervasive that children [and adolescents] feel the need to bring a firearm to school for protection" (Adams 2000, 4).

The U.S. Department of Education's annual report (September 1999) indicates that there is a decline in school violence and victimization. But although violence has declined, students still do not feel safe in the public schools. The report indicates that only "about 7 to 8 percent of the students in grades 9–12 reported that they had been threatened or injured with a weapon while at school (Kaufman *et al.* 1999, vii). The report further stated that some adolescents carry weapons to school to protect themselves, but the majority of students never enter the school building with weapons. The number of students who reported carrying weapons to school in grades nine through twelve fell from 12 percent to 9 percent from 1993 to 1997 (ix). Further, the report indicates that 23 percent of ninth graders were more likely to carry weapons than those in higher grades and 15 percent of twelfth graders reported carrying weapons (26). The report states that male adolescents are three times more likely to carry weapons into school property than females: In 1997, 13 percent of males carried weapons to school, compared to 4 percent of females (26). These data suggest that U.S. schools are safe, but widespread fear, frustration, and overreaction are pervasive.

U.S. schools have experienced major tragedies, and as a result, throughout the country are implementing strict safety precautions in schools, some in the form of prevention programs such as conflict resolution and peer mediation. The primary purpose of these programs is to assist youths with the development of mechanisms to help them resolve feelings of anger nonviolently. Devine (1996) suggests that again adolescents receive the wrong message, because they perceive the conflict resolution and peer mediation of their school curriculum as educators sanctioning violence and teaching them how to respond to it.

Other safety measures have focused on expanding the roles and providing more training for school personnel. Whether U.S. schools are more violent or the students are better armed is not the major concern, because only a small percentage of adolescents carry weapons to school. More important is to ensure that teachers are able and willing to identify adolescents experiencing academic or emotional problems and to work closely with them and their families. School systems should be morally, if not legally, bound to educate and retain all students who do not pose a threat.

Summary

Are students more violent or are they better armed than they used to be in schools? National statistics indicate that students are no more violent, but that students and school systems have become conveniently profitable for sensationalistic news media. School shootings have helped the media sell the public the idea that schools are unsafe and havens for criminals and that students must be treated as felons. School officials have reacted to the sensational media blitz by imposing stringent policies that lack concern for students' procedural due process rights. Many schools have included police officers on their staffs to reduce or prevent violence so that their schools will not become Columbines. Measures such as these have increased the tension between teachers and students. Minority students, especially, may experience enforcement of these policies and a continuation of the lag in their education.

KEY CONCEPTS

corporal punishment	in-school suspension	suspension
expulsion	metal detector	tracking
in loco parentis	school resource officer	

DISCUSSION QUESTIONS

1. What are some rationales for using metal detectors in schools?

2. Explain the concept of tracking.

3. Do you feel that schools are more violent today than when you were in high school or do students have more access to weapons?

4. Discuss your high school's suspension program.

5. Was corporal punishment used in your high school? What methods of discipline were used?

EXERCISES

1. In small groups, discuss the pros and cons of corporal punishment.

2. Invite a school resource officer to class to discuss the role of resource officers in the school system, barriers that they face within the system, and their special training.

3. Discuss the security measures that were taken in your high school with other students in class. Did you feel safe?

4. Visit an area high school and observe the school's safety precautions. During the next class, discuss your visit and some of the school's safety issues.

6 Families and Delinquency

CHAPTER OBJECTIVES

On completing this chapter, the student will have tools to:

- Become aware of the various types of family units
- Gain insight into the role of the departments of social services with delinquents
- Understand changing attitudes about family composition and their impact on delinquency
- Understand the role that families play in the lives of children
- Understand issues, such as parental liability laws, that have an impact on family life and delinquency

Overview of the Family

The family creates the major moral fiber that has an impact on the behavior of the youth in U.S. society. The influence of family values is important to analyzing youths' behavior. Children who excel in school reflect well on their parents (and even on their siblings), who are considered to have played a major role in the process. Within families, children may be expected to be predisposed to certain career choices. For example, in a family of police officers, children may be expected to follow the same path. Likewise, children of criminals may be expected to participate in criminal activities. In reality, however, children of police officers do not necessarily become police officers and children of criminals do not necessarily become felons, because other variables may have an impact on their choices. Even so, the family begins the socialization process that launches the child's developmental career, influencing the child's activities, thinking, and choices.

The concept of the family in U.S. culture is a changing one. A traditional family in the United States for a long period in the twentieth century might have posed for a Norman Rockwell painting: adult parents (one male and one female), two children, and, perhaps, a dog. Ideally, they resided in a quiet, suburban neighborhood in a house with a white picket fence, and drove a station wagon. The father worked at the office every day from nine to five, while the mother stayed home and cleaned house and prepared meals. When the family came home from school and work, they sat down to a home-cooked meal and discussed the events of their day.

In the twenty-first century, the family unit may be composed of individuals who are not biologically related to each other. Children may live with two parents of the same sex or with a single parent who may be a male or a female. The children and the parents may be of varied ethnicities and races. Instead of a single-family dwelling, they may live in a townhouse or an apartment or a condominium. Instead of a station wagon, they drive a sports utility vehicle or a minivan.

Agencies, such as the *DSS* (Department of Social Services), play a vital role in intervening in distressed families in the United States. In considering the changing composition of families in U.S. society, the DSS cannot be overlooked, primarily because of the major role it has played in *parens patriae* intervention for children. The DSS assumes a wide range of responsibilities that include protecting and caring for children when the family system breaks down, and dealing with issues such as adoption, abuse, neglect, and dependency. The DSS works collaboratively with juvenile court counselors and guardians *ad litem,* all of whom work in the best interest of the children and adolescents in their care.

The Derek McStoots Case

Teen charged with killing his parents

Leitchfield, Kentucky. The youngster wanted to be out of the eleventh grade, wanted to be away from his parents in the small Kentucky farming town where his family had lived for generations.

So Derek McStoots, 16, took his father's pickup and ran away from home. He made it as far as Daytona Beach, Florida, before his parents brought him back.

Hours later, Derek ran away again. This time, though, there was no chance his parents would come after him.

He killed them, police say. Bradford McStoots, 45, was shot once in the head as he slept, then beaten with the boy's hunting rifle. Mary Coleen Kerr McStoots, 44, apparently was awakened by the shot and bludgeoned so severely with the rifle that its wooden stock shattered. Her body was found in the hall.

Derek, a small-framed, only child in a family of husky men, was captured Tuesday outside a pawn shop in Sulphur Springs, Texas, about 75 miles from Dallas, while driving his mother's Buick. Authorities think he was trying to sell some items taken from his home in Leitchfield. The boy was charged with murder.

The crime startled Derek's hometown of 5,000 people, about 65 miles southwest of Louisville. His parents belonged to long-established families in the area. Police said there never were any reports of abuse at home. "What would enrage one's mind?" asked coroner Ronald Hudson, who performed the autopsies and had also sold the McStootses' furniture from his store downtown. "How do you beat your mommy and daddy?" No clear motive has emerged, but there were hints of a sometimes stormy relationship between Derek and his parents.

Source: The News and Observer (Raleigh, NC.), Friday, September 8, 1995, p. 8a.

As troubled adolescents commit acts such as murdering their parents, family values become a heated issue and parental liability becomes a major component of debate. Is it the parents' fault that children commit delinquent acts? Do parents demand so much of their youths that adolescents believe their only option is delinquency or parricide?

A Changing Family Concept

As primary socialization agent, the family teaches children morals, spiritual values, and a work ethic. Even if the adults in the home do not openly discuss these topics, children learn by the manner in which the adults practice or fail to practice these values at home.

The concept of the family has seen a gradual but significant change. The family, whose members once traditionally were a closely knit unit with genetic links to each other, seems to be slowly fading from prominence. The major link today seems to focus more on philosophy than blood. The contemporary trend reflects that today's family is linked by commonality more than biological reproduction. The change in attitude about what a family is can be attributed to factors such as technological advances in genetic research, cryogenics, stronger feminist attitudes, and a boom in surrogate parenting.

Technological Advances

With increasing technological strides in human biological reproduction, it has become not only more controlled, but more diverse. When Aldous Huxley published *Brave New World* in 1932, today's technology was near at hand. He described a problem-free, utopian society that was managed by superior technology. In his society, the entire populace reproduced artificially by "genetic manipulation." He challenged society to respond to technological advances by asking to what extent modern technology would sacrifice the individual as it manifested the spiritual bankruptcy of society (Huxley 1932). Described in a book written almost three-quarters of a century ago, Huxley's brave new world is here today.

Modern technology has cast its imprint heavily on the changing sexual role of females, and it did not begin with Dolly, the sheep cloned in 1997, as some might suspect. The female sexual revolution started with Margaret Sanger, who fought for the development of female contraceptives and believed that women should be able to practice birth control (Sanger 2000).

Technological advances not only made it possible to control pregnancies through the use of birth control pills and tubal ligations, but with the development of fertility drugs, women who had once been considered to be infertile were able to have children. Many females who used fertility drugs experienced multiple births, from twins to octuplets—after a Texas woman was treated with fertility drugs, her pregnancy resulted in the birth of eight infants (Santos 1998). Fertility drugs, although controversial because of the dangers of such large multiple births, provide females with another option for making their own decisions. Females having choice about whether and when to have children has been a major impetus in the reformulation of the concept of family. Contemporary feminist philosophy, too, can be attributed to this change.

Feminism and the Changing Family

The notion of equal rights for all individuals has tremendously influenced the changing dimensions of family life in U.S. society. Directly and indirectly, it has had a powerful impact on the family. Its indirect impact is in the labor market, in which females, now more visible, request equal pay for equal jobs. The direct impact of equality in the job market suggests equality in homes and supports the notion that single-parent households, which in the past have received adverse press—being labeled dysfunctional, helpless, and hopeless (Moynihan 1965)—can be as loving, as nurturing, as responsible, and as stable as two-parent households.

Single-Parent Families

Negative attitudes about single-parent families began to change in the last quarter of the twentieth century. During the 1950s and 1960s, single-parent households were considered dysfunctional families because many Americans' perception of the single-parent household was of an African American female with many children subsisting on monthly public welfare checks. Moynihan (1965) labeled these families as infested with a cancerous type of pathology that was eating away at the moral fiber of the United States. However, as the U.S. economy continues to experience positive changes technologically, economically, and socially, single-parent households of both genders, as well as of all races and economic levels, have increased throughout the entire spectrum of U.S. society.

Alvin Toffler, in *Future Shock* (1970), attempted to prepare the U.S. public for the transition of family structure from the two-parent family Rockwell painted, to the single-parent household. He stressed the notion that as Americans focus more on human rights, dignity, and freedom, they would give less attention to sharing, collectivity, and commitment. Toffler suggested that traditional families are held together because of social expectations and not because of family members' commitment to each other. He further notes that this lack of commitment has greatly influenced the creation of the single-parent motif.

Today, both females and males opt to work and have children, but not necessarily to become legally married. Toffler (1970) viewed such singlehood as lack of commitment to the partner. However, members of today's couples commit to themselves as individuals, assessing their living situations and concluding that they will be better off and happier as singles than miserable and dissatisfied as part of couples simply because it is an expected norm. The strain of working and trying to accelerate through the organizational ranks of their career paths has given women, in particular, more self-confidence. As they consider their options in life with strengthened self-confidence, some individuals decide to rear their children alone without reliance on a partner to complete the family structure. Such decisions are changing the composition of families in the United States, as even married couples no longer remain together for the sake of the children, and thus experience high rates of divorce.

Today, divorcing individuals may plan to work and bring up their children without a spouse. Such *broken homes* are nontraditional families in the United States, where the concept of broken homes is considered in a new light. The term *broken* does not usually apply to households in which male and female adults reside with their children.

Even clearly abusive households merely "experience problems." Only divorce defines the broken home, even when it might have been a healthy compromise to maintain the emotional and physical well being of the family. Belsky and Eggebeen (1991) studied more than 5,000 children to determine whether children whose mothers worked outside their homes were different from children whose mothers remained in the home and did not work for pay. They reported that children whose mothers worked away from home showed negative effects. Harvey (1999) replicated Belsky and Eggebeen's 1991 study, using the same group of children, and found no difference between children who had working mothers and those children whose mothers did not work. She concluded that the major important factor is not whether the mothers work but how they spend time with their children.

Much research on youthful offenders reports disproportionately on African-American male youths, as well as youths from divorced homes, and youths of lower socioeconomic status. Limited research studies report on middle- and upper-income offenders, whether black or white, perhaps because children from middle-income families have more community resources available to them and may not find themselves involved with the juvenile justice system as readily as lower-socioeconomic-status youths.

When upper socioeconomic status youths enter the juvenile justice system, they are not studied as frequently as their poorer, black counterparts. The majority of the public schools involved in the violence and shootings of the end of the twentieth century and the beginning of the twenty-first century were in middle- or upper-middle-income communities. Yet, limited information was provided about the communities, the youths, or their families. Systemic issues, such as school security in urban schools and lowering bind-over ages to include younger children, remain in the forefront as societal norms and attitudes change in the twenty-first century.

Two-Parent Families: Experiencing Equality in the Home

In contemporary U.S. society, both parents in most families need to be gainfully employed to maintain a decent standard of living. "Ozzie and Harriet" households rarely exist: no longer is the male the breadwinner, working outside the home, and the female the housewife, cooking, cleaning the house, caring for the children, and waiting in high heels and perfect make-up for her husband. The U.S. economy makes it not only possible, but necessary, for two parents to enter the labor market if they want their family to exist at a middle-income level.

Children of two working parents experience out-of-home care early in their lives. Some couples take advantages of the availability of extended family members, and others use infant day care centers, even for children as young as three months. The impact of early separation of children from their mothers interests researchers who study delinquency. Some study whether the bond between parents and children occurs early enough to strengthen children through their growth and developmental years. Others examine the results of limited and absent adult supervision, especially of *latchkey children,* who go home after school to empty houses because their parents are working. U.S. society accepts that two parents may work away from home, but holds single parents to a different standard.

Changing Attitudes

In the United States, families seem to have fewer children than in earlier years and to recognize that they need to care for aging members of their extended families. A conservative climate in U.S. society espouses conventional family values. National television, print, and billboard campaigns, sponsored by politicians, churches, and interested public and private organizations, encourage parents to talk with their children. Televised antidrug campaigns urge parents to communicate to their children that smoking and taking drugs are not acceptable behaviors. Such campaigns may influence adults as well as children and adolescents.

Many couples either are not having children or are having fewer children because they fear that they will not be able to protect, control, and support them. Schwartz and Albanese have suggested that delinquency will continue to decline in the United States because fewer children will be born (Albanese 1993; Schwartz 1992). Countering their analysis of the impact of the birth of fewer babies in the United States is that many couples adopt babies from countries such as Bosnia, China, and Russia. Infertile U.S. couples may resort to methods such as surrogate parenting.

Laboratory-Created Babies

Sperm banks, which exist throughout the United States, are temporary housing units that hold containers of sperm from sperm donors who either donate their sperm to be used by a person unknown to them, or have it stored in the bank for safekeeping until they are ready to use it themselves. Sperm banks not only house sperm but also may provide male fertility services such as diagnostic and therapeutic components, sperm enhancement, and semen cryopreservation. Cryopreservation protects the semen from protein and membrane damage by the use of cryoprotectants such as saccharide compounds (Towill 2002).

The mission of sperm banks is a major concern. Some sperm banks will accept only sperm from donors with specific physical characteristics, bringing to mind Hitler's plan to create a super-race more than 60 years ago. Many believed that it was immoral, inhuman, and violated the laws of natural selection to biologically manipulate the human species; yet, today sperm banks exist throughout the United States.

Huxley (1932) raised questions about safety, commercialization of reproduction, and the changing nature of family when he made predictions about the future of technological genetic advances. Huxley was concerned about using technology to control and manipulate the human species, without regard to its impact on the future of the human race. Ideally, adults procreate because they desire fulfillment and to share their love with a new life. Children might be created in laboratories for the advancement of science and research, without concern for their best interests, only to see how far genetic manipulation might be taken. The idea of laboratory creation of humans demands consideration of morality, ethics, self-identity, and spirituality (Lemonick & Goldstein 2002, 54).

Is genetic research out of control in the United States? And who are the watchdogs ensuring that ethical standards are met? George Annas, bioethics chair of the Health Law Department at Boston University School of Public Health, expresses concern about the lack of standards and regulations in reproductive medicine, and wonders if the best interest of the child is served by high-tech pregnancies (Lemonick & Goldstein 2002, 52). As technological capabilities increase and provide more scientific capability to manipulate the next generation of citizens, so does the need to consider the implications of those increased capabilities.

Some of the implications, as delineated by Nigel Cameron, are based on his concerns about the future of the human race. Not only could the manufacture of children overpopulate society, but could lead to overpopulation by one kind of individual.

The manipulation of terminology now euphemizes sperm or ova sellers to "donors." Ova, before sperm are inserted, are called "pre-embryos." Cameron suggests that terminological manipulation obscures facts with euphemistic labels to promote the sale of body parts (Cameron 1999). Advertisements for ova and sperm in newspapers and on the Internet mention prices from $3,000 to $50,000, depending on the characteristics desired. Ova from younger women are a highly desired option for older women. White men with high IQs and no genetic medical problems receive high fees for their sperm for intracytoplasmic (ISC) sperm injections.

Creating children through ISC and cloning adds a commercial aspect to reproduction, with very little concern for the growth and development of children. The scientific possibility of creating a being merely because it can be done or for profit ignores the child and the effects that designer children may have on humankind (Cameron 1999).

Intergenerational Parenting

Intergenerational parenting is not a new concept, but has been prevalent in countless minority families in which the extended family is a major force in the family unit (Billingsley 1968, 1994). Researchers term extended family members as "significant others" (Manns 1988), and define them as people who perform a variety of roles and functions within individuals' lives and contribute to the socialization of family members (Manns 1988). Significant others might be related by blood or might be unrelated care providers, but are usually people who are concerned about the best interest of children within the family. An extended family member of an African American family might be the elderly neighbor who sits on the porch and watches out for the neighborhood children as they play. In these families, elderly extended family members care for, supervise, and guide younger members through their formative years. In some Asian American households, the extended family resides in the same household. In intergenerational parenting, older family members are primary care providers for the children in the household. Intergenerational parenting is prevalent and acceptable with the majority population because in some households, both parents are employed, in others, there is a single parent, and in still others, the grandparents are dependents of their adult children or the adult children had children before they were prepared to be independent.

Intergenerational parenting within the same household demands that roles and rules be clearly delineated and consistent. Parents and grandparents must support each other's decisions about the children. Parents and grandparents, whose styles of discipline may differ from extremely strict to remarkably lenient, must agree upon and establish clear disciplinary rules. Otherwise, when grandparents and parents criticize each other for their parental styles, youths may manipulate the discord between the two sets of adults and set them against each other.

The large population of youthful grandparents in their thirties and forties have other issues with intergenerational parenting. Some are not willing to assume responsibility for rearing their children's children because they have raised one family and have no desire to raise another. Some put off meaningful activities to rear their own children earlier in life and only now are able to travel or tend to their own education.

Intergenerational parenting is a practice that continues well into the twenty-first century because the baby boomers, according to the year 2000's U.S. Census predictions, will become 20 percent of the population and will be actively involved in not only families and child-rearing, but also in policy decisions that have an impact on program decisions.

California, Louisiana, New York, North Carolina and Ohio, for instance, have programs in which senior citizen volunteers work with delinquent and at-risk youths. Ohio's foster grandparenting program, a state-sponsored project, matched senior citizens with incarcerated youths. The seniors, who attended a senior citizens' center, were brought to the youth facility. Their interaction with the adolescents included playing games, reading books together, and talking together.

Although not a great deal of research or assessments of the effect of grandparent programs on youths have been done, the Senior Corps (funded by the Corporation for National

A Case to Highlight Grandparenting

Jimmy, a 15-year-old, was incarcerated in a juvenile correctional facility with sentence of a minimum of one year. An insecure but likeable youth, Jimmy was the product of a biracial union and had never met his father and whose mother's family had rejected the boy and his mother. Jimmy was described as "a kid with a chip on his shoulder," and his mother was described as "uncaring, uncooperative, and a mean bitch." Jimmy's institutional adjustment was marginal. In his counseling sessions, Jimmy did not exhibit the openness that was necessary for him to make progress. During most of his sessions, he usually said what he thought the counselor wanted to hear. To encourage more spontaneity, Jimmy was placed in group sessions and was seen less often in individual counseling sessions, but he became guarded, volunteering no input and responding only when directly called upon.

The grandparent program was an important treatment component of the facility. Youths could volunteer to participate or might be referred. Each youth was teamed with a "grandparent" with whom they would engage in individual activities at least twice a week. Jimmy was referred and agreed to participate.

The senior citizens who participated in the grandparent program had received two weeks of orientation. They met once weekly with the program coordinator to consider their interactions with the youths.

After four months with his "grandparent," Jimmy began to speak up more in group and to talk about his anger in individual sessions. Before his discharge from the facility, he was able in group sessions to discuss family issues that concerned him. He brought his grandparent to the group-fest, a leaving party held for each group member who completes his institutional time. Jimmy told his group that the grandparent was the person who had most influenced and changed his thinking. After discharge from the institution, Jimmy continued to write to the program grandparent.

Source: This case is from the author's experience. The youth's name has been changed.

and Community Service Organization) indicates that many adolescents seem to have benefited from their existence (www.cns.gov; www.seniorcorps.org).

Jimmy's youth counselor, his teacher, and his social worker believe that Jimmy's commitment to the juvenile correctional facility could have been avoided if his family had been held more responsible for his behavior and had assumed a more active role in his life. This kind of thinking has led to the implementation of parental liability laws in some states.

Parental Liability Laws

Parental liability laws stipulate that parents are civilly liable for the delinquent behavior of their children. Some sanctions that can be imposed on parents include fines, contempt charges, and incarceration. Colorado, in 1903, was the first state to cite parents for contributing to the delinquency of a minor (Regoli & Hewitt 2000). The purpose of parental liability laws is to make parents more attentive and involved in the lives of their children. Proponents believe that if parents are more involved with their children, the children will be more communicative with parents and less likely to become delinquents. However, some researchers do not believe that holding parents civilly liable for their children's behavior will deter delinquency (Geis & Binder 1991).

Although some states are enacting laws that make parents more accountable for their children's behavior, the issue is rooted in family and values. Some maintain that parents should be treated as accomplices when young children have easy access to guns in the home or use a parent's gun to commit a crime.

In a rural family, the children in the household may be taught how to use a gun to hunt or for protection of the home and family. If one of these children commits a delinquent act using the gun, are the parents responsible? Should the parents be incarcerated? Limited research makes it difficult to determine the effectiveness of parental liability laws in deterring and reducing delinquency. Faltermayer (1998) reports that "parental responsibility law is a gray area. It's a toothless tiger. We have no research on the law's effectiveness at all" (Faltermayer 1998).

Different Types of Families

Families provide children with the knowledge, skills, and motivation that are essential to the development of a strong U.S. society. When family values change, so will overall U.S. values.

The composition of the family changed considerably with the emergence of diverse family types during the twentieth century, in part because of societal changes. Political and economic changes had their impact on families and are responsible partly for the weakening of the traditional family structure. Contemporary U.S. society embraces different types of nontraditional families, based on legal and emotional needs, that include gangs, homosexual families, and multicultural, adopted families.

Gangs.   Children who join gangs do so for various reasons, but primarily because the gang functions as a substitute family. They receive the security, protection, and love that they may not be able to attain in their biological families. Gang members treat the gang as they would treat their genetic families (see Chapter 7).

Homosexual Family.   Traditionally, mothers have been granted custody of children in divorces because women were regarded as the primary caretakers. *Watts v. Watts* (1973), in which the father was granted custody of the child, changed public opinion about simply placing the child with the mother without consideration of other factors regarding whether the father would be the best care provider for the child.

Similarly, as a result of case law such as *Bezio v. Patenaude* (1980), societal taboos about homosexual couples raising children have been all but lifted. It is an accepted practice if courts determine that the relationship does not harm the child and if the couple is able to provide for the care and protection of the child (Brieland & Lemmon 1976). Homosexual couples may use sperm banks, surrogate parents, or adoption to expand their families.

Adoption.   Adoption laws, which differ from state to state, allow the legal placement of children in homes that have been approved by the state. Some states support open adoptions, in which information can be obtained about the natural parents of the child. Many states have closed adoptions, in which information about biological parents is available neither to the adopting couple nor to the children. Consequently, many adopted children who want to find their biological parents must use other resources, such as private investigators.

Adoption policies stipulate that the best interest of the children is the primary concern. The family should be evaluated based on that principle and not on the couple's sexual preference or race. The modifications of old adoption criteria have created heated public debate, not only about homosexual adoption, but also about transracial adoption.

Transracial Adoptions.   The National Association for Black Social Workers (NABSW) believes that black children should be adopted by black families. Only after all other possible alternatives have been exhausted should adoption of black children by white families be considered. NABSW's concern is that black children in biracial adoptions will lose their identity and will not grow to understand and appreciate their black heritage (Ladner 1977).

The opposing argument is that even in a white home, a black child could know love, security, and protection, a far better alternative than growing up in a state-sponsored institution (Steinberg & Hall 2000). Growing up in an institution, lacking the warmth and individual attention of a family, could prompt some to run away and become statistics among the homeless, involved in drugs and prostitution, incarcerated, or dead.

Homosexual Adoptions.   Gay and lesbian families considering adoption have increased, primarily because of changing policies and attitudes toward them. Incidents such as Stonewall in 1969, in which police officers beat people because of their sexual preference, have decreased. The beating and torture murder of Matthew Shepard, a gay college student, in 1998 in Wyoming brought the attention of U.S. society to its own beliefs and practices. Many U.S. citizens do not sanction homosexuality because they believe that it is morally and spiritually wrong, and they believe that homosexual people should not be allowed to adopt children.

At the end of the twentieth century, a number of famous people "came out of the closet" and adopted children. Adoption policies have broadened to include gay and lesbian couples. The primary concern in adoptions now is what is in the best interest of the child, not the legal guardian's sexual orientation.

The Role of Departments of Social Services

The focus on what is best for the child is a controversial issue in adoption. Departments of social services (DSS) must face this issue and continue to offer quality services to children in need.

The primary responsibility of DSS is caring for and protecting children. Hence, the concept of *parens patriae* is one of its underlying principles. In contemporary times, the concept commonly is applied to delinquent children, but it originally emerged over a dispute about placement of children. *Wellesley v. Wellesley* is the first recorded case in which a court declared the state's legal authority to protect children against harm that could result from parental behavior. In 1827, the English Chancery court ruled that the Duke of Wellesley had to give up his children because of his promiscuous behavior (see Chapter 1). The court declared that when parents could not or would not do what was best for their children the state has a responsibility to assume the parental role. The DSS is the states' arm with legal responsibility to intervene on behalf of abused, neglected, and dependent children.

Abuse, Neglect, and Dependency

The first recorded case of the court's interference in child abuse in U.S. history was that of Mary Ellen Wilson, who was reportedly severely beaten by her mother on more than one occasion. In 1874, no agency protected children, although the American Society for the Prevention of Cruelty to Animals (ASPCA) had been established. Etta Wheeler, a humanitarian worker, with the support of Henry Bergh, the founder of the ASPCA, brought Mary Ellen's situation to the attention of the court, which removed the child from the abusive parental home and placed her elsewhere.

Abuse is the repeated infliction of physical or psychological harm on a child. Physical harm can include beatings with the hands or objects—straps, whips, or sticks. Physical abuse may accompany sexual abuse. Psychological harm can include degrading the child with negative labels or with cursing and profanity. Another form of psychological abuse is to keep a child in a state of mental anguish. In the case of Elian Gonzales, well-meaning relatives kept the six-year-old from his father for political reasons. They did not want the boy to return to the unsafe and impoverished life they remembered in Cuba.

Neglect occurs when the primary care provider does not give the child adequate, proper care, including food, clothing, shelter, and protection. Although some researchers use the terms *abuse* and *neglect* interchangeably, they are separate concepts with different intents. The outcome of harm to the child is the same.

Protecting parental rights.
AP/Wide World Photos

The Case of Elian Gonzalez

Elian Gonzalez, a six-year-old Cuban, was rescued in 1999 from a boat off the Miami coast after his mother and other Cubans drowned escaping from Cuba. Elian's father remained in Cuba. Elian was placed with extended family in Miami. The relatives filed for asylum for Elian and for his custody.

The boy's father, Juan Miguel Gonzalez, a Cuban citizen, requested the return of his son. The relatives refused and an extended legal battle that included the INS and Janet Reno, U.S. Attorney General, ensued. On June 1, 2000, a three-judge panel unanimously ruled against the extended family, indicating that only Elian's father, Juan Miguel Gonzalez, could apply for asylum on the boy's behalf. The relatives' appeal to the U.S. Supreme Court was denied.

The extended family's attorneys based their appeal on two points:

1. Opinion letters issued by U.S. government agencies (INS) are not the same as U.S. law.
2. The entire court should reverse an earlier judgement based on case law (*Jean v. Nelson*: noncitizens do not have due process under U.S. law).

Elian and his father returned to Cuba on June 28, 2000.

Source: CNN Report: June 15, 2000. United International Press.

Some parents might not have intended neglect. The single mother who works two menial jobs to feed her family and perhaps to move from a drug-infested neighborhood may be charged with neglect. Neighbors report that she is seldom at home, that the oldest child—perhaps 12 years old—cares for the other children, and that the children are not fed properly and appear dirty most of the time. Clearly the mother's intent is reasonable but her observed behavior may cause her to lose her children.

Neglected children are difficult to identify because, unless their situation is extreme, it is difficult to determine who they are. Gross negligence exists when parents leave children at home alone for days without adult supervision. Not so easily detectable are children whose parents are in the home but do not provide minimal care.

Child Abuse Reporting Laws

Prior to the 1960s, no mechanisms existed for considering or investigating child abuse, and the implementation of sanctions on abusers of children were minimal. C. Henry Kempe (1962) coined the phase, "battered child syndrome," which later became "child abuse syndrome." Kempe studied abuse in children extensively and provided research that supported new rationales and helped to change child-abuse policy. The implementation of reporting laws in 1965 was a major policy change. Reporting laws specify that educators, medical doctors, social workers, day care providers, and police officers are all bound legally to report any incident of suspected child abuse to the proper authority (generally, the local DSS), which must investigate the allegation within 24 hours. Although child-abuse-reporting laws vary from state to state, they all contain the same major components. Brieland and Lemmon (1976:160) list the components:

1. Child's age
2. Definition of abuse
3. Who is responsible for reporting
4. Immunity clause for the individuals who report
5. What agency is responsible for investigating abuse reports
6. Acknowledgment of confidentiality

The reporting law has made it possible to identify and provide assistance to many abused children who otherwise might have gone unnoticed. Public information and public awareness have also made it possible to locate and assist abused children (Kalichman 1999). *In re Frances* [267 N.Y.2d 566 (1966)], the result of a report by hospital staff (Breiland and Lemmon, 1976) is an early case prosecuted under the reporting law. Another noteworthy case is *People v. Schoos* [305 N.E.2d 560 (Ill.App. 1973)] in which Delores Schoos was found guilty of neglect of her 14-year-old daughter who had run away from home.

In 1974, other legislation, the Juvenile Justice Delinquency and Prevention Act and the Child Abuse Prevention and Treatment Act, evolved. The Child Abuse Prevention and Treatment Act ensured that federal funds would be provided to states so that they could provide quality services to children who might be at risk for abuse and their families. The services included training to enhance effective parenting skills, sensitizing parents to effective supervision strategies, and strengthening communication skills between parents and their children. The amended act specifically identifies the criminal elements that should be considered in abuse cases of children under age 18.

Signs and Symptoms of Abuse

Many delinquent children have histories of neglect and physical and psychological abuse (Kacar 1996). They may be supervised under joint custody of DSS and a department of youth services (DYS) when they commit delinquent acts that require a delinquent adjudication. After adjudication, the child serves the DYS commitment, perhaps confinement in a training school, and on release is placed by DSS. Out-of-state placement is sometimes an alternative when relatives in other states are willing to have the child placed in their home. Out-of-state placement requires that an Interstate Compact Agreement must be instituted between the states involved. An *interstate compact agreement,* a contract, is initiated by the sending state to the receiving state, which decides either to reject or to supervise the youth. If the state agrees to the supervision, all parties must sign the agreement before the youth is placed.

Dependent children without primary care providers because their parents are deceased, incarcerated, or otherwise unable to be in the household also come to the attention of DSS. If a dependent child is 16 or older, most states allow a petition to the court to emancipate the child, which means that the child is allowed to function independently of adult supervision with minimal monitoring for a specified period of time.

Of the numerous situations that involve children seeking resolutions to their problems, many that come to the attention of juvenile court do not belong there and should be resolved by DSS. Like the juvenile court system, DSS has legal authorization to make some decisions about the rights and well being of children, and has a procedure for safeguarding the child's constitutional rights. The procedure, administrative hearings, follows guidelines established in *Goldberg v Kelly* [397 U.S. 254 (1970)] and is similar to juvenile court hearings in that it assures that constitutional rights are not violated. Administrative hearings differ in some respects from juvenile court hearings, as Table 6.1 outlines.

A major difference between delinquency cases and cases of abuse, neglect, and dependency is that, in most instances, delinquency can be established by one act committed by the youth, but most cases of abuse, neglect, and dependency require a pattern to establish the abuse. Children may have to endure repeated instances of abuse before any action can be taken to eliminate the problem, and it is not rare for children who have experienced abuse to become delinquent. An early delinquency caused by abuse is running away from home to escape it.

Missing Children

Among the myriad experiences that parents in the contemporary United States endure is finding that their child is missing. Albanese has identified five types of missing children: family abducted, stranger abducted, runaway, thrown away, and lost (Albanese 1993).

TABLE 6.1   Administrative Hearings versus Court Hearings

Similarities	Differences
Right to legal representation.	Judge presides over court hearings. Hearing officer presides over administrative hearings.
Right to written notification of charge.	Court appoints legal representation if client cannot afford one; DSS does not.
Right to written notification of hearing date.	Only court can adjudicate youth delinquent.
	Only court can commit youth to training school.
Right to appeal.	Hearing not necessarily held in courtroom if it is an administrative hearing. It can be held any place in the community acceptable to the hearing officer.
Right to hear testimony and confront witnesses.	Court stenographer must record court proceedings. Court stenographer is not required in administrative hearings but a record of proceedings should be maintained.
	Probation officer is assigned to court case. Social worker is assigned to administrative hearing.

Family-Abducted Children.   In family abductions, a family member, perhaps a noncustodial parent, takes children away from the guardian or custodial parent and relocates them. The family member may change the child's name and physical appearance, give the child a new identity, and even move to other countries. Family abductions usually occur around divorce and custody battles when the court grants custody to one parent (Plass *et al.* 1997).

Stranger–Abducted Children.   Strangers abduct children for reasons that include ransom, replacing a lost child, or pedophilia (Morris 2002). The FBI and local authorities investigate nonfamily abductions. Many children abducted by strangers are found murdered. Speirs (1998) estimates that more than 158 children each year are murdered by strangers. The case of Adam Walsh is representative.

Unsolved Abduction and Murder of Adam Walsh

On July 27, 1981, Adam Walsh, six years old, disappeared from a mall in Hollywood, Florida, where he had been shopping with his mother. She left Adam in the toy department of a store while she shopped for a lamp. When she returned, Adam was gone. Two weeks after Adam's disappearance, his head was found in a canal about 120 miles from the mall, but his body was never recovered and the murder was never solved.

Source: Susan Candiotti: Adam Walsh Back in the Headlines. CNN, February 18, 1999.

Adam Walsh's parents established the Adam Walsh Child Resource Center to sensitize the public to the plight of missing children. The Center merged with the National Center for Missing and Exploited Children (NCMC) in Alexandria, Virginia. The Centers disseminate material on missing children to the public.

Runaway Children.   Children run away from home for reasons that include escaping abuse from a parent, guardian, or relative. Runaway children are youths who leave home and whose parents or guardians do not know their whereabouts. Many youths run away because something in the home seems hopeless. After running away, youths initially experience guilt, sadness, and fear. They seek out relatives or friends whom they trust will not inform on them, but eventually they may turn to strangers who may be recruiting for illegal activities such as pornography, prostitution, and drugs.

Thrown-Away Children.   Thrown-away children are unwanted and discarded by their parents, left at the doorstep of a church or a neighbor, in a hospital waiting room, or in a trash receptacle. Some die before they are discovered. Adolescents may also be put out of their homes by their parents because of misbehavior.

Lost Children.   Some children accidentally become separated from their families. Children may be reported lost when they wander away when the parent is not watching them. They may be preoccupied with something at the same time their parents are preoccupied with something else. Lost children are reported at amusement parks, fairs, and malls. Lost children may be located more readily than other missing children.

Who is responsible?
Bill Aron/PhotoEdit

Internet Abuse

Internet abuse occurs when adults exploit children and adolescents through the Internet. Children and adolescents who spend time in computer chat rooms may encounter adults who entice them into illicit activity. The Regional Task Force on Internet Crimes against Children, sponsored by OJJDP, has as its goal to combat Internet child sexual exploitation by enhancing proactive and reactive investigations of Internet crimes. The Regional Task Force (http://www.ojjdp.ncjrs.org) has reported suspects as young as 16 and as old as 62.

Parents take precautions by sensitizing their children to the abuse they can be subjected to over the Internet and by being more observant of how their children use the computer.

Summary

Few books teach how to bring people with various personalities and needs together to create a family. Families try to remain functional units and deal with these issues, as well as the threat of delinquency, whether they are related biologically or through adoption, are single-parent households, or are homosexual parents.

The major thrust of research in the twentieth century focused on the dysfunctionality of single-parent, broken homes and concluded that a great number of delinquent children are from this type of environment. Minimal research was conducted on children in two-parent homes or on children with access to resources to divert them from the juvenile justice system. It seems logical, then, because more children are nondelinquent than delinquent, that more attention should be paid to youths who are not labeled delinquent to determine what causes them not to become delinquent. That information can be useful to families and to policy makers who create and develop programs to reduce delinquency.

KEY CONCEPTS

abducted children	interstate compact agreement	parental liability
administrative hearing	joint custody	surrogate parent
adoption	latchkey children	transracial adoption

DISCUSSION QUESTIONS

1. Identify some of the pros and cons of the child-abuse reporting laws.

2. Explain how physical and psychological abuse can traumatize children for life if they do not receive help.

3. If there has been a thrust to prevent runaways, why are there shelters for runaway children? Does the existence of the shelters encourage this behavior?

4. Explain to the class why you feel homosexuals should or should not be allowed to adopt children.

5. Discuss some of the critical issues that surrogate parenting may present.

EXERCISES

1. Form two groups and debate the issue of parental liability laws. Should parents be held responsible for their children's behavior? Discuss some issues that parents and transracially adopted children must face. Talk with parents who are single heads of households and parents who live together. Determine if their issues are similar or different. In class, discuss commonalities and differences.

2. List some resources in your community for abused children.

7 Peers, Gangs, and Delinquency

CHAPTER OBJECTIVES

On completing this chapter, students will have tools to:

- Know the warning signs of gang activity
- Learn of specific notorious street gangs they may encounter
- Understand why youths join gangs and participate in gang activity
- Understand gang members' perspectives on gang activity
- Understand how gangs recruit children and adolescents

Gang Activity in the United States: An Overview

Gangs in the United States are not an artifact of the twentieth century. The infamous James gang, one of the most notorious, existed in the Old West of the nineteenth century. Brothers Jesse and Frank James and their companions terrorized the countryside with violence as they robbed banks, stagecoaches, and trains. The James gang was a group of young men no older than 18, who robbed and terrorized the "Yankees" in revenge at the end of the American Civil War (McCorkle & Miethe 2002, 39). The twentieth century saw the rise and fall of the Capone gang, who controlled illegal breweries, speakeasies, prostitution, and numbers running throughout the midwestern city of Chicago. Although the Capone gang was composed primarily of adults, youths on the payroll were lookouts, numbers runners, and delivery boys.

The publication of Frederick Thrasher's *The Gangs: A Study of 1313 Gangs in Chicago* alerted the general public to the activities of youth street gangs in the late 1920s. Thrasher identified gang activities and provided theoretical explanations for them. His definition of the gang, used even today by gang researchers, is

> an interstitial group originally formed spontaneously and then integrated through conflict . . . and characterized by meeting face to face, milling, movement through space as a unit, conflict and planning. The behavior develops a tradition, unreflective internal structure, esprit de corps, solidarity, group awareness, and attachment to a local territory. (46)

Since Thrasher's work, researchers have formulated many definitions of gangs and have conceived theories about gangs and gang activity in U.S. society, focusing primarily on street gangs. Klein's (1971) definition, in part, is "any denotable adolescent group of youngsters who are generally perceived as a distinct aggregation by others in the neighborhood, recognize themselves as denotable, have been involved in a sufficient number of delinquent incidents . . ." (13). Walter Miller (1980) defined the gang as "a self-formed association of peers bound together by mutual interests, with identifiable leadership, well developed levels of authority and other organizational features, who act in concert to achieve a specific purpose . . . which generally include[s] the conduct of illegal activity and control over a particular territory, facility or type of enterprise" (121). Taylor (1990) takes an interesting perspective and states that a group becomes a gang when it is recognized as a gang by the community and another gang. Although researchers do not agree on a specific definition of street gangs in U.S. society, most agree that they can be characterized as having involvement in illegal activities. This chapter describes how street gangs evolve and the activities of gangs, and offers insight into the nature of gangs and gang members.

Youths and violent behavior have become synonymous with gangs and gang activity in the United States. Gang numbers and violence declined in the early 1960s and 1970s but underwent a tremendous upsurge in the 1980s and 1990s.

Regoli and Hewitt (2000) speculate that the decline of youths in gangs occurred primarily because of the war in Vietnam. First, a number of gang members were drafted into the armed forces. Many of them were gang leaders, and their gangs dissolved once they were gone. Second, covert law enforcement officers infiltrated the gang networks. Covert operations were at their height in the 1960s and 1970s under J. Edgar Hoover's FBI regime and Hoover was determined that he would not allow gangs to embarrass him or his office. Officers who successfully infiltrated gangs were able to bring down many of the leaders, which facilitated the dissolution of those gangs and ended their activity. Third, trafficking in heroin was big business: Heroin addiction among gang members negated their usefulness to their gangs and led to their expulsion. Fourth, young citizens of the United States were in a state of rebellion, social disorder, and civil unrest. Throughout the country youths clashed with law enforcement and mounted protests, riots, and episodes of civil disobedience. The entire society appeared to be in a state of disorderly conduct. Gang activity received little media coverage because Vietnam, civil rights marches, and Watergate (the 1972 burglary of the Democratic National Committee offices authorized by then-President Richard Nixon) were more newsworthy.

The media function as a primary socialization agent in U.S. culture (Marger 1997). A stabler U.S. society in the late twentieth century and early twenty-first century gives the media less societal upheaval to report, and teen gangs are important in the media. The media have glamorized gang activity to a new high as movies highlight gang activity and magazines and books about gangs and gang members are published. The drug economy that has evolved and taken hold in the United States is another major reason for the overwhelming reemergence of gangs in the 1980s and 1990s. Drugs are such big business that gangs and gang members have become successful entrepreneurs. Because some illegal drugs are easily accessible and economical to manufacture, many gangs and young gang members find themselves caught up in the drug subculture.

Why Do Youths Join Gangs?

Cloward and Ohlin (1960) are among many researchers who have speculated about why youths join gangs. They theorize that youths join gangs because they cannot experience success in the legitimate world. Miller (1958) suggests that many gang members join in search of a male role model because their female-headed household has not afforded them the opportunity to shape and act out their male role. Gang membership affords them that opportunity. Sutherland's (1934) explanation is that peer pressure plays a major role in youths' joining gangs. His rationale is based on a differential association model. Under these circumstances youths, by association, become fascinated with the idea of gang membership and discuss with their friends how great it would be. Once they are convinced that it is what they want, joining and becoming members is easy.

Abraham Maslow (1987) has summed it up best with his theory of human hierarchical needs. Maslow theorized that all human behavior is motivated by five basic human needs, and regardless of individuals' stations in life, who they are, what race they are, or what gender they are, the same five basic needs must be met. He described those needs as physiological (hunger, thirst, shelter), safety (security, protection from physical and emotional danger), social (belonging, friendship, acceptance), esteem (ego), and self-actualization (ability to accomplish tasks well). Maslow speculated that individuals make every attempt to understand themselves and to perform well. The needs in Maslow's hierarchy are basic components in the struggle to understand self and to be successful. It is reasonable to assume that if adolescents, in their search for identity and success, are unable to have these needs met in the natural family, they may seek gang membership to meet them.

Physiological Needs

Gang membership also provides basic physical needs, such as shelter and food, to youths. Some parents may not be able to provide basic shelter and food for their children because of their own personal conditions (e.g., unemployment, criminal activity, drugs, etc.), so the adolescents find their basic needs of food and shelter within the gang subculture.

Some youths join gangs to establish a better economic base for themselves and their natural family. Many of these youths are from lower socioeconomic family conditions and have experienced poverty all their lives. They may view the gang not only as a way in but also as a way out that will enable them to get money to help their families. When the prospect of monetary gain is available, gang activity is a viable economic venture because many of them are too young to be legally employed elsewhere. Money that they receive as a result of gang activities provides them with supplemental income that may provide food and clothing for family members or pay rent and utility bills.

Safety Needs

Many youths join gangs to satisfy their need for the security and protection that they do not find in the home or in their community. Large numbers of youths live in poverty-stricken, disorganized, and politically powerless neighborhoods that are unable to obtain the resources to provide services for their children and adolescents. As children walk to and from school, they face constant threats and pressure from other youths to join the gangs. With no possibility of adult intervention, they must decide whether to join and avoid the daily threats and taunts, or avoid joining and face and deal with the threats as best they can. Many join gangs, reasoning that their options for security and protection are greater if they do. Now they are part of a group of individuals who will back them up in situations they cannot handle alone. Upon joining, the individual and their biological families are afforded the protection that gang membership offers. Consequently, other family members are not harassed or bothered, but if they do experience problems, the gang members will rally for the family as well.

Social Needs

Many youths join gangs to gain a sense of belonging to a family unit. They may have no cohesive family unit in the home and find that gang membership offers them the chance to experience the closeness of a family. Gangs function like family units. Membership assures youths of a place in the gang, whose members will never turn their backs on one another as long as they remain loyal. Members know that they help each other "through thick and thin, no matter what" (Ice T in Klein, Maxson, & Miller 1995). They express love for each other that many never experienced in their homes. Gang members may express togetherness and belonging by the way they dress or the colors they wear. They may all wear the same type of generic articles of clothing to signify that they are gang members or may wear specific gang insignias. Some get gang tattoos to demonstrate their pride in belonging to the group. They are in search of meaning, trying to figure out who they are and where they fit in the puzzle of life (Erikson 1993; Frankl 1984). Because they have not found their niches in their natural families, they look within the gang, which offers them a distinct identity with specifically defined responsibilities, to discover who they are.

Many of youths who join gangs are considered social deviants and have not faired well in the regular daily activities of their community or school. They may be labeled antisocial, bad, or strange, but the bottom line is that they do not fit in and are unable to function daily as other youths do. The gang offers them the friendships that were not available outside the gang.

Need for Esteem

The gang offers many youths opportunity to find self-respect and achieve personal goals that they might not experience if they did not join. Outside of the gang, they have had no respect, no attention, and no personal recognition from their peers and suffer from low self-esteem. But as gang members, their activities and assignments within the organization bring that attention and recognition. Some youths who were considered shy outside of the gang organization develop high self-esteem within the gang and some aspire to become gang leaders. Even their illegal activities bolster their egos and help them gain greater emotional and physical strength. They move to self-actualized potential when they grow confident that they can accomplish assignments successfully.

Need for Self-Actualization

Some researchers believe that individuals are in a state of constant development and that self-actualization can never be fully achieved. Others believe that individuals become actualized when they have reached a state of achievement or when they have reached their fullest potential. Gang membership offers youths a chance to reach self-actualization or their potential to become self-actualized when they successfully perform their tasks and receive accolades from other members. Gang members may feel that leadership of the set indicates that the gang member has reached the top.

Youths join gangs for as many reasons as there are theories, but whatever reasons they express, youths join gangs because something is missing in their lives that they are not able to find through regular daily interaction with peers and family. The gang recruiter is a strategizer who determines the most effective way to entice youths into the *sets,* which are the various segments of the gang. Recruiters usually hold rank in the gang and are psychologically skillful. They understand basic human needs and target the most vulnerable youths who have something to offer the organization

Factors That May Lead to Adolescent Gang Involvement

Adolescents do not wake up one morning and suddenly decide to be street gang members. Gangs recruit, just as the military and businesses, such as IBM, recruit. The parallel ends there, for gangs are not as discriminating as IBM. Instead of recruiting the best, top-notch students, gangs go after the adolescents who have a void in their lives or youths who are struggling to find meaning in their existence. Among the many factors that may entice youths to gang membership, the four broad categories at the forefront are low self-esteem, family problems, unsatisfactory school experiences, and survival.

Low Self-Esteem

Many gang members experience low self-esteem, a sense of poor self-worth, and negative life experiences prior to joining the gang. They feel that they are excluded from achieving the "American dream" because of bad luck. Cohen (1955) theorizes that they use a middle-class measuring rod, and their feelings of inferiority at not being able to measure up on the middle-class scale generate anger and frustration. Other than gang activities, their lives hold little to build self-esteem. The gang recruiter builds youths' self-esteem magnificently, explaining all the illegal things youths will be able to do and do well. They train the youths and, initially, make them feel as if they are completely unrivaled and extremely important to the production and survival of the organization. Cloward and Ohlin (1960) address youths' attempts to find success through legal or illegal means. They discuss the phenomenon of gang recruiters unblocking blocked opportunities as they open the doors to the illegal world for the youths by building their self-esteem.

Family Problems

Unmanageable stress in the home is another factor that may lead youths to gang membership. Although all families experience stress, in the families of many youths who become gang members excessive stress has its impact. The lack of a positive role model in the household may be the cause of the stress. Families operate more unidimensionally than in previous times, and the extended family has no significance in the lives of youths from homes in which their parents and grandparents are relatively young. The youths are unable to benefit from the wisdom of elders because of the propinquity of the generations. Family structure in U.S. society is rapidly changing, and the change that these youths are living is having an immeasurable effect on them.

Churches once played a pivotal role in the education and socialization of children but contemporary churches seem less receptive to working with these youths. Nevertheless, as one minister explained, it is not that churches are less receptive, but that they are more attentive to the "political correctness of things today than they are to the way they used to be." For example, unlimited access to the church is no longer an option—church doors are open at regulated hours and are locked after Sunday services and Wednesday choir practice. No one is available to meet with troubled children and their families because many ministers are busy working full-time jobs elsewhere. Because of their busy schedules, clergymen do not have time to go out to street corners, malls, or inner city basketball courts to interact with at-risk children. Many churches no longer offer activities for youths (other than perhaps choir and Sunday school) because they do not have funds in their budgets to sponsor extra activities. Consequently, many youths are idle because youth activities are very limited or nonexistent. Historically, churches have been a major institution in the socialization of African American youths. In contemporary U.S. society, churches, especially African American churches, have taken a different role, becoming more entrenched in the political arena, and are less focused on the youths in their communities. Once, when no one else fought for youths, the churches were there, but now even they are not as visible in the fight to protect young people. Gang members indicate that this lack of interest is a major factor in their ability to recruit children easily for gang membership: They have no competition.

Poor School Experiences

The school environment, too, can lead young people to become involved with gangs. The school experience is a very important time in the lives of youths. School is the medium for a socialization process that helps youths to define who they are and who they can become. School is an important socialization tool that greatly influences the youths' chances of success or failure in life.

Academically, youths look to the schoolteacher for cognitive guidance; their rapport with the teacher helps them establish their intellectual identity. Youths who seem to function well academically usually are encouraged by teachers to continue and are provided with all available resources to assure their continued academic successes. But youths who perform poorly (e.g., seldom turn in class assignments, do not read well, do not respond to questions asked by the teacher) are easy targets for gang recruitment. Because of their poor academic performance, many have lost the incentive to try to do better. They base their lack of motivation on their teachers' perception and treatment of them as low achievers, so they begin to believe that they are unable to be successful. When a gang recruiter approaches them and explains the advantages they can reap from their productivity in the gang, they leap at the opportunity because they need to experience success, even though that same success may become a lethal endeavor later.

The school offers social and academic opportunity for youths. Youths are encouraged to engage in extracurricular activities to build their social skills. Youths who are not doing well academically may be able to excel in extracurricular activities and receive some rewards that way. Some students join social clubs such as Scouts and 4-H, while others may play football or basketball or swim competitively. Some youths do not participate in extracurricular activities because they are not accepted by their peers, or do not have the skills and ability to play a sport well, or lack transportation. Whatever the reason, their lack of participation usually is not by preference or choice. The lack of social acceptance in the school setting increases their feelings of inadequacy (Agnew 2001), and when opportunity to join a gang and be part of a group arises, they join, regardless of how deadly the membership may be for them, their families, and others. Gang membership offers them the social acceptability that they did not have in the school setting or in a church, and recruitment of these youths becomes easy.

Survival

Survival, too, may lead youths to become gang members. They may experience direct threats and intimidation, even threats of physical violence to themselves or their families. Where youths live plays a role in determining which gang the youth may be forced to join. For example, in South Central Los Angeles, youths are recruited by the dominant gangs of that region, the Bloods and the Crips, and if they refuse to join, may forfeit their lives (Ice T in Klein, Maxson, & Miller 1995). Gang membership may be an intergenerational affair in families in which numerous members are gang members: The gang members expect other family members to continue the tradition that the family has established. The family may ostracize youths who choose not to continue the family legacy.

Economic survival may affect youths' decisions to join gangs. Gangs offer economic incentives to those with limited financial assets, and youths may join gangs to increase the family income. Distribution and sale of drugs is one productive recruitment tool that many gangs use. Gangs recruit very young children, who are too young to work legally, by showing them that they can earn. Fifty dollars seems like a lot of money to a child. Sometimes children are paid in desirable products: specific athletic shoes or specific designers' clothing. Gang recruiters may offer older adolescents even greater financial incentives. Youths who are employed at fast food restaurants may distribute drugs via the drive-through window for extra money. Although youths may earn very minimal money from the gang, with it they can contribute to the resources of their families.

Children and adolescents join gangs because they are not able to get what they want legitimately. Gang recruiters observe youths, find out what they want, and use various sales pitches to entice them to join. They begin their process gently, building youths' self-esteem, offering them attention and caring, teaching and encouraging them, and finally, offering a small monetary incentive to set the hook.

Recruitment

In the neighborhoods of South Central Los Angeles, recruitment is not meticulous because youths are blatantly confronted with just two choices, "join or die" (Bing 1991). But in rural areas of the United States that are considered virgin territory, recruitment is a very serious matter and a slow and methodical process. In these areas, which have not experienced tremendous gang activity and to which gang members are relocating or migrating, recruitment is well thought out and executed. It begins after the gang has targeted the area for business. Gangs seek college and university locales because they anticipate that college students will be receptive to drugs. Gangs also consider arsenal capabilities, such as nearby military bases and weaponry distribution locations, and easy access to and from major highways. One or two members will relocate to the targeted area and interact with the local residents, socializing with local women and eventually living with them. Ideally, the women are impoverished single parents with limited education. The gang members remain in the relationships while they carefully assess the community and the police patterns. They indoctrinate the women's children, who become the initial recruiters, as they share what they have learned with their friends. Soon, the "stepdad" teaches the children significant, gang-related material. At this point, other members come into the community to assist in recruiting and teaching.

The process is meticulous, and youths advance according to their ability to achieve specific undertakings. They must master all lower-level tasks before they are able take part in the initiation or rite of passage. Recruitment may take about a year, beginning as soon as youths show interest in gang activities. Children may begin as early as age six. In the beginning, gang members will prescribe tasks that must be performed to earn admired articles of clothing, a cap, or athletic shoes. As youths complete each task, they continue to earn articles of clothing or may be allowed privileges, such as sitting in on a meeting or watching higher-ranking members perform a task. Other members carefully observe them as they accelerate through each level of accomplishment. Youths begin as runners, carrying notes and messages. As they advance, they can become lookouts, watching for police officers or for members of other gangs, or mules, carrying drugs and other contraband, such as illegal guns. If by age 14, they have proved themselves to be worthy, they can participate in drive-by shootings. After this slow, painstaking training period, youths who are accepted into the organization are said to be "blessed" or "courted" into the group. Others, who are allowed in the group by reputation or because of the notoriety of family members, may have to complete only one or two acts, and their initiation is different and over shorter period of time.

The formal initiation is short. Observers watch youths perform specific tasks to ensure that they carry them out to the letter. After the jobs have been completed successfully, youths are officially blessed by the other members in a formal ceremony that may include "jumping in," in which youths who have not undergone a strenuous systematic recruitment process are beaten by set members.

Gangs expect their members to be loyal, honor the gang's colors, and participate in the activities of the membership. Although gang members participate in some of the same activities as other youths, the chance of violence is greater because they have taken an oath of protection. If gang members are together at a public place, a simple incident could result in lethal harm to not only gang members but also innocent citizens. Gang members readily involve themselves in the distribution of illegal drugs and protection of turf.

Turf Protection

Turf protection may involve *tagging*, which is the painting of graffiti. This is a form of communication between gangs and among members of the same gang. Gang members spray paint graffiti on areas of walls, houses, buildings, or bridges in their neighborhood with their language to send messages to rival gang members or to communicate among brother members about incidents that have happened to their members. For example, they may mark their turf or write a message that a gang member has been killed by a rival gang. Gang members consider their turf very seriously and are willing to die protecting it. The turf issue not only applies to gang members within their neighborhoods, but in school areas as well: Gang members designate their own areas in the school cafeteria, on the school grounds, or at school activities such as athletic events or dances, and do not allow other students to sit in them. Although tagging may be invisible inside the school, gang members have taught the other students to understand who they are and what their place is in the school. Gang members in schools are known by reputation and visibility. They converse in school nonverbally—graffiti are not common, although some schools have experienced graffiti on the outer walls of the buildings and in bathrooms. Students usually will not tell unless a serious school incident involves gang members.

Graffiti is can be an important means of understanding gangs for law enforcement officers. Graffiti can tell a gang's history and can designate specific activities, such as the arrival of new gang members, a rival gang in the nearby area, or a message sent to a gang member.

That message can be a challenge to which the rival gang responds by issuing their warnings of possible consequences after accepting the challenge. Graffiti is an eminent sign that gangs exist in the area that is marked. Tagging is not simply a show of arrogance, but warns other gangs that they are in alien territory. Tagging also welcomes gang members from another city or state into the area.

Graffiti is an important component in the gang culture and should be removed as soon as it is observed to curtail communication. Graffiti is to gang members what the daily newspaper is to the ordinary citizen. Graffiti contains the latest news of happenings in the gang community. Gang members discover what is going on, right down to obituaries in which the graffiti writer lists an R. I. P. label that not only identifies the slain gang member, but also issues a threat to the killer.

Graffiti is one of gangs' most essential components and one of their most effective means of communicating with each other and with other sets and rival gangs. All members must learn how to use graffiti and it is very important for workers who deal with gangs to learn their alphabet. Each organization has its own alphabet, all of which are similar to each other, yet are unique.

Types of Gangs

African American Street Gangs

The two most notorious street gangs in U.S. society are the Bloods and the Crips. They began in California, and they are distinctly unique and deadly enemies. Although other African American gangs existed prior to the Bloods and the Crips, they did not reach the notoriety of these two groups. Earlier gangs were more territorial, were not as organized as the Bloods and the Crips, and were not as active in illegal drugs and weapons transactions.

Crips International, Inc.   *Crips* is an acronym for *Criminals Running in Packs* or *California Revolution Independent Pistol Slingers.* Crips are said to have originated in Fremont High School in the Watts section of Los Angeles, California, in the late 1960s. They reserve the title "OG" or "Original Gangsta" for leadership positions in their organization. The Crips' color is blue, and their slogan is "beat a person down before they beat you down." Crips are known for their meanness toward their nemeses, the Bloods, and among themselves. They practice tough love with erring members, applying physical pain so that they do not make the same mistake twice. Their war cry is "BK," for "Blood Killa." The Crips dress code includes nothing red, only blues (Ice T in Klein, Maxson, & Miller 1995), and Georgetown Hoya jackets and British Knights tennis shoes are preferred apparel. They adhere to a universal common knowledge of laws that govern their communication. They have their own alphabet in which the letter C is sacred and always replaces the letter B.

Bloods International, Inc.   Bloods began on Piru Street, in Los Angeles, California, in the late 1960s. The acronym stands for *Blood Lords of Our Destiny* or *Black Lords of Our Destiny.* Their leadership title, like that of the Crips, is "OG" for "Original Gangsta." Their gang color is red, to signify blood. In the spirit of brotherhood and brotherly love, the organization stresses what they call "Piru love," and believe that it is easier to teach young recruits what they need to know by walking them through it as many times as it takes to get it right. They do not beat each other, but reserve the violence for their enemies, primarily the Crips. Their war cry is "CK," for "Crip Killa." Their gear is khaki pants and white or black tee shirts, preferring Calvin Klein labels. The governing factor in their communications is their alphabet, in which the letter B is sacred, replacing the letter C.

Folks.   The Folks is another organized gang that has achieved notoriety and become very visible throughout the United States. At about the same time that the Bloods and the Crips were emerging in California, the Midwestern city of Chicago was also experiencing the birth of large scale gang activity with Folks, which stands for *Follow Our Lord King Satan* or *Follow Our Lord King Shorty.* In Folks, the leader's title is Governor. Folks' primary color is black.

Folks has two major subdivisions under its jurisdiction, the GDN (Gangsta Disciple Nation) and the BDN (Black Disciple Nation). The six-pointed Star of David and an upright pitchfork and dagger are their cherished symbols (Sheldon, Tracy, & Brown 2001, 15). Numbers have special meaning to Folks: The number six (6) is held in reverence and the number five (5) is viewed with dishonor. The way they wear their clothing has specific meaning: Caps are worn to the right, pants cuffs are rolled on the right leg, and belts are left hanging to signify that "All is one." Folks incorporate elements of satanic worship, and some members may proclaim Christianity or exhibit hints of both Christianity and satanism. The six-pointed star is used in one of their ceremonial rituals: Members make the star, which is held over their head as they recite a "prayer of eternal commitment" to the organization. The organization is cult-like. Folks' primary nemeses are the Vice Lords.

Vice Lords.   The Vice Lords (also known as the People Nation) emerged in the 1950s as the brainchild of a group of youths in a Chicago training school. With adolescent exuberance they proclaimed themselves to be Lords and Kings of the earth (Sheldon, Tracy, & Brown 2001, 16). Their primary colors are red, black, and gold. They wear hats and caps tilted to the left and roll the left leg of their pants, which signifies that "all is well." Symbols that distinguish them include a crown that bears the numeral 5; the five-pointed star whose points represent letters in the name Allah, which itself implies love, peace, truth, freedom, and justice; the dollar sign that represents the riches of our Lord Allah; and verbal references to Allah, all of which suggest some association with the Muslim religion. The Vice Lords encompass two very interesting components, the Insane Vice Lords and the Latin Kings, which has mostly Hispanic members.

Latin Kings (ALKN or Almighty Latin King Nation).   Hispanic street gangs did not receive a great deal of notoriety until the late 1950s, when they came together to promote unity among Hispanic people. They became well-known in South Chicago, especially in the Southwest area. Their nemeses, the Maniac Latin Disciples (allied with the Folks Nation) are a mixture of Hispanic Americans and African Americans.

The Latin Kings profess to have a formalized rank structure that includes Supreme Crown authorities, Executive Crown Authorities, and Crown Advisors (Grennan *et al.* 2000, 407–409). Their colors are black and gold, symbolizing death and life, respectively. Their emblems include a five-pointed crown, a five-pointed star, a lion's head with a crown, and, recently, a bulldog with a crown. They are known to act very violently against their own members who do not conform to their rules, beating and stabbing them. Their primary source of income is the drug economy (410). The Kings no longer use *monikers* (street names), but now have identification cards and numbers. High-ranking members have bodyguards.

Native American Gangs

Although reports from OJJDP indicate that juvenile crime is on the decrease in the United States (2001), they also report that violent juvenile crime is on the increase on Native American reservations. The number of Native American gangs on reservations has doubled since

1994 (Khoury 1998). Five members of the East Side Crips Rolling Thirties gang on the reservation were convicted of murder under the federal organized crime law (Kelley 1997).

Native American gangs were not discussed until 1992, but since that time their numbers have begun to explode on reservations, where more than 180 gangs have been documented (Buckley 2000). They are very well-organized and have information and weapons far more advanced, in some instances, than those available to tribal law enforcement. Violence on the reservations has increased drastically, in large part because of the Native American youth gangs. Leclaire (1999) in his statement to the Committee on Indian Affairs in the U.S. Senate, stated that youth gangs were able to gain more power on reservations because of ineffective and inefficient law enforcement protocols. He cited the need to assist Native Americans in learning the newest technological advances, discussed problems of violence and poverty with the few criminal justice staff personnel that were assigned, and tried to address the lack of training for personnel to keep abreast of modern intelligence-gathering techniques.

Native American tribal leaders are very much concerned about the increase in gang activity and fear it will escalate because most reservations do not have appropriate tribal law enforcement resources (Leclaire 1999). Unlike other gangs, Native American youth gangs appear to have a greater ability to function with impunity because of the limited law enforcement resources. But because these gangs operate on Native American reservations, their delinquent acts fall under the category of federal crimes and youths are arrested and tried in the federal system. Native Americans are incarcerated at a higher rate than any other group in U.S. society (Badwound 2000). In the Bureau of Prisons (BOP) more than 70 percent of the youth population is Native American (Andrews 2000). One reason for the high incarceration rates is increased gang activity on reservations.

As a result of increased gang activity on Native American reservations, the FBI created the Office of Indian Country Investigations (OICI) in 1997. The primary role of the OICI is to render assistance to tribal law enforcement officers in their efforts to reduce gang violence on reservations (Arrillaga 2001).

The Navajo Nation, the largest Native American tribe, has taken some initiatives to combat their youth gang problem by (1) discussing gangs on the reservation as a primary Native American concern, (2) seeking federal aid by teaming with federal agencies (such as the FBI) to establish gang initiatives, (3) seeking federal dollars to establish gang prevention programs that use cultural approaches to treatment, and (4) establishing community crime coalitions.

The Navajo Nation inhabits land in Arizona, Utah, and New Mexico, in which more than 70 gangs have been identified. One Navajo housing project has been referred to as "Beirut" because of gang violence (Kelley 1997). The Navajo Nation tribal leaders forecast greater increase of gang activity on their reservations because the law enforcement resources are not adequate to reduce the gang activity (*N.Y. Times,* August 16, 1998). The forecast worsens because many of the gang members who were arrested earlier will be released from federal prisons and go back to the reservations, where they are anticipated to attempt to continue their gang activities at an even stronger pace.

Native American youths join gangs for the same reasons as their counterparts— belonging, excitement, and profit—but they also have reasons that are unique to their culture. Kelly (1997) identifies loss of language, losing touch with their culture, and, traditionally, a larger youth population as unique factors that make joining a Native American gang unique. Badwound (2000) discusses the appearance of the Bloods on the reservation and the loss of identity as unique causes for Native American youths joining gangs.

Native American gangs, like Asian gangs, maintain a low profile because the majority of their violent activity is accomplished on the Native American reservations. According to Henderson, Kunitz, and Levy (1999), the gang represents a passage to adulthood and a change from their native customs.

In 1999, Congress appropriated $10 million for the establishment of Tribal Youth Programs (TYP) and $12.5 million for TYP for fiscal year 2000. Congress had never before appropriated funds specifically to target decreasing gang problems by increasing law enforcement resources on Native American reservations (Andrews 2000). There are no comprehensive prevention–intervention programs for juveniles on reservations: "Many of the 1.4 million American Indians living on or near Indian lands lack even the most basic law enforcement services" (Andrews 2000).

White Gangs

Black and Hispanic gangs are the most notorious gangs in the United States, yet gangs in the United States began with a band of white teens organized by Jesse James the mid-1800s. Contemporary white gangs, such as the Skinheads, emerged in reaction to social and economic changes in this country and focus on racial hatred and illegal criminal activities. Their turf encompasses the entire country. They believe in racial cleansing.

Skinheads.   The Skinheads started in England and emerged in the United States in California and other parts of the country during the mid-1980s. They are strong advocates of white supremacy and use violence to accomplish their goals against other races and people whom they deem nonsupporters of their cause. Their appearance through their personal grooming and clothing is unmistakable. Most shave their heads or cut their hair very close, wear plain white tee shirts, black or dark pants, and Doc Martens steel-toed boots. They may tattoo swastikas or iron crosses on their bodies, sew them on their jackets, or wear them as pendants. Skinheads revere Hitler and his notion of the Third Reich and may hang Hitler's picture prominently in the organization's headquarters. Although they operate in illegal activities and fight over turf or communities to keep them white in the name of racial superiority, law enforcement organizations perceive them as political activists and not as street gangs like the Latin Kings, Bloods, or Crips.

A major difference between the white gangs and others is that they take applications, usually keep an ongoing roster of members, and may collect dues from members. They refer to their organizations as "firms" (Leet, Rush, & Smith 1997). White gang members, like other street gang members, may hold legitimate jobs and may openly profess their membership in the firms. African-American gang members in legitimate employment are less likely to admit their involvement in gang activity openly. The U.S. military has experienced incidents of military personnel in skinhead activities. According to Leet, et al. (1997), the Bureau of Organized Crime and Criminal Intelligence (BOCCI) identified four types of Skinheads: white power groups, independents, the Two-Tones, and the wannabes (132–133).

White Power Groups.   White power groups advocate any means, including violence, to accomplish their ultimate goal of white supremacy and the cleansing of the United States of people who are racially, ethnically, or religiously different from themselves. They are very clear about their agenda and support very conservative political views. However, they distrust government officials because they are too liberal on racial and ethnic issues. White people who support equality and equal rights are traitors to their race and are not to be trusted. The Ku Klux Klan (KKK) is one of oldest white supremacy organizations in the United States. After the Civil War, some Southerners organized the Klan to strike back at the economic stronghold by unleashing a rampage of racial bigotry and intimidation, the most obvious of which was burning crosses before a lynching. Black people, former slaves, received the brunt of KKK action because they were a prime component in the economy of the South, were the least organized group in the country because they had been enslaved for a long time, and could be frightened easily because few people in the South supported their rights.

Independents.   Independents believe in white supremacy but are not violent and plan to accomplish their goals legally. They may support the Skinheads financially but do not publicly participate in their rallies. They are "closet Skinheads," professing the same ideologies as Skinheads, but keeping their activities behind closed doors. They may profess that "some of my best friends are black or Jewish, but I don't want to live next door to them."

Two-Tones.   Two-Tones are racial separatists who do not consider themselves racists or bigots, but profess interest in the welfare of the nation. The Christian Bible is the foundation for their ideologies; they cite it to support their beliefs. They are openly opposed to homosexuality to the point of openly physically attacking gay men and lesbians because homosexuality, they believe, violates the dictates of the Bible. Two-Tones want to be seen as nonracists and accept into their ranks some nonwhites who believe in separation of the races and are opposed to homosexuality.

Wannabes.   Wannabes in white power organizations, as in minority street gangs, are on the periphery, observing the activity of the core group of which they are not a part. They might not have been accepted by the core group, might prefer merely to emulate the core group, or have not decided if they want to join, although they have friends or family who are members. As wannabes, they wear the clothes and "talk the talk" of the core group, but, as one core member said, "they cannot walk the walk yet."

The Aryan Youth Movement.   The Aryan Youth Movement recruits youths and children within the ranks of the Aryan Brotherhood. Leet *et al.* (1997) outline the goals of the Aryan Youth Movement (134):

1. To provide a network of strong, young, white supremacist warriors for racial expansion and survival.
2. To use weapons and violence on campuses and in the streets to bring about white power and a white supremacist-based government.
3. To recruit adolescents and young adults into the Aryan Youth Movement, White Student Union, and White Aryan Resistance organizations.

4. To seek and build a separatist Aryan homeland.
5. To encourage sporadic racial violence and anti-Semitic hatred on campuses and in neighborhoods.
6. To work toward the overthrow and destruction of the Zionist Occupational Government (ZOG), which, they believe, is a covert shadow government, in the United States.

White youth supremacy groups have increased tremendously over the last 10 years and have taken on new attitudes and subtle recruiting practices. Their programs, masquerading as social clubs or college fraternities, lure friendless social isolates who do not fit into the daily activities of their peers and who yearn to belong. The groups indoctrinate the vulnerable youths in supremacy philosophies. Subverting the American work ethic (work hard and you will succeed), they suggest that people from minorities might receive the benefits for which the youths have worked so diligently. Some white supremacy organizations receive federal dollars because their programs fit the profile of prevention programs.

White supremacist groups can reach young people through the Internet. Many youths visit the supremacists' colorful Web sites and chat rooms where they find social interaction that they do not experience at school and among their peers. Supremacists also recruit youths in malls and go door-to-door to distribute flyers in neighborhoods.

Asian American Gangs

Filipino, Chinese, Japanese, Korean, and Vietnamese are the most prevalent ethnic Asian youth populations in the United States, although the population includes youths of other Asian nationalities. Changes in U.S. immigration laws, primarily, account for the rapid increase in Asian youths of all nationalities.

As Asians migrate to the United States, they adopt much of U.S. culture. The resulting bicultural integration has, in many instances, led to confusion and a constant struggle to maintain their Asian customs and norms and at the same time try to assimilate into U.S. culture. Asian American gang activity and membership is one of the bicultural adaptations.

Asian youth street gangs are a relatively new phenomenon in the United States. Many emerged in the late 1970s and 1980s (Le 2001). Large numbers of youths belong to Asian gangs, but research provides limited information about them, primarily because most of their victims are of the same ethnic group and the Asian American population does not rely on police intervention to resolve their disagreements and problems. They do not report crimes to the police as readily as other citizens because they have preconceptions about police corruption. In some of the countries from which they immigrated, police were political tools, used to punish political victims and other citizens regardless of guilt or innocence. Police were allowed full authority and decision making about crimes without individual recourse, and in the experience of many Asians, did not support the rights of all individuals and protect the innocent, but used their position to oppress people and seek personal gain.

Many Asian Americans came from countries without constitutions or rules of law to ensure justice. These countries had no mechanisms to check or monitor law enforcement, so corrupt police officers were abundant and were open in their corruption. Although they now live in a democracy, many still perceive law enforcement as corrupt, and when they become victims of a crime in their new country, are reluctant to report it to the police.

*Asian gang members
flashing.
A. Ramey/PhotoEdit*

In addition to negative feelings about law enforcement, many Asian American citizens believe in the Confucian precept that all individuals are responsible for their behavior and the collective is responsible for each other (Cleary 2000). They believe that what happens to them in their community is their responsibility. As victims of crime, they have brought dishonor to the community and failed it and the youths who committed the criminal acts against them. Asian American families who may not only be victims of gangs but who also may have family members in gangs are embarrassed to divulge this information because it is represents failure of the entire family and community (Le 2001).

Asian Americans seek little assistance from outsiders. Victims of gangs succumb to it quietly. Parents whose children are involved in gangs seldom discuss the problem outside of the family. Gangs adhere to the same cultural attitudes. Secrecy and anonymity are major considerations in maintaining a low profile as they go about their business. Other ethnic street gangs also suggest that secrecy and anonymity are important to them, but they publicize their violence and retaliation to advertise their power to their rivals. Asian youth gangs, less concerned about public display of force, do not place as much importance on colors, graffiti, and maintaining specific gang rivalries. American Asian youths join gangs out of consideration of family needs rather than their own. Gang membership is a viable option if the youths' families need protection from violence or financial help.

Asian youths take on added responsibility when they swear allegiance and become gang members. They are expected to not only honor and respect the gang family, but to continue to honor and respect the natural family.

All Asian gangs are not alike. Asian Americans come from strikingly different cultures, and Asian gangs reflect these differences. Le (2001) points out two commonalities among Asian gangs: First, they are connected to organized adult crime, and, second, their method of criminalizing is home invasion within their communities. Le suggests that Asian families invest heavily in gold because it is convenient and requires little English language skill. They keep cash and gold in their homes because they do not trust the banks. Asian American youth gangs break into neighbors' houses, tie them up, and steal these valuables. Although Asian American gangs remain unique and entrenched in their territory victimization, in some instances, they adopt features from other ethnic gangs.

Filipino Gangs. The Los Angeles police department reports that among the Pacific Islanders, including Samoans, Guamanians, Hawaiians, and Filipinos, Samoans in Carson, California, were the first to form street gangs, which they patterned after the Hispanic and African American gangs from which they had split. Filipinos are the largest group of this segment of gang subculture. Filipino gangs are like the African American and Hispanic gangs because Filipinos integrate neighborhoods more quickly than Asians who established their own communities, such as "Chinatowns." Filipino gang members are not necessarily impoverished youths, some come from affluent families.

Filipino youths were recruited for information gathering by the Sige-Sige and Oxo gangs in Manila in the late 1940s. During the 1950s, as Sige-Sige and Oxo became more sophisticated, youth recruitment increased. Eventually the youth gangs became self-sufficient, took on their own identities, and formed their own sets, the Sputniks (offshoot of the Sige-Sige) and the Crossbones (offshoot of the Oxo). New sets developed and sets of Bahala Na and Tres Cantos gangs are highly visible Filipino American entities in the United States (Gang Intelligence 2001).

The pressures of entering a new country with strange customs and unfamiliar language influenced Filipino youths who migrated to the United States to join gangs. Initially the gangs provided emotional support and understanding in a new environment in which youths who entered the U.S. school system felt isolated because they looked different from their school peers and were unable to speak fluent English. They formed Barkada, a social group. Non-Filipino students related to the Filipino Barkada as a street gang. Filipino American youths in Barkada began to act like street gangs for protection and retaliation (Leet, Rush, & Smith 1997). They began to mimic Hispanic and African American gang activities and adopted many of their characteristics.

Although not as distinctive as their Hispanic and African American counterparts, Filipino-American gang members have their own clothing fashions. Some sets wear black, three-quarter-length trenchcoats. Other Filipino American sets wear plain white shirts and pants with no designs or markings. Although many Filipino American gang members do not own cars, those who do favor minipickup trucks or Japanese cars (Leet *et al.* 1997). They modify the vehicles with wild "go faster" designs and add fat polished tires, flared fenders, and tinted windows. Filipino American gang members use tattoos in moderation as identifying marks to proclaim their bravery and commitment. The marks range from initials to cigarette burn marks on their bodies and their hands, on the inside of the index finger or on the calf of the leg. The identifiers provide a history of the individual gang member's activity. A lack of identifiers can indicate a new member with little or no participation in the gang. Numerous identifiers can indicate that the youth has been extremely active in the gang.

Filipino American gangs barter, trading drugs to military personnel for military-issued weapons. Although they prefer semiautomatics, they obtain all sorts of weapons however they can. The more powerful the weapon, the greater their ability to survive. Filipino American gangs emulate their Hispanic and African American counterparts in the use of graffiti to distribute information among members and to send messages to rivals. The gangs use names and cartoon characters in colorful graffiti in the neighborhoods they frequent. Filipino American gangs are as mobile as Hispanic and African American gangs, and have migrated throughout the United States.

Chinese Gangs.   Chinese Americans are the largest Asian American ethnic group in U.S. society. They comprise 4.2 percent of the total U.S. population, numbering more than 2.7 million, approximately 23.8 percent of the Asian American population (U. S. Census 2001). Much Chinese American youth gang activity is contained within the Chinese communities with very little emphasis on a specific nemesis. The Los Angeles police department reports that the Wah Ching, one of the largest Chinese American street gangs, is comprised primarily of Cantonese Chinese who are extremely active in their area. They have become very mobile and are highly visible in the state of Washington and have successfully migrated to establish a stronghold in Canada.

Two Hong Kong born youths, Gene Fong and his brother Joe, began the original Wah Ching in San Francisco in 1964 (Lee 1999). Joe started a rival gang, Chung Ching Yee (or the Joe Boys) in 1972 as a result of dissatisfaction with his brother's style of running the gang. They formed the gangs to protect themselves from American-born Chinese (ABC) youths in Chinatown and non-Asian youths at Samuel Gompers High School (Lin-Chin 2000).

The gang met at a coffee house at 150 Waverly Place (Lin-Chin 2000). They encouraged the business community in Chinatown to use the gang for protection and to use their resources to make community improvements. If businessmen did not agree to their proposals, the gang vandalized their companies. The tongs, organized crime families, hired the Wah Ching youths. Many Wah Ching left to form the Hip Sing Tong youth gang and other gangs, such as the Yau Lay, led by Stephen Chan (Lin-Chin 2000).

The tongs control the youth gangs in Chinatowns throughout the United States and use them to perpetuate their organized criminal activities. They recruit youths primarily to maintain order and create disorder on demand in the communities. The Dragons dominate in Manhattan's Chinatown; Hop Sing and Suey Sing hold the power in San Francisco. The California Justice Department reports that 12 factions of the Wah Ching have members who can be linked to the original Wah Ching. Los Angeles reports 1,800 Wah Ching members. The youth gangs recruit not only young Cantonese Chinese, but are becoming multiethnic, recruiting Taiwanese and Vietnamese youths.

Vietnamese Gangs.   The Vietnamese American population has increased drastically since their influx into the United States when refugees from South Vietnam emigrated in 1975. A second wave of Vietnamese settled in the United States in 1979, bringing with them not only military strategies, but organized criminal structures that many youth fell back on when their efforts to assimilate in U.S. society were unsuccessful (Grannon 2000, 253). Currently the U.S. Census Bureau reports that Vietnamese Americans number more than 700,000. Zhou and Bankston (2000) explain that refugees were settled in poor ethnic and socially deprived areas with inferior schools and infested with street gangs. Vietnamese street gangs were a counter-survival response to a new culture that offered contradictory messages.

Vietnamese street gangs have increased tremendously. Gangs such as Bui Doi, the Natoma Boyz, the Chosen Brothers, and the Viet Ching, with a home base in California, have grown in size (Grennan *et al.* 2000, 251–252). Orange County, California, has the largest Vietnamese population in the United States and estimates over 6,000 gangs in the area. Not only emigrants, but biracial Vietnamese children with Vietnamese and American parents experience isolation, stress, and frustration and form subcultures for physical and psychological protection.

The "new wave" Vietnamese American street gang is young, predominately male, opportunistic, and sophisticated (Leet *et al.* 1997).

They execute missions methodically, carefully planning their attacks. They are not generalists: Their members become specialized and use their specialties accordingly. They rely on the tools of modern technology, planning activities online and making them available for questions and feedback before they carry them out. They engage in drive-by shootings, random shootings, and turf wars infrequently. They do not protect turf or fight about turf issues as do their African American and Latino counterparts (Shelden *et al.* 2000, 46). Grannon, Britz, Rush, and Barker (2001) describe them as "phantom" gangs because they move from location to location within the Vietnamese community as they plan and implement their criminal activities. Recently, Vietnamese gangs began to adopt tattoos and slang expressions and make some modifications to their clothing.

Like other street gangs, the Vietnamese American gangs prefer contemporary, high technology weaponry, such as semiautomatics, Uzis, and submachine guns, which they usually obtain from military personnel. Like Chinese American youth gangs, Vietnamese American gangs do not expend a great deal of time and effort defacing property with graffiti. Like other gangs, though, they do make a commitment to each other as family and are willing to die for each other. Culturally, they embrace the notion of strong family unity with a clear understanding of roles and responsibilities (Grennan *et al.* 2000, 249). Thus, the gang offers them a family structure that is absent in their biological families. Gang leaders adopt the role of parents, and females assume the traditional role of primary care providers. In typical Vietnamese family fashion, the gang pools its resources and distributes the spoils among the members. Vietnamese American gangs have begun to practice the "jump in" ritual like their African American and Latino counterparts, but have a different perspective: The Natoma Boyz, for example limit their beatings to 30 seconds and rule that they be done with integrity, that is, with no blows to the face or groin (Du Phuoc Long 1997) because in their culture honor must be displayed, even in trying times. Uniquely, Vietnamese American gangs allow membership in more than one gang simultaneously (Grennan *et al.* 2000, 250). This practice is culturally based because Vietnamese need to care for each other regardless of prior or current affiliations. Each gang member must succeed so that the gang (regardless of which) will survive and thrive.

Vietnamese American gangs' criminal activities are, primarily, home invasion, extortion, automobile theft, and computer chip theft (Grennan *et al.* 2000, 259). Some sets participate in drug activity, but not yet to the extent of their African American or Latino counterparts.

Korean Gangs.   The passage of the Immigration Reform Act of 1965 led to a sharp increase in the influx of Koreans to the United States. Koreans, with a population of more than a million (Hurn 1998), represent one of the largest Asian groups in this country. Throughout their history, Koreans have been influenced culturally and socially by invaders from Japan, China, and Russia, and with the division of the country into two sovereign entities, its citizens still feel the uncertainty of a people struggling for survival (Kim 2001).

Korean American gangs bear many similarities to Chinese American and Vietnamese American gangs. Korean American gang members quietly go about their duties in the gang and do not boast about membership. Although limited information is available on Korean American youth street gangs, a trend appears to be toward more involvement of females in the business component.

Japanese Gangs.   Japanese Americans are the third largest group of Asian Americans, totaling more than 800,000 according to Grennan et al (2000, 220), but they are not increasing as rapidly as other Asian groups. This slower pace may be attributed to two important factors: that few Japanese immigrate to the U.S. because they prefer life in Japan among familiar surroundings and people, (Trueba, Cheng, & Ima 1993) and the "war brides" syndrome (Mass 1992), in which intermarriages create a population of children who claim a biracial heritage that complicates census counts. The war bride syndrome also creates a breakdown of ethnic boundaries that causes further complexities in categorizing individuals ethnically and culturally.

Adolescent Japanese American street gangs have existed in the United States since the 19th century. The Yakuza, however, an organized crime syndicate, and one of the most feared and productive Asian gangs in the United States, operates legitimate businesses as fronts and makes investments in legitimate companies. The Yakuza is thought to have holdings in major U.S. enterprises and lucrative stock market investments. The Yakuza is thought to be very highly organized with strong ties between Japan and the United States (Leet *et al.* 1997, 113). Although the Yakuza is not a street gang, it uses youths in its activities, especially in pornography, which it imports and exports on a large scale.

U.S. law enforcement does not consider Asian American gangs in the same way as African-American or Hispanic street gangs. Asian gangs are more structured and organized groups, and have different goals. They are involved in extortion, burglary, illegal gambling, prostitution, loan sharking, narcotics trafficking, robbery, and murder. They may be linked with gangs in their home countries and may have established connections between profitable activities in the United States and the home countries. Because of their international connections, their value system is steeped in tradition. Although they are involved in criminal activity, they are still bound by centuries-old codes that dictate respect, honor, and behavioral standards to which they must adhere. Their aims are well-defined and explicit, focusing on group profits rather than individual gains. Like other street gangs, they do not trust the police, and they punish infractions of the rules immediately. They value secrecy and they take care of internal problems themselves. Police find it difficult to infiltrate Asian American gangs or to develop informants among them.

Asian American gangs may contain sets, engage in rivalry, and protect turf to some degree. They are ethnically different from each other, and have values that are unique to their own cultures.

Violence and Gangs

Some researchers believe that youth violence is not increasing, but that youths are political pawns for whom ineffective programs are funded and about whom the public is fed inaccurate information (Schwartz 1992). Others believe that youth violence is increasing and that the increase is associated with drug use and abuse. Whether youth violence is increasing, decreasing, or stable is not a concern. That youths display violent behavior and the determination of the factors that contribute to the violent behavior are concerns.

Major factors that contribute to the adolescents' violent behavior have been the drug economy, easy accessibility of guns, and violence perpetuated by gangs. Inciardi (1992) attributes the adolescent violence reported by the media to the drug subculture. His research revealed that delinquent youths (N = 611) reported drug use at an early age. He reported a mean age for initial drug use at 7.6 years for alcohol and 10.4 years for marijuana, with 93 percent of youths going from marijuana to cocaine by age 13. By age 14.85, the subjects reported regular use of drugs (Inciardi 1992). These youths had a history of drug and repetitive juvenile delinquent activities, with 88.4 percent of the subjects reporting carrying handguns the majority of the time (98–99). Inciardi identified the violence displayed by the drug using adolescents into two distinctive dichotomies, economic compulsive violence and systemic violence.

Economic compulsive violence is perpetuated by individual youths to feed their drug habits. They assault people and take their money and valuables to sell for money to purchase drugs. *Systemic violence* comes with the drug subculture, occurring because of deals that go bad, distrust, or lessons that have to be taught, resulting in physical violence. Regardless of the type of violence, the outcome usually benefits a few gang members within the organization who reap the benefits of drug trafficking, not the total set.

Easy Access to Guns

Youths have easy access to hand guns as criminal organizations provide the weaponry they need to take care of business. Gang members have easy access to guns, which they use for initiation, retaliation, and criminal activity.

Gang Migration and Violence

Gangs are not only an urban phenomenon: Bloods, Crips, and Folks have infiltrated rural communities in the United States and are setting up lucrative operations in many small towns. They migrate to smaller towns when large cities become inhospitable. They choose small towns for their potential for profit, less intensive law enforcement, and less intense competition for drug turf (Jackson 1996).

College towns are great profit makers. College students are eager to experiment with drugs. In small towns, a dearth of social activities to call on their funds allows students to buy drugs. Small towns near military bases are havens for drug deals and are especially important because of the availability of weapons (Jackson 1996).

Personnel in law enforcement organizations in small towns may not be trained or experienced in gang tactics, and small communities tend to deny that they have gangs.

Youths in small rural towns display more serious violent behaviors than previously, much of it enhanced by gang migrations. Even towns' "own" youths bring urban back after they have been away from home for a summer or more. A youth who spends a summer with relatives in a large city might return wearing a different style of clothing and projecting a different attitude. Tremendous physical and emotional transitions might indicate that a youth has joined a gang (Ice T 1995, 152).

Female Gang Members

The general public does not view gang banging—participation in gangs—as an activity of females. The public perceives gangs as violent, male-perpetuated, and male-oriented entities and perceives females as neither capable nor willing to participate in gang activities. When females participate in gang activity, the public expresses as much shock that a female was involved in the act as at the act itself. Arrest rates for females have increased sharply, but society has difficulty accepting that female gang members commit crimes as heinous as those of their male counterparts, perhaps because female gang members are fewer than males and are not as visible.

Although females are capable of committing the same crimes as males, and although feminism has touched the gang subculture, female gang members are viewed by male gang members as second class citizens, incapable of performing important roles. Their treatment reflects the treatment of females in the larger society: Their roles are subservient to those of male gang members. Gangs use females for window dressing and assign them some unimportant, menial tasks, never allowing them decision-making responsibilities concerning gang activities. Yet, they can and do influence the male gang members' decisions, and they do commit violent acts. Arguments about why females join gangs range from women's liberation and the feminist movement to societal stressors such as drugs, changing roles, and advances in the creation of violent images on computers, computerized games, movies, and television, which depict females as violent, promiscuous, and capable. Chesney-Lind (1988) adds that this is no different from the male counterpart: "The 'streets' reflect the strained interplay among race, class, and gender" (72) for both male and female gang members. Bowker and Klein (1983) agree that " . . . in combination, the impact of racism, sexism, poverty, and limited opportunity is likely to be more important in determining delinquency and membership in gangs among women . . . " (745). Whatever the reason, be it the feminist movement or societal stressors, females join gangs for some of the same reasons as their male counterparts. However, some differences between male and female gang members are worthy of note.

Differences between Female and Male Gang Members.   Prior to gang involvement, female gang members are already victim. Incest and other sexual abuse and domestic violence have left their mark, so physically and psychologically debilitating these young women that they believe that within gangs they can express their frustrations, anger, and fears without inhibition by societal norms. Gang membership offers them a form and an opportunity for self-expression in the execution of violent acts in which they are aggressors, not victims.

Researchers find that female gang members may be as or more violent than their male counterparts because their violence is physical, and of greater impact, and of longer duration than that of males. When females "beat down" victims, they may continue the physical attack after the victim is unconscious, and sometimes to the point of total physical disfigurement. Female gang members appear to be less forgiving and more demanding of authority and respect than their male counterparts, perhaps in compensation for a lifetime of lower status in the larger society. Male gang members are secure in their role in society as well as in the gang, so they do not have to "go for the exaggerated respect thing," as one male gang member described it.

Methods of initiation among female gangs vary between sets, ranging from *jumping in* by fighting several gang members simultaneously to prove stamina and loyalty, being *blessed in* by a ritualistic prayer of eternal commitment and obedience, or being *sexed in* by having sex with members. Some are accepted because family members have been affiliated with the set and their loyalty is not questioned. These trusted and honored heirs may be allowed a *walk in.* The gang gives uninitiated females less violent assignments than those delegated to males. Activities that are status offenses, such as being lookouts, are common beginning assignments for females. More serious activities, such as carrying weapons that they are expected to be ready to use, are common early assignments for males. Gangs do not provide females with weaponry assignments even by the age of 14 or 15. Instead, they expect them to get information or set up rival gang members by using sex. Females are not searched by police as often as males. Some law enforcement officers have a paternalistic attitude toward females and allow themselves to be distracted by female gang members who are not wearing their colors.

Female gang members show their colors in their clothing, generally wearing pants and seldom wearing dresses. Asian female gang members, however, may wear short skirts. Female gang members may have tattoos of their gang affiliation, their mates' names, or their own monikers on their body (e.g., face, shoulders, arms, back, ankles, and so forth). African American female gang members use hair clips, bandanas, nail polish, and dress similar to their male counterparts to show their allegiance.

Female gang members do not remain active as long as males because many may become pregnant and their responsibilities change. When they become mothers, they give up their monikers and become active in child-rearing. Gang activities for females are limited by their new responsibilities. Males who become fathers may continue, even escalate, their illegal gangbanging activities to provide for their children.

Adolescent Incarcerated Gang Members

When escalation of illegal activities leads to incarceration, gang members must survive in a prison or juvenile system in which a number of gangs reside. The rules of "gangmanship" change after incarceration. Eisenman (1993) conducted a study of inmates in a treatment program for youthful offenders and discovered that more than 50 percent of them were gang members. Youth authorities grapple with the increasing problems that they encounter with incarcerated adolescents who bring their gang affiliations with them into the juvenile system.

Youths discover that it is not easy to extricate themselves from their gang affiliations even in incarceration. As they attempt to maintain their gang demeanor, they are faced with the rules of the correction system and the rules of different sets. Sets may function differently from one part of a state to another. A Crip from a large city may have different expectations from a Crip from a rural area. Some fundamentals—the colors, the alphabet, and the nemesis—remain the same, but the gang activities and expectations may differ.

Some juvenile correctional systems place gang members in segregated units or dormitories. Other juvenile facilities integrate all the youths in an effort to deter gangs, assigning rivals to work together. Recruitment in facilities is a high priority for gangs. The institutions offer a setting in which recruits can learn the alphabet and history and prepare to recruit more members on their return to the community. In the juvenile correctional facilities, gangs recruit youths who understand that initiated members survive there because the gang protects them.

Beyond the Statistics and the Demographics

Race, ethnicity, and cultural differences dictate gang characteristics, the extent of criminality, and the most effective intervention methods. African American and Hispanic gangs display a flashy, "in your face," demeanor. They publicize their actions through graffiti that issues challenges, reports obituaries, and offers welcomes to newly arriving homeboys. They openly embrace their brotherhood and allegiance to one another and boldly name their enemies and rivals. Although they loudly boast of giving and receiving respect and love, they will quickly dishonor each other and family by engaging in drive-by shootings in their neighborhoods. These encounters result in the deaths of innocent family and community members. Their primary enterprise is drug trafficking and distribution. Their overall goal is self-preservation. Even though they speak about the gang as a family, their primary motivation is the survival of the individual. Each individual's survival contributes to the survival of the gang as a whole.

Hand signs are a primary means of communicating among gang members. A. Lichtenstein/Corbis/ Sygman

Asian street gangs are more secretive and seldom publicize their existence or their activities. They adhere to the importance of honoring the family and seldom become involved in drivebys that would bring family dishonor were innocent individuals killed. They consider the best interest of the collective rather than individual needs. They are less likely to be identified by colors or a particular dress code. Their delinquent activity expands beyond drug trafficking and distribution to include white collar and computer crimes.

White street gangs use threats and intimidation to communicate with outsiders. They show their arrogance through organized, public rallies. They recruit members on college campuses and at parades and festivals. They are precisely uniformed and exhibit military demeanor. They verbalize a collective concern for purity of race. They view the entire United States as their turf and boast about the unfortunate nature of struggles, yet express no remorse for innocent victims—collateral deaths—of their actions. Although they seek monetary gain, their primary goal is to gain supremacy and dominance over people who do not look or act like them. In their communities, they lash out at individuals whom they view as disloyal to their race or who do not support them in their ideology.

Remedies for the Gang Problem

The implementation of new laws is among the remedies that may address the increase in gang activities throughout the United States. One such law is the Street Terrorism Enforcement Protection Act (STEP Act), which was implemented in California in 1988. The purpose of the Act was to reduce gang activity in the state by imposing stricter and harsher punishment on individuals participating in gang activities. As a result of the Act, gang membership became a felony.

Some areas create specialized law enforcement units who hire police officers to target gang members and gang activity. Police officers in community schools establish early identification of gang activity and make recruitment more difficult. These federal- and state-funded projects are called gang units or youth units. The Gang Reporting Evaluation and Tracking (GREAT) system, which collects and dispenses information on gang members throughout the country via computer and specialized training of law enforcement officers on gangs and gang activities are other federal- and state-funded projects (Knox 2000, 381; Sheldon *et al.* 2001, 27). Many states provide such training in their law enforcement academies, too, and others provide ongoing training in dealing with gangs. Even so, gangs continue to grow and develop and relocate their activities all over the country.

Full Employment

If reactive measures such as harsher laws are not the answer to the problem, perhaps proactive measures such as prevention and early intervention, along with legal remedies, may be beneficial. Some proactive remedies for the gang problem are full employment, community-based intervention, fewer students in each school classroom, and less notoriety.

Many youths become gang members because they perceive gang activity as an easy way to increase their financial base. Obtaining legal employment is not easy for youths. Most states issue work permits only to youths 16 or older. Age is a barrier for younger youths who need money and want to work but are too young to obtain the work permit.

Some locales mandate their departments of social services to issue youth work permits. Youths who don't want to provide information about their families are reluctant to apply for work permits from this public body. Schools sometimes provide on-site service for students who want a work permit, but many youths cannot find jobs because work schedules require morning or late evening shifts that would interfere with school or because companies opt for mature adults rather than youths.

Although some critics assume that youths would prefer selling drugs, taking youths' initial response that "I'm not working for nickels and dimes selling burgers" as a final one, youths themselves say that they would rather work in a restaurant than sell drugs because it is less dangerous and, potentially, they can live longer. Youths will work if given the opportunity to do so. They want to work legitimately and earn legitimate money. Many gang members and former gang members are studying on college campuses, are in the military, or are employed by cities and states, earning or preparing to earn through legitimate employment. Full-time employment is not the panacea for resolving the gang activities, but it would assist in reducing the increased gang membership.

Community-Based Intervention

Community-based intervention can be very productive if well thought out and monitored closely. It can have a strong impact on younger children who may become gang members. Many are bored and have limited structured activities. Although communities offer numerous structured programs, they are designed for children who conform to social rules. The programs may not welcome at-risk children simply because they are troubled or at risk. Few programs in communities will accept at-risk children with limited social skills. The programs like to ensure high success rates to ensure continued funding, so they are not likely to admit at-risk children or to encourage them to participate. Programs in the community that are designed specifically to focus on at-risk children are able to accept only a very limited number, who must meet specific criteria that will ensure a high success rate. Program criteria are usually based on how the youths are perceived.

Many community programs are guided by how much funding they can secure, because funds are essential to keep programs functioning. Community programs do not have to cost a great amount of money, but success is necessary to obtain continued funding. Federal or state funds may be the first resources considered, but if public funds were the panacea to the reduction of gang activity, it would have happened long ago. The government continues to fund hundreds of projects, providing thousands of dollars to communities to reduce gang activity. Money in the wrong hands—and used inappropriately—is not the remedy, as the gangs continue to grow and develop and become more lucrative.

Some gang members suggest the need for community-based programs designed with their input. When asked what they would like to see in their communities, they respond: "Teach me how to read better;" "My sister needs a job;" "I want to do something after school." The community-based programs of the 1960s and 1970s, if youths' responses are taken seriously, offer remedies that are applicable in the twenty-first century. The neighborhood houses, community centers, and drop-in centers of the 1960s and 1970s provided youths with places to hang out that provided structured adult supervision and structured activities: evening tutoring, job skills preparation, GED testing, teen pregnancy prevention, and counseling components. These centers were located directly in the neighborhoods, ensuring easy access by community residents. The centers offered adult activities, as well, allowing adults and adolescents to mingle in a social atmosphere. Adult residents of some communities provided tutoring and assisted with youths' school assignments, a very helpful volunteer effort, because large classrooms in the neighborhood schools made it difficult for teachers to reserve time for students who needed additional attention.

Fewer Students per Class

The twentieth century paved the way for indisputable technological advances in the twenty-first century. Students cannot take advantage of this technology if their classes are too large. Many schools and students suffer because poorer quality instruction results from over-crowded classrooms. Youths who need additional instruction are unable to receive it because teachers have to complete assignments within a definite time. In large classes, all students do not have access to computer workstations and disruptive students may have the least opportunity. Few students in impoverished inner city and rural schools have easy access to computers in their homes. Without resources, such as transportation to the library or a home computer, to complete assignments, youths may not do well in school. Consequently, they cannot gain positive attention or rewards in school.

Less Gang Notoriety

The media—television news, motion pictures, books, and records—are prime recruiting tools for gangs. Television news provides information on gang activity throughout the United States, and has helped gangs secure information (McCorkle & Miethe 2001, 79) by identifying locations and activities for gang members and providing intelligence about rival gangs. Gangs strategize with information from news coverage of gang activities (84–87). The motion pictures glorify gang members and depict them as glamorous and respected. Gang members, such as Ice T and the late Tupac Shakur, star in films. Some gang members (Ice T 1994; Scott 1993) publish books about their experiences and discuss them on television. Their warnings to youths against gang membership are outweighed by glamour and excitement. The record industry publishes lyrics that support violence and capitalize on gang rivalry (Klein, Maxon, & Miller 1995, 150).

Summary

Gangs in the United States developed and evolved from Pony Express robbers to high technology entrepreneurs who sell weapons and distribute drugs. From small gangs to large enterprises that include thousands of sets throughout the country, they evolve at such a rapid pace that special federal laws have been enacted to deter their growth.

Arrest rates of female gang members have increased because of their serious violent behavior. The United States looks differently at female gang activity than in the past, but does not yet accept that females are as violent and commit crimes as heinous as do their male counterparts.

Macroprevention efforts to reduce gang activity should vary from state to state, and prevention efforts utilized in urban cities may not be appropriate for rural areas. As gang members migrate from state to state they transport the gang norms, but they find that they must adapt to state norms and customs. Community organization is a major prevention tool that gang members recognize. They cite the need for structured community programs for young children who show interest in gangs because they are bored and have nothing to do.

On a micro, or family, level gang prevention must begin with very young children. Busy parents with stressful jobs and family lives may not offer the supervision and guidance that children need. Prevention programs should focus on strengthening the natural family unit, because many gang members find in their set the family closeness that their natural family lacked. Strengthening the natural family and including positive structured activities could deter youths' receptiveness to gang recruitment and activity.

Youths who experience difficulties in school are ripe for gang recruitment. School systems should become more proactive but not overreactive in addressing the gang issue. Because schools are major recruiting arenas, school personnel should be aware of warning signs in their students. Communities must ensure that school systems are able to hire enough teachers to provide smaller class sizes so that underachieving students can receive positive attention and assistance from teachers. Fewer suspensions and expulsions will be needed if teachers receive periodic, ongoing training about gang activity so they can work with students—and their parents—who are being recruited.

Gang activity in the United States is part of the country's image. Gangs and gang activity play a lucrative part in the capitalist system and will not disappear easily. Will serious, violent gang activity erupt on the urban and rural streets of the United States or will some other issue take the spotlight and refocus the country's attention, thereby reducing gang activity? Will it be the behavior of the stock market? Will it be nuclear weapons in the hands of terrorists? In the 1960s and 1970s, the war in Vietnam and civil rights demanded the country's attention. What will it be in this century?

Although this chapter may have painted a dismal picture of youth gang involvement in all segments of the population, the situation is not entirely hopeless. First, most youths are not violent. Only a small percentage of the youth population participates in violent gang activities. Second, youths do get out of gangs and become positive, productive citizens. Finally, intervention and prevention strategies work if they are comprehensible; involve family, children, and social agencies; and are applied from a culturally based approach. The challenge for communities is to be aware of the problems and to come together to resolve them according to their own cultures, be they Asian, African American, Hispanic, white, or Native American. Silence, indifference, and denial are key factors that can help gangs develop and expand. A proactive community is a primary nemesis to gang activity.

KEY CONCEPTS

blessed in	gang banging	sex in
economic compulsive	graffiti	step act
violence	jump in	systemic violence
gang	moniker	walk in
gang banger	OG	

DISCUSSION QUESTIONS

1. How would you define a gang?

2. Discuss some factors that you believe have attributed to the increase in female gang membership.

3. Discuss some factors that distinguish street gangs from other types of gangs.

4. What are some major differences between "wannabes" and actual gang members?

5. What are some differences between female and male gangs and gang members?

EXERCISES

1. Invite a law enforcement officer to discuss encounters with gang members and the handling of these encounters for the class. How does the law enforcement officer view gang members differently from other individuals who violate penal codes? View a video on street gangs. In small groups, discuss strategies that you would use when approaching gang members.

2. Consider and discuss legal and ethical issues that school systems face in suspending or expelling students because their clothing may indicate gang affiliation.

3. Visit gang Web sites on the Internet and report your findings in class.

CHAPTER OBJECTIVES

On completing this chapter, the student will have tools to:

- Examine factors that place female adolescents at risk of becoming delinquents
- Consider the different methods of the socialization process that create androcentrism
- Examine female arrest rates and how they affect female delinquency
- Consider issues of teen pregnancy and the impact of cross-medication with diet pills
- Examine issues related to capital punishment and female delinquency

Who Is the Female Delinquent and Why Is She Delinquent?

This chapter focuses on female delinquents and female delinquency, specifically emphasizing factors that place females at risk of becoming delinquent. In this chapter, females are discussed as delinquents, and receive neither more nor less consideration than their male counterparts. No comparisons are drawn between male and female delinquents, because both genders have very special gender-specific needs that do not lend themselves to comparison.

In discussion of the female population, some speculations are drawn between female delinquents and nondelinquents. The chapter demonstrates how gender may be a risk factor that leads to delinquency. Just as researchers have demonstrated how risk factors, such as sexual abuse, can lead to delinquency, this chapter highlights certain aspects of the female role in society that can lead to a similar outcome. Androcentrism is a bias that is seldom discussed but is highly prevalent and places the adolescent female at risk of becoming delinquent. Driven by the notion that males are superior to females, androcentrism can and does create feelings of inferiority in females who are socialized at young ages to believe these fallacies. Some females respond to androcentric socialization by doing nothing and refusing to acknowledge that a problem exists. Others are very aware of the problem, but accept androcentrism as part of the female experience and permit the treatment to continue. Still others acknowledge the problem and offer suggestions to remedy the situation. It is impossible to determine the reaction of anyone exposed to adverse circumstances, but some females revert to delinquent behavior to vent their anger or to prove that they can conduct themselves as men do.

Research attempts to identify risk factors that may lead female adolescents to engage in delinquent behavior, the factors that place minor females in jeopardy of becoming delinquent. Risk factors can be as abstract as an ideology or as concrete as sexual abuse. Some of the risk factors most often identified include sexual abuse, physical abuse, poverty, poor academic performance, negative peer associations, and poor parental involvement. Gender is seldom studied as a risk factor for delinquency, yet in discussions about the treatment of females in the juvenile justice system, gender must be a factor, especially in providing placement and treatment programs. Females often are placed in antiquated facilities that are not equipped with appropriate staff or curriculum to treat them or to address their needs.

Studying gender as a risk factor is not feminism. The purpose here is to shed light on the female delinquent. Juvenile delinquency textbooks often grant her only a paragraph or a page or two before the focus shifts back to her male counterpart. Feminist theories, however, must be discussed and considered, in addition to others that may be deemed sexist.

Statistical trends of female delinquent arrest rates over 19 years, using reports from 1977, 1986, and 1996, depict an increase in serious violent delinquent behavior. Some factors that may continue the trend are oppressive rage, attitudinal change within the female and society, and the voices of the offspring of baby boomers. In the twenty-first century, female delinquents will be younger, middle-class, educated, computer-literate, and white. Some of the implications of the new profile will affect female gangs, drug use, teen pregnancy, and the death penalty.

Gendercide

The value of the female, historically, is related directly to her ability to produce offspring, preferably male. However, the depreciation of her value over time has led to severe measures of extermination, which Warren (1985) has termed *gendercide*. Gendercide results from sex selection. Sex selection is practiced extensively in some countries, such as India and China, where male infants are preferred to female. Sex selection can be accomplished in several ways. If modern medicine is available, sex can be identified long before birth and the fetus aborted if it is not male. Gendercide has created a dilemma for the United States because of the conflict between its human rights ideology and its widely practiced androcentricity. Rather than blatantly contradict its human rights ideology, the United States practices a subtle gendercide through selective adoption, sex selection before pregnancy, socializing or conditioning behavior patterns, and inequality of pay and recognition to highly achieving females. These practices reflect the long history of gendercide in the United States. When the government informs the public of a sharp decline in birth rates, especially of males, in this country, the primary purpose of such propaganda is to encourage couples to have children later in life.

Adoptions represent one shrewd method of gendercide. The shortage of male babies for adoption in the United States leads many prospective parents to adopt male babies from other countries—such as Russia, Central America, and South America. Out-of-country adoptions effectively could ensure the male presence in the United States.

A second clever method of gendercide is scientific *sex selection.* Technology advances could allow sex selection to become more common. Amniocentesis is a test in which amniotic fluid surrounding the fetus may be used to determine the sex of the unborn child. Amniocentesis is performed after the latest date that abortion can be done. In the United States, the results of amniocentesis cannot be use for sex selection. Couples do, however, inquire about methods to determine a desired child's sex before conception.

Socialization, in which each new generation is taught that gender differences imply inequality, is a third method of gendercide, and occurs when children and adolescents are taught to value males more and view female roles as minimal and unequal. It permeates society from conception to the end of the life cycle.

The perception of equality between the sexes is the fourth subtle method of gendercide. Females learn that they are not equal and that the experiences and activities that are available to them are limited. If they step outside of the restrictive parameters, they will be punished severely, especially when they press the limits of delinquent behavior.

Ideological perspectives of defined and expected roles, not an epidemic of female delinquency, spark the use of gendercidal techniques. The pressure to conform to the ideology can cause the female population to deviate from defined role expectations, and can lead to delinquency.

Deviant behavior is not new among females but, as a pervasive paternalism would have it, females are naturally pure (Feinman 1981) and submissive and a paternalistic society believes that females should be protected and sheltered. Such attitudes might account for the limited research on female delinquency in the twentieth century. Even contemporary discussions are unidimensional and compare females to males.

Females have evolved from an invisible assertive prototype to a visible aggressive force that will not simply disappear or be added to the endangered list. Only recently have the entertainment media shown females as physically and intellectually powerful and aggressive: New female characters function outside of the defined parameters of traditional female roles (Caplan 2001). For example, television portrays female protagonists in violent and aggressive roles. The 1970s and 1980s *Charlie's Angels* might have been the door opener for female aggressive portrayals that have lead to even more aggressive protagonists, characters who are not only as clever as their male counterpart but as deadly physically.

Legend, Fiction, and History

According to Biblical legend, in the beginning, Eve's aggressive action encouraged Adam to eat the forbidden fruit in the Garden of Eden, leading to their banishment. Some believe that the pains of childbirth are a special punishment that Eve, by her disobedience and moving beyond her submissive role, earned for all the generations of women to come.

Females who act "out of character" and step out of their expected and traditional roles, receive severe punishment. Nathaniel Hawthorne created the unforgettable Hester Prynne, who suffered the social consequences of bearing an illegitimate child, in his 1850 novel, *The Scarlet Letter.* The story reflected the times. Although adultery was unacceptable for both sexes, society dealt—and deals with—female and male offenders by a double standard. Misbehaving or nonconforming women received more severe punishment than men did for the same act. In earlier centuries, females who did not conform were suspected of engaging in witchcraft and were burned alive in public.

Tales from early civilizations, such as Greece and Rome, suggest that women and girls were mindless entities to be owned and used as objects of pleasure. Even the gods of ancient mythology were perceived to be inflexible toward the crimes of women and swift with punishment. Legends describe them as self-righteous, clever men of war, strong and wily enough to outwit and slay their deadliest enemies. Lesser gods who committed acts against the creed of the gods were punished terribly by the god in the upper echelon. Goddesses who erred were banned from the kingdom of the gods and marked physically, like Medusa, who was stripped of her beauty and made so hideous that anyone who saw her face immediately was turned to stone.

Ego and power were denied real women, as well as goddesses. Cleopatra, who inherited the rule of Egypt around 51 B.C., was said to want to become Empress of the world. She allied herself with powerful men in her quest, but in the end, she lost her influence and committed suicide.

Twentieth century society practices male supremacy covertly, through psychological conditioning, resulting in generation after generation of females who believe that they are inferior and need male protection. Female offenders are invisible, not because they do not exist, but because it has served the needs of a male-dominated society to ignore them and pretend that they exist only rarely. Only recently have researchers begun to identify and explain the nature and extent of female juvenile delinquency.

Block (1981) notes that female offenders have been portrayed as isolated victims, "confused, detached and lonely." Yet, he maintains, they have been very aggressive in criminal behaviors and involved in organized crime (such as Mafia activities) and riots. Adler (1975) wonders if females commit more crimes that are not reported and if their criminal acts are really status offenses or are simply labeled as such by law enforcement.

Theories to Consider in Advancing an Understanding of Female Delinquency

Of the many theories about delinquency, most, until recently, were postulated primarily by males. Interested professionals might wonder if the men who formulated many of these theories—from a negative perspective—did not value females greatly and drew conclusions based on limited female data, or if they simply did not consider female data valid? However, theoretical conceptualizations that have focused primarily on male delinquency might be useful in understanding female delinquent behavior. Study of "male" theory might shed light on what does or does not apply to females. Traditional theories do not often propose much about females; most omit females from the populations on which they are based. The omission of research on females, whom Belknap (1997) terms "invisible people," might result from as simple a reason as a researcher's desire to study a population of special interest, or from a subtly paternalistic effort to shelter female delinquency from exposure.

Juvenile workers should be able to understand and apply traditional theories when dealing with females. Freudian theory, as discussed in Chapter 3, voices many negative perspectives about females. Freud theorized that females become delinquent because they have inherently weak egos. He believed that females, as the weaker sex, are at high risk for delinquent behavior. Freud further proposed that women were sex objects and that they used their sexuality in highly promiscuous ways because of penis envy. According to Freudian theory, females cleverly use sexual prowess to achieve a state of equality with males. Women's suffrage was a premier social movement of Freud's time. That Freud's theories reflects the attitudes of the late Victorian and Edwardian periods, just as feminist theory reflects contemporary U.S. society, does not mean, however, that his theories and psychoanalysis are not applicable to some female delinquents.

Gender-Specific Theory

Just as race-specific theories can assist in the comprehension of minorities and delinquency, so can *gender-specific* theories aid in the understanding of both male and female delinquency. Freud's theories, for instance, were clearly gender specific to males (Basow 2001, 126).

However, traditional theories that are not gender specific and seem negative toward females also may have value. Understanding traditional theories is important, because an understanding of what is *not* can lead to an understanding of what *is*. The numerous differences within the female delinquent population make it important to understand and to be able to apply as many theories as possible when studying or working with female delinquents. If juvenile workers are familiar with a broad range of theories, they can apply them appropriately to male and female delinquents. Traditional and classical theories will not be treated in this chapter (see Chapter 3 and Chapter 4), but such theorists and theories, as well as gender-specific theories will be mentioned in discussing female delinquency.

Joanne Belknap (2000) reports that some respected criminological theorists of both sexes have shown bias in their work. She believes Freud and Lombroso to be sexist, Becker and Cohen, Cloward, and Ohlin to have *invisibilized* female offenders, Hirschi to have omitted data on the female offending population, and Simon and Adler to have advanced statistics that were not confirmed by research. Should all theorists be considered racists if they do not include racial minority data in their collection or if they fail to discuss *minority-specific* issues? Juvenile workers must understand the utility of theories whether they are gender specific toward males or toward females. *Gender specific* is used not only to refer to theories that apply to people of one sex or the other, but also to describe issues that apply to them. Perspectives of traditional theorists such as Freud and Lombroso are labeled by some as sexist because they focused primarily on the male gender; but in fact, the research is gender specific to male issues.

Gender-specific theory in this text refers to an integrated set of assumptions about people of either sex. This chapter specifically treats female offenders. Examining theories characterized as gender specific may lead to an answer to the question, "Why do females become involved in delinquent activity?"

Feminist Theories

Renzetti and Curran (1997) trace the feminist movement in the United States as far back as 1830, when females rebelled against paternalistic, oppressive behaviors. They propose that many white females became feminists because they were involved in antislavery issues (14). Studying and speaking for abolition prepared women to speak out against other injustices. Later, involvement in the civil rights movement taught them how to use the courts as a mechanism for change.

Feminists, who may be liberal or radical in perspective, believe in emphasizing issues that center on women and their uniqueness. They do not believe in measuring women's goals and achievements by male baselines. Males, as well as females, can be feminists.

Liberal Feminism. Liberal feminists believe that women have not yet been granted equal rights in U.S. society and are harmed economically, socially, and politically as a result. Women seek equality and argue that if granted equal opportunity, they can become as successful as their male counterparts.

The Civil Rights Act of 1964 and the affirmative action policy enacted by President Johnson were major legislative acts that enhanced equal opportunities for females. The Civil Rights Act made it illegal to discriminate against a person based on gender, as well as race and certain other characteristics. Many females gained greater access to housing and jobs as a result of this legislation. The affirmative action policy, which many people in the United States today believe should be eliminated because of its preferential treatment of minorities and women, primarily benefited women. Affirmative action introduced more females into employment in the criminal and juvenile justice systems, both of which traditionally were dominated by males. More women became politically active and more became elected officials who would serve as policy makers and interpreters of the law, among other responsibilities. In the upper echelons of U.S. government, women in recent years have become Supreme Court justices, Attorney General, Secretary of the Treasury, and Secretary of State. Liberal feminists view every woman who attains prominent and responsible positions as a victory in the quest for equal protection, equal rights, and equal opportunities for females.

Feminists have been strong advocates for the equal rights of women. An equal rights amendment (ERA) was discussed in Congress as far back as 1921, when Alice Paul, a suffragist, wrote the first ERA legislation introduced into Congress. ERA finally passed in Congress in 1972, but was not ratified because only 35 of the needed 38 states voted for ratification by the July 1982 deadline.

Many question the need for an ERA, because all citizens are protected under the fourteenth amendment's equal protection clause. The counter-argument is that the equal protection clause is generalized and nonspecific. The ERA was gender specific and detailed specifically the proposed protections against sex discrimination. Three major provisions of the ERA were:

> Section 1. Equality of rights under the law shall not be denied or abridged by the United States or any state on account of sex.
>
> Section 2. The Congress shall have the power to enforce, by appropriate legislation, the provisions of this article.
>
> Section 3. The amendment shall take effect two years after date of ratification. (Adler 1975)

Some believe that the ERA was not ratified because it was too radical. Others view the denial of its passage as another oppressive measure by male-dominated policy makers.

Radical Feminism.   Radical feminists believe that male domination is central to female oppression. Women do not excel or reach their fullest potential because men have dominated all aspects of their lives and have not allowed them the freedom to self-actualize. Males have been able to maintain this dominance through power, control, and fear, all of which have led to victimization of the female, which is one of the primary tenets of radical feminist theory. People who subscribe to this theory believe that females are victims, and so have a greater tendency toward delinquency.

Subtle victimization occurs in many different forms. Subtle victimization occurs when the person is subjected repeatedly to what may appear to others to be amusing, kindly, or gentle ridicule and patronizing or demeaning remarks that, over time, encourage helplessness and destroy feelings of self-worth. Sometimes this subtle victimization is supported by differences in communication styles between men and women.

Communication is the key to success in U.S. society, but a defective key is useless in unlocking a door. Much research has been conducted on communication styles and differences between male and female language communication patterns. Researchers differ about the effect of communication styles between males and females. Smythe and Meyer (1994) found few differences, if any, between male and female communication patterns. They conclude that responses are situationally based, and that gender does not greatly influence them.

Although researchers differ on their perceptions of differences in communication styles between the genders, gender-biased language prevails in books, games, intelligence tests, standardized tests, and everyday conversation.

An obvious gender bias in language gears it toward masculinity, assuming that the subject of all conversation is male. With absolutely no idea of the gender of a person when speaking generally, referring to that person as "him" or "he" thoughtlessly may be acceptable. For example, mathematics word problems may introduce the test taker to "John," who drives three miles, runs out of gas, and is left to go as far as he can on an empty tank. The math problems rarely mention "Jane." McMinn *et al.* (1994) produced a twelve-item Gender Specific Language Scale (GSLS) to measure amounts of sexist language used. Take the test and review the answers at the end of this chapter.

Gender-neutral language reflects the effort to enhance equality between the genders in microunits and in macrosystems.

From the radical feminist perspective, females fall victim to masculine dominance the moment they are conceived: Sound, one of the simplest forms of communicating, is the means of domination. Research discovered significant changes in the fetuses that were exposed to sound stimulation. Rauscher (1998) exposed rats and then humans *in utero* to a Mozart sonata. He discovered a direct relationship between exposure to complex musical patterns and improved spatial-temporal learning. This relationship increased in magnitude in both the rat research group and the human group over time.

Lafuente et al. (1997) examined the effects of music on the intellectual and physical development of the fetus. They used an experimental and control group of 172 pregnant females who were enrolled in a birth preparation course. The members of the experimental group were exposed to eight different violin sounds through speakers from tape players they wore at their waists. The expectant mothers played the tapes for their growing fetuses an average of 70 hours during the 28 weeks until the babies were born. After the births, the

McMinn et al. (1994) Language Test

Instructions: Read each of the following statements carefully and circle every problem you find, including problems with grammar, spelling, punctuation, and discriminatory language. Work quickly as you will have only five to ten minutes to complete this task.

1. Each persons' alertness was measured by the difference between his obtained relaxation score and his obtained arousal score.
2. The use of experiments in psychology presupposes the mechanistic nature of man.
3. The business executive's learned about domestic tasks from the homemakers.
4. When making an important decision one must first determine how they will be affected and if the outcome is worth the cost.
5. The chairman of the board precided over the meeting.
6. The mailman wasn't never late, no matter how bad the whether.
7. She said she would ask her husband if she could go on the weekend trip with us.
8. The supervisor talked individually with the employees who were to be layed off.
9. The fire fighters' maintained composure when comfronted by the large dog.
10. First the individual becomes aroused by violations of personal space and then he attributes the cause of this arosal to other people in his environment.
11. Evolutionary theory proposes that the human species is evolving through a process of survival of the fittest.
12. Much has been written about the effect that a child's position among his siblings has on his intellectual development.

Source: M. McMinn, P. Williams, and L. McMinn (1994) cited in C. Renzetti and D. Curran (1999). *Women, men, and society:* 124.

---

researchers used an observational scale of development (OSD) to measure the babies' behaviors for six months. The results of the study suggested that the experimental group, who were exposed to the music, were more advanced than the control group, who were not exposed to the music.

Hepper (1991) conducted another study that tested the effects of sound stimulation with music. He suggested that the extent of fetal learning could be assessed before and after birth. He conducted experiments in which 40 fetuses, after 29 to 37 weeks of gestation, were exposed to television theme songs. He reported that fetal heart rate increased and movement became more rapid according to the songs they heard. He conducted a similar experiment with 58 infants and discovered that their behavior changed when they heard the music that had been played for them during their fetal period. Hepper concluded that the changes were not due to genetic factors, but were specific to the musical sounds to which the babies had been exposed during the fetal period.

This research supports the notion that babies can hear and react to sound before birth: It also suggests that sounds affect the child after birth. Thus, every day, mothers, fathers, and significant others communicate with unborn babies. An androcentric country like the

United States may communicate its societal attitudes to fetuses. Whether conscious or unconscious, it affects the way children think, grow, and develop (Basow 2001).

Microvictimization

The socialization process begins in the family unit. Parents and guardians influence children as they formulate their value and belief systems. In the United States, heterosexual, two-parent families, in which the male dominates as protector and provider and the female tends the household and is primary caregiver, was the norm. A family headed by a homosexual couple or a single person would have been labeled dysfunctional by Moynihan (1965). Heterogenic families could oppress their children with impunity because they met the common standard for "family" (Regoli & Hewitt 2000).

Parents may subtly psychologically oppress their daughters by teaching them that boys can fight back and assert their masculinity, but that girls should be understanding and tolerant. Females who see their mothers beaten at home may learn that battering of women is acceptable and that they deserve it. Some states, such as North Carolina and Ohio, have tightened their enforcement of victimization laws to punish domestic violence, although children may witness and become victims of domestic abuse before it comes to the attention of outsiders (Bissada & Briere 2001).

Adolescent females may experience battering by boyfriends. Young females who run away from victimizing homes may take to the streets, where pimps and people who hire them, sexually exploit them (Farley 2001).

Macrovictimization

The media perpetuate the exploitation of females. Movies, music, and videos that are popular with youths, for example, depict females as sexual objects (Pacheco and Hurtado 2001).

Socialization continues as families entrust their children to churches and schools, in which youths continue to experience psychological oppression. Female rabbis, ministers, and priests are rare.

After the primary grades, taught most commonly by women, children encounter more male teachers in secondary schools (Renzetti & Curran 1999, 100). Adolescents' roles in society are reinforced. In high schools, male students learn that they are expected to excel in math and the sciences, and female students learn that they are expected to do well in the humanities and fine arts. Female high school students do not play male-dominated sports, and counselors encourage them to plan for lesser paid "nurturing" careers, rather than engineering or other hard science-related careers (Astin & Lindholm 2001, 17–17).

With more exposure, rules and policies can change to equalize the playing field for female adolescents in math and science. Arenson (1998) concluded that the gap between males and females in math and science is not related directly to intelligence, but to experiences and exposure to them: Typically, males are exposed to games that focus on math and science earlier than females. Males are encouraged and stimulated to continue their interest in math and computers by problems that Crawford (1990) says must be solved with a masculine orientation. Ward and Carruthers (2001) suggest that "video games give boys different messages than girls" (700).

Much of the deviant behavior of nontraditional females is demonstrated by their attempts to escape oppression by running away, a status offense that may lead them into the juvenile justice system. From a feminist perspective, females become delinquent because they live in a male-dominated, male-oriented society and have been victimized through conditioned socialization to perform according to tradition and to limit their goals. Some remain ensnared throughout a lifetime, but others are able to advance beyond their expected roles and elevate themselves to higher levels of functioning.

Arrest Rates

Research provides limited information about female delinquents, but in 1998, the Office of Juvenile Justice and Delinquency Prevention (OJJDP) took a step to ensure funding for projects that will continue to yield data on the female's delinquent activity. OJJDP now provides overview and inventories of efforts of states to focus on at-risk girls and describes efforts in 24 states and the District of Columbia to develop and implement programs for at-risk girls (Budnick & Shields-Fletcher 1998). Through this information, authorities and researchers are able to track female delinquency more rigorously than in the past, when females were protected and not subjected to the criminal and juvenile justice systems as strictly as their male counterparts.

Females' reported arrest rates are lower, so most statistics on female delinquency show a lower arrest rate for *index offenses.* The FBI's eight index offenses are murder and non-negligent manslaughter, forcible rape, robbery, aggravated assault, burglary, larceny-theft, motor vehicle theft, and arson. Female delinquents have not typically experienced high arrest rates for index offenses. However, the arrest rates for status offenses, which are offenses—such as truancy and runaway—that only youths can commit because the laws that they involve were specifically written for the control and benefit of youths, remain high since 1970 (Chesney-Lind & Shelden 1998, 10).

Otto Pollak's theory that females commit just as many crimes as men is controversial. He maintains in *The Criminality of Women* (1978) that women seem to find devious and deceitful ways of committing crimes. Pollak cited what he found to be women's subtle methods of murder that, for instance, rely on such things as hard-to-detect poisons. Insufficient statistics to prove Pollak's argument leave it open to challenge. A plausible rationale for the lack of evidence could lie in the failure of men, who have been primary investigators of crimes, to see the evidence because of their paternalistic, protective attitudes toward women.

A number of rationales address the disparity in arrest rates between men and women. Some researchers believe that females are arrested neither more nor less frequently than males. Others believe that girls' arrest rates are higher for specific crimes. Although numerous females are prostitutes, even the arrest rates for prostitution and similar crimes are low (Steffensmeier & Allan 1998, 6). Statistics for the arrests of females have been lower, in general, than the statistics for males and may be attributed to the way men and societies view females. A general agreement is that a paternalistic attitude toward girls exists in the juvenile justice system.

When researchers compare male and female arrest rates, they may use male rates as a baseline. Although studies do not flesh out the argument that females are engaged in the same amount of delinquent activity as their male counterparts, female gender statistics must be considered on their own merit and not in relation to male statistics, which themselves may be flawed. Hidden and unreported delinquent behaviors skew the statistics about females. Limited data exist, for instance, about the delinquent behavior of females prior to the 1970s and 1980s but it would be difficult to believe that female delinquency is an artifact of the1990s and early twenty-first century.

Arrest rates and punishment for females involved in criminal acts continues to reflect socioeconomic status. Arrest profiles typically include females of low socioeconomic status, high school dropouts, and a disproportionate number of minorities.

In the 1970s and 1980s, OJJDP described the female juvenile delinquent primarily as a black, urban, single head-of-household, a high school dropout with limited skills (Bergsmann 1998, 73). They might have been sexually abused. Runaways or other status offenders were the primary female delinquents. Chesney-Lind (1998) reported that in 1995 27 percent of female arrests were based on status offenses (8). Her report that females are arrested for status offenses at a higher rate falls in line with the theory that women are not very dangerous and are in need of protection. Law enforcement officers attempt to intervene earlier with female delinquents by arresting them for status offenses to discourage them from deviant activity before it gets out of control. Arrest trends suggest an increase in female delinquency, but also that attitudes are changing, and that the role of females in delinquent activity is more closely scrutinized and recorded.

Either female delinquent patterns have remained the same, or reporting systems have remained the same for almost 20 years. Females still are arrested at a high rate for status offenses: Larceny-theft arrests remained about the same for females between 1977 and 1996. Media and public attention on violent crime could account for the increase in index crime arrests for females. The hiring of more female officers by law enforcement may dilute the prevailing paternalistic attitude toward female delinquency and criminality (Britton 2000; Senna & Siegel 2001, 450).

Although the profile of the female offender of the 1990s is similar to those of her sisters in the 1970s and 1980s, the speculative profile of the female offender in the early part of the twenty-first century may be more realistic and the offender less protected. She is younger (under 14), middle-class, educated (not a dropout), involved in serious violent crimes, computer literate, and not a woman of color. Underlying factors that are related distinctly to female delinquency in the United States and support the profile change include oppressive rage, new attitudes about self-identity, and baby boomers.

Oppressive Rage

Oppressive rage is the anger that females experience as a result of victimization and oppression in micro and macrosystems that they could not express outwardly until recently. It is analogous to the *Black Rage* that Grier and Cobbs (2000) identify among black males in the 1970s. As mentioned previously, the female traditionally handles the household and child-rearing responsibilities. Today, in performing those duties, she keeps the house clean, remains sexually attentive, attends PTA meetings and conferences, car pools, and prepares meals. Many women perform all the tasks in addition to being fully employed outside the home.

It should be no mystery, then, why young girls are arrested for running away, but the juvenile system's treatment of arrested females differs greatly from its treatment of arrested males. Girls may be quickly returned home and not processed through the juvenile court system. They are a valued commodity in society, but they are just beginning to understand their own value and power and learning how to use it. Some of this newfound power will be manifested in juvenile delinquent activity and thus result in higher arrest rates and accelerate incarceration (Browne & Lichter 2001).

Juvenile Court and the Female Offender

The next step after arrest is juvenile court processing. Changes in juvenile processing can be expected to increase the incarceration rate of female offenders. As have other government agencies and organizations, the juvenile court system has perpetuated the notion that female crime is virtually nonexistent and serves as a protector of the female offender. Statutory law indicates that the juvenile court system achieves its mission within the constraints of *parens patriae.* Because *parens patriae* does not exclude rehabilitation and protection, the court system should protect females. Spohn (1999), Farnworth et al. (1995), and Curran (1983) argue that the court's protection of females far surpasses *parens patriae,* and demonstrates preferential treatment of female offenders. An example of the leniency of judges toward female offenders is that judges less often commit females to training schools or correctional facilities and more frequently give them probation than they do to males who commit similar delinquent acts (Clark & Kellam 2001).

As female offenders in the United States commit increasing numbers of serious, violent, criminal acts, some states build more correctional facilities to accommodate female offenders and to provide alternative programs, such as boot camps, for them (Clark & Kellam 2001).

Empirical evidence has yet to yield a satisfactory conclusion on the utility of boot camps as successful alternatives to incarceration. The concept of boot camps became popular in 1973 when George Cadwalader, a former marine, established the first youth boot camp on remote, undeveloped Penikese Island, off the coast of Massachusetts (Binder 1997, 306). Cadwalader ran the camp in a tough, challenging military style, believing that this would be effective in altering youths' negative behavior. Boot camps and "get tough" policies became popular in the 1980s. Boot camps typically provide residents a 90-day, intensive program built on a military model. Their goal is to produce a self-disciplined freethinker.

The camps for females require their enrollees to participate in activities to strengthen their physical endurance and agility and to present a uniform physical appearance (Clark & Kellam 2001). Many of the programs are voluntary, in that juvenile judges may permit youths to choose between incarceration and boot camp. Among the pros and cons of voluntary boot camps as an alternative way to sanction female delinquents, the notion of equality tops the list of positive aspects when judges offer the option of attending the boot camp, as males do, to females. The downside is that boot camps are military prototypes (McKenzie *et al.* 1994). In such camps (which are modeled after military training camps) the female is less physically able and unable to survive in this type of environment. Consequently, the female boot camper is prepared to fail upon arrival in entering a system with this philosophy. Because boot camps use androcentric methods of discipline, female soldiers who are compared to male soldiers may fall short of expectation (McKenzie *et al.* 1994). This male-centered view may aid females to fail at the boot camp by leading them to anticipate failure, which may bring them back to the court system and incarceration.

Incarceration of Female Offenders

Inappropriate facilities and programs that do not address the specific needs of females are two of the most outstanding concerns about the incarceration of females. Prior to the nineteenth, twentieth, and twenty-first centuries, female delinquents were incarcerated with adult male and female criminals. Today, juvenile correctional facilities for female delinquents are limited, because females found guilty of delinquency have been few. Females go to facilities designed for males or coeducational facilities. Commonly, the antiquated juvenile facilities available to females were erected decades ago and have not been physically modified or altered and are in poor condition (Senna 2001).

The schedules provided for the rehabilitation of females may be as outdated as the physical facilities. The limited programs commonly consist of GED studies, vocational skills enrichment units, and little or no counseling. The vocational skills component of the programs may be limited to sewing and cooking. Computer training is rare. Counseling may be limited to youths who act out. Seldom do other youths have opportunity to explore personal feelings or to productively work through conflicts. Family sessions are rare and may occur only if an adolescent cannot return to her home. When incarceration ends, juveniles may exist in a limbo—at a standstill—receiving little or no aftercare or follow-up treatment, experiencing another aspect of victimization. They are unable to utilize skills that they may have developed because the skills are nonproductive and not applicable to the information age (Browne & Lichter 2001).

According to the UCR (1997), the female arrest rate is rising. Females are characterized as more violent today than ever before in the history of the United States, being arrested and incarcerated in greater numbers and for more serious, violent crimes, including murder. A greater percentage of violent crimes by females are drug-related. Homicide statistics for female teens have increased sharply and dramatically (Bureau of Justice, 1998), leading to an increase in incarceration numbers.

The incidence of female involvement in criminal activity has increased steadily, according to statistical reports (OJJDP 1998; UCR 1997). Yet, few explanations for this increase are offered other than gang activity and the drug economy, which typically are offered to explain any increase.

Female Gang Members

The gangs (see Chapter 7) of the 1980s and 1990s were macrocosms of the greater society of the United States, not only in violence, but in the female's role, level of participation, and involvement. Even primarily female gangs operate according to societal norms. Female

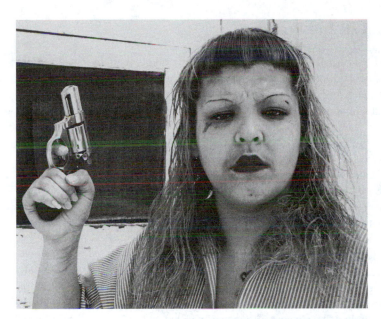

Female gang member.
Getty Images Inc.

gangs rely on males to guide and protect their members and to show members acceptance and approval. Female gangs most often are affiliated with male gangs that keep them under close, paternalistic observation. Females who are peripheral affiliates of male-dominated gangs usually have gained their status by performing sexually (Fishman 1995, 85).

Females in gangs primarily provide sex for the males in the gangs and transport items, generally drugs, for them. In drug activities, the percentage of the profit shared with females is generally very small, if any. Females are usually treated with limited respect. Their suggestions and ideas are not highly regarded, for females are valued only as window dressing. Young females who establish their own set (i.e., organized gang) must rely on male gang members for support and direction (Campbell 1995, 76).

Females join street gangs for many of the same reasons as their male counterparts: They seek protection, belonging, love, and security. Most view the gang as a surrogate family. When brutalized within the gang, women remain loyal because it is family punishment, a necessary component of family life. Women who come from natural home situations in which victimization and brutality occur daily know no alternative. The gang is their escape from terrible home life. Although females experience similar victimization as gang members, they believe that they are making the best choice available (Campbell 1995, 74). Female gang members may emulate male members. In a homogeneous group, females try to master masculine characteristics. Females try to demonstrate prowess, prove physical strength, and prove their aggression, all traditionally male characteristics. Female gang members may be more vicious than males because—according to male gang members—they must prove that they can handle the responsibility of being a gang member (Campbell 1995, 72).

Many females, as they age or become teen mothers, leave the gang. Some no longer need the support of the gang. Others, despite their new roles as mothers, continue to conduct gang business as drug couriers, using their babies as cover (Swart 1995, 81).

Female Teen Drug Use and Its Implications

The United States was concerned with the drug problem for many years before President Ronald Reagan's 1982 declaration of war on drugs. Generally, the U.S. public thinks most often about teenage males using drugs and becomes concerned when confronted with the possibility of young female adolescents experimenting with drugs because it is unladylike and unfeminine. Society wants to protect women from the evils of narcotics, yet the socialization process indicates that drug use would appeal to many females. Pharmaceutical agents, whether prescribed or illegally obtained, offer pain relief, altered consciousness, or escape from reality, Female illegal drug users believe that the substances they ingest will enable them to cope better with the many contradictions and barriers—the overwhelming hurdles—of society (Roberts *et al.* 2000).

The United States socializes its children to use drugs. Prescriptions are provided with the understanding that, within these confines, drug use is acceptable. Children receive distorted and confusing messages about which drugs can be used and under what conditions. In one situation, children learn that some agents are acceptable for other people. For example, parents take pills to relieve headaches, older siblings use pills to gain or lose weight, men take pills to reverse baldness, and esteemed athletes take drugs to improve their performance, but children and adolescents are instructed that they should not use these drugs because they are harmful. Meanwhile, parents maintain ample supplies in the family medicine cabinet (Inciardi *et al.* 1993) indicated that the large numbers of high school students using drugs in the 1960s brought recognition that society needed to change the way it explained drug use to adolescents. It resulted in radical changes in the definition of drug user and in the explanations of the physical and emotional effects of drug abuse. Female students historically have reported higher rates of marijuana use than males (19). As use increased among female adolescents in the 1970s, 1980s, and 1990s, the public saw more emphasis on the reduction and elimination of drug abuse among women, and on drug treatment programs for women. Multifaceted treatment modalities for special populations of females who have escalated their use of legal and illegal drugs are now emphasized (Roberts *et al.* 2000).

Legal Drug Use

Diet pills are a concern in controlling drug use among females. Young girls have been socialized in the U.S. to believe that they must be thin to be attractive. They use over-the-counter diet pills or they share prescriptions without the benefit of professional supervision. Use of diet pills or severe, unsupervised diet control can lead to serious illness, such as anorexia, coma, and death.

Young girls are more prone to use diet pills than young boys because modern women believe that thin and frail female figures are most attractive. The designer clothing industry advertises its products with young, tall, thin models and equates thinness with beauty for young and impressionable girls. Constantly bombarded with propaganda on television, in movies, and in magazines, it is clear to young girls that they must become thin.

Cross-medication is another concern with teens and drugs. For example, a female teen may take diet pills, birth control pills, pills for menstrual cramps, smoke cigarettes and drink alcohol. Because teens may not divulge all of the substances they ingest, doctors may prescribe the wrong treatments.

Some young females use illegal drugs, such as tobacco, alcohol, marijuana, and cocaine. In most states it is illegal for teens to purchase and smoke tobacco products but they do obtain and use them. Because they believe they will not be discovered smoking at school easily, adolescent girls begin their smoking habits there.

Traditionally, society has not supported smoking for females. Ray and Ksir (1999) discuss the evolution of attitudes toward females who smoke from the period of King James, through the feminist movement, and to the contemporary period. In 1908, women could not legally smoke or use tobacco in New York City. Throughout the United States, even in states that did define a legal position on females smoking, females could be expelled and terminated in the workforce if they were caught smoking, in line with the country's paternalistic attitude toward protecting them from themselves (274). Cigarette packaging warns of the health hazard of smoking, recent research links smoking to increased incidences of premature births and spontaneous abortion (Perlman *et al.* 1999), as well as increased incidence of breast cancer.

Concerns about female adolescent drug use have been not only about the detrimental physical and psychological effects on themselves, but also about the effects of their drug use on the children they may bear. Treatment services to help young female drug abusers may not be available. Treatment centers may not be able to provide effective drug treatment services for young female addicts.

Uniqueness in the Drug Subculture

Young females do not often play major roles in drug selling. The drug subculture typically is not a female business, but many female teens become distributors. Young females are valuable commodities, even after they become addicted to drugs. Sexual exploitation, for example, in magazine pornography, X-rated movies, and videos is common. Their usefulness in these businesses is short-lived, and many turn to prostitution to survive. Prostitution, dangerous under any circumstances, increases in danger when it is a part of the drug culture, as "strawberries" trade their bodies for drugs. Teens caught up in prostitution gain new problems when they become pregnant. Some teens attempt to abort without medical attention. Others continue to use drugs until the infant's birth, after which they may sell it for drug money.

Babies born to mothers who used crack cocaine while pregnant have been labeled ***crack babies.*** Crack babies are born addicted and suffer drug withdrawal symptoms soon after birth. Crack baby births early in the 1990s were increasing in epidemic numbers. According to media accounts, crack babies were a lost generation who would be physically and mentally hindered because they began their lives in a state of addiction and the pain of withdrawal from drugs (Scherer 1991).

Some young teens enter drug treatment centers during or after pregnancy. Some of the obstacles they face have been documented extensively in the literature. A major treatment issue that Kirkpatrick (1991) and Kasl (1990) discuss is the continued degradation that females in drug rehabilitation centers must endure under treatment standards, such as 12-step programs, that are designed for males. Kasl (1990), Kirkpatrick (1989), and

Unterberger (1989) argue that females enter drug treatment programs feeling helpless, hopeless, depressed, and with very low self-esteem. Program rules and policies demand that recovering addicts recite the 12 steps daily. Those authors contend that daily repetition of negative concepts, such as "helpless," "hopeless," and "unmanageable lives" reinforce the females' degraded, negative feelings about themselves. Unterberger created a 12-step component specifically for women in alcohol treatment programs.

Men in the drug culture degrade and humiliate females in that milieu. Street names identify people who are involved in the drug culture. Street names for females are insulting—"junkie broad" or "bag bride." Street names for males imply respect—"stand up cat" and "righteous dope fiend" (Inciardi *et al.* 1993, 36).

Female teens are different from other drug populations, so different treatment models may apply for them. Some may respond well to traditional 12-step programs, whereas others may need other intervention models (Roberts *et al.* 2000).

Death Penalty

Capital punishment ranks high among the controversial issues that contemporary U.S. society faces. The debate intensifies when the nation considers capital punishment for children and females. *Capital punishment* is legal execution as punishment for criminal offense. Capital offenses include kidnapping and various degrees of murder. In Mississippi and Georgia, stealing an aircraft is a capital offense, and in California, treason is listed. States vary on the definition of capital offenses and on minimum age at which execution is permitted. All, however, consider alternative methods to execution for females. Hale (1997) notes that gender is the only variable that outperforms race for disparity of treatment in the juvenile justice system. When the focus of observation is narrowed to specific areas of juvenile justice, such as arrest rates and capital offense, females are vastly underrepresented.

Undoubtedly, fewer women than men have been on death row. Streib (1987; 1990; 1995) says that U.S. society screens women from capital punishment. Fletcher *et al.* (1993) maintain that the death penalty is a male construct that is oppressive and gender-biased, although female juveniles who committed horrendous crimes in early U.S. history received capital punishment.

The historical data on capital punishment of female juveniles do not include the slave children who were hanged, mutilated, or flogged to death. The data do not include the females who were stoned or burned at the stake for their suspected participation in witchcraft, although females were accused more often than males of practicing witchery and were tried and punished more often and with equal severity (Browne & Lichter 2001, 613).

Early capital law that allowed women and slaves to be executed came, in part, from interpretations of biblical texts that supported male domination. In the United States, state and church are separate, and U.S. legal authority is separate from religious authority. In contemporary practice, laws are supposed to be gender-neutral. In earlier days, when women were not independent entities protected by the Constitution, laws might be interpreted not to apply to them. Law enforcement might not know what to do with them. The law was even less ambiguous defining sanctions against juvenile offenders.

Streib and Sametz (1989) reported that juvenile executions carried out by the state throughout American history numbered 282 at the time of their study of official statistics. Of them, only 10 were female. The Espy data files record 331 juvenile executions, of which 2.7 percent were female (Hale 1997, 22). The disparity between the numbers of males and females does not mean that juvenile females commit only less serious crimes that are not punishable by capital punishment, but that paternalism, which protects females, permeates the U.S. juvenile justice system (Hale 1997). The ***chivalry hypothesis*** is also used to describe the systemic protection of the juvenile female offender by the justice system (Spohn 1999). Both the paternalism theory and the chivalry hypothesis support the protection of the female from herself so that she will discontinue her deviant behavior, an idea that is enmeshed with the socialization process. In a society where the female is mother, the giver of life, and the primary care provider, to consider taking her life stirs conflicting emotions, and it is up to the male, who has been socialized as protector, to set things right. Males dominate and are primary decision makers in the juvenile justice system, and it is only natural for them to assist with removing female from the capital punishment anomaly. It is difficult to impose capital punishment on mother or sister, as the system views females (Hale 1977).

In the late 1980s, many changes that affected the United States occurred throughout the world. The Berlin Wall fell, the Cold War no longer existed, the United States continued fighting for human rights and equality around the globe, and Americans struggled to put an end to the high domestic crime rate. Greater numbers of children participated in violent criminal activity that would warrant capital punishment, and issues of capital punishment of youthful violent offenders were brought to the Supreme Court.

When the Supreme Court rendered its decision allowing capital punishment in ***Gregg v. Georgia*** (1976), it struck down ***Furman v. Georgia*** (1972), which outlawed capital punishment on the basis that it was unconstitutional because it subjected offenders to cruel and unusual, arbitrarily imposed punishment.

In 1988, in ***Thompson v. Oklahoma,*** the court made age a mitigating factor in capital cases, ruling that children under 16 could not face the death penalty because it would constitute cruel and unusual punishment, violating the eighth amendment. Prior to the Thompson ruling, some states had set ages as low as 10 for capital punishment.

After the Supreme Court's action set age limits for executing juvenile offenders, two cases challenging whether execution of juveniles should be permitted at all were decided. In ***Stanford v. Kentucky*** (1989) and ***Wilkins v. Missouri*** (1989), the Supreme Court decided the issue of whether juveniles who commit capital offenses should be executed. The Court ruled in the two cases, which were argued together, that juveniles could be executed. In both cases, the Court ruled that capital punishment is justifiable in cases involving criminal acts and allowed individual states to set their standards regarding age as long as they did not violate the *Thompson* ruling.

Presently 38 states and the federal government sanction capital punishment for juvenile offenders. Only 14 states and the district of Columbia do not have the death penalty (see Table 8.1).

Of the thirty-eight states that do sanction capital punishment, 14 states (37 percent) have set 18, 4 states (10 percent) have set 17, and 20 states (53 percent) have set 16 as the minimum age for execution (see Table 8.2).

Limited information is available on females who have received the death penalty, and even less information is available about females who committed their capital offenses when

TABLE 8.1   States That Do Not Impose Capital Punishment

Alaska	Michigan	West Virginia
Hawaii	Minnesota	Wisconsin
Iowa	North Dakota	the District of Columbia
Maine	Rhode Island	
Massachussetts	Vermont	

Source: Streib (1987).

they were juveniles. Streib and Sametz (1989) count 10 juvenile females who received the death penalty officially in the United States (see Table 8.3). In 1868, Eliza, a slave teen, was thought to have killed the baby she was watching and was hanged in Henry County, Kentucky (Hale 1997). In 1912, Virginia Christian was executed for killing a woman whose house she cleaned in a fight over a dress supposedly stolen 17 years earlier, according to NAACP records (Hale 1997, 75). Until the present, only 10 other females who committed offenses as juveniles have been officially executed.

That Virginia Christian, in 1912, was the last female to be executed for a juvenile act, provides some indication of how the system struggles with legal ideology versus cultural

TABLE 8.2   Death Penalty States and Minimum Age

Minimum age of 18	Minimum age of 17	Minimum age of 16
California	Georgia	Alabama
Colorado	New Hampshire	Arizona
Connecticut	North Carolina	Arkansas
Illinois	Texas	Delaware
Kansas		Florida
Maryland		Idaho
Nebraska		Indiana
New Jersey		Kentucky
New Mexico		Louisiana
New York		Mississippi
Ohio		Missouri
Oregon		Montana
Tennessee		Nevada
Washington		Oklahoma
federal government		Pennsylvania
		South Carolina
		South Dakota
		Utah
		Virginia
		Wyoming

Sources: Streib (1995); Hale (1997).

TABLE 8.3   Female Juvenile Executions in United States.

Name	Age	State	Year	Crime	Method
*Jane Champion	Unknown	Virginia	1632	Unknown	Hanged
*Marja Lamb	Unknown	Massachusetts	1681	Arson	Burned
**Venus	Unknown	New York	1767	Unknown	
**Hannah Ocuish	12	Connecticut	1786	Murdered six year old	Hanged
**Mary		Missouri	1838		
**Rosan Keen		New Jersey	1844		
**Amy Spain	17	South Carolina	1865	Unknown	Hanged
**Eliza	Unknown	Kentucky	1868	Murdered baby	Hanged
**Mary Wallis		Maryland	1871		
**Caroline Shipp		North Carolina	1892		
**Milbry Brown		South Carolina	1892		
**Virginia Christian			1912	Stole dress	Hanged

Sources: *Fletcher (1993, 78); **Streib and Sametz (1987, cited in Hale, 1997).

norm. However, a shift in the attitude toward capital punishment for minor females can be anticipated because of factors such as the feminist movement, stringent and harsher laws for violent offenders, and tough love, bringing more females into the system.

Although juvenile court judges can impose sanctions on juvenile offenders, capital punishment is still not one of their options. For the juvenile offender to receive capital punishment, the juvenile judge must waive the case to the adult criminal system. States are revisiting the need to revamp their juvenile systems. Some have moved toward criminalizing juvenile delinquency.

The trend may continue in the twenty-first century. As social attitudes in the United States change and the roles of females evolve, the implementation of capital punishment more on females, even juvenile females, who commit capital offenses can be anticipated.

Amnesty International has taken a strong position against the United States for its implementation of capital punishment for juvenile offenders. The international organization raises the issue of the conflicting position of the United States, as it voices its outrage at human rights violations in other countries, yet imposes the death penalty on adolescents. Amnesty International formally states that the U.S. position is not only a blatant contradiction, but that it violates principles of the international treaties and standards of the International Covenant on Civil and Political Rights (ICCPR). The organization cites the United States as barbaric and ranked with Third World countries in its approval of capital punishment for juveniles:

> The USA stands almost alone in the world in still executing offenders who were under eighteen years old at the time of the crime. America has carried out more executions of juvenile offenders than almost any other country in the world, and it probably has the most juvenile offenders

on death row. We are one of only six countries worldwide reported to have carried out such executions in the past five years. The other countries are: Nigeria, Pakistan, Iran, Iraq and one in Saudi Arabia (although Islamic law forbids the execution of under 18 year old offenders).

—Amnesty International Report (www.amnesty.org)

Even with such harsh verbal flogging from the international community, the United States maintains its policy of getting tough at the cost of lives of juveniles, who will include greater numbers of females.

Teen Pregnancy

Females have been viewed as sex objects for centuries and their delinquent behavior has been linked to their fundamental sexual nature (Wulffen 1934). In *Woman as a Sexual Criminal*, Wulffen characterized female criminal activity as a result of sexual acting out because women are born sexual criminals, whereas men are simply criminal types (15). Under this theory, minor females at one time were incarcerated if they became pregnant out of wedlock. Illegitimate pregnancy was a status offense under the category of "incorrigible" behavior. After the 1974 Juvenile Justice Delinquency and Prevention (JJDP) act mandated the deinstitutionalization of juvenile status offenders, it became more difficult to incarcerate females for pregnancy unless they committed a felony while pregnant. Teen pregnancy is not a deviate behavior, but it can be a result of or have an affect on juvenile delinquency. Although teen pregnancy is on the decline (DHHS 1999), teens, either through ignorance or deliberately, are becoming pregnant at younger ages. Adolescent mothers approach borderline risk for delinquency because many drop out of school to have their babies and find it difficult to return. The Personal Responsibility and Work Opportunity Reconciliation Act (P.L. 104-193) of 1996 implemented a change: Teen mothers do not have to quit school because of pregnancy.

The act was part of the ***welfare reform law*** that President William Jefferson Clinton signed in 1996 that included provisions for adolescent pregnant females. The law is a comprehensive welfare reform plan aimed at changing the welfare system to become a time-limited assistance program for people who may need emergency assistance. Some of its goals are to reduce the number of welfare recipients, to break the welfare cycle of families, and to assist pregnant adolescents to cope better by permitting them to remain in school (Straatmann & Sherraden 2001).

Stringent enforcement of child support laws force adolescents to consider their responsibilities and obligations when they assume the role of parent. In order to receive federal assistance, adolescents who become pregnant must adhere to the provisions of the act. Kansas City and the states of California, Colorado, and Maine have submitted their welfare reform plans and are in the process of implementing the plans.

Although welfare reform is intended to keep the female in school, she must face many other difficulties, such as attempting to continue her education, coming to terms with issues within her family, and employment and childcare. Attempting to continue her education is not without its consequences: Some school systems do not allow teen mothers to participate in extracurricular activities.

In *Pfeiffer v. Marion Center Area School District* (1990) the school's chapter of the National Honor Society removed a member who was pregnant. The organization's officials said that the young woman was removed from its activities and its rolls because she had engaged in premarital sex—not because she became pregnant. The young man who admitted having premarital sex with her was not dismissed from the National Honor Society nor did the organization determine how many other members had engaged in premarital sex (Thomas 1991 as cited in Belknap 1997, 221). The Supreme Court, however, did not view this as sex discrimination, because the primary issue was premarital sex, not pregnancy and ruled in favor of the school district.

Coming to terms with family issues is not an easy task for the unwed teen or her family. The pregnancy affects the entire family unit. It unexpectedly changes the composition of the family unit and places the family in crisis, creating a burden of changing household schedules and additional financial responsibilities for the teen's parents. Siblings may be expected to help, and the diversion of parental attention may foster negative attitudes from them toward the pregnant teen and the baby. East (1998) suggests that teen pregnancy in a household that includes younger siblings may socialize the younger ones to perceive early parenthood as acceptable and to begin parenthood early.

Many unwed teen mothers must work to support themselves and their children. Dropping out of school may be necessary, even with the welfare reform law in effect, because many schools do not have childcare facilities for students' children, although some school districts are beginning to provide childcare services to reduce or eliminate dropouts. Even in districts that are sensitive to childcare needs, some staff and faculty are not attentive to the needs of young mothers. Some guidance counselors maintain a traditional attitude that a woman should stay at home with her baby and fail to assist females with gender-neutral career choices.

A public health concern for sexually active youths is sexually transmitted diseases, such as AIDS. Schoeberlein (2000) reports that social behaviors place them at great risk for HIV infection, but she suggests the importance of abstinence as the best method to prevent HIV and STD infections.

Teen pregnancy has forced some females into delinquent behavior and led to the commission of capital offenses through ***neonatacide,*** the killing of a baby within 24 hours after its birth (Kelleher 1998). Phillip Resnick (1970, 13) defined the term in his study of teen pregnancy in which he associated cases of neonatacide with teenage, unwed mothers. In some instances, the father may be involved in the murder or abandonment that leads to an infant's death. One teen couple abandoned a baby at a school dance.

Carlson (1997) notes that many neonatacides occur among adolescents. Like other female statistics, the incidence of neonatacide is unclear because researchers have only

Proms and Babies

In Monmouth County, New Jersey, Amy Grossberg and Brian Peterson dressed up and went to their senior prom, like most of their classmates. What occurred after they arrived made them different from the rest of their classmates: Amy delivered a six-pound, eight-ounce baby boy. She and Brian dumped the newborn infant into a nearby garbage receptacle, returned to the prom, and continued dancing.

Source: Time Magazine, 1997, June 23:42

begun to study female data and UCR is not recording neonatacides. That some cases of neonatacide are categorized as abandonment further skews the statistics. The determinant between simple abandonment and neonatacide is whether the infant dies within 24 hours as a result of the abandonment.

Public concern about youth pregnancy has brought about a number of initiatives that can be separated into diversion and prevention. Diversion measures attempt to stop pregnancies before they occur, and target young females who are at risk of becoming pregnant. Kagan (1991) listed school failure, abusive situations, and values and beliefs that violate social norms as factors that place teens at risk of becoming pregnant. Prevention implies both diversion from the behavior and stopping its repetition.

Diversionary methods include teaching children abstinence early in their lives. One such program is Florida's Education Now and Babies Later (ENABL). The focus of ENABL is to prevent teen pregnancy. The program provides sexual education and the thrust of its teachings is toward abstinence (Arnold *et al.* 1998). Rossi (1997) advocates sexual abstinence, but she indicates that the message may not get through to adolescents who are 15 and older. She suggests early intervention through sex education, beginning in middle schools and throughout school curricula. Addressing female issues such as teen pregnancy is best accomplished through early sex education that includes parental discussions, school curriculum, and media support of abstinence. Sex education should be gender neutral and include both males and females.

Summary

Until the twentieth century, the victimization of women was rarely acknowledged. Women commonly were subjugated and physically and psychologically abused. The proactivity and tenacity of leaders throughout the woman suffrage movement, such as Susan B. Anthony, Elizabeth Cady Stanton, and Sojourner Truth, in 1924 gained women the right to vote and the attendant political responsibilities.

The voices of females in voting booths throughout the country are heard on issues ranging from abortion to capital punishment. Politicians conduct and use the results of polls that include women as they seek information from specific segments of the community. Females use their voting powers to influence legislation.

Many young females fall victim to violence early in their lives, as oppressed entities of society (macrovictimization) and as victims within their families (microvictimization). Familial victimization affects their relationships with males: They accept physical and psychological abuse because such abuse occurred in their parental households, and because it has been reflected in the popular culture of entertainment. However, intelligent, strong, self-sufficient female characters now appear to be positively acknowledged.

As the roles of females change and females experience equal treatment, other changes occur. Changes in the paternalistic attitudes of males in law enforcement may be reflected in the increase in the reported crime rate of female juvenile offenders. More female teens may be subject to capital punishment as reports of serious violent crimes increase and the political climate remains tough on crime. More research is needed on female delinquents as they evolve to reach equity with their male counterparts.

KEY CONCEPTS

affirmative action
androcentrism
boot camps
Civil Rights Act of 1964
crack babies
Equal Rights Amendment
feminist
Furman v. Georgia

gendercide
gender specific
gender-specific language
Gregg v. Georgia
index offenses
liberal feminism
macrovictimization
microvictimization

neonatacide
radical feminism
sex selection
Stanford v. Kentucky
Thompson v. Oklahoma
victimization
welfare reform
Wilkins v. Missouri

DISCUSSION QUESTIONS

1. Discuss how androcentric socialization influenced your life or the life of someone you know.

2. Identify and discuss some strategies that can be used to help create a gender-neutral society.

3. Delinquency is decreasing, yet serious violent behavior among females is increasing. Explain some factors that might contribute to the phenomenon.

4. Should schools be held responsible for child-rearing?

5. Discuss TLO in relation to teens as drug distributors. How is the role of drug distributor outside the parameters of teens' expected role?

EXERCISES

1. Discuss the case of Amy Grossberg and Brian Peterson. List some factors that you feel should be considered in the case. Discuss the major differences between neonatacide and infant abandonment.

2. Form teams and debate the pros and cons of capital punishment for female offenders.

3. Amnesty International has taken a strong position against the U.S. policy on capital punishment for juvenile offenders. Poll the class to determine if any classmates agree with the Amnesty International position. Ask the class to explain why they agree or disagree with that position.

Answers to the McMinn et al. Language Test

1. persons' (person's); his obtained (his or her obtained)—this latter error occurs twice in this sentence

2. mechanistic nature of man (mechanistic nature of humans)

3. executive's (executives)

4. When making an important decision (when making an important decision,); other's (others)

5. chairman (chairperson); precided (presided)

6. Mailman (letter carrier); wasn't never (was never); whether (weather)

7. There are no errors in this sentence.

8. Layed off (laid off)

9. fire fighters' (fire fighters); comfronted (confronted)

10. First the individual (First, the individual); personal space (personal space); and then (Then,); he (the individual); arosal (arousal); in his environment (in his or her environment)

11. There are no errors in this sentence.

12. His siblings (his or her siblings); his intellectual development (the child's intellectual development)

9 Race, Ethnicity, Class, and Delinquency

CHAPTER OBJECTIVES

On completing this chapter, students will have tools to:

- Consider how race and ethnic issues influence the juvenile justice system
- Gain understanding of how racial and ethnic factors influence policy
- Review and explore racial and ethnic data and consider how the data are used to bastardize the system
- Gain a better understanding of how slavery in American history plays a major role in contemporary issues dealing with race and juvenile justice
- Understand the impact of racism and discrimination on the juvenile justice system

Overview of the Enigma of Race and Delinquency

This chapter is designed neither to offer theoretical explanations of race and delinquency, nor to formulate the causal relationships between race and delinquency. It offers information about race and delinquency that will raise questions and help in formulating ideas about this enigma, as well as about the impact of race and ethnicity on the juvenile justice system in the United States.

Race and ethnicity are major variables that directly influence all aspects of daily life in the United States, but many people are uncomfortable discussing them because of the fear that the conversation will become a heated and emotional battle of ideologies and create an uncomfortable and hostile environment. For this reason, when race is a topic of discussion, although some may assert their beliefs, others unconsideringly may assume the position of the majority, and still others may refrain from the discussion. Understanding of terms is important to understanding race and ethnicity. Terms used in the chapter are defined early to clarify any variation from the formal or prevailing definitions. Specific information from states that report data about minority overrepresentation in the correctional system is provided, and incidents and cases that focus on situations that delinquents face as a result of racial and ethnic considerations are presented. The chapter ends with a synopsis of affirmative action and its impact on the juvenile justice system.

Scottsboro Case

Justice begins in contradiction. The notion itself—in theoretical isolation—is an absolute statement of an ideal. Justice supposedly transcends everyday existence. In practice, however, justice is inevitably shaped by social reality. Justice is rarely realized.

—Richard Quinney, 1977

The Scottsboro scandal was one of the most deplorable racial travesties in U.S. history. According to Davis (1981), the Scottsboro case represented the first open challenge to racism in the U.S. court system. Nine young black males, 13 through 21 years of age, were arrested and charged with the rape of two white females at Scottsboro, Alabama, on March 25, 1931.

The youths were tried on April 6, 1931, less than two weeks after their arrest, with a court-appointed defense counsel who had spent very little time with the defendants prior to the trial. The prosecutor's only evidence at the trial was the testimony of the women who accused the youths. The nine were found guilty by an all-white jury. Eight were sentenced to death and the ninth, a 13-year old, was sentenced to life in prison.

Throughout the world, protests erupted. The International Labor Defense Movement (ILD), the National Association for the Advancement of Colored People (NAACP), and the American Communist Party became involved as the case went to three more trials. In the second trial, in 1933, one of the accusers recanted her testimony, but the convictions stood (Davis 1981). The last trial, ending in 1936, resulted in the release of four of the young men. Considered a mockery of justice because of the blatant lack of due process extended to the defendants, the original trial contained many legal and ethical errors that were recognized by the U.S. Supreme Court, which ruled in *Powell v. Alabama* that Ozzie Powell had been denied his constitutional right to counsel and in *Norris v. Alabama* (1935) and *Patterson v. Alabama* (1935) overturned the convictions for Clarence Norris and Haywood Patterson because blacks were prohibited from jury duty. In 1950, the last of the men was released, and in 1976, all were pardoned and their civil rights restored.

The Scottsboro case occurred almost three-quarters of a century ago, yet the intensity of the rage that it created and the use of race to describe juvenile and criminal activity today are as fresh and pervasive as they were then. In October 1989, Charles Stuart reported to police that he and his pregnant wife had been attacked and his wife killed by a black man when they stopped at an intersection in a racially mixed neighborhood in Boston. Stuart, who survived, was shot in the stomach. Based on Stuart's description and identification of the alleged perpetrator, the police arrested a young black male for the crime. As the black and white communities reached the verge of riot, Stuart's brother admitted that the two of them had conspired to commit the murder. Had the black defendant gone to trial, many believe that he would have been tried and convicted rapidly because of Boston's long history of racial prejudice (Ogawa 1999).

In 1994, Susan Smith of Union, South Carolina, told police that a young black male carjacked her and kidnapped her two young sons at gunpoint. The two children were found drowned. Police efforts to locate the killer created tension between law enforcement and the black community. Smith eventually recanted her story, admitting that she had drowned the boys and that the carjacking did not happen (Ogawa 1999).

Ethnicity and race can create violence. Violence is prevalent and ongoing in Northern Ireland, Russia, and Bosnia as a result of ethnic hatred among their populations. People who enter the United States as they flee from their own countries' overt ethnic violence discover that the United States is not without its ethnic-based biases as well. The diverse ethnic groups that enter the United States bring their native cultures, and the differences between their old cultures and the new one of the United States can affect their lives adversely. Children and adolescents may find themselves confused by the perplexing cultural differences that may result in frustration and the instigation of delinquent behavior. It is crucial that everyone have the same definitions of concepts and terminology for discussing issues of ethnicity and race. Emigrants who cannot speak much English may very quickly learn words to express anger and racial and ethnic resentment without understanding their impact in the new culture. When they use the ugly words, they perpetuate the cycle.

Defining Race and Ethnicity

Self-identification is based on how individuals define themselves racially. There are many sources of racial identification. Some individuals may have racial characteristics of one group, but may define themselves as belonging to another racial group. Social identification occurs when societal norms dictate race. The "one-drop rule" stipulates that one drop of African American blood defines an individual as African American. This rule was used extensively in the Antebellum South and Reconstruction primarily to eliminate sexual contact between blacks and whites (Spath 2002). The legal identification of African American is based on U.S. governmental criteria. The Office of Budget and Management (OBM) has the primary responsibility of defining race and racial categories in America. No consistent criteria are utilized by the government to define race, and their criteria are as contradictory and confusing as they are narrowly defined. Race has been defined based on physical characteristics. At one time, people in the United States were categorized Caucasian, Negroid, and Mongoloid.

The racial hierarchy of social equality has been Caucasian, Mongoloid, and Negroid. Physical appearance played a principal role in racial categorizing. Caucasians had light (or *white*) skin, straight hair, long noses, and thin lips. Mongoloids had yellowish skin, black straight hair, slanted eyes, and small-framed bodies. Negroids had black (or dark) skin, curly (wooly or kinky) hair, thick lips, and muscular bodies.

Political pressures from special interest groups forced the U.S. OBM to consider revising its Directive 15, which officially categorizes races for the census. The current racial categories are American Indian or Alaskan Native, Asian or Pacific Islander, Black, Hispanic, and White.

However, the U.S. population grows because of its open-door policy to immigrants, as expressed in the poem on the base of the Statue of Liberty:

> Give me your tired, your poor,
> Your huddled masses yearning to breathe free,
> —*Emma Lazarus* (1849–1887)

Office of Budget Management's Racial/Ethnic Categories Explained

American Indian or Alaskan Native defines a person having origins in any of the original peoples of North America and who maintains cultural identification through tribal affiliation or community recognition.

Asian or Pacific Islander defines a person having origins in any of the original peoples of the Far East, Southeast Asia, the Indian continent, or the Pacific Islands. This area includes China, India, Japan, Korea, Philippine Islands, and Samoa.

Black defines a person having origins in any of the black racial groups of Africa.

Hispanic defines a person of Mexican, Puerto Rican, Cuban, Central or South American, or other Spanish culture or origins, regardless of race.

White defines a person having origins in any of the original peoples of Europe, North Africa, or the Middle East.

Source: Spotlight on Heterogeneity. The Federal Standards of Racial and Ethnic Classification: Summary of a Workshop (1996), p. 65–66; Walker et al. (1996).

This open door has greatly enhanced the development of a diverse society. In addition, technological advances have aided the increase in diversity by making it possible for individuals to change and or modify their racial composition. John Howard Griffin, to enter the U.S. black culture to conduct research for his book, *Black Like Me,* medically changed his skin color to pass as black. Michael Jackson can have treatments to bleach his skin and have cosmetic facial surgery to alter his appearance to appear white. Many groups are proud of their racial heritage. The contemporary notion of multiculturalism or pluralism in which racial groups strive to make others aware of their strengths and contributions to the nation replaces the melting pot concept of blending.

Multiculturalism considers differences and embraces the notion of fostering better understanding between all individuals who compose the society. Thus, not only has the United States' open door to immigrants expanded the heterogeneity of the United States but the healthy economy has also created a more tolerant attitude toward differences. Along with tolerant attitudes come consequences. The United States is so greatly diversified a person's racial or ethnic identity cannot be assumed from physical characteristics. For instance, among African Americans, Haitians, Jamaicans, Cubans, Arabs, Latinos—any might have dark skin. Another consequence of the expanded and diversified U.S. population is the increase in biracial and other racially mixed people. The increase in this segment of the population and its gain in political power stimulates questions and debate about the accuracy of the U.S. census. Some suggest that another category should be added to the census to include individuals of mixed racial heritage.

The importance of this issue is related to the rapidly changing composition of the population of the United States. Minority youths will become a very large segment of the

How do you identify a juvenile delinquent? Michael Newman/ PhotoEdit

population, but the criminal and juvenile justice systems are dominated by white males who make the decisions, interpret the laws, and implement the policies. People entering professions in juvenile justice must understand the issues so they can make intelligent decisions benefiting their clients and effect improvement in systems as they move toward decision making positions. Also, minority youths are arrested and enter the juvenile justice system at a much higher rate than their white counterparts. Although youths from many ethnic groups enter the juvenile justice system, the greatest number who remain in the system are of various minorities within the greater population.

Historical Perspective

Historically, the juvenile justice system reflects society in general in its treatment of children and adolescents. They are commodities of little value, as demonstrated by society's investment in them. In the United States, troubled youths who enter correctional institutions are, for all practical purposes, forgotten. At-risk and delinquent youths are at the mercy of the prevailing political attitude without real consideration for their needs.

The concept of youths as property is not new in the United States. In earlier centuries, children were commonly treated harshly, but African American children and Native American children were separated from their families and used as slave laborers to enhance the production of marketable goods (Barnes 1999). They were not educated and were punished for trying to learn to read. The houses of refuge that emerged in the 1800s were initially reserved for white children. Small numbers of minority youths were placed in the facilities after 1871 (Morton 2000). Although minority and white adolescents become involved in the same types of offenses, there are major differences in how they are treated, in the beginning by the arresting officer and throughout the entire juvenile justice system. Juvenile courts impose more and stricter sanctions for minorities than for whites. Some researchers view the differential treatment not as systemic racism within juvenile justice, but blame it on individuals within the system (Wilbanks 1987). Whatever the cause, minority juveniles are disproportionately represented in the juvenile justice system

Disproportionate Minority Confinement

The Juvenile Justice and Delinquency Prevention Act of 1974 (Public Law 93-415) is important legislation for the juvenile justice system. The act establishes the Office of Juvenile Justice and Delinquency Prevention (OJJDP), which oversees federal funds for delinquency prevention initiatives throughout the United States. Additionally, it deinstitutionalized status offenders, calling for the release of adolescents who were already incarcerated for offenses that are not criminal if done by an adult and declaring that no longer should status offenders be placed in juvenile correctional facilities. The reasoning behind the act was that communities should work with families in providing alternative programs for such adolescents, and that juvenile facilities should be used for serious offenders. Even after the act was passed, however, minority youths continued to be placed in correctional facilities at a rate disproportionate to that of other adolescents.

"Minorities and the Juvenile Justice System," a 1988 report by the University of Wisconsin and Portland State University, alleged bigoted treatment of black adolescents on every level of the juvenile justice system. They reported that "there was substantial evidence that race plays a direct and indirect role in the outcome of many juvenile justice decisions" (Roscoe & Morton 1994). OJJDP looked closely at minority overrepresentation and implemented initiatives to provide more information about it and to gather strategy recommendations from states. Among numerous amendments to the 1974 act, the 1988 amendment (28. F.R. Part 31) focused primarily on race and stipulated studies to address the overrepresentation of minority youths in the juvenile justice system. OJJDP defined disproportionate minority confinement (DMC) as "the proportion of juveniles detained or confined in secure detention facilities, secure correctional facilities, jails, and lockups who are members of minority groups . . . [that] exceeds the proportion such groups represent in the general population" (Roscoe & Morton 1994). OJJDP funded programs to explore racial and ethnic factors and their impact on juvenile justice decisions. As a result, more awareness and sensitivity toward the issue became apparent, but the states' juvenile statistics continued to reveal little action by the states to reduce the problem. OJJDP statistics revealed the following data:

- African American youths were arrested at a higher rate than other races.
- African American youths were disproportionately represented in detention centers.
- In 1991, 43 percent of juveniles in detention centers were black, 19 percent were Hispanic and 35 percent were white.
- In 1991, 44 percent of juveniles in public facilities were black, 18 percent were Hispanic and 34 percent were white (Roscoe & Morton 1994).

As with many issues, it is difficult to change attitudes and behavior about race and ethnicity, until laws dictate the change. Section 223(a)(23) of the Juvenile Justice Delinquency and Prevention Act was amended to stipulate that states should attempt to reduce the proportion of minority juveniles held in secure facilities (e.g., detention centers, jails, training schools, etc.) if the proportion was greater than they represented in the general population. For example, Roscoe and Morton reported that in 1991, as they compared black and white incarceration rates, they found that black juveniles in general comprised only 47 percent of the population but comprised 32 percent of the training school population. (White juveniles made up 57 percent of the training school population.)

In addition to changing and amending laws to change attitudes, incentives may be offered to expedite the changes. All 50 states were asked to assess their juvenile justice systems to determine if minorities were disproportionately represented and to correct the disparity where it existed. The federal government contended that it did not force compliance, but that states would lose 25 percent of their formula grant allocations for that year if they did not correct minority overrepresentation. In 1991, OJJDP issued a request for proposals (RFP) to study disproportionate minority confinement. OJJDP gave five states that submitted proposals (Arizona, Florida, Iowa, North Carolina, and Oregon) funds to study and report on overrepresentation of minority youths in juvenile justice facilities. The OJJDP reported findings of the five initiatives in 1994 that included the following:

- DMC in the juvenile justice system is a reality. Minority youths are arrested and incarcerated at higher rates than white youths.
- More resources are utilized for nonminority youths, and minority youths are sent more often to secure facilities.
- Cultural competency training should be provided throughout the juvenile justice system.

Cultural Competency

Increased diversity within the United States demands that criminal justice professionals be trained in cultural competency. Advanced diversity education and training can enhance the skills and performance levels of juvenile justice professionals.

Cultural competence implies effort to understand, acknowledge, and practice respect for diverse cultures. It implies an appreciation of differences rather than a perfunctory discounting of aspects of the differing culture.

OJJDP suggested that the juvenile justice system openly adopt and address cultural competency. Reports from the OJJDP DMC pilot projects indicate that most key decision makers—police officers, intake workers, defense and prosecuting attorneys, and judges—in the juvenile system are white males. In training schools, the primary counseling staff is white. The report does not imply that the juvenile justice system should require cultural matching, but it stipulates that workers with minority adolescents should receive cultural competency training. Cultural competency training focuses on the perspectives of specific segments of the population, to enhance the trainees' understanding of the cultural differences between themselves and the populations they are studying and to whom they may provide services. If workers have had limited interaction with a minority population, they may make decisions based on misinterpreted behaviors that people from other cultures exhibit.

Cultural awareness is important to understanding why delinquents may speak and act the way they do. It is key to creating better interactions between youths in the justice system and the adults who make decisions about their futures. Armed with cultural knowledge and understanding, courts may be more likely to dispense equal justice to two youths with different social skills and cultural backgrounds who are guilty of the same delinquent act.

Dress for the African American adolescent is a crucial aspect of cultural identity (Pernell-Arnold 1990). Pernell-Arnold reports that some African American adolescents do not attend school because they are unable to wear clothing like that of their peers. Designer clothes and fine jewelry are status symbols, declarations of self-pride (281). When all else in youths' environment is degrading and makes them feel powerless, stylish dress helps them cope and define themselves. Clothing allows the adolescent to make a statement and be heard when no one else listens. Clothing opens doors in the black community. Thus, for African American adolescents, dress is about self-pride, style, and attitude.

The Issue of Class

Some argue that cultural competence is not a relevant training component for juvenile justice personnel because the issue is not race, but economics. Others maintain that regardless of money or status, African Americans are disadvantaged because some continue to treat them with disrespect and as second-class citizens because of their skin color.

Harvard sociologist William Julius Wilson rocked the political environment with the 1987 publication of *The Truly Disadvantaged: The Inner City, the Underclass, and Public Policy* (1987), in part because he, a member of a minority, voiced the opinion that race is not as significant as socioeconomic status. Researchers cite Wilson to make the point that racism is not as blatant as some believe and that class is more important than race in assessing poverty in the United States (McNulty & Holloway 2000). Clarence Thomas, U.S. Supreme Court justice, and Ward Connerly, of the Board of Regents of the University of California, also minorities, some years ago voiced their views against affirmative action, which even now some members of a majority population cite to highlight their own position (Will 2002).

A commonly expressed fallacy is that all U.S. citizens can have the "American dream" if they "pull themselves up by their bootstraps" and work hard to accomplish it. Wealth, however, is synonymous with the concept of power, and those with power will not give it up so easily and do not make it easy for others to join their ranks. Amos Wilson (1990) says that in the United States, wealth and power are held by ethnic whites and white upper and middle classes. These groups have the power to make, interpret, and enforce laws and render sanctions they feel are necessary, while the lower class is subjected to roles defined by the ruling class. Marx labeled the issue as a struggle between two factions of society, the haves and the have nots, which he described as the oppressors and the oppressed. The oppressed encounter the worst of both worlds, not only victimized by the oppressors, but victimized as a result of their low status. For instance, regardless of race, lower income individuals stand greater chances of being victims of a criminal or delinquent (18). Quinney (1977) placed Marx's conclusions into a contemporary framework, viewing the criminal and juvenile justice systems as mechanisms to subdue and control undesirables and protect capitalism (140). In support of his theory, Quinney cites the constant generation and implementation of laws that focus on the lower class, and he emphasizes the use of the justice systems to control the lower class (134).

Youths in the lower and upper socioeconomic ranks commit similar delinquent acts; yet, delinquency is viewed by many to be primarily a problem of lower-class status because:

1. Empirical data suggest that delinquency is a lower-class problem because very limited research is conducted on middle- and upper-class delinquency trends.
2. Media propaganda treat delinquency as a lower-class problem.
3. Capitalism finds that it is profitable and a social control mechanism to define delinquency as a lower-class phenomenon.

Empirical Data

The most widely used instrument for reporting crime statistics in the United States is the Uniform Crime Report (UCR), complied annually by the FBI. The UCR provides statistical data received from law enforcement agencies throughout the country. Even with its numerous limitations, the UCR is still considered the foremost viable tool for understanding and predicting juvenile and criminal information statistically. Some of its limitations were delineated by Samuel Walker, Cassia Spohn, and Miriam DeLone (1996) in *Race, Ethnicity, and Crime in America*:

1. Reporting the data to the FBI is voluntary. All law enforcement agencies do not necessarily comply.
2. Some agencies may over- or underreport criminal activity depending on their political agenda at the time. For example, in an election year, the crime rates may be reported higher because of a push for more arrests.
3. Some crimes are not reported.
4. The people reporting the data may report only part of it or the data may reflect differential treatment to suspects because of race or class.

Walker, Spohn, and DeLone warn about putting too much faith in crime statistics: ". . . the information on offenders gleaned from the UCR is incomplete and potentially misleading because it includes only offenders whose crimes result in arrest" (37). Hamm (1998) indicates numerous concerns about the report. He emphasizes that the report underestimates crime and who commits crimes and suggests that much of the hidden and unreported crime is committed by young white males (244). He suggests that the FBI crime statistics reflect racial and class bias on the part of law enforcement officers more than they represent the actual crime rate. Chorover (1980) supports this opinion by suggesting that the majority of crime in the United States is committed by whites; however, the official crime statistics do not reflect this because white collar crime is not included in their reports. Thus, he suggests that the data shows that minorities, especially black minorities, seem to monopolize criminal activity because criminals are individuals arrested by the police and the majority of the criminals arrested are minorities (Wilson 1990).

The UCR not only reports incidence—number of crimes—but also prevalence—who is committing crimes. After reviewing the yearly UCR, the conclusion that delinquency is a lower-class African American problem could easily be drawn. The UCR data indicate disproportionate minority arrest rates and highlight the crime indexes, which every year reveal lower-class black people at the top of the scale in committing Part 1 Index Crimes in comparison to the general population. It is difficult to argue with statistics and the UCR statistics reinforce the notion that delinquent acts are committed primarily by African-American males.

Media Indoctrination

Media reports and popular entertainment perpetuate the idea that delinquency is a lower-class problem. Programs that focus on delinquency characterize delinquent youths as African American adolescents from impoverished homes, single-parent families, and drug-infested, low-income housing. Seldom are delinquents portrayed as youths from upper-class families.

Capitalism Dictates That Delinquency Is a Lower-Class Phenomenon

Because the lower class is larger than the upper class, given census and UCR date, proportionally more lower-class people commit crimes and create the need for more police officers and juvenile justice personnel to be hired and correctional facilities to be built. Supplying these needs requires more funds, to which the upper class contributes through more taxes. Quinney states, "To reduce crime and thereby reduce the economic costs of crime would be to change beyond recognition the capitalist system" (1977, 130), reflecting on the cycle of social class and delinquency and its capitalist association with profit.

Wilson (1990) maintains that high arrest rates and high incarceration rates reflect the social status of delinquents and not necessarily the seriousness of their offenses if one considers all social classes (24). He explains that the get tough policy or the war on crime is really a war waged against the disadvantaged underclass in society. He accepts that violence exists within the black community, but rejects the notion of a black monopoly on crime and that lower-class black people are more prone to delinquent and criminal behavior (24).

Although OJJDP reports decreasing delinquency (1999, 15), the actions of policy makers do not reflect a decrease. Few media reporters pick up on that news. Why is there a continued urge to change laws so that adolescents can be transferred to the criminal system at a much younger age? Why is there a trend to punish adolescents rather than treating or rehabilitating them? The answer to some of these questions lies in one word, profit. What is most profitable in our society is given higher consideration than investment in the future of delinquent adolescents because they are expendable and because they are primarily lower-class youths who will end up incarcerated in the criminal system.

Incarceration and Minority Juvenile Offenders

At the end of the twentieth century, it was said that more black males were incarcerated than were in college (Wilson 1990). In the twenty-first century, it appears that more African American males are incarcerated than graduate from high school. Jerome Miller, who principally is responsible for the closing of many training schools in Massachusetts in the 1970s, theorizes that institutionalization of all adjudicated offenders is not effective. His approach, which is to send only the most serious offenders to training schools, is cited as an effective reform approach (Miller 1991 & Struckhoff 2000, 171). Miller equates the black male in the juvenile and criminal justice systems as analogous to that of the slave and slave-master relationship. He views training schools and prisons as devices to cripple black males and prevent them from achieving their potential. Just as the slave masters handicapped slaves to prevent their running away (Schiraldi, Kuyper, & Hewitt 1996, 3), so do today's prisons and training schools perpetuate feelings of powerlessness and incompetence (Ogawa 1999, 9).

Minority youths are more likely to be committed to training schools or correctional facilities or transferred to the criminal system than white youths (Agnew 2001, 267; Yablonsky 2000, 41). Agnew (2001) documents that this situation is becoming progressively worse. "About forty percent of confined juveniles are black, even though black juveniles make up just fifteen percent of the juvenile population" (267). He further states, "A recent study of thirty-six states examined the percentage of juveniles in different race/ethnic groups who were confined at some point prior to their eighteenth birthday. The study found that black juveniles were about five times more likely to be confined than whites and three times more likely to be confined than Hispanics" (268).

Agnew's thoughts reflect the trend for incarceration of black youths across the United States. It is believed that this trend will continue well into the twenty-first century (Agnew 2001).

Implications

Young African American males are imprisoned more than any other racial or ethnic group in the world (Wilson 1990). The juvenile institution is a microcosm of larger society and generally, minority youth must function the same in the institution as on the outside. Incarcerated minority youths must deal with a number of issues. In the outside world, decisions about their lives were made for them by people who did not look like them and who did not understand them. In the institution, too, decisions about their lives are made for them by people who do not look like them and who do not understand them. Now, however, locked up in an unfamiliar setting, with no place to hide, incarcerated youths are more exposed and more vulnerable. Youths feel friendless, trapped and isolated from the outside world. They form relationships that are, perhaps, more dangerous than those in the community they left. Youths may identify "homies"—gang members—with whom they can bond in the institution. If they were not members of the neighborhood gang on the outside, they may affiliate with a set in the institution to survive the incarceration (Shakur 1998). Almost all public juvenile correctional facilities, from short-term detention centers that serve as temporary holding units to long-term training schools, have a majority population of minority adolescents (i.e., African American males). Do the facilities rehabilitate youths or are they simply containing them outside the community? Youths may say, "I just do my time, hope that I don't get bruised (raped), and leave."

Are training schools breeding grounds for superdegenerate delinquents, or can they become rehabilitative centers of hope? Since the new breed of exceedingly violent adolescent came into notoriety in the 1990s, the debate continues. Some argue that it is too costly to incarcerate these adolescents and that incarceration does not seem to benefit them because no rehabilitation takes place in the training schools.

Juvenile corrections is like a school system in which achieving each level makes it possible to move to the next level. Probation, the entry level, is like elementary school; the detention center, the second level for the status offender, is like middle school; the training school is like high school; and prison is like college. Students who progress toward college degrees expect to become well rounded and knowledgeable about the world, to enter the job market with pay above minimum wage and with the capacity to earn a respectable living, and to have the potential to continue their education and increase their earning power. Delinquents who progress through the justice system also have agendas. They may expect to gain knowledge about criminal activity so they can become more adept criminals after release, to develop sharper criminal skills that will translate to greater earnings, to establish relationships with criminal role models, and to increase their moneymaking capabilities and gain more power in the criminal world.

Some minority youths age out of delinquency, losing interest in delinquent activities before they become powerful in the criminal world. Systemic pressures, however, ensure that once in the system, the delinquent has little chance to leave it. The enactment of ever-harsher laws requiring ever-harsher punishment for delinquent offenders rapidly pushes them through the justice system. Get-tough rhetoric has escalated the certification of younger offenders to the adult criminal system (Hurst 1990, 49), and by the time they might have aged out, they are already in the adult system.

Some researchers discuss aging out as a positive phenomenon, but is it? What happens to minority youth who age out? Many of them end up dead. "Black teenagers are nine times more likely to be murdered than their white counterparts." (Kennedy 1997, 19–20) Military service is not an option for youths without high school diplomas.

The 1960s and 1970s experienced black males as "invisible" (Ellison 1964), the 1980s and 1990s experienced them as an "endangered species" (Taylor-Gibbs 1976), and the twenty-first century may experience them as a lost generation. Amos Wilson's statistics (1990) support the concept of a lost generation.

> Blacks account for 54.9 percent of those arrested for violent crimes and the highest violent crime rates are demonstrated by young black males. More young black men died from homicide in one year (1977) than died in ten years in the Vietnam War. Black men are six times as likely as white men to be murder victims . . . Over 40 percent of all jail inmates throughout the nation are black—and the percentage is rapidly rising. (Wilson 1990, 1)

This generation of African American males is lost in a sea of super maximum security prisons and high technology jails. Prisons and training schools are rapidly being constructed and supplied with minority youths as quickly as they can be confined, illustrating again that minorities, especially African American males, are an economic commodity. The greater the number of crimes they commit and the higher the incarceration rate, the more money generated to the state and the more jobs created. African American males will not be a part of the labor force that reaps the benefits of the labor market because their criminal behavior originated the labor market.

Minority youths have fewer opportunities for placement in alternative facilities, such as Eckert wilderness camps, or shock probation, such as boot camps. Wilderness camps have specific requirements, such as nonviolence, and will not accept youths who do not meet those criteria. Most African American adolescents are labeled violent, aggressive, and non-compliant. Wilderness camps require a fee and an agreement from the youth that they are willing to participate in the program. Often minority adolescents who are in the juvenile justice system are from single-parent households in which no spare money is available. Urban youths may fear committing to wilderness camps, far away from home and the parent, not only because of a close bond between parent and adolescent, but because the adolescent has assumed responsibilities in the home that cannot be passed on to a younger sibling.

Summary

Race and ethnic issues continue to provoke heated debate among politicians, law enforcement, educators, researchers, and parents. Researchers have the responsibility of providing data as the foundation for arguments to be based on empirical evidence. Yet, the evidence is presented, pilot projects are funded, politicians discuss the issues, and as one youth stated, "The beat goes on." Children and adolescents, especially minorities, continue to have decisions made about them and for them, not just because of class, but because of the color of their skin. Researchers have documented race-based differential treatment in the juvenile justice system in the UCR and continue to document the disproportionate overrepresentation of African American youths in arrest rates. Empirical data also suggest that police officers are more likely to stop and arrest African American youths than any other racial or ethnic group.

Amos Wilson argues that minorities must come to understand their oppressors' history and motives (Wilson 204–205). Great military leaders understood the need to study and know their opponents well, but a first and better strategy might be nonaggression and an understanding of black history and identity. According to Leon Pettiway (1998), many black adolescents born in the late 1980s do not have an understanding of the hardships and suffering that millions of blacks have endured so that they could simply go to the school of their choice (75). They reason that things have always been this way and that if they do not feel like working they do not have to work. Everything will be okay because the United States is prosperous. They deduce that they are born equal, because under the Constitution everyone is equal, but they do not understand the subtleties of that equality. For example, a class was asked, "Have any of you ever experienced discrimination or what you thought was a discriminating experience?" A black male was one of four students who did not respond, even under the encouragement of a friend. The white friend explained that he thought the black friend had been discriminated against when he was barred from a club "because of the club's fire code," but two white friends had been admitted after the black friend was rejected. The black student continued to deny that he had been discriminated against, and explained that he felt the club was overcrowded and trying to adhere to fire safety measures. When challenged, he said that perhaps others in line after him were admitted because he was fatter than the two of them and that race had nothing to do with it.

Younger adolescents in a juvenile correctional facility were asked, "Why are you here [locked up]?" They answered by stating their delinquent offenses (e.g., robbery, auto theft, rape, etc.), but when asked, "Why are you really here [locked up]?" their responses varied but bore prevailing themes of self-hatred, which leads to what Wilson terms "self-annihilation," (1990, 20). Self-annihilation occurs when youths do not have the answers, are not sure why life is going badly for them, and they become angry and upset because they do not understand the chaos around them. They have no positive role models and may experience limited parenting from extremely young and naïve parents. They express frustration and confusion by lashing out at whatever is nearest and most convenient. Such deviant behavior in the black community translates into black-on-black crime. Marcus (1974, 223), describes deviant behavior committed by blacks upon blacks as "a form of insurrection, driven by need and deprivations, an incomplete but not altogether mistaken response to a bad situation, and coming into active existence only by overcoming the resistance of inherited values and internalized sanctions." The youths lash out at themselves without understanding why.

Many African American adolescents seem to take no pride in who they are, nor do they seem to understand or care about the history and circumstances that brought them where they are today. Pettiway (1998) suggests that generational changes within the African-American culture present challenges to their historical memories. He suggests that younger African Americans do not understand their history. Pettiway believes that the suffering and sacrifices that black people have undergone are forgotten by this generation of young black people.

The role of law enforcement is to serve and protect citizens, but without the cooperation of citizens, a higher and more visible police presence will not decrease delinquent activity and reduce crime. African American adolescents, armed with family support and community resources, must reduce or neutralize delinquent activity in their own communities. When this occurs not only will crime rates be reduced statistically, but there will be less probability of losing an entire generation of African American adolescents.

KEY CONCEPTS

confinement	multiculturalism	*Powell v. Alabama*
cultural competent	Office of Budget	race
disproportionate minority	Management	
ethnicity	one drop rule	

DISCUSSION QUESTIONS

1. Why is there a need to discuss race and ethnicity in criminal justice?

2. Discuss some of the strengths and some of the limitations of the UCR data related to race and ethnicity.

3. Why are serious violent crimes reportedly increasing as juvenile delinquency is reportedly decreasing?

4. Why do African American males reportedly experience such a disproportionately high rate of incarceration?

5. Discuss race versus class in juvenile delinquency.

6. Is the role of race in the Scottsboro case any different from the Stewart case or the Smith case? See Brian Ogawa's *The Color of Justice* for the Stewart and Smith cases.

EXERCISES

1. Form small groups and discuss the Scottsboro incident. Students can prepare cases for both sides: one team of students can act as attorney for the defense and the other team of students can be prosecutors. Discuss the case and the facts of the case.

2. Invite a local defense attorney and a local prosecutor to come to class and discuss their roles and to offer their input on the effects of race and ethnicity on the juvenile justice system nationally and locally.

SENSITIVITY EXERCISE

The instructor allows each student to select a classmate whom they do not know. The pairs stand back to back. While in this position, each student describes what the partner is wearing without looking. Then each student changes something (some students will remove an earring, a shoe, unbutton a shirt, or remove eyeglasses). They face each other for ten seconds, then return to the back to back positions and tell the class what change the partner made. Repeat the exercise for three rounds (depending on class time and size). If it is a very large class, instructors can undertake the task by standing in front of the class and then moving to the back of the class and ask the class to describe what they are wearing without turning back to see. Instructors can then change something (remove a tie or pin, remove an earring, and so forth) and ask the students what change they notice.

Point of the exercise. The United States over the years has experienced many racial and ethnic changes that have occurred right in front of our eyes. Some individuals are immediately aware of those changes and able to voice an opinion. Others may take a little longer to detect them and still others may be completely ignorant of them but all will feel their impact eventually.

10 Police and Delinquency

CHAPTER OBJECTIVES

On completing this chapter, students will have tools to:

- Explore the role of law enforcement officers working with delinquent youths
- Examine the historical impact of policing juvenile offenders
- Understand how juvenile justice units evolved
- Examine legal procedures needed when working with juvenile offenders
- Describe police and community initiatives in current practice

The Important Role of the Police

The police play the most significant role of all the criminal-justice professionals who work with youth. They *initiate* juvenile justice. The interactions with every other decision maker—judge, attorney, probation officer, and program specialist—follow from the police encounter. The police have a tremendous power of discretion when dealing with youth: to initiate formal delinquency or criminal proceedings, to refer to other juvenile specialists and programs, to advise and release. At the same time, young people bring pre-existing attitudes toward authority and the police. In many neighborhoods, particularly those of minority populations, there exists a tension between youth and the police. A young person's attitude toward the police will either be confirmed or changed in an encounter with an individual police officer. A police officer who works with youth must be cognizant of the significance that each decision carries.

Some police officers who work with juveniles are designated juvenile specialists. Often municipal police departments have specialized units that work with juveniles; these units typically include detectives assigned to cases that appear in juvenile court. Juvenile officers are assigned to various areas: delinquency prevention, child abuse, school safety, gang violence, and drug-trafficking. Not every police officer who encounters a juvenile is a designated juvenile specialist; for example, they could be a highway patrol officer, a deputy sheriff, or an officer with a special district, such as harbor police or campus police. Not many of these officers have chosen law enforcement as a profession in order to work with troubled youth; for them, police work with juveniles comes close to social work.

Whatever their background or organization, police officers have frequent contact with juveniles. Young people are apt to be in public places, "cruising" the streets and "hanging out" at shopping malls, where their activities are more likely to come to the attention of police (Walker 1992, 122–123). In recent years, community policing has changed the nature of policing, including policing juveniles. Community policing contains several aspects that have the potential for transforming the relationship between police and youth.

This chapter begins with an overview of law enforcement in the United States and describes the operations of juvenile units. The second section ennumerates the legal and procedural encounters as well as other aspects of police diversion. Here, the role conflict in juvenile police work is explored through the example of runaways. In the third section, community policing philosophy and practices as well as community policing strategies for working with juveniles are discussed. In the final section, the difficult relationship between police and black youth is examined through some initiative police relationships with young African American citizens.

The Law and Juveniles

Most juvenile court cases are referred by police. Police accounted for 85 percent of all delinquency cases referred to juvenile court in 1996. Other referrals were made by parents, victims, schools, and probation officers (Snyder & Sickmund 1999, 97). It is difficult to generalize about "the police" because there are more than 17,000 state and local police agencies in the United States (Reaves 1993, 4).

Police in America

Many city police departments have juvenile units or officers specifically designated to work with youth. In addition to the city police departments, there are state, county, and special district law enforcement officials that also have contact with youth. Unlike local police, federal law enforcement officials have relatively little contact with juveniles.

State. State police agencies have statewide jurisdiction for criminal investigation and traffic enforcement. The jurisdiction of highway patrol is limited to enforcement of the state's motor vehicle code and traffic cases. The investigative branches of state agencies include those that regulate alcoholic beverages, fish and wildlife, and transportation. In some states, a single state police department provides both general law enforcement and traffic patrol; in others, there are separate highway patrol, police, and other law enforcement organizations (Bechtel 1995).

In Michigan, a single state agency is charged with the responsibilities of criminal investigation, highway patrol, and general law enforcement. The Michigan Department of State Police consists of two offices—the Office of Director and the Office of Organizational Development—and three bureaus—the Investigative Services Bureau, the Administrative and Information Bureau, and the Uniform Services Bureau. The Office of Organizational

Development includes the Training Division and Michigan Commission on Law Enforcement Standards. The Investigative Services Bureau includes the divisions of Criminal Investigation, Fire Marshal, Forensic Science, and Field Detective. The Uniform Services Bureau includes the Motor Carrier, Special Operations Division, and eight districts of troopers (www.michigan.gov/msp). In North Carolina, these activities are divided among several state agencies. North Carolina has a State Highway Patrol and a State Bureau of Investigation. In addition, the Division of Alcohol Law Enforcement (ALE) enforces alcoholic beverage control laws. ALE agents prepare criminal cases, present evidence in court, conduct permit investigations, and conduct undercover investigations. The Division of Motor Vehicles regulates ownership and operation of motor vehicles registered in the state; the Law Enforcement Section patrols highways and rest areas (Knepper 1999, 83–85).

State police officers come into contact with young people through their law enforcement activities such as traffic patrol and enforcement of alcohol and drug laws. State agencies in conjunction with state police often participate in drug or gang task forces, which focus on the illegal activities of young people.

County.   The sheriff is the principal law enforcement authority in the county. The sheriff's office is charged with the responsibilities that existed under common law: serving civil process, investigating crimes, arresting persons, transporting prisoners and the mentally ill, providing court security, and maintaining the jail. Many sheriff's offices function like municipal police departments, performing basic police tasks and conducting criminal investigations. Although the sheriff's office retains jurisdiction throughout the county, as a practical matter, sheriff's deputies confine their jurisdiction to rural areas outside the boundaries of municipalities.

The Los Angeles Sheriff's Office, with nearly 8,000 deputies, is the largest sheriff's office in the United States. It provides police services for unincorporated areas of Los Angeles county and contracted police services for some incorporated areas (Reaves 1993, 9). The Broward Sheriff's Office, Broward County, Florida, provides 24 hour law enforcement in all of the county's unincorporated areas and in several cities with contracts for protective services. The sheriff's office is also responsible for operating the jail system, protecting the Fort Lauderdale-Hollywood International Airport, the county courthouse, local mass transit, and the county's waterways, including Port Everglades. The Broward County Sheriff's Office has a number of divisions and units organized around these responsibilities. These are: the Aviation Unit, the Civil Division, the Cold Case Unit, the Communications Division, the Crime Lab, the Marine Patrol, the School Resource Officers, and the Strategic Investigations Division (www.sheriff.org).

Law enforcement officers in the county sheriff's office are likely to encounter juveniles who reside in rural areas. These deputies are often assigned to schools in drug prevention programs that put them in frequent contact with youth.

City.   Municipal police departments represent the largest and most important group within law enforcement. Local police departments respond to citizens' calls for service, provide routine patrol services, and enforce traffic laws. The majority of local police departments are the primary investigating agency for crimes occurring in their jurisdiction. The New

York City Police Department is one of the largest municipal police departments in the United States. There are over 38,000 uniformed officers and 9,000 civilians. The police commissioner, appointed to a five-year term, answers directly to the mayor. The department is organized into nine major bureaus: Patrol Services, Detective, Organized Crime Control, Transient, Criminal Justice, Internal Affairs, Housing, Personnel, and Support Services. New York City's five boroughs—Manhattan, the Bronx, Brooklyn, Queens, and Staten Island—are divided into eight Patrol Borough Commands and are further subdivided into 76 precincts (www.ci.nyc.ny.us/nypd).

There are very few large municipal police departments; a typical police department employs only a small number of officers. Of the 12,000 local police departments in the United States, half employ 10 or fewer sworn police officers, and 90 percent employ 50 or fewer. Three-fourths or so serve populations of less than 10,000 (Reaves 1993, 9). The Police Department of Greenville, New Hampshire, has five sworn officers. Located in Hillsborough County, it serves a population of 2,231 residents. The department has the distinction of being the smallest department accredited by the Commission on Accreditation for Law Enforcement Agencies (CALEA). "The pride my employees have in this accomplishment is continually reflected in the work they do," Greenville's Chief of Police David Benedict, has said. "No longer do they have the feeling of being second-class citizens just because they are a small department" (www.calea.org).

Special District.   Special district police include forces located at airports, railroads, harbors, housing developments, mass transit centers, university campuses, and school systems. Special district police enforce the criminal laws of the state on private and public school property, at county and state hospitals, shopping centers, housing complexes and office buildings, golf courses and recreational areas. Many of these officers wear uniforms like those worn by municipal police officers or deputy sheriffs. Others wear "plain clothes." They drive vehicles resembling patrol cars; they carry firearms, handcuffs, and other equipment; and they wear a badge. Although some special district police, such as campus police, have full arrest powers, the powers of other special district police are limited by state statute (Gray 1998, 25–37).

Some special district police, such as school district police, have direct contact with youth. Some of the largest school districts in the United States have their own police departments. The Division of School Police in Dade County, Florida, was established in 1957. The Superintendent of Schools has assigned a School Resource Officer (SRO) to every middle and senior high school within the county school system. The Division of School Police includes about 140 sworn officers who interact with students and staff at 286 schools. The Los Angeles Unified School District Police Department began in 1948 as a security section and grew into a department. The LAUSD Police Department has over 300 sworn personnel and serves 910 schools. The San Antonio Independent School District Police Department includes 75 sworn officers and a dozen non-sworn staff members. They are licensed peace officers within the state of Texas with the same arrest powers, privileges, and immunities as municipal police officers. Two police officers are assigned to each high school and one to each middle school in the district, who remain at the school throughout the day. In addition, there are eight officers assigned to assist elementary schools. These officers, known as "learning community officers," provide educational programs at these schools and they answer police calls. Additional officers are assigned to the detective unit, gang unit, training, and support functions (www.saisd.net).

Juvenile Units

Many city police departments have specialized units for youths, known as a juvenile or youth division. In 1973, The National Advisory Commission on Criminal Justice Standards and Goals recommended that every police department with more than 75 officers establish a youth or juvenile division, and in smaller departments, if community conditions warranted. The *juvenile division* conducts investigations involving juveniles, assists patrol officers in dealing with juvenile problems, and coordinates juvenile activities with other agencies. The juvenile division also provides surveillance of schools, shopping malls, amusement parks, and other areas where youth problems are likely to develop. Juvenile officers gather intelligence about young offenders, particularly about involvement in drug distribution and gang membership. They investigate crimes involving youth, investigate cases involving abused or neglected children, search for missing young people, and provide prevention and intervention programs in conjunction with schools and community organizations (Palmietto 1997, 191–193).

One of the first juvenile units opened in 1909 when Leo Marden of the Los Angeles Police Department took an interest in the needs of children. Marden convinced administrators that particular juvenile programs could prevent delinquents from becoming adult criminals. He gained appointment as the first juvenile probation officer and was charged with developing programs and procedures to handle juvenile matters citywide. A year later, Alice Stebbins Wells, the city's first policewoman, joined Marden and together they organized the Juvenile Bureau. Over the years, the bureau expanded to include a number of more specialized units formed in response to shifting society and juveniles. The Juvenile Narcotics Section and the School Burglary Unit began operation during the 1950s and 1960s. During the 1970s and 1980s, the bureau became the Juvenile Division, and created programs to deal with sexual exploitation of children and drug trafficking in schools (www.lapdonline.org).

The Los Angeles Police Department's Juvenile Division is exceptional for its size and complexity. The Juvenile Division is composed of three basic sections: operations, child protection, and juvenile narcotics. The Juvenile Division consists of more than 100 sworn officers plus non-sworn staff who are responsible for juvenile narcotics enforcement, investigations concerning child abuse and sexual exploitation of children, juvenile court liaison, and a range of prevention and intervention programs, such as DARE (Drug Abuse Resistance Education). In smaller police departments, these duties are performed by a few officers organized within a unit without formal subdivisions. The Juvenile Investigations Unit of the San Jose Police Department conducts child and dependency abuse investigations, missing person investigations for runaways, and criminal investigations involving the city's youth. The officers in the unit are assigned to one of three details: missing persons detail, dependency or abuse detail, or general crimes detail. A sergeant leads each detail. In the smallest police departments across the country, these duties are assigned to a single designated juvenile specialist.

A national survey of law enforcement organizations conducted in 1997 asked large municipal police departments and sheriff's offices (those with one hundred or more sworn officers), about the types of special units they operated. A large proportion reported that they had units devoted to juvenile issues. About 95 percent of local police had units for drug education in schools, 66 percent had juvenile crime units, and 55 percent had gang units. Among sheriff's offices surveyed, 79 percent had drug education programs, 49 percent had juvenile crime units, and 50 percent had gang units. About half of the police departments and sheriff's offices had units for investigation of child abuse. Other units at some agencies were domestic violence, missing children, and youth outreach (Snyder & Sickmund 1999, 139). The Juvenile Division of police departments includes other programs that may be organized into the juvenile unit or as separate units within a youth services division. Typical juvenile programs include drug education, school resource officers, and gang intervention.

Drug Education.   DARE was created in 1983 by the Los Angeles Police Department in partnership with the Los Angeles Unified School District. DARE America is a corporation based in California that controls the curriculum and merchandising. DARE America is directed by Glenn Levant, a former police officer. The DARE program seeks to educate children to resist drug abuse; the DARE motto is "DARE to keep kids off drugs." The program brings uniformed police officers into fifth-grade classrooms for 17 lessons. The DARE program proved popular with law enforcement organizations and many institutionalized the program with specialized units (Carter 1995).

DARE comprises a separate division in the Los Angeles Police Department. The DARE Division provides the curriculum to schools within the city of Los Angeles. Uniformed police officers from the division enter fifth grade classrooms to provide anti-drug curriculum. Police officers assigned to DARE also work with school personnel, parents, and community members to promote a positive relationship between the police and the community. The DARE Division operates the Los Angeles Police Academy Magnet School Program. Established at five schools within the city, this program provides a law enforcement training curriculum to high school students interested in police careers. The program provides the next generation of police recruits and promotes a better understanding of the role of police officers in society. The DARE Division also provides training of DARE officers throughout the nation through the Western Region Training Center (www.lapdonline.org).

School Resource Officers.   School Resource Officers, variously known as Police-School Liaison officers (PSLs) or Juvenile Tactical officers (JTCs), are a common feature in many junior and senior high schools. The first police-school liaison in the United States began in Flint, Michigan, in 1958 at Bryant Community Junior High School. Within seven years, all eight junior high schools and four high schools in the district had PSL officers. Other police-school liaison projects began in Tucson, Arizona (1963), Minneapolis, Minnesota (1966), and Arlington Heights, Illinois (1966). Wisconsin became one of the first states to implement police-school liaison officers statewide through the Wisconsin Juvenile Officers' Association. By 1981, there were 29 police officers located at schools in 14 small and medium-sized cities. Most of these projects began with federal funds or funding through local police or school budgets or both.

The founders of police-school liaison projects placed police officers in schools in order to identify problems with juveniles before they reach the level of serious delinquency; the PSL officers are able to intervene through education, communication, and increased understanding across youth, schools, police, and communities. The School Resource Officer Program in St. Petersburg, Florida, has uniformed police officers in city schools where they serve as law enforcers, counselors, information brokers, and instructors. In addition, the SROs also combine with other community members to sponsor city activities. They distribute admission tickets to "pool parties," which are particularly popular among youth. Although the tickets are given away free of charge, youth must interact with the police to obtain them, promoting a positive relationship. Similar programs operate in over 40 of Florida's 67 school districts (Guarino-Ghezzi & Loghran 1996, 80–81).

Evaluations have generally found that school administrators, teachers, and students support the programs. An evaluation of the SRO program in Birmingham, Alabama, schools found that many of the officers had returned to the high schools from which they had graduated or within the community where they lived. The SRO performed daily security checks (checking doors, patrolling bathrooms and hallways). They developed relationships with students, telling them about police work, and counseled up to a third of the students in the school. They also reported daily contacts with parents, typically related to fights, drugs, and attendance issues. Students reported that they did not resent the increased surveillance but viewed locker searches and the like as necessary to reduce the flow of drugs, to curtail gang-related activities, and to reduce the availability of guns. They also felt that the presence of a uniformed officer in school deterred delinquency and violence. School officials reported decreases in the number of weapons, fights, drug seizures, gambling, sexual incidents, and dress code violations since the program began. The number of misdemeanor and felony arrests stayed the same (Johnson 1999, 173–192).

School Resource Officers typically operate as units within city police departments and county sheriff's departments. North Carolina's SROs began appearing in high schools and middle schools in 1995. By 1999 there were about 450 SROs working in schools in North Carolina. SROs are law enforcement officers permanently assigned to cover a school or set of schools. In Raleigh, North Carolina, the SROs are organized into a School Safety unit within the Juvenile Services section of the Raleigh Police Department's Investigative Division.

Gang Intervention Units.   Some police departments have organized units of investigators who specialize in gangs. Known as "gang intervention," "youth violence," and "gun squads," these units target youth gangs to reduce criminal violence linked to firearms, gangs, and drug-trafficking. The Gang Unit of Orange, California, is part of the Detection Division of the Orange Police Department. The unit consists of one sergeant, two investigators, three "street suppression investigators," and a school resource officer. A deputy district attorney, a district attorney investigator, and a probation officer also work with the unit to provide "vertical prosecution" of gang cases. In vertical prosecution, a single prosecutor handles all stages of proceedings in criminal court (www.cityoforange.org/police). The

Gang Intervention Unit (GIU) of the Fort Collins, Colorado, police department is a four-member team designed to reduce gang-motivated crime and membership. The GIU is part of the Youth Services section, which includes school resource officers and juvenile detectives. The unit began in 1993. GIU members investigate gang-motivated crimes and patrol "hot spots" to suppress gang activity. Officers assigned to the unit have developed expertise in gang identification, gang mentality, and investigation of gang crimes. Team members are frequently called upon to assist other officers with the investigation of gang crimes. The GIU provides community education on gang-related issues, works with parents of "at-risk" juveniles, and actively participate on citizen boards and groups (www.ci.fort-collins.co.us).

The Salinas Police Department in Salinas, California, organized a Gang Task Force during the 1980s in response to an increase in the number of gangs within the city and an escalation in gang violence. The Gang Task Force operated as an independent venture of the Salinas Police Department. In 1995, the department created the Violence Suppression Unit (VSU), an expansion of the Gang Task Force. The VSU includes 15 police officers who use a variety of aggressive patrol strategies to reduce gang-related firearm violence among the city's youth. These strategies include periodic surveillance, probation and parole searches, traffic stops, use of raids and search warrants, use of informants, and development of criteria for determining gang membership. The Violence Suppression Unit developed a Geographic Information System (GIS) that geographically tracks gang activity and firearms use. This system allows Salinas police officers to respond to inquiries about the location of firearm seizures, violent crimes, and gang incidents near school zones (OJJDP 1999, 121).

Other gang units operate as part of task forces that are larger networks of law enforcement, prosecutorial, probation, and other agencies. Police departments in Boston, Minneapolis, Phoenix, Indianapolis, St. Louis, and other cities have gang intervention efforts that join resources of city, state, and federal law enforcement. The Boston Police Department's Youth Violence Strike Force is a multi-agency task force composed of more than 60 sworn officers in collaboration with the Attorney for the Commonwealth of Massachusetts and representatives from various agencies including local, state, and federal law enforcement; probation and parole officers; the mayor's office; city agencies; clergy; and several universities. Through this coordinated effort, the Youth Violence Strike Force intends to communicate to gangs that there would be swift, sure, and severe consequences for violence (OJJDP 1999, 104).

The gang unit of the Minneapolis Police Department participates in several initiatives. In Minneapolis, all police officers within the gang unit participate in the Minneapolis Violence Prevention Initiative, a program modeled after the Youth Violence Strike Force in Boston. The program pairs officers from the gang unit and deputies from the Hennepin County Sheriff's Office with probation officers from the Hennepin County Department of Community Corrections. Police officers and probation officers co-train for two days and then make regular, unannounced visits to the homes of probationers, juveniles, and adults previously identified as gang members. Gang unit police officers, together with patrol officers and agents from the Bureau of Alcohol, Tobacco and Firearms, conduct saturation patrols to remove firearms from the streets through aggressive inspection and consent searches. Gang unit police officers also participate in the State Gang Task Force. Composed of 40 members from local, county, and state police agencies, the task force allows law enforcement to cross jurisdictional boundaries and respond more effectively to statewide gang activities. Members are deputized statewide and have arrest power statewide, and they conduct long-term investigations using the gang database. (OJJDP 1999, 59–60)

Police Encounters with Juveniles

The prevailing social mission of the juvenile court during the 20th century meant that police paid little attention to procedural rights in encounters with juveniles. The focus of the juvenile court was on social workers and intervention, not lawyers and rights, so it was assumed that police had carte blanche authority to do as they pleased with youth. That began to change during the 1970s and the *Gault* era of the juvenile court. Although the *Gault* decision focused on the adjudicatory hearing during delinquency proceedings, the decision extended the due process revolution to juveniles.

Within a decade and a half of the *Gault* decision, two of the most influential organizations in the legal arena recommended a return to adult practices in the administration of arrest, search, and seizure involving youth. In 1980, the Joint Commission on Juvenile Justice and Standards of the Institute of Judicial Administration and the American Bar Association issued a multi-volume publication on legal standards in juvenile law. In the volume entitled *Standards Relating to Police Handling of Juvenile Problems,* the Joint Commission proposed Standard 3.2, which recommends that "police investigation into criminal matters should be similar *whether the suspect is an adult or a juvenile.* Juveniles should receive at least the same safeguards available to adults in the criminal justice system. This standard should apply to: preliminary investigation (e.g., stop and frisk); the arrest process; search and seizure . . . " (Watkins 1998, 104–105). Portions of the Institute of Justice and the American Bar Association Standards have been incorporated into the juvenile codes of some states. The standards serve as guidelines for judges, defense attorneys, prosecutors, and other decision makers as a source for defining due process in juvenile matters (Shepherd, www.abanet.org/crimjust/juvjust).

Law and Procedure

In general, a law enforcement officer may stop an individual for investigative purposes and may detain the individual for a brief period to determine whether or not a crime has been, or is about to be, committed. If the officer has reason to believe the person may be armed or dangerous, the officer may frisk or pat down the suspect. *Arrest* refers to action taken to restrict the freedom of a suspect. An arrest occurs when a law enforcement officer takes a suspect into custody. Patrol officers are responsible, either directly or indirectly, for most arrests. Either they arrest a suspect at the crime scene or they obtain information (description, name of suspect, etc.) from the victim or a witness. Once a suspect has been arrested, the police make an administrative record or *booking.* This process involves recording the suspect's name, address, the time and place of arrest, the charge, and so on. Fingerprints and photographs may be taken at the police department, or the suspect may be transported directly to the jail.

Juvenile case processing of lawbreakers varies from state to state. Some juvenile codes do not use the term "arrest" in defining situations where the police apprehend a juvenile; rather, the phrase "taken into custody" is used. Other juvenile codes contain specific limitations on police interrogation and booking of juveniles.

Investigatory Stops.   As is true with adults, police must have a reason to stop and frisk a juvenile. The juvenile's mere presence in an area where a crime occurred does not justify an investigatory search. The standard is ***reasonable suspicion,*** meaning some minimal level of objective justification for making the stop. Legally, this means something more than a hunch, but less than the probable cause needed for an arrest (Murrell 1996, 3).

This standard of reasonable suspicion has been interpreted broadly by courts, more broadly than for adult suspects; this interpretation is acting in the juvenile's best interest. The Iowa Supreme Court has adopted an expansive view of reasonable suspicion based on the ***totality of the circumstances.*** Based on this view, "seemingly innocent activities may . . . combine with other factors to give an experienced law enforcement officer reason to suspect wrongdoing; all the evidence is taken together regardless of whether each aspect would furnish reasonable suspicion by itself. An officer may, for example, ask a group of youths found in a public bathroom in a park what they are doing, particularly if there are supporting circumstances such as smoke, beer cans, liquor bottles, noise, and so on. Using the totality-of-circumstances doctrine, the Iowa Court of Appeals ruled in *In the Interest of S.A.W.* (1993) that reasonable suspicion justifies a stop in an area where a crime is alleged to have taken place. In this case, the court authorized the investigatory stop of a car leaving the area where shots were reported to have been fired. The fact that there had been a report of shots fired and the fact that the vehicle was leaving the scene at a high speed when the police arrived justified the stop and seizure of a handgun from the passenger's purse.[3]

Interrogations.   Police are prohibited from certain interrogation tactics when questioning youth. In *Haley v. State of Ohio* (1948), a fifteen-year-old boy was arrested for participation in the robbery of a candy store and murder of the owner. The police, "working in relays, questioned him hour after hour, from midnight until dawn." The boy had no attorney and the police denied his mother access for five days. The U.S. Supreme Court reasoned that this method of police interrogation would raise questions of constitutionality if the defendant had been a man, and more so in the case of a 15-year-old boy. The Court held that the fourteenth amendment prohibits police from violating the due process clause in obtaining admissions or confessions from adults or juveniles. Later, in *Gallegos v. Colorado* (1962) the U.S. Supreme Court ruled that isolation of a juvenile for prolonged periods by police may result in confessions involuntarily obtained and in violation of a juvenile's constitutional rights. Prolonged questioning did not occur in this case, rather, a 14-year-old had been detained for five days without access to a lawyer, adult advisor, or even his mother.

[3]*In the Interest of S.A.W.* 499 N.W.2d 739 (Iowa App. 1993).

The court concluded that the length of isolation and the age of the defendant resulted in an inadmissable confession.

On the other hand, the absence of parents does necessarily make a confession involuntary. In some states, statutes require the presence of a parent or lawyer for a juvenile to waive rights, such as the right to remain silent. In the majority of states, the validity of a juvenile's waiver of rights hinges on the "totality of circumstances" surrounding the waiver, and the presence or absence of a parent is only one factor to be considered. In *State v. Sugg* (1995), the West Virginia Supreme Court decided that a juvenile may waive Miranda rights in the absence of his or her parents as long as the juvenile does so knowingly, voluntarily, and intelligently. The court concluded that requiring the presence of a parent in every situation in which juveniles are in custody and are informed of rights would restrict unnecessarily law enforcement (del Carmen *et al.* 1998, 47–48).

Fingerprints.   Traditionally, juvenile codes have discouraged fingerprinting of juveniles upon arrest. Some state statutes require that a judge approve the fingerprinting of a juvenile defendant; others provide for the destruction of fingerprints under certain circumstances.

More recently, state statutes have granted greater authority to law enforcement in fingerprinting and photographing juveniles. North Carolina's Juvenile Justice Reform Act of 1998 allows police to fingerprint and photograph juveniles at least 10 years of age alleged to have committed a felony offense, or under some circumstances, a nondivertible offense. The prints are transferred to the State Bureau of Investigation following adjudication. Both prints and photos must be destroyed, however, if the court finds no probable cause for the arrest, if the court does not find the juvenile to be delinquent, or if no petition is filed with juvenile court within one year.

Federal courts have authorized greater authority to law enforcement in this area as well. In *United States v. Miller* (1972), the U.S. Court of Appeals for the Fourth Circuit decided that a juvenile may voluntarily provide fingerprints after waiver of rights with no adult guidance or legal advice. If, after having been informed of constitutional rights and intelligently waiving them, a juvenile submits to fingerprinting and handwriting samples, these may be used in delinquency proceedings in juvenile court (del Carmen *et al.* 1998, 28–29). In *United States v. Sechrist* (1981) the Court of Appeals for the Seventh Circuit held that fingerprints may be taken, based on less than probable cause, if the juvenile is legally detained. The court decided that no probable cause was needed to take fingerprints because the juvenile was already in lawful custody at the time pursuant to a federal magistrate's order. The court ruled that lawful custody of the juvenile satisfied the fourth amendment's search-and-seizure requirement of reasonableness (del Carmen *et al.* 1998, 33–34).

Discretion and Diversion

A majority of youths who are arrested are sent to juvenile court. In 1996, 69 percent of juvenile arrests were referred to juvenile court, 6 percent to criminal court. About 23 percent of juvenile arrests eligible for referral to juvenile court were handled within the law enforcement agency and the youth was released. The others were referred to a social service agency or another police agency (Snyder 1997, 6). Most police encounters with juveniles do not, however, result in arrest.

For the most part, on-the-street encounters between police officers and juveniles resemble those involving adults. Many of these encounters are the result of a telephone call, and involve maintenance rather than criminal activity. The resultant crimes reported are minor rather than violent felonies. Unlike encounters with adults, however, police-juvenile contacts may involve running away, truancy, alcohol use, curfew violations, or other status offenses. In 1996, less than one half of 1 percent of all persons between the ages of 10 and 17 in the United States were arrested for a violent index offense (murder, forcible rape, robbery, aggravated assault) (Snyder 1997, 4).

The range of police responses is wider when dealing with juveniles than adults. Police officers may:

1. Take "no action," or no formal action against the juvenile even though probable cause may exist for an arrest.
2. Take the youth into custody, but then release him or her at the police station. Although technically an arrest, there may be no formal record of the apprehension.
3. Refer the youth to a parent or guardian, or if no responsible parent can be located, refer the youth to a county social service agency.
4. Refer the juvenile to juvenile court intake. The intake officer prepares a petition for juvenile court and arranges for detention of the youth (Walker 1993, 124).

The ability to make a choice between courses of action or inaction is known as *discretion.* Police discretion with youth is not unlimited of course; the police may not legally arrest a young person under any circumstances. But as a government official acting in an official capacity, a police officer retains the authority to make a decision on the basis of official judgment (Walker 1992, 198).

A number of factors, including state laws, help to determine which option is used. The Institute of Judicial Administration of the American Bar Association Standards require the *least restrictive alternative.* The least restrictive alternative principle holds that the response that intrudes less on a juvenile's constitutional rights ought to be tried before invoking a more intrusive course of action. The standards require decision makers, including the police, to provide a written reason for not choosing the least restrictive alternative (Sheperd). State legislatures have rewritten this language, however. Until 1998, North Carolina law required police officers who had taken a juvenile into custody to follow the least restrictive approach. The Juvenile Justice Reform Act of 1998 removed the least restrictive language and directed officers to take the action "most appropriate" to the situation, the needs of the juvenile, and the protection of public safety (*North Carolina Juvenile Colde and Related Statutes* 1999).

Police departments and commissions whose job is to recommend effective police practices have for years had disdain for "in-house" alternatives to juvenile court. Police officers do not feel qualified to counsel or personally supervise a juvenile on the grounds that the police officer is not a psychologist or social worker. Rather, the police should refer those youth who can benefit from alternatives to juvenile court to social service and other community-based agencies outside of law enforcement (Rubin 1985, 96). This is known as police diversion or adjustment. "Community adjustment" or "station adjustment" is an alternative to juvenile court, made at the discretion of police, for less serious offenses. The term *adjustment* is often used in conjunction with intake and refers simply to a decision to refer the juvenile to some other agency. The officer may release the offender to a parent or guardian with follow-up by the police or a community agency.

Adjustments are made by the officers, or in some cities, by a panel of decision makers (Chaiken 1998, 24). The Pasadena Police Department Youth Accountability Board allows minors who have committed their first criminal offense to receive an intervention before their behavior escalates into a more serious crime. To be eligible, the youth must be 17 years of age or younger, reside in Pasadena or attend a Pasadena Unified School, possess no prior arrest record, and have been charged with a minor offense, such as vandalism. The Youth Accountability Board is composed of city residents who have completed the Citizens Police Academy; each board has a chairperson and two members. The diversion process has several steps:

1. Once the minor is accepted, Pasadena Mental Health does an assessment of the minor and the family. The board then meets with the youth, the parents, the counselor, and the officer handling the case.
2. The Board then proposes an accountability contract written to respond to the minor's criminal behavior and any underlying issues. The youth and the youth's parents must agree to the contract, to meet on a weekly basis, and to complete six months of counseling.
3. The Board monitors the case by assessing improvement in school and in the home. The Board meets with the youth, the parents, the counselor, and the police officer handling the case once every two months during the six month period. The Youth and Family Services Unit monitors compliance with the contract.
4. After six months, the youth graduates from the program and the case is closed. The purpose of the program is to hold the youth accountable for his or her actions by providing swift and appropriate sanctions (www.ci.pasadena.ca.us/police).

Police Officers or Social Workers?

Not many law enforcement personnel have chosen their careers in order to work with youth. Within police departments, detective is typically ranked as the most prestigious position, whereas juvenile specialists have lower prestige positions. Many police officers prefer to work on cases not involving juveniles. They avoid juvenile and domestic cases in favor of "real" crimes. Not surprisingly, some officers believe that working with runaways, truants, and other juvenile offenders is akin to "social work," or something that detracts from what many law enforcement officers see as their primary role—the suppression of crime (Walker 1992, 123). The conflict between the "law enforcement" and "social work" roles of juvenile police work raises practical and professional dilemmas for police.

The Women's Bureau.   The view that juvenile work is outside the boundaries of "real police work" has deep roots in American policing. Historically, development of the juvenile specialization in police departments coincided with the introduction of women officers. When police departments first hired women in the late nineteenth century, they hired them to do juvenile work, which was considered to be an unsuitable job for a man. Mary Owens, the first woman to become a police officer in the United States, worked with juveniles. The Chicago Police Department hired Owens as a "policeman" in 1893; she made visits to juvenile court and assisted detectives on cases involving women and children. Owens came to police work in the same way as many of the other women who followed—as a widow. Her husband, a Chicago police officer, had been killed in the line of duty, and because she had no income or death benefits from the city, the department gave her a job (Schulz 1995, 26).

During the first decade of the twentieth century, the police departments of other cities, including Portland, Los Angeles, and Denver, hired women to work with juveniles as well. These policewomen, or "police matrons" as they were sometimes called, were assigned to suppress vice and juvenile delinquency. Many of the first juvenile bureaus were known as *women's bureaus.* The women's bureau established in Washington, D.C., in 1918 was the model for many police departments between 1918 and 1928. The departments hired women with social service backgrounds as directors, and they in turn hired women to work with women and youth. The policewomen supervised dance halls, theatres, skating rinks, and other places frequented by youth. They met with the families of delinquent youth in the probation system and also looked for runaways and missing girls. The policewomen assisted the male officers in interviewing and searching women offenders, in addition to arranging for medical exams and pregnancy tests for those girls who were arrested. These women officers also referred to juvenile court foster children who had been arrested.

Role Conflict.   The law enforcement and social work roles of juvenile police work also raises a practical dilemma. Samuel Walker, a professor of criminal justice at the University of Nebraska, observes that police work with juveniles involves *role conflict,* that is, the officers are asked to do both law enforcement and delinquency prevention. The police are caught between legal requirements on the one hand and public expectations on the other. Young people have the right to "hang out" on the street corner or city park provided their behavior does not violate the law. Yet their presence offends other citizens who may be fearful and demand that the police do something in the interest of public safety. Even when the law is broken, the dilemma remains. An argument can be made for a strictly law enforcement role, for pursuing formal action whenever the police have legal grounds for an arrest. Others insist that the police should maintain a delinquency prevention role, concentrating on the most serious crimes only and emphasizing advice and counseling for young people in trouble. The International Association of Chiefs of Police (IACP) recommends a middle-of-the-road position, noting that most police departments operate juvenile programs that combine the law enforcement and delinquency prevention roles, and that police ought to pursue that combination most suitable for their community (Walker 1992, 123).

At the same time, juveniles demonstrate unfavorable attitudes toward the police. In part, these attitudes are the nature of police encounters with juveniles. In addition, the imposition of legal authority within particular neighborhoods engenders a pervasive resentment toward the law and those who enforce it (Leiber, Nalla, & Farnworth 1998, 151–174). Proactive policing and delinquency prevention programs may be viewed by the youths themselves as harassment.

The traditional police-juvenile encounter takes place through a patrol car window. The patrol car pulls up to a corner where several youths have gathered. The officer stares at the youths, the youths stare back. The officer calls one over and the youth walks toward the car, determined to show his peers that he is not intimidated. The officer poses the questions, "Do you live around here?" and "What are you up to?" The officer then admonishes the youth to stay out of trouble; the youth answers, "Yeah," "Nothing," and "Sure." Meanwhile, the other boys laugh and joke at the officer's expense and the officer cannot be sure what has been said. The police officer has learned nothing in the exchange, but the youths have learned that the police represent a repressive force to be challenged (Wilson & Kelling 1982, 29–38).

Community Policing and Juveniles

In the last 20 years, the majority of police departments have moved to community policing. Community policing has shifted the emphasis from reactive law enforcement to prevention and problem-solving methods. It has been suggested that community policing may alter the antagonistic dynamic between police and juveniles (Guarino-Ghezzi 1994, 131–153).

Community Policing

"A quiet revolution is reshaping American policing," observes George L. Kelling. That quiet revolution is community policing (Kelling 1988, 1). By 1993, about half of 2,000 local law enforcement organizations reported they had either implemented or were in the process of implementing community policing. Community policing was most common among departments in the West, followed by the South, Midwest, and Northeast (National Institute of Justice 1995). By 1997, an estimated 16 percent of local police departments had a formally written community policing plan. A majority of departments serving populations of 50,000 or more residents had a fulltime community policing unit (Bureau of Justice Statistics 1999, 2). In Houston, Texas, the community policing program is known as "neighborhood-oriented policing," in Baltimore County, Maryland, "citizen-oriented police experiment," in Newport News, Virginia, "problem-oriented policing" and in Kansas City, Missouri, as "target-oriented policing."

Community Policing Philosophy.   As the various labels for community policing suggest, this philosophy encompasses police practices ranging from assignment of officers to foot patrol beats to police cooperation with civic officials in order to raze abandoned buildings that provide havens for drug activity. Community policing has also been associated with problem-oriented and neighborhood policing (Oliver 2000).

Community policing has been defined as "a philosophy and an organizational strategy that promotes a new partnership between people and their police. It is based on the premise that both the police and the community must work together to identify, prioritize, and solve contemporary community problems such as crime, drugs, fear of crime, social and physical disorder, and overall neighborhood decay, with the goal of improving the over-all quality of life in the area" (Trojanowicz & Bucqueroux 1990, 2). Community policing efforts involve specific programs, organizational arrangements, and citizen participation. Programs and practices include neighborhood-based offices or substations, designated "community" police officers, foot patrol assignments, regular meetings with community groups, interagency involvement in identification of community problems, and use of codes to combat drugs and crime, such as enforcement of housing codes to shut down operation of crackhouses. Organizational arrangements include decision making tied to specific geo-graphical areas, beat or patrol boundaries that coincide with these areas, decentralized field services, and special units for problem solving and crime prevention. Citizen participation in community-policing areas includes neighborhood watch programs and volunteer citizen patrols (National Institute of Justice 1995).

The idea of community policing came from an article in the *Atlantic Monthly*. James Q. Wilson, a political scientist, and George L. Kelling, a former Newark police officer, sug-gested that although Newark's foot patrol experiment failed to reduce crime, it did reduce citizens' fear of crime. The citizens appreciated police efforts to deal with disorderly peo-ple, namely, the beggars, drunks, and rowdy teenagers. This was significant because foot patrol officers had addressed the physical and psychological ingredients of crime, the "bro-ken windows" that invited criminals to break others because it suggested that no one cares. Fear of crime led to a reluctance on the part of citizens to participate in public life, which in turn led to a surrender of public areas to lawbreakers. Wilson and Kelling suggested that reducing the citizens' fear of crime and listening to their concerns about problems of disor-der would have an impact (Wilson & Kelling 1982, 29–38).

Lee P. Brown, who served as director of the Law Enforcement Assistance Adminis-tration and as chief in the Atlanta, Houston, and New York City police departments, became one of the first to implement community policing. While Brown was chief of the Houston Police Department, he implemented a program called Directed Area Responsibility Team (DART), which emphasized decentralized management and community involvement. The plan paired police officers with civilian community service officers and established com-munity command stations and storefront police stations in Houston neighborhoods. The storefronts became a model for other projects across the country (Brown 1989, 1–12). Brown later became Commissioner of Police in New York City where he began to imple-ment community policing strategies. When William Bratton, who had developed commu-nity policing initiatives in Boston, became commissioner, he established a department-wide community policing strategy. Bratton initiated a series of periodic meetings of senior man-agers. Using comparative crime analysis known as compstat, the system required each manager to devise strategies to solve particular crime and quality of life problems (Bratton & Knobler 1998). Other community policing initiatives began in other cities under other police leaders: Paul Evans in Boston, William Finney in St. Paul, Dennis Nowicki in Char-lotte, and Norm Stamper in Seattle.

Federal support during the 1980s and 1990s helped make community policing a national initiative. In 1985, the Criminal Justice Policy Management Program at the John F.

Kennedy School of Government at Harvard University, with funding from the National Institute of Justice and foundation grants, brought 30 police executives and professors together for a series of meetings to discuss the status of policing in the United States. They met several times a year for the next several years. In 1993, the Bureau of Justice Assistance, U.S. Department of Justice, created the Community Policing Consortium, composed of the International Association of Chiefs of Police (IACP), National Sheriff's Association (NSA), Police Executive Research Forum (PERF), Police Foundation, and National Organization of Black Law Enforcement Executives (NOBLE). The Consortium provides training and technical assistance to police departments and sheriff's offices with community policing programs. In 1994, Congress passed the Violent Crime Control and Law Enforcement Act of 1994. The act authorized $8.8 billion over a six-year period in grants to local law enforcement agencies to add community-policing officers to the streets. President William Jefferson Clinton, who had pledged to add 100,000 community-policing officers, signed the act into law September 13, 1994. Attorney General Janet Reno created the Office of Community Policing Services (COPS) to implement the 100,000 police officers initiative in October 1994.

Community Policing and Youth   Community policing initiatives with youth can take a variety of forms. Community police officers of the Pequannock Police Department in Pequannock Township, New Jersey, work out of a substation in the Boys and Girls Club. They counsel students who come to the center for after-school activities, give talks in area schools about drugs and alcohol, participate in school activities, and sponsor teen night activities to provide an alternative to street activities. The youth appreciate the access to police officers and come to them to share problems and seek advice. "We try to help kids before a little problem becomes a big one," Sergeant Rick Jennings explains. "It is much easier for a kid to talk to an officer on his turf than to walk into a police station." Parents also drop by the substation to let officers know about problems that have developed in their neighborhoods. The "Cops 'n Jocks" program was started by the Pequannock Police Department in New Jersey as part of its community policing effort. The program seeks to build trust between young athletes and the police. Officers attend games and practices offering support, advice, and counsel. (Office of Community Oriented Policing Services 1999).

Gordon Bazemore and Scott Senjo of Florida Atlantic University studied community policing in one south Florida city. They found that the community-oriented policing officers impacted three areas in police encounters with juveniles: law enforcement, prevention, and order-maintenance.

1. COP officers do not abandon the law enforcement focus. "A lot of people think community police officers are soft on crime," said one COP officer, "That's not it at all. We don't make any exceptions for people who break the law. We try to spend time with the kids playing basketball, and do stuff for the kids so we can prevent them from getting into the system in the first place" (Bazemore & Senjo 1997, 67). From the officers' perspective, spending time with the youth makes the job of gathering intelligence and deterring delinquent activity easier. "We want to be like Mayberry, R. F. D. with Andy Griffith and Barney because they knew everyone in Mayberry. So we consider [our city] to be another Mayberry. When we get to know everyone, it makes our job easier" (Bazemore & Senjo 1997, 68).

Police officers join teachers in classrooms after the introduction of DARE in 1983. Michael Newman/ PhotoEdit

2. Community policing includes prevention efforts. These efforts worked to establish a visible presence (primary prevention) and to reach out through specialized police programs such as DARE, police-school, and midnight basketball league liaison (secondary prevention). The prevention aspect also includes monitoring and surveillance of known offenders, typically on probation or aftercare. One COP officer in South Florida explains that he does "a lot of 'street counseling' (more like lecturing) with kids—often telling them that he doesn't care whether their mother is on crack and father is long gone, they still have to have respect for themselves and other people" (Bazemore & Senjo 1997, 73).

3. Community policing incorporates problem solving and diversion. One officer described a creative solution to the problem of fighting between Haitians and African Americans. The COP officers sponsored a flag football game of police versus teams of both Haitians and African Americans offering to sponsor a pizza party if the kids won. If the police won, the youths would have to agree to stop fighting "Well we won and they stopped fighting," the officer observed, "and we gave them a pizza party anyway . . ." (Bazemore & Senjo 1997, 74).

Evaluations of other youth-oriented community policing projects have also had positive results (Chaiken 1998; Thurman, Giacomazzi, & Bogen 1993, 554–564). In 1999, the Youth-Focused Community Policing initiative was begun. A joint project of the Office of Juvenile Justice and Delinquency Prevention, the U.S. Department of Justice's Community Relations Services, and the Office of Community Oriented Policing Services, the initiative is designed to assist local jurisdictions in improving relationships between youth, police, community, and local government agencies. Eight cities received funds through this initiative: Boston; Chicago; Houston; Kansas City; Los Angeles; Oakland; Mound Bayou, Mississippi; and Rio Grande, Texas.

The Problem-Solving Process

Problem solving is an important aspect of community policing. The problem-solving approach is a step-by-step process for reducing the impact of social disorganization that leads to crime and delinquency. One of the most popular problem-solving models is *SARA*—Scanning, Analysis, Response, Assessment.

The SARA Model.   SARA is a four-step process used in community policing efforts.

1. *Scanning.* The identification of a cluster of similar, related incidents through a preliminary review of information. The selection of a crime or disorder problem from among competing priorities to address.

2. *Analysis.* The use of several sources of information to determine why a problem occurs, who is responsible, who is affected, where the problems occurs, when the problem occurs, and what form the problem takes. Sources of information typically include police arrest and other data, victim interviews, environmental surveys, resident and business surveys, social service and other data, and insurance information.

3. *Response.* The implementation of coordinated actions that address the most important findings of the analysis and focus on at least two of the following: (1) preventing future occurrences by deflecting offenders, (2) protecting likely victims, and (3) making crime locations less conducive to criminal behavior. Responses are designed to have a long-term impact and not require a major amount of police resources.

4. *Assessment.* The measurement of the responses on the targeted crime/disorder problem using information from multiple sources, both before and after the response has been implemented (www.usdoj.gov/cops/).

SARA and Youth Disorder.   In 1995, the town of Danvers, Massachusetts, took the problem-solving approach in response to vandalism in the downtown business district. Many residents, particularly elderly citizens, feared being injured by skateboarders and inline skaters. Skaters had done considerable damage to steps, benches, and railings in the downtown area. Elected officials formed the Skateboard-Inline Skating Committee. Police officers conducted interviews with merchants, customers, and youth in the downtown area. Much of the vandalism occurred during after-school hours; the incidents involved youths who used the downtown area to ride skateboards because they did not have a convenient location or facilities made for this purpose.

The town developed a two-fold response: it decided to build a skateboard park in a recreational area near downtown Danvers and it passed a local ordinance prohibiting inline skating and skateboarding within the downtown business area. The park provided a safe location for skateboarding and inline skating and is overseen by the recreation department. Assessment of the response revealed a lower level of fear among customers and no reports of skating downtown. (Office of Community Oriented Policing Services 1999).

Prevention and Intervention Programs

Because community policing is an elastic concept encompassing a broad range of ideas, it can offer many delinquency prevention and intervention programs. These programs may also be offered through crime prevention and police-community relations efforts.

Police Athletic League.   PAL stands for "police athletic league" or "police activities league." It is a juvenile crime prevention program that provides educational, recreational, and athletic programs to young people. With the help of police officers and community volunteers, PAL seeks to improve attitudes among the youths. The programs aim to promote a positive relationship between youths and police officers while bringing youths under supervision of responsible adults who serve as mentors, tutors, and positive role models. In this way, young people learn values and skills needed to become productive citizens.

What eventually became the PAL program began in Sacramento, California, in 1914 by providing sports programs for youth. Captain John Sweeney insisted that participation in recreational programs provided a deterrent to juvenile delinquency. His idea followed the English model of the early nineteenth century whereby organized sports became a standard at schools to provide an alternative to stealing, bullying, and drinking. In the 1930s, police departments all over California and across the country began to develop PAL programs. In 1974, a group of Sacramento police officers formally organized the Sacramento Police Athletic League with 15 children and a boxing program in one of the city's poorest neighborhoods (www.sacpal.com).

More recently, PAL programs have expanded to include a wide range of activities in recreation, arts, and education. The Sacramento Police Athletic League offers painting, drawing, coloring, computer learning, web page design, and other activities. The Center has two computer labs, a library, and an after-school homework assistance program. The Minneapolis Police Athletic League is a nonprofit organization sponsored by the Minneapolis Police Department. The program offers a wide range of sports activities for boys and girls, including football, basketball, soccer, weightlifting, softball, baseball, golf, volleyball, and hockey along with outdoor recreational events, such as camping, swimming, and fishing. In addition to the athletic programs, cultural and academic enrichment activities are offered through the Children's Theatre Company, Walker Art Center, and Children's Museum of Minnesota. The Back-on-Track program is a remedial reading program for PAL junior high students who are referred by a police officer (www.ci.minneapolis.mn.us/police).

Police Explorer Programs.   Explorer programs provide an opportunity for young men and women between 15 and 21 years of age who are interested in a law enforcement career to participate in various police activities. Explorers participate in community service and crime prevention activities and have the opportunity to learn first aid and CPR training. If qualified, Explorers ride along with patrol officers to learn aspects of criminal law, building searches, crime scene investigation, felony and traffic stops, working traffic collisions, and firearm safety.

The Pasadena Police Department's Explorer Program offers a 22-week Explorer Academy. Graduates receive the title of Police Explorer. Participants meet twice a month and participate in weekend activities featuring work details, competitions, and social events. Work details provide the city with volunteers for civic events held at the Rose Bowl, City Hall, and Civic Center. In addition to softball, volleyball, and basketball, competitions are held in building searches, foot pursuits, driving skills, drug raids, and drill team. Social events include trips to Disneyland, Dodger Stadium, picnics, ice skating, and other activities. The program also offers scholarships toward college (www.ci.pasadena.ca.us/police). The Phoenix Police Department's Explorer Post, part of the Boy Scouts of America, operates as a co-educational, young-adult program developed and supervised by the Phoenix Police Department along with community organizations, businesses, and individuals. Participants may become a probationary Explorer after passing the entrance exam and an oral interview. Explorers ride with patrol officers; compete in the annual Explorer Academy competitions; take part in out-of-state trips and sporting events; provide community service, such as crowd control at parades and neighborhood cleanup; receive training for personal fitness; and participate in outdoor activities, such as backpacking, hiking, and camping (www.ci.phoenix.az.us/police).

Police and Minority Youths

The tension between police and young people is greatest between the police and minority youth, especially young African American people. Community policing seeks to improve police relations with residents of black majority neighborhoods, yet tension remains. Black men charge that police single them out for scrutiny, harassment, and mistreatment. This suggests that community policing, while ubiquitous, has not completely replaced conventional police organization.

Police Subculture

Academy training represents the initial step in the process of professionalization. During this process, police officers begin to acquire the knowledge and skills needed to enter the profession of law enforcement. Through professionalization, police officers begin to internalize the standards, values, and ethics necessary for self-regulation. A professional need not be watched directly by a supervisor who must constantly enforce work rules because professionals carry these work rules within themselves. Academy training also initiates the process of socialization. This is a complex process that "contributes to the individual's personality, permits participation in group life, and acceptance of the beliefs and values of the group" (Albert & Dunham 1992, 88).

Socialization shapes what has been called the ***police subculture.*** Police officers share many of the attitudes and beliefs of the American culture, the customary way of acting prevalent in the larger society. Police officers, however, develop beliefs, traditions, and values owing to their vocation that differ from the larger culture. Curiously, the meaning of subculture comes closer to the root word for culture than the contemporary understanding of the word culture. The word originated from the idea of *cult,* that of a tightly knit group committed fervently to an idea or a person. Dale Bowlin, who served as chief of the Miami-Metro Dade Police Department, describes officers who adopt the police subculture as persons who "become cynical in a few years and tend to isolate themselves within the police culture. Their friends are police officers; they talk primarily about job-connected interests and concern themselves to a great degree with the stupidity displayed by anyone who is not a police officer. As a result, a feeling of 'us against them' dominates their lives and robs them of any real or prolonged happiness . . . " (Albert & Dunham 1992, 89). Chief Bowlin is not saying that all police officers share the police personality; he is saying police officers can develop cultlike devotion to the profession owing to the nature of police organizations.

Citizens have not always respected law enforcement officials, whether county sheriffs, municipal police, or provost marshals in early colonial times. Lawmakers in colonial North Carolina abolished the office of provost marshal in favor of the county sheriff due to the neglect of duty "which hath occasioned great Murmurs and Discontents among the Inhabitants of this Province . . . " (Campbell 1986, 6–7). Sheriffs did not fare any better, held in disdain by attorneys and the well-to-do who attempted to shield themselves from appointment to the office. By 1841, when several towns had organized paid watches, the North Carolina *Standard* quipped, "Of all the tyrannies in the world, that of the city police is the most ridiculous and absurd" (Campbell 1986, 8).

As a result, police organizations have developed an organizational culture that engenders formation of a subculture. Police organizations have pursued a bureaucratic structure requiring a chain of command, written policies, and formal communication. Goals come from the top of the organization; mission, values, and status come from within. Activities are expressed in written directives, and communicated down through the ranks; police officers communicate with one another, from superior to subordinate, in a language foreign to non-police officers. Police have sought professional status through credentials and statutory authority. This emphasizes a distinction between sworn and nonsworn personnel, between insiders and outsiders. In addition, the constant threat of personal danger while on patrol—the backbone of police work—encourages solidarity with those who have been there. Given the pattern of public criticism, police organizations avoid external scrutiny, whether from media, other government officials, or even rival law enforcement organizations. They limit information about activities, decisions, and practices to those thought capable of making appropriate judgments—other police officials, and preferably, colleagues, who really understand.

Community policing attempts nothing less than a transformation of police culture. Joseph Santiago, Director of Police in Newark, New Jersey, describes the shift to community-policing strategies as a work in progress more than two decades after the Foot Patrol Experiment described by Wilson and Kelling. Immediately after assuming the top post in 1996, Santiago began a plan to change the way the department does business. The plan sought to improve response time to calls and reduce open-air drug trafficking within the city. Santiago's plan helped reduce crime, curb corruption within the ranks, and improve the city's image. It also sought to change the organizational culture from reactive to proactive. "Changing the organizational culture," he concludes, "represents the most challenging aspect of the new direction. The process of creating a high-performance organization which embraces integrity and community values and welcomes the active participation of a wide range of collaborative partners continues to represent our greatest internal struggle" (Santiago 2001, 11). Santiago points to compstat as an effective means of organizational renewal because it can bring accountability to police managers. COMPSTAT is a computerized crime-mapping system, developed by the New York City Police Department, to provide performance measures in police management.

The difficulty in transforming the organizational culture of a police department helps explain why community policing does not necessarily lead to improved police relations with minority youths, particularly African Americans. The tension between youths and police is most visible between black youth and white police officers. "Many of us have observed for some time what is best described as a growing polarization between the police and the African American Community. . . ." Lee P. Brown has said, "If those of us in leadership positions saw this polarization happening and did not do something about it, then we would not be serving those that we represent very well" (Baker Institute for Public Policy 1997).

Delores Jones-Brown, a professor at John Jay College of Criminal Justice, analyzed surveys completed by 125 African American youths who resided in five towns in a suburban county in central New Jersey. She asked them about direct contact with police, indirect contact (reports from friends), and attitudes toward police. A majority of those surveyed viewed the police as a repressive rather than a helpful agency. Although few of the young men had involvement with juvenile court, about half had five or more encounters with the police. About half of the direct encounters and indirect encounters left unfavorable impressions. The respondents attributed these unfavorable encounters to the officer's attitude, to physical handling by the officer, or to perceived racial motivation, "They stopped us because we were black." Jones-Brown concluded that increasing the frequency of police contacts with citizens, a primary goal of community policing, will not lead to improved attitudes toward police among black youth (Jones-Brown 2000, 209–229).

Driving While Black

Jones-Brown's research contributes to decades of research exploring the influence of race on police decision making. During the 1960s, researchers found that young black men who dressed like tough guys received more attention from police than other youths. This increased surveillance led to more police intervention, questioning, and harassment. They noted that the black youth stopped by police received relatively severe dispositions when they displayed a hostile demeanor. The youth responded with indifference or increased hostility and the police responded with increased surveillance and greater numbers of referrals to juvenile court (Pillalvin, Irving, & Briar 1964, 206–214).

More recently, Janice Joseph, a professor of criminal justice at Richard Stockton College in New Jersey, surveyed black youth. She reported that 60 percent of black youth surveyed claimed that the police harassed them. The harassment included unnecessary stops, unjustified seizures of jewelry and other personal property, and verbal insults using racial slurs. Several youths reported being taken to the police department for questioning for possessing a large amount of cash. The police viewed carrying cash as a sign of drug dealing, and if the young black male could not provide an adequate explanation for the source of the money, the police seized the money even though no arrest was made. Others reported being stopped and frisked for hanging out with their friends. The police justify their methods by arguing that certain urban neighborhoods are hot spots for crime and that young black men in these areas are likely to engage in delinquency and crime. The black males view this as unwarranted harassment and react by being uncooperative when questioned. The police in turn interpret this behavior as a sign of badness and are more likely to increase their surveillance and make arrests in the area (Joseph 1995, 76).

Katheryn Russell, a criminologist at the University of Maryland, conducted focus groups with young black men. She observes that young black men report being pulled over by police and that the the practice has acquired its own acronym: DWB or "Driving While Black" (Russell 1998, 33). Russell reviewed computer records of motorist stops collected by the Maryland State Police as part of a settlement in the case of a Washington, D.C., lawyer. The black professional had been stopped while returning with his family from a funeral in Chicago because he fit the profile of a drug courier. Between 1995 and 1997, Maryland troopers conducted 533 searches along a 50-mile stretch of Interstate 95 between Baltimore and the Delaware line. Seventy-seven percent (409) of the searches conducted by Maryland troopers involved vehicles driven by black motorists, 18 percent involved white drivers, and 1 percent were Hispanic motorists. The troopers found drugs on 33 percent of the black motorists and 22 percent of the white motorists. While the police relied on the percentage difference between those found with drugs to justify the pattern of traffic stops, Russell notes the larger percentage of black motorists stopped for which no contraband was found. This greater scrutiny of blacks by police engenders unfavorable attitudes. As Robert Wilkins, the plaintiff in the case explained, "[There] is no compensation for the type of humiliation and degradation you feel when for no other reason than the color of your skin . . . you're charged and placed in the category of a drug trafficker" (Russell 1998, 33).

The judiciary has supported the use of racial profiling in traffic stops in the "out of place" doctrine. This doctrine allows for the use of race as the basis for a stop if that person is in an area where another race predominates. Russell notes the large number of well-known black men who fit the profile and have been stopped. These include: Marcus Allen (athlete), LeVar Burton (actor), Calvin Butts (pastor, university president), Wynton Marsalis (musician), Will Smith (actor), Wesley Snipes (actor), Roger Wilkins (professor), and William J. Williams (professor). Mae Jemison, the first African American woman astronaut, was stopped in her hometown and arrested for an outstanding parking ticket. Jemison's close-cropped hair has led some to surmise that she was stopped because the officer mistook her for a black man. In 1999, when Representative Conyers introduced the Traffic Stops Statistics Act in Congress the Fraternal Order of Police lobbied against the measure, while the National Organization of Black Law Enforcement Executives issued a policy statement supporting the measure. The legislation would require the Attorney General to conduct a nationwide study on racial bias in traffic stops.

The Victims of Crime

The tragedy of difficult police–minority community relations is that black youths suffer the highest victimization rate from violent crime (Bastian & Taylor 1994). Researchers from the John F. Kennedy School of Government at Harvard University analyzed youth homicide in Boston from 1990 to 1994. The researchers found that youth homicide was confined almost entirely to the city's poor, African American neighborhoods, and that black men between the ages of 15 and 21 committed most of the homicides. Firearms were the weapon of choice. The researchers also reviewed emergency room visits for nonfatal gunshot and sharp instrument wounds. They reviewed data on 155 youth murder victims and 125 known youth offenders who committed gun or knife homicides. They found that both victims and offenders had had some degree of prior criminal involvement including court actions ranging from arraignments to sentences of probation (OJJDP 1999, 27).

Nationally, young African American men experience the highest homicide victimization rate of any race or gender. Homicides involving firearms have been the leading cause of death for African American males between the ages of 15 and 19 since 1969. Although black juveniles accounted for only 15 percent of the juvenile population, more black juveniles than white juveniles were murdered between 1988 and 1995. In the early 1980s, the juvenile homicide rate for black youths was four times the white rate. In 1993, the black rate peaked at seven times the white rate, and by 1997 had declined to five times the white rate. Between 1980 and 1997, in homicides where the race of the offender could be determined, 92 percent of juveniles were murdered by a member of the same race. The percentage of same race homicides was slightly higher for blacks (94 percent) than for whites (91 percent) (Snyder & Sickmund 1999, 18).

Summary

The name and idea, "police," encompasses a variety of law enforcement organizations. There are state police agencies, county sheriff's offices, city police departments, and special district police. A juvenile's contact with police may involve a patrol officer who has no special training or interest in juvenile matters. Many city police departments, particularly those in medium-sized and large cities, do have specialized units of officers assigned to juveniles. Officers assigned to juvenile units search for missing young people, investigate cases of abuse and neglect, and generally assist other officers in cases involving young people. Juvenile units typically include proactive policing programs such as drug education, school resource officers, and gang intervention.

Police encounters with juveniles resemble those with adults in several ways. Since *In Re Gault,* the judiciary has generally found that juvenile suspects are entitled to at least the same due process safeguards as adult suspects. In some policework, such as investigatory stops, interrogations, and fingerprinting of youths, special rules apply. The police retain a great deal of discretion in responding to the juveniles they encounter. Police may pursue several courses of action in dealing with a juvenile suspect including diversion to a social service or community-based program. Policework with juveniles involves a certain degree of role strain, that is, confusion between the law enforcement and social work aspects of policework with juveniles. This tension between the role of the police officer who works with juveniles as a social worker rather than a police officer has deep roots in American policing. Historically, the policework with juveniles and the creation of juvenile units coincided with the introduction of women to policing and the creation of women's bureaus to deal with wayward youth.

Community policing has the potential to redefine the police–juvenile role. Community policing has transformed policework in general and policework with youth in particular. Community policing emphasizes proactive activities designed to solve neighborhood problems in partnership with citizens. Problem solving is an important aspect; it involves scanning, analysis, response, and assessment. Prevention and intervention are other important aspects of community policing. Two of the most widely used programs in working with youth are the police athletic league (PAL), and the police explorer posts.

Youths tend to have a difficult relationship with police; this is particularly true in the case of black youths. During the 1990s, DWB, or Driving While Black, came to the attention of the media and courts as young black men were stopped more often than their white counterparts. The phrase captures the sense of being singled out that many young black men experience in their encounters with police. Tragically, it is young black men who need police protection the most. Young black men experience the highest victimization rate for violent crime, particularly homicide. There are several strategies to improve police relations with the African American community; these include deployment of black officers in black neighborhoods, deployment of the same police officer in the same neighborhood, and police serving as mentors for young black people.

KEY CONCEPTS

adjustment	discretion	role conflict
arrest	gang intervention	SARA model
booking	juvenile division	school resource officer
community policing	least restrictive alternative	totality of circumstances
custody	police subculture	women's bureaus
DARE	reasonable suspicion	

DISCUSSION QUESTIONS

1. What qualifications should a juvenile specialist in a police department possess?

2. Should police exercise greater discretion in their encounters with juveniles?

3. Does community policing provide a meaningful way of reducing the tension between police and minority youth?

LEARNING ACTIVITY: SMALL GROUPS

Because police initiate the juvenile justice process, police officers are often the ones to implement public policy concerning juveniles. When the public cannot agree on the appropriate response, police officers must make difficult decisions. This is the case with runaways, who occupy a status in public policy somewhere between victim and lawbreaker. First, divide into groups of four or five; next, read the information below and formulate your response. Finally, choose one member of the group to report to the class.

Runaways create a legal and a practical dilemma for police. California law, similar to that of other states, prohibits the secure detention of runaways. If the police cannot locate a parent or guardian, the child may be taken to juvenile hall. The juvenile hall must keep runaways confined separately from those convicted of a criminal offense. These halls with limited space are reserved for detention of youth in varying time periods: up to 12 hours to determine whether there are outstanding warrants; up to 24 hours to locate a parent and arrange family reunification; or up to 72 hours to arrange unification with a parent out of state. San Francisco, a destination for many interstate runaways, has only three residential facilities with a total capacity of less than forty. California police officers complain that they are placed in the role of temporary babysitters; that "they're driving around for hours. They don't know what to do with these kids. Nobody wants them. And nobody will take them. These kids are displaced. What are we supposed to do with them?" (Joe 1995, 50).

There is tension between the police and shelter care workers. "There's always some tension because the kids are on one side, and the police are on the other, and the center is in the middle," one shelter care worker explains. "The center has to obey the laws, yet we want to help the kids. We don't want the word getting around that we're siding with the police." The counselors know about the streets, about drug trafficking and prostitution, but do not want the kid to talk to police because then the child's life will be in danger. Some shelter care workers complain that the police "barge into the place, looking for certain kids." "They think we're only interested in busting and convictions," observed one California detective, and there is a lack of communication because "the counselors want to protect certain kids." But because the shelters are not secure and invoke strict program rules, many youth simply "walk in the front door" and "out the back door." The police worry that their own efforts contribute to a system that does not work (Joe 1995, 50).

Until the 1970s, the police had a wide variety of legal and practical options in dealing with runaways. Beginning with the Juvenile Justice and Delinquency Act of 1974, legislators began a rethinking of law enforcement's response. The act called for the deinstitutionalization of status offenders (DSO movement), meaning a general reluctance to place runaways in detention facilities. The JJDP Act contained the Runaway and Homeless Youth Act, which specified federal funding for runaway programs through the Department of Health and Human Services. Deinstitutionalization called for placement of youth into community-based programs rather than detention, noting that juveniles have a right to freedom from custody. Many states enacted statutes prohibiting or limiting secure custody for status offenders. Most states passed restrictions on dealing with runaways. Law enforcement authorities do not have power to arrest, nor does the juvenile court have the power to detain runaways.

Beginning with the Reagan Administration, federal policy shifted. The Juvenile Justice and Delinquency Act came under attack for failing to deal with the fact that youths accounted for a disproportionately high percentage of violent crimes. The National Advisory Committee for Juvenile Justice and Delinquency Prevention in 1984 recommended that federal efforts get tough with the serious, violent, and chronic young offenders. That same year, the Office of Juvenile Justice and Delinquency Prevention issued a report insisting that the DSO movement had backfired. The policy had emancipated children, from both the authority of the police and juvenile court and from their parents, releasing too many from safe environments to exploitation on the streets. Children on the streets become prey for those drawing them into lives of drug dealing, prostitution, and pornography. The law made the police mere bystanders, preventing them from interventions that would protect youth from more serious criminal victimization.

In addition to the policy shift and legal restrictions, there are resource limitations. At the same time that federal funding for community diversion programs ended there was the demise of the Law Enforcement Assistance Administration. Because many states and counties were unwilling or unable to assume the costs for alternative programs, the number of alternatives to detention has diminished. Although funding through Health and Human Services has increased over the years, there are too few runaway shelters and youth homes available. As one director in California describes shelters for runaways "The residential programs want to help the less risky ones, the first and second time runners. Those kids are easier to work with. While there is some benefit in trying to get the kids at the early stages of street life, this still leaves a set of kids out of the picture" (Joe 1995, 49).

11 The Juvenile Court Process

CHAPTER OBJECTIVES

On completing this chapter, students will have tools to:

- Improve their understanding of the role court systems play in America
- Examine the roles of the prosecutor and the defense attorneys in juvenile court
- Understand the juvenile court process
- Know the stages in processing a juvenile offender through the system

Evolution of the Juvenile Court System

The founders of the juvenile court might not recognize it today. It began as a social rather than a legal institution, emphasizing informality and discretionary justice. A judge or court clerk convened hearings involving youths and their parents. Attorneys for either side seldom appeared. Since the United States Supreme Court's *In Re Gault* (1967) decision, many of the due process procedures used in criminal court have been extended to juvenile court. *Gault* prosecutors routinely appear, so judges must protect the rights of the accused, which includes appointment of legal counsel, and in some states, a jury trial. State legislatures have adopted statutory guidelines designed to limit the discretion once thought to be at the center of the juvenile court. Even the presumption of private, confidential proceedings has changed as legislators respond to demands for accountability and public safety.

This chapter explores the juvenile court, its workings and organization. The first part reviews the structure of courts, the organization of juvenile court, and two alternative structures—family court and juvenile drug court. The second section examines the role of three major decision makers in juvenile court: prosecutors, defense attorneys, and judges. Part three explains the major steps in delinquency proceedings, beginning with intake, transfer, adjudication, and disposition.

Organization of Juvenile Court

For a hundred years, juvenile court has been a part of the American court system. The juvenile court grew out of Progressive Era reforms that led to specialized courts in cities. Later, they were incorporated into state court systems during the movement for court unification. More recently, two alternative courts for juveniles have appeared: family court and drug court.

America's Courts

The United States has a dual court system, that is, a federal system and the systems of the 50 states. Although the nation's court system began with the federal system, federal courts have a limited role in juvenile justice. Juvenile court originated as a specialized court within state court systems. Since unification, which began in 1940, juvenile court has become part of the system of trial courts in the states.

Federal Courts.   The Constitutional framers who met at Independence Hall in Philadelphia provided for a federal court system but left the details to the legislature. Congress devoted its entire first session to this issue and eventually enacted the Judiciary Act of 1789, which, along with the Reorganization Act of 1801, established the federal court system. Unlike the maze of specialized courts in England, the founders created a simple, three-tiered system. At the lowest level are district courts: one district covers each state and serves as the trial courts. At the highest level sits the court of last resort. It is staffed by associate justices and a chief justice and resolves appeals surrounding the trial judges' application of the law. On the middle level are the circuit courts, now known as circuit courts of appeal, which relieve case pressure on the court of last resort.

Because the delegates to the First Congress feared that creation of a national court system would intrude on the authority of the states, they were careful to create courts of limited jurisdiction. For criminal activity to be within federal jurisdiction, it must arise under a specific statute enacted by the U.S. Congress. Some crimes, such as counterfeiting, racketeering, blackmail, treason, mail fraud, and illegal immigration are prohibited by federal law and can be prosecuted only in federal courts. Congress left the bulk of criminal prosecutions, including those involving juveniles, to the states.

There is no separate juvenile justice component within the federal system. Federal courts did not receive legal authority to distinguish between adults and juveniles until the Federal Juvenile Delinquency Act of 1938. The act included provisions for hearing cases promptly, privately, and without a jury; for detention apart from adult criminals; and authorized flexibility in the treatment of youths. Federal law requires that U.S. attorneys restrict proceedings against juveniles unless there is a substantial federal interest and the state does not have jurisdiction, lacks adequate programs and services, or the offense is a violent felony, drug-trafficking, or firearms offense. In 1997, there were less than 200 juveniles in federal custody. Federal jurisdiction in Indian Country accounts for most of these. The U.S. District Court has jurisdiction over all felony and some misdemeanor crimes committed in Indian Country as well as all delinquent acts committed in Indian Country. (Probation/Pretrial Service 1997; Scalia 1997).

State Courts. Constitutions drafted in the various states followed the federal example by providing for the appointment of justices of the peace in each county. These justices resolved matters individually and sat as a county court. The state constitutions created appellate courts called courts of appeals or supreme courts. These courts were set up mostly to resolve land disputes and provide clear titles. Judges were appointed by the governor. Any other disputes that might need to be resolved were left to the legislature, to create additional courts as needed.

The legislatures created a confusing array of courts, which carried the names of English courts, but not necessarily their function. Kentucky's general assembly created three different court systems. Lawmakers created courts of quarterly sessions to handle civil matters other than land titles, county courts to deal with administrative matters within the county, and courts of oyer and terminer, which had criminal jurisdiction (Ireland 1972). To cope with the increasing volume of cases, state legislatures created new courts by splitting existing courts along more specific geographic boundaries. There were superior courts, justice of the peace courts, magistrate's courts, county criminal courts, and courts of common pleas. In addition, home rule provisions under state law allowed cities to create their own courts as they saw fit. City councils and commissioners added mayor's courts, city courts, police courts, municipal courts, and recorder's court to the county courts and city-county courts. Justices of the peace were eager to trade favorable decisions for additional business. Some maintained an office, others decided cases part-time on a front porch, over a butcher shop counter, or at a fairground ticket booth.

Around 1900, court reformers began to talk about court unification. The unplanned and rather sudden growth of courts led to tremendous confusion. Jurisdiction overlapped so that cases might by heard in several courts depending on the choice of the litigants. These courts suffered from inadequate financing, lax court procedures, inadequate facilities, and unbalanced caseloads. Organizations such as the American Judicature Society and the American Bar Association advocated a consolidated state courts structure to deal with the variety of problems. ***Court unification*** involves a simplified court structure, centralized administration and rule-making, and statewide financing. In 1947, New Jersey passed a new state constitution that allowed the chief justice to appoint an administrative director for state courts. By 1952 14 other states enacted similar measures (Peak 1995, 62).

The system that emerged in most states follows a ***four-tiered structure,*** consisting of two levels of trial courts and two levels of appellate courts. The first level of trial courts, or the court of limited jurisdiction, is variously known as justice of the peace, city, county, magistrate, and municipal courts. These typically hear misdemeanor cases, civil cases of limited amounts, preliminary stages of felony cases (arrest and search warrants, probable cause hearings), ordinance violations, traffic matters, domestic and family-related issues, and infractions related to alcohol, boating, and game and fish violations. The second level of trial courts, or the court of general jurisdiction, is known as superior, circuit, common pleas, district, and in New York, supreme court. This is the state court of original jurisdiction for felony cases, civil cases above a certain amount, and some appeals from lower courts which are heard *de novo* (tried again).

The first level of appellate courts, or intermediate court of appeal, hears appeals from both levels of trial courts as well as administrative agencies. The judges rarely sit *en banc* (altogether), but typically in panels of three across the state. At the top, there is the court of last resort, or state supreme court. The state supreme courts hear cases of significance to the state as a whole. It is the ultimate review for all matters concerning the state constitution. Two states, Texas and Oklahoma, have separate supreme courts for civil and criminal matters. But in most states, there is a single supreme court to handle the two types of cases. Cases come to the supreme court when the court grants a petition for discretionary review. Some cases come by right, meaning that they are heard automatically. Murder cases in which the defendant has been sentenced to death or life imprisonment are appealed by right directly to the state supreme court.

Unification made courts the responsibility of state government. Prior to unification, counties had extensive responsibility for the financing and operation of courts. Now, virtually all the costs of operating the court are paid by the state, along with the salaries of judges, prosecutors, public defenders, clerks, and other court personnel. The counties retain some responsibilities, however. Counties, and cities in some states, must provide space and furniture for courts. Typically county sheriff's departments provide bailiffs. The bailiff opens and closes the courts, assists jurors, and provides security.

The Juvenile Court

The juvenile court first appeared in 1899 during the specialization of courts in the Progressive Era. The Illinois legislature enacted the first juvenile court law on April 21, 1899. Enthusiasm among Progressive Era reformers led to the establishment of other juvenile courts modeled after Chicago's. In Colorado, Judge Ben Lindsey, using the models of the Illinois act and that of Massachusetts, succeeded in having the Colorado juvenile court statute passed in 1903. By 1923, every state except for Connecticut and Wyoming had enacted juvenile court statutes establishing special courts for juveniles (Roberts 1998, 125).

The reformers organized these juvenile courts as separate organizations. In form and function, they resembled social institutions removed from the court system. Some cities housed juvenile court in courtrooms separate from the county courthouse. Juvenile matters were heard in separate courtrooms, roped off from criminal courts. Other cities combined juvenile courts with domestic relations courts, or they created city-county courts with overlapping jurisdiction. Court unification efforts, beginning in the 1940s, led to the incorporation of juvenile courts within state court systems.

Organizationally, juvenile court may be a division of the state's trial court of limited jurisdiction, general jurisdiction, or a separate entity. Juvenile court structure differs from state-to-state; within some states the structure differs from county-to-county, so that juvenile court may be part of one court structure in one part of the state and be located in a different court structure in another part. H. Ted Rubin summarizes the variation in juvenile court structure:

General jurisdiction trial courts are upper-level courts or the only trial courts within a state. Jurisdiction is unlimited, except where other, more specialized trial courts have been created to hear other cases. The judicial caseloads of these courts include adult felonies, civil suits, and juvenile cases.

Limited jurisdiction trial courts are lower-level courts whose jurisdiction is limited by law. Judicial caseload includes misdemeanors, ordinance violations, preliminary stages of felony proceedings, and limited civil cases. In some states, juvenile court is a division of this category.

Special jurisdiction trial courts are autonomous, that is to say, separate from other trial courts. They are granted jurisdiction over subject matter or categories of persons. These include juvenile, family, probate courts (Rubin 1996, 42).

In many urban jurisdictions, juvenile court occurs in a building separate from the county courthouse downtown. Juvenile court centers, located in suburban areas, typically include the office of juvenile probation and a juvenile detention center. In other areas, particularly rural counties, juvenile court is held in a courtroom in the same courthouse where other courts are held. Juvenile cases may be docketed for one afternoon every week, one day per week, or more frequently, depending on the size of the jurisdiction. Because juvenile proceedings are confidential, persons unrelated to the case may not be present in the courtroom. In these situations, when the judge is ready to hear the juvenile *docket,* the bailiff clears the courtroom and the judge announces the first case.

Some juvenile courts, such as Denver's, are mandated by state constitution, but that is the exception. Juvenile courts are statutory courts. State statutes determine the type of cases that can be brought to the court, the age of youths whose cases are to be heard, the procedures used in processing delinquents, and the authority of judicial officers at each stage in the proceedings. State legislatures fund some of the costs, local government entities fund others. Local governments may enact curfew and traffic ordinances whose violations are heard in juvenile court. A state supreme court may promulgate rules concerning juvenile procedure, but state law determines the court's primary subject matter (Rubin 1996, 41).

From its inception juvenile court jurisdiction has extended to an array of child welfare and child-protection cases, such as those dealing with orphaned and abandoned children. ***Child protection proceedings*** refer to those proceedings in juvenile court that may lead to emergency removal of a child from the home, placement of the child into foster care or some other out-of-home placement, and termination of parental rights and adoption. Although serious physical or sexual abuse may lead to proceedings in criminal court against one or both parents, the typical finding in juvenile court child protection proceedings is dependency. A dependent child is in need of state care because there is no parent or caretaker responsible for the child, or the parent is unable to provide adequate care for the child due to a physical or mental incapacity.

The juvenile court's responsibility in these cases has traditionally been to determine the facts of the case, to ensure the child's protection, and to protect the rights of parents. During the last two decades, the juvenile court's responsibility has been enlarged. The courts must now ensure that child welfare agencies are responsive to families. Juvenile courts are now authorized to place children removed for abuse, neglect, or dependency into permanent homes. Child protection proceedings begin with a petition alleging abuse, neglect, or dependency. Petitions are screened by the state's child welfare agency, typically the county department of social services. An emergency removal or shelter care hearing is held before the juvenile court judge to determine whether temporary removal of the child from the home is justified. An adjudication hearing follows, to determine whether the abuse or neglect occurred as alleged in the petition, followed by a dispositional hearing to decide whether the child can be returned home and if not, to order some other permanent placement for the child.

Alternative Juvenile Courts

Family Court.   The family court began about the same time as the juvenile court, as reformers turned their attention to families. Starting in Cincinnati, Ohio, in 1914 courts with jurisdiction over both children and families began to appear in cities, including Des Moines, St. Louis, Omaha, Portland, Gulfport, and Baton Rouge. In 1959, three working groups collaborated to produce the Standard Family Court Act to assist states interested in family courts. After publication of the Act, several states created family courts. Rhode Island began its family court in 1961, New York a year later, and Hawaii in 1965 (Babb 1998, 32:35–37).

Since 1961, when Rhode Island first adopted a statewide unified family court system, five other states have started unified family courts, four others have started regional family courts, and eight have pilot programs. The Family Court of Jefferson County, Kentucky, was piloted by a grant from the Edna McConnell Clark Foundation. In 1995, the Robert Wood Johnson Foundation of Princeton, New Jersey, approved a grant to the American Bar Association Standing Committee on Substance Abuse to fund demonstration family court projects in Atlanta, Baltimore, Seattle, Washington, D.C., and San Juan, Puerto Rico (Barnes 1996, 22).

The central idea of *family court* is that, rather than shuffle family matters from court to court to resolve disputes that stem from a single source, such as domestic violence or drug abuse, all matters related to a single family would be heard by a family court judge according to the "one judge—one family" principle. If there are no family courts, judges may issue a ruling without the knowledge of another court's ruling, or a judge may need to wait to make a decision until another court has decided an particular aspect of the case. Lack of coordination and duplication of services creates higher costs and delays in resolving issues. As Roscoe Pound, Dean of Harvard Law School and an early advocate of family court explains, "Treating the family situation as a series of single controversies may often not do justice to the whole or the several parts. The several parts are likely to be distorted in considering them apart from the whole, and the whole may be left undetermined in a series of adjudications of the parts" (Pound 1959, 164).

Family court models differ, but their jurisdiction may include: marital actions, juvenile proceedings, adoptions, paternity actions, civil commitments, protection orders, and criminal cases resulting from domestic violence. Family court jurisdiction may extend to intrafamily criminal cases and lawsuits between family members. The broadest jurisdiction for family court would include abuse and neglect, adoption, child custody, child support, divorce, domestic violence, paternity, and termination of parental rights as well as juvenile delinquency and status offenses (truancy, runaway, and so on). Concurrent adult criminal jurisdiction over crimes involving family members is the furthest extent of family court jurisdiction. This jurisdiction has been controversial in the area of domestic violence because critics fear that incorporating these crimes into family court will lessen the perception of the severity of the crimes (Barnes 1996, 23).

If unresolved, family problems tend to develop into larger problems of delinquency and family violence. A three-site study has found that a minimum of 64 percent of abuse and neglect cases, 48 percent of delinquency cases, and 16 percent of divorce cases involving children had a different family matter adjudicated by these courts during the past five years (Rubin 1996, 6:43). When family courts have included jurisdiction over delinquency cases, they have been active in nonadversarial means of dispute resolution. Delinquency matters within the family context have been dealt with through the use of judicial conference, neighborhood dispute committees, intake service conferences, and programs featuring youth juries. Intake conferences are frequently used in resolution of status offenses involving truancy, incorrigibility, and runaways (Page 1993, 44:33).

While family courts have been funded in urban areas, many *de facto* family courts exist in rural areas where a single judge serves the county or several counties. In such one-judge courts, problems with coordination, duplication, or conflicting court orders do not arise. There remains, however, a difference in resources. Urban family courts can afford programs and professionals that rural areas lack. In an urban setting, a highly trained judge handles all matters that relate to a family with the assistance of court staff and social workers.

Juvenile Drug Courts.   The movement to establish specialized drug courts began in the 1980s. In 1989, the first ***drug court*** opened in Miami, Florida (Harrell, 1998, 1). Other juvenile drug courts appeared in 1995 in Birmingham, San Jose, Tulare (California), Las Vegas, Reno, and Salt Lake City. By 1998, juvenile drug courts had been initiated in 33 states (Drug Court Clearinghouse 1998).

The term *drug court* includes not only specialized courts, but programs featuring case management, pre-trial diversion, and treatment programs for drug offenders. Drug courts concentrate expertise in a single courtroom in order to reduce drug use and criminal activity among drug-using offenders; they also help reduce the caseloads of general felony courts. Drug courts feature early intervention, judicial involvement in the offender's progress, frequent drug testing, and immediate access to drug test results. Drug courts follow a "therapeutic jurisprudence" model that implements five elements: immediate intervention, nonadversarial adjudication, active judicial involvement, treatment programs, and clear rules and goals. They also follow a team approach that brings together the judge, prosecutor, defense attorney, treatment provider, and correctional staff (Hora, Schma, & Rosenthal 1999, 453).

The drug court judge works with the other team members to select appropriate treatment; address issues of housing, employment, and other barriers to program completion; and to monitor the offender's progress. In Miami's drug court, the defendant is charged, tried, and found or pleads guilty. The judge defers the sentence and refers the defendant to a treatment program. The judge monitors the defendant with periodic status hearings. If the defendant graduates, the charge may be dismissed or the sentence reduced. If not, the sentence is imposed (Goldkamp 1994, 110–116). The Birmingham Treatment Alternatives to

Street Crime program identifies drug-using defendants at the point of arrest and diverts them to drug court. The drug court program judge releases the defendant on bond and refers the defendant to a treatment program. The defendant appears before the judge periodically in order to monitor progress toward the treatment plan and for drug testing at each court appearance. The judge has a range of graduated sanctions, including jail time and increased frequency of drug testing. Sanctions are applied soon after program violations. The judge may dismiss the charges for those who graduate successfully from the program (Harrell, Cook, & Carver 1998, 9–13).

A juvenile drug court focuses on juvenile delinquency matters and status offenses that involve substance abusing juveniles. In a typical juvenile drug court, delinquents and status offenders who meet certain criteria are offered the option of participation in drug court as an alternative to juvenile court. To be eligible, the juvenile must have a substance abuse problem and not have committed a violent offense. The judge maintains close contact with the juvenile through weekly status hearings. The juvenile and other family members are required to participate in intensive drug treatment programs. Sanctions range from community service to detention and are used along with rewards to encourage the juvenile's completion of treatment. At the center of the juvenile drug court is a team consisting of the judge, prosecutor, treatment provider, and probation officer all working collaboratively to encourage the juvenile's rehabilitation (Kimbrough 1998, 5:11–12).

Prosecution, Defense, and the Judiciary

In 1967, the U.S. Supreme Court fundamentally changed proceedings in juvenile court with the landmark *In re Gault* case. It held that many of the due process requirements granted adults in criminal proceedings are also required in juvenile proceedings. The ruling brought defense attorneys and prosecutors to juvenile court to complete the balance of adversarial justice. Emphasis now shifted away from judges as the most important persons in the juvenile court to juveniles and their rights.

Prosecution

Although prosecutors represent the state's interest in criminal cases, few prosecutors are employees of state government. The attorney general is the state's chief law enforcement official who is allowed to prosecute offenses in any of the state's courts. The bulk of criminal prosecutions are handled by the local prosecutor known as district attorney, county attorney, state's attorney, prosecuting attorney, or commonwealth's attorney. Virtually all prosecutors are elected in county-wide elections. In most states, prosecutors have jurisdiction within the county, although in rural areas, prosecutorial districts may include two or more counties (DeFrances 1998, 2).

As elected officials, prosecutors represent important political figures. This means that for a lawyer interested in a political career, the prosecutor's office makes an excellent springboard. Many politicians, including governors, legislators, and judges, began their public careers as prosecutors. It also means that prosecutors exercise great discretionary power. They operate without the oversight of a board of commissioners and are answerable directly to the voters. The selection of cases to prosecute reflects the prosecutor's personal philosophy, community standards, and organizational resources. In cases that involve serious charges and strong evidence (several eyewitnesses), the decision to prosecute is straightforward. More often the decision requires case screening based on a combination of seriousness and evidence. The criteria used in case screening is seldom written policy. Few prosecutors have written guidelines. When asked to explain the rationale for their decisions, prosecutors suggest that case screening, like medical diagnosis, involves both "science and craft" (Forst 1983).

The prosecutor in a large city may have a staff of a hundred or more assistant prosecutors. The largest office, the District Attorney for Los Angeles County, has more than 500 assistant prosecutors. The majority of prosecutor's offices across the country, however, are much smaller, with only two or three assistant prosecutors as well as an office manager, investigator, and one or more victim's advocates. In rural areas, prosecutors are part-time public officials who practice law on the side to supplement their income (DeFrances 1998, 2–3).

Prosecutors and Juvenile Court.   Prosecutors had no role in the first 60 years of juvenile court. The Illinois Juvenile Court Act of 1899 authorized any reputable person having knowledge that a child appeared delinquent to file a petition in writing with the clerk of the court setting forth the facts. Although prosecutors likely exercised some informal case screening, the absence of the prosecutor from the formal process was consistent with the *parens patriae* juvenile court. The juvenile court had extensive informality, broadly defined jurisdiction, and unchecked authority. The mystique and authority of the court allowed probation officials to structure conferences with parents and work out a variety of informal approaches. In many communities, the juvenile court granted automatically those police, school, and parental requests for petitions, so long as the offense occurred within the court's geographic jurisdiction and the child was within the age prescribed by statute (Rubin 1980, 300–301).

Prosecutors followed defense attorneys into juvenile court. The *In Re Gault* decision in 1967 produced the adversarial model for the juvenile court that inevitably led to a breakdown of the former model of a judge assisted by probation officers. In order to balance defense counsel's entry and deal with growth in juvenile crime, prosecutors developed a parallel approach of screening police reports and criminal charges for juveniles just as they had done for adult cases. Police criticism of probation officer intake decisions also led to increased prosecutor involvement. Police officers better understand a prosecutor's decision not to file a petition due to a faulty police report than a probation officer's decision not to file a petition due to an assertion that the juvenile has become "cooperative." At the same time, defense attorneys did not object to the role of the prosecutor. Although their goals are different, they share with the prosecutor a legal background, legal language, and interest in the present offense rather than the juvenile's social background. They prefer a working relationship with prosecutors as a means of advocating for their clients rather than a probation officer's uncertain criteria (Rubin 1980, 311–312).

Prosecutor involvement in juvenile cases varies with the court system. The prosecutor reviews all complaints for sufficient probable cause before the petition can be processed. State statutes have given the prosecutor this responsibility in the interest of protecting the community. Two versions may be described as second-level and first-level prosecutor screening. In second-level screening, the prosecutor reviews petitions filed by an intake officer. The referral flows from police, to intake officer, to prosecutor. This model, which first appeared in the 1970s, initiated a trend toward prosecutor sign-off for each petition filed. This occurred as the intake function became more specialized and was assigned to a specific probation official or intake division. In these states, the intake function remains a responsibility of the judiciary, and the intake workers. In first-level prosecutor screening, the prosecutor receives all referrals directly from law enforcement and makes the decision without benefit of an intake officer. First enacted in Colorado in 1973, this model eliminates intake officials, such as probation officers, altogether, or reduces their role to detention screening. This represents the furthest evolution of prosecutor involvement. Second-level screening has become the major model and all national juvenile justice standards suggest the second-level review and petition preparation function for prosecutors (Rubin 1980, 311–312).

The introduction of prosecutors in juvenile court coincided with the adversarial model in juvenile court. Within ten years of *In re Gault,* prosecutors regularly appeared at major stages of proceedings, including detention, probable cause, adjudication, disposition, review, probation violation, and other hearings (Shine & Price 1992, 101–133). As in adult court, prosecutors have a major role in plea negotiation. A survey for the National Center for State Courts found that plea bargaining occurred in 85 percent of the largest 150 juvenile courts. In 80 percent of these, negotiations occur exclusively with prosecutors; in another 16 percent, the prosecutor is joined by a probation officer (Rubin 1985, 267).

Prosecutors also exercise tremendous influence over juvenile justice policy and practice. At the local level, they shape diversion policy and practice. In some communities, prosecutors control this decision-making process, determining which youngsters may be diverted to community agencies. In all communities, the prosecutor's influence over decision policy affects the flow of referrals to particular agencies. The prosecutor's office communicates with juvenile police officers on legal issues surrounding arrest, detention, preparation of petitions, and referrals to community programs. In many juvenile courts, the prosecutor's office advises probation officers, provides standard forms for intake, and assists in the preparation of petitions and interpretation of juvenile statutes. At the state level, prosecutors use their tremendous influence with legislatures to lobby for changes in juvenile law. Prosecutors, speaking either as representatives of large urban counties or through the voice of state organizations, such as district attorneys associations and bar associations, have a major voice whenever legislatures contemplate changes in juvenile codes.

Organization of Juvenile Prosecution.   In most jurisdictions, an assistant prosecuting attorney conducts juvenile prosecution. The size of prosecutors' offices expanded rapidly in the decade after *In re Gault.* In California, the number of attorneys in the district attorney's office had by 1977 doubled in most counties. The majority had created a separate division or designated a specific assistant district attorney to juvenile court (Sagatun & Edwards 1979, 18–19).

Assistant prosecutors serve at the pleasure of the elected official. Assistants may be assigned to prosecute cases on a variety of bases. Some prosecutors assign new assistant district attorneys to juvenile court, then move them up to adult felony court. In other districts, assistant district attorneys prosecute all types of cases on a rotating basis, prosecuting in juvenile court for several weeks or months before moving to other courts. In larger districts, one or more prosecutors may specialize in juvenile and family court, prosecuting delinquency as well as abuse, neglect, and dependency cases. Although there are assistant prosecutors who are well-trained and committed to child welfare, they are few and far between. Juvenile court often becomes a proving ground for inexperienced prosecutors because the stakes are considered to be lower than those for criminal cases (Herring 1993, 24:608).

In most jurisdictions there is no requirement for a juvenile prosecutor other than a law degree. Juvenile prosecutors need legal skills. Law school courses in criminal law provide graduates with a general knowledge of criminal law, but only a small percentage of law schools offer courses in juvenile justice. Where these courses are available, they are offered as electives. Clinical programs in law schools enable motivated law students to obtain some experience before prosecuting cases, but the juvenile prosecutor should have experience in criminal court before serving in juvenile courts. "Prosecutors see juvenile court as demeaning but end up enjoying the experience," commented one Philadelphia prosecutor. "We have to handle all types of matters from routine to very interesting and difficult crimes." But after two years, "I burned out and asked to be reassigned." Not only did the job require being in court nine days of every ten, but "it seemed that whenever the system gave a kid a break or I gave a kid a break he would come back in later on a reoffense." (Rubin 1985, 262)

Defense

Public Defense.   The defense attorney who represents the defendant may be paid by the defendant or by the government. Retained counsel, paid for by the defendant, have always been allowed in juvenile court. Those paid by the government, the court-appointed attorneys, are appointed to represent indigent defendants. *Indigents* are those defendants too poor to pay for an attorney themselves who are then entitled to legal counsel at government expense.

In *Gideon v. Wainwright* (1963), the U.S. Supreme Court held that a defendant charged with a felony, including state crimes, had the right to counsel. The Court later extended the indigent's right to counsel to all criminal prosecutions, felony and misdemeanor, which carry a sentence of imprisonment (*Argerslinger v. Hamilton* 1972). The Court essentially mandated the development of systems for indigent defense, but left the method of financing and delivery to the states and counties. Three systems have emerged throughout the country to provide legal services to indigent defendants:

(1) Public defender programs are public or non-profit organizations with salaried staff. Some states operate statewide programs in which an individual appointed by the governor, a commission, council, or board maintains a system of representation in each county. The public defender programs are the primary method in 30 states.

(2) Assigned counsel systems involve the appointment by the courts of private attorneys from a list or panel of available attorneys. In ad hoc systems, judges appoint individual attorneys on a case-by-case basis. In coordinated assigned counsel systems, an administrator oversees appointment of counsel within guidelines established for program administration.

(3) Contract attorney systems involve governmental units that secure agreements with private attorneys, bar associations, or private law firms to provide indigent services for a specific contractual period (Smith & DeFrances 1996, 1–2).

Public defender and contract systems are common in urban areas, assigned-counsel in rural areas. Prior to assignment of counsel, the defendant fills out an affidavit of indigency which the courts use to assess the defendant's financial need. Using this information, along with questions from the bench, the judge makes a finding that the defendant is indigent and appoints counsel at public expense (or in rare cases, finds that the defendant can afford private legal counsel).

Indigent Juveniles.   With *Gault* (1967), the U.S. Supreme Court determined that juveniles were entitled to the right to counsel in delinquency cases in which there was a possibility of commitment to an institution. Following the decision, state courts and legislatures extended this provision to dependency proceedings, delinquency, and in some states, to the parents of indigent defendants (Davis 1993–94, 32:817–822) beyond adjudication proceedings.

Despite these provisions, many juveniles appear in court without benefit of defense counsel. In 1993, the American Bar Association Presidential Working Group on the Unmet Legal Needs of Children and Their Families found that, "Each year, thousands of American children and youth are arrested, tried, and convicted and incarcerated in facilities that often resemble adult prisons and jails, without benefit of counsel, despite the Supreme Court's landmark 1967 decision in *In re Gault*" (ABA 1993, 60). In 1995, the American Bar Association's Juvenile Justice Center published *A Call for Justice,* a national assessment of representation of youth in juvenile court. "One of the most disturbing findings of the assessment," the researchers observed, "is that large numbers of youth across the country (Puritz *et al.* 1995, 7).

The dark secret of juvenile court, as University of Minnesota law professor Barry Feld describes it, is that counsel is routinely waived after an advisory colloquy—a meaningless technicality. In Minnesota, less than half of the juveniles adjudicated delinquent received the assistance of counsel to which they are constitutionally entitled. In only 6 of the state's 87 counties were even a majority of defendants represented; in 68 counties less than one third had counsel. Across the state, one third of juveniles were removed from their homes and a quarter of those placed in secure detention were not represented (Feld 1989,

1189). Representation ranged from 100 percent in one county to less than 5 percent in several others. "The reason they sent me up to adult," reported a Kentucky 16-year-old from county jail, "is because the judge doesn't like me and he said he is going to do all he can to get me tried as an adult. I didn't have a lawyer so I stood there all by myself" (Brooks *et al.* 1996, iv).

Among those who receive a court-appointed attorney, the quality of legal advocacy remains an issue. The ABA report cites research showing that even using "the most basic criteria of effectiveness" only 4 percent of panel attorneys provide effective representation. The ABA found "serious gaps in the training available to juvenile defenders" (Puritz *et al.* 1995, 23). The majority of training programs overlooked pretrial motions, transfer to adult court, and dispositional alternatives. *A Call for Justice* found several reasons for the ineffectiveness of counsel. The size of caseloads seriously limited the ability of lawyers to represent their clients. Although the public defender program provided training, contract attorneys lacked adequate training in juvenile law. Judges did not allow lawyers adequate time to prepare a defense; often, they did not appoint counsel until arraignment. The attorneys' lack of preparation for trial and motions, and lack of contact with the child after disposition was cited as another reason for ineffective counsel (Cooper, Puritz, & Shang 1998, 658–660).

The Role of Counsel.   Few attorneys specialize in juvenile court law. Public defense in juvenile court does not attract the most experienced attorneys. The average starting salary for juvenile defenders is among the lowest in the legal profession. A 1996 study found the average starting salary for fulltime juvenile defenders in Kentucky was $22,833 per year (Brooks *et al.* 1996, 7). Many are new attorneys, fresh from law school, who receive an assignment to juvenile court when hired by the public defender program. More than half of the public defender officers report hiring beginning lawyers to work in juvenile court. Representing children in juvenile court provides one means of establishing a law practice. Contract attorneys are primarily solo practitioners who have been in law practice for less than five years. Public defender's offices do not have budgets to send lawyers to training, nor do they have a section of the office training manual devoted to juvenile delinquency practice. "Moreover, there are significant gaps in public defender trainings" (Puritz *et al.* 1995, 11).

Juvenile court places attorneys in a professional dilemma. The ***advocate model*** of representation in juvenile court follows the lawyer's traditional role. In this model, attorneys possess a professional duty to represent their clients according to the client's point of view. This model is reflected in the Juvenile Justice Standards developed by the Institute for Judicial Administration and American Bar Association in the 1970s. The ***guardian model*** is geared to assisting the court in its decision making process; as the eyes and ears of the court, the attorney investigates and provides information to the court in both legal and social matters. The attorney advocates for the best interest of the child regardless of the child's expressed desire. When the juvenile is too young to articulate self-interest, this distinction remains philosophical. But when the juvenile can express a desire, these dual roles create a practical and ethical dilemma for the attorney, particularly in plea negotiations. (Long 1982–83, 607; Guggenheim 1996, 1399)

Programs in several states have overcome this sort of role ambiguity by pairing lawyers with social workers in juvenile cases. Maryland's Office of the Public Defender created the Juvenile Client Services Division in 1992 to improve the quality of legal representation in juvenile court. Lawyers in the Youthful Defendant Unit work with juveniles charged as adults to transfer their case to juvenile court, while social workers in the Client Assessment Recommendation and Evaluation Unit provide psychosocial assessments of clients at the request of attorneys. The Detention Response Unit, a unit of assistant public defenders and social workers, works with juveniles in detention. While the attorney investigates the situation from a legal perspective, the social worker researches alternative residential and community placements. The New York Legal Aid Society, the primary public defender agency in New York City, developed the Bronx Office of the Delinquency Unit in 1997 to maintain focus on delinquency cases. The office combines six attorneys, social workers, and a paralegal. The attorneys develop expertise in juvenile law and share trial strategies and legal expertise, while the social workers interview clients at intake and begin work on a dispositional plan. Later, the social worker appears as a witness to present the dispositional plan to the court (Puritz & Shang 1998).

Judiciary

The Judiciary.   In most states, judges are elected. In other states, judges are appointed by the governor with legislative approval; and in a dozen states commissions to recommend appointments to the governor or make appointments themselves (called merit selection). Even where the law provides for election, most judges attain office by appointment. When a vacancy occurs other than at the end of the term, such as a mid-term retirement, state statutes allow the governor to appoint a judge to fill the vacancy until the next general election. Vacancies typically occur this way. In a general election, the appointee runs for office as an incumbent and incumbents almost always prevail in judicial elections.

Although judicial reform organizations encourage specialization, most judges who hear juvenile matters are not specialists. The juvenile court exists as a division of the state's trial courts with general or limited jurisdiction; judges often remain generalists who hear cases on a periodic basis. In North Carolina, juvenile court operates as a division of district court, the state's trial court of limited jurisdiction. In judicial districts with more than one judge, the chief judge determines which judge will hear juvenile cases. In some districts, judges choose to hear juvenile cases and specialize as juvenile judges. Often judges choose not to hear any juvenile cases. In one-judge districts, typically in rural areas encompassing more than one county, the judge tries the juvenile docket along with criminal, traffic, and other dockets.

A majority of the judges who sit in juvenile court possess no special qualifications. They usually possess a law degree, although there are still a few judges holding juvenile court without a law degree. Currently, some juvenile matters may be decided by a judicial officer, known as a magistrate, referee, or commissioner. Magistrates are judicial officers who do not necessarily possess a law degree, but who are supervised by a judge.

National and state organizations exist to foster expertise among juvenile court judges. The National Council of Juvenile and Family Court Judges (NCJFCJ), headquartered in Reno on the campus of the University of Nevada, began in 1937 when a group of judges organized to focus attention on the concept of a separate court for children. The NCJFCJ provides continuing education programs at the Reno headquarters and nationwide on a variety of court management, child protection, and family-related issues. NCJFCJ also seeks to influence legislation concerning juvenile issues by testifying to Congress and submitting amicus briefs to appellate courts in juvenile cases. In North Carolina, the Administrative Office of the Courts has established a juvenile court certification process to increase the qualifications of judges who hear juvenile cases. Training provided by the Institute of Government at the University of North Carolina in Chapel Hill provides instruction in juvenile law, child development, educational issues, family dynamics, and medical signs of abuse and neglect. By statute, certification requires that the judge preside over at least 100 juvenile hearings within 12 months of completing the training (Knepper 1999, 192).

The Role of the Juvenile Judge.   Many roads led to the juvenile court bench. In states with specialized juvenile courts, such as Utah, judges come to the bench with an interest in hearing juvenile matters. Where juvenile court is a division of the state's misdemeanor or felony court, juvenile cases are assigned to judges. The duration of this assignment and the percentage of time dedicated to the judicial workload varies. Judges are either elected or appointed for a four- or six-year-term. In the most populous jurisdictions, judges take turns hearing the juvenile docket according to a rotation. Judges may work a rotation as often as once every four months, but the typical rotation lasts one year. A trend in the assignment of judges to juvenile cases appears to be heading for longer terms of two or three years. This is in response to the increased knowledge and responsibilities of the judge in juvenile proceedings. In Chicago and Los Angeles, juvenile judges specialize in particular types of juvenile cases, either delinquency or dependency. In other cities, such as Cincinnati, Denver, and Baltimore, juvenile cases are heard by magistrates, not judges. These quasi-judicial officers are attorneys appointed by the chief judge to hear certain types of cases on behalf of the court (Rubin 1996, 46–47).

"The most important person in the juvenile court is the juvenile court judge," explains Leonard P. Edwards (1992, 25), superior court judge, Santa Clara County, California. The role of the judge in juvenile court includes many nontraditional functions and combines judicial, administrative, and advocacy elements. Juvenile delinquency proceedings are complex events involving troubling matters related to family dissolution. Issues concerning the evilness of the act, youthfulness of the defendant, mental health, and other issues are difficult to sort out. In addition to the prosecutor and public defender, there may be social workers, school officials, police officers, psychologists, and others who give testimony.

The judge must ensure that the parties appearing before the court receive the legal and constitutional rights to which they are entitled. The judges' decisions set standards for systems connected to the court. They must ensure that these systems work properly when relying on information from social service agencies, probation departments, and attorneys. In addition to providing due process, judges act as fiscal managers for the court. They must

Juvenile Court requires a nontraditional role for the judiciary.
Joel Gordon/Joel Gordon Photography

ensure that an adequate number of attorneys is available to complete the work of the court. Often, the juvenile court judge is the sole administrator of the juvenile probation department and court personnel who work in the system. This role may include supervision of detention facilities, court clinics, and other placements. Judges also serve as community advocates for children, making sure that community resources are available to children and their families who come to court. In order to do this, judges must maintain knowledge of social service programs and provide information to the community about how the court is working. "This may be the most untraditional role for the juvenile court judge," concludes Judge Edwards, "but it may be the most important"(Edwards 1992, 25–29).

Not surprisingly, few judges come to the bench with a background or interest in juvenile law. Many judges sit for a rotation in juvenile court that is frequently too short to be effective. Attracting competent judges to the juvenile court bench is one of the most serious challenges facing the juvenile court. Judges avoid juvenile court for several reasons. Traditionally, the substance of the juvenile court has been regarded more as a social than a legal institution. Partly because of this, juvenile court dockets possess low status within the legal community. Juvenile law is held in low esteem by bar associations, as well as many law schools in which finance law is held in higher regard than the practice of law dealing with issues of family, privacy, and liberty. Law school curriculum does not include a course in juvenile law. Finally, the juvenile court is typically located away from the courthouse and the center of activities. The physical isolation of a juvenile court near detention facilities, probation departments, and social service buildings further diminishes the attractiveness of the juvenile court bench (Edwards 1992, 25–29).

Delinquency Proceedings

As Howard N. Snyder, director of the National Center for Juvenile Justice in Pittsburgh explains, juvenile court proceedings can be understood as a series of decision-making points. All juvenile courts are making the same basic sets of decisions; what differs from state to state is who is making those decisions. The decision makers are: the police, prosecutor, clerk, judge, or probation officer, depending on the jurisdiction (Snyder 1996, 55–56).

Intake

Intake is the first step for defendants in juvenile court. At intake, a decision is made whether to begin formal proceedings. Many states employ *intake officers,* who are called by different titles depending on the state. Some of these titles are: court-designated worker, juvenile court counselor, and juvenile probation officer. Intake officers may be employed by the state administrative office of the courts, the department for social services, or a separate department within the executive branch. The police, private citizens, business people, school administrators, and parents may also file a formal complaint with the juvenile intake worker.

The Police.   When juveniles enter the court system, the process usually begins with the police, who may decide to arrest the young person. Police must exercise a great deal of discretion in dealing with young people; their options range from a simple verbal warning to taking the juvenile into custody and making a referral to juvenile court. In most jurisdictions, the officer is free to adjust the case as necessary. A perception exists that police officers prefer not to work with juveniles. These officers may regard their contact with juveniles as more appropriate to social work; they don't consider dealing with rowdy youths to involve "law enforcement."

The police officer may decide to warn the youth, return the youth home, release the youth after arrest, or take the youth to a detention facility. If a police officer takes a juvenile into custody and is unable to release him or her, the officer then contacts a juvenile intake officer. In most states, the decision whether to prepare a delinquency petition and file the case with the juvenile court, or to resolve the case informally and divert the youth away from the court and the formal delinquency process, is made by the juvenile intake officer. Intake workers interview the youths, review the charges that have been filed, and advise them of their rights. Uniform criteria under state statutes determine which cases must be taken to juvenile court and which are eligible for informal processing. Typically, the intake worker must receive the prosecutor's approval to begin proceedings.

Informal Processing. Once a juvenile has been taken into custody by the police, the case is referred to an intake officer for processing. The intake official, who may confer with the prosecutor, decides the ***legal sufficiency*** of the case. Legally sufficient means that the prosecutor believes that he or she can reasonably substantiate the allegations against the juvenile by use of admissible evidence at trial (Shine & Price 1992, 109). If the case lacks legal sufficiency, the matter is dismissed. If the case has legal sufficiency, the intake official may decide that the juvenile is eligible for informal processing. If eligible for informal processing, the juvenile intake worker may release the child to his or her parents, relatives, or an emergency shelter.

The purpose of informal processing is to divert from juvenile court those youths who are not a threat to the public and for whom adequate resources exist outside the court within the community. The goals are to rehabilitate the youths, to prevent future delinquent behavior, and to protect the public. Cases are eligible for informal processing if the juvenile admits wrongdoing, if the act is the juvenile's first offense, or if the charge is not serious. A formal conference is held and the young person may enter into a diversion agreement with the intake officer. This agreement is a voluntary contract negotiated between the intake worker and the juvenile that serves to resolve the complaint. In some jurisdictions, the victim may be asked about the terms of the agreement. The terms of agreement may include restitution, community service, seminar attendance, letters of apology, counseling, drug and alcohol assessment, or other appropriate terms. If the youth fulfills the contract, the charge is dismissed.

Detention. If the initial allegation is a serious public offense, or if the youth fails to complete the diversion agreement, the juvenile would not be allowed to return home to parental custody. Instead, the intake worker may order the juvenile be placed in a secure detention facility. ***Juvenile detention*** refers to the "temporary confinement of children within a physically restricting facility pending adjudication, disposition, or implementation of disposition" (del Carmen *et al.* 1998, 85). In some jurisdictions, juveniles are confined in county jails and they are usually kept separate from adults. In other states, juveniles are confined in regional detention centers or in a nonsecure detention program. Nonsecure detention programs are for those youth who do not present a danger to the community or themselves. These programs meet the need for juveniles who require supervision but not custody.

Statutes governing juvenile detention in most states require that an early detention hearing be held. A ***detention hearing*** must be held by a juvenile court judge within 48 to 72 hours to determine further action on a case. Laws in most states authorize the court to release youths from detention except in the following circumstances: the court determines that the juvenile is a fugitive from another jurisdiction; the young person constitutes a danger to self or others; if released, the juvenile is likely to abscond; the youngster has no parent, relative, or guardian who will return him or her to court for trial; the juvenile lacks suitable parental supervision; or the offense for which the juvenile is charged is serious, such as murder (NCJFCJ 1990, 15). In *Schall v. Martin* (1984) the U.S. Supreme Court recognized the constitutionality of pretrial detention. The Court held that although a juvenile must be protected from unlimited preventive detention, preventive detention is constitutional because it protects both the juvenile and society from crime. What harm might be done to the juvenile while being detained does not outweigh the greater harm that could be inflicted on the community by an unsupervised juvenile for whom there is probable cause to believe he has committed a serious offense (del Carmen *et al.* 1998, 88–89).

In practice, however, juveniles are detained for various reasons. Detention has been, and remains, a highly discretionary decision making process (Frazier & Bishop 1985, 1132–1152). Some states have implemented measures to reduce judicial discretion at intake detention. In 1990, the Florida legislature mandated new discretion intake screening procedures intended to reduce overcrowding and rational use of detention facilities. Juvenile court judges reluctantly supported the measure (Bazemore 1994, 429–452). The National Coalition on Crime and Delinquency estimates that if the reasons for detention were objectively followed at the detention stage, no more than 10 percent of all arrested youth would be detained. The juvenile system has become more punitive, however, and courts in recent years have increasingly turned to detention. In California, the state with the highest juvenile detention rate in the country, detained youths amount to a third of all youths detained in the United States, yet only about 10 percent of the nation's young people reside in that state (NCJFCJ 1990, 15).

Transfer

If the juvenile is charged with a serious public offense, such as rape or murder, they may be transferred to criminal court. There are three basic mechanisms by which juveniles may be transferred to criminal court: judicial waiver, prosecutorial discretion, and statutory exclusion. (Torbet *et al.* 1996; Feld 1987)

1. Judicial waiver In almost all states, juvenile court judges may waive jurisdiction over a case and transfer it to criminal court. The judge may decide to waive a case at the prosecutor's request, or in some states, at the request of the juveniles or their parents. Several states have also enacted statutes providing for ***presumptive waiver.*** In these states, some juveniles must be waived to criminal court unless they can prove that they are amenable to rehabilitation. This type of waiver shifts the burden of proof from the prosecutor to the juvenile (Torbet *et al.* 1996, 4).

2. Prosecutorial discretion Some states authorize prosecutors to file certain cases in either criminal or juvenile court. "Concurrent jurisdiction" or "direct file" statutes allow the prosecutor to file the case for certain juveniles in criminal court without a probable cause hearing. This means of transfer to criminal court remains controversial because the prosecutor's decision is not subject to judicial review, nor is it required to be based on detailed criteria. State courts have determined that this form of prosecutorial discretion compares to the discretion available to prosecutors in routine charging decisions in criminal court. In some states, legislatures have mandated that prosecutors develop guidelines for filing juvenile cases in criminal court. Florida law requires that each state attorney develop written guidelines and policies to govern determinations for filing a juvenile case in criminal court. State attorneys must submit these policies annually (Torbet *et al.* 1996, 8).

3. Statutory exclusion Available in more than half of the states, this form of transfer has received the most attention in recent years. In many states, statutes exclude from juvenile court jurisdiction certain cases involving a person who by age alone would be considered a juvenile and require that these cases be retained by criminal court. Essentially, this form of transfer places juveniles into the adult criminal court at the point of arrest, bypassing juvenile court decision makers altogether. Legislative waiver, also known as automatic waiver, exists in two variations. One variation is called offense exclusion, which excludes some juvenile offenses from juvenile court jurisdiction, typically murder and other crimes against persons. The other excludes from juvenile court juveniles who possess a combination of prior record and present offense (Torbet *et al.* 1996, 4).

Of the three mechanisms, judicial waiver is the least controversial and most common. Judicial waiver has received support from professional organizations, including the American Bar Association. Almost half of the states have enacted *reverse waiver* provisions that allow the criminal court, on a motion from the prosecutor, to transfer excluded or direct-file cases back to the juvenile court for adjudication or disposition. Somewhat less than half of the states have "once an adult, always an adult," provisions, which stipulate that once juvenile court jurisdiction has been waived, or the juvenile has been sentenced in criminal court subsequent to direct-filing or statutory exclusion, all subsequent cases involving the juvenile fall under criminal court jurisdiction (DeFrances & Strom 1999, 4).

Judicial Waiver. Judicial waiver has always been permitted in most states, but the practice was quite rare until the late 1960s. Judicial waiver is governed by the rules outlined in *Kent v. United States* (1966). In *Kent,* the Supreme Court extended due process rights to juveniles faced with transfer to criminal court. The Court held that juveniles are entitled to a hearing, to be represented by counsel at the hearing, to receive access to records considered by the juvenile court, and to receive a statement of the reasons for support of the waiver order. The court held that the decision to transfer a juvenile to adult court required a full hearing and established the juvenile's right to counsel at the hearing (del Carmen *et al.* 1998, 137–139). State statutes provide for a probable cause hearing in juvenile cases involving felonies before transfer can be made. Similar to a probable cause hearing in criminal court, the hearing is held to determine whether it is more likely than not that the juvenile committed the offense as alleged. If probable cause is found, the prosecutor may move to transfer to criminal court. If probable cause is not found, the court may dismiss the case or move to an adjudicatory hearing in juvenile court.

By 1970, every state allowed some form of transfer process. Between 1971 and 1981, use of transfers increased 400 percent, from less than 1 percent of juvenile arrests to more than 5 percent, and have continued to increase (Fritsch & Hemmens 1995, 23). Waiver of juveniles has increased as the focus has shifted to chronic and serious juvenile offenders, and as states have enacted get-tough strategies. Between 1992 and 1995, several states modified their waiver statutes to loosen requirements: 11 states lowered the age limit, 10 states added crimes, and 2 states added prior record provisions (Torbet *et al.* 1996, 4). Despite the attention generated by judicial waiver in the past few years, transfer of juveniles to criminal court by means of judicial waiver rarely occurs. Between 1985 and 1994, judges waived only about 1.4 percent of juvenile cases to criminal court (DeFrances & Strom 1997, 4).

The transfer of juveniles to criminal court, despite its popularity with legislatures, remains controversial. There is ongoing disagreement about which juveniles are sent to criminal court. Several researchers have concluded that the majority of juveniles transferred to criminal court are violent offenders. A study comparing samples of juveniles certified and not certified for transfer to criminal court during 1993 in St. Louis found that the majority (55.8 percent) of those certified had been arrested for a violent crime, whereas the non-certified sample was more likely to have been arrested for drug-related crime (40.5 percent) (Kinder *et al.* 1995, 39–40). Kevin J. Strom and Steven K. Smith, statisticians at the Bureau of Justice Statistics, have analyzed data for the period 1990 to 1994 from criminal courts in the nation's largest 75 counties. They conclude that juveniles transferred to criminal court were generally violent offenders. Violent offenses (murder, rape, robbery, and assault) comprised the most serious charge for 66 percent of those juvenile felony defendants in criminal courts. Property offenses (burglary, theft) accounted for 17 percent and drug offenses for 14 percent (Strom & Smith 1998, 1–2).

Other researchers have reached the opposite conclusion. Rick Ruddell and associates at the University of Missouri–St. Louis analyzed juvenile court data for 1986 to 1994 collected by the National Center for Juvenile Justice in Pittsburgh. They conclude that violent offenses (homicide, rape, robbery, aggravated assault, sex offenses) represent about a third of all transfers. Although the percentage of youths transferred for violent offenses increased during this period, the majority of youths transferred to criminal court were charged with nonviolent offenses (Ruddell *et al.* 1998, 6–7). Other researchers have reached the same conclusion. (Feld 1987; Hamparian *et al.* 1982; Bishop *et al.* 1989)

There is more agreement about the race of juveniles transferred to criminal court. A number of studies have concluded that a disproportionate number of African American defendants are sent to criminal court. One study found that 73 percent of those transferred in New Jersey during the first year after revised waiver statutes were black youths (Thomas & Bilchik 1985, 439–479). In their study of juvenile felony defendants in the criminal courts of the nation's largest 75 counties, the Bureau of Justice Statistics statisticians Kevin Strom and Steven Smith found that 67 percent were black (Strom & Smith 1998, 1).

What happens to juvenile defendants in criminal court is less controversial. Nearly two-thirds of those juvenile defendants tried in criminal court were convicted. In those cases in which the defendants were not convicted it was because the prosecutor or the court dismissed the charges. Overall, 68 percent of convicted juveniles in criminal court were sentenced to state prison or local jails. The criminal courts in most states impose adult correctional sanctions. Some states provide for a blend of juvenile and adult sanctions, and in others, the criminal court can transfer the case back to juvenile court for sentencing. Persons under age 18 who serve time in juvenile institutions until the age of majority are later transferred to adult facilities.

Adjudication

The majority of juvenile cases are not transferred to criminal court but remain in juvenile court. The intake officer files a petition with the juvenile court asking the court to adjudicate the young delinquent. *Adjudication* is the process of determining guilt or innocence; the adjudicatory hearing in juvenile court resembles a trial except that it is less adversarial than a criminal trial.

Adjudicatory Hearings.   Traditionally, juvenile court emphasized informality of proceedings. The Chicago Juvenile Court's Judge Julian Mack, writing in the *Harvard Law Review* in 1904, explained that the child in juvenile court should understand the authority of government, but at the same time feel like the object of the government's care. "The ordinary trappings of the courtroom are out of place in such hearings. The judge on the bench, looking down upon the boy standing at the bar, can never evoke a proper sympathetic spirit. Seated at a desk, with the child at his side, where he can on occasion put his arm around his shoulder and draw the lad to him, the judge, while losing none of his judicial dignity, will gain immensely in the effectiveness of his work" (Mack 1909, 104, 107). Juvenile courts have followed evidentiary and procedural rules less rigorously, and in practice, the proceedings are less adversarial and more casual than criminal court. This has led to juvenile court being nicknamed "kiddie court." Trial in juvenile court seldom means a jury trial. Most juvenile court trials are bench trials heard by the juvenile court judge.

The attempt to provide both legal proceedings and social service has meant that the defendant receives neither (Sanborn 1994; Ainsworth 1996). In 1966, the U.S. Supreme Court emphasized that *parens patriae* philosophy is not an invitation to procedural arbitrariness. In *Kent v. United States* (1966), the Court observed that lax courtroom procedures, along with inadequate personnel and facilities, meant "that the child receives the worst of both worlds: that he gets neither the protections accorded to adults nor the solicitious care and regenerative treatment postulated for children." The Court responded with its' decision in *In re Gault* a year later, leading to rejection of a pure *parens patriae* model in favor of an approach balancing due process protections.

Sanborn concluded that the *parens patriae* ideology still prevails in juvenile courts and interferes with a young offender's ability to receive access to effective counsel. In a 1994 survey of 100 juvenile court judges, lawyers, and probation officers, a majority of those interviewed described judicial conduct they believed compromised the ability of juvenile defendants to get a fair trial. This judicial conduct included forcing unprepared parties to proceed with trial or admission of guilt, interrupting the lawyer's examination of witness with their own questions, and abruptly ending examination or cross-examination. Two thirds of court workers surveyed reported that judges had pretrial knowledge of a juvenile record and the probation officer's recommended disposition. Almost half of the respondents believed that juvenile court judges found juveniles guilty when evidence did not meet the legal requirement. Many observed that juvenile hearings were conducted too quickly, the atmosphere was not serious, and the treatment of juvenile court regulars interfered with the juvenile's ability to get a fair trial. (Sanborn 1994; Ainsworth 1996)

Jury Trials.   A few juvenile petitions are decided by trial and some of these are jury trials. In most states, there is no right to trial by jury. Those cases that go to trial are decided by a ***bench trial,*** that is, by a judge who renders a verdict after hearing evidence introduced by prosecuting and defense attorneys.

Most states follow the U.S. Supreme Court's lead in *McKeiver v. Pennsylvania* (1971) and prohibit jury trials in juvenile court. The *McKeiver* decision held that juveniles do not have a constitutional right, under either the sixth or the fourteenth amendment, to a jury trial in juvenile proceedings. The Supreme Court listed several reasons for not extending the right of jury trial to delinquency proceedings:

- The introduction of a jury would make the process into a fully adversarial proceeding and end the informal, protective features of juvenile proceedings.
- Jury trial would add delay and formality to court proceedings, and might entail a public trial.
- A jury trial would not improve significantly the juvenile court's fact-finding function, nor remedy the juvenile court's defects.

Adding a jury trial to juvenile court might end juvenile court altogether. (del Carmen *et al.* 1998, 180–181)

Since *McKeiver* advocates of jury trials for juveniles have tried to find a way to establish a constitutional right to a jury in juvenile court trials. They have looked for federal constitutional protections other than those considered in *McKeiver.* One argument put forth states that changes in juvenile court proceedings since 1971 require a second consideration of the application of the due process clause and sixth amendment to juvenile court. Until recently, the only state courts that had recognized a constitutional right to jury trial for juveniles were the Alaska and New Mexico Supreme Courts. These states had found grounds in their constitutions for juvenile jury trials prior to the U.S. Supreme Court's decision. Advocates for youths have urged other state courts to interpret their constitutions in order to reach a contrary decision to the *McKeiver* case. In 1998, the Louisiana Supreme Court decided in favor of jury trial on due process grounds. (Guggenheim & Hertz 1998, 554–555)

Janet Ainsworth, a professor at Seattle University School of Law, advocates for juvenile jury trials on several grounds. Juries acquit more readily than judges, so juveniles are more likely to be convicted by bench trial than if they could choose a jury trial. Judges hear hundreds of cases a year and through frequency and familiarity, they become less careful and more cynical in weighing the evidence. Additionally, attorneys in a jury trial have the opportunity to exclude biased decision makers from the jury. Jurors must go through a *voir dire* examination in which the attorneys can move not to seat those with attitudes, beliefs, or life experiences that might bias their judgment. There is no such opportunity in a bench trial. Finally, bench trials provide less opportunity for appeal. In a jury trial, jurors receive instruction in points of law from the judge that can later be examined for error. In a bench trial, the judge does not make these points of law explicit, but simply rules, reducing the opportunity to find error in the judge's interpretation of the law on appeal (Ainsworth 1996, 67–68).

Plea Bargaining. Juries have significance procedurally, but not practically. Even in states where they are available, they are seldom used. Jury trials occur in fewer than 5 percent of cases (Feld 1993, 220–221). The great majority of petitions result in an admission by the juvenile to the facts of the petition, otherwise known as a ***plea bargain.***

Plea bargaining is not supposed to happen in juvenile court. Juvenile defendants are not entitled to jury trial in most states, so there should not be caseload pressure forcing juvenile courts to rely on negotiating pleas. Both prosecutors and defense attorneys are supposed to be committed to *parens patriae;* they should be doing what is best for the young juvenile rather than pursuing their own career goals of obtaining convictions. The legal court officers should try to presume the least restrictive sentence for a client in every case (Sanborn 1993, 510). Nevertheless, plea bargaining does occur in juvenile court.

Judges and lawyers surveyed in Kentucky in 1996 reported that over 60 percent of the cases in juvenile court ended in plea bargaining agreements. About 10 to 12 percent of cases went to trial (Brooks *et al.* 1996, 19). Defense attorneys, prosecutors, and judges have incentives to plea bargain. For the defense attorney, plea negotiation provides a means to minimize the youth's court record and reduce the disposition. For prosecutors, plea bargaining ensures a conviction for the government and spares witnesses the ordeal of testifying at trial. For defense attorneys, prosecutors, and judges, plea bargaining offers a means to conserve resources. Negotiating pleas helps the court deal with the overwhelming number of cases on the juvenile docket. Agreeing to a plea enables the court to extend resources to the juvenile more quickly, and the admission of guilt provides a good start toward rehabilitation (Sanborn 1993, 514–517).

In *Boykin v. Alabama* (1969), the U.S. Supreme Court established some guidelines for negotiated pleas in criminal court. Guilty pleas may be entered by defendants who know what they are doing (the intelligence requirement) and who freely do so (the voluntariness requirement). The Supreme Court has not yet determined that the *Boykin* requirement applies to juvenile court, and has left the issue of guidelines to state law. A 1992 study found that in 10 states, neither statutory provisions nor appellate courts provided guidelines concerning plea bargaining in juvenile court. In the remaining 40 states, there was some regulation, mostly through juvenile courts' rules or specific statutory provisions. In a few states, defendants are required to talk with their parents, legal counsel, or both before pleading, but that is the exception. In some courts juveniles receive an advisory colloquy from the judge to determine that the defendant's plea meets, in effect, *Boykin* requirements (Sanborn 1992, 127–150).

Disposition

For those youths found delinquent, whether by adjudicatory hearing or guilty plea, the next step in the proceedings is disposition. Disposition in juvenile court parallels the sentencing hearing in criminal court, although disposition implies more than a sentence. ***Disposition*** is the point at which the court decides what is to be done with the child. The decision must balance the need for public safety against the young individual's needs.

The Dispositional Hearing.   A dispositional hearing is held almost immediately following the juvenile's admission of guilt. State law usually requires that adjudication and disposition are separate events in order to allow time for an investigation to assist the court in deciding the best disposition. To assist the court in its determination, a ***predispostional report*** is prepared. This investigation is conducted for the court by the intake officer, juvenile probation officer, or social worker. Research suggests that juvenile court judges follow the recommendations of probation officers in 90 percent of the cases. A predispositional report (or social history) may contain social, medical, psychiatric, psychological, and educational information and includes a recommendation and a case plan or treatment plan.

Using information in the report, the judge prepares a ***dispositional order,*** to explain the facts found by the court, the specific disposition, and who is responsible for carrying it out. The judge may order that the juvenile be examined by a physician, psychiatrist, psychologist, or other expert to determine the juvenile's needs. If the juvenile needs medical, psychological, or other treatment, the court may allow the parents to arrange for it, appoint a guardian, or order the parents to pay for it. If the judge finds that the youth is mentally disabled or has mental retardation, the case is referred to mental health services. The court may continue the case to allow for evaluation. If so, the juvenile may be returned home under parental supervision, be placed in a special school or detention facility, with a relative, or in public foster care. The range of alternatives ordered by the judge may include full or partial restitution, imposition of a fine, supervised community service, a day treatment program, a community-based academic or vocational program, confinement to a detention facility, or probation.

Juvenile court has traditionally attempted to individualize dispositions. After a determination of delinquency, state statutes provide juvenile court judges with a wide array of dispositional options. The least restrictive alternative, a product of the Juvenile Justice and Delinquency Prevention Act of 1974, emphasized the use of community-based sanctions instead of training school commitments. In Los Angeles County, following the recommendations of probation officers, judges usually sent youths home on probation after the first few court appearances. "Home on probation" tested whether the family could straighten out the juvenile. Only after it became apparent that the probation had failed in this matter did the court refer the youths for placement in a camp, a youth home, or a facility operated by the California Youth Authority (Greenwood & Turner 1993, 231).

Sentencing. State legislatures have recently redefined the purpose of juvenile court to emphasize public safety, punishment, and accountability. Many of these legislative initiatives have been passed in response to concerns about serious, violent, and chronic juvenile offenders. As a result, the principles of least restrictive alternative and individualized justice have been replaced by an offense-based model followed in criminal court.

A number of states have replaced statutory provisions allowing broad discretion at the dispositional stage of delinquency proceedings with determinate sentencing schemes. Washington became the first state to break from the juvenile court's traditional emphasis on individualized, indeterminate sentencing. The Washington State Juvenile Justice Act of 1977 overhauled the practice of juvenile dispositions in that state. The act introduced presumptive sentencing to juvenile court. This means that there is a presumptive or expected sentence for each offense identified in the juvenile code. The Washington code created three categories of juvenile offenders—serious, middle, and minor—with presumptive sentences and standard ranges for each. The legislation provided that judges calculate the presumptive sentence from the juvenile's age, present offense, and prior record based on guidelines developed by a sentencing commission. The guidelines specify the security level and length of stay. Judges may order a disposition other than the presumptive sentence, but only to avoid a manifest injustice supported by clear and convincing evidence (Guarino-Ghezzi & Loughran 1996, 116–117).

In 1995, the Texas legislature enacted into law a system of progressive sentencing guidelines. Intended to balance public protection, offender accountability, and rehabilitation, the guidelines describe seven levels of sanctions, each more restrictive than the last. The first four sanction levels are administered by local probation departments and range from counseling, to informal probation, intensive probation, and placement outside the home. Levels five and six refer commitment to the Texas Youth Commission, the state agency responsible for the state's most serious delinquent and disturbed youth. Sanctions include up to a year in a residential program and supervised parole. Judges may commit youth to the Texas Youth Commission for an indeterminate period, and the Commission determines the minimum length of stay based on its policy, or for a determinate period up to 40 years (Briscoe 1997, 9–10).

Three new disposition or sentencing options have emerged: blended sentencing, mandatory minimum sentences, and extended jurisdiction.

Blended Sentencing.   Blended sentencing provisions allow the juvenile court judge to mix adult and juvenile sanctions for serious and violent juvenile offenders. These are based on age or a combination of age and offense. New Mexico's youthful offender provision allows the juvenile court the authority to impose a sanction involving either the juvenile or the adult corrections systems. But in the majority of states with blended sentencing, the juvenile court has original jurisdiction and responsibility for adjudication of the case, and it may impose a sanction to remain in force beyond the age of the juvenile court's jurisdiction. At this point, various procedures are invoked to transfer the case to the adult correctional system. In Texas, a youth sentenced to incarceration under its blended sentencing provision goes to a facility operated by the Texas Youth Commission. If the youth is not released by the age of 17 years and 6 months, the juvenile court holds a transfer hearing to decide whether to release the juvenile on parole or transfer the youth to the Texas Department of Corrections (Torbet *et al.* 1996, 13–14).

Mandatory Minimums.   Since 1992, 15 states, including Florida, Ohio, Colorado, and Georgia, have added or amended statutes that provide for mandatory minimum periods of incarceration for juveniles convicted on violent or other serious crimes. Legislation enacted by the Louisiana legislature in 1993 provides that for certain violent felony-grade delinquent acts, the judge must order the juvenile committed to the Department of Correction, to be placed in a secure facility until 21 years of age without benefit of parole, probation, modification, or furlough (Torbet *el al.* 1996, 14–15).

Extended Jurisdiction.   State legislatures have also increased the maximum age of the juvenile court's continuing jurisdiction over juvenile offenders. Since 1992, 11 states have extended the age for juvenile commitments; in several states, juvenile court jurisdiction now extends to youths aged 21, 25, and 4 states have indefinite jurisdiction (Torbet *et al.* 1996, 15).

Summary

The juvenile court has been part of the American court system for more than a hundred years. The juvenile court emerged from Progressive Era reforms that led to specialized courts in cities. Following the court unification movement that began in 1940, the juvenile court was incorporated into state court systems. The juvenile court may occupy a place within the state's general jurisdiction trial courts, limited jurisdiction trial courts, or exist as a special jurisdiction trial court. Most recently, two alternative legal forums for juveniles have appeared: family court and drug court. Family court aims to bring all disputes and issues that occur within a single family within a single court according to the "one judge—one family" principle. Juvenile drug courts feature case management, pre-trial diversion, and judicially-monitored treatment programs for substance-abusing juveniles and their families.

In 1967, the U.S. Supreme Court changed fundamentally proceedings in juvenile court in its landmark decision *In re Gault*. The court held that many of the due process requirements granted to adults in criminal proceedings are also required in delinquency proceedings. The ruling brought prosecutors and defense attorneys to the juvenile court to complete the balance of adversarial justice. Prosecutorial screening of juvenile cases occurs on a first-level or second-level basis, that is, either before or after the intake officer's decision. Defense work in juvenile court invokes the dual roles of the advocate model and the guardian model. Juvenile court requires many non-traditional roles for the judge, including administrator, policy maker, and child advocate. Overall, emphasis has now shifted away from judicial discretion and toward ensuring legal rights in juvenile court proceedings.

Juvenile court proceedings can be understood as a series of decision-making points. These include: intake, transfer, adjudication, and disposition. At intake, the court decides whether to initiate formal proceedings. In many jurisdiction, the decision is made by a juvenile intake officer. If the juvenile is charged with a serious public offense, such as rape or murder, a decision is made about whether to transfer the juvenile to adult court. There are three transfer mechanisms: juvenile waiver, prosecutorial discretion, and statutory exclusion. Adjudication is the process of determining guilt or innocence; the adjudicatory hearing resembles to trial stage in criminal court. However, adjudicatory hearings are bench trials; juveniles do not possess a constitutional right to a jury trial. Disposition is the point at which the court decides "what is to be done" with the juvenile; it resembles the sentencing stage in criminal court. Three sentencing reforms have emerged in recent years: blended sentencing, mandatory minimums, and extended jurisdiction.

KEY CONCEPTS

adjudication	court of last resort	docket
advocate model	court of limited jurisdiction	drug courts
bench trial	court unification	family court
blended sentencing	detention hearing	four-tiered structure
child protection proceedings	disposition	guardian model
court of general jurisdiction	dispositional order	indigents

judicial waiver	plea bargain	prosecutorial discretion
juvenile detention	predispositional report	reverse waiver
legal sufficiency	presumptive waiver	statutory exclusion

DISCUSSION QUESTIONS

1. Should proceedings in juvenile court be kept secret?

2. How does the role of prosecutor in the juvenile system differ from that of the criminal system?

3. What are some factors to consider when transferring a youth to the adult system?

LEARNING ACTIVITY: DEBATE

Should what happens in juvenile court be kept secret? Juvenile court has traditionally operated under the banner of confidentiality, but that is beginning to change. Recently, the debate over confidentiality has occurred among juvenile justice professionals, police, judges, legislators, victims, and citizens. Divide the class into two groups. One side should find three arguments in the discussion below in favor of maintaining confidentiality; the others must find and support arguments for abolishing it. Flip a coin to decide which group takes which position.

Many of the original juvenile court acts did not provide for confidentiality of juvenile court proceedings and records, but most practiced confidentiality. In an effort to maintain a separate court for young people and to avoid stigmatizing them as lawbreakers, judges routinely cleared juvenile courtrooms. The Standard Juvenile Court Act of 1959 emphasized the need to maintain a "casework relationship, and avoidance of the spectacle of a public criminal trial." Only those with "a direct interest in the work of the Court," namely, the prosecutor, defense counsel, bailiff, clerk, probation officer, social worker, along with the youth's parents needed to be there. Gradually, state legislatures provided for the confidentiality of records, allowing for disclosure of juvenile court records only to those with a legitimate interest. While police, prosecution, and defense counsel, and other courts routinely had access to juvenile court records, outsiders such as the public, media, or researchers did not have access. Most state statutes also protected the confidentiality of agency records, such as those for detention and treatment facilities, or agencies performing evaluations for the court, mandating that they be restricted to the agency and the client. Those juvenile workers with professional credentials, such as social workers, also adhered to confidentiality of client records based on their professional code of ethics (Etten & Patrone 1994, 65–66). Social workers also operate according to the agency policy, informed by the code of professional ethics for social workers, which limits sharing of information to persons who have a need to know. The National Association of Social Workers Code of Ethics (1996) limits disclosure of confidential information "when appropriate with valid consent from a client or a person legally authorized to consent on behalf of a client."

Beginning in the 1970s with the perception of increased juvenile crime, critics of the juvenile court called for relaxation of confidentiality practices. They charged that confidentiality practices jeopardized public safety and impinged on the public's right to know. The U.S. Supreme Court, while preserving some confidentiality provisions, never upheld a constitutional right to confidentiality for an adjudicated delinquent (Kfoury 1983, 135–144). Since 1992, a number of state legislatures have called for the presumption of open proceedings and the release of juvenile defendants' names. The National Council of Juvenile and Family Courts Judges resolved in 1995 that "traditional notions of secrecy and confidentiality should be re-examined and relaxed to promote public confidence in the court's work. The public has a right to know how courts deal with children and families." The Council recommended that court be open to the media and the public, to make itself accountable and to encourage community involvement (NCJFCJ 1995, 3).

During the 1990s, many states passed laws that would either open general juvenile court proceedings or proceedings for specific violent juvenile offenders. The critics had challenged the juvenile court to open records based on the public's right to know and to promote accountability to the community. This erosion of the traditional juvenile courts as a separate social institution toward a court with due process protections within a single criminal justice system has inevitably led to a relaxation of traditional prohibitions (Martin 1995, 393–410). By 1995, 39 states permitted the release of a juvenile's name, photograph, or both to the media or general public in certain juvenile cases. California, Florida, and Virginia enacted legislation to promote sharing of juvenile court information among juvenile courts, law enforcement agencies, and schools in order to rehabilitate offenders and lessen the potential for drug use, violence, and other forms of delinquency. California's legislation, enacted in 1995, specifically allows for court personnel (the district attorney, city attorney, county prosecutor, judges, referees, and other judicial officers), the minor's parents and retained counsel, probation officers, law enforcement officers, school superintendent, child protection agencies, members of child multidisciplinary teams, treatment and others supervisory personnel, as well as any other person designated by court order, to have access to juvenile records involving serious juvenile offenders (Torbet *et al.* 1996, 39). Yet because of the exceptions built into such laws, information is shared by police, courts, schools, social welfare, medical, and mental health service providers. The various juvenile agencies practice information territoriality that hampers exchange of information in particular cases and has prevented development of statewide computerized management systems. In juvenile court, juvenile offenders with treatment needs may not receive treatment until after disposition because such information was not previously available to the court. Among those transferred to criminal court, repeat juvenile offenders are seen as first-time recidivists because the court does not have the juvenile record.

Although there is support for information sharing among agencies, there is also a concern about the quality of the information to be shared. Juvenile court records typically provide information about arrest and intake, but less frequently include adjudication and disposition information. Sharing information about juvenile arrest without disposition can be misleading. At the same time, case files maintained by child welfare agencies are "notorious repositories of opinion, hearsay and gossip," subject to the views of social workers who create them (Etten & Petrone 1994, 75–76). Many juvenile court officers retain reservations about opening proceedings to media and the general public. Juvenile court judges should have the right to close proceedings to protect the victim or the offender whenever there are specific security concerns. All states authorize the use of the defendant's juvenile record at sentencing for those youth transferred to criminal court. However, a finding of guilt in juvenile court is not a criminal conviction because it is not derived through the means of adjudication. Generally, the finding of guilt in juvenile court is not based on trial by jury, nor is it based on the rules of evidence practiced in a criminal court (Redding 1999, 50:5).

12 Juvenile Corrections

CHAPTER OBJECTIVES

On completing this chapter, students will have tools to:

- Understand juvenile training schools
- Clarify the differences between training schools and detention centers
- Examine the role of camps, ranches, and farms in delinquency
- Develop a better understanding of rehabilitation

Deinstitutionalization versus Secure Correctional Facilities

Since 1971 or so, deinstitutionalization has become a major goal. Deinstitutionalization involves placing juvenile offenders, particularly status offenders, in facilities and programs other than secure correctional facilities. States have shifted juveniles from training schools to a variety of programs ranging from wilderness adventures to military-style boot camps. About half of the states operate at least one ranch, camp, or farm; about half operate at least one group home. About a third have at least one state-administered residential facility, foster care facility, and diagnostic facility. The type and number of juvenile corrections facilities varies with the organization of juvenile corrections within the state. Unlike the adult system, private facilities have a larger role.

Rehabilitation no longer serves as the guiding model for juvenile corrections. State legislatures and juvenile justice policymakers emphasize accountability, responsibility, and community safety. Yet the issue of program effectiveness remains. Since the nineteenth century, when institutions for juveniles first opened, they have been criticized for failing to teach young people to live responsibly in the community following release. Alternative programs, however, face similar scrutiny. Few public officials are willing to fund programs that do not show that they are effective. Defining and measuring success represents an important issue in juvenile justice. The first section of this chapter describes the origins of juvenile corrections, beginning with the house of refuge. The second section looks at the three types of corrections institutions for juveniles: detention centers; training schools; and camps, farms, and ranches. The third section explores the issue of rehabilitation and the efforts of researchers to document what works. The fourth section reviews aftercare services.

Origins of Juvenile Corrections

Juvenile correctional facilities in the United States are extensions of the nineteenth-century house of refuge and its institutional ancestor, the English poorhouse. The *house of refuge* developed into the juvenile reformatory, which represented the basis of juvenile corrections throughout most of the twentieth century.

The House of Refuge

In the American colonies during the eighteenth century, it was common for youthful law-breakers to be sent home for a whipping administered by a parent. Others were confined in county jails with adults. Colonial jails amounted to local lockups for detention of suspects awaiting trial and convicted lawbreakers sentenced to corporal punishment. They were exclusively county responsibility and did not cost the public any money. They were something like boarding houses; the jailer lived with his family on site and the prisoner's lot depended on personal finances or handouts from friends and relatives. Some children found relative safety in the keeper's house, but others faced grim exploitation at the hands of adult inmates. The practice of confining juveniles in adult jails continued in some states longer than others and to some extent continues today, although jail facilities have changed.

In 1819, the Society for the Prevention of Pauperism found evil conditions at New York City's Bellevue Prison. The group took particular interest in young lawbreakers confined there. Thomas Eddy, who had organized the city's first penitentiary and served at its first warden, was an influential leader of the group. The society reorganized as the Society for the Reformation of Juvenile Delinquents and set about creating an institution reserved for juveniles. The reformers knew about the Poor Law of 1601 and England's practice of sweeping young paupers from London streets into poorhouses. During the Elizabethan Age, the English poorhouse did not differentiate among delinquent, abused, neglected, and abandoned children and confined them all together. London's oldest poorhouse, Christ's Hospital, contained orphaned, impoverished, and among delinquent children. Youths were sent from poorhouses to work as apprentices in the countryside. The purpose of these apprenticeships was not so much to teach a complex trade as to keep them from returning to a life of vagrancy and crime. Boys were sent to farmers and girls to work as domestics. Others were transported to the American colonies as indentured servants (Mennel 1973).

The society established the New York House of Refuge, which became the first juvenile institution in the United States. It selected a site for the institution about a mile beyond the last row of houses in New York City, an airy space surrounded by farms and fields of wildflowers (near the present location of Madison Square Garden) (Bernard 1992, 62, 67). The institution, which opened New Year's Day 1825, became a model for similar institutions in other cities, including the Boston House of Reformation (1826) and the Philadelphia House of Refuge (1828). Thirteen additional institutions appeared between 1841 and 1856 (Pisciotta 1984, 1985). By 1868, there were more than 20 houses of refuge throughout the country.

The American house of refuge combined a reform school and orphanage. Their founders hoped to remake street children and delinquents into law-abiding citizens by instilling values of self-control, discipline, and respect for authority. The house of refuge relied on a strict schedule and labor to teach young inmates the values of self-control, discipline, and respect for authority. It implemented a program featuring labor, education, and religious instruction. Labor was the most important activity. At the New York House of Refuge, boys worked seven to eight hours each day in workshops where they caned chairs, made shoes, fashioned wire sofa springs, and hewed wood for barrels. Other boys labored on institution farms. They also cleaned the building and sewed clothing. Some boys worked for private contractors who paid the institution managers on a per diem or per piece basis. Education and religious instruction were secondary activities. For about four hours a day, Monday through Friday, boys attended classes where they learned to "read, write, and cipher." On Sundays, the boys attended Sabbath school. Bible classes were also offered on Sunday afternoons (Pisciotta 1985).

The goal was to train young people for life as self-sufficient productive citizens and avoid sending them back to the streets. The house of refuge classified youthful inmates into one of four sections distinguished by clothing and privileges. Troublemakers lost time for play, went to bed without dinner, spent time in solitary confinement, or received a spanking. Boys who behaved well appeared before an indenture committee, which decided whether to return boys to their parents or place them in the indenture system. The practice of indenture, also known as apprenticeship or outplacing, discharged youths to masters who agreed to provide them with food, clothing, and shelter until age 21. To protect the boys from vices, the committee did not place boys in the city or with tavern keepers. The New York House of Refuge indentured most boys to farmers in upstate New York, Connecticut, and New Jersey. Others were put on trains headed west. The *orphan trains,* operated by the Children's Aid Society of New York City beginning in 1854, brought orphaned youth to farms in Ohio, Indiana, and Illinois. When the train stopped in a town, the children would stand on the station platform to be selected by local farmers. Those not chosen returned to the train and moved on to the next town. The phrase "put up for adoption" comes from this practice; over 50,000 children left New York City this way (Bernard 1992, 65–66).

The Juvenile Reformatory

The *juvenile reformatory* developed in the early twentieth century alongside the juvenile court. Juvenile reformatories were separate institutions for juvenile delinquents sentenced to confinement by juvenile courts. The juvenile reformatory borrowed ideas from the emerging new science of penology followed at Elmira, New York. Zebulon Brockway, who had been appointed the first superintendent in 1876, established the first reformatory for young adults. It became a model for other reformatories across the country. There were 6 reformatories for young adults by 1890, 12 by 1901, and 18 by 1913 (Pisciotta 1993).

Brockway's prescription for reformation made use of individualized treatment, indeterminate sentencing, classification, military training, and parole. His mark system used a carefully planned progressive classification designed to employ rewards and sanctions. Prisoners earned marks for school performance, labor, and general deportment; they progressed through three divisions distinguished by uniforms and caps. Brockway's ticket of leave system allowed inmates who had a job to be released, subject to positive monthly reports from their supervisor. The key was the indeterminate sentence. An act passed by the New York legislature in 1877 stated that the immediate behavior of the offender, not the punishment for past offense, determined the date of release. Indeterminate sentences remained on statute books until well into the twentieth century (Pisciotta 1985, 616–618).

Juvenile reformatories melded the reformatory model with the house of refuge. Reformatories for children were meant to replicate conditions in the home. Placed in the country, they followed the cottage plan. The founders intended them to be small institutions, with about 40 children placed in each, and houses for the youngest children were staffed exclusively by women. Juvenile reformatories aimed to educate children by moral training, religion, and labor. Children would learn simplicity in dress, diet, and surroundings through regular exercise and constant supervision. They would receive basic education and vocational instruction emphasizing industrial and agricultural trades. And, the founders hoped, they would learn the values of sobriety, thrift, industry, and prudence as taught by honest New England families (Platt 1977).

The nation's first cottage/family reformatory for boys, the Ohio Reform School, opened in 1857 at Lancaster, Ohio. The Ohio Reform School introduced the cottage or family plan to the United States. Prior to this school, state institutions were indistinguishable from the early houses of refuge. They were large congregate institutions featuring strict work regimens. The cottage or family system emphasized agricultural labor over industrial labor and group living rather than congregate dormitory housing. Each house was to be a family under direction of a mother or matron. Cottage reform schools, some located on farms, spread across the United States (Mennel 1973).

In later years of the nineteenth century, juvenile reformatories added regimens of industrial education, military drill, and parole. Industrial education at New York's House of Refuge in 1888 featured knitting and hosiery-making, typesetting and printing, carpentry, horticulture, tailoring, painting, gas and steam fitting, and baking. Under the military plan, boys were divided into squads of cadets, received uniforms, and marched to and from dormitories, shops, school, and chapel services. In 1894, the indenture committee hired Bradford K. Pierce as chaplain and assigned to him the additional duty of home examinations. Pierce investigated the homes of parents prior to return of a child and those of masters to ensure they fulfilled the terms of their contract. Pierce and his successors implemented the first juvenile parole system (Pisciotta 1985).

Of Girls and African Americans

The founders overlooked girls and African Americans when they created juvenile reformatories. In 1860, "ladies of the highest respectability" petitioned the New York legislature to include girls who were released or otherwise sent to jails, workhouses, and penitentiaries in the house of refuge. The Western House of Refuge in Rochester, New York, opened a division for female delinquents in 1876. Like the boys, girls were to learn order, discipline, and self-control. They attended Sabbath school and learned to read and write. The goal of training was not to teach them to support themselves but to become good wives and domestic servants. While boys learned how to operate machines and farm implements, girls learned cooking, cleaning, washing, ironing, and sewing.

The first reformatory for girls, the Industrial School for Girls, opened in 1857 at Lancaster, Massachusetts, about 50 miles from Boston. The first cottage was a two-story red brick building. Both as the first reform school for girls and as the first family-style institution, the founders intended it to be a model. The cottage gathered together about 30 girls who lived together as sisters under a mother or matron. The founders selected Bradford K. Pierce to serve as superintendent and chaplain. Pierce implemented a training program of domestic science and common school curriculum. The program trained girls for jobs with families as domestic servants (Brenzel 1983).

The experience of African American children in nineteenth-century juvenile institutions differed from their white counterparts. African American youths at the Western House of Refuge in Rochester, New York, were indentured to sea captains for whaling voyages rather than to farms because masters did not want to include them as part of their families. White masters often rejected black girls as domestics for the same reason (Pisciotta 1984, 82).

The founders never intended to extend the benefits of juvenile institutions to African Americans. The nineteenth-century reformers excluded black youths from their institutions; they went to separate institutions or to county jails. The Philadelphia House of Refuge refused to admit black youths. Shortly after admitting "a colored boy" in 1829, the managers decided to open a separate institution for black children. Philadelphia's Colored House of Refuge opened in 1848. The regimen in these institutions reflected the same bigotry that had precluded integrated settings. The managers discouraged education for black youths and emphasized manual labor instead. The managers of the House of Reformation and Instruction for Colored Children in Baltimore stressed that African American youths confined there must learn the importance of work through basic agricultural and animal husbandry. African American girls should learn household chores and domestic service (Pisciotta 1983, 260–261).

Elsewhere, the founders of juvenile reformatories overlooked black youth altogether, and opening institutions for them became the responsibility of the African American community. The first institution for African American boys in North Carolina opened in 1925 following a campaign by Thaddeus Tate, an African American civic leader in Charlotte. Tate convinced Judge Heriot Clarkson of Charlotte of the need for a training school for black delinquents, and their efforts led to the state's purchase of Governor Cameron Morrison's 400-acre farm for the school. The school was later named the Cameron Morrison school (Alley & Wilson 1994, 3–4). Similarly, the first institution for African American girls resulted from the efforts of Charlotte Hawkins Brown, a doctor and president of the State Federated Negro Women's Club, who set up the Efland Home for girls near Hillsboro in 1925. The home 20 twenty girls who were taught domestic science and sewing. Club members received Lawrence Oxley's help in lobbying the legislature, and the home operated until 1942. Not until 1943 did the state legislature open the State Training School for Negro Girls in Rocky Mount, North Carolina. The new school, directed by Mae D. Holmes, sought to teach marketable skills for financial independence, including economics, agriculture, cosmetology, home care, and food service. The school also offered religious services, farming, and physical education (Alley & Wilson 1994, 13–14).

Detention Centers and Training Schools

Detention centers are basically jails for juveniles who have been arrested and are awaiting trial. Designed as an alternative to adult jails, they have come to have a central place in the juvenile justice system. *Training schools* are the juvenile justice equivalent of prisons; they are secure residential facilities designed to provide confinement and treatment for youths. Training school programs seek to rehabilitate youths through programs designed to teach acceptable standards of behavior, academic subjects, and vocational training. Although a few states have closed large facilities, many states continue to operate training schools, many of which were built before 1900.

Detention Centers

Individuals in detention centers are thought to be the most dangerous or most likely to flee prior to court hearings. In the past few years, detention centers have come to occupy a place in the juvenile justice system that jails occupy in the adult system. Their use as places of secure confinement postadjudication is increasing. Ethnic minority populations make up the majority of admissions. Detention for status offenses has decreased, but detention for violation of court orders had increased (Schwartz & Willis 1994, 15).

There are 422 public juvenile detention centers in the United States and about 500,000 admissions to these centers every year. The rate and number of youths in detention vary by state. The detention rate ranges from a low of 44.7 per 100,000 youths in North Dakota to a high of 4,734 per 100,000 in California. In 1989, about 56 percent of admissions to detention centers occurred in five states: California, Ohio, Texas, Washington, and Florida; these five states accounted for 52 percent of admissions and only 29 percent of all eligible youth (Schwartz & Willis 1994, 13–15).

The Purpose of Detention.   The National Juvenile Detention Association (NJDA) defines *detention* as "the temporary and safe custody of juveniles who are accused of conduct subject to jurisdiction of the court who require a restricted environment for their own or the community's protection while pending legal action" (Dunlap & Rosch 1995, 4). There have been two somewhat contradictory types of detention: *preventive* detention and *therapeutic* detention. Preventive detention aims at restricting liberty through placement in a secure, locked institution. Therapeutic detention seeks to provide helpful programs for diagnosis, remediation, and rehabilitation of the youth. Detention centers have served as a catchall for youths who need to be restrained, for youths who need assistance, and for youths no one is quite sure what else to do with. Judges also place youths in detention postdisposition, which is intended as a sanction. Confusion over the purpose of detention has led to an overreliance on detention as a policy in general and to overcrowded facilities and lawsuits for violations of civil liberties in particular. Judge Sharon McCully of the Third District Juvenile Court in Salt Lake City, Utah, explains that the juvenile bench must first recognize an inherent evil in juvenile detention. Detaining a child in a secure facility means a serious deprivation of liberty and a significant loss of personal dignity. Secure detention is not a beneficial substitute for parental custody, especially when detention mixes youths in need of care with the most serious juvenile criminals. She urges judges to adhere to basic standards for detention found in the juvenile statutes of most states:

1. *Failure to Appear.* There must be an objective basis for believing a child will fail to appear as the rationale for detention. Commission of a status offense or minor delinquent act is not sufficient if the offense charged would not result in a detention order.

2. *Preventive Detention.* The decision to detain a youth to protect the public by preventing further delinquent activity prior to adjudication should be based on objective criteria, such as risk prediction instruments or guidelines established by the court. Judges need to remember that alternatives to secure detention could be just as effective at preventing further criminal activity as secure confinement.

3. *Protection of the Juvenile.* Preventing juveniles from harming themselves (suicidal behavior), from their own self-destructive and immoral behaviors (such as prostitution), and from an abusive or neglectful home environment are worthy goals, but secure detention is not the best place to accomplish them (McCully 1994).

Judge McCully recognizes that the trend toward postadjudication detention is likely to continue because judges have no other alternatives for youths who repeatedly defy, ignore, and refuse to obey court orders. She urges communities to involve themselves in providing alternatives.

Cuyahoga County Juvenile Detention Center. Detention practices in Cuyahoga County (Cleveland), Ohio, reveal shifts in the rationale. By 1965, the old dormitory-style facility had become overcrowded. The rated capacity was 150 between 1966 and 1971; its population averaged 172 and frequently reached as high as 225 juveniles. In 1965, the county opened a new Court Annex facility which included a detention area with 78 beds. In 1973, Judge W. G. Witlatch of the Cuyahoga Juvenile Court initiated a detention control program to reduce detention of youths for reasons other than a danger to self or others or likelihood of absconding. In 1969, Cuyahoga County's detention policy was written into Ohio law, and by 1971, the detention population had declined 60 percent (Martin 1994).

The detention population increased in 1971 to a high of 117 in 1980, not because more juveniles were going in, but because those that did stayed longer. In 1981, the court established a home detention program as an alternative to secure detention, and in 1981, the first shelter care beds became available. By 1983, annual admissions to these two programs totalled 900, reducing the detention center admissions from 1980 levels. In 1985, with the detention center population rising, the juvenile court made plans to renovate and expand the facility. Instead, the county hired a new administrator committed to minimizing use of secure detention. The new administrator developed written policies for intake and reduced admissions. In 1988, the administrator appointed the manager of the court's home detention and shelter care program to monitor detention policies. The monitor established a 24-hour emergency shelter care program for unruly juveniles apprehended on warrants and coordinated 24-hour transportation to shelters so that youths assigned to shelter care did not need to spend a single night in secure detention (Martin 1994).

Since 1989, admissions to the Cuyahoga County Juvenile Detention Center have increased. The court received nearly triple the number of drug violation complaints, and the court instituted a policy of mandating secure detention for all juveniles charged with felony drug violations or commission of a crime with a firearm. Changes in the juvenile court bench and personnel at the center have also led to an increase (Martin 1994, 40–42).

Training Schools

Following the nineteenth-century philosophy, many training schools continue to be set up on the cottage system. Residents are housed in small cottages of 20 to 40, originally made of wood, but later of brick, stone, and concrete. Training schools are located in rural areas, and some deliver specialized programs and services. Diagnostic and reception centers are extensions of training schools. Juveniles are assigned to these centers for the first 30 to 90 days of their total commitment to a training school, primarily for diagnosis. Based on this diagnosis, they are routed to an appropriate facility to complete their disposition (Lozano *et al.* 1990, 25). Other training schools offer specialized academic, vocational, and therapy programs, such as sex offender treatment.

Stonewall Jackson School. Stonewall Jackson School at Concord is the oldest training school in North Carolina. The Division of Youth Services, North Carolina Department of Health and Human Services, currently operates five training schools. During 1969, two years after the National Council on Crime and Delinquency's national survey, North Carolina had 2,595 admissions (both status offenders and delinquents), the highest number of juveniles in training schools in the United States (Division of Youth Services 1997, 11).

Founded in 1909, the school resulted from a 17-year campaign led by James P. Cook, editor of the Concord *Standard*. Cook became a lifetime advocate of a state reform school for wayward boys after seeing a destitute 13 year old sentenced to 3 and a half years at hard labor on a chain gang for stealing $1.30. Cook teamed up with the King's Daughters, a group of club women, who began to raise funds for the school. Together they convinced Governor R. B. Glenn of the need for a school, and the governor convinced the legislature. There were several Confederate soldiers in the state assembly, and the bill needed their support for it to pass. When the sponsor amended the bill so that the school would be named after General Thomas "Stonewall" Jackson, the Confederate senators voted for the bill, and it passed by a margin of four votes (Concord Telephone Company 1995, 25).

Walter Thompson, who headed the Concord Schools, became the first superintendent. Before he left in 1913, two cottages went up, along with an administration building and a barn. There were 56 boys. By 1943, there were three other training schools, and the state legislature created the Board of Correction and Training to administer a unified training school system. Stonewall Jackson School and Cameron Morrison School, near Charlotte, were designated for older boys and specialized in high school and marketable vocational subjects. At Stonewall Jackson in 1943, there were 17 cottages, a refurbished administration building, and buildings housing trades, laundry, bakery, infirmary, dairy, textile plant, ice plant, gym (with swimming pool), and school building. Vocational instruction included shoe making, machine repair, sewing, printing, barbering, textile manufacture, and dairying. The school reached its largest population in 1954 when more than 500 boys were confined there (Concord Telephone Company 1995, 28). In 1972, the North Carolina Bar Association conducted a comprehensive analysis of the state's training schools. The report concluded that the deficiencies of the training school system should "spark concern, indignation—*even outrage*—among the people of North Carolina" and urged "phasing out of the present large institutions which are relics of our past" (Penal System Study Committee 1972, 3). In 1975, the general assembly passed an act to provide community-based alternatives to state training schools. In 1980, the legislature passed a revised juvenile code. The code provided that the maximum term in training school could be no longer than an adult would serve for the same offense and established a uniform statewide treatment program for children in training schools.

Presently, the typical training school stay begins with a two-week orientation. After completion of social, psychological, and academic testing, each student is assigned to a living cottage, a treatment team, and a school program. For most, the stay is nine months. For those with special treatment needs (sex offenders, substance abusers, serious offenders) and those with behavior problems, the stay is longer. About half of the students receive remedial math and reading programs, about a fifth receive special education services. The vocational education instruction allows students to gain work experience in traditional fields, such as barbering and horticulture, as well as areas of automotive technology, computer applications, and graphic communications (Division of Youth Services 1997). Table 12.1 shows a typical day in a North Carolina training school.

Except for the racial/ethnic background of the youths sent to Stonewall Jackson school, the profile has not changed over the years. The majority are male (86 percent), between the ages of 14 and 15 (65 percent), have had two or more previous adjudications (67 percent), come from a single parent family (72 percent), and have some history of substance abuse (55 percent). The racial composition of Stonewall Jackson's population has changed dramatically. The school was specifically opened for white boys, and the population remained white until 1965 when the Board of Juvenile Correction officially adopted a plan to desegregate all training schools. In 1997, the population at North Carolina training schools reached 64 percent minority, the majority of which were African American (Division of Youth Services 1997, 135).

Ethan Allen School. Ethan Allen School in Delafield, Wisconsin, is one of three juvenile correctional institutions for males operated by the Division of Youth Services. The school delivers a sex offender treatment program aimed at developing responsible, productive persons able to meet life's challenges.

TABLE 12.1   Daily Routine in a North Carolina Training School

6:00 A.M.	Awaken for showers, chores, medical call, breakfast.
8:00 A.M.–3:00 P.M.	Attend academic and vocational classes.
3:00 P.M.–6:00 P.M.	Return to cottage for treatment team activities, counseling sessions, mail call, dinner.
6:00–9:00 P.M.	Participate in recreational, counseling, religious, volunteer, or leisure activities; perform chores, eat snack, prepare for bed.
10:00 P.M.	Lights out.

The Stout Serious Sex Offender Treatment Program (SSOP) was developed in 1984 in response to the increase in commitments of juvenile sex offenders. The program is based on the cottage treatment principle in which all staff who interact daily with the youths participate in the delivery of treatment services. SSOP staff includes two full-time social workers, a group facilitator, seven youth counselors, six teachers, and a section manager. The team employs an intensive six-phase group therapy approach along with a four-level behavioral system through which the offender is expected to progress (Millard & Hagan 1996, 92).

Phase 1. The entry phase orients the youth to the cottage environment. The youth participates in an educational group and completes a group therapy interview by admitting sexual assaults.

Phase 2. The youth participates in group therapy. All begin in the intake group and after completing a written assessment are assigned to the regular or fast-track groups.

Phase 3. Group therapy focuses on each youth's personal sexual history and issues of anger and control. Youths write and present a sexual autobiography.

Phase 4. Group therapy focuses on issues such as family, chemical abuse, victimization, feelings of anger and powerlessness, and self-concept. Youths move to phase 5 when they have completed their answers and have successfully incorporated the critique of their autobiography.

Phase 5. The final group therapy phase seeks to integrate previous learning and enable youths to plan for the future. Youths prepare and present one-year and five-year goals.

Phase 6. Reintegration planning prepares the youth to leave SSOP. Before returning to the community, youths must have attained level three or four status within the behavioral system demonstrating consistent social skills. Others may remain in the institution and participate in additional treatment programs (Millard & Hagan 1996, 94–95).

Chapter 980 of the Wisconsin statutes requires review of certain classes of sex offenses by the attorney general's office. The attorney general's office must determine whether a juvenile may be released or requires further treatment. The Sexually Violent Person Act Committee meets each month at Ethan Allen School to review cases of those reaching the final 120 days of their scheduled release. The committee makes a recommendation to the Office of Juvenile Offender Review, the releasing authority for juvenile corrections, and the office forwards a copy to the attorney general's office for final decision. SSOP participants have been tracked since the program's inception. Follow-up studies report failure rates (return juvenile/adult institution or probation/parole violation for new sexual offense) of 10 percent. The program graduates about 20 each year (Millard & Hagan 1996, 95–96).

Deinstitutionalization

Since 1971 or so, states have sought to reduce their detention center and training school populations. Four years earlier, the National Council on Crime and Delinquency (NCCD) surveyed juvenile detention and corrections facilities at the request of the President's Commission on Law Enforcement and the Administration of Justice. The NCCD survey found that the average daily population in juvenile correctional facilities was 42,000. Nearly half the state facilities were overcrowded, and rehabilitation programs were limited. The survey concluded that although training schools represented specialized facilities for rehabilitating hardened juvenile delinquents, there was such a wide discrepancy between planned and available services that they amounted to little more than warehouses. As a result, juvenile policymakers feared that juvenile institutions might be doing more harm than good (Howell 1998).

Massachusetts took the lead in closing large institutions for juveniles. In 1971, Jerome Miller, Commissioner of the Massachusetts Department of Youth Services, abruptly removed most of the youth from the state's training schools and placed them in community-based programs. Juveniles requiring secure detention were placed in small facilities of 20 to 30 beds each. Massachusetts continues to operate with only a fraction of the beds used in other states, and the majority of youths are placed in small, privately managed programs. Over the past two decades, other states, including Maryland, Pennsylvania, and Utah, have moved to deinstitutionalize juvenile corrections as well. Colorado, Oklahoma, Oregon, and Pennsylvania have followed the lead of Massachusetts and Utah and rely on a network of private agencies to provide community-based residential and nonresidential services (Greenwood 1996, 75–76).

In 1972, the same year the last training school was closed in Massachusetts, U.S. Senator Birch Bayh introduced the Juvenile Justice and Delinquency Prevention Act. The JJDP Act, enacted in 1974, called for deinstitutionalizing status offenders (DSO) nationwide. The act required states to move all status offenders from detention and correctional facilities to shelter-care facilities. Four years later, the mandate was clarified with the "substantial compliance standard," which gave states two years to reduce status offender populations in corrections facilities by 75 percent. Should a state fail to make sufficient progress, it could become ineligible for federal funding through the act. By 1992, 5 states achieved full compliance and 29 others reached full compliance with minimal exceptions (Holden & Kepler 1995).

The Massachusetts DSO model followed the observation that warehousing young lawbreakers in large training schools was counterproductive. Training schools swept up status offenders who would otherwise not have been incarcerated. They also returned with the enduring stigma of a reform school, prepared for little else other than institutional living. Rural training schools not only separated young people from corrupting influences of the city but also from family members and friends. The demise of the indenture system resulted in returning those who had been confined to the environment from which they had come, and they returned to a delinquent lifestyle.

Deinstitutionalization has its critics as well. Although status offenders are much less likely to be found in secure detention or training schools today, many have been relabeled and placed in private mental health or other child care institutions. The result has not been "deinstitutionalization," but rather, "transinstitutionalization," substituting hospital stays for commitments to training schools. Inpatient psychiatric and chemical dependency units in nonprofit and for-profit hospitals and free-standing residential settings have been described as the "hidden system" of institutionalization, the nouveau training schools for the affluent. Deinstitutionalization of status offenders left a void in the care of troubled juveniles, especially where alternative services have not been developed. Where the network of community services did not develop sufficiently, runaways and others are at risk of serious victimization by adult offenders on the streets (Aliosi 1992, 238).

Training Delinquents, but for What?

Training schools are defended on the grounds that community programs have not proven more effective and that institutional environments are necessary to protect the public. Training schools alert delinquents to the painful consequences of violating the law and deter future delinquent behavior. Correctional facilities also serve to incapacitate delinquents by removing the small portion of chronic, serious juvenile criminals from public circulation. On the other hand, confinement in a training school or other secure corrections facility may do more harm than good. Bringing delinquents together in any unsupervised or unstructured setting is particularly risky. Peer pressure appears to be strong toward continued delinquency. Since they first appeared, training schools have been shadowed by the issue of what sort of training they provide: training for living as self-sufficient, productive members of society or training in the craft of hardened criminals (Greenwood 1996, 82–83).

Education researchers distinguish between the written curriculum and the learned curriculum. The written curriculum is found in the teacher's lesson plans, the textbook, and the ancillary materials teachers distribute to students. The learned curriculum is what students actually learn; it includes all elements of the classroom environment, whether planned or not. In the written curriculum of training schools, students learn vocational skills, academic subjects, and life skills through a controlled environment and academic, vocational, and counseling programs. In the learned curriculum version, students learn from other students as well as instructors. The difference between written and learned curriculum is important for understanding the value of training schools because there is a great deal of evidence that training schools do not deliver the written curriculum. The negative effect of confinement helps explain the paradox of juvenile justice: Most juveniles adjudicated in juvenile court do not become adult criminals, but most of those confined in juvenile corrections facilities do.

Most training schools are overcrowded, and it is difficult to say what portion of the written curriculum is delivered in this environment. A recent OJJDP study of conditions of confinement within juvenile corrections facilities found that nearly half (47 percent) were overcrowded. The study surveyed 984 public and private juvenile detention centers, reception centers, training schools, ranches, camps, and farms (Office of Juvenile Justice and Delinquency Prevention 1994). In Ohio, overcrowding reached 175 percent in 1992 and prompted the Ohio Department of Youth Services to rethink the usefulness of its correctional institutions. The Ohio DYS had 2,500 youthful offenders in aging institutions designed to hold only 1,400. Such overcrowding limited meaningful programming, increased assaults on staff and youths, and decreased public safety, which led to a major overhaul of juvenile corrections within the state (Natalucci-Persichetti & Rapp-Zimmerman 1997, 15–16).

The learned curriculum in institutional environments raises serious questions about the effectiveness of training schools. Confinement in a juvenile corrections facility represents a stop on the road to a criminal career. Utah decided to close its large institution, the 166-bed Youth Development Center, after realizing the institutional approach was not working. Three out of four "graduates" from the center went on to commit new offenses after release. Most of these youth had been confined for nonviolent offenses and had been turned into hardened criminals while confined. "We were creating good inmates," explained C. Ronald Stromberg, superintendent of the Youth Development Center. "We got the youth out of bed every morning, taught them how to pick up a tray, go through a food line three times a day, how to line up and 'march' to school, the cafeteria, the gymnasium, and we conducted head counts. When they left our facility we knew they'd be able to adapt quickly to prison life. What we were not doing was teaching them to be good productive citizens" (Donziger 1996, 139).

Critics charge that training schools tend to offer stale and unimaginative programs, are inappropriate surroundings to foster rehabilitation, and allow abuse and mistreatment of residents. Placing youths, who are adolescents in the formative stages of personality development, into secure custodial facilities risks the development of youths with "institutional" personalities. These youths will know little about the outside world, and instead develop behaviors and values consistent with the values that prevail at the institution. Community-based alternatives are favored because they provide more realistic settings in which youths can learn needed social skills and maintain contact with families, schools, and employers (Forst, Fagen, & Vivona 1989, 1–4).

Carl S. Taylor (1996, 36), an ethnographic researcher at Michigan State University, explains how the environment within juvenile corrections facilities may foster criminality:

1. *Confinement disrupts the family unit.* The male youth who winds up in a detention facility often provides economic support, which places the remaining members of the family under greater stress and younger siblings at greater risk of delinquency.

2. *Negative identity formation.* Once the youth has been confined, identity forms around negative images of bad and outcast. Youth are more likely to view their life chances negatively.

3. *Physical and emotional detachment.* The physical separation from family members can lead to emotional detachment. This disinvestment in others retards social skills and produces feelings of loneliness, depression, and powerlessness.

4. *Socialization within a criminal subculture.* Within institutions, the process of victimization and vengeance solidifies a delinquent outlook. Juveniles exchange information, criminal skills, and the values and outlook of delinquent subcultures.

One training school veteran, a 33-year-old gang warlord who had spent time in Detroit's Wayne County Youth Home, put it this way: "The Youth Home is where you learn the basics, it's like basic training before you become a full-time gangster. They'll teach you in the Home, plenty of s— to make you street smart, make you hard . . . yeah, that's the first place to learn 'bout what the rest of your life is gonna be . . ." (Taylor 1996, 36).

Training school is a lot like sunshine on a clear day: A little produces a pleasant effect on the skin, but too much results in a serious burn. Training schools represent a valuable resource for those youths who have histories of violent behavior and severe emotional problems and who pose a danger to the public. However, training schools represent a serious liability when they become a means to forget about the unwanted troublemakers.

The DMC Issue

The chances of confinement for African American youths is much higher than for others. The problem of locking up large numbers of black juveniles has become such an issue that the Office of Juvenile Justice and Delinquency Prevention gave it an acronym, DMC, for disproportionate minority confinement.

Numerically speaking, the problem of ***disproportionate minority confinement*** means that a larger percentage of African American youth are confined than their percentage of the youth population. OJJDP-sponsored research examined the prevalence of minority youths in juvenile corrections facilities in 16 states. These studies revealed that African American youths had the highest prevalence rates of all segments of the population in 15 of the 16 states. In two states, it was estimated that 1 in 7 African American males, compared with 1 in 125 white males, would be incarcerated before the age of 18. Across the county in 1995, minority youths represented about 32 percent of the youth population and about 68 percent in juvenile corrections facilities, such as training schools. This was a significant increase over 1983, when minority youths constituted 56 percent of the population in juvenile corrections facilities (Hsia 1998, 1).

The problem of disproportionate minority confinement cannot be understood with reference to numbers. Rather it must be viewed in terms of its impact on African Americans. The consequence of DMC over the decades is a belief that doing time in a corrections facility is a normal part of growing up; it is a milestone comparable to high school graduation. DMC became a national issue with the Coalition for Juvenile Justice's report, *A Delicate Balance* (1988). The report prompted the National Council of Juvenile and Family Court Judges to undertake an intensive analysis of minority youths in the juvenile justice system. In 1989, the council convened a national conference in St. Louis, Missouri, "The Disproportionate Incarceration of Minority Youth in America: A National Forum," and issued a report documenting disparate outcomes for minority youth at each stage of proceedings. The report found that minority youths were incarcerated in public institutions at a rate three to four times that of white youths. Furthermore, minority youth were not placed in private facilities at the same rate as they were placed in public facilities. Minorities represented only 35 percent of youths in private facilities, and whites represented 65 percent of this population (National Council of Juvenile and Family Court Judges 1990, 7).

In 1988, Congress amended the Juvenile Justice and Delinquency Prevention Act to address the overrepresentation of minorities in the juvenile justice system. Congress required that states seeking JJDP formula grants address efforts to reduce disproportionate incarceration of minority youth. If the proportion of minority youths detained or confined in secure detention and correctional facilities, jails, and lockups exceeded the proportion of such groups in the general population, the act required those states to develop a strategy to reduce those proportions. Phase I of the initiative required studies of overrepresentation. Phase II required states that found problems to develop program strategies and models to eliminate disproportionate confinement of minority youths.

In 1992, disproportionate minority confinement became a core requirement, with future funding tied to state compliance. Core requirement meant that states that did not comply risked loss of federal funds for juvenile delinquency research and programs. OJJDP selected five pilot states for further analysis of the disproportionate minority confinement issue: Arizona, Florida, Iowa, North Carolina, and Oregon. Although the minority proportion varied by state, each of the five pilot sites found overrepresentation of minority youth in secure confinement. Disproportionality was true not only for confinement but also at every step of the juvenile justice process: complaint, arrest, intake, detention, petition, adjudication, and waiver to adult court. In other words, the disparity between minority and majority youth increased as youths proceeded through the legal process. This process is known as accumulated disadvantaged status. The effects of decisions at early stages culminate at the "back end" of the system—that is, confinement to an institution (Mann 1994).

Janice Joseph (2000, 233–234) at Richard Stockton College in New Jersey offers a fourfold prescription for reducing racial discrimination within the juvenile justice system:

1. *States should develop comprehensive, culturally sensitive training programs for all juvenile justice personnel.* Training programs should focus on racial and ethnic differences and how insensitivity to these distinctions can lead to discriminatory treatment.

2. *States should increase the number of minorities employed at all levels of the juvenile justice system.* The recruitment of minority police officers, attorneys, and judges will not ensure sensitivity to racial and ethnic differences but will lead to better understanding of minority youths and help restore minority confidence in the system.

3. *States should mandate that all agencies of juvenile justice monitor, evaluate, and review decisions for discrimination.* States should provide clear guidelines for decision making and monitor each stage to determine where changes are needed.

4. *States should establish procedures for reporting, recording, and investigating discrimination in the system.* States should establish formal reporting procedures, similar to those for sexual harassment, for responding to those who engage in discrimination within the system.

Alternatives to Training School

Each state has a juvenile corrections agency. The organization of these agencies varies with state government. In about a third of the states, juvenile correctional agencies function as a subdivision of the state's department of health and human services. Colorado, Connecticut, Delaware, Kansas, Missouri, New Mexico, and Wisconsin are organized this way. In about a third, there are freestanding juvenile agencies that answer directly to the governor. This method of organization occurs in Arizona, Florida, Georgia, Idaho, Maryland, Nebraska, New York, Tennessee, and Texas. In other states, juvenile corrections functions as part of the state department of corrections. Illinois, Indiana, Louisiana, Maine, Minnesota, and North Dakota operate juvenile corrections as part of adult corrections. Still other states have different arrangements. In New Jersey, there is a Division of Juvenile Operations within the Department of Corrections for juvenile institutions and a Division of Juvenile Services within the Department of Human Services, which has responsibility for residential and day programs (Dedel 1998). In addition to state facilities, there are local and private facilities. Local facilities are operated by cities and counties. Private facilities are more common. State juvenile justice agencies contract with private vendors, particularly for group homes

and residential facilities. California, Kansas, Minnesota, Ohio, Tennessee, and Virginia operate county-based systems. In these states, the capacity at county facilities amounts to a third
or half of state facilities. In Minnesota, the majority of juvenile corrections facilities are
county-based; there are more than 1,076 beds at locally operated facilities and about 315 at
state-operated facilities. Florida, Maryland, Michigan, Oregon, Pennsylvania, Tennessee,
Utah, West Virginia, and Wisconsin operate large private juvenile corrections facilities.
Some states have privatized nearly all of juvenile corrections. In Pennsylvania, the capacity
at privately operated facilities is 6,309, with only 745 at state facilities (Dedel 1998, 523).

Camps, Ranches, and Farms

Camps, ranches, and farms developed in response to the perceived negative effects of placing youth in a prison atmosphere. Forestry and wilderness camps, ranches, and farms offer
open settings without the gates, guns, and bars that are found in urban areas. *Camps,
ranches,* and *farms,* which feature a series of physically challenging outdoor activities for
small groups, are designed to meet youth's desire for thrill and adventure in a socially
approved way. These programs provide a middle ground between sending a youth to a
prison or reformatory, which lack rehabilitative services, and returning the youth to the
community without providing treatment services. They are intended to instill self-control,
build self-esteem, encourage self-reliance, and develop basic academic and vocational
skills (Roberts 1988, 1998). Judge Samuel R. Blake, Kenyon Scudder, and Karl Holton
lobbied the legislature for a program for transient boys. The California legislature passed
legislation establishing forestry camps for delinquent boys to be run by the county. These
programs operated for boys only, and they stayed for about six months. These early forestry
camps were soon to be modeled after the Civilian Conservation Corps camps that operated
between 1933 and 1943. The goal was to provide treatment that included conservation of
natural resources and vocational training. Early forestry camps emphasized work in the
nursery, reforestation, brush clearance, and fire suppression. Most camps had a nursery
where youths learned to gather seeds from mountainous areas, grow seedlings, and trans-
plant young plants in areas scorched by fires. They also included counseling and group
activities. Night school classes featured remedial education in academic subjects (Roberts
1998).

Last Chance Ranch.   The Florida Environmental Institute (FEI), popularly known as
"Last Chance Ranch," targets Florida's most serious juvenile lawbreakers. The FEI is operated by Associated Marine Institutes, a network of affiliated programs operating in seven
states. Located in a remote area of the Florida Everglades, it has a capacity of 40: 20 in a
residential component and 20 in the nonresidential aftercare component. The average
length of participation is 18 months with a residential stay of at least 9 months. Although
FEI handles serious delinquents, it is not a locked facility. Surrounded by forests and
swamp, it is considered a secure facility.

The FEI program philosophy focuses on education as a means of reducing recidivism
and views hard work as a therapeutic means of teaching vocational skills. The program
employs a system of rewards for positive behavior and sanctions for inappropriate behavior.

It promotes bonding with staff role models and includes a strong aftercare component. The program begins with a three-day orientation. During orientation, treatment plans are devised, work projects assigned, and the bonding process begins. The youth help clear land, cook food, tend animals, and attend school within a strict environment; those that do not follow the program receive a work assignment featuring physical labor (Kahler 1993, A4). Phase 1 emphasizes work and education. Students must earn points to move on to Phase 2, where they can participate in paid projects and earn money to meet restitution agreements. Near the end of Phase 2, students return to their communities; the program assists in job placement and rebuilding family relationships. In the third phase, students live in their community but maintain weekly contact with aftercare staff. If they break curfew or engage in criminal activity, they return to the residential portion of the program (Howell 1995, 155–156).

The Associated Marine Institutes began in 1969 when Judge Frank Orland and businessman Bob Rosof took some boys declared wards of the court on Rosof's marine research vessel. Pleased by the progress, Judge Orlando continued to refer children, and six programs were eventually organized. AMI's programs serve youths between the ages of 14 and 18. They seek to help them meet their responsibilities, develop employable skills, increase their self-confidence, and encourage further education. The programs draw on the geographic features of each community, using the ocean, wilderness, rivers, and lakes to develop exciting programs. Programs feature oceanography, earth sciences, diving, seamanship, aquatics, physical education, and academic and vocational education. After completing the program, each youth is placed in school, a job, or the armed forces.

VisionQuest.   One of the most widely known wilderness programs is VisionQuest, an outdoor adventure program established by Robert Burton in Tucson, Arizona, in 1973. Burton, a controversial figure who invokes loyal praise and bitter criticism, operates several types of programs, including wilderness programs in Pennsylvania and New Mexico. Burton's programs feature a blind walk in which youth are blindfolded and a solo that requires each participant to spend three days alone with limited food and water. Youths do rock climbing, rappelling, and a six-mile run. VisionQuest also operates the wagon train program. A wagon train takes youths 15 to 20 miles a day in a caravan of covered wagons. Youths must work together to keep the wagon train on its scheduled course; each "family" of youths has responsibility for its own wagon, horse, mule, and equipment. Youths establish camp each night, and after chores, participate in an educational program (Roberts 1998, 335–336).

In 1977, VisionQuest began incorporating buffalo soldiers into the wagon train program. Buffalo soldiers refer to certain all-black military units within the U.S. armed forces. The name originated in the nineteenth century, following creation of the all-black cavalry and infantry regiments by the U.S. Congress in 1866. The Cheyenne called the African Americans who served in the 10th Cavalry Buffalo Soldiers out of respect for their fierce fighting on the Great Plains. Many of the men who served in segregated units of the U.S. Army during World War II and the Korean War are still alive and participate in the Buffalo Soldiers program. VisionQuest's Buffalo Soldiers program teaches youth the history of all-black cavalry regiments along with precision marching drills and horseback formations. In the final stages of the program, youth reenact the history and educate the community by performing these drills in parades for elementary schools.

Eckerd Camps.   The Eckerd Foundation underwrites theraputic wilderness camps. The foundation was established by Jack Eckerd, who made a fortune through his chain of pharmacies. The foundation established it first program in Brooksville, Florida, in 1968. Since then, camps have opened in North Carolina, Georgia, New Hampshire, Tennessee, Rhode Island, and Vermont.

The camps serve children of ages 10 to 17; most participants are between the ages of 13 and 15. The camps emphasize helping children find better methods of dealing with their emotions and teaching them realistic problem-solving skills. The Eckerd Foundation seeks to provide children's services throughout the state based on concepts of individual dignity, self-esteem, and self-improvement. In North Carolina, the foundation's funds were matched by state funds and other private foundations. Each camp is designed to treat 60 boys, age 7 to 17, who live year-round in small residential therapy groups of ten participants and two staff members. Length of stay is about 12 months. Units for girls were added at two sites in 1983 and 1984 (Alley & Wilson 1994, 45). The camping program features a four-week precamp experience in which youth participate in hikes, rope courses, and swimming tests to assess physical agility and emotional adjustment. The campers are assigned tents and activity groups based on staff observations. During the camp, participants experience a trail life program featuring a variety of outdoor activities including; rock climbing, hiking, whitewater rafting, horseback riding, and cave exploring. During the final week, each participant completes a solo experience, in which they spend a night alone in the wilderness. In addition, juveniles observe staff perform activities that model positive behaviors (Roberts 1998, 342–343).

Boot Camps

During the 1980s, boot camps became a popular program for juveniles. ***Boot camps*** offer a military-style environment, separation of participants from regular inmates where programs are housed in correctional facilities, and some form of hard labor (Peters *et al.* 1997, 2–3). The term *boot camp* is also used along with *shock incarceration* to describe programs aimed at shocking youth into acceptable behavior. Zebulon Brockway pioneered the original military-style program at Elmira, New York, more than a hundred years ago; modern boot camps began in 1983. They have proved popular for both juvenile and adult offenders. By 1991, boot camp programs had been established in 23 states, not counting programs established by cities and counties and numerous juvenile boot camps (MacKenzie & Souryal 1991, 90). Most boot camp programs range from 90 to 120 days. The programs are styled after the military model for basic training. Participants are usually nonviolent, first-time offenders. Boot camp participants are not mixed with regular inmates; they reside in separate housing units and participate in military drills, physical training, and treatment-oriented activities. Elements of boot camp include drills, ceremonies, and physical training, as well as substance abuse education, drug/alcohol treatment, physical labor, and basic education. The programs are designed to instill respect for authority, promote discipline, improve confidence, reduce criminal behavior, and promote positive social behaviors. Some boot camp programs include treatment intervention such as group counseling, individual counseling, or milieu therapy. Youth may receive an option of boot camp participation or commitment to more traditional training school programs. Most programs are brief, ranging from three to six months (Peters, Thomas *et al.* 1997).

Multi-ethnic group of teen wards in gray sweats marches at L.A. City Youth Authority.
Copyright A. Ramsey / Photo Edit—All rights reserved.

Boot camps rely on the basic premise that military discipline is just what young offenders need to straighten them out. Roger Redd, who began a military-style physical training program in 1991 in Fayetteville, North Carolina, for juveniles on probation, explains that his aim is to teach personal responsibility and break young men of their "I am a victim" mentality. "If you're using your conscience every day, then you're not going to go out and do something stupid," Redd tells the young men. "By the time you leave here, you should be remorseful for what you've done." Redd explains that most of the young men he works with have never learned discipline or respect; they get into trouble because they are followers. The military training teaches good habits, which bring about good attitudes and help them to act independently (Loconte 1977). "Boot camps . . . are not intended to make a young person into a fully functional soldier," the director of special alternative incarceration at the Michigan Department of Corrections explains, "Rather, they provide a foundation of discipline, responsibility and self-esteem the military can build on during the advanced training that follows" (Hengesh 1991, 106). Correctional boot camps "provide a strong foundation parole and probation officers can build on in guiding young offenders into necessary community-based programs that will help them" (Hengesh 1991, 106). Young offenders have a false sense of pride stemming from criminal lifestyles and have resentment for authority. This must be stripped away before they can develop self-esteem, self-discipline, personal responsibility, and a work ethic. Through succeeding in educational programming, physical conditioning, and work programs, juveniles experience personal growth and development. They begin to understand how good it feels to achieve (Hengesh 1991, 106, 108).

On the other hand, critics have asked, "Why would a method that has been developed to prepare people to go into war, and as a tool to manage legal violence, be considered as having such potential in deterring or rehabilitating offenders?" (Morash & Rucker 1990, 206). At the same time, the popular appeal of boot camps is based on an overly simplified and exaggerated notion of military training, now outdated and rejected by the military itself. The negatively oriented model that relies on aggressive tactics to train people to act prosocially is founded on a contradiction: the idea of using hostile and intimidating tactics to teach people not to get what they want by using hostile and intimidating tactics. There is also a "distorted image of masculinity embodied in the idea of boot camp" (Morash & Rucker 1990, 215). Boot camp philosophy based on making men out of boys links masculinity with power and aggression. Boot camps contain a disproportionate number of minorities and underclass members (Morash & Rucker 1990). Margaret Beyer, a Washington, D.C., psychologist, argues that "juvenile boot camps don't make sense" because they violate basic principles of adolescent development. Teenagers are "fairness fanatics" who see group punishment as unfair; they reject imposed structure and react with "authority problems" to attempts to control their lives. Teenagers respond to encouragement, not punishment (Beyer 1996).

In 1995, the federal government appropriated $24.5 million for boot camp programs. By 1997, however, the wave of enthusiasm for boot camps had crested. Arizona and Maryland closed boot camps programs due to high costs, reports of incidents involving abuses by staff, and the lack of aftercare services. In Arizona, a study found that almost 70 percent of 1,253 youths sent to boot camp during a 3-year period were back in custody within 7 years either for new crimes or technical violations of parole (Davidson 1997, A20).

The Rehabilitation Question

The whole idea of juvenile justice is to rehabilitate young lawbreakers and keep them from becoming criminals as adults. Rehabilitation programs fell on hard times during the 1980s, and legislators, policymakers, administrators, and others demanded to know what works. But determining what works isn't easy.

Searching for What Works

During the 1970s, a debate occurred among researchers about whether anything in juvenile justice really worked. In 1974, Robert Martinson published a widely cited report which asserted that "nothing works." After reviewing hundreds of evaluations of correctional treatment programs, Martinson concluded that "with few and isolated exceptions, the rehabilitative efforts that have been reported so far have had no appreciable effect on recidivism" (Martinson 1974, 25). Other researchers took issue with Martinson's report, arguing that some programs work for some offenders. Basically, the counterargument to Martinson insisted that it was not fair to lump all programs together. Rather, finding effective treatment programs was a matter of identifying those offenders who could benefit from specific kinds of programs. Other researchers identified successful programs (McCollum 1977; Palmer 1975).

The debate continues today, although "nothing works" has become the conventional wisdom and "some programs do work" is a perennial challenge. In part, the debate was about philosophy. Some legislators, policymakers, social critics, and others who favored a shift away from rehabilitation simply disagree with rehabilitation. The argument is that young lawbreakers deserve punishment or their "just deserts," not treatment and a second chance. Others favor the end to rehabilitation based on the observation that there is no cure for delinquency. Juvenile offenders cannot be successfully rehabilitated, so the best that can be done is keep them from harming someone else. The issue is about exactly how to define "success."

Recidivism: The Acid Test?   When legislators, administrators, and others ask, "Does it work?" the discussion usually involves reference to recidivism. **Recidivism** can be conceptually defined as a "return to crime" or "repeated criminal behavior." It is a slippery concept operationally and raises difficult issues for program evaluations.

Evaluations of recidivism do not really measure recidivist behavior at all. They actually measure whether a person is caught again. Those individuals who complete a program, or who are part of the control group, who engage in further illegal activity but are not caught are not counted as recidivists because no one knows about them. Evaluators cannot be faulted for not counting behavior no one knows about, of course, but to say that a program must reduce recidivism to be successful when recidivism cannot be measured raises a dilemma. Imagine medical researchers trying to find out if a particular drug was a cure for cancer without knowing whether the disease was in remission or not among those who took the drug. It may seem not worthwhile to do the study, but that is the situation evaluation researchers in juvenile justice face.

In any study of program effectiveness using recidivism as an outcome measure, the definition of recidivism must be specified, and the particulars are extremely important. How recidivism is defined by the researcher determines what is actually measured, given that repeat illegal behavior cannot really be measured. There are a number of ways to define recidivism, and researchers must decide which is the most meaningful within the context of the research and the program:

- *Researchers must decide if failure to complete program is due to recidivism.* If youths fail to meet the conditions of program attendance because they don't show up for classes or because they do not complete assignments, is that recidivism? Does recidivism mean failure to complete the program or getting in trouble with the law again?

- *Is any violation of the law recidivism?* If a youth referred to a substance abuse program remains drug-free but is rearrested for assault within the follow-up period, is that a failure? Is the program successful in terms of drug addiction but not successful in terms of keeping juveniles out of trouble? Does recidivism mean free of the behavior that led to referral to the program or trouble-free in general?

- *Researchers must decide the jurisdiction.* These are arbitrary definitions for the most part. Rarely, if ever, do researchers have access to national records. Most studies must rely on local records, and those who relocate or offend outside the jurisdiction of interest are simply not counted as recidivists. Is a youth who does not violate the law in the same county or city but moves away to commit another violation in a neighboring state a success?

■ *Similarly, researchers must decide the length of follow-up.* How long does it take to say that a person is rehabilitated? Is a person who remains trouble-free three years rehabilitated? For a year? For six months?

Finally, there is a conceptual problem with the way recidivism is measured. James Q. Wilson has observed that studies that report recidivism rates really do not report rates at all; they merely report the percentage who fail. Rate means the incidence of delinquency within a given population over a particular period of time—that is, the overall level of delinquency within a community or population. For example, if 40 of the 50 participants in a shoplifting prevention program shoplifted an average of twice a month during the follow-up period compared to an average of five times a week prior to participation in the program, the program would appear to be successful in reducing shoplifting behavior. Using the traditional understanding of recidivism, however, these 40 would be counted as program failures, and the recidivism rate would be reported at 80 percent, which suggests the program failed dramatically (Wilson 1983, 171).

This misunderstanding of recidivism rate has profound implications for deciding which programs "work" and which are not effective. However, rarely do researchers have access to this kind of information about the youths under study, and the majority mistakenly report the "recidivism rate" when they mean to say "the percentage who failed." As important as it is to know the impact a program has on the behavior that those delivering the program seek to change, researchers simply lack the measurement tools. Deciding what programs are effective using this formulation of recidivism is something like looking for a pair of shoes in a store that has no half sizes. Because the pair that fits "just right" cannot be found, the decision is made to settle for avoiding those that are "too big" or "too small."

Selection Bias. Another troubling issue for evaluation of programs is trying to decide whether the results obtained were in fact due to the program or to some characteristic of the group selected for participation in the program. To put it another way, the question of whether a program works for a group of young offenders cannot be separated from the question of which young offenders participate in the program. This problem of a stacked deck is known as ***selection bias.***

There are at least two sides to the selection problem. First, whenever a juvenile intake worker or other juvenile justice official decides which offender to send to a particular program, selection bias affects the outcome of any study designed to figure out whether the program is effective. To say that a program for first-time offenders is successful because the majority of those who complete the program do not go on to commit more serious offenses is not saying much when the youths referred to the program—those youths who commit the least serious offenses—are the most likely to avoid getting into more serious trouble anyway. The program appears to work only because all the "good kids" were sent to that particular program.

Second, anytime juvenile offenders are allowed to choose for themselves which program to participate in, self-selection will affect the outcome of a study designed to find out whether it works. This is because the program participants differ in at least one important way from those who do not participate—they are by definition more motivated to succeed. It is difficult to say the program turned around the youths when those youths who participated had already decided to turn themselves around (Knepper 1989, 113–114).

The problem is not that program administrators consciously stack the deck to make themselves look good; the problem is that however the deck is stacked, it's hard for evaluators to separate program effects from selection effects when examining evaluation findings. In biology, chemistry, medicine, and other fields, researchers counter the selection bias problem with random assignment. All of the cancer patients willing to try a new drug and who fit the criteria for study (have the type of cancer under study, do not possess other health problems, and so on) are randomly assigned to receive either the new drug or a harmless substitute (placebo). Because those who received the new drug were randomly assigned to the study group, the researchers can attribute any positive effect on the cancer to the drug and not to some difference in motivation, physical health, and so on. Random assignment is, however, seldom possible in juvenile justice. It would be unfair to young offenders, their families, and their victims for researchers to experiment with young lives. Juvenile justice professionals are legally and ethically obligated to do their best for each young person despite the scientific knowledge that might be gained from regarding some as human guinea pigs.

Unintended Effects.   Another conundrum in evaluation research is ***unintended effects.*** Even when programs are delivered as designed, the impact may be other than the goals. Although programs are intended to have positive effects, they may have unintended negative effects. In the simplest terms, a juvenile sent to juvenile court for truancy may as a result no longer fear court and return to school with a lack of respect for authority at school and the court. Net widening, one of the most intractable unintended effects in juvenile justice, is a problem with programs established as alternatives. Many community-based programs are intended to reduce overcrowding in secure detention, residential, and other institutional settings. Juveniles whose offenses fit a category eligible for placement in a new community program are referred to a program such as intensive probation rather than a group home or other institutional setting. The intended effect is that the 50 youths on intensive probation relieve the strain on the state's institution population. However, if at the end of the new program's first year the institutional population is more overcrowded than before and the new intensive probation program is filled to capacity, the program has succeeded only in increasing the overall juvenile justice population by 50, not decreasing it. This overall increase is known as "net widening," one of the most visible unintended effects of alternative programs.

Defining Success.   Finding a cure for delinquency is more difficult than finding a cure for cancer. Finding a cure for cancer is a serious challenge, but medical researchers have one advantage over delinquency researchers: They can recognize a cure when they see one. Deciding whether a proposed drug works can be done by looking at whether it puts cancer in remission. If cancer patients who take the new drug live longer, the drug works. But delinquency research is less clear. If recidivism is not a valid measure, then what constitutes success? The challenge for evaluation researchers is to decide what constitutes success. If an alternative program boasts a low recidivism rate, but at the same time catches more young people in the net of juvenile justice control than would otherwise be caught, in what sense is the program effective? In what sense is the program an alternative?

There are several characteristics of successful programs—some are borrowed from the medical community:

■ *Above all, do no harm.* Delinquency programs, like medical procedures, should help, not hurt, the target populations. Therapies or programs that promise great rewards but that negatively impact young people should be avoided.

■ *Do the benefits outweigh the side effects?* Every program, just like every medicine, has side effects. Although sometimes necessary, surgical procedures cause stress to the body, and it is best to try a less invasive procedure before surgery. Similarly, programs that cause less disruption to the lives of young people should be tried before those that represent greater risk. The same is true of expenses. If less expensive programs seem to have results as good as more expensive programs, policymakers should rely on the less expensive programs.

■ *Overlapping strategies overcome gaps.* Rather than search for a "miracle cure," a single program that works for everything, it makes more sense from a program standpoint to use a combination of strategies. If a program appears to have good results, even if researchers are not sure exactly why it works, it is wise not to rely on it exclusively, but use it in combination with other programs. OJJDP and several states have developed comprehensive strategies. If one programs works with some youths and a different program works with others, the chances of overall positive effects are improved.

The Shape of Success

One way to find promising programs is through meta-analysis. **Meta-analysis** is a statistical technique that allows reviewers to compare results across programs while controlling for differences in sample size and evaluation methods. Meta-analysis provides for systematic assessments of evaluation results for large numbers of programs. To reach a conclusion about the effectiveness of a particular program or approach, it is best if the results from several evaluations of individual programs are aggregated and then systematically analyzed (Greenwood 1996, 77).

The Cognitive Model.   Meta-analysis has been used to isolate the essential ingredients of rehabilitation. Carol J. Garrett (1985) conducted a meta-analysis of the effects of residential treatment on adjudicated delinquents. She concluded that treatment of delinquents in institutional or community settings does work. She found that programs pursuing a cognitive-behavioral approach appeared more successful than any other.

Robert Ross and his colleagues at the University of Ottawa carried out a meta-analysis of 317 studies. They concluded that "although most successful programs were multi-faceted . . . one type of treatment was common to most of them: some technique that could have an impact on the offender's *thinking*" (Izzo & Ross 1990, 139). The *cognitive model* holds that altering the way juveniles think about themselves and their place in society is the key to effective treatment. Since "criminogenic thinking" puts young people at risk for engaging in delinquent acts, it is necessary to change the way they think.

The cognitive model insists that many delinquents experience developmental delays in the acquisition of cognitive skills needed for appropriate social behavior. Many are ego-centric, nonreflective, concrete-thinkers who are impulsive and action-oriented. Juveniles faced with personal crisis or conflict act impulsively or without a knowledge of alternatives. They do not understand the consequences of their actions. In social perceptions, these youths have not developed the capacity to comprehend the perspectives of other people. Being extremely self-centered and lacking empathy, they misinterpret the actions, intentions, and messages of others. This culminates in social perceptions that are negative (Izzo & Ross 1990, 140).

From this perspective, treatment approaches must change two aspects of the way offenders think to be effective. Offenders should be taught to "think logically, objectively, and rationally" without overgeneralizing, exaggerating, or externalizing blame and they should be taught to "stop, think, and analyze consequences before taking action" (Izzo & Ross 1990, 141). They need to learn how to formulate plans and better conceptualize the ways in which their needs can be met. Ross and his associates designed a "comprehensive cognitive program" (Ross *et al.* 1988). The 80-hour program was delivered by 5 trained probation officers to 62 adult and adolescent probationers. The cognitive component included the following techniques: structured learning therapy, lateral thinking, critical thinking, values education, assertiveness training, negotiation skills training, interpersonal problem solving, role playing, modeling, and other techniques to improve the offenders' social-cognitive development. After a nine-month follow-up period, those in the cognitive group had dramatically lower reconviction and reincarceration rates (Ross *et al.* 1988).

Effective Techniques. Based on a meta-analysis of 400 studies, Mark Lipsey contends that no one approach is better than another. Rather than isolating what works in changing delinquent behavior, Lipsey identifies the characteristics of programs that reduce recidivism:

- Treatment in public facilities, custodial institutions, and the juvenile justice system had smaller effect on recidivism than community-based programs.
- Structured approaches that trained subjects in new behaviors and skills were associated with greater effect on recidivism than less structured programs such as counseling and supervision.
- Higher levels of involvement of the researcher in the treatment program produced greater effects, suggesting that operating the program consistent with its design is important.

These characteristics have been expanded by James O. Finckenauer (1992), who has summarized basic issues in treatment effectiveness:

- *Individual treatment plans.* Effective programs develop a plan of action with participation of the youth. The plan is tailored to the youth's specific situation and often takes the form of a behavioral contract.
- *Consistent point of contact.* The single point of contact principle means that the same treatment person maintains contact with the youth throughout all phases of the

treatment. This maximizes the positive relationship between the adult and the youth, role modeling, and internalization.

- *Progressive behavioral environment.* Program phasing begins with a highly restrictive setting, continues through a less restrictive setting, and culminates in a nonrestrictive setting.
- *Aftercare.* Reintegration and follow-up services are important to treatment success and are a weak component of many treatment programs. Aftercare programs should combine both supervision and assistance, including educational, vocational, mental health, and crisis intervention.
- *Staffing.* The main ingredient is a sufficient number of committed staff. A high ratio of staff to participants improves security and reduces fear for personal safety, a factor that is counterproductive to successful treatment.
- *Structure.* The rules, mechanisms, and regulations that govern the program should be clear. Participants should receive unambiguous, goal-oriented expectations concerning their plan, what they must accomplish, and the relationship between their behavior and overall completion of the program. Rewards and privileges should be consistent with this performance.

Aftercare

Transition or **aftercare services** are a key to successful institutional treatment programs. Whatever behavioral, educational, and theraputic gains are made while confined, they are lost once youths return to their community. Aftercare services are consistent with goals of public protection and treatment.

In 1987, the Office of Juvenile Justice and Delinquency Prevention announced its Intensive Community-Based Aftercare Programs Initiative. The IAP initiative was designed to enable public and private correctional agencies to implement effective aftercare programs for chronic and serious juvenile offenders. The model provided for seven years of research and development into existing programs, the formulation of prototypes, and pilot testing of model programs. In 1994, pilot projects began in Colorado, Michigan, Nevada, New Jersey, North Carolina, Pennsylvania, Texas, and Virginia. The IAP projects in these states all incorporate elements of the basic model featuring overarching case management, enhanced technology for electronic monitoring and drug testing, and collaboration among agencies providing services to IAP youth in the community (Altschuler & Armstrong 1996).

In Nevada, the project is operated by the Youth Parole Bureau, Division of Nevada Youth Corrections Services. The project operates in Clark County (Las Vegas), which has the highest concentration of serious juvenile offenders committed to confinement in the state. Youths are screened for IAP program eligibility and randomly assigned to an experimental group. Selected youths are sent to the Nevada Youth Training Center in Elko for three weeks of assessment. Afterward, they are transferred to Caliente Youth Center, about 150 miles from Las Vegas. The Caliente Youth Center houses all IAP program participants in a single cottage. The program has several features:

- *Transition.* Participants receive prerelease curriculum about one month prior to their release from Caliente. The course focuses on social skills training. An aftercare worker at

Caliente serves as liaison between the institution and the community, and an educational liaison worker at the Clark County School District serves as liaison between the institution and the school system.

■ *Team Approach.* Participants are supervised by a team of juvenile parole officers. Three officers supervise about 45 IAP parolees on a 24-hour basis. The team uses a system of positive sanctions and graduated sanctions, with consequences ranging from community service to house arrest.

■ *Additional Activities.* Additional personnel supplement the parole officers. Two community outreach trackers provide expanded hours of supervision during evenings and weekends. These workers blend surveillance with life skills training and supervised recreation (Altschuler & Armstrong 1996, 18–19).

If the IAP model proves effective in Nevada and other demonstration sites, it may serve as the basis for changes in juvenile corrections in states across the nation.

Summary

Institutions for youth first opened in the nineteenth century. The house of refuge, patterned after the English poorhouse, housed both orphans and delinquents. The house of refuge developed into the juvenile reformatory, which first opened in 1857. The juvenile reformatory emphasized familylike surroundings and academic and vocational rehabilitation. It remained the model for juvenile corrections until well into the twentieth century. Training schools are secure residential facilities designed to provide secure confinement for youth. Some offer specialized academic, vocational, and therapy programs. Detention centers function like adult jails; they detain juveniles awaiting court appearances. Detention centers are used for preventive and therapeutic detention.

Beginning in 1971, states have moved to decrease training school and detention center populations and shift youths in custody into different types of facilities and programs. These include camps, ranches, farms, military-style boot camps, and other residential facilities. Alternative facilities include wilderness programs, forestry camps, and residential camps; some of the best-known are operated by VisionQuest, Associated Marine Institutes, and the Eckerd Foundation. Boot camps appeared during the 1980s; they feature a military-style regimen used to "shock" youths into acceptable behavior. Other residential programs, such as Paint Creek Youth Center, feature school and work activities and a positive peer community treatment approach.

Although lawmakers and public officials rarely mention rehabilitation as a juvenile justice goal, the effectiveness of correctional programs for juveniles remains an important issue. The bottom line for many public officials is recidivism, which literally means "return to crime," but recidivism cannot be measured with precision. In addition to finding a usable measure of recidivism, selection bias and unintended effects represent major issues in evaluation of correctional programs. Before effectiveness can be measured, it is necessary to formulate a meaningful definition of success. Meta-analysis represents one technique for identifying effective programs. The cognitive approach represents one effective element in correctional programs.

KEY CONCEPTS

aftercare services

boot camp

camps, ranches, and farms

cognitive model

deinstitutionalization

detention

detention center

disproportionate minority

   confinement

house of refuge

juvenile reformatory

meta–analysis

recidivism

selection bias

training school

unintended effects

DISCUSSION QUESTIONS

1. What was the original purpose of juvenile confinement? How has it changed?

2. Can juveniles be rehabilitated? What is the best measure of success?

3. Should the United States follow the international community in abolishing executions of juvenile offenders?

A DEATH AT CEDAR KNOLL: SMALL GROUPS

Divide the class into small groups. One group will serve as an ad hoc committee established by the legislature to look into resident suicide at Cedar Knoll. Each of the other groups will represent teams of consultants. Each consultant group should formulate a plan for reducing the risk of resident suicide. The plan should respond to the discussion questions that follow. After hearing from each consultant group, the committee should identify the best plan and explain its selection rationale.

Sixteen-year-old Stephen entered the Receiving Home for Children, in Washington, D.C., a few weeks before Christmas. The Youth Services Administration (YSA) has responsibility for providing care, custody, and treatment to youths who enter the juvenile justice system of the District of Columbia. The YSA operated three institutions: Oak Hill Youth Center, Cedar Knoll Youth Center, and the Receiving Home for Children. The Receiving Home had 38 beds, although it was overcrowded during most years, holding as many as 54 youths. Due to staff shortages on many shifts, general lockdown of youth was not uncommon at YSA facilities. Two years before Stephen arrived, the District had entered into a consent decree to improve conditions of confinement at these facilities. The consent decree provided for improved delivery of educational and mental health services, improved staff-to-youth ratios, limited use of general lockdown, and a suicide prevention program.

    When Stephen arrived at the Receiving Home for Children in December, he had already spent most of the past two years in Youth Services Programs facilities and programs. Stephen had a prior psychiatric history. Not long after his arrival, he told his probation officer at the facility that he would hang himself with bed linen if he was returned to isolation at Cedar Knoll Youth Center. Stephen was placed on suicide watch and evaluated by a staff psychiatrist. The psychiatrist found that Stephen "appeared to be in distress" and that his "depression and anxiety appear severe enough for him to entertain suicidal fantasies." Stephen insisted that he could not stay at Cedar Knoll, where an older boy would hit him, and asked to stay at the Receiving Home until his court appearance.

    Stephen was transferred to Cedar Knoll, and he remained under suicide watch until his court hearing. At disposition, the sentence ordered him to the Receiving Home, and he was later released to a shelter program. Two months later, Stephen was arrested again, this time for PCP distribution. He was initially held at the Receiving Home and then transferred to Cedar Knoll the following day. The following afternoon, Stephen and all the other youths at the facility were locked in their rooms due to staff shortage. When staff began distributing meals room by room, they found Stephen's body hanging from a bed sheet from the window grate of the door to his room.

An investigation into Stephen's death found that he had been improperly screened and classified on arrival. Staff had been unaware of his prior suicidal threats, psychiatric evaluations, and fear of returning to Cedar Knoll. A superior court judge who held hearings regarding Stephen's death and compliance with the consent decree ordered the District to develop and present a comprehensive suicide prevention plan to the court by August, to end use of lockdown, and to hire additional security staff. Eight months later, the judge found that the District had failed to implement a comprehensive suicide prevention plan. That same month, 15-year-old Peter, confined at Cedar Knoll, hanged himself with a bed sheet from his door. He and other residents had been on lockdown due to staff shortage (Hayes 1994, 67–68).

13 Preventing Delinquency

CHAPTER OBJECTIVES

After studying this chapter, students will have tools to

- Examine juvenile delinquency prevention strategies
- Examine various diversionary and intervention strategies used in the juvenile justice system
- Describe federal efforts to prevent delinquency
- Gain a better understanding of the teen court model
- Develop an understanding of conflict resolution

Approaches to Prevention

Prevention is the most widely endorsed and infrequently used response to delinquency. Few would disagree with the goal of delinquency prevention. If young people can be prevented from beginning delinquent lifestyles, then the juvenile justice system can avoid expensive court procedures and detention. But many disagree about the means of prevention. Deciding what prevention programs to fund remains one of the most contentious issues in juvenile justice. "Everybody likes prevention," explains Peter Greenwood, Director of the Criminal Justice Program at the RAND Corporation. "Police, prosecutors, and corrections officials are all in favor of it, until it comes to putting up resources, or knowing how to do it" (Greenwood 1995, 112). For this reason, delinquency prevention has not always been a national priority. During the 1970s, when the United States experienced a surge in crime, Congress invested in delinquency prevention. During the 1980s, the priority shifted from preventing delinquency to dealing with chronic, violent juvenile offenders. During the 1990s, the Office of Juvenile Justice and Delinquency Prevention renewed the prevention emphasis with a comprehensive program to reduce youth violence.

The first section of this chapter discusses the logic of delinquency prevention. The second section identifies five major prevention strategies: deterrence, diversion, intervention, public policy and public health. The third section reviews federal efforts to prevent delinquency with emphasis on the Juvenile Justice and Delinquency Prevention Act of 1974 and subsequent amendments. The fourth section recalls the prevention strategies of the eugenics movement. The fifth section describes three promising prevention programs: law-related education, conflict resolution, and teen court. Finally, the future of delinquency prevention is discussed.

The Logic of Prevention

Both delinquency prevention and juvenile corrections seek to reduce the number of juvenile offenders who go on to become adult criminals. The difference between corrections and prevention is that correctional efforts to rehabilitate juvenile offenders focus on *changes after the fact,* whereas the goal of prevention is to alter the pathway to delinquency *before delinquent behavior becomes a fact.* Correctional treatment attempts to correct or reduce delinquent behavior among those who have already engaged in delinquent behavior. Juvenile institutions, such as training schools, and programs, such as wilderness experience programs, attempt to redirect young people away from a life of crime. *Delinquency prevention* aims at stopping delinquency before it starts. Prevention strategies aim to interrupt the formation of delinquency in its early stages before habits form that are associated with lawbreaking behavior. In a sense, the whole concept of juvenile justice is about prevention. The juvenile justice system exists as a separate entity from the adult criminal justice system. If more young people can be dealt with effectively by the juvenile justice system, fewer delinquents will grow up to become criminals. The juvenile court, juvenile corrections, and laws prescribing procedures for intake, detention, adjudication, and confinement of juveniles are designed to control delinquency before it becomes crime. This same logic applies to delinquency prevention. If more young people can be prevented from becoming delinquents, less juvenile justice is necessary.

Prevention efforts range from governmental efforts to improve the juvenile justice process to youth policies enacted by legislatures to programs and facilities operated by non-profit organizations. Delinquency prevention strategies can be divided into two broad categories. *Primary prevention* strategies are aimed at the general youth population. These include education campaigns, conflict resolution training, after-school programs, and job training programs. Primary prevention efforts also include public policy approaches to delinquency prevention, such as curfews and traffic safety laws designed to discourage teenage drinking and driving. *Secondary prevention* strategies target specific at-risk youth populations. These include remedial education programs, violence prevention training, and employment programs in impoverished and high-crime areas. Secondary prevention also includes programs designed to divert first-time and minor juvenile offenders away from the formal court process. Whether primary or secondary, delinquency prevention constitutes an essential first response to delinquency similar to the practice of medicine. The medical profession operates according to an ethic: "Above all else, do no harm." Procedures with the least risk of further injury and minimal side effects should be tried first. Only if these fail are invasive procedures, such as surgery, used. It works the same way with juvenile delinquency. Prevention programs represent less expensive, first-step methods of responding to juvenile crime. The worst that can be said about a prevention program is that it does not work to prevent delinquency. On the other hand, the worst that can be said about training schools is that not only do these institution fail to reduce criminality among young people, but they may increase criminality. In addition to the behaviors that led young people to the institution, those who have been confined in training schools now have had experiences and learned institutional behaviors that accelerate their delinquent behavior.

The issue is not about whether public safety or prevention should be a top priority; that is, whether there should be training schools or prevention programs. Clearly, there should be both. Some juveniles need to be incarcerated in secure detention facilities to protect the community. The issue is about resources and whether it makes more sense to confine a young robber for an additional year at $40,000 or to use that same money to hire a staff person to run an after-school recreational program that serves hundreds of young people (Greenwood 1995, 117). The issue is about spending for programs and institutions at the front end of life or the back end.

Delinquency prevention offers a proactive response to juvenile crime. Rather than waiting for young people to break the law before intervening, prevention efforts seek to identify at-risk youth and extend beneficial services. Often, prevention efforts extend the traditional boundaries of juvenile justice. Creative prevention programs require thinking about prevention not solely as matters of juvenile justice or law enforcement but as civic, social, and economic development as well. Economic development of impoverished urban neighborhoods, for example, represents a form of delinquency prevention. As Robert Woodson of the National Center for Neighborhood Enterprise explains, researchers and policymakers need to study "living models of success." More can be learned by studying the successes of inner-city residents than by studying their failures. For too long it has been the failures that provided the focus for juvenile justice (Sulton 1996).

Delinquency prevention represents an investment. Prevention programs seek to improve lives of young people by giving them more choices. Prevention programs teach young people about their rights and responsibilities, offer positive experiences to enhance self-confidence, and seek to enrich communities. Investing in delinquency prevention is a lot like investing in the stock market. Financial planners suggest a balanced portfolio and a long-term strategy. A diversified or balanced portfolio of stocks offers a hedge against overall loss. Losses in one or more sectors of the economy are offset by gains in others. A diversified portfolio is also the key to making money. Because it is impossible to foresee technological or product developments, wise investors spread their holdings over a variety of industries. That way, the investor is in a position to profit from a gain in any sector. It works the same way in delinquency prevention. A wise approach is to pursue a variety of prevention strategies. Rather than rely on a particular program to reduce juvenile crime, it is better to encourage development of a range of prevention measures. The OJJDP's *comprehensive strategy* follows this approach in principle because it emphasizes the support of several programs within an overall strategy. What works for one community may not work for another.

Delinquency Prevention Strategies

There are five delinquency prevention strategies. The first two, deterrence and diversion, rely on the juvenile justice system itself. The third attempts to target potential delinquents through early intervention; it relies on programs outside the juvenile justice system. The fourth uses public policy to limit opportunities for delinquent conduct. The fifth and newest strategy attempts broad-based change by integrating elements of the first four.

Deterrence

From the deterrence perspective, the juvenile justice system itself prevents delinquency. Generally speaking, there are two strands of *deterrence:* specific deterrence and general deterrence. *Specific deterrence* is focused on the individual. Individuals who receive appropriate punishment for misbehavior and learn a lesson are less likely to commit a second offense. *General deterrence* maintains that by punishing actual lawbreakers, potential lawbreakers will decide not to break the law. General deterrence aims at sending a message to young people to think twice before breaking the law.

Deterrence theory is premised on the concept that young persons are rational thinkers. Young people make decisions that they believe will improve their lives. This approach borrows from theory developed by economists and mathematicians who use the language of costs and benefits to describe decision making. No matter what the decision, whether to try a new restaurant for lunch or settle for a hamburger and french fries, whether to break into one house or the house next door, it is based on weighing the expense and risk of loss (the costs) against the potential gain (the benefits). If a potential delinquent's calculations suggest the benefits of breaking the law outweigh the risk and consequences of getting caught, then the young person will choose to break the law. On the other hand, if the fear of getting caught and being punished is greater than the perceived gain, then the young person will choose not to break the law. Deterrence ups the ante on would-be delinquents. By raising the stakes associated with getting caught and punished, deterrence seeks to discourage young people from making the wrong choice and thereby prevent delinquency.

Scared Straight.   One of the best known delinquency prevention projects to use the deterrence approach was *Scared Straight. Scared Straight* is a documentary that originally aired on national television in 1979. That same year it received an Academy Award for best film documentary. The filmmakers followed a group of 17 teenagers on a visit to New Jersey's Rahway State Prison. All of the teens were described as frequently and seriously delinquent. At the prison, the teens listened to graphic stories of assault, rape, and murder told by inmates trying to change the teens' perceptions of prison life. As a result of this dramatic program and its national visibility, legislators in several states seized on the idea that fear of punishment suppresses delinquency. Similar programs appeared. But although the original program at Rahway reported that 16 of the teens had become law-abiding citizens, the other programs could never replicate that success rate. Nor did the Rahway program itself sustain that kind of success. Later groups to Rahway had failure rates as high as 40 percent, and some began to question inmates' use of exaggeration and the fondling of the teenagers as persuasion techniques (Lundman 1993).

Sending a Message.   From the deterrence perspective, delinquency prevention is a matter of making punishment certain, swift, and severe. Deterrence theory has influenced a rewriting of juvenile justice systems across the country. Between 1991 and 1996, 47 states and the District of Columbia have made a fundamental shift in statutes governing juvenile justice

(Torbet & Snyder 1998, 8). The statutory changes have made it easier to prosecute juveniles in adult courts, have lowered the age of waiver or certification to adult court, or have excluded certain offenders from juvenile court jurisdiction. Other states have stiffened penalties for juvenile lawbreakers by mandating minimum terms of incarceration or enacting sentencing guidelines. These statutory changes have redefined the purpose of juvenile court. Although juvenile court decisions have been historically based on the needs of the juvenile and judges have been able to exercise discretion in the imposition of penalties, legislatures since 1992 have emphasized accountability. Accountability is a worthwhile goal. Legislatures have interpreted accountability as punishment and confinement according to a rationale that is offense based rather than offender-based (Torbet & Snyder 1998, 8). This is consistent with a pure deterrence model, which seeks to apply the amount of punishment necessary to deter repeat offenders (specific deterrence) and send a message to potential juvenile offenders (general deterrence).

Diversion

From the diversion perspective, the juvenile justice system is the problem, not the solution. The idea of diversion insists that formal processing of young troublemakers creates juvenile delinquency, and therefore, by avoiding those processes that label delinquents, delinquency can be prevented. In a sense, diversion is as old as the juvenile court itself. Juvenile court exists as a separate entity to channel young lawbreakers away from adult criminal court. Diversion also exists informally in the form of discretion. Police officers who choose not to file a petition but, instead, issue a warning and send the youth home are using diversion. In a formal sense, *diversion* refers to the channeling of cases to community or other noncourt programs, where these cases would otherwise have received an adjudicatory hearing by the court (Roberts 1998).

Diversion Theory.   Diversion draws theoretical support from social psychology and sociology. Social psychologists have described the concept of *self-fulfilling prophecy.* The self-concept is not an objective portrait but rather a prophecy about oneself that a person fulfills. Thus, individuals reinforce their self-concept, whether positive or negative, by adjusting their perceptions so that they are consistent with that sense of self. Persons with high self-esteem arrange successes for themselves, and persons with low self-esteem arrange their own failures (Calhoun & Acocella 1978, 76). Psychological research in educational and mental health settings has made much of self-fulfilling prophecy. Researchers have found that children regarded as "slow learners" by their teachers perform less well than their counterparts. Rather than place "special needs" students in special education classes, the goal is to mainstream these students by keeping them in the classroom.

Sociologists have contributed *labeling theory.* From the labeling perspective, a crucial step in development of a delinquent career is the process of being caught by the police and formally labeled "a delinquent" by the court. Others see the delinquent label and expect the worst. This experience creates a wholesale change in the individual's identity as the individual creates an image of self as delinquent and chooses to behave consistently with the label. As the self-image becomes more entrenched, youths labeled delinquent select friends with the same delinquent image, and together they try more extreme lawbreaking behavior (Becker 1963; Chambliss 1996; Lemert 1951; Schur 1973; Tannenbaum 1938).

From this perspective, the juvenile justice system creates delinquents in two ways. First, the system processing provides young persons with a delinquent self-image. Whereas prior to arrest, most juvenile see themselves as basically good kids, being treated as delinquent causes some to view themselves as delinquent and results in more, not less, delinquent behavior. Second, juvenile justice system processing stigmatizes juveniles in the eyes of significant others. Schoolteachers, police officers, and employers, along with potential employers, friends, and spouses, hesitate to build relationships with those possessing formal records of delinquency. This hesitation hampers the transition from adolescence to adulthood, and prolongs the delinquent career (Lundman 1993, 89).

Youth Service Bureaus.   During the 1970s, the federal government initiated a national experiment with diversion. In 1973, the Law Enforcement Assistance Administration's National Advisory Commission on Criminal Justice Standards and Goals expressed the belief that many of the problems considered delinquent should be defined as family, educational, or public welfare problems. The commission encouraged each state to establish youth service bureaus (YSBs) with the goal of minimizing the involvement of young people in the juvenile justice system and diverting young troublemakers away from juvenile court and into short-term community-based programs (Roberts 1998).

Omni Youth Services in suburban Chicago became the first YSB in Illinois and one of the first in the nation. Funded by a grant from the Illinois Law Enforcement Commission in 1972, Omni Youth Services, or Omni House Youth Service Bureau as it was known then, was established to enable diversion of youths from the juvenile justice system by providing the police and courts with a local means of intervention in the lives of young people. The organization has offered group and individual counseling, work and recreational programs, and remedial education. Omni Youth Services has historically provided a place for police to refer youthful troublemakers with emotional or family problems. Police also use Omni Youth Services as a form of indirect diversion for more serious delinquents by referring the case to court "to get the kid's attention," knowing that the court would refer the case to Omni anyway. In addition to diversion, Omni Youth Services provides a range of family support and delinquency prevention programs (Seng & Bensinger 1994).

Theater in Diversion.   One of the most innovative diversion programs began in Kenton County, Kentucky, when Sue Larison, a juvenile justice worker, read an article about Peg Phillips's THEATER INSIDE program. Peg Phillips, an accomplished actor perhaps best known for her role as storekeeper Ruth Anne on the CBS television series *Northern Exposure,* had conducted the program for five years. Theater Inside featured weekly drama workshops for the residents of a maximum security juvenile facility in Snoqualmie, Washington. Phillips brought Larison to Washington to see the program, and after Larison returned to Kentucky, she teamed up with the manager of the local community theater. Together they created Theater in Diversion. The program allowed a group of young troublemakers, 5 girls and 6 boys, the option of attending a 12-week drama program instead of appearing in juvenile court. During the following weeks, the young people learned acting techniques from volunteer actors culminating in a live performance. The program offered young people the opportunity to reaffirm their importance in the community, to experience positive relationships, to take pride in their accomplishment, and to gain a sense of self-respect (Larison *et al.* 1994).

Intervention

Intervention approaches do not rely on the juvenile justice system but seek to reduce the effect of the correlates of delinquency. These approaches attempt to intervene with juvenile populations at risk of delinquent behavior due to the prevalence of drug use, family violence, or gang behavior within these populations. The goal is that if professionals can intervene early enough, the path to delinquency can be blocked. Some programs attempt to target specific at-risk populations; others take a shotgun approach using schools, health departments, or other institutions.

Education Campaigns.   First Lady Nancy Reagan's "Just Say No" campaign combined fear arousal and moral appeal. Many of the public service announcements (PSAs) that appear in print also rely on these two ideas. The Partnership for a Drug Free America funds full-page ads in major daily newspapers and television spots about the negative effects of drugs. One of the most memorable of these ads pictured a man holding an egg. "This is your brain," he said as he cracked the egg into a frying pan. "This is your brain on drugs," he said as the egg began to sizzle. Shortly after its inception, MTV ran spots from Rock Against Drugs (RAD) featuring pop music personalities who party without abusing drugs (Walker 1994, 267). "Take a bite out of crime" is the slogan of the McGruff campaign. McGruff, the bloodhound in a trenchcoat, is the creation of the National Crime Prevention Council (NCPC) of the Crime Prevention Coalition (CPC). The CPC consists of more than 130 national, state, and federal organizations involved in delivering the National Citizen's Crime Prevention Campaign. The NCPC was formed in 1982 to promote crime prevention in the United States. With support from the U.S. Department of Justice, the Advertising Council, and the Crime Prevention Coalition, NCPC has made McGruff one of the most recognizable symbols of crime prevention. Market researchers in 1987 found that 3 of 4 adults, 9 of 10 teenagers, and 99 percent of all children aged 6 to 12 recognized the McGruff figure. In addition to crime prevention videos and classroom-based puppet curriculum, McGruff has been featured on a postage stamp, popular magazines, and television spots. State and local chapters of the NCPC hand deliver public service announcements for use by local television stations (Crime Prevention Coalition 1990, 95–97).

DARE.   One of the most popular recent approaches to anti-drug education is DARE (Drug Awareness Resistance Education). Created by the Los Angeles Police Department in 1983, DARE is a copyrighted drug prevention program for children in kindergarten through the twelfth grade. It has become the the the most widely used delinquency prevention program in the world. More than 22,000 police officers from 7,000 communities across the country have taught the program to more than 25 million elementary school students (Bureau of Justice Assistance 1995, 1, 4). DARE is a collaborative program between school and law enforcement. Sworn police officers deliver an educational program to schoolchildren designed to prevent substance abuse and develop resistance to gangs and violence. The core curriculum targets fifth- and sixth-grade students to prepare them to resist substance abuse and violence as they enter adolescence. DARE officers are usually selected from community-oriented law enforcement projects. The uniformed officers work in the classroom along with certified teachers who are required to be present at all times. DARE training is offered at five regional training centers, which are organized by DARE America, a nonprofit corporation that holds the DARE copyright. The centers are funded by grants from the Bureau of Justice Assistance, U.S. Department of Justice (Bureau of Justice Assistance 1995, 3).

DARE is popular among schoolchildren, teachers, and police officers. In a Gallup Poll Survey of 2,000 DARE graduates conducted in July 1993, 90 percent felt that the program had assisted them in avoiding drugs and alcohol. A study funded by the National Institute of Justice and conducted by the Research Triangle Institute found strong support for DARE among school staff, students, parents, and the community. Although other substance abuse prevention programs were rated highly, ratings for DARE were substantially higher (Bureau of Justice Assistance 1995, 4). Some initial research, however, suggests that DARE is no more effective in reducing drug use than other education approaches. Samuel Walker (1994, 268), professor of criminal justice at the University of Nebraska at Omaha, concludes "there is no evidence that drug education, by itself, substantially reduces drug use." It may be that the lessons are too brief to overcome the social pressures youths experience to experiment with drugs. Or perhaps many of the youths at greatest risk do not respect police officers.

The Public Policy Approach

The *public policy approach* relies on legislation and policies outside the juvenile justice system itself to limit the opportunity for delinquent behavior. Through restrictions on firearm purchase, curfews ordinance, and the design of public facilities, policymakers attempt to protect youths from participating in activities that could lead to delinquent conduct.

Firearms. The federal law concerning youth and firearms is straightforward. No person under the age of 18 may purchase a firearm in the United States. Federal law mandates that a person must be at least 18 years old to purchase a shotgun or rifle and at least 21 years old to buy a handgun. State laws vary regarding the legality of youths possessing firearms if ownership is transferred to them following a legal purchase. Despite the provisions of federal and state law, a significant number of young people carry guns that they have purchased or otherwise acquired illegally. From 1983 through 1995, the proportion of homicides in which a juvenile used a gun increased from 55 to 80 percent (Greenbaum 1997, 3).

One of the most promising public policy approaches to reducing the availability of firearms seeks to reduce the source of firearms. Some young people possess firearms to enhance their status, but many do so for their own protection from other young people who carry firearms. Many youths that possess guns report that they stole the weapon; many more acquire weapons from family members and friends. In some instances, juveniles "borrow" these weapons without the owner's permission. This suggests that policies designed to discourage laxity and negligence in the care of legally purchased firearms would decrease their availability to youth. Policies such as extending civil liability for injury inflicted while a minor is in possession of a legally owned firearm may help reduce availability. This would be similar to prohibitions about a minor driving one's automobile (Smith 1996, 365–366). A related policy approach would require adults who purchase a firearm to provide evidence that they have made reasonable efforts to provide a safe, secure place for storing the weapon. This approach would urge gun owners to demonstrate responsible ownership of their firearms and discourage laxity or negligence in the care of legally purchased firearms.

Curfew.   In recent years, curfews have become an important delinquency prevention measure. More than three-fourths of the major cities in the United States have curfew ordinances. Between 1990 and 1994, half of major American cities either enacted a curfew ordinance or revised an existing ordinance. Some of these ordinances are simple and straightforward; they apply to one age group and have the same curfew hours every night, such as 10 P.M. until 6 A.M. for all persons aged 17 or younger. Other curfew ordinances vary the times for different ages, or vary the days of the week, for different weeks or seasons of the year (Ruefle & Reynolds 1995, 360–361).

Curfew ordinances remain a controversial crime policy. Using juvenile crime statistics, it is not clear whether curfew ordinances decrease crime. Those who favor curfews argue that they serve as a tool for both police and parents. Curfews help the police by keeping nondelinquents from associating with delinquent peers and give delinquents less opportunity to commit crime. They allow police to disperse unruly crowds, stop and question youths, and keep youths off the streets and out of harm's way. Curfews help parents by supporting their restrictions on late night activities. It is easier for parents to enforce their own rules about not staying out late at night if the law requires other parents to do so as well (Ruefle & Reynolds 1995, 349).

At the same time, there are those who contend that curfew enforcement is ineffective, discriminatory toward minority youth, and on doubtful legal ground. The Board of Trustees of the National Council on Crime and Delinquency (NCCD) published a policy statement in 1972 opposing adoption of new curfews and urging the appeal of existing juvenile curfew ordinances. Since then, many curfew laws have come under legal attack from minors and their parents (Ruefle & Reynolds 1995, 347). So far, the judiciary has not provided a clear answer. General curfew ordinances are clearly an invalid infringement on the rights of adults. In the case of juvenile curfews, however, the U.S. Supreme Court has held that certain constitutional rights apply differently to children and adults. In *Belloti v. Bell* (1979), the U.S. Supreme Court provided criteria for determining whether the government has an interest compelling enough to justify an infringement of a minor's constitutional rights, but the criteria fail to address the extent to which curfew infringement on a minor's fundamental rights is constitutionally permissible. Lack of judicial precedent means that curfew ordinances are subject to challenge in local courts (Marketos 1995, 17).

Professor Marketos offers one solution to the curfew debate, and particularly to concerns about equal protection, overbreadth, and vagueness of curfews in the Loitering and Prowling Act of the Model Penal Code. The section provides that "a person commits a violation if he loiters or prowls in a place, at a time, or in a manner not usual for law-abiding individuals under circumstances that warrant alarm for the safety of persons or property in the vicinity." Loitering and vagrancy laws, although not immune to challenge, are already on the books in all 50 states. They do not unconstitutionally infringe on a minor's rights. Although the Loitering and Prowling Act may pass constitutional muster, questions about the effectiveness of curfews as a means of preventing delinquency remain (Marketos 1995, 24).

The Public Health Model

The ***public health model*** for delinquency prevention is based on the public health strategy to prevent the spread of contagious diseases. From this perspective, the goal of prevention is not merely to stop young people from negative behavior but, at the same time, to encourage positive behavior.

Risk-Focused Prevention. The University of Washington's J. David Hawkins, one of the leading proponents of this perspective, explains the rationale for the approach with reference to disease control. To reduce cardiovascular disease, public health researchers first identified risk factors. These are factors that increase a person's chances of contracting the disease, such as tobacco use, high-fat diet, sedentary lifestyle, high levels of stress, and family history of heart disease. Then they identified certain protective factors, such as aerobic exercise and relaxation techniques that helped prevent the development of heart problems. The goal of the public health campaign that followed was to halt the onset of heart disease to avoid costly, and risky, medical procedures such as angioplasty and bypass surgery. If risk factors could be reduced within the population, then the incidence of cardiovascular disease could be reduced. Hawkins reasoned that the same prevention principles could be applied to reduce violent behavior (Hawkins 1995, 10). The public health approach does not represent a specific prevention program but rather seeks to redirect available community resources through partnerships among agencies. Community leaders begin with a needs assessment to identify those ***risk factors*** that put youth at risk for delinquency. Hawkins explains that these risk factors arise within neighborhoods, families, and schools. Neighborhood risk factors include the availability of guns, community norms favorable to crime, media portrayals of violence, community disorganization, and extreme economic deprivation. Family risk factors include poor family management practices, family conflict, and parental attitudes and involvement in criminal behavior. Two of the most important school risk factors are antisocial behavior in primary grades and association with peers who engage in problem behaviors (Hawkins 1995).

A related approach has been developed by Norma Wright at the Center for Civic Education. She describes risk factors and two sets of responses: resiliency factors and protective factors. Resiliency factors, including social competence, problem-solving skills, and a sense of autonomy make youth resistant to delinquency. Protective factors are those that decrease the damage of risk factors and increase the development of resiliency factors. They are not merely the opposite of risk factors. The "protective shield" that families, schools, and communities can develop includes providing care and support, positive expectations, and ongoing opportunities for participation (Wright 1997).

Community leaders then take an inventory of ***protective factors*** to provide a buffer against the risk factors. Three categories of protective factors have been identified from research into resiliency, which is the ability of youth who have been exposed to risk to avoid delinquency and make positive contributions. Individual characteristics are those aspects of young people that enable them to make a positive contribution, such as positive social orientation, gender, and intelligence. Bonding involves the presence of some adult in the community, such as a parent, grandmother, teacher, or youth worker, who took an interest in a child. Healthy beliefs/clear standards include consistent family prohibitions against drug and alcohol use, demands for good school performance, and disapproval of problem behaviors (Hawkins 1995). The key in developing a communitywide approach is forging long-term collaborative relationships across institutional boundaries. Community leaders develop a communitywide plan that coordinates use of resources such as parks, teen centers, youth employment programs, churches, and other organizations.

The Youth Assistance Program.   The Oakland County Probate Court Youth Assistance (YA) Program is a prevention effort that employs features of the risk-focused prevention model. Located north of Detroit, Michigan, Oakland County is a suburban setting with a few outlying areas. In 1953, Chief Probate Judge Arthur E. Moore began a community collaborative effort to provide services to youths and families before trouble occurred, and it became the YA program. During the past 40 years, the program has expanded. YA-sponsored programs exist within each of the county's 26 school districts. The probate court provides professional staff support, and the school district, city government, and probate court deliver programs. Each community within the county has a local YA board of directors to coordinate the services. Services include free counseling and education for children and their families through the probate court. Individuals may choose counseling themselves, or police or school authorities refer them. Other programs include parent education sessions, supervised teen recreation, summer camp scholarships, and People Listening, Understanding, and Sharing (PLUS), a one-to-one mentoring program that matches adults with youths (Howitt, Moore *et al.* 1998, 40–41).

Federal Efforts to Prevent Delinquency

Although the act was not the first federal law to address juvenile delinquency, the Juvenile Justice and Delinquency Prevention Act of 1974 was the first federal response to delinquency to deliver a comprehensive approach. In the words of Ira M. Schwartz, who administered the OJJDP from 1979 to 1981, "The Juvenile Justice and Delinquency Prevention Act of 1974 is the most important piece of federal juvenile justice legislation ever enacted" (Schwartz 1989, 124).

Early Federal Initiatives

Prior to the Kennedy-Johnson years, there was little federal interest in juvenile justice and delinquency prevention. In 1912, Congress charged the Children's Bureau, U.S. Department of Health and Human Services, with investigating the operation of juvenile courts. But even during President Franklin D. Roosevelt's New Deal, Congress enacted no new legislation dealing with juvenile justice. Roosevelt held an attitude of limited government action in social affairs, and the public viewed delinquency as a state and local problem (Binder & Polan 1991, 243–244). In 1948, President Harry Truman convened the Mid-Century Conference on Children and Youth to explore methods of improving juvenile courts, improve police services to juveniles, and examine the prevention aspects of social service providers. The election of John F. Kennedy led to new federal efforts. Within a week of the 1960 elections, Kennedy and the man who would become his attorney general, Robert Kennedy, asked a member of their campaign organization to head a national effort to reduce juvenile delinquency. Robert Kennedy began a crusade against poverty, and the delinquency prevention effort was part of the crusade. At Kennedy's urging, Congress enacted the Juvenile Delinquency and Youth Offenses Control Act in 1961. This legislation directed the Department of Health, Education, and Welfare (HEW) to provide funds to state, local, and nonprofit agencies to develop demonstration projects on improved methods of preventing and controlling crime. The federally funded programs sought to improve social conditions within the nation's cities through community action. Many of these projects, such as Neighborhood Youth Corps, Legal Services Corporation, and Head Start, served as models for the programs Lyndon B. Johnson would initiate after the assassination of John F. Kennedy. They brought community resources to prevention through combating the sources of delinquency; Lyndon Johnson's war on poverty included community action plans to reduce delinquency on a large scale (Binder & Polan 1991, 249–251). By the time Johnson arrived in the White House, delinquency had become a national issue. Juvenile arrests rates for murder, rape, and robbery had increased year after year, as did arrest rates for property crime, such as burglary and auto theft. Johnson began to implement what Kennedy had initiated: a war on poverty that included a war on crime. A Democrat who had represented an impoverished district of Texas, Johnson urged Americans to build a great society. He used the power of the presidency to direct federal spending toward reducing poverty and malnutrition and improving education and medical care. In his effort to uncover the root causes of crime, President Johnson created the Commission on Law Enforcement and the Administration of Justice in 1966. The Commission's Task Force on Juvenile Delinquency proposed six major strategies to reduce juvenile crime that would guide federal juvenile justice policy for the next 30 years:

1. Decriminalization of status offenses; that is, not considering acts as juvenile crimes that would not be considered crimes if committed by adults, such a truancy
2. Diversion of youths from courts to alternative treatment programs
3. Extension of due-process rights to juveniles
4. Deinstitutionalization, or using community treatment centers and nonresidential treatment facilities rather than large, secure training schools
5. Diversification of services from state services to community-based and nonprofit organizations (small community-based facilities instead of large warehouse institutions)
6. Decentralization of control (Raley 1995, 12)

Two years later, Congress passed the Juvenile Delinquency Prevention and Control Act (1968). This legislation provided $150 million to state and local governments to implement the commission's recommendations in the area of juvenile delinquency. The 1968 act also anticipated the Juvenile Justice and Delinquency Prevention (JJDP) Act of 1974.

The Juvenile Justice and Delinquency Prevention Act of 1974

The legislative process culminating in the JJDP Act began in 1969, when the U.S. Senate Subcommittee to Investigate Juvenile Delinquency began to look at the nation's juvenile justice system. The subcommittee, chaired by Senator Birch Bayh of Indiana, heard from dozens of witnesses, including juvenile court judges, professors, child advocates, prosecutors, public defenders, parents, and children. The subcommittee concluded that large numbers of juveniles confined in training schools, detention centers, and county jails were status offenders and victims of parental neglect. They found overcrowded and understaffed juvenile courts, training schools, and social services unable to provide adequate treatment. "The juvenile justice system is a failure," Bayh's subcommittee concluded, "not only from the child's point of view but also from the point of view of our society" (Schwartz 1989, 110).

Bayh's subcommittee discovered that although the federal government had numerous juvenile justice programs, lack of coordination hampered their impact. Five federal departments and at least 116 federal programs were involved in juvenile delinquency, but the overall federal effort lacked focus (Saucier 1995, 19–20). In hearings leading up to passage of the legislation, Milton Rector, president of the National Council on Crime and Delinquency, advised Bayh's subcommittee that a "major weakness [in the federal effort] is the lack of a structure present where Federal juvenile and criminal justice planning can be coordinated with other human service agencies" (Saucier 1995, 19).

The act that Congress passed in 1974 established two themes that guided subsequent federal delinquency legislation. First, financial assistance alone was an insufficient federal response to delinquency. The federal government had to provide comprehensive planning and coordination of services as well. Second, some practices, such as confining juvenile offenders with adults, did more harm than good (Raley 1995). Even more important, the JJDP Act provided a federal focus on delinquency prevention. Senator Bayh urged Congress to provide a one-word description of the JJDP Act: *prevention* (Saucier 1995, 20).

The goals of the JJDP Act were, however, more limited than the strategies identified by Johnson's Commission on Law Enforcement in 1966. Although the new law did not decriminalize status offenses, it did encourage the use of nonsecure treatment alternatives. The act provided federal funds to divert juveniles from correctional settings into restitution and other community programs and discouraged large warehouse institutions. The act did require removal of status offenders from secure incarceration. Specifically, the law required states to remove status offenders from secure confinement and separate adult and juvenile offenders in order to receive federal funds. Further, the law required that states dedicate three-fourths of federal funds they received to community-based programs to encourage diversification of services and decentralization of control. When juveniles were placed in residential facilities, they had to be the least restrictive alternative appropriate to the needs of the child and be in reasonable proximity to their families (Raley 1995).

Passage of the JJDP Act meant that juvenile justice had finally become a national priority. Congress established the Law Enforcement Assistance Administration (LEAA) in 1968 and in 1974 assigned to it responsibility for the JJDP Act. The LEAA provided funds to states (based on population) and directly to organizations for various crime reduction strategies. As it turned out, the JJDP Act survived longer than the LEAA. LEAA funded programs ranging from juvenile diversion to computerized recordkeeping, and critics charged that the agency threw money at the crime problem without sense or strategy. Congress abolished LEAA in 1984 and assigned its responsibilities for federal grants to a new Bureau of Justice Assistance within the U.S. Department of Justice. The JJDP Act would also survive a change in presidential leadership and garner more than two decades of congressional support.

The 1980 Amendments. During the 1980s, the focus for juvenile justice shifted from delinquency prevention to incarceration of serious, violent delinquents. Congress revised the act through a series of amendments in response to interest group lobbying and the priorities of a new presidential administration.

In 1980, Congress revised the JJDP Act. OJJDP Administrator Ira Schwartz testified that between 1975 and 1977, the total number of cases referred to juvenile courts had decreased, as did the number of status offenders to juvenile court and the detention of status offenders. The National Council of Juvenile and Family Court Judges (NCJFCJ), however, asked Congress to repeal the provision requiring removal of status offenders from secure incarceration. Congress approved a compromise that allowed incarceration of juveniles for violations of court order. Many national organizations viewed the court order compromise as a retreat from the goals of the act (Raley 1995).

The amendments passed that year included a major initiative that required removal of all juveniles from adult jails within five years. The Carter administration had supported the initiative, noting that 12,000 children were detained in adult jails on any given day. With the election of President Reagan, the federal focus shifted from delinquency prevention to prosecution of serious juvenile offenders. The Reagan administration's war on crime aimed at redirecting the criminal justice system from its failed strategy of rehabilitation toward accountability and incapacitation. Ronald Reagan's juvenile justice administrator established a different set of priorities emphasizing mandatory sentencing laws, programs to prevent school violence, efforts against drugs and pornography, and the plight of missing children (Regnery 1986).

One of the top juvenile justice priorities during the Reagan years was missing children. The U.S. Department of Justice convened the National Symposium on Child Molestation in 1984 to focus national attention on heinous crimes committed by strangers who molested children. The president signed into law the Missing Children's Assistance Act that same year (Abell, 1989). Senator Hawkins, a supporter of the act, told his Republican colleagues in the Senate, "President Reagan and you and I ran on the slogan of family, home, neighborhood, peace, and freedom. This [act] strengthens all aspects of that pledge" (Fritz & Altheide 1987, 477). In 1984, Congress revised the JJDP Act again. The amendments created Title V, the Missing Children's Assistance Act, designed to promote research for aid in finding missing children.

The abduction and murder of Adam Walsh by a stranger in Florida in 1981 and the TV docudrama *Adam,* which followed in 1983, led to widespread concern about missing children. Although the actual number of stranger abductions was fewer than 100 per year according to the FBI (35 in 1981, 49 in 1982, and 67 in 1983), the docudrama reported that "1.5 million children vanish, disappear, or are abducted each year," implying that there were thousands, even a million Adam Walshes. (The 1.5 million statistic has been traced to a Louisville study cited by a 1979 U.S. Department of Health and Family Services report. The figure was generated by multiplying the Louisville figure to account for the rest of the country and multiplying it again to quantify cases not reported to police (Fritz & Altheide 1987, 477). The docudrama featured news photos of missing children but did not explain that most of these children had been taken by parents involved in custody disputes rather than strangers. The docudrama led to regular news features on local TV stations showing missing children, photos of missing children on milk cartons at grocery stores, and a popular weekly television series, *America's Most Wanted,* featuring John Walsh, Adam's father. The public concern with missing children triggered the Reagan Administration's funding of

$1.5 million for the National Center for Missing and Exploited Children and drew attention away from preventing delinquency (Fritz & Altheide 1987).

The 1990 Amendments.   During the 1990s, federal efforts renewed the focus on prevention despite concerns about a new generation of superpredators. The increase in juvenile homicides was particularly troubling. During the period between 1987 and 1994, the total annual number of murders by juveniles doubled (Snyder & Sickmund 1999, 56). Social critics charged that society had produced a new breed of juvenile offender. The superpredator concept suggested that unlike the violent juvenile offenders prior to the 1980s, the new strain of youthful criminals engaged in more lethal violence more often than ever before. Research has not supported this assertion, and the increase is more likely due to drug markets and the escalating use of firearms by drug traffickers (see Chapter 2).

Unlike the missing children campaign, public concern over superpredators did not distract federal prevention efforts. In 1992, Congress passed extensive amendments to the JJDP Act. These amendments added initiatives addressing juvenile gangs, youth development, mentoring, and prevention. They added youth development activities and made them eligible for state formula grants. Congress also rewrote Title V to establish incentive grants for local delinquency prevention programs. These grants covered a wide variety of activities, including recreation, tutoring, remedial education, substance abuse prevention, and work skills development (Raley 1995).

In 1994, President Bill Clinton appointed Shay Bilchik as administrator of the OJJDP. Bilchik has emphasized the importance of the JJDP Act's core requirements: deinstitutionalizing status offenders, separating juveniles from adults in corrections, removing juveniles from adult jails, and addressing the disproportionate confinement of minority juveniles. Bilchik points out that talk about superpredators fails to recognize that only less than one-half of 1 percent of juveniles ages 10 to 17 were arrested for a violent crime (in 1996), and only 6 to 8 percent can be considered serious, chronic, or violent offenders. The majority of youths are good citizens who have never been arrested for any crime. "Talk of superpredators is tabloid journalism that distorts the facts" (Appleby 1997, 2).

Bilchik has also renewed the focus on prevention. "We cannot afford to lose the critical opportunities we have to intervene in the developmental paths of at-risk youth and status offenders through proven programs . . ." (Appleby 1997, 7). Bilchik insists that prevention not only interrupts the processes that would otherwise lead to delinquent behavior, but it keeps juveniles from being processed by the system, which saves public money, prevents individuals from being victimized, and helps keep the next generation of young people from delinquency (OJJDP 1995).

A Comprehensive Strategy for Preventing Delinquency

In 1993, the OJJDP initiated a *comprehensive strategy* for dealing with serious, violent, and chronic juvenile offenders. The strategy is founded on the public health prevention approach developed by J. David Hawkins. John J. Wilson, acting administrator of OJJDP, and James C. Howell, director of research and program development at OJJDP, advanced the comprehensive strategy by saying that "delinquency prevention [is] the most cost-effective approach to dealing with juvenile delinquency" (Wilson & Howell 1994, 4). The prevention measures outlined in the plan have a higher probability for success because they are positive in orien-

The resiliency of youth makes prevention a worthy goal.
© *CORBIS*

tation. They promote positive social development rather than merely responding to antisocial behavior.

Guidelines for Prevention Intervention.   OJJDP's comprehensive strategy consists of two components: prevention and intervention. Prevention, recognized as the most cost-effective means to deal with delinquency, is based on a risk-factor approach. It recognizes that programs must be developed to counter six major risk factors: (1) delinquent peer groups, (2) poor school performance, (3) high-crime neighborhoods, (4) weak family attachments, (5) lack of consistent discipline, and (6) physical or sexual abuse. This risk-factor approach seeks to intervene according to children's age and level of development, beginning with prenatal care. It calls on communities to assess their delinquency problem, identify local risk factors, and implement programs to counter them. The comprehensive strategy can be replicated at the state, county, and local levels (OJJDP 1993).

Communities That Care.   The Communities That Care (CTC) approach is a model for implementation of the comprehensive delinquency prevention strategy at the community level. OJJDP selected the CTC approach in 1994 as a model to assist communities in developing comprehensive juvenile violence prevention strategies. The approach involves four steps:

1. Key community leaders meet to devise common goals for the community, to commit to a risk-focused prevention strategy, and to decide who should sit on the community prevention board.

2. The community prevention board is created to reflect diverse groups within the community. The board then develops as a team through a series of training events.

3. The community prevention board directs an assessment of the risk factors within the community, inventories existing programs and services designed to meet those risks, and identifies overall prevention strategies.

4. The community prevention board develops a risk-focused action plan and establishes appropriate methods of evaluation.

The CTC approach was developed by Developmental Research and Programs, a corporation founded in 1984 by J. David Hawkins and Richard F. Catalano. Hawkins and Catalano founded the corporation to translate current research findings concerning delinquency prevention into community programs. CTC provides a series of training and community-planning events to assist communities who wish to design a comprehensive approach (Developmental Research and Programs 1993).

In 1997, the North Carolina Department of Public Safety and Crime Control, a cabinet-level agency, received $1 million from the governor's Crime Commission to fund CTC projects throughout the state. The department established a Center for the Improvement of Juvenile Justice within the Department of Public Safety and Crime Control to oversee development of about 10 CTC sites throughout the state. Training of key leaders in each community is provided through an agreement with Developmental Research and Programs.

The Color of Delinquency Prevention

An understanding of delinquency prevention in the United States would be incomplete without realizing that prevention efforts have never been color-blind. The history of delinquency prevention in the United States includes a meaner, more sinister side. Early in the twentieth century, before the federal government took interest, the eugenics campaign defined delinquency prevention in the United States.

Eugenics and Scientific Racism

Eugenics represented a collection of theories about the connection between behavior and the physical shape of the skull (phrenology), between intelligence and the physical size of the brain (craniology), and the hereditary transmission of criminality (criminal anthropology). Eugenics researchers set out to identify families in which criminality, alcoholism, and feeblemindedness had been transferred from generation to generation. H. H. Goddard, director of research at the Vineland Training School for Feeble-Minded Girls and Boys in New Jersey, published a study in 1914 of the Kallikak family. Goddard hoped to show how "feeblemindedness" had been passed genetically to generations of the Kallikak clan and had produced a large portion of criminal behavior. Goddard invented the pseudo-scientific term *moron* to categorize persons of low intelligence (Gould 1981).

Eugenics gave prejudice against immigrants and minorities a scientific veneer. **Scientific racism** is a belief that cultural, historical, and behavioral differences among members of social groups are due to biological or genetic differences. Eugenics researchers sought to identify the criminal race, and they were quite sure that the color of this race would not be white. Cesare Lombroso, whose book *The Criminal Man* found support among eugenicists after its publication in the United States in 1911, wrote, "There exist whole tribes and races more or less given to crime." Lombroso taught that persons of African and Oriental ancestry were prone to commit murder, whereas the hereditary crimes of fraud, forgery, and prostitution characterized Jewish people. Earnest Hooton, a Harvard anthropologist, carried out a well-funded study to identify a distinct criminal race. He believed that the criminal race contained fewer "pure racial types" and more "mixed racial types" than among normal, noncriminal persons (Hooton 1979; Lombroso-Ferrero 1979). This kind of scientific racism led to two attitudes about delinquency prevention. Eugenicists themselves pursued the first. To prevent delinquency, it was necessary to identify (by means of body measurements or IQ testing), institutionalize (into institutions, colonies, etc.), and sterilize (whenever practical) degenerate persons before they could pass on crime-prone genetic material to their offspring. Pennsylvania, an early leader in the eugenics movement, opened an institution for the feebleminded at Polk in 1897 and additional facilities in 1911 and 1918. The Pennsylvania legislature passed legislation to identify the criminal race among school, prison, and workhouse populations, and a research program aimed at limiting the "liberty and power of degenerates to transmit criminal propensities to unfortunate progeny" began in 1907 at Eastern State Penitentiary in Philadelphia (Jenkins 1984). Indiana became the first state to enact legislation providing for sterilization of social defectives in 1907, and between 1911 and 1930, 33 states followed suit. Meanwhile, eugenicists in Congress succeeded in passing legislation in 1924 intended to restrict the immigration of "inferior races" from southern and eastern Europe to the United States (Beckwith 1985).

The eugenics campaign in the United States ended in the aftermath of World War II. Policies advocating sterilization of those with low IQs and restriction of immigration based on race sounded too much like what Americans had helped fight to end in Nazi Germany. But eugenics policies remained on the books and continued to influence the lives of minorities long after the public campaign ended. More than 60,000 sterilizations occurred after 1930. Between 1960 and 1968, for example, the Eugenics Board of North Carolina sterilized 1,620 persons, mostly young African American women (Beckwith 1985, 315). The scientific racism that fueled eugenics social policy engendered another attitude toward delinquency prevention: It is better to do nothing about minority crime, particularly when black lawbreakers select black victims.

Control, Not Prevention

This version of scientific racism holds that it is pointless to try to prevent delinquency among black youths. After all, "what do you expect of *those* people." "Deliberately withholding protection against criminality . . . ," observes Harvard law professor Randall Kennedy, "is one of the most destructive forms of oppression that has been visited upon African-Americans" (1997, 29). In his discussion of American legal history, Kennedy explains how government has not only failed to protect African Americans from the racially motivated violence of whites (e.g., lynching) but also has failed to protect blacks from ordinary criminality, much of it perpetrated by other blacks.

Child welfare officials in North Carolina, for example, simply overlooked the black citizens of the state in developing programs. If it had not been for Lawrence A. Oxley, one of the first African American social workers in the state, there would have been no delinquency prevention efforts directed at young black North Carolinians. In 1925, the State Board of Charities and Public Welfare made Oxley head of the Bureau of Work among Negroes, funded by a grant from the Laura Spelman Rockefeller Memorial Fund and money raised in local African American communities. Oxley centered his efforts on broken homes, truants, and delinquent children. He studied child welfare among the state's African Americans and found that in Appalachian counties no black youths had been declared wards of the county and delinquent black children were sent home to be whipped by their parents, a disposition never given to white children (Burwell 1995, 1996). In 1929, Oxley surveyed local officials about their attitudes toward legal enfranchisement of African Americans. Few of those surveyed desired blacks to achieve an education or perform anything other than farm labor. The clerk of court in Burke County put it this way: "The white people should not be taxed in order to put money into something that is of no value. 'Educate' a negro and you ruin a good servant" (Crowe *et al.* 1992, 138). This same attitude persisted after legal equality had been achieved in the politics of race and crime control. Since 1964, every major political candidate has had a position on crime, and the only position worth having is to appear tougher on crime than one's opponent. Appeals in political campaigns address anxieties that stem not only from fear of crime but fear of black criminality in particular. Candidates express the attitude that delinquency among urban minority youths can be "controlled" but not "prevented" and that prevention programs amount to wasteful government spending, but additional institutions are needed for confining delinquents.

This same attitude also persists in juvenile court decision makers who refer fewer minority juveniles to diversion programs than their white counterparts. An advisory committee to the National Council of Juvenile and Family Court Judges on the disproportionate incarceration of minority youth in 1986 found a three-track juvenile justice system in California. There was a public system, a private system, and a hidden system. The first operated for Latinos, and the second two were for whites. The result produced an underrepresentation of minorities in educational and private treatment programs and an overrepresentation of minorities in the more punitive public facilities (National Council of Juvenile and Family Court Judges 1990). In 1988, Congress took an interest in the issue of disproportionate confinement of minority juveniles. An amendment to the JJDP Act required states receiving federal funds to report on the race of children in state custody. Following completion of the reports in 1992, the JJDP Act was amended to require assurance that states would treat youth equitably on the basis of gender, race, family income, and mental, emotional, or physical disabilities.

Promising Prevention Programs

No longer is the chief prevention issue a matter of getting the attention of policymakers. The public is interested, and politicians will respond. The major challenge is to get policymakers to select those programs that have proven effective. There is a wide variety of potential prevention strategies, but few have been seriously evaluated (Greenwood 1998). Several promising prevention programs have survived the test of time.

Law Related Education

The founders of the *law related education (LRE)* movement intended to provide civic education, not delinquency prevention. The LRE movement began after the Soviet launch of Sputnik in 1957 as an effort to teach young people the principles of citizenship in a free society. The first LRE programs appeared in schools. Teachers invited lawyers, judges, law students, and police officers to their classrooms to teach students about the law and legal principles. In the words of the Isidore Starr, the movement's founder, LRE aims "to improve the citizenship education of American youngsters by teaching them about the law, legal processes, and the legal system . . . to give them another way of understanding our society and some tools with which they can participate in the making and shaping of laws" (Starr 1985). In 1970, there were close to 100 LRE programs in schools across the county and a handful of statewide programs. Eight years later, the movement had expanded to nearly 300 projects and 35 statewide programs. Today, an LRE coordinator exists in every state, and programs operate in secondary and primary schools from coast to coast (Knepper 1997).

Kids and the Law.   California's LRE effort has recently expanded with the support of the state bar. The State Bar of California has produced a booklet entitled *Kids and the Law: An A-to-Z Guide for Parents.* The booklet offers relevant, easy-to-understand information on a wide range of legal issues involving children. The state bar association teamed up with 4,000 local Parent-Teacher Associations (PTAs) and local bar associations to distribute the booklet to schools, parent groups, law enforcement agencies, and courthouses. The goal is to encourage young people to talk with their parents about the law.

The Kids and the Law project was triggered by a statewide survey of 600 California youngsters (ages 10 to 14) commissioned by the bar association. The survey suggested that most children are unclear about what is, and what is not, against the law and about the consequences for breaking the law. Youngsters would prefer to ask their parents about legal issues, but they do not. Rather, what they think they know about the law they learned from school and television. The book describes current California law concerning alcohol, curfew, drugs, police, school, and other rights and responsibilities relevant to young people. This California approach is modeled after the Street Law program offered by the University of San Francisco Law School (Nazario 1996).

LRE and Delinquency Prevention.   Delinquency prevention represented a logical extension of citizenship education: If youth appreciated the principles underlying the nation's laws and government, they would be less likely to commit delinquent acts. Beginning with the JJDP Act of 1974, Congress funded a number of LRE programs. In an evaluation funded by OJJDP, Robert Hunter at the University of Colorado explored the delinquency prevention aspect of LRE. Using self-report delinquency data, Hunter evaluated programs in classes from grades six through twelve in California, Colorado, Michigan, and North Carolina between 1979 and 1984. He found that when properly implemented, LRE had a positive effect on students' knowledge of law and legal principles, attitude toward authority, and antisocial behavior (Hunter 1987). Following Hunter's evaluation, OJJDP established the National Training and Dissemination Program (NTDP) with the five principal LRE organizations: The American Bar Association's Special Committee on Youth Education for Citizenship, the Center for

Civic Education, the Constitutional Rights Foundation, the National Institute for Citizen Education in the Law (now known as Street Law), and the Phi Alpha Delta Public Service Center. In NTDP's first year, OJJDP and the five organizations worked to distribute resource materials to teachers. OJJDP also experimented with LRE for juvenile justice populations in a variety of settings. LRE projects appeared in diversion, detention, and community corrections programs; training schools; and group homes. In 1990, NTDP embarked on a three-year initiative to introduce LRE programs in juvenile justice by offering coordination, public information, training, and technical assistance, in addition to program development and assessment through its cooperating organizations. Sixteen pilot sites—institutional schools and diversion, detention, and community settings—in 14 states were selected.

Recent evaluation research confirms the promise of LRE as a delinquency prevention tool. Researchers at Eastern Kentucky University evaluated seven groups of LRE students across five sites in Kentucky completing an LRE-based diversion program. They compared students who participated in the LRE program with a comparable group of students who had not completed the program. They found that although the diverted youth were significantly less positive in their social and self-perceptions prior to participation in the program, there were no significant differences between the two groups after completion of the LRE program. In other words, the LRE program raised the social and self-perception of delinquent youth to a level comparable with nondelinquents (Fox *et al.* 1994).

Conflict Resolution

Conflict resolution programs began in schools during the 1960s, when teachers began incorporating dispute resolution lessons into their curricula. In 1981, Educators for Social Responsibility (ESR) organized these efforts into the first national association. The central question for this organization was: "How can students find alternative ways of dealing with conflict?" (Miller 1994, 2). Today, conflict resolution in schools has been referred to as "The Fourth R" (Bradley & Henderson 1994).

Four approaches to conflict resolution have emerged:

1. *Process curriculum.* An approach in which teachers devote time to teaching principles of negotiation and mediation as a separate course, specific curriculum, or daily lesson plan.
2. *Mediation program.* A program in which teachers and students are trained in conflict management. Then selected students serve as mediators to assist other students in solving their problems.
3. *Peaceable classroom.* A whole classroom approach in which conflict resolution education is incorporated into all core subjects and forms the basis of conflict management strategies used in the classroom.
4. *Peaceable school.* A comprehensive whole-school approach in which conflict resolution principles are learned and used by every member of the school community—librarians, teachers, counselors, and parents (Crawford & Bodine 1996; deJong 1994).

Peer Mediation.   Mediation is a process of conflict resolution. In mediation, a neutral third party, the mediator, intervenes in a conflict to enable the disputants to resolve it, but has no authority to impose a decision. The mediator's task is to help the disputants find a solution to their conflict. Peer mediation programs seek to empower students by teaching them skills necessary to resolve interpersonal conflicts. Students learn that although conflict is inevitable and cannot be eliminated, it can be effectively managed. Conflict can be managed unproductively by means of avoidance and fighting or productively through informal and formal means. Formal means range from school disciplinary systems to the juvenile justice system, and informal means include various forms of alternative dispute resolution, including peer mediation.

Peer mediation programs in schools encourage students to question violence as a means of conflict management and to analyze problems critically. When students understand conflict resolution techniques, they cultivate valuable life skills, learn nonviolent responses to conflict, and develop an experiential need for rules. While learning how to identify sources of conflict and discuss them in an organized forum, students realize their own power to resolve conflict. They learn how to take ownership of their conflicts, to take an active role in their resolution, and to accept responsibility for their behavior. The mediation process allows each student to understand how his or her own behavior led to the conflict and to identify changes in behavior that will make things right. These skills allow students to become proactive problem solvers and more responsible citizens.

Evaluations of mediation programs in schools in New York, Illinois, New Mexico, and Florida have reported positive results (Crawford & Bodine 1996). One recent study used an experimental design with random assignment to evaluate the impact of a school mediation program. Fifty-two students who had been referred to the assistant dean for interpersonal conflict were assigned by coin toss to the assistant dean for traditional disciplinary methods (warnings, demerits, suspensions) or mediation. The researchers found that mediation was more effective than traditional school discipline in reducing the number of interpersonal conflicts. Also, the researchers found that the total number of referrals for interpersonal conflict dropped during the year the program was implemented; students began to avoid conflict on school grounds and during school time (Tolson *et al.* 1992).

Conflict Resolution and the Arts.   Peer mediation programs are not the only form of conflict resolution programs in schools. The arts are a natural forum for teaching, modeling, and using conflict resolution processes. The OJJDP and the National Endowment for the Arts (NEA) joined together to create the Partnership for Conflict Resolution in the Arts. This national program provides support for community-based arts programs for youth at risk of drug abuse and violence. The partnership supports professional development workshops on conflict resolution education for program administrators, artists, and youth workers. In 1997, the National Center for Conflict Resolution Education conducted on-site workshops for nine arts programs. The two-day workshops enabled artists to make use of conflict resolution principles in their work with youth, including understanding conflict, negotiation processes, and group problem solving. At Stopover Services of Newport, Rhode Island, an arts-based conflict resolution program, troubled youths participated in a creative writing workshop. Their writing tended to be graphic, and several students felt that their work had been censored when only certain works were published. The students themselves were divided over a poem about sexual abuse that contains one student's fantasy about killing the abuser. The program manager used the disagreement to teach group problem solving. The students discovered several solutions, including protecting the program's interest in choosing works for publication and the students interest in learning by agreeing to inform students about other outlets for publishing their work (Klink & Crawford 1998).

Teen Court

Teen courts have existed since the late 1980s (Seyfrit *et al.* 1987). The idea behind teen court is reverse peer pressure: to turn peer pressure into a source for positive change rather than a force for negative behavior. In *teen court,* known as youth court or peer court in some parts of the country, first-time juvenile offenders plead guilty and face a jury of their peers for constructive sentencing. Except for the judge, all participants in teen court—the clerk, the bailiff, the jury, and prosecuting and defense attorneys—are teenagers.

The Teen Court Model.   In 1983, Natalie Rothstein, a social worker in Odessa, Texas, suspected that a significant portion of the city's juvenile delinquency problem resulted from the response to young lawbreakers. Many of the city's youth developed habits leading them to delinquency because the juvenile court gave them little incentive to change their behavior. Those apprehended for misdemeanors, such as shoplifting and intoxication, listened to a lecture from the judge and then returned home to commit second and third offenses. If the system held them accountable for their behavior by involving them in the judicial system before crime had become a habit, Rothstein reasoned, the pattern could be interrupted. She encouraged the city to create a new program emphasizing "diversion and accountability" (Rothstein 1987a, 1987b).

The program Rothstein developed was teen court. Although there is some variation among teen courts, in all courts based on the Odessa, Texas, model, the participants are between the ages of 12 and 18, except for the judge. Defendants are sentenced by a jury of peers. Teen courts do not determine guilt or innocence; rather, they fix a disposition for defendants who plead guilty and agree to appear in teen court. Teen court defendants are youths who plead guilty to minor offenses, such as vandalism, shoplifting, drug/alcohol use, assault/fighting, and traffic-related crimes. The programs generally meet the goal of diversion, and they may also function as a dispositional alternative. Youths who complete the constructive sentence assigned to them do not receive a formal court record (Williamson *et al.* 1993).

Teen courts developed across Texas and other parts of the country. Headquartered at Tyler, the Texas Teen Court Association has more than 30 programs. Many of these are volunteer projects funded by local junior action leagues in cooperation with cities and other organizations. A 1995 survey conducted by the American Probation and Parole Association (APPA) had located 250 teen court programs in 30 states and the District of Columbia. The operation and administration of teen courts vary; juvenile probation departments, law enforcement agencies, private/nonprofit agencies, and schools administer teen courts (Godwin 1996).

Bay County Teen Court.   Bay County Teen Court is one of about 20 teen court programs in Florida. Bay County includes Panama City and several smaller municipalities. The program began in 1994, when a Bay County administrative judge urged several circuit and county judges to volunteer to sit on the bench.

Now, on Tuesday evenings, about a half dozen defendants wait in the hallways of the Bay County Juvenile Court Building. The young attorneys meet with the program coordinator to discuss the evening's docket prior to 5 P.M., when the judge arrives. The participants file into the courtroom, and the bailiff, a member of Bay County Sheriff's Explorer Program, administers the oath of confidentiality. The attorneys make opening statements and then the defendant takes the stand to answer questions. They probe the defendant for information about school performance, grades, attitude, and any mitigating circumstances surrounding the offense. The jury deliberates, arrives at a constructive sentence, and the judge reminds the young person that teen court is a privilege. Failure to complete the sentence will result in the case being transferred to juvenile court. The defendant meets with the Panama City Police Department's community services division to sign a community service contract. Defendants have 30 days to complete their sentence. Each defendant is invited to return to court for jury service (Zehner 1997).

About 40 percent of the defendants who complete the program volunteer for jury service. More than 90 percent of those sentenced in Bay County complete the program, and fewer than 10 percent reoffend within a 12-month postcompletion tracking period. Bay County's success rate mirrors that of other teen court programs. Generally, youths who offend and complete teen court reoffend at a lower rate than do youths tried and sentenced in juvenile courts. The North Carolina Administrative Office of the Courts completed an extensive evaluation of three pilot teen courts. The researchers compared overall recidivism rates for a sample of teen court participants with a matched sample of preprogram juveniles and found that teen court participants had lower rates of recidivism. The researchers found that older juveniles had higher rates of recidivism in general, although higher rates of recidivism may be a function of offense type than age, given that older juveniles tend to commit nonviolent and property offenses. When the researchers controlled for age and offense type, no significant differences were found (North Carolina Administrative Office of the Courts 1995).

The Future of Delinquency Prevention

Delinquency prevention is not about finding a miracle cure for youth misbehavior. Too often, prevention programs have appeared, gathered tremendous enthusiasm, and then withered away as another program appears. Despite about 25 years of federal prevention efforts, no single prevention program has been found to inoculate young people from breaking the law. Then again, delinquency prevention is not about supporting a particular program or strategy. The significance of understanding the history of the JJDP Act is the commitment to prevention over the long term. Federal support for prevention provides the continuity with the seed money that makes the development of local prevention programs possible.

Several prevention programs currently underway that have the potential to prevent delinquency if developed on a wider scale include:

- *WritersCorps.* Funded by the National Endowment for the Arts, WritersCorps places volunteer writers at community sites. The writers teach literary arts through classes, workshops, public readings, and publication projects. Current projects are located in

San Francisco, Bronx, New York, and Washington, D.C. In its initial 3 years, the program has supported 183 writers at 213 host sites serving over 10,000 city residents.

- *Pathways to Success.* Pathways to Success is a collaborative effort of the OJJDP, the Bureau of Justice Assistance, and the National Endowment for the Arts. An afterschool program for at-risk youth, Pathways to Success promotes vocational skill building, entrepreneurial activities, recreation, and arts education. At the local level, the program foster collaboration among existing youth-serving agencies and the education, business, and arts groups within the community. Program sites are located in Anchorage, Washington, D.C., Miami, New York, and Newport County, Rhode Island.
- *SafeFutures.* A program sponsored by the U.S. Department of Justice, SafeFutures seeks to use existing federal, state, and local partnerships to develop graduated sanctions to hold delinquents accountable to the community, develop a more efficient service delivery system, expand and diversify funding sources for community efforts, and determine what outcomes have been achieved. The program currently operates in six communities: Contra Costa County, California; Imperial County, California; Boston, Massachusetts; St. Louis, Missouri; Fort Belknap Indian Community, Harlem, Montana; and Seattle, Washington.
- *Youth Environmental Service.* This program is a collaborative effort of the OJJDP and the U.S. Department of the Interior's Office of National Service and Educational Partnerships. The program establishes a nationwide network of small, specialized programs using federal lands. These programs include residential and nonresidential conservation work and educational initiatives. The program seek to recruit youths who reside in underserved communities and those serious and violent offenders in confinement.
- *Youth Fair Chance.* Youth Fair Chance, funded by the U.S. Department of Labor, concentrates diverse resources for employment and job training within impoverished areas. YFC supports local initiatives such as school-to-work transition programs, alternative schools, and case management strategies. There are 17 sites at present. Two are located in rural areas, one on a Native American reservation, one is in a migrant farmworker community, and the rest are urban.

Ultimately, prevention is about enriching the lives of young people. Prevention programs make it worthwhile for young people to stay out of trouble by improving their life chances, by enhancing their community life, and by helping them make wise choices.

Summary

Delinquency prevention aims at stopping delinquency before it starts. Delinquency prevention is an investment; it is an essential first-step response to juvenile crime. The five major strategies are deterrence, diversion, intervention, public policy, and public health. Prior to the JJDP Act of 1974, the federal response was unorganized. The JJDP Act focused federal efforts on prevention and established guidelines for federal juvenile justice initiatives since then. The comprehensive strategy, sponsored by the OJJDP, is the current federal approach. The primary issue now is not whether prevention should be tried but which strategies should be pursued. Several promising strategies include law related education, conflict resolution, and teen court. The best prevention approach does not gamble on finding a single miracle program but seeks an array of prevention strategies.

KEY CONCEPTS

comprehensive strategy	JJDP Act of 1974	risk factors
conflict resolution	labeling theory	scientific racism
delinquency prevention	law related education	secondary prevention
deterrence	primary prevention	self-fulfilling prophecy
diversion	protective factors	specific deterrence
general deterrence	public health	teen court
intervention	public policy approach	

DISCUSSION QUESTIONS

1. Which would have a bigger impact on public safety: building more training schools or establishing more delinquency prevention programs?

2. Does listening to a police officer talk about drugs, as schoolchildren do in the DARE program, really keep them from experimenting with drugs?

3. Are juvenile curfews an appropriate method of delinquency prevention?

4. What circumstances led to the Juvenile Justice and Delinquency Prevention Act of 1974?

5. According to the comprehensive strategy's risk-focused approach, what factors place young people at greatest risk of becoming delinquent?

6. Did the ideas behind the eugenics campaign really end in the 1940s or do they still influence juvenile justice decision making today?

7. If young people have a better understanding of law, legal processes, and the legal system will they be more likely not to break the law?

8. Are peer mediation programs in school an effective means of reducing school violence?

14 Community Response to Delinquency

CHAPTER OBJECTIVES

After studying this chapter, students will have the tools to:

- Be sensitive to the relevance of community corrections
- Examine the impact of community response to delinquency
- Gain a better understanding of community's alternatives
- Examine electronic monitoring and its impact on the community
- Better understand the different community service work programs in communities

Diversion, Intermediate Sanctions, and Restorative Justice

Although dispositions within the community have always been part of the juvenile court, they have acquired new importance during the past three decades. The deinstitutionalization movement began in Massachusetts in 1971. During the 1970s, Massachusetts initiated a statewide effort to develop community-based alternatives to secure confinement. Federal policy, expressed in the Juvenile Justice and Delinquency Prevention Act of 1974, promoted diversion of delinquents away from secure confinement and toward community-based placements where the chance for successful reintegration would be greater. During the 1980s, legislators began to place emphasis on intermediate sanctions—that is, on the development of sanctions between probation and secure confinement. During the 1990s, interest in balanced and restorative justice emerged as legislators began to take victims and communities into account along with the offender's needs. Although the rationales of diversion, intermediate sanctions, and restorative justice conflict, they have produced a range of community-based alternatives.

Probation, the most common justice court disposition, has been upgraded to include intensive probation, school probation, and police-probation partnerships. In addition, legislatures have created a range of dispositions, including restitution, community service, and work programs, electronic monitoring programs, day treatment, group homes and residential placements, victim-offender mediation, and family group conferencing. As diverse as these programs are, they share the element of community response. They are in the broadest sense intended to retain, establish, and strengthen the young person's ties to the community. Some, such as restitution and house arrest, reflect ancient practices. Others, such as group homes and electronic monitoring, represent more recent experiments.

This chapter reviews the community response to delinquency. The first section describes three rationales for community corrections: diversion, intermediate sanctions, and balanced and restorative justice. The second section reviews probation including recent versions, such as intensive supervision probation. The third section surveys the range of alternatives to confinement and standard probation. These are restitution, community service and work programs, victim-offender mediation, family group conferencing, house arrest/electronic monitoring, day treatment, and group homes and residential placements. The final section reviews sanctions in the Jewish tradition.

Community Corrections for Juveniles

The diversity of community corrections programs in place today reflects several rationales of juvenile justice. Deinstitutionalization in the 1970s occurred within an overall philosophical framework of rehabilitation. The 1970s rationale for community-based corrections was diversion. During the 1980s and 1990s, when the overall philosophy shifted to accountability, new rationales emerged. The accountability-oriented rationales have been intermediate sanctions and the balanced approach.

Diversion

Training school ceased to be the first option at disposition in about 1971. Four years earlier, the National Council on Crime and Delinquency (NCCD) surveyed juvenile detention and corrections facilities at the request of the President's Commission on Law Enforcement and the Administration of Justice. The NCCD survey found that the average daily population in juvenile correctional facilities was 42,000. Nearly half the states' facilities were overcrowded, and rehabilitation programs were limited. The survey concluded that although training schools represented specialized facilities for rehabilitating hardened juvenile delinquents, there was such a wide discrepancy between available and actual services that they amounted to little more than warehouses. As a result, juvenile policymakers feared that juvenile institutions might be doing more harm than good (Howell 1998).

Diversion Theory. Although diversion practices vary, the concept generally involves a decision to turn a youth away from the official system and toward alternative procedures and programs. At disposition, *diversion* typically means the youth is sent to a program or facility other than a secure corrections facility for juveniles, known as a training school. The Massachusetts model followed the observation that warehousing young lawbreakers in large training schools was counterproductive. Training schools swept up status offenders who would otherwise not have been incarcerated. Those incarcerated returned with the enduring stigma of a reform school, prepared for institutional living and little more. Rural training schools not only separated young people from corrupting influences of the city but also from family members and friends. The demise of the indenture system resulted in returning those who had been confined to the environment from which they had come, and they returned to a delinquent way of life.

Diversion became national policy with the Juvenile Justice and Delinquency Prevention Act of 1974. The JJDP Act prohibited secure placement of status offenders. The act, as amended, states that "juveniles charged with or who have committed offenses that would not be criminal if committed by an adult or offenses which do not constitute violations of valid court orders . . . shall not be placed in secure detention facilities or secure correctional facilities." The JJDP Act also prohibited juveniles, either status offenders or those adjudicated delinquent, from being confined (or detained) "in any institution in which they have contact with adults incarcerated because they have been convicted of a crime or are awaiting trial on criminal charges . . ." (Snyder & Sickmund 1999, 207–208).

At the same time, the "least restrictive alternative" doctrine found its way into juvenile justice. The *least restrictive alternative* concept proposes that the court look to the least restrictive sanction in terms of custodial management. It follows from the idea that the deeper an individual juvenile goes in the corrections system, the more difficult it will be for the youth to emerge as a productive citizen. The concept appears in the Institute of Justice Administration/American Bar Association *Juvenile Justice Standards* of 1980: "In choosing among statutorily permissible dispositions, the court should employ the least restrictive category and duration of disposition that is approximate to the seriousness of the offense . . . the imposition of a particular disposition should be accompanied by a statement of the facts relied on in support of the disposition and the reasons for selecting the disposition and the less restrictive alternatives" (Watkins 1998, 199–200). State juvenile codes written during the 1970s reflected this concept. North Carolina's Juvenile Code Revision Committee, created by the state legislature in 1977, recommended similar language concerning the court's decision making at disposition. "A juvenile should not be committed to training school if he can receive help in his community" (Carlton 1979, 227).

Diversion has been practiced since the beginning of the juvenile court more than a hundred years ago. Police, court intake workers, judges, and probation officers had broad discretion under the *parens patriae* philosophy of the court, and juveniles went to whichever alternative programs the officials wanted to send them. Beginning in the 1960s, juvenile professionals believed that the court should concentrate its resources on the small number of serious and violent juvenile offenders by sending the others to alternative programs. Following the recommendations of the President's Commission on Law Enforcement and the Administration of Justice, federal funds became available for state and local programs. As a result, formal diversion programs appeared alongside traditional practices of informal adjustment. Formal diversion programs created during this period included youth service bureaus, job training and placement programs, alternative schools, and family counseling. Since the 1980s, when the philosophy of juvenile justice shifted from rehabilitation to accountability, diversion programs have emphasized restitution and work programs for diverted youth (Ezell 1992).

Diversion programs have confronted the challenge of net widening. *Net widening* describes a situation in which a program set up to divert offenders away from confinement has the unintended effect of drawing more juveniles under court supervision. A true diversion program would actually reduce the number of commitments to training school because youths who would have been sent to training school are diverted to community-based programs instead. Net widening occurs when the number of commitments to training school remains the same or increases, and additional youths are sent to the "diversion" program. Rather than reduce the number of training school commitments, diversion has produced an increase in the total number of juveniles processed. In other words, diversion should divert youths bound for training school and not those who would otherwise be released without any intervention (Lundman 1993, 99). Concerns about net-widening miss the mark. Although juvenile justice policymakers generally view diversion as a failure because of net widening, a different criticism suggests that net widening per se—the failure to leave children outside the system—is not really the problem. Rather than restricting government nets, community nets should be widened. Programs founded with diversion as the primary purpose fail to distinguish between programs that enhance or build links between youths and the community and those that isolate young people from the community. The goal of community corrections should be to increase the community's role in sanctioning, not to limit the government's role in sanctioning. As Gordon Bazemore, director of the Community Justice Institute at Florida Atlantic University, puts it: "The problem with juvenile justice intervention, therefore, has not been with government itself, but with a failure to define a suitable role for government" (Bazemore 1998, 77).

Massachusetts and Afterward.   Massachusetts took the lead in closing large institutions for juveniles. In 1971, Jerome Miller, then head of the Department of Youth Services in Massachusetts, abruptly removed most of the youths from the state's training schools and placed them in community-based programs. Juveniles requiring secure detention were placed in smaller facilities with between 20 and 30 beds. Massachusetts continues to operate with only a fraction of the beds used in other states, and the majority of youths are placed in small, privately managed programs (Miller 1998).

Over the past two decades, other states have moved in the same direction. Maryland, Pennsylvania, Utah, Colorado, Oklahoma, and Oregon have created networks of community-based residential and nonresidential services following Massachusetts' lead (Greenwood 1996). In Oklahoma and Utah, deinstitutionalization resulted from agreements to settle lawsuits. Deinstitutionalization in Oklahoma followed a federal lawsuit, *Terry D. v. Rader,* filed in federal district court in Oklahoma City in 1978. The suit alleged abusive practices, unconstitutional use of isolation and restraints, a lack of adequately trained staff, and mixing of offenders with nonoffenders. The Oklahoma Department of Human Services closed a number of institutions and implemented a variety of community-based programs for children, including residential and nonresidential facilities. In 1994, the Oklahoma legislature passed the Juvenile Reform Act, creating the Office of Juvenile Affairs. OJA had authority over juvenile matters and, in April 1996, met the federal court requirement for dismissal of the *Terry D.* lawsuit.

In Utah, a class-action lawsuit, *Manning v. Matheson* (1975), challenged conditions of confinement at the state industrial school. The suit alleged that a juvenile's stay in solitary confinement led to or contributed to the young man's mental illness. Two years later, Governor Scott Matheson's Blue Ribbon Task Force recommended that youths should be placed in the "least restrictive setting" consistent with public safety. The Governor also convened meetings of juvenile justice leaders in the state to make recommendations for settling the suit and, a year later, obtained an $800,000 grant to begin development of a network of community-based, privately operated residential programs. This led to the creation of the Division of Youth Corrections in 1981 to administer secure care, detention, and alternatives to secure placement along the lines of the Massachusetts experience (Division of Youth Corrections 1998).

Other states pursued deinstitutionalization without encouragement from the federal judiciary. Ohio developed an innovative strategy for reducing the number of youths in secure placements based on a market approach. In 1993, the state legislature approved RECLAIM Ohio, a funding system to encourage development of community-based options. RECLAIM—Reasonable and Equitable Community and Local Alternatives to the Incarceration of Minors—originally began as part of Governor George Voinovich's Family and Children First Initiative.

Prior to 1993, county governments in Ohio had no control over funds used for juvenile incarceration. Judges could order commitment to a facility operated by the state Division of Youth Services (DYS) "for free." Under the RECLAIM program, counties receive a yearly allocation from the DYS for treatment of youthful offenders. The DYS in turn charges each county a daily rate for every day a juvenile spends in a DYS facility. There is "no charge" for violent juvenile offenders; DYS allocates "public safety beds" to the counties for use in cases of murder, kidnapping, rape, and other serious offenses. DYS charges a reduced rate for every day a juvenile spends in a community corrections facility to encourage use of these resources when appropriate. RECLAIM funds may also be used by the counties to develop prevention and diversion programs for status offenders, traffic offenders, and other at-risk youths. These include day treatment, alternative schools, intensive probation, electronic monitoring, and residential treatment. RECLAIM Ohio began as a pilot program in nine counties in 1994; it became statewide in 1995 (Natalucci-Persichetti & Zimmermann 1997).

Intermediate Sanctions

Intermediate sanctions refer to a continuum of punishments that provides for graduated levels of supervision and harshness. Standard probation occupies one end of the continuum and training school the other, with a range of community-based sanctions, such as work programs, electronic monitoring, and community service in the middle (DiMascio 1995). In 1990, Norval Morris and Michael Tonry pointed out that judges face an either/or choice at sentencing due to the lack of sanctions between the extremes of incarceration and community supervision. They argued for a graduated system of sanctions, including fines, community service, house arrest, intensive probation, and electronic monitoring. Only with such a range of sanctions could judges match the consequences to the seriousness of the offense (Morris & Tonry 1990). The idea began in adult corrections and found its way into juvenile corrections.

Georgia's Intensive Supervision Program.   Legislative interest in intermediate sanctions began during the 1980s when overcrowded prisons and a poor economy fueled interest in cost-saving alternatives to incarceration. Georgia developed an intensive supervision probation program with a 2-person team assigned to supervise 25 offenders in the community. The team consisted of a surveillance officer, who monitored the offenders, and a probation officer, who counseled the offenders and retained legal authority over the case. While under intensive supervision, each offender was seen five times a week, did community service, paid a supervision fee, and had to be employed or participating in an educational program. An evaluation showed that the program had an extremely low failure rate of about 5 percent, and in 1985, Georgia Corrections Commissioner David Evans announced that the program saved the cost of building two new state prisons (Petersilia 1999).

Illinois, Massachusetts, New Jersey, and Florida adopted the program along with a number of other states, and developing intermediate sanctions became a national corrections initiative. The National Institute of Justice and the Edna McConnell Clark Foundation, a private foundation, helped make Georgia's approach a national approach. Between 1985 and 1995, hundreds of intermediate programs began across the country. Probation departments developed intensive surveillance programs, electronic monitoring, drug testing, and other sanctions. About half of the states had passed community corrections laws by 1995. Advocates of intermediate sanctions argued that using the graduated sentencing scheme would reserve expensive prison cells for violent criminals, and less expensive community-based sanctions could be used for nonviolent and low-risk offenders. At the same time, restitution-focused community programs would teach offenders accountability for their actions and heighten their chances for rehabilitation. By expanding the range of sentencing options, judges have greater discretion in selecting the punishment that most closely fits the crime and the criminal. As William M. DiMascio, writing for the Edna McConnell Clark Foundation, put it: "The approach treats prison as the backstop, rather than the backbone, of the corrections system" (DiMascio 1995, 34).

Because intermediate sanctions have sprouted up at the local rather than at the state or federal level, describing them on the national level is difficult. Goals for particular types of intermediate sanction vary from one program to the next. Individual programs often pursue multiple and sometimes conflicting goals; a strategy can be a useful means of attracting broad political support for particular initiatives. Some legislators, for example, support intermediate sanctions as alternatives for prison-bound offenders, whereas others support them as harsher punishment for offenders considered insufficiently punished by regular probation. On the other hand, ambiguous and confusing goals for a program translate into inconsistent operating policies and can result in multiple and conflicting outcomes such as "adding on" restitution to a probation sentence or "stacking" community service on home detention (Parent *et al.* 1997).

OJJDP's Comprehensive Strategy.   Intermediate sanctions have been introduced to juvenile justice through the efforts of the Office of Juvenile Justice and Delinquency Prevention. In 1993, OJJDP published its *Comprehensive Strategy for Serious, Violent and Chronic Juvenile Offenders*. The strategy has two program development facets: prevent delinquency through prevention programs targeting at-risk youths and improve the juvenile justice response through development of "graduated sanctions" organized along the lines of an increasing level of supervision.

The graduated sanctions model provides a continuum of diverse programs, including immediate sanctions within the community for first-time, nonviolent offenders and intermediate sanctions for more serious offenders. There are secure care programs for the most violent offenders and after-care programs that provide high levels of surveillance and treatment.

Juveniles should move along the continuum through a well-structured system of phases that addresses both their needs and the safety of the community. At each level, the juvenile should be subject to sanctions of increasing severity, and the most violent juvenile offenders should be waived into criminal court. Juvenile intake workers and treatment providers should rely on risk assessments and classification schemes to determine the most appropriate sanctions for each young person. These assessments should be based on the risk to society, the seriousness of the offense, the number of prior offenses, and the presence of other risk factors. Programs should remain small so that each youth receives individual attention (Howell 1995).

Many states have adopted the comprehensive strategy. The California legislature allocated $50 million for probation programs requiring that both surveillance and treatment be part of any funded program (Petersilia 1999). Intermediate sanctions programs include intensive supervision, boot camps, wilderness programs, and community-based residential programs. Model programs have appeared in South Carolina, Ohio, Michigan, Tennessee, Illinois, and Maryland (Howell 1995).

Balanced and Restorative Justice

Balanced and Restorative Justice (BARJ) represents a new way to look at the goals of community corrections for juveniles. The BARJ approach suggests that justice is done when the interests of the community, offender, and victim receive balanced attention. The BARJ model relies on two key concepts: restorative justice and the balanced approach.

Restorative Justice.   *Restorative justice* emphasizes that when a young person commits a crime, there is injury to another person—the victim—as well as to the community. Consequently, the youth incurs an obligation to repair the harm done and "restore" the victim and the community, to the extent possible, to the state of being that existed before the criminal act. What became the balanced and restorative justice approach to juvenile corrections began with restorative justice.

Howard Zehr, a professor at Eastern Mennonite University in Virginia, outlined the theology of restorative justice in his book *Changing Lenses.* Zehr draws on three Hebrew words for justice found in the law of Moses. *Tsedeq* means "straight" or "righteous." It is the standard of behavior that humans should conform to in their relationships with each other and God. *Mishpat* refers to justice in the judicial or legal sense; it refers to the rights and responsibilities that are enforced under the law of the land in court. *Shalom* is the word for peace, completeness, fulfillment, and wholeness. Peace (*shalom*) is the result of people treating each other the way they should (*tsedeq*), which the law and courts (*mishpat*) uphold. Zehr called this "covenant justice," the Judeo-Christian alternative to contemporary practice and what he calls "retributive justice" (Zehr 1990).

From the restorative perspective, the concept of crime is much broader than the concept based on the criminal law that identifies certain harms and conflicts as crimes. *Retributive justice,* the prevailing philosophy of criminal justice, makes the government into a victim and puts punishment of the lawbreaker at the center of proceedings. The restorative view of crime includes civil wrongs as well as crimes—all violations of the standard of righteousness. Crime represents a violation of human relationships and the standard to which people should adhere to in their relationships. It also includes a social dimension because crime spreads fear and mistrust. In this sense, the ultimate victim of crime is peace. Restorative justice defines crime as harm caused to a person; putting individual lives and their relationships back together is the center of the justice process (Zehr 1990).

The restorative justice perspective has three key principles:

1. Crime results in injuries to victims and communities; the goal of criminal justice should be to repair them.
2. The government is not the victim—the person who suffered the harm is the victim. Relationships between people, the offender, and the community are also victims of crime.
3. In promoting justice, the government is responsible for order; the community is responsible for peace. It is up to the members of the community, not the government, to do justice to one another (Van Ness 1990).

When the criminal justice system promotes punishment rather than reconciliation, there is further injury. Not only is the victim injured and left without reparation, but the offender is left without an opportunity to make reparations and be restored within the community.

The Balanced Approach.   The ***balanced approach*** holds that the system should give "balanced" attention to the goals of public safety, accountability of juvenile offenders, and correcting juvenile offenders so that they will not reoffend. The balanced approach does not require proportional amounts of "treatment" and "punishment" but rather that the juvenile justice process devotes sufficient time and resources to each of the three goals.

In 1987, the National Council of Juvenile and Family Court Judges outlined a balanced approach to juvenile probation. The balanced approach insists that the juvenile justice system serves three populations, not one: the offender, the victim, and the community. The emphasis is on restitution negotiation and problem solving, an approach that finds its most direct application to property offenses (Umbreit 1995). As of 1997, 14 states had balanced approach language written into their juvenile codes. A much larger number of local juvenile courts have adopted the balanced approach or have issued policies requiring probation staff to follow a balanced approach (Bazemore 1997).

Pennsylvania adopted the balanced and restorative justice model in 1994 when the race for governor highlighted juvenile crime. Governor Tom Ridge (later appointed by President George W. Bush to head the White Office of Homeland Security), fulfilling a campaign promise, called for a special session on crime the day after his inauguration. During that summer, the Juvenile Court Judges Association drafted a proposal to include the principles of community protection, youth and system accountability, and competency development. The Juvenile Court Act of 1995 redefined the purpose of Pennsylvania's juvenile justice system from providing a system of "supervision, care and rehabilitation" to giving "balanced attention" to community protection, offender accountability, and competency development enabling children to become responsible members of the community. Pennsylvania's BARJ model requires development of partnerships at the state and local level, among schools, the police, community service providers, local employers, and churches. The partnerships will rely on new sources of funding. Victim services, not traditionally included as juvenile court services, will need to be funded through the new law (Torbet & Thomas 1997).

The Canadian government has also made a commitment to the balanced approach. In March 1999, the government of Canada enacted the Youth Criminal Justice Act, new legislation that replaced the Young Offenders Act. The new legislation is one of the most important aspects of Canada's "renewed youth justice strategy" launched in May 1998. *A Strategy for the Renewal of Youth Justice* refers to "A Need for Balance" and outlines a response to youth violence promoting crime prevention and effective alternatives to the formal youth system, ensuring meaningful consequences for offenses committed by youth, and emphasizing rehabilitation and reintegration. The strategy promotes a number of restorative justice approaches, including youth justice committees, family group conferencing, and victim-offender mediation (Department of Justice Canada 1999).

In 1997, the Office of Juvenile Justice and Delinquency Prevention funded the Balanced and Restorative Justice Project, a joint project of the Community Justice Institute at Florida Atlantic University and the Center for Restorative Justice and Mediation at the University of Minnesota. The BARJ project sponsors restorative justice projects in Palm Beach County, Florida; Allegheny County, Pennsylvania; Dakota County, Minnesota; and Deschutes County, Oregon. The project requires every sanction involving juveniles to include consideration of public safety, accountability to victim and community, and the development of competency by offenders (Lipkin & Abelson 1997–1998).

Restorative justice began as an application of Judeo-Christian principles, although not all programs operate on a Judaic or a Christian basis. There is a secular analog to the emphasis on confession, repentance, and reparation. This makes the term *restorative justice* rather vague and can lead to confusion and misunderstanding (Quinn 1998). Although it is too early to assess the effects of the victims' rights and restorative justice movements on the juvenile correctional populations, the movement has aroused suspicion over several issues. Critics argue that restorative language is a new guise for "get-tough" policies. Rhetoric concerning victims' rights becomes a rationale for stiffening the sentence given the offender. At the same time, the flurry of victims' rights legislation does not necessarily translate into practice. Most state legislatures have written victims' rights language, but these rights are difficult to enforce (Shapiro 1990).

Probation

Probation is the most common disposition ordered by juvenile courts. In 1994, 54 percent of all cases adjudicated for a delinquency offense received probation as the most severe disposition; 29 percent were placed in a residential facility, 15 percent received some other disposition (restitution, fine, community service), and 4 percent were dismissed (Sickmund 1997, 2). Probation has been described as the "backbone," the "workhorse," and the "catch basin" of the juvenile justice system.

Juvenile Probation.   The word **probation** comes from the Latin word *probare,* meaning "to prove." It allows the youth to prove himself or herself worthy of remaining in the community rather than being confined (Roberts 1998a, 132). Under a sentence of probation, the offender lives at home but receives some supervision, such as meeting with the probation officer a certain number of times per month or keeping a journal of activities.

The Beginnings of Probation. Probation began in 1841 when a Massachusetts bootmaker, John Augustus, convinced a judge to suspend for three weeks the sentence of a drunkard. Augustus assured the court that he could keep the man sober and risked forfeiting a personal bond if he could not. Augustus succeeded, and after returning with the man to the court three weeks later, the judge replaced the sentence of imprisonment with a small fine. Augustus never worked as a paid employee of the state. He was a volunteer and eventually involved himself in more than 5,000 cases. He helped both men and women, adults and children. In 1878, the Massachusetts legislature enacted legislature making probation a state function and provided for the hiring of a paid probation officer. Within a few decades, other states passed similar legislation and probation became a common penalty for both adults and juveniles (Durham 1994, 172–173).

By 1927, almost all states had enacted juvenile court laws, and a juvenile probation system developed in every state except Wyoming. Probation became the legal means for judges to allow juveniles to be sanctioned in their own homes. The Juvenile Court of Cook County, Illinois, began in 1899 with Judge Richard S. Tuthill as presiding judge and Timothy D. Hurley as chief probation officer. Cook County furnished a courtroom, clerk, prosecuting attorney, and office facilities. The city of Chicago paid the salaries of 16 police officers who were appointed by the court to act as juvenile probation officers. The majority of juvenile courts did not, however, employ probation officers. In these courts, probation often meant "signing the book" and assigning youths to their parents for probation or relying on citizens who volunteered to serve as probation officers. Volunteers served as probation officers in rural areas and small cities in some states until the 1950s (Roberts 1998a, 128).

Within a few years of passage of probation legislation, most states created positions for salaried probation officers. Massachusetts, Rhode Island, Indiana, Minnesota, and New Jersey passed laws creating the position of paid state probation officer within three years of Illinois. Other states followed, although training standards were not in place for several decades. In New York, the first probation officers consisted of "kindly ex-policemen or retired subway guards with political pull." In 1928, New York mandated that probation officers possess a high school diploma as a minimum. During the 1930s, the U.S. Children's Bureau devised and promoted professional standards for probation officers working with juveniles. The standards recommended a college degree in social work, at least a year of experience in case work, and a salary comparable to social workers in other service areas. By the 1960s, probation departments had been established in all 50 states and in hundreds of counties across the nation. Although a 1967 study by the National Council on Crime and Delinquency found no juvenile probation services in many rural counties of four states, the nation's largest jurisdictions had developed a professional probation staff (Roberts 1998a, 132–133).

Standard Probation. Probation can be either voluntary or court-ordered. Some juveniles are ordered to probation after an adjudication of delinquency. For these offenders, probation represents an alternative to institutional confinement. Other juveniles, who are not adjudicated delinquent, agree to abide by certain probation conditions on the condition that if they successfully complete their probation, the case will be closed without filing a delinquency petition. These juveniles are first-time, low-risk offenders. **Standard probation** supervision includes contact with a probation officer once a week or once a month depending on the risk level and needs of the youth. In addition, probation officers monitor the youth's out-side activities, such as school attendance, and refer the youth to needed services, such as drug and alcohol counseling.

Juvenile courts have latitude in determining the conditions of probation. North Car-olina law, for example, provides that "the court may impose conditions of probation that are related to the needs of the juvenile and that are reasonably necessary to ensure that the juve-nile will lead a law-abiding life." State statutes specifically require that the juvenile remain on good behavior, not violate any laws, and "shall not violate any reasonable and lawful rules of a parent." The juvenile must attend school regularly, make passing grades in at least four courses, or be employed if not attending school. The juvenile must abide by curfew, not associate with specified persons, refrain from use or possession of drugs and alcohol, pos-sess no firearm or explosive device, and make restitution as specified by the court. The law also provides "that the juvenile satisfy any other conditions determined appropriate by the court" (North Carolina General Statutes 1999).

In about half of the states and the District of Columbia, probation services are admin-istered by the local juvenile court or the administrative office of the courts. In 14 states, pro-bation is administered by a combination of organizations, typically by juvenile courts in urban counties and by the executive branch in rural counties. In 10 states, probation is admin-istered statewide through a branch within the executive branch. A national survey of proba-tion officers found that caseloads ranged from 2 to 200, with an average caseload of 41. The probation officers surveyed suggested an optimal caseload of 30. Probation officers working in urban jurisdictions tended to report higher caseloads than those working in suburban and rural areas. Probation officers in rural areas tended to report that they carried a mixed case-load of juvenile and adult cases (Torbet 1996, 2–3).

In Texas, probation is administered at both the state level and the county levels. There are 168 local juvenile probation departments. The county juvenile board makes policy and budgeting decisions at the local level and hires the chief probation officer. The chief proba-tion officer is responsible for the day-to-day administration of the probation department and, in smaller counties, supervises probationers. The Texas Juvenile Probation Commis-sion (TJPC) is a state agency. The legislature created the TJPC in 1981 to bring consistency to probation services throughout the state. The TJPC is overseen by a nine-member board appointed by the governor. It distributes funds appropriated by the legislature, carries out a strategic planning process, makes and enforces statewide standards, provides education and training, provides legal and technical assistance, and certifies juvenile probation and deten-tion officers. Juvenile probation officers must possess a baccalaureate degree and have completed one year of graduate study or related work experience and 40 hours of basic pro-bation training to be certified. There are more than 2,300 certified juvenile probation offi-cers in Texas (Texas Juvenile Probation Commission Web site, www.tjpc.state.tx.us).

Nationally, the majority of cases placed on probation involve property offenders. In 1994, 51 percent of cases in which the juvenile was adjudicated delinquent involved a prop-erty offense; 22 percent of these cases involved a crime against a person, 9 percent involved drugs, and 19 percent were public order offenses (Sickmund 1997, 2). Between 1985 and 1994, however, the percentage of cases involving offenses against a person grew from about 15 percent to about 22 percent (Sickmund 1997, 2). There is also a growing perception among probation officers that the work of juvenile probation has become increasingly dangerous. Almost one-third of probation officers surveyed reported that they had been assaulted at least once in their careers; 42 percent reported that they were always or usually concerned about their safety (Torbet 1996, 4). Balancing the safety of probation officers and the public with the needs of juveniles is a major challenge. This increasing proportion of violent juvenile offenders on probation does not reflect a shift in judicial philosophy so much as a lack of resources. Probation represents the only alternative in jurisdictions within crowded juvenile facilities. Probation represents the "catch basin" of the juvenile justice system. It is the thing to do with a juvenile when there is nothing else to do (Torbet 1996, 4).

Probation Plus

Standard probation services have undergone relatively few changes in the past three decades from traditional emphasis on office visits, occasional referrals to specialized providers, and enforcement of conditions, such as curfew (Bazemore 1991, 28). Probation, however, is the backbone of services and approaches. Collectively, these approaches and services are known as *community-based services* or *community-based alternatives* because they provide alternatives to training school and incarceration.

Intensive Probation.   During the 1980s, the *intensive supervision probation* (ISP) approach to programs and services emerged. ISP programs generally emphasize use of various surveillance techniques, such as team supervision and *saturation surveillance* (24-hour monitoring), high-tech surveillance (electronic monitoring, random drug testing), classification to determine risk levels, and specialized treatment programs (Armstrong 1991, 2). Intensive probation is an enhancement of traditional probation services. A youth sentenced to intensive probation receives traditional probation services and, in addition, more frequent face-to-face meetings with a probation officer, greater scrutiny of the youth's outside activities (home, school, and employment), and more frequent assessments of the youth's progress (Clouser 1996, 1).

In some states, ISP has been promoted as a relevant approach for chronic, high-risk juvenile offenders. ISP programs for juveniles emerged in the 1980s during the get-tough movement because it offered control, surveillance, and enforcement. It also provides a "solution" to prisons and jails packed to capacity: a "tough new probation program to deal with persons who should be incarcerated but for whom there is no room." "This aspect of the new intensive probation programs," comments Todd Clear (1991, 31), "is based on desperation—something has to be done." The rationale for intensive supervision of juveniles is simple: probation supervision is good, and more supervision is better. ISP programs have a twofold purpose: punishment and risk control. They attempt to blend these two. The basic strategy includes frequent contact (semi-monthly or weekly), specialized assessment for service delivery, and emphasis on surveillance and treatment. Common risk control strategies include random or surprise home visits, electronic monitoring, home detention, curfew requirements, search and seizure, residential day treatment, big brother/volunteer, and referrals to treatment services. Common punishment strategies include work crews, community service, restitution, victim-offender conferences, and fines (Clear 1991).

Erie County initiated the first intensive juvenile probation program in Pennsylvania in 1977. The program was designed to provide the habitual or chronic offender with one last chance before residential placement. The program, which became a model for intensive probation programs throughout Pennsylvania, begins with seven days of house arrest. During this time, the juvenile must contact his or her probation officer every evening and receive instructions about completing the program (Clouser 1996, 2). To complete the program, the juvenile must pass through four phases:

1. *Phase I.* The juvenile keeps a daily record of progress toward goals, obtains weekly progress reports from teachers, attends a weekly self-help group session offered by the probation department, and reports to her or his probation officer, in person, twice a week. In addition, the probation officer makes weekly visits to the juvenile's home and school, makes 3 curfew checks each week, and requires the juvenile to submit to drug screenings every 10 days.
2. *Phase II.* For 60 days, the juvenile receives slightly less supervision and less frequent checks by the probation officer. Only two curfew checks are done each week, and drug screens and progress reports are completed every two weeks.
3. *Phase III.* During this phase, also 60 days, drug screens are given randomly and daily reporting requirements are reduced. Reporting of goals and school progress reports are less frequent.
4. *Phase IV.* During the final 30 days, the juvenile is "weaned" from the probation officer. The probation officer tailors the requirements placed on the juvenile to remaining needs and parental responsibility for supervision of the youth (Clouser 1996, 2).

Erie County's program began in 1977 with 33 youths. Eighteen had successfully completed the program by the end of the first year and 15 others remained under supervision. In 1984, the Pennsylvania Juvenile Court Judges Commission provided funds for additional programs. Eleven programs began during that first year, and by 1995, intensive probation programs operated in 39 of Pennsylvania's 67 counties (Clouser 1996, 4).

Probation Innovation.   School probation and police-probation partnerships represent two innovations in juvenile probation. School probation began in Pennsylvania. The Lehigh County Juvenile Probation Department, in conjunction with the Allentown School District, developed ***school-based probation*** to provide for closer monitoring of juvenile behavior and assist the school in dealing with misbehavior by juvenile probationers attending public schools. In 1990, the school-based probation program became the first program to locate a full-time juvenile probation officer in a public school. School-based probation officers develop treatment plans and monitor the day-to-day behaviors of youths on their caseloads. They are responsible for attending all court proceedings on behalf of school-based probationers. In addition, they coordinate community service and other programs for students suspended from school and arrange reentry conferences for students returning to school following placement in a juvenile justice facility. Since the Lehigh County program began, about 35 programs have developed in 20 other counties with support from the Pennsylvania Commission on Crime and Delinquency. In some programs, a probation officer is assigned to a specific school, and in others, the probation officer divides his or her time between schools (Clouser 1995).

Boston's Operation Night Light combines police and probation services to provide around-the-clock surveillance. The project began in 1992 as a partnership between probation officers in Dorchester, Massachusetts, district court, and police officers within the Anti-Gang Violence Unit of the Boston Police Department. Boston's ***probation/police partnership*** pairs one probation officer with two police officers to make surprise visits to the homes, schools, and work places of high-risk probationers. Rather than make these visits during the day, the traditional time for probation visits, the visits occur between 7 P.M. and midnight. The partnership means that police report violations of curfew and firearms-possession restrictions to probation officers, police have information on conditions of probation, and the court serves warrants for violations. The police attend joint training seminars, participate in strategic planning sessions, and participate in research projects. Police, probation, and members of the community—clergy, youth workers, parents, and school personnel—participate in monthly meetings. Police also help probation officers monitor probationers in school programs to reduce truancy. The program has spread from Boston to a dozen other jurisdictions within Massachusetts (Corbett *et al.* 1998).

Community Corrections Alternatives

Since 1971 and the beginning of deinstitutionalization, alternatives to institutional confinement for juveniles have flourished. Whether guided by a specific rationale of intermediate sanctions, restorative justice, or a general interest in deinstitutionalization and diversion, community-based programs have been developed in every state. These include restitution, community/work service, victim-offender reconciliation, family group conferencing, and house arrest/electronic monitoring.

Restitution

The requirement for juveniles to pay back their victims for property losses or damage has become a frequent disposition in juvenile court. As a sanction imposed by the court, a ***restitution*** order requires the offender to make a payment by performing a service for the victim or, most frequently, by paying money. Juvenile restitution may be used at the intake stage of juvenile court processing in conjunction with diversion agreements. Restitution orders are most commonly applied by the juvenile court at the disposition stage, typically as a condition of probation. Restitution may be ordered as the sole sanction or in conjunction with commitment to a community corrections program, such as day treatment, residential setting, or drug/alcohol treatment program (Hudson & Galaway 1989). Under Texas law, the judge may order the young person to pay restitution as a condition of probation or to pay restitution independently of probation. Alternatively, the judge may order the parents to pay restitution.

The Principle of Restitution.   Victims have always had a common law right to restitution for criminal harm. This right was codified as early as the seventh century, when Ethelbert of

Kent issued his Laws of Ethelbert. The laws contained detailed restitution schedules: Front, side, and back teeth each had their specified value as did each finger and fingernail (Van Ness 1986, 65). American courts never fully enforced restitution claims, however, and the laws fell into disuse during the nineteenth and early twentieth centuries. Restitution reemerged in the 1930s when a few states enacted laws allowing for restitution in cases with suspended sentences and probation. During the 1970s, various commissions recommended a return to restitution, including the National Commission on Criminal Justice Standards and Goals, the Council of Judges of the National Council on Crime and Delinquency, and the American Bar Association. Restitution returned in full only after the Victims' Rights Movement. Following the election of Ronald Reagan in 1980, restitution became a major goal of victims' rights legislation. In 1982, Congress enacted the Victim and Witness Protection Act that required federal judges to order full restitution in criminal cases or provide written reasons for not doing so. That same year, the President's Task Force on Victims of Crime recommended that judges across the country order restitution in all cases in which the victim suffered a financial loss. In 1994, Congress responded with the Violent Crime Control and Law Enforcement Act, which included provisions for mandatory restitution in federal cases of sexual assault or domestic violence (Office for Victims of Crime 1998b, 2).

Within 10 years of the Victim and Witness Protection Act of 1982, every state passed legislation addressing restitution. As of 1995, 29 states followed the federal model and mandated restitution in all cases unless the judge has compelling reasons for not doing so. Some states, however, mandate restitution only in cases involving violent crimes, whereas others mandate restitution only in cases involving property crimes (Office for Victims of Crime 1998a, 2).

Juvenile Restitution.   The Utah Juvenile Court operates a structured juvenile restitution program that includes both financial and community service. The court encourages victims to claim restitution and orders it in almost every case in which a claim is made. During the 1980s, the amount of restitution ordered and paid to victims doubled from $250,000 to $500,000. In recent years, as much as two-thirds of restitution money collected by the Utah Juvenile Court has been collected and paid to victims (Butts & Snyder 1992, 2). In the majority of restitution cases, juveniles were ordered to make restitution in the form of direct financial payments. Utah state law also allows the juvenile court to order a youth to "repair, replace, or make restitution for victims' property and other losses" in cases where no petition of delinquency has been filed. In these cases, which amount to about 10 percent of restitution orders, probation officers develop restitution or community service plans, consent agreements are signed by the youth and his or her parents, and restitution is paid directly to the victim (Butts & Snyder 1992, 2).

In about a third of restitution orders, juveniles are required to participate in community service programs to earn money to make restitution payments. Also, Utah's restitution policy, established by state statute in 1979, allows the court to withhold a substantial portion of fines paid by juveniles to underwrite a work restitution fund. This fund allows juveniles otherwise unable to pay restitution to work in community service projects in the public or private sector to repay victims. The juvenile's earnings are paid from the fund directly to the victims (Butts & Snyder 1992, 2).

Juvenile restitution has received renewed emphasis for several reasons. Arguments can be made that restitution fulfills all the aims of criminal justice, including rehabilitation, retribution, and deterrence. Although it is not clear why restitution works, it has been found to lower recidivism. A key element in restitution, whether ordered to achieve the aim of retribution or rehabilitation, is that the offender takes a step toward reconciliation. One criticism of restitution, however, is that when ordered by the court, it relies on the authority of the government. The "moral contract" between the delinquent and the victim is lost when the government becomes a collection agency. At the same time, when viewed as an alternative to conventional approaches, restitution is seldom implemented in this manner. Rather than ordered as the sole disposition, juvenile courts typically "add on" restitution to probation or another sentence. As an add on, the emphasis on monitoring is lost (Staples 1986, 182).

Community Service/Work Programs

During the 1990s, judges began ordering *community restitution* in which convicted or adjudicated youth "pay back" the community through service.

Community Service.   The Earn-It program, developed in Quincy, Massachusetts, has become a national model. Judge Albert Kramer, who along with Andrew Klein established the Earn-It program at the Quincy District Court in 1975, expressed a philosophy of "no restitution, no second chance." Kramer started Earn-It because he was faced with offenders who could not pay restitution. He met with business owners and merchants and succeeded in getting commitments from them to hire defendants at minimum wage to work and pay restitution. Offenders keep one-third of their earnings, and the other two-thirds are paid to their victims. For juvenile offenders, the Earn-It program requires *community service* in place of monetary restitution. The Earn-It program at Keene, New Hampshire, juvenile court began in 1988. Youth in the Keene program earn money to pay back their victims and perform community service work. The program aims to hold youthful offenders accountable for their conduct and compensates victims for their losses. Juveniles have taken responsibility for their behavior and have increased the community's respect for the court system. The Earn-It program has been replicated by other juvenile courts across the country (Sadaski 1999).

Work Programs.   Employment and work experience interventions have been spinoffs of juvenile restitution programs. Programs that began with the intent of locating money-earning opportunities for youth with restitution agreements gradually developed into programs with more comprehensive objectives. *Work programs* include a variety of approaches including subsidized individual placements into public sector jobs, private sector job banks based on agreements with local small businesses to reserve spaces for clients, and projects involving supervised work crews paid through contracts with government agencies or subsidy funds. In recent years, the "crew-type" programs with 6 to 10 offenders working with a trained supervisor have become popular (Bazemore 1991).

A model crew-type program is that of Youth Conservation Corps (YCC). Modeled after the depression-era California Conservation Corps, YCC programs focus on environmental, community improvement, and high-demand social service projects. These involve contracts with county, state, and other government agencies as well as public and private nonprofit agencies, which pay the salaries of the youths and their supervisors. The YCC model has been developed in California and several Oregon counties. Other crew-type programs have been developed in Ohio counties. The program offers several benefits:

- Accomplishes productive work to improve community and business climate
- Rewards youths with earned income and work experience that makes it possible to restore victims
- Provides a means of incapacitating offenders through programmed activities
- Provides active, specific behavioral requirements for youths under community supervision
- Offers a new image of youths as potential resources rather than as threats to public well-being (Bazemore 1991, 40–41)

Utah's Genesis Work Program is a community-based, residential work program operated by Division of Youth Corrections. Governor Leavitt initiated the program in 1993, and it formally began in 1994. Located at Draper, the program provides 72 beds as an alternative to confinement. It provides services for all youths under probation supervision through the juvenile court, for youths placed in Youth Corrections with Community Alternatives placement, and for youths in Youth Corrections custody on parole or aftercare. Genesis programming is guided by the balanced approach to restorative justice model. Genesis residents have the opportunity to learn work ethics and good work habits. They learn about the use of power tools, lawn equipment, and the basics of landscaping. Regular work projects include grounds maintenance at the Utah State Capitol, governor's mansion, and other public buildings; maintaining hiking trails in the national forest; community service projects in area civic service organizations; and work in the Genesis kitchen preparing meals and cleaning. In 1999, the Genesis facility added a maintenance shop and greenhouse to provide additional learning opportunities (Division of Youth Services 1999).

There are several keys to developing and operating successful work programs. Successful programs pay attention to community needs as well as the needs of young people who learn and benefit from the work experience. Finding projects that are useful and valuable to communities is not difficult. In rural areas, youth crews have constructed mosquito abatements, cleaned streams and river banks, built ski shelters, restored fairgrounds, and painted recreational access signs. In cities, youth have repaired park play sets, plowed community gardens, and landscaped senior citizen centers (Bazemore 1991, 35–36). Because much of the needed work in social services, public works, and conservation never gets done, work crews create value in communities. To establish community ownership, economic advisory committees of local business leaders, civic leaders, and tourism members have been established. The committees ask for recommendations for projects that would improve the quality of community life and enhance the economic development of regions. One variation of these is for youths to comprise "transition teams" in which the youths perform "adjunct tasks" for private companies under project supervision (Bazemore 1991, 35–36).

A second key is insistence on high-quality standards. Given public scrutiny, it is necessary to have a high attrition rate rather than sacrifice the integrity of the work program. Strictly enforced regulations and consistent discipline are vital to ensuring control of offenders and reassuring citizens about the potential risk of offenders working in their neighborhoods. Rules such as program termination for three late arrivals or two "no shows" regardless of excuses are common. Programs require prompt payment of restitution, and they reinforce regular attendance and good behavior on the job with positive incentives. Some programs build in recreational activities around work activities (Bazemore 1991, 37–38).

Victim-Offender Reconciliation

Victim-offender reconciliation is a restorative approach to justice. Victim-offender reconciliation began in Canada, near Kitchener, Ontario, in 1974. Two young men, under the influence of alcohol, went on a Saturday night vandalism spree that resulted in 22 counts of willful damage. Vandalism is not an unusual delinquent activity; it was the response to it that became the Kitchener experiment and spread across the United States. Mark Yantzi, a juvenile probation officer assigned to the case, envisioned a response that would require the two boys to meet the victims, be held accountable to the victims, and take responsibility for their misbehavior. Yantzi, a member of the Mennonite church, along with David Worth, coordinator for volunteer service of the Mennonite Central Committee, convinced the provincial court judge to give it a try. The judge remanded the case for one month to allow time for the two boys to meet with victims and assess losses. Accompanied by Yantzi and Worth, the two young men retraced their steps on that Saturday night. They visited each place where they had damaged property, slashed tires, and broken windows of homes, two churches, and a liquor store. They spoke to 21 victims in all and calculated the damage at $2,189.04. Returning to court, the judge ordered a fine and a probation sentence contingent on restitution. Three months later, the youths had visited each victim and handed them a certified check for their losses (Peachey 1989).

Since then, hundreds of victim-offender reconciliation programs have appeared in Canada and the United States. In 1998, there were victim-offender mediation programs in about 150 cities and towns across the United States (Bazemore & Day 1998, 6). Victim-offender reconciliation, or victim-offender mediation (VOM) as the programs became known, involve a face-to-face meeting between the victim and the offender facilitated by a trained mediator. The program offers victims an opportunity to hear the facts, express their feelings, and receive restitution. For the offender, VOM offers an opportunity to learn first-hand about the harm caused, to acknowledge responsibility for wrongdoing, and to make amends. During the mediation session, the offender agrees to a contract that typically involves paying restitution, although victims may request other conditions such as the offender repairs the property damage, donates community service hours, or agrees to attend counseling for alcohol abuse or other life problems. The mediator represents the community. The original VOM in the United States began at Elkhart, Indiana; the process was administered by a nonprofit agency outside the system that worked in cooperation with the court.

In the United States, victim-offender mediation programs operate for both adults and juveniles. The Mediation Center of Asheville, North Carolina, operates a victim-offender mediation program. During 1997, the center accepted 36 cases, and of the 30 cases mediated to completion, there was 100 percent reconciliation. Restitution involved direct compensation paid to the victim (money or work), community service agreed upon by the victim and offender, or both. "My goal," wrote one of the victims who had participated, "was to have the boys learn responsibility for their actions . . . they spent time working off a debt that I paid to repair the damage. [One of the boys] told me personally that he appreciated the opportunity to work and show me he was sorry for his actions" (Fink-Adam 1998, 5). The Mediation Center at Asheville operates as one of 27 mediation centers throughout North Carolina, a number of which offer victim-offender mediation programs. The Center for Restorative Justice and Mediation was established in the School of Social Work at the University of Minnesota in St. Paul to provide training, technical assistance, and research for victim-offender mediation programs in Minnesota and across the country.

The victim-offender mediation program of York County, Pennsylvania, began in 1995 as a partnership between the York County Probation Department and Mediation Services for Conflict Resolution, a nonprofit agency organized to provide dispute settlement services. The program began with funds from the Pennsylvania Commission on Crime and Delinquency, which established a grant program to implement balanced and restorative justice throughout the state. The program receives referrals from the juvenile probation department for appropriate cases involving felony or misdemeanor property offenses and simple assaults. Preliminary meetings are held with the offender and the victim to explain the program, obtain willingness to participate, and arrange for the mediation session. During the session, the mediator allows each person to share facts and feelings. The victim goes first. The storytelling phase guides the development of the restitution contract agreeable to both. The outcome is reported to the juvenile probation department, and the probation department monitors the contract (Kurlychek 1999).

Family Group Conferencing

Family group conferencing represents a broader, more extensive variation of victim-offender mediation by bringing more participants to the table. Those involved include not only the offender and the victim, but the families and supporters of both and any other adults who can voice the community's concerns about the offense and speak to the reintegration of the offender.

The New Zealand Model. Family group conferencing was imported to the United States from Australia and New Zealand. Family group conferencing began in New Zealand after passage of the Children, Young Persons and Their Families Act (1989) that attempted to provide a culturally appropriate juvenile justice response to the aboriginal Maori people. The Maori have practiced negotiation among extended family members as a means of conflict resolution for centuries. The 1989 act required that all juvenile offenders over the age of 14 (except the most serious cases) participate in a family group conference. The *family group conference* "is a meeting at a time and place chosen by the family and attended by the young person, the family (including the wider family), the victim, the police, the youth advocate (young person's lawyer), where one has been appointed and any other people whom the family wish to be present" (Maxwell & Morris 1994, 18). The primary purpose of the new system is to make young people accountable for their lawbreaking behavior by encouraging them to take responsibility for their actions, to make good the damage done, or to accept a penalty.

Several routine features of family group conferences can be identified as practiced in New Zealand, although the act allows for the family to develop its own procedures. The process begins with introductions, and in Maori areas, there is a prayer or blessing followed by a traditional welcome. The program coordinator explains the process and invites the Youth Aid officer to read a summary of the facts. The officer asks the youth if the facts are accurate. If the young person denies the charges, the case may be referred to Youth Court. If the young person admits the offense, the coordinator then asks the victim or victim's representative (such as the Youth Aid officer) to speak. A general discussion among all the participants follows about possible outcomes. At some point, the Youth Aid officer and other officials leave the room and allow the family to discuss in private how best to respond to their youth's lawbreaking. Once the family has produced a plan, the coordinator seeks agreement from the victim and police, and the agreed plan is recorded. Most likely, the young person apologizes, pays restitution or makes a donation to charity, performs some kind of community service work, or agrees to a restriction on liberty, such as grounding, curfew, or loss of driving privileges. The meeting closes, sometimes with a prayer (Maxwell & Morris 1994, 27–28).

In Australia, the practice spread to five states by 1994. Family group conference programs operate in New South Wales, Western Australia, South Australia, Victoria, and Canberra. The family group conference is intended to be an informal meeting in which the offender and his or her extended family are brought together along with the victim and her or his supporters, along with any other invited participants, to discuss the youth's offense and negotiate an appropriate response. The programs fit into the policy of diversion and the policy goal of diverting young people from the formal court process, although the program fits the "back-to-justice" rather than the "welfare" approach to juvenile justice policy. The victim's involvement in the process is an important element in promoting accountability. Family group conferencing in Australia seeks to make young people accountable for their actions and to provide restitution for victims of youth lawbreaking. It relies on the direct involvement of parents. The conferences provide a means for ensuring that families take more responsibility and are held accountable for their children's behavior. John Braithwaite, a criminologist at Australia National University, states that the emphasis of the program should be on successful "reintegration" of the offender and suggests that a more appropriate term for the Australian practice might be "community accountability conferences" (Adler & Wundersitz 1994, 7–8).

Community Mediation Panels. In the United States, family group conferencing has been adapted in several formats. The Illinois Juvenile Justice Reform Act of 1998 created ***community mediation panels*** to make the minor aware of the harm caused to the victim, the minor's family, and the community. Participants on the panels reflect the ethnic makeup of the community and include community members with diverse backgrounds. Minors diverted to these panels, either by station adjustment, probation adjustment, or as a diversion by the state's attorney, are required to face community representatives. The panel has a number of sentencing options, including mandatory school attendance, up to 100 hours of community service, substance abuse screening for the minor and the minor's parents, and restitution either through direct payment or work service (Stevenson 1999b, 1).

The Illinois legislature created community mediation panels as part of the Juvenile Justice Reform Act of 1998. The act, reflecting balanced and restorative justice principles, created a community-oriented response to crime that places the primary focus on restoring the well-being of the victim and repairing the harm done to the community. The act resulted from work that began in 1994 when the Legislative Committee on Juvenile Justice convened to revamp the state's juvenile code. Rather than be based solely on the notion that juvenile court decisions are made in the "best interest of the child," holding the juvenile accountable, building competency in delinquent children, and protecting the community became the primary principles. The act attempts to promote three broad goals of juvenile justice: (1) hold each offender accountable for his or her conduct, (2) have a mechanism for juvenile justice professionals to intervene early in a juvenile's "delinquent career," and (3) increase the community's participation in the juvenile justice process, including the offender's victims. The act made several changes in juvenile procedures to provide for increased accountability, early intervention, and increased community and victim involvement. The act increased the rights of victims of juvenile offenders, bringing them in line with the rights afforded victims of adult offenders (Stevenson 1999).

House Arrest/Electronic Monitoring

House arrest is an old practice in the administration of criminal law. Individuals including Galileo Galilei and Tsar Nicholas II of Russia lived under house arrest. In the United States, house arrest became a sentencing option during the 1970s. House arrest, or home confinement, has been implemented in conjunction with parole and probation (Durham 1994, 187). During the 1980s, *electronic monitoring* became a means of enforcing house arrest.

The concept of enforcing house arrest with the aid of an electronic monitoring device began with New Mexico District Court Judge Jack Love in 1983, who came up with the idea after reading a Spiderman comic strip. During the 1980s, two electronic monitoring devices had been developed: continuously signaling/monitoring and the programmed contact. The continuously signaling device requires a transmitter, a home receiver unit, and a central computer. When the person is in range of the transmitter (within 150 feet), the transmitter receives the signal; when they leave the residence, the signal is interrupted and a message is sent to the central computer. The programmed contact technology generates random telephone calls to the offender's house, and the offender must insert the encoder device into the verifier box to receive the signal. Some programmed contact devices incorporate video, photograph, or voice verification technology to determine the offender's presence in the house. Although electronic monitoring programs for adults developed rapidly, the program came more slowly to juveniles. Electronic monitoring programs developed for adults in the late 1980s. In 1986, there were 10 programs in the United States; by 1987, there were 50 programs in 21 states. By 1998, there were 83 programs. But juveniles raised special concerns. Some feared juveniles would damage the equipment or simply run away, resulting in a high failure rate. Others had concerns that the technology would amount to an unnecessary intrusion on the youth's family and that the equipment would stigmatize youth. Others had doubts about whether the program could adequately ensure public safety. The first electronic monitoring programs for juveniles opened in rural North Carolina and middle Indiana. By 1988, there were 11 programs across the country (Vaughn 1989, 4).

The Supervised Electronic Confinement Program in Orange County, California, began in 1986 as a one-year pilot project. It was an alternative to jail for inmates eligible for work furlough. In 1987, the Orange County Probation Department initiated an electronic home confinement program in response to crowding at Juvenile Hall. The Probation Department obtained equipment to monitor 25 juveniles across 3 programs: Home Supervision Program, Home Confinement, and Community Transition Furlough. The programs provided for discretionary release under California law of juveniles detained or committed to secure facilities. Probation officers experienced with the technology received caseloads including the juveniles to be electronically monitored. After a successful trial, the department made electronic monitoring a formal part of probation programs. The department has found that although there are some problems with juveniles not encountered with adults, such as parents' trustworthiness and cooperation, these can be resolved with adequate planning, screening, and supervision. Rather than stigmatize youth, the department found that the bracelet could be easily concealed under a cuff or pants leg. Some juveniles requested wearing the bracelet after completing the program so they could use it as an excuse for declining activities suggested by peers (Whittington 1989).

Since the 1980s, enthusiasm for electronic monitoring has waned. In 1998, less than 0.01 percent of the criminal justice population in the United States was on electronic monitoring (Connelly 1998, 10). Electronic monitoring received negative media and several well-publicized accounts of program failures (such as when one man committed manslaughter while being monitored electronically). Corrections policymakers accepted the technology as an "easy alternative": just clip the bracelet on the offender's ankle and the computer does the rest. The equipment has proved more complex to operate, resulting in down systems and false positives. Rather than reduce staff caseloads, the program required additional staff time. At the same time, the companies marketing electronic monitoring technology resisted industry regulation and refused to develop standardized equipment, leaving an array of devices and conflicting claims about what various devices could and could not do. Companies competed to win bids, oversold the product, and left a question mark in the minds of many corrections policymakers. In October 1997, industry representatives met in Lexington, Kentucky, at the headquarters of the National Probation and Parole Association to develop polices and plans for public education (Connelly 1998, 10–11; Paporozzi & Wicklund 1998, 8–9).

Legal Sanctions in Jewish Tradition

The reference to *"an eye for an eye,"* explains Rabbi Morris N. Kertzer (1978), is one of the most misused and misunderstood in Jewish scripture. The phrase *ayen tachat ayen* in Hebrew does not direct the victim of a wrong to take vengeance on the wrongdoer. Retaliatory eye-gouging has never really been part of Jewish tradition.

The phrase comes from the Torah, the five books of Moses given at Mount Sinai. The Torah comprises the center of the Jewish way of life. Torah portions are read aloud in synagogues throughout the world at the beginning of the twenty-first century, just as they have been for centuries. Each congregation keeps its Torah scrolls, written in exquisite Hebrew calligraphy, in a small chest or opening in the wall known as the Ark. The text of the Torah, however, is not the sole basis for Jewish tradition. Along with written scripture there is the oral law, the teachings of the rabbis over the centuries. The oral law had been preserved by word of mouth until the first century of the common era (C.E.), when the Roman occupation threatened to destroy it. In the year 73 C.E., the Roman Tenth Legion crushed the last zealots at Masada and initiated the Diaspora, the scattering of Jewish people throughout the world.

Judah the Prince compiled the Mishnah, the first written version of the oral law, around 200 C.E. Rabbinical commentary on the Mishnah yielded the Talmud several centuries later. The Talmud has been the primary source of Jewish teaching since the medieval era taught at yeshivas—that is, schools combining Talmud study with secular subjects.

The law of Moses provided for the death penalty for certain crimes. Few executions occurred because of safeguards built into the sentence by rabbinical authorities. Not only would the judgment require the testimony of two witnesses, but the eyewitnesses would have had to warn the wrongdoer about the consequences of the act and have heard the wrongdoer express the desire to carry out the wrongful act despite a full understanding of the sentence. Capital cases required a panel of 23 judges, and the national court, or Sanhedrin, a court of 71 judges, decided cases unresolved by regional courts (Appleson 1991). In the case of the *ben sorah ou'moreh,* the "disobedient and defiant child," to be put to death under the law of Moses, the Mishnah built so many restrictions into the law it was virtually impossible to carry out. Both parents had to be willing to accuse their child of the offense. The mother and father had to enjoy a good marriage; they had to share a common approach to raising the child. An unsuccessful marriage could contribute to a son's misbehavior and deflect some of the blame to the family. In addition, neither parent could have a physical disability that would have prevented seeing or hearing the child (Weiss 1998).

There is within Jewish tradition an intimate connection between "law" regulating social interaction and "law" as a guide to the moral way of life. The Judaic concept of law, *halakhah,* often translated as "Jewish law," literally means "that path one walks." The *halakhah* describes the rules and practices that describe the Jewish way of life: studying the Torah, observing holy days, and adhering to dietary practices. It includes the commandments or *mitzvot* in the Torah. It also includes the teachings of rabbis, who instituted various practices to prevent people from accidentally violating a commandment. The Jewish boy who reaches his thirteenth birthday is *bar mitzvah* (*bat mitzvah* for girls), a "man of duty" obligated under the *halakhah.* The ceremony itself marks the first occasion the young person is called up to read the Torah in the synagogue, an act only adults can perform. In the broader sense, the occasion marks the passage of a young person into the adult world of the Jewish community.

Restitution is the operative principle of justice within halakhic law. The Mishnah understood that the wrongdoer should compensate the victim. Nonfatal injuries had to be repaid in terms of lost wages (due to incapacitation), the cost of medication or therapy, and the intrinsic value of the injury (measured in lost future earning power). The requirement also extended to compensation for pain and embarrassment. The wrongdoer who could not pay became an *eved* to the victim. The Mishnah clarifies that the Jewish person who steals and is unable to repay the loss is given to the victim as a servant. Unlike a slave, servanthood was not permanent; the servant was freed during the seventh year. The *eved* also retained important rights and would be freed if intentionally injured by the victim (Appleson 1991). In practice, then, as Rabbi Kertzer explains, the phrase has been understood to mean "the *cost* of an eye for the *cost* of an eye."

The practice of restitution expresses the halakhic understanding of walking rightly. The Psalm that begins, "The Lord is my shepherd," traditionally read at Jewish funerals, includes the phrase "He leads me in right paths." The Hebrew word translated "right" is the root word for *tzedakah,* meaning "good deeds" or charity. Giving to the poor, helping those in need, and supporting worthy causes is a requirement in Judaism, not an option. To refuse to do *tzedakah* would mean straying from the right path. It would be a sin. The Hebrew word translated "sin" literally means to "miss" or "go astray." Jewish tradition distinguishes two kinds of sin: a sin against God and a sin against another person. To return to the right path, one must do *t'shuvah,* or repent—to "return" or "turn back." The practice of *t'shuvah* in Judaism depends on the kind of sin. To repent of a sin against God, the person must acknowledge the wrong, pray for forgiveness, and determine to change. On Yom Kippur, or Day of Atonement, the rabbi leads the congregation in a prayer seeking forgiveness from the Almighty. To repent of a sin against another requires something more: the person must ask the person wronged for forgiveness and make restitution. In the ten days between Rosh Hashanah, the Jewish New Year, and Yom Kippur, Jewish people are to remember wrongs they committed against family members, friends, and others throughout the year and ask forgiveness. And in Jewish tradition, the person wronged must forgive when restitution is made as part of seeking forgiveness.

Although the practice of "restorative justice" comes from a psychologist and not a rabbi, it expresses many elements of the Jewish way of justice (Norman 2000). David Lerman, a prosecuting attorney who also produces a Jewish radio program in Milwaukee, provides an account of Jewish restorative justice. In Des Moines, Iowa, two young people desecrated a synagogue with swastikas and Nazi slogans. They were arrested and plead guilty to felony crimes. Neither had prior records. A local prosecuting attorney approached the rabbi about meeting with the pair to explain the damage and possibly work out a sentence. The congregation agreed and sent several representatives, two Holocaust survivors and a former Israeli military officer among them. They encountered a thin young man with a hearing disability. The boy had found a place to stay among members of a hate group after running away from home. It was his first "public action." His girlfriend had gone along for "something to do" without much thought about what it meant. Several members of the congregation demanded the prosecutor "throw the book at them," but others feared that jail time would only embitter the pair and crystallize their ideology. After much discussion, the congregation offered a sentence the court accepted: the vandals received 100 hours of community service to the synagogue supervised by the custodian and 100 hours of study in Judaism with the rabbi. The sentence further specified that the young man remove the Nazi tattoos from his arms, referred him to a hearing specialist, and provided that both pursue completion of high school requirements. The young man completed his sentence, as did the young woman. They decided to marry and invited both the custodian and the rabbi to their wedding (Lerman 1998).

Summary

Although every state has at least one training school or other secure corrections facility for juveniles, training school no longer serves as the paradigmatic disposition in juvenile court. Beginning in 1971 or so, community-based sanctions became the best answer to the question: "What is to be done with juvenile delinquents?"

Three broad rationales for the community response to delinquency can be identified: diversion, intermediate sanctions, and balance and restorative justice. Diversion of youths to programs and facilities other than training school is based on the idea that confinement may do more harm than good. Juvenile justice decision makers should choose the "least

Bud Almassy applies a chemical remover to a spray-painted swastika on the gate of the Jewish Passaic Junction Cemetery in Saddle Brook, N.J., Friday, Nov. 3, 1995. Officials of the Anti-Defamation League of B'nai B'rith have asked for harsher penalties for this type of anti-Semitic graffiti. AP/Wide World Photos

restrictive alternative" in deciding dispositions for delinquents and place the offender within the community to the extent possible. Intermediate sanctions have to do with a range of dispositions between standard probation at one end and confinement in training school at the other. The idea of graduated sanctions is to provide juvenile court judges with a continuum of dispositions, graduated by level of supervision and harshness, to match with the juvenile's needs and seriousness of offense. The balanced and restorative justice holds that the purpose of disposition is to repair the harm done to the victim and to the community by the delinquent's act. Juvenile justice decision makers should balance their attention to the goals of public safety, accountability, and correcting juvenile offenders.

Probation has been the most common disposition in juvenile court since the court's founding in 1899. Under a sentence of probation, the juvenile lawbreaker lives at home but receives some supervision such as meeting with a probation officer a certain number of times each month. Juvenile courts have wide latitude in determining conditions of probation, such as assigning the juvenile to attend school and rehabilitative programs. In recent years, intensive supervision probation has appeared, which emphasizes more frequent face-to-face meetings with the probation officer, greater scrutiny of the youth's activities, and more frequent assessments of the youth's progress in addition to traditional probation services. Recent probation innovations include school probation, in which probation officers work out of offices in schools to monitor the youths on their caseloads, and police-probation partnerships, which pair probation officers and police officers to make surprise visits to the homes of probationers.

In addition to probation, community-based dispositions include restitution, community service, victim-offender reconciliation, family group conferencing, house arrest/electronic monitoring, day treatment, and group homes/residential placement. Diversion options typically include probation, day treatment, and group homes. Intermediate sanctions include fines, community service, house arrest, intensive probation, and electronic monitoring. Balanced and restorative responses include restitution, community service, victim-offender reconciliation, and family group conferencing.

KEY CONCEPTS

"an eye for an eye"	family group conferencing	probation/police partnerships
balanced approach	group homes	residential facilities
community mediation panels	intensive supervision	restitution
community service	probation	restorative justice
day treatment	intermediate sanctions	school-based probation
deinstitutionalization	least restrictive alternative	standard probation
diversion	net widening	victim-offender mediation
electronic monitoring	probation	work programs

DISCUSSION QUESTIONS

1. Is net-widening good or bad when it comes to community-based programs?

2. Why is standard probation the typical sentence in juvenile court? How can it be enhanced?

3. Restitution is an ancient practice. Is it a realistic, practical approach today?

LEARNING ACTIVITY: ROLE PLAY

Should juvenile probation officers carry firearms? It is a complex question that raises a variety of issues. Divide the class into groups of three. One person should role play a probation officer thinking about carrying a firearm from the standpoint of personal safety. Another should role play the supervisor considering the issues involved in formulating an agency policy on firearms. The third member should serve as a reporter; the reporter relates the discussion to the class when the class comes together after each group has finished. Before beginning, read the following.

Betsy Johnson works with the legislative liaison section of the Ohio Department of Youth Services.
Ever since the introduction of House Bill 1, I've wondered to myself whether it was a good idea to allow parole officers to carry firearms. I had the opportunity to hear expert testimony on both sides of the issue during the General Assembly's consideration of the legislation, yet I was still not convinced one way or the other. I knew that the only way I could form an opinion would be to go on the road with a parole officer (PO).

On July 20th, I met Chuck Wyss at the Columbus Regional Office at 9:00 A.M. While we waited to see if Bill (a longtime parolee on Chuck's caseload) would show up for community service, we had a chance to get acquainted. I asked Chuck to tell me about the most successful and the most difficult youth he has on his caseload. It was an easy question. Jeff, who was committed for complicity to induce panic, is doing exceptionally well after a rocky start living with his father, Chuck told me. After moving home with his mother and stepfather, he has taken on a full time job at Dairy Queen, he's pursuing his GED, he's staying out of trouble, and most importantly, he appears genuinely happy.

Jason, on the other hand, has been a constant challenge for Chuck since the day he arrived at DYS. "He's been very labor intensive, often taking me away from the office for a whole day at a time because he was acting up in the institution," Chuck explained. "In fact, I have a letter from him I haven't had a chance to read. He mailed it to me from Colorado where he's being held in jail." Chuck opened the letter and noted that it was quite long. Instead of reading it, he handed it to me, telling me we could read it on the road. It was time to head out on the streets. Bill was a no show.

Our first stop was at John's on the west side of Columbus. It was 10:30 A.M. John answered the door wearing a pair of shorts and no shirt. He had been lying on the couch watching Sally Jesse Raphael. The curtains were drawn and the house was hot and quiet. Chuck asked John several questions about how he was progressing on finding a job, applying to the GED program, and writing his letter of apology. John reported little progress on all fronts. When asked how his parents were getting along, John stated emphatically, "a lot better!" Chuck, who later explained that he had a long talk with John's father about the need to curb his abusive treatment of his wife, couldn't hide the smile on his face having heard that things improved. Before leaving, Chuck made it clear to John that he expected some serious progress by the following week.

Just before 11:00 A.M., we arrived unannounced at Bill's house to find out why he didn't show up for community service. Bill answered the door in his shorts and no shirt. He, too, had been lying on the couch watching Sally Jesse Raphael. The curtains were drawn and the house was hot and quiet. Chuck asked Bill why he had not shown up for community service, and Bill explained that he hurt his back at work the previous day. The back injury claim was challenged by Chuck, but he never received an answer on how it all happened. Chuck asked Bill many of the same questions he asked of John. His manner, however, was much more forceful than it had been with John. It was evident that Chuck was extremely annoyed by Bill's lack of initiative, especially when Bill was unable to produce any recent pay stubs. At the end of the visit, Chuck made it clear that if Bill did not make serious progress by the following week, he would face serious consequences.

When we got back into the car, I couldn't help but remark on what was beginning to appear as a recurring theme. "Oh yeah," said Chuck, "apathy is the biggest roadblock these kids have to overcome."

"Let's hurry to the next house," I joked, "I want to see the end of Sally Jesse Raphael."

The third visit, however, was unlike the first two. This time we stopped by the house of the ailing father of Alfred, a youth who had been locked up for nearly five years. Alfred's father had phoned Chuck the previous week to check up on his son, who is currently enrolled in a Civilian Conservation Corp program in Northwest Ohio. Since the gentleman did not have a phone, Chuck returned this call in person. It was a short visit, but one that was clearly appreciated by the sick, worried father.

After the final visit of the morning, which went much like the first two, Chuck and I headed back toward his office. During the drive back, I asked him about the possibility of carrying a firearm. He said he didn't think that it was necessary. As we started to part ways, I remembered I still had his letter from Jason. Before handing it back, I skimmed the last paragraph. "Chuck," I said, "you ought to read this."

You can bet you're a— I'm going to get my revenge. My a— is covered, is yours? (Johnson 1999)

15 The Future of Juvenile Justice

CHAPTER OBJECTIVES

After studying this chapter, students will have tools to:

- Examine the pros and cons of abolishing the juvenile court system
- Consider the impact of abolishing the juvenile court system
- Understand the philosophy of policy makers about the future of juvenile court
- Consider alternative visions of the juvenile court
- Review the pros and cons of hearing juvenile cases in criminal court

The Juvenile Court in 2010

In *Crime and Justice in the Year 2010,* leading criminologists explore the future of criminal justice in the United States. Carl Pope, of the University of Wisconsin at Milwaukee, discusses the future of juvenile justice. "Perhaps the major consideration as we move into the twenty-first century," Pope begins, "is whether there will, in fact, be a separate system of juvenile justice" (1995, 268).

During the 1990s, legislatures in virtually every state enacted legislation to curtail the juvenile court's jurisdiction and limit the discretionary power of juvenile court judges. Legislation has redefined nearly every aspect of the juvenile court's operation, including jurisdictional authority, sentencing authority, confidentiality provisions, and correctional programs. Pope observes that, since the 1960s, the juvenile court has begun to resemble criminal court in procedure so that it may cease to be distinguishable. The juvenile court as it existed in Chicago and Denver is definitely a relic of the past (1995, 271). In 1997, the School of Social Work at the University of Pennsylvania cosponsored a symposium with the University's law school on the future of the juvenile court. Two years later, the T. C. Williams School of Law at the University of Richmond hosted a symposium on the future of the juvenile court.

Whether the juvenile court will survive, and if so, what form it should take, is the topic of this chapter. The first section reviews changes in the Illinois juvenile court. The second section explores the debate about whether the juvenile court ought to be abolished. The third section explores themes and trends in juvenile justice and some alternative visions for the twenty-first century juvenile court. The fourth section reviews the legacy of the twentieth-century juvenile court and larger issues of juvenile justice policy.

The Illinois Juvenile Court Centennial

The first juvenile court in the world began in Cook County, Illinois, in 1899. The original juvenile court building, which doubled as a detention center for delinquent and abandoned children, stood across the street from Hull House on Halsted Avenue in Chicago. Hull House has been preserved. It became the Jane Addams Hull House Museum at the University of Chicago. The original juvenile court building no longer stands. Where the building once stood is now a parking lot for the Chicago campus of the University of Illinois. The University of Illinois installed a plaque at the Hull House Museum on June 29, 1999, during the centennial celebration of the juvenile court, to commemorate the location of the original juvenile court (National Council of Juvenile and Family Court Judges 1999a, 8).

The juvenile court in Illinois today is very different from the original court the plaque commemorates. Beginning in 1966, the U.S. Supreme Court rejected the juvenile court's lower standard of due process. In a series of cases, including *Kent v. United States* (1966), *In re Gault* (1967), *In re Winship* (1970), and *Breed v. Jones* (1975), the U.S. Supreme Court extended due process rights to juveniles and greatly increased the formality of juvenile court proceedings. The U.S. Supreme Court began to converge juvenile court procedure with criminal court procedure, initiating the erasure of the distinction between the two courts in the direction of a single criminal justice system for adults and juveniles. "Lawmakers cannot put the genie back in the bottle," Jeffrey A. Butts and Adele V. Harrell, of the Urban Institute, have observed, "The informal, social welfare approach of the original juvenile court has been lost. In its place, the nation has inherited a network of junior criminal courts, with preliminary hearings, motions for the appointment of counsel, subpoenas to appear, speedy trial rules, and sentencing guidelines" (1998, 8).

Not only have state lawmakers not attempted to restore the original juvenile court approach, they have enacted legislation to further restrict the jurisdiction of the juvenile court. During the 1980s and the first part of the 1990s, the Illinois legislature, with the legislatures of virtually every other state in the country, enacted a series of laws to further restrict the jurisdiction of the juvenile court and the discretionary authority of juvenile court judges. Responding to concerns that juveniles convicted of serious and violent offenses served relatively short sentences, lawmakers concluded that more juveniles should be tried in criminal court. The first automatic transfer statute passed in 1982. The law required that juveniles age 15 or older who are charged with murder, rape, robbery with a firearm, or certain sexual assaults be automatically transferred to criminal court. Three years later, the Illinois legislature expanded its automatic transfer law to include juveniles of 15 years of age or older who are charged with committing drug or weapons violations within 1,000 feet of school. In 1990, the legislature further expanded its automatic transfer provision to include juveniles charged with felonies "in furtherance of gang activity" and juveniles 15 years of age or older who are charged with committing drug violations within 1,000 feet of public housing. In 1995, juveniles 15 years of age or older who were charged with aggravated vehicular hijacking were automatically transferred to criminal court (Stevenson 1999a, 10–11).

In 1998, the Illinois legislature overhauled the entire juvenile court. The Juvenile Justice Reform Act enacted that year shifted the purpose of juvenile court altogether. For the first 100 years of its existence, the juvenile court in Illinois had jurisdiction over minors accused of criminal violations for the purpose of rehabilitating them. The Act replaced rehabilitation with multiple goals of accountability, competency development, and community safety. The act also replaced the language of the juvenile court with that of the criminal court. Under the old statute, a juvenile was "taken into custody," given an "adjudicatory hearing," and if found "delinquent," was sanctioned at a "dispositional hearing." Under the new act, the juvenile is "arrested," has the right to a "trial," and if found "guilty" is subject to a "sentencing hearing."

Catherine M. Ryan of the Cook County State's Attorney's Office explained that these are the terms professionals who work in the court and youth in the system use already. The general public understands these terms, if only from television and media. Those who favored the change in terminology suggested that it enables the public, such as victims and witnesses, to better understand what is happening in juvenile court and enable the youths themselves to follow the proceedings. Critics of the new terminology insist that it makes it harder for those involved in the juvenile court to understand the difference from adult criminal court. Betsy Clarke, juvenile justice counsel at the Cook County Public Defender's Office, argues that "merely substituting adult terminology for the juvenile justice phrases used in the past does not fully convey the special nature of court proceedings—it merely encourages all present to think of minors as mini adults and of court proceedings as mini adult trials."

In Cook County, the home of the world's first juvenile court, juvenile justice decision makers have abandoned the specialized terms of the juvenile court as "phrases used in the past." With a few exceptions, basic juvenile court procedures in Illinois have come to resemble those in adult court. The philosophy of *parens patriae* has been replaced by a due process model of criminal court. At the same time, the rationale for the juvenile court has been abandoned. The court no longer takes as its *raison d'être* the rehabilitation of young people: Community safety has become its purpose. Meanwhile, lawmakers increasingly believe that a larger and larger portion of juveniles belongs in criminal courts. The transformation of the juvenile court in Illinois raises an obvious question: *Is the end of the juvenile court's first century the beginning of the end of the juvenile court altogether?*

The End of the Juvenile Court?

At present, national debate concerns the future of juvenile justice, and specifically, whether the juvenile court ought to be abolished. "Abolitionists" question the whole juvenile court experiment, noting that juvenile offenders never should have been placed in a noncriminal court. They recommend doing away with the concept of delinquency and returning young offenders to the jurisdiction of criminal courts with complete due process rights. "Preservationists" want to maintain the juvenile court as a noncriminal, quasicivil court with exclusive jurisdiction over young people. They view the juvenile court as essential because young people are developmentally different from adults and because the juvenile court's limited due process requirements afford the court wide latitude to intervene. The debate features a clash of titans: legislators and preeminent law professors versus juvenile court judges and the nation's premiere juvenile justice organizations.

Abolish the Court

Several arguments have been made for abolishing the court. Some abolitionists suggest that the concept of a social welfare institution dressed in legal clothing was flawed from its beginning. Others reason that if due process for juveniles is a good thing, then all juveniles should be tried in criminal court with full due process and procedural safeguards. Still other abolitionists argue that juvenile court is based on a outdated concept of youthfulness and question the definition of delinquency.

The Fundamental Flaw

Barry Feld, professor of law at the University of Minnesota School of Law, is probably the most outspoken abolitionist. He rejects the rationale established by the founders 100 years ago. Feld insists that the failure of the juvenile court to deal effectively with young people during its first century represents a failure of conception, not implementation. The original juvenile court, conceived as "a social service agency in a judicial setting," simply does not work. The fusion of social welfare and judicial coercion represents the inescapable clash of very different rationale for government intervention (1993a, 256).

Feld argues that the juvenile court confuses the social welfare role and the judicial role. The founders of the court envisioned the use of government coercion to achieve social welfare objectives. This attempt to combine social welfare and criminal social control into a single institution constitutes the *fundamental flaw* of the juvenile court. Social welfare is a social responsibility, Feld insists, not a legal one. The juvenile court does not represent the best, or even a good, mechanism to achieve the goals of child welfare. Feld raises two significant questions about the concept of intervention embodied in the juvenile court:

1. *Why should criminality be a prerequisite for receipt of services?* Some children may have needs that are not being met by their families or communities and ought to receive government services. But it makes no sense to wait until a child has broken the law, nor does it make sense to withhold services unless a child breaks the law. A child in need ought to receive social services based on the need and not based on a finding of criminality.
2. *How does the fact of youth crime confer on the juvenile court any competency as a provider of youth services?* Young people may in fact break the law for different reasons than adults; delinquency may represent a different social phenomenon than crime. But the concept of delinquency does not give the court any special expertise as a provider of services. There are better ways to organize the delivery of social services to children than a legal institution (Feld 1999b, 18–19).

In questioning the rationale for the juvenile court, Feld revived some classic criticisms of the juvenile court as social welfare institution in a legal setting. Roscoe Pound, dean of Harvard Law School from 1916 to 1936, noted that the juvenile court represented "the illegitimate issue of an illicit relationship between the legal profession and the social work profession, and now no one wants to claim the little bastard" (Shepherd 1999b, 20). Or as John Henry Wigmore, dean of Northwestern University School of Law and founder of the prestigious

Journal of Criminal Law and Criminology put it, "the social workers and the psychologists and the psychiatrists know nothing of crime and wrong . . . these people need to have the moral law dimned [*sic*] into their consciences every day of the year. The juvenile court does not do that. And to segregate a large share of daily crime into the juvenile court is to take a long step toward undermining the whole criminal law. . ." (Watkins 1998, 104–105).

The argument for not confusing social service intervention with criminal law adjudication has also been made by Travis Hirschi and Michael Gotffredson, two of the nation's foremost criminologists. Abolishing the juvenile court would eliminate an artificial restriction on dealing effectively with youthful criminals. Legislatures, responding to what they believe the public wants, have created transfer mechanisms for dealing with young people who commit serious, criminal, and heinous acts. From Hirschi's and Gottfredson's perspective, these acts ought to be dealt with by a system of justice that holds the offender accountable, but without the pretense of a court devoted primarily to child welfare and rehabilitation. At the same time, there are the children whose only "crime" is to have been neglected by their families. These cases should be dealt with by a system of public welfare that provides care and support for the child, but without the pretense of a crime-prevention function (Hirschi & Gottfredson 1990, 484).

No Parens Patriae, *No Court.* Since 1967 an "adultification" of the juvenile court has occurred as the U.S. Supreme Court extended more due process rights to juveniles. The notion that the juvenile court represents a substitute parent, or *parens patriae,* broke down 30 years ago with the U.S. Supreme Court's decision in the *Gault* case. Given that the standards reject the "medical model" of the juvenile court in favor of a "criminal juvenile court," Feld raises the obvious question: "As juvenile courts converge procedurally and substantively with criminal courts, is there any reason to maintain a separate court whose only remaining distinctions are procedures under which no adult would agree to be tried?" (Feld 1993a, 257).

Feld points to the model of the juvenile court found in the American Bar Association's Institute of Judicial Administration's juvenile justice project. The ABA/IJA *Juvenile Justice Standards* envision the juvenile court as the mechanism to ensure due process rights. The project recommended repeal of jurisdiction over status offenders, use of proportional and determinate sentences, and use of regular criteria to standardize pretrial detention and judicial waiver to criminal court, along with the provision of nonwaivable counsel and jury trials. The ABA/IJA standards specifically reject the welfare oriented juvenile court and its paternalism. Broad discretion under the guise of well-meaning paternalism translates into a violation of constitutional rights. The ABA/IJA standards replicate the adult procedure, but there is no rationale for doing so in a separate court system.

Janet E. Ainsworth, a professor of law at the University of Puget Sound School of Law, concludes that the juvenile court, even in its "constitutionally domesticated" version, violates core notions of due process. Denying young people a jury trial sacrifices the notion of equal protection under law to a welfare state paternalism. Abolishing the juvenile court would have three practical consequences:

1. *Jury trial availability.* Juveniles would be entitled to jury trials and to the prospect of a judicial factfinder that tends to acquit more often than judges.
2. *Effective assistance of counsel.* Although the U.S. Supreme Court decided to guarantee assistance of counsel for juveniles, the quality of that legal assistance remains

inadequate given the juvenile court's status as a "kiddie court." Given the uncertainty of the juvenile court's mission, many lawyers feel ambiguity about their role, and are too willing to cooperate with prosecutors.

3. *Dispositional needs of juveniles.* Abolishing the juvenile court would not ignore the special dispositional needs of juveniles; there is no more need for a special court guaranteeing juvenile offenders to be confined in juvenile institutions than there is for a special court for women to be confined in women's institutions. Without a juvenile court and the distraction of the "transfer" issue, juvenile defendants from the least serious to the most serious could routinely receive the most appropriate sanction (Ainsworth 1991, 1095–1097).

Because of this "fundamental flaw" in the conceptualization of the juvenile court, reforming the juvenile court is impossible. But, Feld observes, "For more than two decades since *Gault,* juvenile courts have deflected, coopted, ignored, or accommodated constitutional and legislative reforms with minimal institutional change" (Feld 1993a, 252).

The Demise of Delinquency

Ainsworth suggests that the juvenile court be abolished because the idea of delinquency, and specifically, the image of childhood on which it is based, are no longer current. Ainsworth suggests that academics and social reformers during the Progressive Era of the late nineteenth and early twentieth centuries reconstructed the image of childhood. They invented the word ***adolescence*** to describe a developmental stage between childhood and adulthood. By categorizing the adolescent as a subclass of child rather than as a young adult, the Progressives formulated a juvenile justice system centered around the idea that adolescents are not morally accountable for their behavior. They viewed juvenile lawbreaking as a condition requiring government intervention. They compared social deviance to a physical disease, which if not treated in its early stages of delinquency would mushroom in advanced stages to fullblown criminality (Ainsworth 1991, 1083–1132).

During the late twentieth century, the model of adolescence as a developmental stage of childhood gave way to a view of life as a continuum. Psychologists have broken the life cycle into an increasing number of phases or stages, identifying life events such as "midlife crisis." Adolescence ceased to have any distinguishing characteristics, and the distinction between childhood and adulthood blurred. From Ainsworth's perspective, the U.S. Supreme Court's extension of due process rights to defendants in juvenile court followed this change in American society's view of young people. In *Gault,* the court determined that "the condition of being a boy does not justify a kangaroo court." They might well have said, Ainsworth contends, that the condition of a boy makes no difference in the scope of his constitutional rights. In other words, if the conceptions of rights did not differ from child to adult, then why should the judiciary maintain the conception that the reasons for lawbreaking differ for children than from adults (Ainsworth 1991, 1118)? Or as Feld (1993a, 420–421) puts it: "A society that regards young people as fundamentally different from adults easily justifies an inferior justice system and conveniently rationalizes it on the grounds that children are entitled only to custody, not liberty."

Travis Hirschi, a sociologist at the University of Arizona, and Michael Gottfredson, a professor of public administration, have developed the most extensive attack on the concept of delinquency. They have insisted the juvenile court be abolished based on their general theory of crime. Essentially, they contend that "juveniles" and "adults" break the law for the same reason: ***low self-control.*** Self-control is taught by parents, and to some extent, in schools. The level of social control stays relatively stable throughout the life course. Those with low self-control engage in activities that require little cognitive complexity, learning, planning, or skill—activities available to everyone not constrained by fear of long-term consequences. Acts include recklessness, school misconduct, delinquency, and crime. When crime rates are calculated by age, they tend to peak at age 17 then decline thereafter. Rates decline with age with or without intervention. This suggests to Hirschi and Gottfredson that there is no justification for a separate juvenile court. "Changing from juvenile to adult sanctions has no apparent impact on the rate (which begins to decline before juveniles legally become adults)." The distribution, which varies for individuals depending on the level of self-control, would remain the same if the juvenile court were abolished (Gottfredson & Hirschi 1990; Hirschi & Gottfredson 1996, 478).

Hirschi and Gottfredson challenge seven justifications for the juvenile court:

1. *The criminal behavior of children is less serious.* The evidence, Hirschi and Gottfredson contend, suggests otherwise. Offenders do not escalate their offenses as they age.
2. *Young people, unlike adults, are not responsible for their acts.* This is another way of saying that young people cannot or do not anticipate the consequences of their acts. Hirschi and Gottfredson agree—it is a matter of low self-control. But if low self-control excuses young people from responsibility for their acts, then it would excuse adults with low self-control for their acts as well.
3. *Young people are more malleable than adults.* Hirschi and Gottfredson deny that young people are more receptive to being treated and more capable of being rehabilitated. Individual differences in self-control are established before the age of intervention by juvenile court.
4. *There is a distinct class of deviant behaviors for children.* These are the status offenses—behaviors considered deviant for children; but not for adults. Hirschi and Gottfredson challenge the logic of this distinction. Alcohol and drugs are the most frequent cause of arrests for adults and children. The behavior is the same; how the court responds is the difference.
5. *Juvenile court allows for treatment of behavior without stigmatizing the child.* Juvenile court records have been unavailable to adult courts. Hirschi and Gottfredson point out that legislatures have begun to rethink this position and that separate systems of court records compound the problem of gathering the information needed for constructive sentencing. At the same time, if offenders avoid further contact with the court over a period of time, there should be no point in maintaining a file on them, but this is true regardless of age.
6. *Young people need the care and attention of responsible adults.* Young people are dependent on adults until the time when they should be free to take care of themselves. The juvenile court does care for, and should continue to care for, abused, neglected, and abandoned children. But the rationale for care of these children ought not be confused with the rationale for dealing with juveniles who break the law.
7. *The juvenile justice system provides separate facilities for youth.* Children ought to be isolated from the corrupting influences of hardened criminals. Prisons, it is said,

are schools of crime. Hirschi and Gottfredson contend that the opposite is true—the age distribution of crime suggests that adults are less criminal than young people (Hirschi & Gottfredson 1996, 479–482).

Preserve the Juvenile Court

The primary argument of the preservationists for preserving the juvenile court attributes the failings of the juvenile court to faulty implementation: The founders were right and it is a matter of devoting adequate resources to the juvenile court strategy of intervention. Other preservationists contend that the abolitionists exaggerate the benefits of the criminal court: Trial courts, they believe, will be no better in the extension of due process rights. Others argue that it makes no sense to throw away the juvenile court, which deals effectively with most young lawbreakers, in an effort to deal more effectively with the few serious and violent youth.

The Legacy of the Juvenile Court.   During the Centennial Celebration in 1999, the National Council of Juvenile and Family Court Judges reaffirmed the nineteenth-century reformers' beliefs. The court was founded in recognition that children and adolescents are "developmentally different" from adults and these differences make youth "less culpable and more amenable to intervention and treatment." Juvenile courts were created 100 years ago because children have different needs than adults and need adult protection and guidance. From the beginning, the juvenile court has been committed to the "recovery and rehabilitation of children rather than their punishment and incapacitation" (Mildon 1998, 5). Centennial activities promoted several key messages:

1. Children have constitutional and human rights and need adult involvement to ensure those rights.
2. Very few children are beyond redemption.
3. Children are everyone's responsibility. Family, community, volunteer programs, and financial support are needed from public and private sources to enable the court to do its job well (Mildon 1998, 5).

Robert E. Shepherd, professor of law at the University of Richmond and a chair of the American Bar Association's Juvenile Justice Committee, put the argument succinctly: "Overall, the juvenile or family court of the twenty-first century should not be fundamentally different in design and jurisdiction from the court as it has been throughout most of the twentieth century. But it should receive significantly more of society's attention and resources" (1999, 1). The juvenile court is not fatally flawed, but like many institutions for youth, requires some fine tuning and greater support to carry out its mission.

Judge J. Dean Lewis has reviewed seven achievements of the juvenile court during its first century to defend the court's place in the American judicial system:

1. The juvenile court represents the first court established that recognizes that children are developmentally distinct from adults.
2. The juvenile court represents a forerunner of the unified family court and the idea that children's needs are best met through a court with jurisdiction over family issues.

3. The juvenile court introduced a different response to children, a response that treated each child as a unique human being based on the concept of "individualized justice."
4. The juvenile court introduced the "medical model" that focused on the need for diagnosis and treatment in disposing of cases.
5. The juvenile court introduced the use of alternative methods for resolving conflicts and pioneered alternative dispute resolution techniques.
6. The juvenile court emphasized community and family-oriented dispositions for youth rather than institutions.
7. Juvenile and family court judges have taken a leadership role in areas of children and the law (Lewis 1999, 3–7).

"The juvenile court should remain a critical societal institution, principally because there is no alternative," insists Leonard P. Edwards of the Superior Court of Santa Clara County, California, and a prominent spokesperson for the National Council of Juvenile and Family Court Judges. Edwards contends that the juvenile court remains "society's means of holding children accountable for their conduct and parents accountable for raising their children to be productive members of the larger community" (Edwards 1996, 131–139).

Leaving Bad Enough Alone.   Irene Merker Rosenberg, a law professor at the University of Houston, contends that the abolitionists exaggerate the ability of the criminal court to guarantee due process rights. As bad as the juvenile court might be, it is still better than criminal courts would be if they were to have jurisdiction for all juveniles. "It seems to me," Rosenberg reasons, "that underlying the views of the abolitionists, at least unconsciously, is a somewhat idealized or romanticized version of adult courts in which the criminal guarantees of the Bill of Rights are meaningfully enforced" (Rosenberg 1993, 162).

Gary L. Crippen, a senior judge on the Minnesota Court of Appeals, agrees with Rosenberg. Crippen observes that nearly all the proposals for abolition of the court boil down to a preference for general laws over judicial discretion. He argues that this preference for the administration of criminal law by adult courts to the model of judicial discretion afforded by the juvenile court amounts to "mere speculation." Crippen insists that the model of judicial discretion exercised within the juvenile court is not really a modern invention at all. The court's child-protective role actually began many years earlier than Chicago; acting as *parens patriae* has been part of Anglo-American law for at least three hundred years. It has a tie to common law courts of equity that individualized justice represents a noble tradition in American courts and the most ambitious effort toward rehabilitation (Crippen 1998, 1–19).

Robert O. Dawson, a law professor at the University of Texas, writes that "The case against abolition is based on three clusters of arguments:

1. *The notion that minors have less responsibility for their misconduct than do adults.* Children should be held to a lower standard of responsibility than adults. The juvenile court avoids applying the label of criminal to youth misconduct to allow for rehabilitation. If the criminal court annexed the juvenile court, this philosophy of lessened responsibility would have to change. Childhood would still be taken into account by judges, but the labeling would remain that of adults and lessen the chances for rehabilitation.

2. *The greater rehabilitation potential of minors.* Dawson also points out that children attract resources. The big difference between the adult and juvenile justice systems is the greater reliance on private resources by the juvenile justice system. The juvenile justice system includes a network of private, charitable, and religious institutions and programs. There is no counterpart to this network within the adult system, and if the juvenile justice system were dismantled, it is likely that these resources would not be captured by the criminal justice system

3. *The avoidance of inappropriate legal rules.* Dawson argues that maintaining the juvenile court avoids applying inappropriate legal rules to young people. The whole-sale transfer of young people to adult criminals would make them subject to the bail system. In juvenile court, bail is simply ignored and juvenile courts avoid the influence of bail-bonding agencies. Many states are moving toward pretrial services to remove the influence of bail bondsmen from the system. Bail bonds are not appropriate for adults, and even less appropriate for young people. Pretrial release would depend on a young person's family to post bond and the willingness of a bonding agent to write a bond. Introducing a whole generation of defendants to commercial bail bonding would be a step backwards in criminal court reform (Dawson 1990, 136).

Juvenile Crime Revisited. Other preservationists argue that juvenile crime is not the problem people think it is. Judge Cindy S. Lederman, presiding judge of the Miami-Dade Juvenile Court, observes that although juvenile crime remains at a higher level than a decade ago, it is declining. She also refers to OJJDP research to show that although more juveniles are being arrested for violent acts, youth do not commit more acts of violence with greater regularity than earlier generations. "This means that the 'superpredator epidemic' does not exist," Lederman concludes.

Some in the juvenile justice system merit classification as serious, violent, and chronic juvenile offenders, but as a group they constitute a small minority of the juvenile population. These offenders may need to be confined to receive long-term treatment and to ensure the safety of the community. But at the same time, the juvenile justice system should not be redesigned to overemphasize its response to this small number of offenders. "It is essential to avoid creating a one-dimensional juvenile justice system with rules, laws, practices and goals designed to adjudicate Billy the Kid," Lederman insists, "when most of the juveniles in the system more closely resemble Dennis the Menace" (Lederman 1999, 24). In other words, the juvenile court should not be abolished in favor of a criminal court model with an eye toward developing a better response to a small percentage of young lawbreakers. Lederman's point resembles the maxim: "If it ain't broke, don't fix it."

The Lawmakers and the Public

Congress has, in recent years, stood on the brink of a major overhaul of the juvenile court. The lawmakers in Washington are responding to their perceptions of what citizens want, and they have perceived that the public wants fundamental change in the way this nation deals with young lawbreakers.

The Lawmakers. There was a great deal of momentum early in the 105th Congress to enact juvenile justice legislation in response to headlines across the country about mass murderers at schools. Several juvenile justice bills were proposed, but the only bill to receive serious attention was S. 10, the Violent and Repeat Juvenile Offenders Act of 1997. The Act, cosponsored by Republican Senators Orrin Hatch of Utah and Jeff Sessions of Alabama, contained numerous provisions ranging from allowing the Ten Commandments to be posted in public school classrooms to eliminating the requirement that states assess the extent of disproportionate minority confinement in juvenile institutions. During Senate debate of the 1997 act, several members of Congress expressed skepticism about the role of the juvenile court. "It is not hard to see why state legislatures around this country are proposing bills to get rid of the juvenile justice system altogether," commented Senator Ron Widen. "Today we are living with a juvenile justice system that was created around the time of the silent film," quipped Senator John Ashcroft, who later became United States Attorney General (Butts & Harrell 1998, 1).

The 1997 act, which drew fire from Democrats, the ACLU, and the NAACP, was not brought out of the Senate floor before the end of the session. During the final days of the 105th Congress, attention turned to a new-and-improved version of the legislation, S. 254, the Violent and Repeat Juvenile Offender Accountability and Rehabilitation Act, also led by Hatch. Negotiation between the Senate, the House of Representatives, the Department of Justice, and the White House continued into the 106th Congress.

Like its predecessor S. 10, the Violent and Repeat Juvenile Offender Accountability and Rehabilitation Act of 1999 contained provisions to earmark federal funds to state and local governments for prevention and law enforcement, regulation of Internet and television displays of violence, stiffer penalties for juvenile firearms violations, and safer, more secure school environments. Hatch's act amended the federal juvenile code, the Juvenile Justice and Delinquency Prevention Act, and provided funds for prevention through block grants. "People are expecting us to do something about these violent teenagers," Hatch urged his colleagues, "We've got to move on this" (Shiraldi & Soler 1998, 591). The Senate enacted the Violent and Repeat Juvenile Offender Accountability and Rehabilitation Act on May 20, 1999. The following month, the House passed a separate bill sponsored by Representative Bill McCollum of Florida, H.R. 1501 Consequences for Juvenile Offenders Act, and the two bills went to conference committee.

Public officials appear more willing than ever to support the end of the juvenile court. In 1996, Arizona citizens gave the state legislature permission to abolish the juvenile court. The "Stop Juvenile Crime" initiative contained a provision that amended the Arizona constitution so that juvenile courts no longer have "exclusive" and "original" jurisdiction over lawbreakers under 18 years of age. The initiative, endorsed by 63 percent of Arizona voters, led Arizona's governor to form an advisory committee to recommend a new system for handling young offenders. Although the governor's plan stopped short of abolishing juvenile court jurisdiction altogether, it did reflect an abandonment of the founder's rationale for a separate juvenile court. The presiding judge of the Phoenix juvenile court said that the governor's plan reflected a philosophy that "punishment is the only thing that changes human behavior" (Butts & Harrell 1998, 8).

What Does the Public Think?   What does the public think about juvenile justice reform? In 1991, the Survey Research Center at the University of Michigan's Institute for Social Research conducted a national telephone survey about juvenile crime. Generally, people are very concerned about juvenile crime. The researchers found that although there is popular support for trying juveniles who commit violent felonies in adult courts, the public does not support sending juveniles to adult prisons. The majority wanted juveniles who committed serious crimes to be punished, but wanted them treated and rehabilitated if at all possible (Schwartz 1992b, 124–125). A 1995 survey of Virginia citizens commissioned by the Virginia Commission on Youth found that the majority (63 percent) believed that the main purpose of the juvenile court should be to rehabilitate youth (Shepherd 1996, 1–3). In 1998, a national telephone survey asked citizens about several provisions of the Violent and Repeat Juvenile Offender Act of 1997. That survey found:

- A majority of citizens (67 percent) disagreed with housing children in adult jails after arrest. The majority (74 percent) also disagreed with housing status offenders in adult jails for up to 24 hours.
- The majority (70 percent) disagreed with making felony arrest records of juveniles available to colleges to which they are applying for admission even when not convicted of the offense for which they were arrested.
- The majority (74 percent) agreed that part of the money set aside for new detention facilities and drug testing should also be used for prevention programs, including recreational, job, and parenting programs.
- About half (56 percent) disagreed with the idea of giving federal prosecutors complete discretion to try juveniles as adults for all felonies (Shiraldi & Soler 1998, 590–601).

The Koch Crime Institute in Topeka, Kansas, surveyed citizens and juvenile justice professionals statewide to find out what Kansans think about the juvenile court. The poll followed legislation enacted by the Kansas legislature creating a commission for the reform of the state's juvenile justice system. In Kansas:

- Citizens ranked rehabilitation and education as the most important goals of the system. However, nearly 75 percent of those surveyed do not believe the current system rehabilitates juveniles. Respondents reported that they are willing to spend twice as much to rehabilitate juveniles and prevent juvenile crime than on adult crime prevention and rehabilitation (Clements 1996, 3).
- Most believe that juvenile offenders get off too easily. About 72 percent of those surveyed believed that juvenile offenders receive less punishment than they ought to have received. Nearly all those surveyed (93 percent) believed that juveniles who commit rape or murder should be tried as adults. About 46 percent reported that juveniles should be treated as adults for minor crimes.
- Citizens believe strongly that juveniles and their parents should be accountable for criminal acts. About 91 percent felt that juveniles should be accountable for criminal acts and believed that poor parenting is a fundamental cause of juvenile crime (Clements 3–4).

The survey results have led to different claims about what the public really wants. Commenting on the Michigan survey results, Ira M. Schwartz concludes that "The public does not support the current movement to abandon the historical mission and purpose of the juvenile court" (Schwartz 1992b, 222). Former Attorney General Edwin Meese III, on the other hand, has argued that the public has lost confidence in the juvenile justice system. Meese and his colleague, Robert O. Heck, cite Gallup polls conducted during the 1990s that revealed similar public sentiments: 49 rehabilitation programs for juveniles are not successful, 52 percent believe that punishments juveniles receive should be the same as those for adults, and 83 percent believe that juveniles who commit two or more crimes should receive the same sentences as adults. Meese and Heck point out that over 93 percent of teenagers themselves believe that juveniles accused of murder or rape should be tried as adults and that these lawbreakers should not receive special consideration because of their age (Wootton & Heck 1997, 126). The public, it would appear, supports delinquency prevention and elements of a separate juvenile justice system. At the same time, the public supports holding serious juvenile offenders accountable, approving of increased punishments for serious offenders in juvenile court, and the transfer of some juveniles to criminal court.

Citizens' views of juvenile justice can also be interpreted alongside citizens' views of courts in general. Based on research using citizen surveys and focus groups of court users in Louisiana and North Carolina, the public thinks:

- *The courts are too soft on crime.* A court survey in Louisiana found that the majority of court users, with the exception of criminal defendants and court employees, felt that the courts were too soft on crime. Even jurors, who are generally the most positive court users, shared this sentiment. Of those surveyed in North Carolina, 55 percent thought that the courts had an "extremely or very serious problem" with leniency for criminals.
- *It takes too much time from arrest to trial.* Court users in Louisiana expressed particular concern about court delay from arrest to trial. About 82 percent agreed that too much time passes from arrest to trial; only 28 percent agreed that cases are processed in a reasonable time. About 50 percent of North Carolina survey respondents felt that the time from arrest to trial for felonies was an extremely or very serious problem.
- *Unequal treatment is a problem.* The majority of court users in Louisiana reported that unequal treatment was a problem in state courts, particularly unequal treatment based on economic status and political connections. Only 14 percent of those surveyed believed that wealthy and poor are treated alike in the system, and 91 percent agreed that people with political connections receive differential treatment. In North Carolina, 52 percent thought that the courts had an extremely or very serious problem with treating people differently based on their wealth; another 20 percent thought that such treatment was a "moderately serious problem" (Crowell 1996, 33; Howell 1998, 19).

If citizens feel about the juvenile court the way they feel about courts in general, there may be public support for major change in the response to juveniles. There are at least two factors, however, that complicate reaching a simple conclusion that the public favors abolition of the juvenile court. On the one hand, most citizens know very little about the courts. Citizens surveyed in North Carolina thought that the courts consumed between 18 to 20 percent of the state budget when in fact the proportion is less than 3 percent. North Carolinians estimated that about 250,000 cases are filed each year; in reality, the figure is about 10 times that at more than 2.5 million case filings a year. Most thought that the justices on the state supreme court were appointed, although state statutes provide for election of state supreme court justices. On the other hand, people who have been to court express greater dissatisfaction than those who have not been to court. Just more than half of the citizens in North Carolina's state opinion poll had been to court in a traffic, domestic, small claims, or civil case and about 20 percent had served on a jury. Generally, these citizens had a more unfavorable impression of the courts, believed the courts treated people differently based on wealth, and that judges were biased in their decision making. People with experience in domestic cases were the most dissatisfied (Crowell 1996).

The Twenty-First Century Juvenile Court

At the end of the juvenile court's first century, the winds of change are blowing harder than they have at any time before in the court's first century. No one doubts that the juvenile court of the twenty-first century will look much different than the juvenile court of the twentieth century. However, there are several different versions of what the juvenile court should look like. Predicting the future is impossible, of course, but it is possible to identify several themes and trends.

Reaffirming Juvenile Justice

The Juvenile Court's Centennial occasioned the reaffirmation of the juvenile court's original mission.

The U.N. Declaration.   Shepherd has invoked the United Nation's Convention on the Rights of the Child to shore up the nation's commitment to the juvenile court as an institution. The U.S. government has never formally ratified the Convention, which was originally adopted by the United Nations in 1952. The American Bar Association has supported the United State's ratification of the Convention. Expect for Somalia, every other nation of the world has ratified the Convention. Although the United States has signed the Convention, Shepherd contends that formal ratification by the U.S. Congress would reassert the importance of childhood in society (Shepherd 1999a).

Judge Ernestine Gray of Orleans Parish Juvenile Court has outlined a vision of juvenile court based on the United Nation's Convention on the Rights of the Child. Judge Gray points to several provisions:

1. Principle Two of the Convention establishes the "best interest of the child" as the rationale for affording "special protection" to juveniles under law. The declaration also establishes "the best interest of the child standard" as the basis for decision making in juvenile court.
2. Principle Four establishes a right to social security and "adequate nutrition, housing, recreation, and medical services."
3. Principle Six affirms that children should grow up in the care of their parents and that young children should not be separated from their mothers except for "exceptional circumstances." Payment of government assistance toward the maintenance of children and families is "highly desirable."

4. Principle Seven entitles children to receive a free but compulsory education based on the "best interest of the child."
5. Principle Nine provides that all children be protected against "all forms of neglect, cruelty, and exploitation," including engaging in any form of labor that would interfere with the child's education, health, or physical, mental, or moral development (Gray 1999, 29–30).

Gray envisions a juvenile court playing a role in guaranteeing that the provisions of the Convention are extended to children. She anticipates an increase in the number of unified family courts and the proliferation of specialized courts such as drug courts, gun courts, and community courts. Because the court will continue to lack resources to carry out its mission, the juvenile court will need to develop more partnerships with private sector and voluntary organizations. "The Court must take the initiative to work with communities in organizing the communities to work with courts on behalf of children. Through this effort, more community-based services will be developed," Gray concludes (1999, 31).

Comprehensive Juvenile Justice.   Shay Bilchik, who administrated the Office of Juvenile Justice and Delinquency Prevention under President Bill Clinton, described a "juvenile justice system for the twenty-first century." Bilchik insisted that the founders of the juvenile court had made substantial progress in achieving their aims and urged juvenile justice providers and state lawmakers to remain faithful to the founders' vision. "Considerable progress has been made since the birth of the juvenile justice system at the end of last century . . ." Bilchik (1998, 1) writes, "To create an effective juvenile justice system for the twenty-first century, we must take to heart the lessons learned from this century . . . and redouble our efforts on behalf of America's children."

Bilchik outlines a "juvenile justice system for the twenty-first century" drawing on the *Comprehensive Strategy* introduced in 1993 and elements of the Balanced and Restorative Justice approach. An effective juvenile justice system combines prevention with early intervention and graduated sanctions. To implement such a system, state and local governments should: (1) include the overall principles of prevention, early intervention, and graduated sanctions in the purpose clause of the state's juvenile code, (2) provide for appropriate interagency oversight and management structures to support delivery of juvenile justice, and (3) provide adequate funding at both the state and local levels. An effectively managed juvenile justice system should include:

- A state-level interagency coordinating committee that focuses on juvenile justice matters
- Regional/local advisory boards and regional offices within the state juvenile justice agency responsible for developing and implementing local juvenile justice plans
- A uniform funding mechanism for city and county juvenile justice system facilities, programs, and services that encourages pooling of juvenile justice funds (Bilchik 1998, 5–6)

Bilchik's strategy for the twenty-first century envisions an integrated juvenile justice system that cuts across health, education, social services, courts, and corrections. It calls for state legislatures to update juvenile justice planning and policy making to create a framework that provides for cross-jurisdictional and coordinated responses to juvenile crime.

To overhaul the juvenile court along these lines, OJJDP developed test sites in California and Florida. Juvenile justice planners in San Diego County, California, and Jacksonville, Florida, received intensive, on-site assistance to build a continuum of services including prevention, early intervention, and graduated sanctions. In San Diego County, planners began by identifying gaps in the existing system. They aimed to create a seamless web of integrated services for youth. Programs and strategies developed included a family-focused assessments program through the probation department and neighborhood-based community assessment centers. The California approach also included a state-funded program targeting high-risk, repeat juvenile offenders and a program using county funds to provide health, education, recreation, and skill development programs for middle-school youths. The Jacksonville approach began with private funds granted the city by the Jessie Ball DuPont Fund and extensive data collection on risk factors such as economic deprivation, academic failure, and drug use throughout the city. Criminal justice officials implemented SHOCAP, the Serious Habitual Offender Comprehensive Action Program, which identifies and tracks repeat juvenile offenders. The strategy directs juvenile justice programs to the few juvenile offenders responsible for the majority of juvenile arrests. The Jailed Juvenile Program is a mentoring program that matches institutionalized juveniles with a mentor after release. The program operates as part of the state attorney's office overall strategy for identification, intervention, and prosecution of serious, habitual juvenile offenders.

The Janiculum Project.   In 1997, the National Council of Juvenile and Family Court Judges, along with the Office of Juvenile Justice and Delinquency Prevention and the State Justice Institute, convened a panel of juvenile justice experts to assess the past, present, and future of the juvenile court. The project took its name from Janiculum Hill, the highest point near the city of Rome and the site of a watchtower from which observers could anticipate invasions from every direction. Juvenile court judges, prosecutors, defense attorneys, court administrators, probation officials, and professors developed *The Janiculum Report: Reviewing the Past and Looking Toward the Future of the Juvenile Court* (National Coucil of Juvenile and Family Court Judges 1998, 105–126).

The report contains four sets of recommendations for a "juvenile and family court that is more open, user friendly, and sensitive to crime victims":

1. *Jurisdictional and structural recommendations.* The report advises that juvenile and family courts have broad jurisdiction over the range of legal issues confronting families, including delinquency prevention.
2. *Procedural recommendations.* Youth ought to have an unwaivable right to effective and well-compensated legal counsel in juvenile court cases involving criminal and noncriminal behavior as well as abuse and neglect.
3. *Programmatic recommendations.* The juvenile court should develop and rely on a continuum of program options for neglected, abused, and dependent youth.
4. *System accountability recommendations.* The juvenile court should acquire and use the best available technology to enhance effective operation (Appleby 1999, 11).

The report reaffirmed the juvenile court as "society's official means of holding itself accountable for the well-being of children and the family." Children are "developmentally different" from adults and need a separate court and this "simple truth that children are not little adults and should not be treated as adults gave rise to the juvenile court almost a century ago. . . ." The Janiculum authors went on to insist that "there is a fundamental difference in philosophy between juvenile courts and adult criminal courts." The juvenile court seeks to rehabilitate young lawbreakers because they are more malleable and receptive to rehabilitation while the criminal court is primarily devoted to inducing law-abiding behavior by punishing wrongdoing (NCJFCJ 1998, 109).

Alternative Visions of the Juvenile Court

What would an alternative to juvenile court look like? Both abolitionists and preservationists have offered alternative visions of the twenty-first century juvenile court: family court, family bankruptcy court, and the youth discount and multicourt youth justice system.

The Family Court.   Judge Leonard P. Edwards, Superior Court of Santa Clara County, California, insists that the most significant proposal for structural changes in the juvenile court is the unified family court. Under the family court model, juvenile court would become part of a court with integrated jurisdiction over most or all legal issues that relate to a family. Robert Shepherd at the University of Richmond also favors the unified family court.

The family court makes "family" the organizing principle for the court's jurisdiction. The family court would be able to deal "holistically" with the youth who come from dysfunctional families. As envisioned by Edwards, family court would collapse specialized courts devoted to juvenile delinquency and juvenile dependency (abuse and neglect cases) into a single court along with domestic relations (custody, child support, property division), paternity, domestic violence, adoptions, guardianships, termination of parental rights, and child support enforcement. Jurisdiction could extend to criminal and civil cases involving family members, such as drugs and lawsuits involving family members (Edwards 1996, 132).

The first family court appeared in Cincinnati, Ohio, in 1914, less than two decades after the establishment of the first juvenile court. The concept languished until 1959 when it was revived by the National Council on Crime and Delinquency, the National Council of Juvenile and Family Court Judges, and the Children's Bureau, U.S. Department of Health and Human Services. These organizations published a "Standard Family Court Act" that established the creation of family court.

The National Council of Juvenile and Family Court Judges recommends that the state's enabling legislation for family court should provide for statewide implementation and give the state's supreme court authority to adopt rules of procedure for court proceedings. Family court jurisdiction should include:

- Family dissolution matters including divorce, child custody, property division, and visitation
- Child dependency matters including child abuse and neglect, termination of parental rights, family violence protective orders, and children in need of protection and adoption
- Juvenile delinquency proceedings including traffic offenses and liquor offenses (such as driving while intoxicated)
- Adult and juvenile guardianships, issues related to civil commitment of mentally ill persons, and other family-related legal issues, including abortion, right to die, emancipation, and name change (Moore & Wakeling 1997, 275–276)

Family Bankruptcy Court.   Mark H. Moore and Stewart Wakeling at the John F. Kennedy School of Government, Harvard University, contend that the family court as envisioned by Judge Edwards and the NCJFCJ judges resembles the current model of juvenile court. As such, it does not serve as a genuine alternative to contemporary thinking about juvenile court structure. They have sketched a vision of a family court model that would make it comparable to bankruptcy court.

The family court would intervene when a family declares that it is going "bankrupt" or when society determines that things are not going sufficiently well in the area of child rearing. Faced with signs of family bankruptcy, the family court would pursue two lines analogous to financial bankruptcy. The court could "liquidate" the bankrupt family's assets by transferring the children to a stable caretaker. Or, the court could decide to "restructure" by explaining to the "creditors" that although the parents have not been successful in child rearing it would not be in their best interests to break apart the family. To serve the creditors' interests, the court would place someone in the role of "special master" to monitor the family, such as a social worker or juvenile probation officer. The family bankruptcy court would reflect three basic ideas about the role of the court and the role of families in society:

1. Despite its desire to see children remain in their families, society has acknowledged that child rearing is a public responsibility.
2. Parents of children have a responsibility to the broader society and are subject to supervision by the state.
3. Intervention when breakdowns occur in child-rearing reflect not only children's rights but the imposition of duties on parents (Moore & Wakeling 1997, 290–294).

Moore and Wakeling admit that the level of government intervention they propose is frightening but insist that the view they propose is consistent with political doctrines that have developed over time (Moore 1996, 140–146).

An Integrated Criminal Court.   Barry Feld insists that juveniles should be tried in criminal courts along with adult defendants. Before returning juveniles to criminal courts, however, the legislature should create a rationale to sentence young offenders differently than their adult counterparts. Feld argues that juveniles should receive shorter sentences than adults given that youths should be punished for their mistakes but not forfeit their life chances altogether. "Shorter sentences for young people do not require that they be tried in separate criminal courts," Feld (1993, 417) concludes.

Feld envisions returning juveniles to criminal courts operating according to principles of "diminished responsibility" when sentencing youth. Diminished responsibility is a function of age. It is not that being young reduces the level of harm, but Feld insists, it should alter the extent of culpability or blameworthiness. At 14 years of age, a person knows "right from wrong" in the abstract, but ought not be considered as blameworthy or as culpable as an adult guilty of the same offense. Statutes in some states already recognize "youthfulness" or "immaturity" as a mitigating factor in sentencing. Louisiana statutes, for example, refer to "the youth of the offender at the time of the offense"; North Carolina's statutes recognize "the defendant's age, immaturity, or limited mental capacity" as mitigating factors (Feld 1999a, 326). Feld's system would eliminate juvenile transfer hearings and related issues of fairness and add, by definition, the right to jury trial. Young people should be tried in criminal courts with full procedural safeguards extended to adults. Young people should receive additional safeguards, not less, as is the case in the traditional juvenile court (Feld 1993a, 417–418).

Criminal courts should recognize diminished responsibility of youth in the form of a *youth discount,* that is, a fractional reduction in sentence length. For example, a 14-year-old would receive 33 percent of the adult penalty, a 16-year-old 66 percent of the penalty and an 18-year-old, the full penalty without discount. The principle of associating the severity of sanction with age is already a recognized principle in juvenile justice. The ABA/IJA's *Juvenile Justice Standards* provide that "The age of the juvenile is also relevant to the determination of the seriousness of his or her behavior. In most cases, the older the juvenile, the greater is his or her responsibility for breaking the law" (1999, 317–318). This graduated age-culpability scheme should be implemented within an overall system of humane, realistic, and determinate adult sentencing practices.

Sentencing young people in this way would not mean confining them in adult correctional facilities. Departments of corrections already classify inmates by age and young people sentenced in criminal courts in this way could still be sent to existing juvenile detention facilities. Other practical issues within implementing the youth discount, Feld insists, can be solved. The difficulty is political (Feld 1999a, 420). Further, an integrated juvenile and criminal justice system would entail a number of advantages. An integrated system would provide for better record keeping and reduce the number of youth who "fall through the cracks" between juvenile and criminal court. It would also allow courts to divert the bulk of "kid stuff" cases and concentrate on the more criminally deserving youth (Feld 1999a, 325).

Multi-Court Youth Justice. Jeffrey A. Butts and Adele V. Harrell at the Urban Institute believe that the original informal, social welfare approach to the juvenile court has been lost forever. The nation has already replaced juvenile courts with a network of "junior criminal courts." As juvenile and adults courts converge in rationale and procedure, it will become increasingly more difficult to retain a separate juvenile court. They believe that states should fashion a new youth justice system before the concepts of delinquency and juvenile courts are abandoned (Butts & Harrell 1998; Merlo, Benekos, & Cook 1999, 7–8).

The Butts and Harrell version of the future would replace the juvenile court with a network of other specialized courts. Rather than a distinction between adult and juvenile court, there would be a number of specialized courts for young people. Many of these courts are already in place, including drug courts, gun courts, teen courts, community courts, and alternative dispute resolution programs. Many of these alternative courts share rationale and procedures that suit an emerging youth justice system:

- Treatment programs are matched to individual needs.
- Judges personally negotiate written agreements and monitor compliance.
- The court process involves a combination of penalties and rewards to shape behavior.
- The court relies on community-based programs for delivering services and sanctions (Butts & Harrell 1998, 12).

The emergence of the multi-court youth justice system enlarges to debate between those who favor abolishing the juvenile court and those in favor of preserving it. Policymakers can draw on these innovative courts to construct a youth justice system of the twenty-first century.

Butts and Harrell acknowledge that a new youth justice system built around numerous courts would require an effective intake process. The multi-court youth justice model would require "a sophisticated intake process to determine the most appropriate court for each matter referred by law enforcement." After the initial intake interview, the youth would be referred to a conventional trial court, treatment-oriented drug court, weapons court, peer-justice-oriented teen court, voluntary mediation court, or family conferencing agency. The decision would be based on the defendant's situation and prior record, not whether the defendant meets the statutory definition of a "juvenile." "After all, the central issue in the fight against juvenile crime is not whether these young offenders are called delinquents or criminals," Butts and Harrell (1998, 13) conclude, "The central issue is what happens to young people following arrest."

Themes and Trends

Will one of these alternatives become the model for the juvenile court of the twenty-first century? It is difficult to predict with certainty whether one of these alternative models, or some other model, will emerge as the paradigm. It is possible to identify several themes and trends that will shape juvenile court reform during the next few years. Important themes in juvenile justice are accountability, prevention, community, integration, convergence, and juvenile crime.

Accountability

Juvenile justice philosophy has shifted from individualized justice based on notions of "the best interest of the child" to that of punishing criminal behavior. Changes in state statutes during the 1990s reflect a belief that young lawbreakers ought to be held accountable for their actions. Accountability has been defined as period of confinement with less emphasis on the activities during this confinement. The dispositions provided for state statutes reflect the goal of punishment rather than rehabilitation (Torbet *et al.* 1996, xi).

New York and Florida became the first states to legislate criminal responsibility for juveniles. In 1976, New York enacted a felony statute that enabled juvenile courts to sentence juveniles charged with designated felonies with up to five years incarceration. Two years later, New York passed legislation redefining as criminal offenders anyone 13 years of age or older charged with a Class A or B felony. Florida became the first state to authorize direct filing in criminal court. Hunter Hurst IV, Director of the National Center for Juvenile Justice in Pittsburgh, observed as early as 1982 that pursuit of due process in juvenile court proceedings would inevitably raise the issue of responsibility. The introduction of the due process model to juvenile court brought a view of criminal responsibility on the part of young people that brought additional change (Hurst 1999, 22). There will likely be increasing number of transfers to adult court and legislation increasing the range of juvenile defendants eligible for transfer.

The 1990s also introduced legislation to make parents accountable. Parents have been made accountable for ensuring that children receive services. North Carolina's Juvenile Justice Reform Act of 1998 extended juvenile court jurisdiction over the parents of juveniles in juvenile court. Juvenile court judges may send parents a summons holding parents in contempt for failing to attend scheduled court hearings, for failing to bring the juvenile before the court for a hearing, or for noncompliance with a court order. In addition, parents can be required to provide transportation to juveniles on probation; attend parental responsibility classes; or pay fees for detention, probation, or attorneys' services (North Carolina Juvenile Code 1999).

In addition, juvenile offenders are being made increasingly accountable to victims. Since 1992, nearly half of the states have enacted laws that increase the roles or rights of victims of juvenile crime. State statutes in every state currently contain specific provision in their juvenile codes for victims' rights. These rights, more than 20 in all, contain provisions to attend hearings and to restitution from juveniles (Hurst 1999, 24).

Prevention

Despite the overall emphasis on accountability, prevention will continue to be a theme. Former Attorney General Janet Reno put the argument for prevention succinctly: "I think the greatest crime problem we face in terms of violence is the problem of youth violence. One of the reasons that it exists is because we have failed to make an investment in the juvenile justice system because we'd rather wait and build expensive prisons down the road" (Reno 1996, 3). The nation's war on crime requires an investment up front—in young people, in opportunities for young people, and in their communities.

In a speech at the Baker Institute at Rice University in Houston, Texas, Reno explained how she came to the position that an effective response to youth crime requires prevention and punishment. As a prosecutor in Miami, she recalled how she had adjudicated a young person delinquent for armed robbery and noticed in the file "four or five points along the way where we could have intervened and have made a difference in that child's life." She helped develop a dropout prevention program with local middle schools and discovered it was not enough. So she developed an early intervention program focused around Head Start. Then she visited the hospital to see babies of cocaine addicts who had no mothers to hold them and who did not display basic human emotions. She learned that people develop the concept of reward and punishment, a conscience, during their first three years of life. "It became clear to me that what good would all the prisons be years from now if that child never learned what punishment was all about or if that child never developed a conscience." She concluded that early investment, and a continuing investment, in communities was critical (Reno 1996, 2).

Community

Community remains a pervasive theme in juvenile court. Probation, the supervision of young offenders within the community, has always been the mainstay of juvenile justice. Since the Juvenile Justice and Delinquency Prevention Act of 1974 and a deemphasis on training schools, juvenile court sanctions have emphasized community-based programs. Community-based programs also remain on the forefront of prevention and early intervention efforts.

In *Emerging Criminal Justice,* Xavier University's Paul Hahn identifies a community-oriented response to juvenile crime. This community-oriented response parallels the similar transitions in corrections and law enforcement: community corrections and community policing. The movement reflects a new concept of crime as injury to all members of the community rather than an affront to the government. It requires that all efforts be designed

Improved educational opportunities are viewed as key to many juvenile justice reforms.
Chuck Savage/Corbis/Stock Market

to promote "community healing" the restoration of relationships broken by the criminal act. Hahn notes the role of community-based "criminal justice councils" to ensure participation of all participants. The councils provide for a community-based level of planning and coordination of juvenile justice interventions, a pillar of a proactive juvenile justice system (Hahn 1998, 60).

Illinois's Juvenile Justice Reform Act of 1998 authorized creation of such councils to advise county boards on the statutes of juvenile delinquency prevention programs. The legislation, which authorized but did not mandate creation of the councils, anticipated that the council would formulate a comprehensive county juvenile justice plan to be used by the county board. The council could also have a major role in coordinating various youth service agencies and develop pilot programs with public and private partners (Illinois Criminal Justice Authority 1999, 15). North Carolina's Juvenile Justice Reform Act of 1998 created similar councils known as juvenile crime prevention councils or JCPCs. The JCPCs replaced youth service advisory committees (YSACs) originally created in 1975. After a finding that North Carolina had the highest rate of commitment to training schools, the state legislature created the Community-Based Alternatives program through the Division of Youth Services. Under the program each YSAC received state monies, known as CBA funds, to develop local delinquency prevention programs based on an annual needs assessment. The JCPCs will have a similar role, including needs assessment, planning, and coordinating youth service initiatives. County-based planning councils provide for community-based decision making and improved coordination of juvenile justice initiatives at the local level.

Integration

Efforts toward integration of juvenile justice and youth services have occurred at the federal and state levels. Shay Bilchik, former administrator of the Office of Juvenile Justice and Delinquency Prevention (OJJDP), sought to integrate federal initiatives on behalf of children. Bilchik arranged for a meeting between representatives of OJJDP and the Administration on Children, Youth and Families (ACYF), to identify common strategies for delinquency prevention and early intervention. The agencies identified four programs—Family Preservation and Support Services (ACYF), State Court Improvement Program (ACYF), Children's Justice Act (ACYF), and the Delinquency Prevention Initiative (OJJDP)—that represented areas for collaboration between child welfare and juvenile justice systems. Bilchik left OJJDP in 1999 to lead the Child Welfare League (Chemers 1995).

State legislatures have attempted to provide for coordinated, cross-jurisdictional responses to juvenile crime. The National Conference of State Legislatures has called for *comprehensive juvenile justice* that cuts across health, education, social services, and corrections. Comprehensive calls for "integration of policies that affect those agencies and their handling of children in contact with, or at-risk of being in, the child welfare, mental health, juvenile justice, or adult criminal justice systems." The Connecticut legislature enacted a comprehensive juvenile reform law in 1995 incorporating five components: prevention in early childhood, intervention for at-risk youth, graduated juvenile justice sanctions, juvenile detention and corrections, and treating juveniles similar to adults. The law provided for changes in organizational structure and budgets and established the role for the judicial branch in coordinating the agencies to carry out new programs and services other than incarceration for juveniles (National Conference of State Legislatures 1999, 3).

Several states have created new organizational structures to coordinate juvenile justice initiatives. In Pennsylvania, Governor Tom Ridge convened the state legislature into a special session the day after his inauguration to deal with issues of crime. Ridge also recognized the need for improved planning and coordination of the state's juvenile justice system. He challenged the Juvenile Advisory Committee to develop "a strategic plan to take Pennsylvania's juvenile justice system into the next century." The committee envisioned a unified system organized around a single mission statement for all youth-serving agencies in the state (Kurlychek 1998, 1–2).

Several states, including Kentucky, North Carolina, and Kansas, have created new juvenile justice agencies. In North Carolina, responsibility for juvenile justice was divided between the Juvenile Services Division, the Administrative Office of the Courts, and the Division of Youth Services, Department of Health and Human Services until 1999. Legislation merged these agencies within a new Office of Juvenile Justice with a director appointed by the governor. Kentucky created the Department of Juvenile Justice within its Justice Cabinet in 1996. The Kansas legislature created the Criminal Justice Coordinating Council in

1994 to study and make recommendations about the state's juvenile justice system. A year later, the legislature created the Juvenile Justice Authority. In 1997, all of the responsibilities for juvenile offenders previously retained by the Department for Social and Rehabilitation Services transferred to the Juvenile Justice Authority.

Delinquency

The rhetoric of the juvenile court as a "kind and just parent" and of the juvenile court dispensing "rehabilitation" and "healing" have been replaced by "you do the crime, you do the time" (Crawford 1998, 62–64).

George W. Bush, who became governor of Texas in 1994, made crime a central feature of his campaign. Early in 1994 he sat down with Harold C. Gaither, Jr., a Dallas district court judge, to map out a series of reforms. Bush's 17-point proposal included many of the changes sought by state legislatures across the country between 1992 and 1995 that targeted violent and serious juvenile crime. Bush advocated lowering the age at which a minor could be tried as an adult, fingerprinting every youth apprehended for a misdemeanor, and opening juvenile records to the public. When a journalist with a Dallas newspaper challenged Bush's use of the word "thugs" when referring to young lawbreakers, Bush explained: "I tend to speak off my gut. There are thugs and there are not thugs. There are nice little kids lost for all kinds of reasons who need to be surrounded with love, who can be saved. And then there are those *thugs* who walk into people's *homes and blow people's heads off*" (Mitchell 2000, 302–303). Bush's language may have riled a few, but his emphasis on juvenile crime took him to the statehouse. And, as a result, the Texas legislature produced during 1995 "some of the nation's toughest responses to violent juvenile crime" (Torbet *et al.* 1996, 57).

Will the Juvenile Court Survive?

Whether the court *should* survive is one question, whether it *will* survive is another. The trends influencing juvenile court will likely shape the court in ways unanticipated by the reformers. The juvenile court may survive regardless of the abolitionists arguments or legislative efforts to dismantle it, but for reasons other than what the preservationists would want.

"Will there be a separate juvenile justice system in the year 2010? Probably so," Professor Pope concludes. Pope observes that the juvenile court is a matter of substantial history and tradition, and these are hard to overcome. Even if the court has not fulfilled the goals of rehabilitating youth, this remains a worthwhile goal and it is unlikely to be completely abandoned. There is also an entrenched bureaucracy of programs and services devoted to the juvenile justice system. Once created, government bureaucracies demonstrate tremendous staying power (Pope 1995, 271).

At the beginning of the twenty-first century, probably the most significant major difference between the juvenile court and criminal court is the large network of private, charitable, non-profit and allied programs that serve the juvenile court. Children in trouble attract resources that adults in trouble do not, and over the years, the juvenile court has enmeshed itself in a large array of private, private-like, and quasi-governmental agencies. This significant amount of society's resources will not simply evaporate as legislatures rewrite juvenile codes. Even if juvenile court procedure became completely indistinct from that of the criminal court—the U.S. Supreme Court authorized jury trials for juveniles, for example—the juvenile court as an institution would remain supported by the large conglomeration of child welfare oriented programs and services (Dawson 1990, 148). The juvenile court, without its conception of childhood, survives by "sheer institutional inertia." Dismantling the system would encounter vested interests of an entrenched bureaucracy. ". . . Inertia might not be an insupportable basis for maintaining the juvenile court," concludes Professor Janet Ainsworth, "After all, dismantling the system would entail at least some political and economic costs. Indeed, overcoming the vested interests of such an entrenched institution could take a heroic effort of will" (Ainsworth 1991, 118).

Schwartz and his colleagues at the University of Pennsylvania School of Social Work contend that the juvenile court will survive into the next century. From its inception, the juvenile court has been subjected to criticism from within and without. The juvenile court has survived as an institution primarily by outlasting its critics rather than by implementing meaningful reforms. Juvenile court leaders have pursued a "paranoid" style of management, leading to some of the harshest criticism of the court, but this management style is also responsible for its capacity to persist. The juvenile court probably will survive, and it will survive without fundamental change (Schwartz 1998, 533–552).

The court has retained a state-of-siege posture, protecting its failures with a "culture of secrecy" that pervades juvenile justice. Despite legislative attempts to encourage the sharing of information across youth-serving agencies, juvenile justice professionals avoided public accountability in favor of protecting the lives of youth (Hughes 1999, 27). This posture has been maintained due to the "down-and-dirty nature of the politics of kids." When children are involved, all the players claim the high moral ground, which opens the door to bitter, partisan attacks from all sides while each side claims particular knowledge of children's best interest. Through the years, juvenile court leaders have been able to silence the critics calling for major reforms through a continual process of definition and redefinition. The broad, ambiguous mission established by the founders of the juvenile court a hundred years ago has given the court a chameleon-like quality: It can become, without fundamentally changing, whatever it needs to be at the moment. "It makes no difference which direction the public and political winds might be blowing," Schwartz (1998, 551) insists, "the juvenile court can bend without breaking."

Juvenile Reform and the Big Picture

History provides a perspective that transcends the precise moment and provides a larger perspective. From a historical perspective, many of the current themes and trends in juvenile justice sound familiar. Just as the critics of juvenile court at the beginning of the twenty-first century propose to reform the response to juvenile lawbreakers, the founders of the juvenile court proposed to reform the way juveniles were treated in criminal courts. As historian David Rothman puts it, "Reform is the designation that each generation gives to its favorite programs" (Rothman 1980, 4).

Several observers have identified a cyclical quality to juvenile justice reforms (Bernard 1992; Ferdinand 1989, 79–106; Schultz 1973, 457–476). At each stage of the cycle, Pennsylvania State University's Thomas Bernard insists, juvenile justice authorities generally believe that juvenile crime is at an exceptionally high level, that the present response makes the problem worse, and that shifting to new policies will reduce juvenile crime. From Bernard's perspective, juvenile justice policy has no impact on juvenile crime. Juvenile crime rates generally remain high as a consequence of urbanization, industrialization, and the breakdown of informal social controls. The perception that juvenile crime is exceptionally high, however, drives a shift between harsh and lenient responses:

1. The cycle begins when juvenile crime is thought to be high and there are many harsh responses and a few lenient responses. Decision makers are thought to have their options limited to punishing harshly or doing nothing at all.
2. The "forced choice," of either punishing too harshly or too leniently, is identified as the source of juvenile crime. That is, both harsh punishments and lenient punishments are thought to cause juvenile crime.
3. A major reform introduces lenient treatment for juvenile offenders. This creates a middle ground for juvenile justice decision makers.
4. Juvenile crime is thought to be unusually high and is blamed on lenient treatments. Harsh punishments gradually expand and lenient treatments contract, and the cycle repeats itself (Bernard 1992, 4).

Bernard doubts that the problem of juvenile crime will ever be solved because improving the life chances of children would require more resources than American society is willing to expend. Americans live with juvenile crime because they are not willing to expend the resources to do something meaningful about it. Bernard's cycle predicts that in the next few decades juvenile justice policy in the United States will turn to more lenient punishments.

There is no inevitability to history, no grand determinism to the course of human events. There is at the same time lessons that can be learned from looking at history and the history of juvenile justice in particular.

Rothman interprets the "success" of the movement to establishment juvenile courts at the beginning of the twentieth century as a matter of both "conscience" and "convenience." The reformers of the Progressive Era, who have been referred to as "the Child Savers," genuinely represented "benevolent and philanthropic-minded men and women." They proposed to solve the problems of youth crime by a case-by-case approach and promoted a legal mechanism, the juvenile court, to deliver it. That the juvenile court as an institution gave tremendous discretionary authority to public officials to bring the power of the government to bear upon youth and their parents did not matter. They believed that the juvenile court judge, along with a staff of probation officers and social workers, could deliver both sanction and intervention at the same time. Their reforms succeeded in the sense that they were widely accepted by juvenile court judges, probation officers, and administrators who welcomed increased authority and fewer legal restrictions on their authority; their reforms were "convenient" to implement. The convenience aspect of the juvenile court led to its own undoing by the U.S. Supreme Court about half a century later.

Summarizing the reformers' efforts, Rothman writes: "In the end, when conscience and convenience met, convenience won. When treatment and coercion met, coercion won" (Rothman 1980, 10). Commenting on the creation of *parens patriae* juvenile justice and its later demise, the University of Alabama's John C. Watkins comments: "What is so amazing is that it took the judiciary nearly seventy years to come to the realization that even benevolent power can be egregiously misused" (Watkins 1998, 250).

Summary

The juvenile court founded in Cook County, Illinois, a century ago no longer exists. Beginning in 1967, the U.S. Supreme Court began a process that has made juvenile court procedures virtually indistinguishable from criminal court. The Illinois legislature has overhauled the state's juvenile court, replacing the court's mission of rehabilitation with that of community safety. State statutes also replaced the language of juvenile court with the more familiar language of criminal court.

Currently there is a national debate about whether the juvenile court ought to be abolished altogether. The abolitionists argue:

- The conception of the juvenile court as a social welfare institution in a legal setting is fatally flawed.
- Juveniles are entitled to due process and would receive greater due process in criminal court anyway.
- The concept of "delinquency" and the view of "adolescence" on which it was based no longer exists.

The preservationists defend the court: They argue:

- The failure of the juvenile court can be attributed to incomplete implementation, not conceptualization.
- As bad as the juvenile court might be in promoting due process, the criminal court will not do any better.
- The court works for most juveniles and ought not be abolished in an attempt to deal more harshly with the few violent juvenile offenders.

The public appears to agree with arguments from each side; many citizens favor prevention efforts and transfer of some juvenile offenders to adult court. The public does want change and lawmakers are responding to what they perceive as a willingness to abandon the juvenile court altogether.

The Juvenile Court's Centennial in 1999 occasioned a re-affirmation of the juvenile court. Preservationists have argued that the United States ought to ratify the United Nations Conventions on the Rights of the Child; adopt a comprehensive approach to juvenile justice uniting the efforts of social service, mental health, and juvenile court interventions; and expend greater resources on the juvenile court to carry out needed reforms. Both abolitionists and preservationists have offered alternative visions of the twenty-first century juvenile court including family court, family bankruptcy court, an integrated criminal court, and multi-court youth justice. Which of these models will emerge as the model for the juvenile court's next century is impossible to say. It is possible to identify several themes and trends that will shape juvenile court reforms in the next few years, which are: accountability, prevention, community, integration, convergence, and youth crime.

Most likely, the juvenile court will survive if for no other reason than "bureaucratic inertia"—the juvenile court is enmeshed in an array of government and private interests that make abolishing it an act of tremendous political will. From a historical perspective, the current changes proposed by reformers are not unique. To some extent, the reforms follow a predictable cycle. One lesson that can be learned from the court's history is that power, even benevolent power, can be misused.

KEY CONCEPTS

accountability
adolescence
community
comprehensive juvenile
  justice
family bankruptcy court
family court

fundamental flaw
integrated criminal court
integration
Janiculum project
juvenile crime
juvenile justice standards
low self-control

multi-court youth justice
prevention
U.N. Declaration
Violent and Repeat Juvenile
  Offender Accountability
  & Rehabilitation Act
  of 1999

DISCUSSION QUESTIONS

1. Will the juvenile court survive? Explain your thinking.

2. What does your community think about the future of juvenile court?

3. Discuss what an alternative to juvenile court would be if the court were abolished.

EXERCISE

Disposition

You have graduated and taken a position as a juvenile probation officer. Tamra, one of the juveniles on your caseload, is due to appear for disposition at a hearing in juvenile court tomorrow. Prepare your recommendation for the judge. Make it as practical and realistic as you can. Be prepared to answer questions from the judge about what you recommend. Then, prepare a second recommendation describing the ideal situation. In this recommendation, describe your vision of an ideal juvenile court.

Fifteen-year-old Tamra has been picked up by the sheriff's department for the third time in two months for behavior "beyond parental control." Twice she stayed out all night with "a friend" until law enforcement found her and brought her home. She was intoxicated on both occasions. She was intoxicated on the third occasion when a sheriff's deputy found her at a trailer belonging to a single man.

Tamra performs poorly in school and expresses hostility toward teachers and authority figures. She had a reputation among other students for being promiscuous and angry. After being suspended for fighting, she ran away for two days. Tamra's mother Jackie is well-known to the sheriff's department. They have been to her home three times during the past year in response to domestic violence. Jackie received a domestic protection order prohibiting her spouse of seven years, Mark, from returning home. She has filed for divorce from Mark with the help of Legal Services. Jackie appears to care for Tamra, and two younger children. She has told the Department for Social Services that Mark physically abuses Tamra and the children but the DSS investigation could not substantiate her claims. Jackie admits to alcohol abuse and to a boyfriend who stays in her home overnight several nights a month. She has agreed to attend a 12-step program because she might be pregnant.

Tamra has hostile feelings toward Jackie. She says that her mother has no reason to know her business and has threatened Jackie with physical violence in the presence of a social worker. She says she wants to live with her dad Mark and will run away again in an attempt to find him. Tamra denies that Mark has ever abused her. She says the only friend she has is the man she stayed with on at least the one occasion.

REFERENCES

Abadinski, A. (1991). *Law and justice.* Chicago: Nelson-Hall.

Abell, Richard B. (1989). A federal perspective on victim assistance in the United States of America. In Viano, Emilio C. (ed.), *Crime and its victims: International research and public policy issues.* New York: Hemisphere.

Adams, Anthony Troy (1994). *The economic determinants of high school punishment: A travesty of justice.* Paper presented at the annual meeting of the Eastern Sociological Society, March 17–20, 1994, Baltimore.

———. The status of school discipline and violence. *Annals of the American Academy of Political and Social Science, 567,* 140.

Adler, Christine, and Wundersitz, Joy (1994). New directions in juvenile justice reform in Australia. In Adler, Christine and Wundersitz, Joy (eds.), *Family conferencing and juvenile justice: The way forward or misplaced optimism.* Canberra: Australian Institute of Criminology.

Adler, Freda (1975). *Sisters in crime.* New York: McGraw-Hill.

Ageton, Suzanne, and Elliott, Delbert (1978). *The incidence of delinquent behavior in a national probability sample.* Boulder, CO: Behavioral Research Institute.

Agnew, Robert (2001). *Juvenile delinquency: Causes and control.* Los Angeles: Roxbury.

———. (1995). Controlling delinquency: Recommendations from general strain theory. In Barlow, Hugh D. (ed.), *Crime and public policy: Putting theory to work.* Boulder, CO: Westview.

Agnew, Robert, and White, Helen Raskin (November 30, 1992). An empirical test of general strain theory. *Criminology,* 475–499.

Ainsworth, Janet E. (1991). Re-Imaging childhood and reconstructing the legal order: The case for abolishing the juvenile court, *North Carolina Law Review 69* 1083–1132.

———. (1996). The court's effectiveness in protecting the rights of juveniles in delinquency cases, *The future of children* [David and Lucille Packard Foundation] 6 67–68.

Albanese, Jay (1993). *Dealing with delinquency: The future of juvenile justice* (2nd Ed.). Chicago: Nelson-Hall.

Albert, Geoffrey P., and Dunham, Roger (1992). *Policing urban America.* Prospect Heights, IL: Waveland Press.

Albrecht, Hans-Jörg (1997). Juvenile crime and juvenile law in the Federal Republic of Germany. In Winterdyk, John (ed.), *Juvenile justice systems: International perspectives.* Toronto: Canadian Scholars Press, 236–239.

Alex, Nicholas (1996). *Black in blue: A study of the negro policeman.* New York: Appleton-Century-Crofts.

Aliosi, Michael F. (1992). Emerging trends and issues in juvenile justice. In Hartjen, Clayton A., and Rhine, Edward E. (eds.), *Correctional theory and practice.* Chicago: Nelson-Hall.

Allen, Harry, and Simonsen, Clifford. (1992). *Corrections in America* (6th Ed.). New York: Macmillan.

Alley, Betty Gene, and Wilson, John T. (1994). *North Carolina juvenile justice system: A history 1868–1993.* Raleigh: North Carolina Administrative Office of the Courts.

Allport, Gordon (1954). *The nature of prejudice.* New York: Addison-Wesley.

Alpert, Geoffrey P., and Dunham, Roger G. (1966). *Policing urban America.* Prospect Heights, IL: Waveland Press.

———. (1999). The force factor: Measuring and assessing police use of force and suspect resistance. In *Use of force by police.* Washington, DC: National Institute of Justice/Bureau of Justice Statistics.

Altschuler, David M., and Armstrong, Troy L. (1996). Aftercare, not afterthought: Testing the IAP model. *Juvenile Justice 3,* 15–17.

American Bar Association presidential working group on the unmet legal needs of children and their families. *America's children at risk: A national agenda for legal action.* Chicago: American Bar Association, 1993, 60.

American Correctional Association (1993). *Female offenders.* Baltimore: United Book Press.

Amnesty International (1989). *When the state kills . . . The death penalty: A human rights issue.* New York: Amnesty International Publications.

Anderson, Bjorkqvist, Niemela, Kaj, and Niemela, Pirkko (1992). *Of mice and women.* New York: Academic Press.

Andrews, Chyrl (2000). OJJDP tribal youth program. *Journal of the Office of Juvenile Justice and Delinquency Prevention. VII 2,* 9–30.

Appleby, Earl E. (1999). An evolving juvenile court: On the front lines with Judge J. Dean Lewis, *Juvenile Justice 6,* 11.

———. (1997). Making a difference: On the front lines with OJJDP administrator Shay Bilchik, *Juvenile Justice 4*, 2, 5.

Appleson, Robert (1991). *Comments on "Crime and its victims."* Highland Heights: Northern Kentucky University.

Argerslinger v Hamillin 407 U.S. 25 (1972).

Armstrong, Troy L. (1981). *Intensive interventions with high-risk youths: Promising approaches.* Monsey, NY: Criminal Justice Press.

Arnold, Elizabeth, Smith, Thomas, Harrison, Dianne, and Springer, David (1998). The effects of an abstinence-based sex education program on middle school students' knowledge and beliefs. *Research on Social Work Practice 9*(1), 10–24.

Asante, Molefi (1988). *Afrocentricity.* Trenton, NJ: African World Press, Inc.

Ascher, Carol (1994). Gaining control of violence in the schools. *ERIC Digests.* Report #EDO-UD. 94(6), 1. Washington, DC: NEA.

Asquith, Stewart (1998). Juvenile justice and juvenile delinquency in central and eastern Europe, *Children's Legal Rights Journal 18*, 39.

Astin, Helen, and Lindholm, Jennifer (2001). Academic aspirations and degree attainment of women. In Worell, Judith (ed.), *Encyclopedia of women and gender: Sex similarities and differences and the impact of society on gender.* San Diego: Academic Press. Vol. I, 15–27.

Austin, Regina (1992). The black community, its lawbreakers, and a politics of identification, *Southern California Law Review 65*, 1769–1817.

Babb, Barbara (1998). Where we stand: An analysis of America's family law adjudicatory systems and the mandate to establish family courts, *Family Law Quarterly 32*, 35–37.

Badwound, Barbara (2000). American Indian youth outnumber others in justice system. *Indian Country News.* Washington, DC: Aboriginal Youth Network.

Bandura, Albert (1977). *Social learning theory.* Englewood Cliffs, NJ: Prentice Hall.

Barnes, Jessica, and Bennett, Claudette (2001). Census 2000 brief. Washington, DC: U.S. Web site of Department of Commerce: www.census.gov

Barnes, L. Diane (1999). Southern artisans, organizations, and the rise of a market economy in antebellum Petersburg. *The Virginia Magazine of History and Biography 107*(2), 159–188.

Barnes, Patricia (1996). It may take a village . . . or a specialized court to address family problems, *American Bar Association Journal 82*, 22.

Basow, Susan (2001). Androcentrism. In Worell, Judith (ed.), *Encyclopedia of women and gender: Sex simi-*

larities and differences and the impact of society on gender. San Diego: Academic Press. Vol. I, 125–135.

Bass, L. (1995). *African American nurturing program.* Park City, UT: Family Development Resources, Inc.

Bass, L., and Moody, D. (1993). *African American nurturing.* Park City, UT: Family Development Resources, Inc.

Bastian, Lisa A., and Taylor, Bruce M. Young black male victims. *National crime victimization survey.* Washington, DC: Bureau of Justice Statistics, 1994.

Bavolek, Stephen (1984). *Adult-adolescent parenting inventory.* Park City, UT: Family Development Resources, Inc.

———. (1988a). *Nurturing program for parents and adolescents.* Park City, UT: Family Development Resources, Inc.

———. (1988b). *Nurturing programs for parents and adolescents: Adolescent handbook.* Park City, UT: Family Development Resources, Inc.

———. (1989). *Research and validation report of the Adult-Adolescent Parenting Inventory (AAPI).* Eau Claire, WI: Family Development Resources, Inc.

———. (1990a). *Research and validation report of the nurturing programs: Effective family-based approaches to treating and preventing child abuse and neglect.* Eau Claire, WI: Family Development Resources, Inc.

———. (1990b). *Research validation report of the nurturing programs.* Eau Claire, WI: Family Development Resources, Inc.

Bazemore, Gordon (1991). New concepts and alternative practice in community supervision of juvenile offenders: Rediscovering work experience and competency development. *Journal of Crime and Justice 14*, 27–52.

———. (1994). Understanding the response to reforms limiting discretion: Judges' views of restrictions on detention intake, *Justice Quarterly 11*, 429–452.

———. (1997). What's new about the balanced approach? *Juvenile and Family Court Journal 48*, 1.

———. (1998). A vision for community juvenile justice, *Juvenile and Family Court Journal 49*, 77.

Bazemore, Gordon, and Day, Susan E. (1998). Restoring the balance: Juvenile and community justice. *Juvenile Justice 3*, 6.

Bazemore, Gordon, and Feder, Lynette (1997). Judges in the punitive juvenile court: Organizational, career and ideological influences on sanctioning orientation, *Justice Quarterly 14*, 87–114.

Bazemore, Gordon, and Senjo, Scott (1997). Police encounters with juveniles revisited, *Policing 20*, 67.

Bechtel, H. Kenneth (1995). *State police in the United States.* Westport, CT: Greenwood Press.

Becker, Howard. (1963). *Outsiders: Studies in the sociology of deviance.* New York: Free Press.

Beckwith, Jon (1985). Social and political uses of genetics in the United States: Past and present. In Marsh, Frank H., and Katz, Janet (eds.), *Biology, crime, and ethics.* Cincinnati: Anderson.

Bedau, H. (1997). *The death penalty in America.* New York: Oxford University Press.

Belknap, Joanne (2000).*The invisible woman: Gender, crime, and justice* (2nd Ed.). Belmont, CA: Wadsworth.

Belsky, Jay, and Eggebeen, David (November 1991). Early and extensive maternal employment and young children's socioemotional development: Children of the national longitudinal survey of youth. *Journal of Marriage and the Family 53*(4), 1083–1098.

Bernard, Thomas J. (1992). *The cycle of juvenile justice.* New York: Oxford University Press.

Berryman-Fink, Cynthia (1994). In Turner, L. H., and Sterk, H. M. (eds.), Communication competencies of women employees: A comparison of self-ratings with other ratings, *Differences that make a difference: Examining the assumptions in gender research.* 5–11. Westport, CN: Greenwood.

Berube, Lionel. (1999). Dream work: Demystifying dreams using a small group for personal growth. *Journal for Specialists in Group Work 24*(1), 88–101.

Beyer, Margaret (1996). Juvenile boot camps don't make sense, *Criminal Justice 10,* 1–3.

Bierne, Piers (1993). *Inventing Criminology.* Albany: State University of New York Press.

Bilchik, Shay (1998). A juvenile justice system for the twenty-first century. *Juvenile justice bulletin.* Washington, DC: Office of Juvenile Justice and Delinquency Prevention.

Billingsley, Andrew (1968). *Black families in white America.* Englewood Cliffs, NJ: Prentice Hall.

———. (1994). *Climbing Jacob's ladder: The enduring legacy of African American families.* Westport, CT: Touchstone.

Binder, Arnold, Geis, Gilbert, and Bruce, Dickson (1997). *Juvenile delinquency.* Cincinnati: Anderson.

Binder, Arnold, and Polan, Susan L. (1991). The Kennedy-Johnson years, social theory, and federal policy in the control of juvenile delinquency. *Crime and Delinquency 37,* 243–244.

Bing, Leon (1991). *Do or die.* New York: Harper-Collins.

Bishop, D., Frazier, C., and Henretta, J. (1989). Prosecutorial waiver: Case study of a questionable reform, *Crime and Delinquency 35,* 179–201.

Bissada, Angela, and Briere, John (2001). Child abuse: Physical and sexual. In Worell, Judith (ed.), *Encyclopedia of women and gender: Sex similarities and differences and the impact of society on gender.* San Diego: Academic Press. Vol. I, 219–231.

Block, Nadine (2000). Abandon the rod and save the children. *Humanist 60*(2), 4–5.

Blumstein, Alfred P., Farrington, David P., and Moitra, Soumyo. (1985). Delinquency careers: Innocents, amateurs, and persisters, *Crime and Justice: An Annual Review 6,* 187–220.

Blustein, Jeffrey (1983). On the doctrine of *parens patriae. Criminal Justice Ethics* 2(2), 39–47.

Bowker, L., and Klein, Malcolm (1983). The etiology of female juvenile delinquency and gang membership: A test of psychological and social structural explanations. *Adolescence 18*(72), 739–751.

Bowker, Lee H. (1981). *Women and crime in America.* New York: Macmillan.

Bradley, Scott, and Henderson, Frances (1994). A calm approach to violence in the schools, *Popular Government* [Institute of Government, University of North Carolina at Chapel Hill], *59,* 35, 37.

Bratton, William, and Knobler, Peter (1988). *Turnaround: How America's top cop reversed the crime epidemic.* New York: Random House.

Brenzel, Barbara M. (1983). *Daughters of the state: A social portrait of the first reform school for girls in North America, 1856–1905.* Cambridge, MA: MIT Press.

Brieland, Donald, and Lemmon, John (1976). *Social work and the law.* St. Paul, MN: West.

Briscoe, Judy (1997). Breaking the cycle of violence: A rational approach to at-risk youth, *Federal Probation 62,* 9–10.

Britton, Dana (2000). Feminism in criminology: Endangering the outlaw. *Annals of the American Academy of Political and Social Science 571,* 57–76.

Brondino, M. J., Henggeler, S. W., Rowland, M. D., Pickrel, S. G., Cuningham, P. B., and Schoenwald, S. K. (1997). Multisystemic therapy and the ethnic minority client: Culturally responsive and clinically effective. In Wilson, D. K., Rodrigue, J. R., and Taylor, W. C. (eds.), Health-promoting and health-compromising behaviors among minority adolescents. Washington, DC: APA Books, 229–250.

Brooks, Kim Crone, and Earl, James (1996). *Beyond In Re Gault: The status of juvenile defense in Kentucky.* Covington, KY: Children's Law Center.

Brown, Lee P. (ed.) (September 1989). Community policing: A practical guide for police officials, *Perspectives on Policing 12,* 1–12.

Browne, Angela, and Lichter, Erika (2000). Imprisonment in the United States. In Worell, Judith (ed.), *Encyclopedia of women and gender: Sex similarities and differences and the impact of society on gender.* San Diego: Academic Press. Vol. I, 611–623.

Browne, Zambga (1999). School suspension stats reveal startling racial disparities nationwide. *New York Amsterdam News 90*(52), 40.

Brownstein, Henry (1996). The media and the construction of random drug violence. In Inciardi, James (ed.). *Examining the justice process.* NY: Harcourt Brace College Publishers.

Brunetiere, Herve, Leguay, Denis, and Depond, Eric (January 1986). Some stages in the Freudian definition of proof of reality. *Psychologie Medicale 18*(1), 99–102.

Buckley, Ray (2000). *Dancing with a brave spirit: Telling the truth about native America 1999–2000.* Washington, DC: Native American Communications Office: www.naco.umcom.org.

Budnick, Kimberly, and Shields-Fletcher, Ellen (September 1998). What about girls? OJJDP fact sheet #84. Web site: www.ncjrs.org (for free copy: 1-800-851-3420).

Bureau of Justice Assistance (1995). *Drug abuse resistance education (D.A.R.E). Bureau of Justice Assistance fact sheet.* Washington, DC: U.S. Department of Justice.

Bureau of Justice Statistics (1993). *Highlights from twenty years of surveying crime victims.* Washington, DC: U.S. Department of Justice, 36–37.

———. (1999). *Local police departments, 1997.* Washington, DC: US Department of Justice.

Burwell, N. Yolanda (1995). Shifting the historical lens: Early economic empowerment among African Americans. *Journal of Baccalaureate Social Work 1,* 25–37.

———. (1996). Lawrence Oxley and locality development: Black self-help in North Carolina, 1925–1928. In Carlton-Laney, Iris, and Burwell, N. Yolanda (eds.), *African American community practice models: Historical and contemporary responses.* New York: Haworth Press.

Butts, Jeffrey A., and Halemba, Gregory (1994). Delays in juvenile justice: Findings from a national survey, *Juvenile and Family Court Journal 45,* 31–46.

Butts, Jeffrey A., and Harrell, Adele V. (1998). *Delinquents or criminals: Policy options for young offenders.* Washington, DC: The Urban Institute, 8.

Butts, Jeffrey A., and Sickmund, Melissa (1992). *Offenders in juvenile court 1989.* Washington, DC: U.S. Department of Justice.

Butts, Jeffrey A., and Snyder, Howard N. (1992). Restitution and juvenile recidivism. *OJJDP update on research.* Washington, DC: Office of Juvenile Justice and Delinquency Prevention.

Caldwell, Robert (1965). *Criminology.* New York: Ronald Press.

Calhoun, James F., and Acocella, Joan R. (1978). *Psychology of adjustment and human relationships.* New York: Random House.

Campbell, Anne (1995). Female participation in gangs. In Klein, Malcolm, Maxson, Cheryl L., and Miller, Jody (eds.), *The modern gang reader.* Los Angeles: Roxbury.

Campbell, James M. (1986). Is there historical evidence of respect for the police in North Carolina? *North Carolina Criminal Justice Letter and Review 4,* 6–7.

Caplan, Paula (2001). Motherhood: Its changing face. In Worell, Judith (ed.), *Encyclopedia of women and gender: Sex similarities and differences and the impact of society on gender.* San Diego: Academic Press. II, 783–794.

Carlson, Margaret (June 23, 1997). Prom nightmare. *Time,* 42.

Carlton, J. Phil (1979). *The final report of the Juvenile Code Revision Committee.* Raleigh, NC: Governor's Crime Commission.

Carter, Dan (1984). *Scottsboro: A tragedy of the American South* (2nd Ed.). Baton Rouge: LSU Press.

Carter, David L. (1995). Community policing and D.A.R.E.: A practitioner's perspective, *Bureau of Justice Statistics Bulletin.* Washington, DC: U.S. Department of Justice.

Cecelski, David, and Tyson, Timothy (eds.) (1998). *Democracy betrayed: The Wilmington race riot of 1898 and its legacy.* Chapel Hill: University of North Carolina Press.

Chaiken, Jan R. (1998). Kids, cops, and communities, *NIJ Issues and Practices.* Washington, DC: National Institute of Justice.

Chambliss, William J. (1996). The saints and the roughnecks. In Berger, Ronald J. (ed.), *The sociology of juvenile delinquency.* Chicago: Nelson-Hall.

Chemers, Betty M. (1995). Bridging the child welfare and juvenile justice systems, *Juvenile justice bulletin.* Washington, DC: Office of Juvenile Justice and Delinquency Prevention.

Chesney-Lind, Meda, and Shelden, Randall G. (1998). *Girls, delinquency, and juvenile justice* (2nd Ed.). Belmont, CA: Wadsworth.

Chilton, Roland, Teske, Raymond, and Arnold, Harold (1995). Ethnicity, race, and crime: German and non-German suspects, 1960–1990. In Hawkins, Darnell F. (ed.), *Ethnicity, race and crime: Perspectives across time and place.* Albany: State University of New York Press.

Chin, Ko Lin (2000). *Chinatown gangs: Extortion, enterprise, and ethnicity.* New York: Oxford University Press.

Chodorow, Nancy (1978). *The reproduction of mothering: Psychoanalysis and the sociology of gender.* Berkeley: University of California Press.

———. (1991). Psychoanalytic feminism: Family structure and feminine personality. In Kourany, J., Sterba, J., and Tong, R. (eds.). *Feminist philosophies.* Englewood Cliffs, NJ: Prentice Hall. 309–322.

Chorover, Stephen (1980). *From Genesis to genocide: The meaning of human nature and the power of behavior control.* Cambridge: MIT Press.

Church, Thomas (1985). Examining local legal culture, *American Bar Foundation Research Journal.* 449–518.

Clarke, Cheryl, and Kellam, Leslie (2001). These boots are made for women. *Corrections Today 63*(1), 50–54.

Clarke, Leslie, Schmitt, Karla, Bono, Christine, Steele, Joann, and Miller, Michael (August 1998). Norplant selection and satisfaction among low-income women. *American Journal of Public Health 88*(8), 1175–1181.

Clarke, Stevens. (1998). At last, some good news about violent crime, *Popular Government 63,* 6.

Clear, Todd R. (1991). Juvenile intensive probation supervision: Theory and rationale. In Armstrong, Troy L. (ed.). *Intensive interventions with high-risk youths: Promising approaches to juvenile probation and parole.* Monsey, NY: Criminal Justice Press.

Cleary, Thomas (2000). *The essential Confucius.* New York: Harper Collins.

Clements, Robin (1996). *The Koch Crime Commission recommends changes to the Kansas juvenile justice system.* Topeka, KS: Koch Crime Institute, 3.

Clouser, Megan (1995). School-based juvenile probation. *Pennsylvania Progress* [Pennsylvania Commission on Crime and Delinquency], *2,* 1–6.

———. (1996). Intensive probation: An alternative to placement. *Pennsylvania Progress* [Pennsylvania Commission on Crime and Delinquency], *3,* 1.

Cloward, Richard, and Ohlin, Lloyd (1960). *Delinquency and opportunity.* New York: Free Press.

Clynch, Edward, and Neubauer, David (1981). Trial courts as organizations: A critique and synthesis, *Law and Policy Quarterly 3,* 69–94.

Cohen, Albert (1955). *Delinquent boys.* New York: Free Press.

Cohen, Albert, and Short, James (1968). Research on delinquent subcultures. *Journal of Social Issues 14* (20), 22.

Cole, George F. (1970). The decision to prosecute, *Law and Society Review 4,* 313–343.

Community policing strategies (1995). National Institute of Justice, Washington, DC: U.S. Department of Justice.

Comprehensive juvenile justice: A legislator's guide. Washington, DC: National Conference of State Legislatures, 1999.

Concord Telephone Company (June 1995). The training school prior to 1959. *Progress,* 25.

Conley, Darlene J. (1994). Adding color to a black and white picture: Using qualitative data to explain racial disproportionality in the juvenile justice system, *Journal of Research in Crime and Delinquency 31,* 135–148.

Connelly, Linda (1998). What happened to electronic monitoring? *Perspectives* [American Probation and Parole Association], *22,* 10.

Cooper, N. Lee, Puritz, Patricia, and Shang, Wendy (1998). Fulfilling the promise of *In Re Gault*: Advancing the role of lawyers for children, *Wake Forest Law Review 33,* 658–660.

Corbett, R., Fitzgerald, B., and Jordan, J. (1996). Boston's Operation Night Light: An emerging model for police-probation partnerships. In *Invitation to change: Better government competition on public safety.* Boston: Pioneer Institute for Public Policy Research.

Costellano, Thomas (1986). The justice model in the juvenile justice system: Washington state's experience. *Law and Policy 8,* (4).

Cothern, Lynn (2000). Juveniles and the death penalty. *Coordinating council on juvenile justice and delinquency prevention.* Washington, DC: Office of Juvenile Justice and Delinquency Prevention.

Crawford, Donna, and Bodine, Richard (1996). *Conflict resolution education: A guide to implementing programs in schools, youth-serving organizations, and community and juvenile justice settings.* Washington, DC: Office of Juvenile Justice and Delinquency Prevention.

Crawford, Kay (Fall 1998). More than "broken windows": A house in danger of collapse, *American Outlook,* 62–64.

Crime Prevention Coalition (1990). *Crime prevention in America: Foundations for action.* Washington, DC: National Crime Prevention Council.

Crippen, Gary L. (1998). The juvenile court's next century—Getting past the ill-founded talk of abolition, *Journal of Constitutional Law 2,* 1–19.

Crowe, Jeffrey J., Escott, Paul D., and Hatley, Flora J. (1992). A *history of African Americans in North Carolina.* Raleigh: Division of Archives and History, North Carolina Department of Cultural Resources.

Crowell, Michael (Summer 1996). What do North Carolinians think of their court system? *Popular Government* [Institute of Government, UNC-Chapel Hill], *61,* 31–33.

Cubberley, E. P. (1962). *Public education in the United States: A study and interpretation of American educational history.* Cambridge, MA: Riverside Press.

Culliver, Concetta (1993). *Female criminality.* New York: Garland.

Cummins, Jim. (September 1988). Teachers are not miracle workers: Lloyd Dunn's call for Hispanic activism. *Hispanic Journal of Behavioral Sciences 10* (3), 263–272.

Curran, Debra (1983). Judicial discretion and defendant's sex. *Criminology 21*(1), 41–58.

Dahl, E. Kirsten (1996). The concept of penis envy revisited: A child analyst listens to adult women. *Psychoanalytic Study of the Child 51*, 303–325.

Davidson, Joe (April 18, 1997). Boot camps for young criminals lose favor as costs, abuse claims and recidivism pose problems. *Wall Street Journal*, A20.

Davis, Angela Y. (1981). *Women, race, and class*. New York: Vintage Books.

Davis, Samuel L. (1993–1994). The role of the attorney in child advocacy, *Journal of Family Law 32*, 817–822.

Dawson, Robert O. (1990). The future of juvenile justice: Is it time to abolish the system? *Journal of Criminal Law and Criminology 81*, 136.

Dedel, Kelly (1998). National profile of the organization of state juvenile corrections systems. *Crime and Delinquency 44*, 509–511.

DeFrances, Carol J. (1998). *Prosecutors in state courts, 1996*. Washington, DC: Bureau of Justice Statistics.

DeFrances, Carol J., and Strom, Kevin J. (1997). *Juveniles prosecuted in state criminal courts*. Washington, DC: Bureau of Justice Statistics.

DeJong, William (1994). School-based violence prevention: From the peaceable school to the peaceable neighborhood. *National Institute for Dispute Resolution Forum 25*, 8–14.

Del Carmen, Rolando V., Parker, Mary, and Reddington, Frances P. (1998). *Briefs of leading cases in juvenile justice*. Cincinnati: Anderson.

Department of Justice Canada (1999). A *strategy for the renewal of youth justice*. Ottawa, Ontario: Department of Justice.

Developmental Research and Programs (1993). *Risk-focused prevention using the social development strategy*. Seattle: Developmental Research and Programs.

Devine, John (1996). *Maximum security: The culture of violence in inner city schools*. Chicago: University of Chicago Press.

DiIulio, John J. (November 27, 1995). The coming of the super-predators, *Weekly Standard* [Washington, DC], 23.

DiMascio, William M. (1995). *Seeking justice: Crime and punishment in America*. New York: Edna McConnell Clark Foundation.

Division of Youth Corrections (1998). *DYC annual report*. Salt Lake City: Utah Division of Human Services.

Division of Youth Services (1997). *DYS sourcebook*. Raleigh, NC: Department of Health and Human Services.

———. (1999). *DYS annual report*, Raleigh, NC: Department of Health and Human Services.

Donziger, Steven R. (ed.) (1996). *The real war on crime: The report of the National Criminal Justice Commission*. New York: Harper Perennial.

Douglas, Marie C. (1992). Ausländer raus! Nazi raus! An observation of German skins and jugendgangen, *International Journal of Comparative and Applied Criminal Justice 16*, 133.

Drowns, Robert, and Hess, Karen (1995). *Juvenile justice*. St. Paul, MN: West.

Drug Court Clearinghouse (1988). *Juvenile and family drug courts: An overview*. Washington, DC: Drug Courts Program Office.

Du Phuoc Long, Patrick (1997). *The dream shattered*. Boston: Northeastern University Press.

Dulaney, W. Marvin (1996). *Black police in America*. Bloomington: Indiana University Press.

Dunlap, Earl L., and Roush, David W. (1995). Juvenile detention as process and place. *Juvenile and Family Court Journal 46*, 4.

Durham, Alexis M. (1994). *Crisis and reform: Current issues in American punishment*. Boston: Little, Brown.

Durkheim, Emile (1933). *The division of labor in society*. New York: Free Press.

East, Patricia (1998). Impact of adolescent childbearing on families and younger siblings: Effects that increase younger siblings' risk for early pregnancy. *Applied Developmental Science 2*(2), 62–74.

Edwards, Leonard P. (1992). The juvenile court and the role of the juvenile court judge, *Juvenile and Family Court Journal 43*(1), 25–29.

———. (1996). The future of the juvenile court: Promising new directions. *The Future of Children 6*, 131–139.

Eggebeen, David (1992). Family structure and intergenerational relations. *Research on Aging 14*(1), 427–447.

Eggleston, Carolyn (1989). *Zebulon Brockway and Elmira Reformatory: A study of correctional/special education*. Dissertation: Virginia Commonwealth University.

Eisenman, R. (Fall 1993). Characteristics of adolescent felons in a prison treatment program. *Adolescence 28*(111), 695–699.

Eisenstein, James, and Jacob, Herbert (1977). *Felony justice: An organizational analysis of criminal court process*. Boston: Little, Brown.

Empey, LaMar, and Stafford, Mark (1991). *American delinquency* (3rd Ed.). Belmont, CA: Wadsworth.

Erikson, Erik (1993). *Childhood and society*. New York: Roxbury.

Erikson, Erik, Erikson, Joan, and Kivnick, Helen (1989). *Vital involvement in old age*. New York: W. W. Norton.

Etten, Tamryn J., and Petrone, Robert F. (1994). Sharing data and information in juvenile justice: Legal, ethical, and practical considerations. *Juvenile and Family Court Journal*, 65–66.

Ezell, Mark (1992). Juvenile diversion: The ongoing search for alternatives. In Schwartz, Ira M. (ed.), *Juvenile justice and public policy: Toward a national agenda*. New York: Lexington Books, 48–49.

Faltermayer, Charlotte (April 6, 1998). What is justice for a sixth-grade killer? *Time*, 36.

Farley, Melissa (2001). Prostitution: The business of sexual exploitation. In Worell, Judith (ed.), *Encyclopedia of women and gender: Sex similarities and differences and the impact of society on gender, Vol. II.* San Diego: Academic Press, 879–891.

Farnworth, Margaret, and Eske, Raymond (1995). Gender differences in felony court processing: Three hypotheses of disparity. *Women and Criminal Justice 6* (2), 23–44.

Federal Bureau of Investigation (1997). *Uniform crime reports for the United States 1996*. Washington, DC: U.S. Department of Justice.

Federal Standards of Racial and Ethnic Classification (2000). *Executive Summary: Spotlight on Heterogeneity*, 65–66.

Feinman, Clarice (1998). *Women in the criminal justice system*. New York: Praeger.

Feld La. Rev. Stat. Ann § 905.5(f) [West 1997]; N. Car. Gen. Stat. § 15A-1340.16(e) (4) [1996].

Feld, Barry (1987). Juvenile court meets the principle of offense: legislative changes in juvenile waiver statutes, *Journal of Criminal Law and Criminology 78*, 471–533.

———. (1989). The right to counsel in juvenile court: An empirical study of when lawyers appear and the difference they make, *Journal of Criminal Law and Criminology 79*, 1189.

———. (1992). Criminalizing the juvenile court: A research agenda for the 1990s. In Schwartz, Ira, (ed.), *Juvenile justice and public policy*. New York: Lexington Books.

———. (1993a). Criminalizing the American juvenile court. In Tonry, Michael (ed.), *Crime and justice: A review of research*. Chicago: University of Chicago Press.

———. (1993b). Juvenile (in)justice and the criminal court alternative, *Crime and Delinquency 39*, 417.

———. (1995). Violent youth and public policy: A case study of juvenile justice law reform, *Minnesota Law Review*, 79.

———. (1999a). *Bad kids: Race and the transformation of the juvenile court*. New York: Oxford.

———. (1999b). Will the juvenile court system survive? The honest politician's guide to the juvenile justice in the twenty-first century, *Annals* [American Academy of Political and Social Science] *564*, 18–19.

Ferdinand, Theodore N. (1989). Juvenile delinquency or juvenile justice: Which came first? *Criminology 27*, 79–106.

Finckenauer, James O. (1992). Juvenile criminals: Punishment or reform? In Hartjen, Clayton A., and Rhine, Edward E. (eds.), *Correctional theory and practice*. Chicago: Nelson-Hall.

———. (1995). *Russian youth: Law, deviance, and pursuit of freedom*. New Brunswick, NJ: Transaction.

Fink-Adams, Kim (Spring/Summer 1998). Asheville's victim offender mediation program, *The North Carolina Mediator*, 5.

Firestone, Shulamith. (1974). *The dialectic of sex: The case for feminist revolution*. New York: William Morrow.

———. (1991). Radical feminism: The dialectic of sex. In Kourany, J., Sterba, J., and Tong, R. (eds.), *Feminist philosophies*. Englewood Cliffs, NJ: Prentice Hall.

Fishman, Laura (1995). The vice queens: An ethnographic study of black female gang behavior. In Klein, Malcolm, Maxson, Cheryl L., and Miller, Jody (eds.), *The modern gang reader*. Los Angeles: Roxbury.

Fletcher, Beverly, Shaver, Lynda Dixon, and Moon, Dreama G. (1993). *Women prisoners: A forgotten population*. Westport, CT: Praeger.

Forst, Brian (1983). Managing prosecution, *Popular Government* [Institute of Government, University of North Carolina-Chapel Hill] *48*, 1–10.

Forst, Martin, Fagan, Jeffrey, and Vivona, T. Scott (1989). Youth in prisons and training schools: Perceptions and consequences of the treatment-custody dichotomy. *Juvenile and Family Court Journal 40*, 1–15.

Fox, James W., Minor, Kevin I., and Pelkey, William L. (1994). The relationship between law-related education diversion and juvenile offenders' social and self-perceptions. *American Journal of Criminal Justice 19*, 61–77.

Frankl, Viktor (1984). *Man's search for meaning*. New York: Washington Square Press.

Frazier, Charles E., and Bishop, Donna M. (1985). The pretrial detention of juveniles and its impact on case dispositions, *Journal of Criminal Law and Criminology 76*, 1132–1152.

Fritsch, Eric, and Hemmens, Craig (1995). Juvenile waiver in the United States 1979–1995: A comparison and analysis of state waiver statutes, *Juvenile and Family Court Journal*, 23.

Fritz, Noah J., and Altheide, David L. (1987). The mass media and the social construction of the missing children problem, *Sociological Quarterly 28*, 477.

Gallegos v Colorado 370 U.S. 49 (1962).

Galton, Francis (1988). Natural abilities and the comparative worth of races. In Benjamin, Ludy Jr. (ed.), *A history of psychology: Original sources and contemporary research.* New York: McGraw-Hill, 248–252.

Gang intelligence. *Police training manual* (2001). Gang awareness training, Vance-Granville Community College, NC Justice Academy.

Gang resistance education and training, *Promising Strategies.* OJJDP, 59–60.

Gangs 2000 Report. California Department of Justice, Bureau of Investigation, Intelligence Operations Program. Sacramento, CA: California Department of Justice.

Garrett, Carol J. (1985). Effects of residential treatment on adjudicated delinquents: A meta-analysis. *Journal of Research in Crime and Delinquency 22,* 7–44.

Geden, E., Lower, M., Beattie, and S., Beck, N. (1989). Effects of music and imagery on physiologic and self-report of analogued labor pain. *Nursing Research 38*(1), 37–41.

Geis, Gilbert, and Binder, Arnold (1991). Sins of their children. Parental responsibility for juvenile delinquency. *Notre Dame Journal of Law, Ethics, and Policy 5,* 303–322.

Georges-Abeyie, Daniel (1984). Black police officers: An interview with Alfred W. Dean, Director of Public Safety, City of Harrisburg, Pennsylvania. In Georges-Abeyie, Daniel (ed.), *The criminal justice system and blacks.* New York: Clark Boardman, 161–162.

Giallombardo, Rose (1974). *The social world of imprisoned girls.* New York: John Wiley and Sons.

Gibbs, Nancy (April 17, 2000). Give me back my son. *Time 15,* 24–33.

Gideon v Wainwright 372 U.S. 335 (1963).

Glasser, William (1965). *Reality therapy.* New York: Harper and Row.

———. (1972). *The identity society.* New York: Harper and Row.

Glueck, Sheldon, and Glueck, Eleanor (1950). *Unraveling juvenile delinquency.* Cambridge, MA: Harvard University Press.

Godwin, Tracy (1996). *Peer justice and youth empowerment: An implementation guide for teen court programs.* Washington, DC: American Probation and Parole Association.

Goldkamp, John S. (1994). Miami's treatment drug court for felony defendants: Some implications of assessment findings, *Prison Journal 73,* 110–116.

Golub, Andrew L., and Johnson, Bruce D. (1997). *Crack's decline: Some surprises across U.S. cities.* Washington, DC: U.S. Department of Justice.

Gottfredson, Michael R., and Hirschi, Travis (1990). *A general theory of crime.* Stanford, CA: Stanford University Press.

Gould, Stephen Jay (1981). *The mismeasure of man.* New York: W. W. Norton.

Government of Japan (1997). *Summary of the white paper on crime 1996.* Tokyo: Ministry of Justice.

Gray, Ernestine S. (1999). Juvenile court system as it enters the twenty-first century: What should it look like, *Juvenile and Family Court Journal 50,* 29–30.

Gray, Jeffrey P. (1998). Company police in North Carolina: Much more than "rent-a-cops," *Popular Government* [Institute of Government, UNC-CH] *62,* 25–37.

Greenbaum, Stewart (1997). Kids and guns: From playgrounds to battlegrounds. *Juvenile Justice 3,* 3.

Greenberg, David (1999). Students have always been violent: They're just better armed today. *Slate.* Web site: www.slate.com.

Greenwood, Peter W. (1995). Juvenile crime and juvenile justice. In Wilson, James Q., and Petersilia, Joan (eds.), *Crime.* San Francisco: ICS Press.

———. (1996). Responding to juvenile crime: Lessons learned, *The future of children* [The David and Lucile Packard Foundation], *6,* 75–76.

———. (1998). Investing in prisons or prevention: The state policy makers' dilemma. *Crime and Delinquency 44,* 139.

Greenwood, Peter W., and Turner, Susan (1993). Private presentence reports for serious juvenile offenders: Implementation issues and impacts, *Justice Quarterly 10,* 231.

Grenfield, Patricia. (1998). The cultural evolution of IQ. In Neisser, Ulric (ed.), *The rising curve: Long-term gains in IQ and related measures.* Washington, DC: American Psychological Association.

Grennan, Sean, Britz, Marjie, Rusk, Jeffrey, and Barker, Thomas (2001). *Gangs: An international approach.* Upper Saddle River, NJ: Prentice Hall.

Grier, William H., and Cobbs, Price M. (2000). *Black rage* (2nd Ed.). New York: Basic Books/Harper Collins.

Guarino-Ghezzi, Susan (1994). Reintegrative police surveillance of juvenile offenders: Forging an urban model, *Crime and Delinquency 40,* 131–153.

Guarino-Ghezzi, Susan, and Loughran, Edward J. (1996). *Balancing juvenile justice.* New Brunswick, NJ: Transaction Publishers, 1996, 80–81.

Guggenheim, Martin (1996). A paradigm for determining the role of counsel for children, *Fordham Law Review 64,* 1399.

Hadr, Uri (1999). Bold analysis and associative dialogue: Freedom and continuity in analytic dialogue. *Psychoanalytic Dialogues 9*(1), 109–127.

Haghighi, Bahram, and Lopez, Alma (1993). Success/failure of group home treatment programs for juveniles. *Federal Probation 57,* 53–58.

Hahn, Paul (1998). *Emerging criminal justice: Three pillars for a proactive system*. Thousand Oaks, CA: Sage.

Hale, Robert (1997). A *review of juvenile executions in America*. Lewiston, NY: The Edwin Mellen Press.

Haley, John O. (1989). Confession, repentance and absolution. In Wright, Martin, and Galaway, Burt (eds.), *Mediation and criminal justice: Victims, offenders and community*. Newbury Park, CA: Sage, 195–196.

Hamm, Mark (1998). Images of crime and punishment: The laundering of white crime. In Mann, Coramae, and Zatz, Majorie (eds.), *Images of color, images of crime*. Los Angeles: Roxbury, 244–270.

Hamparian, D., Estep, L., Muntean, S., Priestino, R., Swisher, R., Wallace, P., and White, J. (1982). *Youth in adult courts: Between two worlds*. Washington, DC: Office of Juvenile Justice and Delinquency Prevention.

Haney, Craig, and Zimbardo, Philip (June 1975). It's tough to tell a high school from a prison. *Psychology Today 26,* 29–30.

Harrell, Adele (1998). *Drug courts and the role of graduated sanctions*. Washington, DC: National Institute of Justice.

Harrell, Adele Foster Cook, and Carver, John (1998). Breaking the cycle of drug abuse in Birmingham, *National Institute of Justice Journal 236,* 9–13.

Hartmann, Heidi (1992). The unhappy marriage of Marxism and feminism: Towards a more progressive union. In Kourany, J., Sterba, J., and Tong, R., *Feminism philosophies*. Englewood Cliffs, NJ: Prentice Hall, 343–355.

Harvey, Elizabeth (1999). Short term and long term effects of early parental employment on children of the national longitudinal survey of youths. *Journal of Developmental Psychology 35*(2), 445–459.

Hawkins, J. David (1995). Controlling crime before it happens: Risk-focused prevention. *National Institute of Justice Journal 229,* 10.

Hawkins, J. David, Herrenkohl, Todd I., Farrington, David P., Brewer, Devon, Catalano, Richard F., Harachi, Tracy W., and Cuthern, Lynn (April 2000). Predictors of youth violence, *Juvenile Justice Bulletin.* Washington, DC: Department of Justice.

Hayes, Lindsay M. (1994). Juvenile suicide in confinement: An overview and summary of one system's approach. *Juvenile and Family Court Journal 45,* 67–68.

Henderson, Eric, Kunitz, Stephen, and Levy, Jerrold (1999). The origins of Navajo youth gangs. *American Indian Culture and Research Journal 23*(3), 243–364.

Hengesh, Donald J. (October 1991). Think of boot camps as a foundation for change, not an instant cure. *Corrections Today,* 106.

Henggeler, S., Schoenwald, S. K., Borduin, C., Rowland, M. D., and Cuningham, P. B. (1998). *Multisystemic treatment of antisocial behavior in children and adolescents*. New York: Guildford Press.

Henggeler, Scott (1997). Treating serious antisocial behavior in youth: The MST approach. *Juvenile Justice Bulletin.* Washington, DC: U.S. Department of Justice, Office of Juvenile Justice and Delinquency Prevention.

Hepper, P. G. (1991). An examination of fetal learning before and after birth. *Irish Journal of Psychology 12* (2), 95–107.

Herrenstein, Richard, and Murray, Charles (1994). *The bell curve: Intelligence and class structure in American life*. New York: The Free Press.

Herring, David J. (1998). Legal representation for the state child welfare agency in civil child protection proceedings: A comparative study. *University of Toledo Law Review,* 608.

Hill, Robert (1992). Strengths of the black family. In Billingsley, Andrew, and McAdoo, Harriette (eds.). *The black family* (2nd Ed.). Newbury Park, CA: Sage Publications.

Hirschi, Travis (1969). *Causes of delinquency*. Berkeley: University of California Press.

Hirschi, Travis, and Gottfredson, Michael (1996). Rethinking the juvenile justice system. In James A. Inciardi (ed.), *Examining the justice process*. Fort Worth: Harcourt Brace College Publishers.

Hirschi, Travis, and Hindelang, Michael (1977). Intelligence and delinquency: A revisionist review. *American Sociological Review 42,* 471–587.

Holden, Gwen A., and Kepler, Robert A. (1995). Deinstitutionalizing status offenders: A record of progress. *Juvenile Justice 2,* 3–10.

Hooton, Ernest A. (1979). The American criminal. In Joseph E. Jacoby (ed.), *Classics of criminology.* Prospect Heights, IL: Waveland Press.

Hora, Peggy F., Schma, William G., and Rosenthal, John T. (1999). Therapeutic jurisprudence and the drug treatment court movement: Revolutionizing the criminal justice system's response to drug abuse and crime in America, *Notre Dame Law Review 74,* 53.

Howell, James C. (ed.) (1995). *Guide for implementing the comprehensive strategy for serious, violent and chronic juvenile offenders*. Washington, DC: Office of Juvenile Justice and Delinquency Prevention.

———. (1998). National Council of Crime and Delinquency survey of juvenile detention and correctional facilities, *Crime and Delinquency 44,* 102–109.

Howell, Susan (1998). Citizen evaluation of Louisiana's courts, *Court Column* [Supreme Court of Louisiana], *1*, 19.

Howitt, Pamela S., Moore, Eugene A., and Gaulier, Bernard (1998). Winning the battles and the wars: An evaluation of comprehensive, community-based delinquency prevention programming. *Juvenile and Family Court Journal 49*, 40–41.

Hsia, Heidi M. (1998). *Disproportionate minority confinement: 1997 update.* Washington, DC: Office of Juvenile Justice and Delinquency Prevention.

Hudson, Joe, and Galaway, Burt (1989). Financial restitution: Toward an evaluable program model. *Canadian Journal of Criminology 31*, 1–18.

Huff, Ronald (1996). *Gangs in America.* Newbury Park, CA: Sage Publications.

Hughes, Samuel (May/June 1999). The children's crusaders, *Pennsylvania Gazette*, 27.

Hunter, Robert (1987). Law-related education practice and delinquency theory. *International Journal of Social Education 2*, 52–64.

Hurn, Won Moo (1988). *The Korean Americans.* Westport, CT: Greenwood.

Hurst, Hunter (1990). Turn of the century: Rediscovering the value of juvenile treatment. *Corrections Today*, 47–50.

———. (1999). Juvenile court—As we enter the millennium, *Juvenile and Family Court Journal 50*, 22.

Ice T (1994). *The Ice opinion.* New York: St. Martin's Press.

———. (1995). The killing fields. In Klein, Malcolm, Maxson, Cheryl L., and Miller, Jody (eds.), *The modern gang reader.* Los Angeles: Roxbury.

Illinois Criminal Justice Information Authority (1999). The Juvenile Justice Reform Act of 1998, *The Compiler*, 10–11.

In re C. B. 708 So. 2d 391 (La. 1998). Guggenheim, Martin and Hertz, Randy (1998). Reflections on judges, juries, and justice: Ensuring the fairness of juvenile delinquency trials, *Wake Forest Law Review 33*, 554–555.

In the Interest of S. A. W. 499 N.W.2d 739 (Iowa 1993); del Carmen et al., *Briefs of Leading Cases*, 41–43.

Inciardi, James (1992). Drug use can cause youth violence. In Bender, David, and Leone, Bruno (eds.), *Youth violence.* San Diego: Greenhaven.

Intelligence Operations Bulletin. *Gangs 2000 Report.* Part II. Vol. 10 (April 1993). Sacramento, CA: California Department of Justice.

———. *Gangs 2000 Report.* Part. III. Vol. 10 (April 1993). Sacramento, CA: California Department of Justice.

International Association of Chiefs of Police (1929). *Uniform crime reporting: A complete manual for police.* New York: IACP.

Ireland, Robert M. (1972). *The county courts in antebellum Kentucky.* Lexington: University Press of Kentucky.

Izzo, Rhena, and Ross, Robert (1990). Meta-analysis of rehabilitation programs for juvenile delinquents: A brief report. *Crime and Delinquency 17*, 139.

Jackson, Mary S. (1996). *Public safety in a multicultural society.* New York: McGraw-Hill.

James A. Baker Institute for Public Policy (1997). *Police and the African-American community: Building bridges for the future.* Houston: Rice University.

Jenkins, Philip (1984). Eugenics, crime and ideology: The case of progressive Pennsylvania. *Pennsylvania History 51*, 64–78.

Jensen, Arthur (1969). *The g factor: The science of mental abilities.* Westport, CN: Praeger, 1998.

Joe, Karen (1995). The dynamics of running away: Deinstitutionalization policies and the police. *Juvenile and Family Court Journal 46*, 50.

Johnson, Betsy (Summer 1999). On the road with a parole officer, *DYS Today* [Ohio Department of Youth Services], *1*, 4.

Johnson, Ida M. (1999). School violence: The effectiveness of a school resource officer program in a southern city. *Journal of Criminal Justice 27*, 173–192.

Johnson, J., and Secret, P. (1990). Race and juvenile court: Decision making revisited, *Criminal Justice Policy Review 4*, 159–187.

Jones-Brown, Delores D. (2000). Debunking the myth of officer friendly: How African American males experience community policing, *Journal of Contemporary Criminal Justice 16*, 209–229.

Joseph, Janice (1995). *Black youths, delinquency, and juvenile justice.* Westport, CT: Praeger.

———. (2000). Overrepresentation of minority youth in the juvenile justice system: Discrimination or disproportionality of delinquent acts. In Markowitz, Michael W., and Jones-Brown, Delores (eds.), *The system in black and white.* Westport, CT: Praeger, 233–234.

Junger, Patrick (1983). The serious young offender under Vermont's juvenile law. *Vermont Law Review 8*(1), 173–202.

Kagan, Jerome (1991). Etiologies of adolescents at risk. *Journal of Adolescent Health 12*(8), 591–596.

Kahler, Kathryn (January 14, 1993). Last chance is hard work, love. *New Orleans Times-Picayune*, A4.

Kaiser, Günther (1992). Juvenile delinquency in the Federal Republic of Germany, *International Journal of Comparative and Applied Criminal Justice 16*, 189.

Kakar, Suman (1996). *Child abuse and delinquency.* Lanham, MD: University Press of America.

Kalichman, Seth (1999). *Mandated reporting of suspected child abuse: Ethics, law and policy.* Washington, DC: American Psychological Association.

Kaplan, John, Skolnick, Jerome, and Feeley, Malcolm (1991). *Criminal justice: Introductory cases and materials* (5th Ed.). Westbury, New York: The Foundation Press.

Kasl, Charlotte (1990, November/December). The twelve-step controversy. *Ms. Magazine,* 80–81.

Kaufman, Phillip, Chen, Xianglei, Choy, Susan P., Ruddy, Sally, Miller, Amanda, Chandler, Kathryn, Chapman, Christopher, Rand, Michael, and Klaus, Patsy (1999). *Indicators of school crime and safety, 1999.* U.S. Department of Justice, National Center for Education Statistics, Bureau of Justice Statistics. NCJ-178906. Washington, DC: GPO.

Kelleher, Michael (1998). *When good kids kill.* Westport, CT: Praeger.

Kelling, George L. (1988). Police and communities: The quiet revolution. In *Perspectives on policing* (1). Washington, DC: National Institute of Justice.

Kelly, Matt (September 19, 1997). Reservation crime wave blamed on gang influence. *News Times,* Salt River, Arizona.

Kempe, C. Henry (1972). *Helping the battered child and his family.* Philadelphia: Lippincott, Williams, and Wilkins.

Kempf-Leonard, Kimberly (1998). Equity and juveniles: What is justice? *Corrections Management Quarterly 2,* 31.

Kennedy, Randall (1994). The state, criminal law, and racial discrimination: A comment, *Harvard Law Review 107,* 1255.

———. (1997). *Race, crime and the law.* New York: Vintage Books.

Kent v United States, 383 U.S. 541 (1966).

Kermode, Jennifer, and Walker, Garthine (1994). *Women, crime and the courts in early modern England.* Chapel Hill: The University of North Carolina Press.

Kertzer, Morris N. (1978). *What is a Jew?* New York: Collier Books.

Kfoury, Paul R. (1983). Confidentiality and the juvenile offender, *New Hampshire Bar Journal 24,* 135–144.

Khoury, Kathy (1998). Fighting back against Indian gangs. *Christian Science Monitor.* Web site: www.csmonitor.com.

Kim, Bryan Soo Kyung (2001). Cultural diversity and Asians. *The Korean Americans.* ERIC counseling and student services Web site: ericcass.uncg.edu.

Kimbrough, Robin J. (1998). Treating juvenile substance abuse: The promise of juvenile drug courts, *Juvenile Justice 5,* 11–12.

Kinder, Kristine, Veneziano, Carol, Fichter, Michael, and Azuma, Henry (1995). A comparison of the dispositions of juvenile offenders certified as adults with juvenile offenders not certified, *Juvenile and Family Court Journal,* 39–40.

Kirkpatrick, Jean (1989). Cited in Unterberger, Gail (December 6, 1989), Twelve steps for women alcoholics. *The Christian Century,* 1150–1152.

Klein, Ellen (1996). *Feminism under fire.* Amherst, NY: Prometheus Books.

Klein, Malcolm (1971). *Street gangs and street workers.* Englewood Cliffs, NJ: Prentice Hall.

Klinger, David A. (1996). More on demeanor and arrest in Dade County, *Criminology 34,* 61–82.

Klink, Marianne, and Crawford, Donna (1998). Conflict resolution and the arts, *OJJDP fact sheet,* Washington, DC: Office of Juvenile Justice and Delinquency Prevention.

Knepper, Paul (1989). Selective participation, effectiveness and prison college programs. *Journal of Offender Counseling, Services and Rehabilitation 14,* 113–114.

———. (1996). Race, racism and crime statistics, *Southern University Law Review 24,* 104.

———. (1997). Three decades of law related education. In Williamson, Deborah, Minor, Kevin I., and Fox, James (eds.), *Law related education and juvenile justice.* Springfield, IL: Charles C. Thomas.

———. (1999). *North Carolina's criminal justice system.* Durham, NC: Carolina Academic Press, 83–85.

Knepper, Paul E., and Barton, Shannon M. (1997). The effect of courtroom dynamics on child maltreatment proceedings, *Social Service Review 71,* 288–308.

Knepper, Paul, and Potter, David M. (1998). Crime, politics and minority populations: Use of official statistics in the United States and Japan, *International Journal of Comparative and Applied Criminal Justice 22,* 2–12.

Knox, George (2000). *An introduction to gangs* (5th Ed.). Peoria, IL: New Chicago School Press.

Kocourek, Albert, and Wigmore, John (1951). Source of ancient and punitive law, *Evolution of law: Selected readings on the origin and development of legal institutions.* Boston: Little, Brown.

Kourany, Janet, Sterba, James P., and Tong, Rosemarie (1991). *Feminist philosophies: Problems, theories, and applications.* Englewood Cliffs, NJ: Prentice Hall.

Kramer, S. N. (1963). *The Sumerians.* Chicago: University of Chicago Press.

Kriegel, Robert, and Kriegel, Marilyn (1984). *The C zone.* New York: Doubleday.

Kurlychek, Megan (1998). A new mission: Guiding Pennsylvania's juvenile justice system into the twenty-first century, *Pennsylvania Progress* [Pennsylvania Commission on Crime and Delinquency], *5,* 1–2.

———. (1999). Victim-offender conferencing in the juvenile justice system. *Pennsylvania Progress* [Pennsylvania Commission on Crime and Delinquency], *6,* 1–6.

Ladner, Joyce (1977). *Mixed families.* Garden City, NY: Anchor Press.

Lafuente, M. J., Grifol, R. R., Segarra, J., Soriano, J., Gorba, M., and Montesinos, A. (1997). Effects of the Firstart method of prenatal stimulation on psychomotor development: The first six months. *Pre- and Peri-Natal Psychology Journal 11*(3), 151–162.

Lakeoff, R. (1990). *Talking power: The politics of language in our lives.* NY: Basic Books.

———. (1991). You are what you say. In Ashton-Jones, E., and Olson, G. A. (eds.). *The gender reader,* Boston: Allyn and Bacon, 292–298.

Larison, Sue, Williamson, Deborah, and Knepper, Paul (1994). Dress rehearsal for citizenship: Using theatre to teach law related education to diverted youth. *Juvenile and Family Court Journal 45,* 55–64.

Lawrence, Richard (1998). *School, crime, and juvenile justice.* New York: Oxford University Press.

Le, Binh (2001). *Asian gangs: A bibliography.* The Pennsylvania State University, Abington-Ogontz Campus Web site: www.community.policing.org.

Leary, Mark (1999). The scientific study of personality. In Derlega, Valerian, and Winstead, Barbara (eds.), *Personality: Contemporary theory and research.* Chicago: Nelson-Hall, 3–26.

Leclaire, Thomas (February 24, 1999). Testimony of Thomas Leclaire, Director of Tribal Justice, before the U.S. Senate Committee on Indian Affairs, concerning Indian budget for fiscal year 2000. U.S. Department of Justice.

Leclerc, Annie (1991). Woman's word. In Kourany, J., Sterba, J., and Tong, R. (eds.), *Feminism Philosophies.* Englewood Cliffs, NJ: Prentice Hall, 362–371.

Lederman, Cindy S. (1999). The juvenile court: Putting research to work for prevention, *Juvenile Justice 6,* 22–31.

Lee, Bill (1999). *Chinese playground.* San Francisco: Bill Lee Associates.

Leet, Duane, Rush, George, and Smith, Anthony (1997). *Gangs, graffiti, and violence.* Cincinnati: Copperhouse.

Lehnen, Robert G., and Skogan, Wesley (eds.) (1984). *National crime survey: Working papers, Vol. 2.* Washington, DC: U.S. Department of Justice, v.

Leiber, Michael J., Nalla, Mahesh K., and Farnworth, Margaret (1998). Explaining juveniles' attitudes toward the police, *Justice Quarterly 15,* 151–174.

Leinen, Stephen (1984). *Black police, white society.* New York: New York University Press, 226–239.

Lemert, Edwin M. (1951). *Social pathology.* New York: McGraw-Hill, 1951.

Lemonick, Michael, and Goldstein, Andrea Q. (April 22, 2002). At your own risk. *Time 159*(16), 46–47.

Lerman, David (1998). Restorative justice and Jewish law. *VOMA Quarterly 9,* 2.

Lester, D. (1998). *The death penalty: Issues and answers.* Springfield, IL: Charles C. Thomas.

Lewis, J. Dean (1999). America's juvenile and family courts: 100 years of responding to troubled youth and their families, *Juvenile and Family Court Journal 50,* 3–7.

Lipkin, Rachel, and Abelson, Lillian (1997–1998). BARJ model site news, *Balanced and restorative justice project update* [Community Justice Institute, Florida Atlantic University], *2,* 4–5.

Livingstone, David (1995). For whom the bell curve tolls. *Alberta Journal of Educational Research 41*(3), 335–341.

Loconte, Joe (1977). Redd scare: A drill sergeant's brilliant assault on juvenile crime. In Meese, Edwin, and Moffit, Robert E. (eds.), *Making America safer.* Washington, DC: Heritage Foundation, 139–144.

Lombardo, Paul (April 1985). Three generations, no imbeciles: New light on *Buck v Bell. New York University Law Review 60*(1), 30–62.

Lombroso-Ferrero, Gina (1972). Criminal man, according to the classification of Cesare Lombroso. Glen Ridge, NJ: Patterson Smith.

———. (1979). Criminal man. In Jacoby, Joseph E. (ed.), *Classics of criminology.* Prospect Heights, IL: Waveland Press.

Long, Linda (1982–1983). When the client is a child: Dilemmas in the lawyer's role. *Journal of Family Law 21,* 607.

Loury, Glenn C. (1994). Listen to the black community, *The Public Interest 117,* 33–37.

Lozano, Antionette R., Mays, G. Larry, and Winfree, L. Thomas (1990). Diagnosing delinquents: The purposes of a youth diagnostic center. *Juvenile and Family Court Journal 41,* 25.

Lundman, Richard J. (1993). *Prevention and control of juvenile delinquency.* New York: Oxford University Press.

Mack, Julian (1909). The juvenile court, *Harvard Law Review 23,* 104, 107.

MacKenzie, Doris Layton, and Souryal, Claire C. (October 1991). Boot camps: Rehabilitation, recidivism reduction outrank punishment as main goals. *Corrections Today,* 90.

MacKinnon, C. (1989). *Toward a feminist theory of the state.* Cambridge: Harvard University Press.

MacKinnon, Catharine A. (1991). Pornography, civil rights, and speech. In Kourany, J., Sterba, J., and Tong, R. (eds.), *Feminist philosophies.* Englewood Cliffs, NJ: Prentice Hall.

Maltz, Michael D. (1977). Crime statistics: A historical perspective. *Crime and Delinquency 23,* 34.

Mann, Coramae Richey (1994). A minority view of juvenile justice. *Washington and Lee Law Review 51,* 468–472.

Manns, Wilhelmina (1988). Supportive roles of significant others in black families. In McAdoo, Harriette Pipes (ed.). *Black families* (2nd Ed.). Newbury Park, CA: Sage.

Marger, Martin (1997). *Race and ethnic relations.* Belmont, CA: Wadsworth.

Marketos, Alexander (1995). The constitutionality of juvenile curfews. *Juvenile and Family Court Journal 46,* 17.

Martin, Charles H. (Spring 1985). The international labor defense and black America. *Labor History,* 26.

Martin, G. (1995). Open the doors: A judicial call to end confidentiality in delinquency proceedings, *New England Journal of Criminal and Civil Confinement 21,* 393–410.

Martin, Teri K. (1994). Determinants of juvenile detention rates. In Schwartz, Ira M. and Barton, William H. (eds.), *Reforming juvenile detention: No more hidden closets.* Columbus: Ohio State University Press, 30–42.

Martinson, Robert (1974). What works? Questions and answers about prison reform. *The Public Interest 35,* 25.

Maslow, Abraham (1987). *Motivation and personality* (3rd Ed.). New York: Harper and Row.

Mass, Amy (1992). Interracial Japanese Americans: The best of both worlds or the end of the Japanese American community? In Root, Maris (ed.), *Racially mixed people in America.* Newbury Park: Sage.

Matza, David (1964). *Delinquency and drift.* New York: John Wiley and Sons.

Maxwell, Gabrielle M., and Morris, Allison (1994). The New Zealand model of family group conferences. In Adler, Christine, and Wundersitz, Joy (eds.), *Family conferencing and juvenile justice: The way forward or misplaced optimism?* Canberra: Australian Institute of Criminology.

McCarthy, F. B., and Carr, James (1980). *Juvenile law and its processes.* New York: Bobbs-Merrill.

McCleary, Richard, Neinstadt, Barbara C., and Erven, James M. (1982). Uniform crime reports as organizational outcomes: Three time-series experiments, *Social Problems 29,* 361–372.

McCollum, Sylvia (1977). What works! A look at effective correctional education and training experiences. *Federal Probation 41,* 32–35.

McConnell, James (1994). *Understanding human behavior.* New York: Thomson.

McCorkle, Richard, and Miethe, Terance (2002). *Panic: The social construction of the street gang problem.* Upper Saddle River, NJ: Prentice-Hall.

McCully, Sharon (1994). Detention reform from a judge's viewpoint. In Schwartz, Ira M. and Barton, William H. (eds.), *Reforming juvenile detention: No more hidden closets.* Columbus: Ohio State University Press, 162–173.

McMinn, M., Williams, P., and McMinn, L. (1994). Assessing recognition of sexist language: Development and use of the gender specific language scale. *Sex Roles 31,* 741–755.

McNulty, Thomas, and Holloway, Steven (2000). Race, crime, and public housing in Atlanta: Testing a conditional effect hypothesis. *Social Forces 79*(2), 707–729.

Mennel, Robert (1973). *Thorns and thistles: Juvenile delinquents in the United States, 1825–1940.* Hanover, NH: University Press of New England.

Merida, Kevin (1996). Proposals push to try juveniles as adults, *Emerge 8,* 26–27.

Merlo, Alida V., Benekos, Peter J., and Cook, William J. (1999). The juvenile court At 100 years: Celebration or wake? *Juvenile and Family Court Journal 50,* 7–8.

Merlo, Alida, and Pollock, Joycelyn M. (1995). *Women, law, and social control.* Boston: Allyn and Bacon.

Merton, Robert (1957). *Social theory and social structure* (Rev. Ed.). New York: Free Press.

Messner, Steven, and Rosenfeld, Richard (1997). *Crime and the American dream* (2nd Ed.). Belmont, CA: Wadsworth.

Meyers, Kristen, Anderson, Cynthia, and Risman, Barbara (1998). *Feminist foundations.* Thousand Oaks, CA: Sage Publications.

Mildon, Marie (1998). Centennial celebration of the founding of the juvenile court, *Juvenile and Family Justice Today 7,* 5.

Millard, Dianne and Hagan, Michael (August 1996). Ethan Allen School rehabilitates juvenile sex offenders. *Corrections Today 58,* 92.

Miller, Jerome (1998). *The last one over the wall: The Massachusetts experiment in closing reform schools.* Columbus: Ohio State University Press.

Miller, Walter (Summer 1958). Lower-class culture as a generating milieu of gang delinquency, *Journal of Social Issues 14,* 12.

———. (1980). Gang, groups, and serious youth crime. In Schichor, David, and Kelly, Delos H. (eds.).

Critical issues in juvenile delinquency. Lexington, MA: D. C. Heath.

Mills, James (1999). Cocaine, smoking and spontaneous abortion. *New England Journal of Medicine 340*(5), 380–381.

Mitchell, Elizabeth (2000). *W: The revenge of the Bush dynasty.* New York: Hyperion.

Moore, Mark H. (1996). The future of the juvenile court: A theoretical framework that fits, *The Future of Children 6,* 140–146.

Moore, Mark H., and Wakeling, Stewart (1997). Juvenile justice: Shoring up the foundations, *Crime and Justice: An Annual Review of Research 22,* 275–276.

Morash, Merry, and Rucker, Lila (1990). A critical look at the idea of boot camp as a correctional reform. *Crime and Delinquency 36,* 206.

Morris, Jill (1998). Unconscious conflicts in the pre-Oedipal mother-daughter relationship as revealed through dreams. In Fenchel, Gerd (ed.), *The mother-daughter relationship: Echoes through time.* Northvale, NJ: Jason Aronson.

Morris, Lyn (March 28, 2002). *Who are strangers?* Indianapolis: The lost child emergency broadcast system. Web site: www.lostchild.net.

Morris, Norval, and Tonry, Michael (1990). *Between prison and probation: Intermediate punishment in a rational sentencing system.* New York: Oxford University Press.

Morton, Marian (Fall 2000). Institutionalizing inequalities: Black children and child welfare in Cleveland 1859–1998. *Journal of Social History 34*(1), 141–162.

Moynihan, Daniel Patrick (1965). *The negro family: The case for national action.* U.S. Department of Labor. Washington, DC: G PO.

Murray, Charles, and Herrenstein, R. (1994). *The bell curve.* New York: The Free Press.

Murray, Hugh (1967). The NMCP v the Communist Party: The Scottsboro Rape Case. 1931–1932. *Phylon,* 28.

Murrell, Dan S. (1996). *Constitutional law outline for the Fourth and Fifth Amendments of the United States Constitution.* Durham, NC: Carolina Academic Press.

Murrell, Dan S., and Dwyer, William O. (1991). *Constitutional law and liability for park law enforcement officers* (3rd Ed.). Durham, NC: Carolina Academic Press.

Myers, Alice, and Wright, Sarah (1996). *No angels.* San Francisco: Harper Collins.

N.C. State Bureau of Investigation, *Uniform Crime Report 1996.*

Natalucci-Persichetti, Geno, and Zimmermann, Carol Rapp (1997). Managing multidimensional change: A perspective on changing juvenile corrections in Ohio. *Corrections Management Quarterly 1,* 15–21.

National Association of Social Workers (1999). *Code of Ethics.* Washington, DC: NASW.

National Conference of State Legislators (1999). *Comprehensive Juvenile Justice: A Legislator's Guide.* Washington, DC: NCSL.

National Council of Juvenile and Family Court Judges (1990). Minority youth in the juvenile justice system: A judicial response, *Juvenile and Family Court Journal 41.*

———. (1995). *Children and family first: A mandate for America's courts.* Reno, NV: National Council of Juvenile and Family Court Judges.

———. (1998). Recommendations from a national symposium, *Juvenile and Family Court Journal 49,* 105–126.

———. (1999). Centennial celebrations, *Juvenile and Family Justice Today 8.*

———. (1999). Plaque marks site of first juvenile court building, *Juvenile and Family Justice Today 8,* 8.

Nazario, Thomas A. (1996). *Kids and the law: An A-to-Z guide for parents.* San Francisco: State Bar of California.

Neubauer, David W. (1996). *America's courts and the criminal justice system.* Pacific Grove, CA: Brooks/Cole.

Norman, Alma (2000). *Tzedek tzedek tirdorf: Jewish values and criminal justice.* Ottawa: Correctional Service of Canada.

Norris v Alabama, 294 U.S. 587 (1935).

North Carolina General Statutes § 7B-2510 (a)(1)–(14) (1999).

North Carolina juvenile code and related statutes §7B-2100 (1999).

Office for Victims of Crime (1998a). Victims' rights and services for the twenty-first century: Restitution. *OVC bulletin: New directions from the field.* Washington, DC: U.S. Department of Justice, 2.

Office of Community Oriented Policing Services, Pequannock, New Jersey, *COPS in action.* Washington, DC: U.S. Department of Justice, 1999.

Office of Community Oriented Policing Services (1999). Tackling youth disorder in Danvers, Massachusetts, *What Works.* Washington, DC: U.S. Department of Justice.

Office of Juvenile Justice and Delinquency Prevention (1988). A *private-sector corrections program for juveniles: Paint Creek Youth Center.* Washington, DC: U.S. Department of Justice.

———. (1993). Serious, violent and chronic juvenile offenders: A comprehensive strategy. *Office of Juvenile Justice and Delinquency Prevention fact sheet.* Washington, DC: U.S. Department of Justice.

———. (1994). *Conditions of confinement: Juvenile detention and corrections facilities.* Washington, DC: U.S. Department of Justice.

———. (1995). *Delinquency prevention works.* Washington, DC: U.S. Department of Justice.

———. (1997). *Juvenile offenders and victims: Update on violence.* Washington, DC: US Department of Justice.

———. (1999). *Promising strategies to reduce gun violence.* Washington, DC: Office of Justice Programs.

Ogawa, Brian K. (1999). *The color of justice.* Boston: Allyn and Bacon.

Ohio Community Service Council (2002). *Foster grandparent programs in Ohio.* www.state.oh.us/ohiogcsc.

OJJDP Research (August 1999). *Making a difference for juveniles.* U.S. Department of Justice. Shay Bilchik, Administrator. Report 15.

———. (May 2001). *2000 OJJDP Report.* Washington, DC: U.S. Department of Justice.

Oliver, William M. (ed.). *Community policing: Classical readings.* Upper Saddle River, NJ: Prentice Hall.

On Indian reservations in the West, violent crime soars, (August 16, 1998). *New York Times, 28.*

Overview: Toward comprehensive juvenile justice. National Conference of State Legislatures Web site: www.ncsl.org.

Pacheco, Sandra, and Hurtado, Aida (2001). Media stereotypes. In Worell, Judith (ed.), *Encyclopedia of women and gender: Sex similarities and differences and the impact of society on gender.* San Diego: Academic Press. II, 703–708.

Page, Robert W. (1993). The justification for a family court, *Juvenile and Family Court Journal 44, 33.*

Palmer, Ted (1977). Martinson revisited. *Journal of Research in Crime and Delinquency 12, 133–152.*

Palmiotto, Michael J. (1997). *Policing: Concepts, strategies, and current issues in American police forces.* Durham, NC: Carolina Academic Press, 191–193.

Paporozzi, Mario, and Wicklund, Carl (1998). Electronic supervision tools: Lessons learned, *Perspectives 22,* 8–9.

Parent, Dale, Dunworth, Terence, McDonald, Douglas, and Rhodes, William (1997). Key legislative issues in criminal justice: Intermediate sanctions. *NIJ: Research in Action.* Washington, DC: National Institute of Justice, 1–2.

Park, Robert, Burgess, Ernest, and McKenzie, Roderick (1928). *The city.* Chicago: University of Chicago Press.

Patterson v Alabama, 294 U.S. 600 (1935).

Peachey, Dean E. (1989). The Kitchener experiment. In Wright, Martin and Galaway, Burt (eds.), *Mediation in criminal justice: Victims, offenders and community.* Newbury Park, CA: Sage.

Peak, Kenneth J. (1995). *Justice administration: Police, courts, and corrections management.* Englewood Cliffs, NJ: Prentice Hall, 1995.

Pearlman, Deborah, Clark, Melissa, Rakowski, William, and Ehrich, Beverly (1999). Screening for breast and cervical cancers: The importance of knowledge and perceived cancer survivability. *Women and Health 28*(4), 93–112.

Penal System Study Committee (1972). *As the twig is bent.* Raleigh: North Carolina Bar Association.

Pernell-Arnold, Anita (January 10, 1990). *Everything you need to study to become culturally competent.* Hunter College Intensive Case Management Training Program. Handout.

Peters, Michael, Thomas, David, Zamberlan, Christopher, and Caiber Associates (1997). *Boot camps for juvenile offenders.* Washington, DC: Office of Juvenile Justice and Delinquency Prevention, 1997.

Petersilia, Joan (1999). A decade of experimenting with intermediate sanctions: What have we learned? *Perspectives* [American Probation and Parole Association], *23,* 39–40.

Pettiway, Leon (1998a). Images of African Americans: Voices of two black men. In Mann, Coramae and Zatz, Majorie (eds.), *Images of color, images of crime.* Los Angeles: Roxbury.

———. (1998b). *Every road has an end.* Los Angeles: Roxbury.

Piliavin, Irving, and Briar, Scott (1994). Police encounters with juveniles, *American Journal of Sociology 70,* 206–214.

Pisciotta, Alexander W. (1983a). Race, sex, and rehabilitation: A study in differential treatment in the juvenile reformatory. *Crime and Delinquency 29*(2), 254–269.

———. (1983b). Scientific reform: The new penology at Elmira. *Crime and Delinquency 29*(4), 613–630.

———. (1984). Parens patriae, treatment and reform: The case of the Western House of Refuge, 1849–1907. *New England Journal on Criminal and Civil Confinement 10,* 65–86.

———. (1985). Treatment on trial: The rhetoric and reality of the New York House of Refuge, 1857–1935, *American Journal of Legal History 59,* 151–181.

Plass, Peggy, Finkelhor, David, and Hotaling, Gerald (1997). Risk factors for family abductions: Demographic and family interaction characteristics. *Journal of Family Violence 12*(3), 333–348.

Platt, Anthony (1969). *The child savers.* Chicago: University of Chicago Press.

———. (1974). The triumph of benevolence: The origins of the juvenile justice system in the U.S. In Quinney, Richard (ed.), *Criminal justice in America.* Boston: Little, Brown.

———. (1977). *The child savers: The invention of delinquency.* Chicago: University of Chicago Press.

Pollak, Otto (1978). *The criminality of women.* Westport, CT: Greenwood.

Pollock-Byrne, Joycelyn M. (1993). *Women, prison, and crime.* Pacific Grove, CA: Brooks/Cole.

Pope, Carl E. (1995). Juvenile justice in the next millennium. In Klofus, John, and Stojkovic, Stan (eds.), *Crime and justice in the year 2010.* Belmont, CA: Wadsworth.

Porterfield, Austin (1946). *Youth in trouble.* Austin, TX: Leo Potishman Foundation.

Potter, David M., and Knepper, Paul (1996). Comparing official definitions of race in Japan and the United States, *Southeast Review of Asian Studies 18,* 103–118.

Pound, Roscoe (1957). The place of the family court in the judicial system, *National Probation and Parole Association Journal 5,* 164.

Public law 104-193. August 22, 1996[HR 3734] Personal responsibility and work opportunity reconciliation act of 1996 42 USC 1305.

Puritz, P., Burrell, S., Schwartz, R., Soler, M., and Warboys, L. (December 1995). *A call for justice: An assessment of access to counsel and quality of representation in delinquency proceedings.* Washington, DC: American Bar Association.

Puritz, Patricia, and Shang, Wendy Wan Long (1998). *Innovative approaches to juvenile indigent defense,* Washington, DC: Office of Juvenile Justice and Delinquency Prevention.

Puzzanchera, Charles M. (2000). *Self-reported delinquency by 12-year-olds, 1997, OJJDP Fact Sheet.* Washington, DC: Office of Juvenile Justice and Delinquency Prevention.

Quinn, Thomas (1998). Restorative justice: An interview with Visiting Fellow Thomas Quinn. *National Institute of Justice Journal 235,* 14.

Quinney, Richard. (1977). *Class, state and crime. On the theory and practice of criminal justice.* New York: David McKay.

Raley, Gordon P. (1995). The JJDP Act: A second look. *Juvenile Justice 2,* 12.

Rauscher, F. H., Robinson, K. D., and Jens, J. J. (1998). Improved maze learning through early music exposure in rats. *Neurological research 20*(5), 427–432.

Ray, Oakley, and Ksir, Charles (1999). *Drugs, society, and human behavior.* New York: McGraw-Hill.

Reaves, Brian A. (1993). *Census of state and local law enforcement agencies, 1992.* Washington, DC: Bureau of Justice Statistics.

Redding, Richard E. (Winter 1999). Juvenile offenders in criminal court and adult prison: Legal, psychological, and behavior outcomes. *Juvenile and Family Court Journal 50,* 1–20.

Regnery, Alfred S. (1986). A federal perspective on juvenile justice reform, *Crime and Delinquency 32,* 39–51.

Regoli, Robert, and Hewitt, John (1997). *Delinquency in society* (3rd Ed.). New York: McGraw-Hill.

———. (2000). *Delinquency in society* (4th Ed.). New York: McGraw Hill.

Reno, Janet (1996). Urban crime and violence: Keynote address at the 1996 Baker Institute Annual Conference. Houston: James Baker Institute.

Renzetti, C., and Curran, D. (1999). *Women, men, and society.* Boston: Allyn and Bacon.

Report on the teen court programs of North Carolina (1995). Raleigh, NC: North Carolina Administrative Office of the Courts.

Rest, James, Narvaez, Darcia, Bebeau, Muriel, and Thomas, Stephen (1999). *Postconventional moral thinking: A neo-Kohlbergian approach.* Mahwah, NJ: Lawrence Erlbaum Associates.

Roberts, Albert R. (1988). Wilderness programs for juvenile offenders: A challenging alternative. *Juvenile and Family Court Journal 39,* 1–2.

———. (1998a). The emergence and proliferation of juvenile diversion programs. In Roberts, Albert R. (ed.), *Juvenile justice: Policies, programs and services.* Chicago: Nelson-Hall.

———. (1998b). Wilderness experiences: Camps and outdoor programs. In Roberts, Albert R. (ed.), *Juvenile justice: Policies, programs and services.* Chicago: Nelson-Hall, 327–346.

Roberts, Amelia, Jackson, Mary S., and Laney-Carlton, Iris (Fall 2000). Revisiting the need for feminism and Afrocentrism theory when treating African American female substance abusers. *Journal of Drug Issues 30*(4), 901–918.

Roe, Keith (1995). Adolescents' use of the socially disvalued media: Towards a theory of media delinquency. *Journal of Youth and Adolescence 24*(5), 617–631.

Roscoe, Mark, and Morton, Reggie (1994). *Disproportionate minority representation fact sheet: No. 1.* Office of Juvenile Justice and Delinquency Prevention. Washington, DC: FS-9411.

Rosenberg, Irene M. (1993). Leaving bad enough alone: A Response to the juvenile court abolitionists, *Wisconsin Law Review,* 163.

Rosenman, Ray, and Friedman, Meyer (1974). *Type A behavior and your heart.* New York: Knopf.

Ross, Robert, Fabiano, Elizabeth, and Diemer-Ewies, C. (1988). Reasoning and rehabilitation. *International Journal of Offender Therapy and Comparative Criminology 32,* 29–35.

Rossi, Alice (1998). The impact of family structure and social change on adolescent sexual behavior. *Children and Youth Services Review 19*(5–6), 368–400.

Rothman, David (1980). *Conscience and convenience: The asylum and its alternatives in progressive America.* Glenview, IL: Scott Foresman.

Rothstein, Natalie (February 18, 1987). Teen Court. *Corrections Today 18* (20), 22.

Rothstein, Robert (1987). Teen court: A way to combat teenage crime and chemical abuse. *Juvenile and Family Court Journal 38,* 1–3.

Rubin, H. Ted (1980). The emerging prosecutor: Dominance of the juvenile court intake process, *Crime and Delinquency*, 300–301.

———. (1985). *Juvenile justice: Policy, practice and law.* New York: McGraw-Hill.

———. (1996). The nature of the court today, *The Future of Children 6,* 41.

Ruddell, Rick G., Mays, Larry, and Giever, Dennis M. (1998). Transferring juveniles to adult courts: Recent trends and issues in Canada and the United States, *Juvenile and Family Court Journal 49,* 6–7.

Ruefle, William, and Reynolds, Kenneth M. (1995). Curfews and delinquency in major American cities. *Crime and Delinquency 41,* 360–361.

Russell, Katheryn (1998). *The color of crime.* New York: New York University Press.

Ryan, William (1976). *Blaming the victims.* New York: Random House.

Sadoski, Judith (December 15, 1999), Earn-It program manager, unpublished correspondence to Paul Knepper.

Sagatun, Inger J., and Edwards, Leonard P. (1995). *Child abuse and the legal system.* Chicago: Nelson-Hall.

Sampson, Robert J., and Laub, John H. (1993). *Crime in the making: Pathways and turning points through life.* Cambridge, MA: Harvard University Press.

Sanborn, Joseph B. (1992). Pleading guilty in juvenile court: Minimal ado about something very important to young defendants, *Justice Quarterly 9,* 127–150.

———. (1993). Philosophical, legal and systemic aspects of juvenile court plea bargaining, *Crime and Delinquency 39,* 510.

———. (1994). Remnants of *parens patriae* in the adjudicatory hearing: Is a fair trial possible in juvenile court? *Crime and Delinquency 40,* 599–615.

Sanger, Margaret (2002). *Motherhood in bondage.* Columbus: Ohio University Press.

Santiago, Joseph J. (2001). *A new direction in policing: Changing old perceptions with a new reality,* Heritage Lecture #709. Washington, DC: Heritage Foundation.

Santos, Michael Chan (1998). Octuplets draw attention to fertility drugs. *Austin American Statesman,* E1. [Lexis Nexis Academic Universe.]

Saucier, Michael (1995). Birth of partnership. *Juvenile Justice 2,* 19–21.

Scalia, John (1997). *Juvenile delinquents in the federal criminal justice system,* Washington, DC: Bureau of Justice Statistics.

Schall v Martin 104 S.Ct. 2403 (1984).

Scherer, Jane (1991). *Crack babies.* Belmont, CA: Professional Publishing.

Schultz, J. Lawrence (1973). The cycle of juvenile court history, *Crime and Delinquency 19,* 457–476.

Schulz, Dorothy M. (1995). *From social worker to crime fighter: Women in United States municipal policing.* Westport, CT: Praeger.

Schur, E. M. (1973). *Radical non-intervention: Rethinking the delinquency problem.* Englewood Cliffs, NJ: Prentice-Hall.

Schwartz, Ira M. (1989). *(In)justice for juveniles: Rethinking the best interests of the child.* Lexington, MA: D. C. Heath.

———. (1992a). *Justice for juveniles: Rethinking the best interests of the child.* Lexington, MA: Lexington Books.

———. (ed.). (1992b). *Juvenile justice and public policy: Toward a national agenda.* New York: Lexington Books.

———. (1992c). The problem of youth violence. In Bender, David, and Leone, Bruno (eds.), *Youth violence.* San Diego: Greenhaven.

———. (1991d). Juvenile crime-fighting policies: What the public really wants. In Schwartz, Ira M. (ed.) (1992). *Juvenile justice and public policy.* New York: Lexington Books.

Schwartz, Ira, and Albanese, Jay (1993). *Dealing with delinquency: The future of juvenile justice.* Chicago: Nelson-Hall.

Schwartz, Ira M., Weiner, Neil A., and Enosh, Guy (1998). Nine lives and then some: Why the juvenile court does not roll over and die, *Wake Forest Law Review 33,* 533–552.

Schwartz, M., and Willis, Deborah A. (1994). National trends in juvenile detention. In Schwartz, Ira M., and Barton, William H. (eds.), *Reforming juvenile detention: No more hidden closets.* Columbus: Ohio State University Press.

Schwitzgebel, R. K. (1979). *Legal aspects of the enforced treatment of offenders.* Washington, DC: U.S. GPO.

Seidman, David, and Couzens, Michael (1974). Getting the crime rate down: Political pressure and crime reporting. *Law and Society Review 8,* 457–493.

Seng, Magnus J., and Bensinger, Gad J. (1994). Juvenile diversion as an agency policy: A twenty-year perspective. In Pallone, Nathaniel J. (ed.), *Young victims, young offenders*. New York: Haworth Press.

Senna, Joseph, and Siegel, Larry (2001). *Essentials of criminal justice*. Belmont, CA: Wadsworth.

Sergeyev, Victor (1998). *The wild East: Crime and lawlessness in post-Communist Russia*. Armonk, NY: M. E. Sharpe.

Serious and Violent Juvenile Offenders (May 1998). *Juvenile Justice Bulletin*. Washington, DC: Department of Justice.

Seyfrit, Carole, Reichel, Philip, and Stutts, Brian L. (1987). Peer juries as a juvenile diversion technique. *Youth and Society 18*, 302–316.

Shakur, Sanyika (1993). *Monster: The autobiography of an L.A. gang member*. New York: Penguin Books.

Shannon, Lyle (1982). *Assessing the relationship of adult career criminals to juvenile careers: A summary*. Washington, DC: US GPO.

Shapiro, Carol (1990). Is restitution legislation the chameleon of the victims movement? In Galaway, Burt, and Hudson, Joe (eds.), *Criminal justice, restitution and reconciliation*. Monsey, NY: Criminal Justice Press.

Shaw, Clifford, and McKay, Henry (1942). *Juvenile delinquency and urban areas*. Chicago: University of Chicago Press.

Shelden, Randall, Tracy, Sharon, and Brown, William (2001). *Youth gangs in American society* (2nd Ed.). Belmont, CA: Wadsworth.

Shelley, Louise I. (1980). Crime and delinquency in the Soviet Union. In Pankhurst, Jerry G., and Sacks, Michael Paul (eds.), *Contemporary Soviet society: Sociological perspectives*. New York: Praeger.

Shepherd, Robert E. (1999). A celebration or wake: The juvenile court after 100 years. *The Advocate* [Kentucky Department of Public Advocacy], *21*, 1–3.

———. (1999).The juvenile court at 100 years: A look back, *Juvenile Justice 6*, 20.

———. (Spring 1996).What does the public really want? *Criminal Justice* [American Bar Association], 1–3.

———. (1999). The juvenile court of the twenty-first century, *Criminal Justice*. [American Bar Association].

Sherman, Janet S., Christensen, Jon, and Henderson, Joel (1984). Reorganized crime: The creation of the Uniform Crime Reports. In Spitzer, Steven, and Simon, Rita J. (eds.), *Research in law, deviance and social control* Greenwich, CT: JAI Press.

Shine, James, and Price, Dwight (1992). Prosecutors and juvenile justice: New roles and perspectives. In Schwartz, Ira M. (ed.), *Juvenile justice and public policy*. New York: Lexington Books.

Shiraldi, Vincent, and Soler, Mark (1998). The will of the people? The public's opinion of the Violent and Repeat Juvenile Offender Act of 1997, *Crime and Delinquency 44*, 591.

Shoda, Yuichi (1999). Behavioral expressions of a personality system: Generation and perception of behavioral signatures. In Cervone, Daniel (ed.), *The coherence of personality: Social-cognitive bases of consistency, variability, and organization*. New York: The Guilford Press.

Shoeberlein, Deborah (2000). *Everybody: Preventing HIV and other sexually transmitted diseases among young teens*. Carbondale, CO: RAD Educational Programs.

Sickmund, Melissa (1997). The juvenile delinquency caseload. *Fact sheet*. Washington, DC: Office of Juvenile Justice and Delinquency Prevention.

Siegel, Larry, and Senna, Joseph (1997). *Juvenile delinquency: Theory and practice*. Pacific Grove: Brooks/Cole.

Sigurdson, Ola (March 1997). Silence reigns! A communitarian critique of the ethics of Lawrence Kohlberg. *Scandinavian Journal of Educational Research 41*(1), 5–13.

Singer, Simon, Levine, Murray, and Jou, Susyan (August 1993). Heavy metal music preference, delinquent friends, social control, and delinquency. *Journal of Research in Crime and Delinquency 30*, 317–329.

Skinner, Nicholas (June 1997). Failure to support a test for penis envy. *Psychological Reports*. 80(3, pt. 1), 754.

Smith, Beverly (1988). Military training at New York's Elmira Reformatory. *Probation 52*(1), 33–40.

Smith, Ian K. Ritalin for toddlers. Hyperactive kids are being given stimulants at younger and younger ages. Can this be good? *Time*. March 6, 1984, vol. 155.

Smith, J. David (August 1993). Institutionalization, involuntary sterilization, and mental retardation: Profiles from the history of the practice. *Mental Retardation 31*(4), 208–214.

Smith, M. Dwayne (1996). Sources of firearm acquisition among a sample of inner-city youths: Research results and policy implications. *Journal of Criminal Justice 24*, 365–366.

Smith, Steven K., and Defrances, Carol J. (1996). *Indigent defense*. Washington, DC: Bureau of Justice Statistics.

Smythe, M., and Meyer, J. (1994). On the origins of gender-linked language differences: Individual and contextual explanations. In Turner, L. H. and Sterk, H. M. (eds.), *Differences that make a difference*, Westport, CT: Bergin and Garvey.

Snyder, Howard N. (1996). The juvenile court and delinquency cases, *The future of Children* [David and Lucille Packard Foundation], *6*, 55–56.

———. (1997). *Juvenile arrests 1996*. Washington, DC: Office of Juvenile Justice and Delinquency Prevention.

Snyder, Howard N., and Sickmund, Melissa (1999). *Juvenile offenders and victims: 1999 national report*. Washington, DC: Office of Juvenile Justice and Delinquency Prevention.

———. (2000). Challenging the myths. In *1999 National Report Series: Juvenile Justice Bulletin*. Washington, DC: US Department of Justice.

Spath, Stefan (2002). What's wrong with reparations for slavery. *Ideas on Liberty 52*(4), 44–47.

Speck, Nancy (1968). Parental responsibility laws reviewed. *Juvenile Court Journal 19*(3), 90–97.

Speirs, Verne L. (January 1989). Preliminary estimates developed on stranger abduction homicides of children. *OJJDP Juvenile Justice Bulletin*.

Spelman, Elizabeth V. (1992). Gender in the context of race and class: Notes on Chodrow's reproduction of mothering. In Kourany, J., Sterba, J., and Tong, R. (eds.), *Feminist philosophies*. Englewood Cliffs, NJ: Prentice Hall.

Spengel, Irving (1995). The youth gang problem. New York: Oxford University Press.

Spohn, Cassia (1999). Gender and sentencing of drug offenders: Is chivalry dead? *Criminal Justice Policy Review 9*(31), 365–399.

Staff of U.S. Probation/Pretrial Services Office (1997). Federal juvenile corrections in South Dakota, *Federal Probation 61*, 38.

Staples, William G (1986). Restitution as a sanction in juvenile court. *Crime and Delinquency 32*, 182.

Starr, Isidore (1985). Reflections on the law studies movement in our schools. In White, Charles, and Gross, Norman (eds.), *The bulwark of freedom: Public understanding of the law*, Chicago: American Bar Association.

State of North Carolina: Uniform Crime Report 1996 (1997). Raleigh: N.C. State Bureau of Investigation.

State v Sugg 456 S.E.2d (W.Va. 1995); del Carmen et al., *Briefs of Leading Cases*.

Steffensmeier, Darrell, and Harer, Miles D. (1991). Did crime rise or fall during the Reagan presidency? The effects of an "aging" U.S. population on the nation's crime rate, *Journal of Research in Crime and Delinquency 28*, 330–359.

Steinberg, Gail, and Hall, Beth (2000). *Inside transracial adoption*. Indianapolis: Perspectives Press.

Stevenson, Phillip (1999a). The cycles of response to juvenile delinquency, *The Compiler* [Illinois Criminal Justice Information Authority], *19*, 10–11.

———. (1999b). The Juvenile Justice Reform Act. *Trends and issues update* [Illinois Criminal Justice Information Authority], *1*, 1–4.

Stinchcombe, Arthur (1964). *Rebellion in a high school*. Chicago: Quadrangle Press.

Straatmann, Shelia, and Sherraden, Margaret (2001). Welfare to self-employment: A case of the first step fund. *Journal of Community Practice 9*(3), 73–94.

Streib, V. L. (1987). *Death penalty for juveniles*. Bloomington, IN: Indiana University Press.

———. (1988). Imposing the death penalty on children. In Haas, K. C. and Inciardi, J. A. (eds.), *Challenging capital punishment*. Newbury Park, CA: Sage Publications.

Streib, Victor, and Sametz, Lynn (1998). Executing female juveniles. *Connecticut Law Review 22*(1), 3–59.

Strom, Kevin J., and Smith, Steven K. (1998). *Juvenile felony defendants in criminal courts*. Washington, DC: Bureau of Justice Statistics.

Stuckhoff, David R. (ed.) (2000). *Juvenile delinquency*. Guilford, CT: Dushkin/McGraw-Hill.

Sulton, Anne T. (1996). Preventing crime through economic development of urban neighborhoods. In Sulton, Anne T. (ed.), *African American perspectives on crime causation, criminal justice administration and crime prevention*. Boston: Butterworth-Heinemann.

Sutherland, Edwin (1934). *Principles of criminology* (2nd Ed.). Philadelphia: J. B. Lippincott.

———. (1939). *Principles of criminology*. Philadelphia: J. B. Lippincott.

Sutphen, Richard P., Kurtz, David, and Giddings, Martha (1993). The influence of juveniles' race on police decision making: An exploratory study, *Juvenile and Family Court Journal*, 69–78.

Swart, William (1995). Female gang delinquency: A search for acceptably deviant behavior. In Klein, Malcolm, Maxson, Cheryl L., and Miller, Jody (eds.), *The modern gang reader*. Los Angeles: Roxbury.

Sykes, Gresham, and Matza, David (December 1967). Techniques of neutralization: A theory of delinquency. *American Sociological Review 22*, 664–670.

Tannenbaum, Frank (1938). *Crime and the community*. Boston: Ginn.

Tatum, Becky (1999). The link between rap music and youth crime and violence. *Justice Professional 11*(3), 339–353.

Taylor, Bruce (1989). *New directions for the National Crime Survey*. Washington, DC: Bureau of Justice Statistics, 3–5.

Taylor, Carl (1990). *Dangerous society*. East Lansing: Michigan State University Press.

Taylor, Carl S. (1996). Growing up behind bars: Confinement, youth development, and crime, *Journal of the Oklahoma Criminal Justice Research*, 36.

Taylor, W., Lewis, C., and Nicholas, C. (1978). The Americanization of *parens patriae*: A right to treatment for juvenile offenders. *Journal of Humanics 5*(2), 119–135.

Thomas, Charles W., and Bilchik, S. (1985). Prosecuting juveniles in criminal courts: A legal and empirical analysis, *Journal of Criminal Law and Criminology 76,* 439–479.

Thomas, Stephen, and Quinn, Sandra (November 1991). The Tuskegee Syphilis Study, 1932 to 1972: Implications for HIV education and AIDS risk education programs in the black community. *American Journal of Public Health 81*(11), 1498–1505.

Thompson, M. Guy (October 1998). The fundamental rule of psychoanalysis. *Psychoanalytic Review 85*(5), 697–715.

Thornton, Robert Y., and Endo, Katsuya (1992). *Preventing crime in America and Japan: A comparative study.* Armonk, NY: M. E. Sharpe.

Thrasher, Frederick (2000). *The gang: A study of 1313 gangs in Chicago.* Peoria, IL: New Chicago School Press.

Thurman, Quint C., Giacomazzi, Andrew, and Bogen, Phil (1993). Research note: Cops, kids, and community policing—An assessment of a community policing demonstration project, *Crime and Delinquency 39,* 554–564.

Toffler, Alvin (1970). *Future shock.* New York: Random House.

Tolson, Eleanor R., McDonald, Shirley, and Moriarty, Anthony R. (1992). Peer mediation among high school students: A test of effectiveness. *Social Work in Education 14,* 86–93.

Torbet, P., Gable, R., Hurst, H., Montgomery, I., Szymanski, L., and Thomas, D. (1996). *State responses to serious and violent juvenile crime.* Washington, DC: U.S. Dept. of Justice, Office of Juvenile Justice and Delinquency Prevention.

Torbet, Patricia (1996). Juvenile probation: The workhorse of the juvenile justice system. *Juvenile Justice Bulletin.* Washington, DC: Office of Juvenile Justice and Delinquency Prevention.

Torbet, Patricia, and Snyder, Howard (1998). Juvenile violence: A new perspective. *Juvenile and Family Justice Today* [National Council of Juvenile and Family Court Judges], 7, 8.

Torbet, Patricia, and Thomas, Douglas (1997). Balanced and restorative justice: Implementing the philosophy. *Pennsylvania Progress* [Pennsylvania Commission on Crime and Delinquency], 4, 1–6.

Towill, Leigh Edward (ed.) (2002). *Cryopreservation of plant germplasm* II: *Biotechnology in Agriculture and Forestry, 50.* New York: Springer Verlag.

Trojanowicz, Robert, and Bucqueroux, Bonnie (1990). *Community policing: How to get started.* Cincinnati: Anderson.

Trueba, Henry, Cheng, Li Rong, and Ima, Kenji (1993). *Myth or reality: Adaptive strategies of Asian Americans in California.* Washington, DC: The Falmer Press.

U.S. Census Bureau (2000). National population projections. Web site: http://www.census.gov/population/projections.

Umbreit, Mark S. (1995). Holding juvenile offenders accountable: A restorative justice perspective. *Juvenile and Family Court Journal 46,* 31.

United States v Miller 453 F.2d 634 (4th Cir. 1972); del Carmen et al., *Briefs of Leading Cases,* 28–29.

United States v Sechrist 640 F.2d. 81 (7th Cir. 1981); del Carmen et al., *Briefs of Leading Cases,* 33–34.

Unterberger, Gail (December 6, 1989). Twelve steps for women alcoholics. *The Christian Century,* 1150–1152.

Validation of the nurturing programs. Received from the Nurturing Center of North Carolina, June 2, 2000.

Van Ness, Daniel (1986). *Crime and its victims.* Downer's Grove, IL: Intervarsity.

———. (1990). Restorative justice. In Galaway, Burt, and Hudson, Joe (eds.), C*riminal justice, restitution, and reconciliation.* Monsey, NY: Criminal Justice Press.

Vaughn, Joseph B. (1989). A survey of juvenile electronic monitoring and home confinement programs. *Juvenile and Family Court Journal,* 4.

Wald, Matthew (August 3, 1999). EPA bans pesticide to protect children. *New York Times* reported in the *Daily Reflector,* Greenville, North Carolina, 1, 7a.

Walker, Samuel (1992). *The police in America.* New York: McGraw Hill.

———. (1994). *Sense and nonsense about crime and drugs.* Belmont, CA: Wadsworth.

Walker, Samuel, Spohn, Cassia, and Delone, Miriam (1996*). The color of justice: Race, ethnicity, and crime in America.* Belmont, CA: Wadsworth.

Wallerstein, James, and Wyle, J. C. (1947). Our law-abiding law-breakers, *Federal Probation 25,* 107–112.

Ward, L. Monique, and Caruthers, Allison (2001). Media influences. In Worell, Judith (ed.), *Encyclopedia of women and gender: Sex similarities and differences and the impact of society on gender.* San Diego: Academic Press. Vol. II, 697–702.

Warren, Marguerite (1982). *Comparing female and male offenders.* Beverly Hills: Sage Publications.

Watkins, John C. Jr. (1998). *The juvenile justice century.* Durham, NC: Carolina Academic Press.

Web site of Amnesty International: www.amnesty.org.

Web site of Boston Police Department: www.cityofboston.com/police.

Web site of Broward County Sheriff's Office: www.sheriff.org.

Web site of CALEA: www.calea.org.

Web site of Community Oriented Policing Services: www.usdoj.gov/cops/.

Web site of Corporation for National and Community Service Organization: www.cns.gov.

Web site of Fort Collins Police Department: www.ci. fort-collins.co.us.

Web site of Los Angeles Police Department: www. lapdonline.org.

Web site of Michigan State Police: www.michigan.gov/ msp.

Web site of Minneapolis Police Department: www.ci. Minneapolis.mn.us/citywork/police.

Web site of New York City Police Department: www.ci. nyc.ny.us/nypd.

Web site of Pasadena [CA] Police Department: www.ci. pasadena.ca.us/police.

Web site of PBS on Line Report: www.pbs.org/wgbh/ pages/frontline/shows/fertility.

Web site of Phoenix [AZ] Police Department: www.ci. phoenix.az.us/police.

Web site of Regional Task Force on Internet Crimes against Children: www.ojjdp.ncjrs.org.

Web site of Sacramento [CA] Police Athletic League: www.sacpal.com.

Web site of the San Antonio Independent School District: www.saisd.net.

Web site of Senior Corps: www. seniorcorps.org.

Web site of Texas Juvenile Probation Commission: www. tjpc.state.tx.us.

Web site: www.mstservices.org/text/how/diff.html.

Web site: http://zebu.uoregon.edu/1998/ph101/glossary/ malthus.html.

Web site: www.alumni.cc.gettsburg.edu.

Web site: www.ci.keene.nh.us/police/occupations.html.

Web site: www.nyu.edu/projects/Sanger.

Weiss, Avi (1998). *Parshat ki tetze.* Riverdale, CA: Hebrew Institute.

West, D. J., and Farrington, David (1977). *The delinquent way of life.* London: Heinemann.

Westerman, Ted W., and Burfeind, James W. (1991). *Crime and justice in two societies: Japan and the United States.* Pacific Grove, CA: Brooks/Cole.

Whitaker, Catherine J. (1989). *The redesigned National Crime Survey: Selected new data.* Washington, DC: U.S. Department of Justice.

Whittington, Marie (1989). Supervised electronic confinement in Orange County, California. In Russell, Ken and Lilly, Robert (eds.), *The electronic monitoring of offenders.* Leicester Polytechnic Law School Monograph. Department of Law, Leicester Polytechnic.

Wilbanks, William (1987). *The myth of a racist criminal justice system.* Monterey, CA: Brooks/Cole.

Wilkinson, Sallye (April 1993). The female genital dress rehearsal: A prospective process at the oedipal threshold. *International Journal of Psycho-Analysis 74*(2), 313–330.

Will, George (March 25, 2002). Dropping the one-drop rule. *Newsweek 139*(12), 64.

Williamson, Deborah, Chalk, Michelle, and Knepper, Paul (1993). Teen court: Juvenile justice for the twenty first century? *Federal Probation 57,* 54–58.

Wilson, Amos (1990). *Black-on-black violence.* New York: Afrikan World Infosystems Publishers.

Wilson, James Q. (1985). *Thinking about crime.* New York: Basic Books.

Wilson, James Q., and Kelling, George (March 1982). Broken windows: The police and neighborhood safety, *Atlantic Monthly,* 29–38.

Wilson, W. Julius (1987). *The truly disadvantaged.* Chicago: University of Chicago Press.

Wisconsin Juvenile Officers' Association (1981). *Police/ school liaison program development.* Mequon, WI: Wisconsin Juvenile Officers' Association.

Wolfgang, Marvin, Figlio, Robert, and Sellin, Thorsten (1972). *Delinquency in a birth cohort.* Chicago: University of Chicago Press.

Wolford, Bruce, Jordan, Forrest, and Murphy, Kathryn (1997). Day treatment: Community-based partnerships for delinquent and at-risk youth. *Juvenile and Family Court Journal,* 35–42.

Wootton, James, and Heck, Robert O. (1997). How state and local officials can combat violent juvenile crime. In Meese, Edwin III, and Moffit, Robert E. (eds.), *Making America Safer.* Washington, DC: Heritage Foundation.

Worden, Robert E., and Shepard, Robin L. (1996). Demeanor, crime and police behavior: A reexamination of the police services study data, *Criminology 34,* 83–106.

Wright, Norma (1997). From risk to resiliency: The role of law related education. In Williamson, Deborah, Minor, Kevin I., and Fox, James (eds.), *Law related education and juvenile justice.* Springfield, IL: Charles C. Thomas.

Wubbolding, Robert E. (1981). Balancing the chart: Do it person and positive symptom person. *Journal of Reality Therapy 1*(1), 4–7.

———. (Fall 1984). Using paradox in reality therapy. *Journal of Reality Therapy 4*(I), 3–9.

———. (January 1985). Reality therapy: Principles and steps, *The WVSCA newsletter,* 6.

Wulffen, Erich (1934). *Woman as a sexual criminal.* New York: American Ethnological Press.

Yablonsky, Lewis (2000). *Juvenile delinquency into the twenty-first century.* Belmont, CA: Wadsworth.

Yeager, Matthew G. (1997). Immigrants and criminality: A cross-national review, *Criminal Justice Abstracts* 29, 153–154.

Youth Advocate Program International (1999). Juvenile justice in the United States. *Youth Advocate Program International Report 4,* 1–2.

Youth violence, guns, and illicit drug markets (1995). National Institute of Justice. Washington, DC: U.S. Department of Justice.

Zaplin, Ruth T. (1998). *Female offenders.* Gaithersburg, MD: Aspen.

Zastrow, Charles, and Kirst-Ashman, Karen. (1994). *Understanding human behavior and the social environment.* Chicago: Nelson-Hall.

Zehner, Sharon J. (1997). Teen court. *FBI law enforcement bulletin 66,* 1–7.

Zehr, Howard (1990). *Changing lenses: A new focus for crime and justice.* Scottsdale, PA: Herald Press.

Zhou, Min, and Bankston, Carl (2000). *Cultural diversity for Asian students: The biculturalization of the Vietnamese student.* ERIC Clearinghouse on Urban Education.

INDEX